LARSON, BOSWELL, KANOLD

Passport
to **Algebra** and **Geometry**

Complete
Solutions Manual

Complete Solutions Manual includes step-by-step solutions for all exercises in the Student Edition.

McDougal Littell
A HOUGHTON MIFFLIN COMPANY
Evanston, Illinois • Boston • Dallas

ISBN: 0-395-89681-9

23456789-DWI-02 01 00 99 98

Chapter 1
Exploring Patterns

ONGOING ASSESSMENT

1. 8, 12, 17

2. 8, 13, 21

3. 7, 11, 13

EXERCISES

1.–4. *Sample answers:*

1. Mathematics is the study of numbers and their uses.

2. Phone numbers, house numbers, auto license plates

3. Heights of people in feet and inches, weights of packages in pounds and ounces, speeds of cars in miles per hour, liter, yard, second

4. Hat sizes: $7, 7\frac{1}{8}, 7\frac{1}{4}, 7\frac{3}{8}, 7\frac{1}{2}$, and so on. Each number is $\frac{1}{8}$ more than the preceding number.

5. Pattern: Add 2 to the preceding number.

$1 + 2 = 3$ $\qquad$ $7 + 2 = 9$

$3 + 2 = 5$ $\qquad$ $9 + 2 = 11$

$5 + 2 = 7$ $\qquad$ $11 + 2 = 13$

Solution: 9, 11, 13

6. Pattern: Subtract 5 from the preceding number.

$80 - 5 = 75$ $\qquad$ $65 - 5 = 60$

$75 - 5 = 70$ $\qquad$ $60 - 5 = 55$

$70 - 5 = 65$ $\qquad$ $55 - 5 = 50$

Solution: 60, 55, 50

7. Pattern: Add 2, add 3, add 4, and so on, to preceding number.

$1 + 2 = 3$ $\qquad$ $10 + 5 = 15$

$3 + 3 = 6$ $\qquad$ $15 + 6 = 21$

$6 + 4 = 10$ $\qquad$ $21 + 7 = 28$

Solution: 15, 21, 28

8. Pattern: Subtract 3, subtract 4, subtract 5, and so on, from preceding number.

$63 - 3 = 60$ $\qquad$ $51 - 6 = 45$

$60 - 4 = 56$ $\qquad$ $45 - 7 = 38$

$56 - 5 = 51$ $\qquad$ $38 - 8 = 30$

Solution: 45, 38, 30

9. Pattern: Add 1 to both numerator and denominator of preceding number.

$$\frac{1}{2} \to \frac{1+1}{2+1} = \frac{2}{3} \to \frac{2+1}{3+1} = \frac{3}{4} \to \frac{3+1}{4+1} = \frac{4}{5} \to \frac{4+1}{5+1} = \frac{5}{6} \to \frac{5+1}{6+1} = \frac{6}{7} \to \frac{6+1}{7+1} = \frac{7}{8}$$

Solution: $\frac{5}{6}, \frac{6}{7}, \frac{7}{8}$

10. Pattern: Add 2 to both numerator and denominator of preceding number.

$$\frac{2}{3} \to \frac{2+2}{3+2} = \frac{4}{5} \to \frac{4+2}{5+2} = \frac{6}{7} \to \frac{6+2}{7+2} = \frac{8}{9} \to \frac{8+2}{9+2} = \frac{10}{11} \to \frac{10+2}{11+2} = \frac{12}{13} \to \frac{12+2}{13+2} = \frac{14}{15}$$

Solution: $\frac{10}{11}, \frac{12}{13}, \frac{14}{15}$

11. Pattern: Add $\frac{3}{2}$ to preceding number.

$2 = \frac{4}{2}, 5 = \frac{10}{2}$;

$\frac{4}{2} + \frac{3}{2} = \frac{7}{2}$

$\frac{7}{2} + \frac{3}{2} = \frac{10}{2}$

$\frac{10}{2} + \frac{3}{2} = \frac{13}{2}$

$\frac{13}{2} + \frac{3}{2} = \frac{16}{2} = 8$

$\frac{16}{2} + \frac{3}{2} = \frac{19}{2}$

$\frac{19}{2} + \frac{3}{2} = \frac{22}{2} = 11$

Solution: $8, \frac{19}{2}, 11$

12. Pattern: Name next smaller perfect square; or subtract 19, subtract 17, subtract 15, and so on, from previous number.

$10^2 = 100, 10 - 1 = 9$

$9^2 = 81, 9 - 1 = 8$

$8^2 = 64, 8 - 1 = 7$

$7^2 = 49, 7 - 1 = 6$

$6^2 = 36, 6 - 1 = 5$

$5^2 = 25, 5 - 1 = 4$

$4^2 = 16$

Solution: 36, 25, 16

13. Pattern: Multiply preceding number by 3.

$2 \times 3 = 6$ $\qquad$ $54 \times 3 = 162$

$6 \times 3 = 18$ $\qquad$ $162 \times 3 = 486$

$18 \times 3 = 54$ $\qquad$ $486 \times 3 = 1458$

Solution: 162, 486, 1458

14. Pattern: Divide preceding number by 4; or name next small power of 4; or name next smaller even power of 2.

$4096 \div 4 = 1024$ $\qquad$ $64 \div 4 = 16$

$1024 \div 4 = 256$ $\qquad$ $16 \div 4 = 4$

$256 \div 4 = 64$ $\qquad$ $4 \div 4 = 1$

Solution: 16, 4, 1

15. Pattern: Give the letter two letters after the previous letter.

<u>A</u> B <u>C</u> D <u>E</u> F <u>G</u> H <u>I</u> J <u>K</u> L <u>M</u> ...
Solution: I, K, M

16. Pattern: In every odd-numbered position except the first: Name the letter of the alphabet that precedes the letter in the preceding odd-numbered position. In every even-numbered position except the first: Name the letter of the alphabet that follows the letter in the preceding even-numbered position.

Z last letter

A first letter

Y 2nd to last letter

B 2nd letter

X 3rd to last letter

C 3rd letter

Solution: W, D, V

17. Pattern: In every odd-numbered position except the first: Name the letter of the alphabet that follows the letter in the preceding odd-numbered position. In every even-numbered position except the first: Name the letter of the alphabet that follows the letter in the preceding even-numbered position.

A   1st letter

N   14th letter

B   2nd letter

O   15th letter

C   3rd letter

P   16th letter

D   4th letter

Solution: C, P, D

18. Pattern: In every odd-numbered position: Name the letter of the alphabet in that position. In every even-numbered position: Subtract the position number from 27 and name the letter of the alphabet in that numbered position.

A   first letter

Y   2nd to last letter

C   3rd letter

W   4th to last letter

Solution: E, U, G

19.
$50 - 3 = 47$

$47 - 3 = 44$

$44 - 3 = 41$

$41 - 3 = 38$

$38 - 3 = 35$

Solution: 50, 47, 44, 41, 38, 35

20. 1, 3, $1 + 3 = 4$; $3 + 4 = 7$; $4 + 7 = 11$; $7 + 11 = 18$

Solution: 1, 3, 4, 7, 11, 18

21.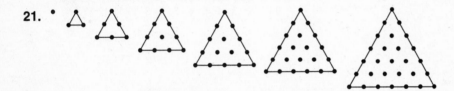

22. The figure is rotating clockwise.

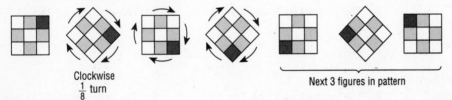

Clockwise
$\frac{1}{8}$ turn

Next 3 figures in pattern

23. You win.

24. You win; 14 ft 3 in. − 13 ft 11 in. = 13 ft 15 in. − 13 ft 11 in. = 4 in.

25. They get smaller and smaller.

26. *Sample answer:* Identify objects: Rides and buildings numbered on displayed maps, cars of roller coasters and Ferris wheels numbered on their sides. Measure objects: Time it takes to run a film, maximum number of people (or maximum weight) allowed in a car on a ride.

27. B;
Eighth: 29
Seventh: $29 - 3 = 26$
Sixth: $26 - 3 = 23$
Fifth: $23 - 3 = 20$
Fourth: $20 - 3 = 17$
Third: $17 - 3 = 14$
Second: $14 - 3 = 11$
First: $11 - 3 = 8$

28. D;
First: 2
Second: $2 \times 2 = 4$
Third: $4 \times 2 = 8$
Fourth: $8 \times 2 = 16$
Fifth: $16 \times 2 = 32$
Sixth: $32 \times 2 = 64$

29. a. Shows start every 45 min. The earliest show you can see after 1:00 P.M. is at 1:30 P.M.

b. Shows end every 30 min. Your show will end at 2:00 P.M.

30. Answers vary.

1.2 *Number Operations*

ONGOING ASSESSMENT

1. 2×7 or 7×2

2.

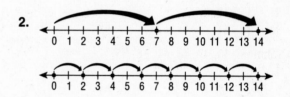

EXERCISES

1. Addition, subtraction, multiplication, division

2. $+, -, \times$ or $\cdot$ or $(\ )$, $\div$ or $/$

3. Answers vary.

4. *Sample answer:* A cash register adds the prices of various products bought in a store.

5. The product of 6 and 8 is 48.

6. The quotient of 25 and 5 is 5.

7. The sum of 3 and 14 is 17.

8. The product of 9 and 7 is 63.

9. The difference of 111 and 56 is 55.

10. The quotient of 12 and 4 is 3.

11. The product of 2 and 54 is 108.

12. The quotient of 132 and 11 is 12.

13.
$$\begin{array}{r} 659 \\ +\ 23 \\ \hline 682 \end{array}$$

14.
$$\begin{array}{r} 350 \\ +211 \\ \hline 561 \end{array}$$

15.
$$\begin{array}{r} 746 \\ -\ 27 \\ \hline 719 \end{array}$$

16.
$$\begin{array}{r} 858 \\ -349 \\ \hline 509 \end{array}$$

17.
$$\begin{array}{r} 75 \\ 40 \\ +\ 98 \\ \hline 213 \end{array}$$

18.
$$\begin{array}{r} 352 \\ 67 \\ +\ 20 \\ \hline 439 \end{array}$$

19.
$$\begin{array}{r} 10.9 \\ -\ 8.6 \\ \hline 2.3 \end{array}$$

20.
$$\begin{array}{r} 112.7 \\ -\ 72.9 \\ \hline 39.8 \end{array}$$

21. $\frac{5}{6} + \frac{1}{6} = \frac{6}{6} = 1$

22. $\frac{3}{8} + \frac{1}{8} = \frac{4}{8} = \frac{1}{2}$

23. $\frac{9}{12} - \frac{5}{12} = \frac{4}{12} = \frac{1}{3}$

24. $\frac{6}{13} - \frac{3}{13} = \frac{3}{13}$

25.
$$\begin{array}{r} 16 \\ \times\ \ 7 \\ \hline 42 \\ 7 \\ \hline 112 \end{array}$$

26.
$$\begin{array}{r} 21 \\ \times\ 14 \\ \hline 84 \\ 21 \\ \hline 294 \end{array}$$

27.
$$\begin{array}{r} 17 \\ 31\overline{)527} \\ 31 \\ \hline 217 \\ 217 \\ \hline 0 \end{array}$$

28.
$$\begin{array}{r} 41 \\ 35\overline{)1435} \\ 140 \\ \hline 35 \\ 35 \\ \hline 0 \end{array}$$

29.
$$\begin{array}{r} 4.7 \\ 8.9 \\ \hline 423 \\ 376 \\ \hline 41.83 \end{array}$$

30.
$$\begin{array}{r} 13.2 \\ 5.1 \\ \hline 132 \\ 660 \\ \hline 67.32 \end{array}$$

31.
$$\begin{array}{r} 321 \\ \times\ \ 156 \\ \hline 1\ 926 \\ 1\ 60\ 5 \\ 3\ 2\ 1 \\ \hline 5\ 0,076 \end{array}$$

32.
$$\begin{array}{r} 497 \\ \times\ \ 38 \\ \hline 3\ 976 \\ 14\ 91 \\ \hline 18,886 \end{array}$$

33.
$$\begin{array}{r} 8 \\ 32\overline{)\ 256} \\ -256 \\ \hline 0 \end{array}$$

34.
$$\begin{array}{r} 16 \\ 64\overline{)\ 1024} \\ -64 \\ \hline 384 \\ -384 \\ \hline 0 \end{array}$$

35. $3 \cdot \frac{4}{6} = \frac{12}{6} = 2$

36. $7 \cdot \frac{1}{8} = \frac{7}{8}$

37. $4.3\overline{)76.97} =$
$$\begin{array}{r} 17.9 \\ 43\overline{)769.7} \\ 43 \\ \hline 339 \\ 301 \\ \hline 38\ 7 \\ 38\ 7 \\ \hline 0 \end{array}$$

38.
$$\begin{array}{r} 4.4 \\ 33\overline{)145.2} \\ 132 \\ \hline 13\ 2 \\ 13\ 2 \\ \hline 0 \end{array}$$

39.
$$\begin{array}{r} 131.8 \\ 15\overline{)1977.0} \\ 15 \\ \hline 47 \\ 45 \\ \hline 27 \\ 15 \\ \hline 12\ 0 \\ 12\ 0 \\ \hline 0 \end{array}$$

40.
$$\begin{array}{r} 62.5 \\ 34\overline{)2125.0} \\ 204 \\ \hline 85 \\ 68 \\ \hline 17\ 0 \\ 17\ 0 \\ \hline 0 \end{array}$$

41. $2 \times 4 = 8$

42. $3 \times 3 = 9$

43. 3×9 or $9 \times 3 = 27$

44. 4×6 or $6 \times 4 = 24$

45. 442 million

46.
$$\begin{array}{r} 723 \\ -273 \\ \hline 450 \end{array}$$ million more CDs

47.
$$\begin{array}{r} 723 \\ -408 \\ \hline 315 \end{array}$$ million more CDs

48. More and more CDs, and fewer and fewer cassettes, will be sold.

49.
$$\begin{array}{r} 14 \\ \times\ 5 \\ \hline 70 \end{array}$$

The storage unit holds 70 CDs.

50.

First number	Operation	Second number	Result
Odd	+	Even	Odd
Odd	+	Odd	Even
Odd	×	Even	Even
Odd	×	Odd	Odd

Examples:
$3 + 2 = 5$
$3 + 3 = 6$
$3 \times 2 = 6$
$3 \times 3 = 9$

51. C;

$$\begin{array}{r} 72 \\ \times \ \ 60 \\ \hline 4320 \end{array}$$

52. D;

$$\begin{array}{r} \$527 \\ - \ \ \ 58 \\ \hline \$469 \end{array}$$

53. a. Answers vary.
   b. Answers vary.

1.3   *Powers and Square Roots*

ONGOING ASSESSMENT

1. Yes; $47{,}961 = 219^2$; answers vary.

2. 2; $35^2 = 1225$ and $36^2 = 1296$

EXERCISES

1. base, exponent

2. 3 raised to the 4th power is 81.

3. 4

4. 7

5. 9

6. The square root of 36 is 6.

7. 6 raised to the fourth power is 1296.

8. 2.9 squared is 8.41.

9. The square root of 1.21 is 1.1.

10. The square root of 2.25 is 1.5.

11. 12^2; 144

12. 8^5; 32,768

13. 3.4^3; 39.304

14. 9.7^4; 8852.9281

15. 3^6; 729

16. $\left(\frac{3}{5}\right)^5$, 0.07776

17. 13

18. 21

19. 10.82

20. 19.29

21. 2.35

22. 2.87

23. $8 \cdot 8 \cdot 8 = 512$; the answer is 8.

24. $5 \cdot 5 \cdot 5 \cdot 5 = 625$; the answer is 5.

25. $2.1 \cdot 2.1 = 4.41$; the answer is 2.1.

26. $3.5 \cdot 3.5 \cdot 3.5 = 42.875$; the answer is 3.5.

27. $9^2 = 81$; the answer is 81.

28. $17^2 = 289$; the answer is 289.

29. $2^3 = 8$, $3^2 = 9$; $2^3 < 3^2$

30. $2^4 = 16$, $4^2 = 16$; $2^4 = 4^2$

31. $4^3 = 64$, $3^4 = 81$; $4^3 < 3^4$

32. $5^2 = 25$, $2^5 = 32$; $5^2 < 2^5$

33. $10^2 = 100$, $2^{10} = 1024$; 2^{10}

34. 5^6; Keeping track of the number of fives, press 5 and then press $\times$ and 5 repeatedly until the result is over 20,000. The power of five is one less than the number of fives pressed.

35. a. Since the room is to be square, the length and width are the same. Therefore, you can take the square root of the area of the room. $\sqrt{506.25} = 22.5$; each side is 22.5 ft.

b. $4(22.5) = 90$ ft

c.

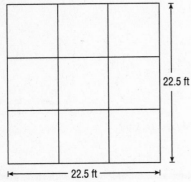

22.5 ft

22.5 ft

$506.25 \div 9 = 56.25$ ft

d. 7.5 ft; $\sqrt{56.25} = 7.5$

36. a. A cube has 6 faces.

b. Area of one face: $7 \times 7 = 49$ in.^{2}

c. Surface area is area of one face multiplied by the number of faces. $49 \times 6 = 294$ in.^{2}

37. No; $6(14^2) \neq 2[6(7^2)]$; the surface area is 4 times larger when you double the length.

38. D

39. B; $11.2 \times 11.2 = 125.44$

40. a. $\sqrt{4840} \approx 69.57$ yards

b. 278.28 yards

Spiral R E V I E W

1. $\frac{2}{4} = \frac{1}{2}$

2. $\frac{6}{3} = 2$

3. $\frac{12}{8} = \frac{3}{2}$ or $1\frac{1}{2}$

4. $\frac{6}{20} = \frac{3}{10}$

5.
$$\begin{array}{r} 0.5 \\ 2\overline{)1.0} \\ \underline{1\,0} \\ 0 \end{array}$$

6.
$$\begin{array}{r} 0.25 \\ 4\overline{)1.00} \\ \underline{8} \\ 20 \\ \underline{20} \\ 0 \end{array}$$

7.
$$\begin{array}{r} 0.375 \\ 8\overline{)3.000} \\ \underline{2\,4} \\ 60 \\ \underline{56} \\ 40 \\ \underline{40} \\ 0 \end{array}$$

8.
$$\begin{array}{r} 0.4 \\ 5\overline{)2.0} \\ \underline{2\,0} \\ 0 \end{array}$$

9. Pattern: Add 2 to preceding number.

$2 + 2 = 4$ $8 + 2 = 10$
$4 + 2 = 6$ $10 + 2 = 12$
$6 + 2 = 8$ $12 + 2 = 14$

Solution: 10, 12, 14

10. Pattern: Subtract 3 from previous number.

$30 - 3 = 27$ $21 - 3 = 18$
$27 - 3 = 24$ $18 - 3 = 15$
$24 - 3 = 21$ $15 - 3 = 12$

Solution: 18, 15, 12

11. Pattern: Add 2 to both numerator and denominator of preceding number.

$$\frac{1+2}{2+2}=\frac{3}{4} \qquad \frac{7+2}{8+2}=\frac{9}{10}$$

$$\frac{3+2}{4+2}=\frac{5}{6} \qquad \frac{9+2}{10+2}=\frac{11}{12}$$

$$\frac{5+2}{6+2}=\frac{7}{8} \qquad \frac{11+2}{12+2}=\frac{13}{14}$$

Solution: $\dfrac{9}{10}, \dfrac{11}{12}, \dfrac{13}{14}$

12. Pattern: Add 5, then add 6, then add 7, and so on, to preceding number.

$$1+5=6 \qquad 19+8=27$$

$$6+6=12 \qquad 27+9=36$$

$$12+7=19 \qquad 36+10=46$$

Solution: 27, 36, 46

13. **a.** $\$2.75 + \$2.75 + \$2.75 = \$8.25$

  b. $\$10.00 - \$8.25 = \$1.75$

14. $5^7 = 78,125$

15. $(3.9)^2 = 15.21$

16. $\sqrt{22} \approx 4.690 \approx 4.69$

Using a Calculator

1. Guess, check, and revise to obtain 4.64 feet.

2. You could double the volume so it holds 2000 gallons of water or you could double the length of each side. These two meanings do not describe the same size aquarium.

1.4 *Order of Operations*

ONGOING ASSESSMENT

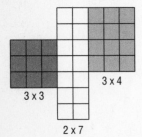

3 x 4

3 x 3

2 x 7

1. $3^2 + (2 \times 7) + (3 \times 4)$

2. 35 units^2

EXERCISES

1. To always get the same results. Examples vary. *Sample answer:* The total number of pencils in 3 boxes of 12 pencils each and 2 boxes of 10 pencils each is $3 \times 12 + 2 \times 10$ or 56, not 380.

2. Evaluating powers, multiplications and divisions, and additions and subtractions; to always get the same results.

3. a. $18 - 4 \times 3 = 18 - 12 = 6$

b. $48 \div 6 \times 3 = 8 \times 3 = 24$

c. $12 + 4^2 - 3 \times (5 - 2) = 12 + 4^2 - 3 \times 3$
$$= 12 + 16 - 3 \times 3$$
$$= 12 + 16 - 9$$
$$= 28 - 9$$
$$= 19$$

4. a. $4 \div 2 \times (8 + 2) = 4 \div 2 \times 10$
$$= 2 \times 10$$
$$= 20$$

b. $3 \times (4 + 8) - 2 = 3 \times 12 - 2$
$$= 36 - 2$$
$$= 34$$

5. $7 + 12 \div 6 = 7 + 2$
$$= 9$$

6. $12 - 3 \times 4 = 12 - 12$
$$= 0$$

7. $5 \cdot 3 + 2^2 = 5 \cdot 3 + 4$
$$= 15 + 4$$
$$= 19$$

8. $5^2 - 8 \div 2 = 25 - 8 \div 2$
$$= 25 - 4$$
$$= 21$$

9. $11 + 4 \div 2 \times 9 = 11 + 2 \times 9$
$$= 11 + 18$$
$$= 29$$

10. $21 - 1 \cdot 2 \div 4 = 21 - 2 \div 4$
$$= 21 - \tfrac{1}{2}$$
$$= 20\tfrac{1}{2}$$

11. $14 - 8 + 4 \cdot 2^3 = 14 - 8 + 4 \cdot 8$
$$= 14 - 8 + 32$$
$$= 38$$

12. $3^3 - 8 \cdot 3 \div 12 = 27 - 24 \div 12$
$$= 27 - 2$$
$$= 25$$

13. $(9 + 7) \div 4 \times 2 = 16 \div 4 \times 2$
$$= 4 \times 2$$
$$= 8$$

14. $6 \div (17 - 11) \cdot 14 = 6 \div 6 \cdot 14$
$$= 1 \cdot 14$$
$$= 14$$

15. $4 - (5)(5) + 13 = 4 - 25 + 13$
$$= -21 + 13$$
$$= -8$$

16. $16 \div 4 \cdot 2 - 7 = 4 \cdot 2 - 7$
$$= 8 - 7$$
$$= 1$$

17. $3[16 - (3 + 7) \div 5] = 3[16 - 10 \div 5]$
$$= 3[16 - 2]$$
$$= 3[14]$$
$$= 42$$

18. $(6 + 32)(4 - 2) = (38)(2)$
$$= 76$$

19. 79

20. 50

21. 2

22. 110

23. about 19.33

24. 113

25. 600

26. 18

27.

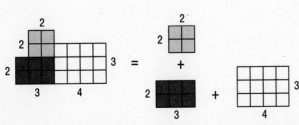

$(2 \times 2) + (2 \times 3) + (4 \times 3) = 4 + 6 + 12 = 22 \text{ units}^2$

28.

$$(4 \times 3) + (4 \times 2) + (3 \times 2) = 12 + 8 + 6 = 26 \text{ units}^2$$

29. $6 + 21 \div 3 = 6 + 7 = 13$; the statement is false.
True statement: $(6 + 21) \div 3 = 9$

30. $6 \cdot 3 - 2 \cdot 5 = 18 - 10 = 8$
The statement is true.

31. $6 + 3^2 \div 3 = 6 + 9 \div 3 = 6 + 3 = 9$
The statement is false.
True statement: $(6 + 3^2) \div 3 = 5$

32. $8^2 - 1 \cdot 3 - 5 = 64 - 1 \cdot 3 - 5$
$$= 64 - 3 - 5$$
$$= 61 - 5 = 56$$
The statement is true.

33. $7 + 7 \cdot 2 + 6 = 7 + 14 + 6 = 27$
The statement is false.
True statement: $7 + 7 \cdot (2 + 6) = 63$

34. $36 \div 9 - 6 \div 2 = 4 - 3 = 1$
The statement is false.
True statement: $36 \div (9 - 6) \div 2 = 6$

35. $5 \times 0.5 + 3 \times 2.25 + 5.99$; $15.24

36. D; $5^2 - 3^2 \times 2 = 25 - 9 \times 2 = 25 - 18 = 7$

37. C; $(3 + 3)^2 + 44 \div 11 = 36 + 44 \div 11$
$$= 36 + 4$$
$$= 40$$

38. $2(2.05 + 2 \times 2.05)$; 12.3 billion

39. a. Answers vary.
b. Answers vary.

Mid-Chapter ASSESSMENT

1. *Sample answer:* height, weight, area

2. Pattern: Add 3 to the previous number.
$3 + 3 = 6$
$6 + 3 = 9$
$9 + 3 = 12$
$12 + 3 = 15$
$15 + 3 = 18$
$18 + 3 = 21$
Solution: 15, 18, 21

3. Pattern: Subtract 9 from previous number.
$90 - 9 = 81$
$81 - 9 = 72$
$72 - 9 = 63$
$63 - 9 = 54$
$54 - 9 = 45$
$45 - 9 = 36$
Solution: 54, 45, 36

4. Pattern: Give the squares of the counting numbers.
$1^2 = 1$
$2^2 = 4$
$3^2 = 9$
$4^2 = 16$
$5^2 = 25$
$6^2 = 36$
$7^2 = 49$
Solution: 25, 36, 49

5. Pattern: Add 1 to the denominator of the previous number.

$$\frac{1}{1+1} = \frac{1}{2} \qquad \frac{1}{5+1} = \frac{1}{6}$$

$$\frac{1}{2+1} = \frac{1}{3} \qquad \frac{1}{6+1} = \frac{1}{7}$$

$$\frac{1}{3+1} = \frac{1}{4} \qquad \frac{1}{7+1} = \frac{1}{8}$$

$$\frac{1}{4+1} = \frac{1}{5}$$

Solution: $\frac{1}{6}, \frac{1}{7}, \frac{1}{8}$

6. The pattern is of a dial rotating counterclockwise over 2 stationary dots, one dark and one light.

7. The pattern is of upside-up odd numbers alternating with upside-down even numbers.

7 8 9

8. The product of 22 and 4 is 88.

9. 4 raised to the 5th power is 1024.

10. The square root of 289 is 17.

11.
$$\begin{array}{r} 12 \\ \times\ 4 \\ \hline 48 \end{array}$$

12.
$$\begin{array}{r} 176 \\ \times\ 12 \\ \hline 352 \\ 176 \\ \hline 2112 \end{array}$$

13.
$$\begin{array}{r} 9 \\ 41\overline{)\,369} \\ -369 \\ \hline 0 \end{array}$$

14. $5^8 = 5 \cdot 5 \cdot 5 \cdot 5 \cdot 5 \cdot 5 \cdot 5 \cdot 5$
$= 390,625$

15. $(4.3)^2 = 4.3 \cdot 4.3$
$= 18.49$

16. $\sqrt{256} = 16$

17. $\sqrt{795.24} = 28.2$

18. $\sqrt{19} = 4.36$

19. $28 - 21 \div 7 = 28 - 3$
$= 25$

20. $8 \div 2 \cdot 4^2 = 8 \div 2 \cdot 16$
$= 4 \cdot 16$
$= 64$

21. $40 + \frac{15}{3} - 6 = 40 + 5 - 6$
$= 45 - 6$
$= 39$

22. $6 + 9 \div 3 - 1 = 6 + 3 - 1$
$= 9 - 1$
$= 8$

23. $9 \times (3 + 4) - 7 = 9 \times 7 - 7$
$= 63 - 7$
$= 56$

24. $48 \div [2 \cdot (12 - 4)] = 48 \div [2 \cdot 8]$
$= 48 \div 16$
$= 3$

25. $(21 - 8) \times 2 = 26$

26. $24 - 20 \div (4 + 6) = 22$

27. $24 - (12 - 4) \cdot 2 = 8$

28. $505 \times 255 = 128,775$

29. $255 \div 13 \approx 19.6$ feet

30. $19.6 \times 7 \approx 137$ feet

Lab 1.5

Part A

1.

Pattern for 5: $2 + 2(5)$
Pattern for 6: $2 + 2(6)$

2. $2 + 2(10) = 22$

3. To find the perimeter of any figure, multiply the figure number by 2, and add 2.

4. $2 + 2(41) = 84$

Part B

5.

6.

Figure	1	2	3	4	5	6
Perimeter	3	4	5	6	7	8
Pattern	$1+2$	$2+2$	$3+2$	$4+2$	$5+2$	$6+2$

7. 11

8. To find the perimeter of any figure, add 2 to the figure number. n = figure number, P = perimeter; $P = n + 2$

9. 34th figure: $P = 34 + 2 = 36$

1.5 ALGEBRA CONNECTION: Variables in Expressions

ONGOING ASSESSMENT

1. Perimeter;

$P = l + l + w + w$
$= 2l + 2w$

2. Perimeter $= 2 \cdot \text{length} + 2 \cdot \text{width}$

EXERCISES

1. An algebraic expression is a collection of numbers, variables, operations (such as addition or division), and grouping symbols.

2. Find its numerical value.

3. n

4. 3

5. $4 + n$

6. 7

7. $3a + b = 3 \cdot 5 + 3$

$ = 15 + 3$

$ = 18$

8. $(b^2 + 6) \div a = (3^2 + 6) \div 5$

$ = (9 + 6) \div 5$

$ = 15 \div 5$

$ = 3$

9. $5 + x = 5 + 4$

$ = 9$

10. $32 \div x = 32 \div 4$

$ = 8$

11. $12x = 12(4)$

$ = 48$

12. $x \cdot 3x = 4 \cdot 3(4)$

$ = 4 \cdot 12$

$ = 48$

13. $3x^2 + 9 = 3(4^2) + 9$

$ = 3(16) + 9$

$ = 48 + 9$

$ = 57$

14. $2x^2 \cdot 3x = 2(4^2) \cdot 3(4)$

$ = 2(16) \cdot 12$

$ = 32 \cdot 12$

$ = 384$

15. $(x + 3)6 = (4 + 3)6$

$ = (7)6$

$ = 42$

16. $(x - 2) \div 4 = (4 - 2) \div 4$

$ = 2 \div 4$

$ = \frac{1}{2}$

17. $(9 - x)^2 = (9 - 4)^2$

$ = 5^2$

$ = 25$

18. $(7 - x)^3 = (7 - 4)^3$

$ = 3^3$

$ = 27$

19. $(8 - x + 8) \div x = (8 - 4 + 8) \div 4$

$ = (4 + 8) \div 4$

$ = 12 \div 4$

$ = 3$

20. $x^2 - 3 \cdot x = 4^2 - 3 \cdot 4$

$ = 16 - 12$

$ = 4$

21. $b - a = 7 - 2$

$ = 5$

22. $ab = (2)(7)$

$ = 14$

23. $3b - a = 3(7) - 2$

$ = 21 - 2$

$ = 19$

24. $5a + 2b = 5(2) + 2(7)$

$ = 10 + 14$

$ = 24$

25. $3a^2 \cdot b = 3(2^2) \cdot 7$

$ = 3(4) \cdot 7$

$ = 12 \cdot 7$

$ = 84$

26. $(4b) \div (2a) = [4(7)] \div [2(2)]$

$ = 28 \div 4$

$ = 7$

27. $(24a - 6) \div b = [24(2) - 6] \div 7$

$ = (48 - 6) \div 7$

$ = 42 \div 7$

$ = 6$

28. $b(9 - a) = 7(9 - 2)$

$ = 7(7)$

$ = 49$

29. $(b - a)^3 = (7 - 2)^3$

$ = 5^3$

$ = 125$

30. $(5 + b)^2 + a = (5 + 7)^2 + 2$

$ = 12^2 + 2$

$ = 144 + 2$

$ = 146$

31. $(a + b) \div (b - 2a) = (2 + 7) \div [7 - 2(2)]$

$ = 9 \div (7 - 4)$

$ = 9 \div 3$

$ = 3$

32. $6(b - a) \div (3a) = 6(7 - 2) \div [3(2)]$
$$= 6(5) \div 6$$
$$= 30 \div 6$$
$$= 5$$

33. $x + y - z = 5 + 8 - 9$
$$= 13 - 9$$
$$= 4$$

34. $x + (z - y) = 5 + (9 - 8)$
$$= 5 + 1$$
$$= 6$$

35. $z \div (y - x) + z = 9 \div (8 - 5) + 9$
$$= 9 \div 3 + 9$$
$$= 3 + 9$$
$$= 12$$

36. $y(z - x) + x = 8(9 - 5) + 5$
$$= 8(4) + 5$$
$$= 32 + 5$$
$$= 37$$

37. B

38. D

39. C

40. A

41. $30 \ \cancel{\text{min}} \times \dfrac{50 \text{ ft}}{\cancel{\text{min}}} = 1500 \text{ ft}$

42. $2600 \ \cancel{\text{ft}} \times \dfrac{\text{min}}{50 \ \cancel{\text{ft}}} = 52 \text{ min}$

43. $x = 4$
$$4 \cdot 4 + 2 = 16 + 2 = 18$$

44. $n = 10$
$$5 \cdot 10 - 3 = 50 - 3$$
$$= 47$$

45. a. $6p + 2p$
b. $6p + 2p = 6(3) + 2(3)$
$$= 24$$
You will spend $24 for you and your friends.

46. C

47. B

48. a. $30 \ \cancel{\text{mi}} \times \dfrac{1 \text{ hr}}{20 \ \cancel{\text{mi}}} = 1.5 \text{ hr}$

$1.5 \ \cancel{\text{hr}} \times \dfrac{60 \text{ min}}{1 \ \cancel{\text{hr}}} = 90 \text{ min}; \ \dfrac{1}{4} \text{ h or } 15 \text{ min}$

b. $105 \ \cancel{\text{min}} \times \dfrac{1 \text{ hr}}{60 \ \cancel{\text{min}}} = 1.75 \text{ hr}$

c. Answers vary.

1.6 *Exploring Data: Tables and Graphs*

ONGOING ASSESSMENT

1. *Sample answer:* 1991; the score was close.

2. *Sample answer:* similar—both graphs show winning and losing scores; different—a bar graph uses bars to represent the data and a line graph uses points.

EXERCISES

1. *Sample answer:* table, bar graph, line graph

2. a. Answers vary.
   b. Answers vary.

3. $44 + 32 + 25 = 101$ medals, United States

4. Total gold $= 44 + 26 + 20 + 16 + 15 = 121$
Total silver $= 32 + 21 + 18 + 22 + 7 = 100$
Total bronze $= 25 + 16 + 27 + 12 + 15 = 95$
As a group, there were more gold medals won.

5. Russia, $26 - 10 = 16$

6. France, $15 - 8 = 7$

7.

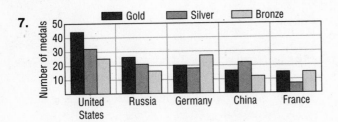

A bar graph is preferable because there are no connections among the numbers of medals won by the various teams.

8. 300 ft

9. 1980 difference: $299 - 224 = 75$
1984 difference: $284 - 228 = 56$
1988 difference: $276 - 245 = 31$
1992 difference: $294 - 224 = 70$
1996 difference: $289 - 223 = 66$
The least-difference year: 1988
The greatest-difference year: 1980

10. *Sample answer:* Representing the data with a table would show the distances as numbers. This would enable you to interpret the data more accurately than you could with a graph.

11. Perimeter:

$4(1) = 4 \qquad 4(2) = 8 \qquad 4(3) = 12 \qquad 4(4) = 16$

$4(5) = 20 \qquad 4(6) = 24 \qquad 4(7) = 28$

Area:

$1 \times 1 = 1 \qquad 2 \times 2 = 4 \qquad 3 \times 3 = 9 \qquad 4 \times 4 = 16$

$5 \times 5 = 25 \qquad 6 \times 6 = 36 \qquad 7 \times 7 = 49$

Side Length	1	2	3	4	5	6	7
Perimeter	4	8	12	16	20	24	28
Area	1	4	9	16	25	36	49

12.

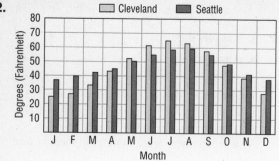

13. *Sample answer:* Cleveland: 49°, Seattle: 50°; by adding the highest and lowest average monthly temperatures and dividing by 2.

14. Answers vary.

15. C

16. a. Monday: 400; Tuesday: 700; Wednesday: 750; Thursday: 600; Friday: 500

   b. *Sample answer:* Monday because it is less crowded.

Lab 1.7

Part A

1. $\frac{1}{2}$ unit^2

2. 1 unit^2

3. $\frac{1}{2}$ unit^2; the shaded rectangle is 2 unit^2. The two blue triangles are the same size as triangles *B* and *C*. So, $2 - \frac{1}{2} - 1 = \frac{1}{2}$.

Part B

4. Answers vary.

5. Answers vary.

6. Answers vary.

7. The area of the large quadrilateral is 10 units^2. The area of the small figure is 5 units^2.

Part C

8. Answers vary.

9.

Drawing	I	II	III	IV
Area of large quadrilateral	20	30	40	50
Area of small quadrilateral	10	15	20	25

10. The area of the small quadrilateral is half that of the large quadrilateral.

11. 10; the small quadrilateral is half the large quadrilateral.

12. Answers vary.

13. Look at the table in exercise 14.

14.

Drawing	I	II	III	IV
Area of large triangle	2	8	18	32
Area of small triangle	0.5	2	4.5	8
Related	$\frac{1}{4}$	$\frac{1}{4}$	$\frac{1}{4}$	$\frac{1}{4}$

Answers vary.

15. 5; area of small triangle is $\frac{1}{4}$ as large as the large triangle.

1.7 GEOMETRY CONNECTION: Exploring Patterns in Geometry

ONGOING ASSESSMENT

1. Heptagon: $T = \dfrac{n(n-3)}{2}$

$\qquad = \dfrac{7(7-3)}{2}$

$\qquad = 14$

2.

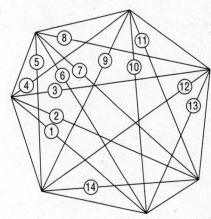

EXERCISES

1. *Sample answer:* a polygon is a figure formed by line segments that are connected at their ends so that they close in an area.

2. F: decagon; I: quadrilateral or rectangle; T: octagon; Y: nonagon

3. 2 diagonals

4. Answers vary.

5. Yes; quadrilateral

6. Not a polygon. The figure is not closed.

7. Yes; hexagon

8. Yes; pentagon

9. Not a polygon. All sides are not line segments.

10. Yes; heptagon

11. Yes; octagon

12. Yes; hexagon

13. Area of triangle = base × height ÷ 2

14. $A = b \cdot h \div 2$

15. $A = b \cdot h \div 2$
$= 16 \cdot 8 \div 2$
$= 128 \div 2$
$= 64 \text{ in.}^2$

16. No; its sides are not all straight.

17. Yes; octagon

18. Yes; quadrilateral

19. Yes; pentagon

20. Yes; quadrilateral

21. Yes; nonagon

22. No, because all sides are not segments.

23. Yes; pentagon

24. Yes; triangle

25. Yes; hexagon

26. 20;

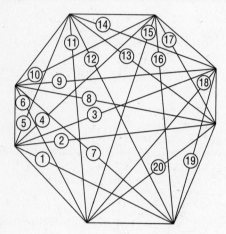

27.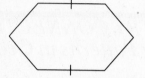

28.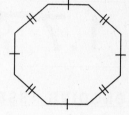

29. B

30. *Sample answer:*

a.

b. 4; quadrilateral

c.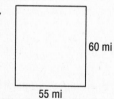
60 mi
55 mi

31. $55 \times 60 = 3300 \text{ mi}^2$

Spiral R E V I E W

1.
$$\begin{array}{r} 14.2 \\ \times\ \ \ 6 \\ \hline 85.2 \end{array}$$

2.
$$\begin{array}{r} 8.45 \\ \times\ \ \ 5 \\ \hline 42.25 \end{array}$$

3.
$$\begin{array}{r} 1.444 \approx 1.44 \\ 9\overline{)13.000} \\ \underline{9} \\ 40 \\ \underline{36} \\ 40 \\ \underline{36} \\ 40 \end{array}$$

4.
$$\begin{array}{r} 32.35 \\ 20\overline{)647.00} \\ \underline{60} \\ 47 \\ \underline{40} \\ 70 \\ \underline{60} \\ 100 \\ \underline{100} \\ 0 \end{array}$$

5. $7^5 = 16,807$

6. $\sqrt{155} \approx 12.4499$
≈ 12.45

7. a. 6×20
b. $6 \times 20 - 50; 70$

8. $2y = 2(5)$
$= 10$

9. $4z - x = 4(2) - 4$
$= 8 - 4$
$= 4$

10. $(x + y)^2 = (4 + 5)^2$
$= 9^2$
$= 81$

11. $5x(x - 4) = 5(4)(4 - 4)$
$= 5(4)(0)$
$= 0$

12. $x + y \times z = 4 + (5 \times 2)$
$= 4 + 10$
$= 14$

13. $2x \div z^2 = 2(4) \div 2^2$
$= 8 \div 4$
$= 2$

14. $(y - z)^2 - x = (5 - 2)^2 - 4$
$= 3^2 - 4$
$= 9 - 4$
$= 5$

15. $(y - x) \div z = (5 - 4) \div 2$
$= 1 \div 2$
$= \frac{1}{2}$

Communicating About Mathematics

1. $2,200,000 - 800,000 = 1,400,000$ acres
Subtract the number of acres burned from the total number of acres.

2. $370 + 1200 = 1570$
There are 1570 miles of trails and paved roads in Yellowstone National Park.

3. *Sample answer:* on a trail; there are more than three times as many miles of trails as roads.

4. No; In the last paragraph, the book states Yellowstone has about 10,000 geysers and hot springs, more than the rest of the world combined.

5. *Sample answer:* $2,200,000 - 1,300,000 = 900,000$;
Rhode Island has 900,000 acres.

1.8 Exploring Patterns with Technology

ONGOING ASSESSMENT

1. 7th triangular number:

$$T = \frac{n(n + 1)}{2} = \frac{7(7 + 1)}{2} = \frac{7 \cdot 8}{2} = 28$$

2.

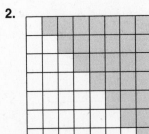

7-by-8

EXERCISES

1. 0; 1

2. $n = 1$: $\frac{1}{11} = 0.\overline{09}$

$n = 2$: $\frac{2}{11} = 0.\overline{18}$

$n = 3$: $\frac{3}{11} = 0.\overline{27}$

$n = 4$: $\frac{4}{11} = 0.\overline{36}$

$n = 5$: $\frac{5}{11} = 0.\overline{45}$

The decimal repeats a two-digit pattern. The sum of the two digits is 9. The repeating decimal is $0.09n$.

3.

$$\begin{array}{r} 192 \\ 1)\overline{192} \\ \underline{1} \\ 09 \\ \underline{9} \\ 02 \\ \underline{2} \\ 0 \end{array} \qquad \begin{array}{r} 96 \\ 2)\overline{192} \\ \underline{18} \\ 12 \\ \underline{12} \\ 0 \end{array} \qquad \begin{array}{r} 64 \\ 3)\overline{192} \\ \underline{18} \\ 12 \\ \underline{12} \\ 0 \end{array} \qquad \begin{array}{r} 48 \\ 4)\overline{192} \\ \underline{16} \\ 32 \\ \underline{32} \\ 0 \end{array}$$

n	1	2	3	4
$192 \div n$	192	96	64	48

4.

$$\begin{array}{r} 75 \\ \underline{\times 0} \\ 0 \end{array} \quad \begin{array}{r} 75 \\ \underline{\times 1} \\ 75 \end{array} \quad \begin{array}{r} 75 \\ \underline{\times 2} \\ 150 \end{array} \quad \begin{array}{r} 75 \\ \underline{\times 3} \\ 225 \end{array} \quad \begin{array}{r} 75 \\ \underline{\times 4} \\ 300 \end{array} \quad \begin{array}{r} 75 \\ \underline{\times 5} \\ 375 \end{array} \quad \begin{array}{r} 75 \\ \underline{\times 6} \\ 450 \end{array} \quad \begin{array}{r} 75 \\ \underline{\times 7} \\ 525 \end{array} \quad \begin{array}{r} 75 \\ \underline{\times 8} \\ 600 \end{array}$$

n	0	1	2	3	4	5	6	7	8
$75n$	0	75	150	225	300	375	450	525	600

5. $\frac{1}{3} = 0.\overline{3}$, $\quad \frac{2}{3} = 0.\overline{6}$, $\quad \frac{3}{3} = 1$, $\quad \frac{4}{3} = 1.\overline{3}$, $\quad \frac{5}{3} = 1.\overline{6}$, $\quad \frac{6}{3} = 2$, $\quad \frac{7}{3} = 2.\overline{3}$, $\quad \frac{8}{3} = 2.\overline{6}$ $\quad \frac{9}{3} = 3$

n	1	2	3	4	5	6	7	8	9
$\frac{n}{3}$	$0.\overline{3}$	$0.\overline{6}$	1	$1.\overline{3}$	$1.\overline{6}$	2	$2.\overline{3}$	$2.\overline{6}$	3

6. $\frac{0^2}{2} = 0$; $\frac{1^2}{2} = \frac{1}{2} = 0.5$; $\frac{2^2}{2} = \frac{4}{2} = 2$; $\frac{3^2}{2} = \frac{9}{2} = 4.5$; $\frac{4^2}{2} = \frac{16}{2} = 8$; $\frac{5^2}{2} = \frac{25}{2} = 12.5$; $\frac{6^2}{2} = \frac{36}{2} = 18$

n	0	1	2	3	4	5	6
$\frac{n^2}{2}$	0	0.5	2	4.5	8	12.5	18

7. $\frac{1}{1+1} = \frac{1}{2} = 0.5$; $\frac{2}{2+1} = \frac{2}{3} = 0.\overline{6}$; $\frac{3}{3+1} = \frac{3}{4} = 0.75$; $\frac{4}{4+1} = \frac{4}{5} = 0.8$; $\frac{5}{5+1} = \frac{5}{6} = 0.8\overline{3}$

n	1	2	3	4	5
$\frac{n}{n+1}$	0.5	$0.\overline{6}$	0.75	0.8	$0.8\overline{3}$

8. $\frac{2}{1} = 2$, $\frac{2}{2} = 1$, $\frac{2}{3} = 0.\overline{6}$, $\frac{2}{4} = 0.5$, $\frac{2}{5} = 0.4$, $\frac{2}{6} = 0.\overline{3}$

n	1	2	3	4	5	6
$\frac{2}{n}$	2	1	$0.\overline{6}$	0.5	0.4	$0.\overline{3}$

Repeating decimals are produced when n equals 3 and 6.

9. $8(2) + 2 = 16 + 2 = 18$
$8(23) + 3 = 184 + 3 = 187$
$8(234) + 4 = 1872 + 4 = 1876$
$8(2345) + 5 = 18,760 + 5 = 18,765$
$8(23,456) + 6 = 187,648 + 6 = 187,654$
$8(234,567) + 7 = 1,876,536 + 7 = 1,876,543$
$8(2,345,678) + 8 = 18,765,424 + 8 = 18,765,432$

Each number, after the first, is 10 times the preceding number plus 1 less than the units digit of the preceding number.

10. $\frac{5}{6} + 9\left(\frac{1}{3}\right) = \frac{5}{6} + 3 = 3.8\overline{3}$
$\frac{5}{6} + 9\left(\frac{2}{3}\right) = \frac{5}{6} + 6 = 6.8\overline{3}$
$\frac{5}{6} + 9\left(\frac{3}{3}\right) = \frac{5}{6} + 9 = 9.8\overline{3}$
$\frac{5}{6} + 9\left(\frac{4}{3}\right) = \frac{5}{6} + 12 = 12.8\overline{3}$
$\frac{5}{6} + 9\left(\frac{5}{3}\right) = \frac{5}{6} + 15 = 15.8\overline{3}$
$\frac{5}{6} + 9\left(\frac{6}{3}\right) = \frac{5}{6} + 18 = 18.8\overline{3}$
$\frac{5}{6} + 9\left(\frac{7}{3}\right) = \frac{5}{6} + 21 = 21.8\overline{3}$

Each number, after the first, is 3 more than the preceding number.

11. $77(1443) = 111,111$
$154(1443) = 222,222$
$231(1443) = 333,333$
$308(1443) = 444,444$
$385(1443) = 555,555$
$462(1443) = 666,666$
$539(1443) = 777,777$

Each number, after the first, is 111,111 more than the preceding number.

12. $T = n \times (n + 1) \div 2$
$= 8 \times (8 + 1) \div 2$
$= 8 \times 9 \div 2$
$= 72 \div 2$
$= 36$

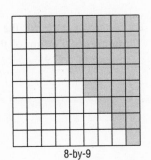

8-by-9

13. 45

14. 210

15.

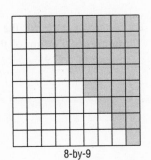

$4 \times 4 \times 4$

The cubic number is 64.

16. Verbal model: nth cubic number $=$ (edge length)^3
Algebraic model: $C = n^3$

17. C; $P = 10 + 10 + w + w$
$32 = 20 + w + w$
$w = 6$
$A = l \times w = 10 \times 6 = 60 \text{ m}^2$

18.
$1 + 1 = 2$
$1 + 2 = 3$
$2 + 3 = 5$
$3 + 5 = 8$
$5 + 8 = 13$

Pattern: Each number, except the first two, is the sum of the two preceding numbers.

19.
$8 + 13 = 21$
$13 + 21 = 34$
$21 + 34 = 55$
$55 + 34 = 89$
Solution: 21, 34, 55, 89

20. Answers vary. The ratios get closer and closer to 1.61803 . . . .

Chapter **REVIEW**

1. Pattern: Multiply the preceding number by 2.
Solution: 32, 64

2. Pattern: Subtract 7 from the preceding number.
Solution: 22, 15

3. Pattern: Divide the preceding number by 2.
Solution: 12, 6

4. Pattern: Add 4, add 5, add 6, and so on, to preceding number.
Solution: 23, 31

5. Pattern: Subtract 15, 14, 13, and so on, from preceding number.
Solution: 51, 40

6. Pattern: Except for the first two numbers, each number is the sum of the preceding numbers.
Solution: 59, 95

7.
$$\begin{array}{r} 105 \\ +\ \ 8 \\ \hline 113 \end{array}$$

8.
$$\begin{array}{r} 46 \\ -\ 19 \\ \hline 27 \end{array}$$

9.
$$\begin{array}{r} 125 \\ -\ 42 \\ \hline 83 \end{array}$$

10.
$$\begin{array}{r} 359 \\ 154 \\ +\ \ 12 \\ \hline 525 \end{array}$$

11.
$$\begin{array}{r} 50 \\ \times\ \ 6 \\ \hline 300 \end{array}$$

12.
$$\begin{array}{r} 17 \\ 9\overline{)153} \\ 9 \\ \hline 63 \\ 63 \\ \hline 0 \end{array}$$

13.
$$\begin{array}{r} 16 \\ \times\ \ 4 \\ \hline 64 \end{array}$$

14.
$$\begin{array}{r} 13 \\ 5\overline{)65} \\ 5 \\ \hline 15 \\ 15 \\ \hline 0 \end{array}$$

15. $2^9 = 512$

16. $9^5 = 59{,}049$

17. $7^3 = 343$

18. $(2.4)^2 = 5.76$

19. $\sqrt{421} \approx 20.52$

20. $\sqrt{729} = 27$

21. $\sqrt{2088.49} = 45.7$

22. $\sqrt{500} = 22.36$

23. $4 + 3 \times 3 = 4 + 9 = 13$

24. $15 - 6 \times 4 \div 8 = 15 - 24 \div 8$
$= 15 - 3$
$= 12$

25. $12 \div 3 \cdot 2 + 1 = 4 \cdot 2 + 1$
$= 8 + 1$
$= 9$

26. $50 - 20 \times 2 - 1 = 50 - 40 - 1$
$= 10 - 1$
$= 9$

27. $2 + (9 - 6) \div 3 = 2 + 3 \div 3$
$= 2 + 1$
$= 3$

28. $12 \cdot 3 - (2 + 5) = 12 \cdot 3 - 7$
$= 36 - 7$
$= 29$

29. $(16 + 2^2) \div 4 = (16 + 4) \div 4$
$= 20 \div 4$
$= 5$

30. $2[20 - (10 + 4)] = 2[20 - 14]$
$= 2[6]$
$= 12$

31. $(8 - 3)^2 = 5^2 = 25$

32. $3 - 2(5) + 2 = 3 - 10 + 2$
$= -7 + 2$
$= -5$

33. $d = rt = (55)(3) = 165$ mi

34. Arizona, Maryland, Washington

35. Maryland

36. Washington

37. No; the figure is not closed.

38. Not a polygon, because all the sides are not segments.

39. Yes; pentagon

40. Yes; triangle

41.

```
 105    105    105    105    105    105    105    105    105
 × 1    × 2    × 3    × 4    × 5    × 6    × 7    × 8    × 9
 ────   ────   ────   ────   ────   ────   ────   ────   ────
 105    210    315    420    525    630    735    840    945
```

Pattern: Add 105 to the previous number.

n	1	2	3	4	5	6	7	8	9
$105n$	105	210	315	420	525	630	735	840	945

Chapter ASSESSMENT

1. $a \cdot c = 8 \cdot 5 = 40$

2. $b^2 = 3^2 = 9$

3. $\dfrac{a}{4} = \dfrac{8}{4} = 2$

4. $3c^3 = 3(5^3)$
$= 3(125)$
$= 375$

5. $4(a + 1)^2 = 4(8 + 1)^2$
$= 4(9)^2$
$= 4(81)$
$= 324$

6. $\sqrt{(a + 1)} = \sqrt{(8 + 1)}$
$= \sqrt{9}$
$= 3$

7. Pattern: Each number is 2 less than the previous number.
Solution: 7, 5, 3

8. Pattern: Multiply the preceding number by 2.
Solution: 48, 96, 192

9. Pattern: Each number is a perfect square.
$3^2 = 9 \qquad 7^2 = 49$
$4^2 = 16 \qquad 8^2 = 64$
$5^2 = 25 \qquad 9^2 = 81$
$6^2 = 36$
Solution: 49, 64, 81

10. $3 + 5 \cdot 2 + 4 = 3 + 10 + 4 = 17$

11. $10 - 4 + 5 \div 4 = 10 - 4 + 1.25$
$= 7.25$

12.
$$(6+2) \cdot 2 + 3^2 = 8 \cdot 2 + 9$$
$$= 16 + 9$$
$$= 25$$

13.
$$14 \div (9-2) + 2^3 = 14 \div 7 + 8$$
$$= 2 + 8$$
$$= 10$$

14.

n	0	1	2	3	4	5	6	7	8
$21n$	0	21	42	63	84	105	126	147	168

Pattern: The tens' digit increases by two each time, while the units' digit increases by one. The tens' digit (sometimes the hundreds' digit and tens' digit) is found by multiplying the whole number by 2, while the units' digit is the whole number itself.

15. Yes; pentagon

16. Yes; hexagon

17. No, all sides are not segments.

18. 52

19. Atlanta Hawks and Detroit Pistons

20. Bulls: $72 - 10 = 62$
Pacers: $52 - 30 = 22$
Cavaliers: $47 - 35 = 12$
Hawks: $46 - 36 = 10$
Pistons: $46 - 36 = 10$
The Chicago Bulls had the greatest difference between wins and losses.

21.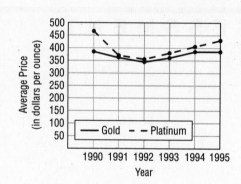

Standardized Test Practice

1. C

2. B;
$$10 - 2^3 \div 2 = 10 - 8 \div 2$$
$$= 10 - 4$$
$$= 6$$

3. B

4. C

5. D; $5(98765) = 493,825$

6. B; $\sqrt{8100} = 90$

7. D; $15^2 = 225$

8. B

9. A

10. B;
$$6^2 - 2(6) = 36 - 12$$
$$= 24$$

Chapter 2
Investigations in Algebra

Lab 2.1

Part A

1. **a.** $4x + 3$
   b. $3x + 7$
   c. $x + 7$

2. (figure: tiles) 8

3. (figure: tiles) $2x$

4. (figure: tiles) $3x + 9$

5. (figure: tiles) $2x + 5$

6. (figure: tiles) $x + 3$

7. (figure: tiles) $4x + 7$

8. No; the tiles model $4x + 10$.

Part B

9. A, F; $2(2x + 1) = 4x + 2$

10. D, G; $2(3x + 1) = 6x + 2$

11. C, H; $4(x + 1) = 4x + 4$

12. B, E; $3(2x + 3) = 6x + 9$

13. $n(ax + b) = (nax + nb)$

14. (figure: tiles)

15. (figure: tiles)

16. $3x + 12$
    (figure: tiles)

17. $6x + 10$
    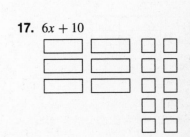

18. $2(x + 3)$

19. $3(x + 1)$

2.1 The Distributive Property

ONGOING ASSESSMENT

1. $4(3x + 1) = 12x + 4$

2. $4(3x + 1) = 4(3 \cdot 5 + 1) = 64;$
$4(3x + 1) = 12x + 4 = 12 \cdot 5 + 4 = 64$
Both expressions yield the same solution.

3. *Sample answer:* $12x + 4$; it's easier to not have to deal with the parentheses.

EXERCISES

1. Value of x for last column varies.

	$x = 0$	$x = 1$	$x = 3$	$x = 10$	$x = 15$
$2(x + 2)$	$2(0 + 2) = 4$	$2(1 + 2) = 6$	$2(3 + 2) = 10$	$2(10 + 2) = 24$	$2(15 + 2) = 34$
$2x + 4$	$2(0) + 4 = 4$	$2(1) + 4 = 6$	$2(3) + 4 = 10$	$2(10) + 4 = 24$	$2(15) + 4 = 34$

The two expressions are equivalent because numerical expressions result in the same answer.

2. **A.** Incorrect. $2(3 + 5) = 2(3) + 2(5)$
B. Correct.
C. Correct.
D. Incorrect. $2(a + 6) = 2a + 2(6)$

3. **a.** True; $3(5x) = 3 \cdot 5 \cdot x = 15x$
b. False; $4(9x) = 4 \cdot 9 \cdot x = 36x$
c. False; $2(5 + 6) = 2(11) = 22$

4. Dimensions: 2 by $x + 4$
Area $= 2(x + 4) = 2x + 2(4) = 2x + 8$

5. Dimensions: 2 by $3x + 2$
Area $= 2(3x + 2) = 2 \cdot 3 \cdot x + 2(2) = 6x + 4$

6. $4(x + 2) = 4(x) + 4(2)$
$\qquad = 4x + 8$

7. $2(x + 1) = 2(x) + 2(1)$
$\qquad = 2x + 2$

8. $2(5x + 3) = 2 \cdot 5 \cdot x + 2(3)$

$\quad\quad = 10x + 6$

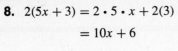

9. $5(2x + 3) = 5 \cdot 2 \cdot x + 5(3)$

$\quad\quad = 10x + 15$

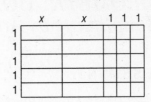

10. $9(8 + 7) = 9(8) + 9(7)$

$\quad\quad = 72 + 63$

$\quad\quad = 99$

11. $11(10 + 5) = 11(10) + 11(5)$

$\quad\quad = 110 + 55$

$\quad\quad = 165$

12. $4(x + 9) = 4(x) + 4(9)$

$\quad\quad = 4x + 36$

13. $16(z + 3) = 16(z) + 16(3)$

$\quad\quad = 16z + 48$

14. $5(y + 20) = 5(y) + 5(20)$

$\quad\quad = 5y + 100$

15. $8(4 + q) = 8(4) + 8(q)$

$\quad\quad = 32 + 8q$

16. $0(x + 12) = 0(x) + 0(12)$

$\quad\quad = 0 + 0$

$\quad\quad = 0$

17. $a(b + 4) = a(b) + a(4)$

$\quad\quad = ab + 4a$

18. $r(s + t) = r(s) + r(t)$

$\quad\quad = rs + rt$

19. $4(6 + 10 + 12) = 4(6) + 4(10) + 4(12)$

$\quad\quad = 24 + 40 + 48$

$\quad\quad = 112$

20. $3(5 + 8 + 9) = 3(5) + 3(8) + 3(9)$

$\quad\quad = 15 + 24 + 27$

$\quad\quad = 66$

21. $12(s + t + w) = 12(s) + 12(t) + 12(w)$

$\quad\quad = 12s + 12t + 12w$

22. $3(1.21 + 5.48) = 3(1.21) + 3(5.48)$

$\quad\quad = 3.63 + 16.44$

$\quad\quad = 20.07$

$3(1.21 + 5.48) = 3(6.69) = 20.07$

23. $10(6.81 + 9.06) = 10(6.81) + 10(9.06)$

$\quad\quad = 68.1 + 90.6$

$\quad\quad = 158.7$

$10(6.81 + 9.06) = 10(15.87) = 158.7$

24. $525(11.19 + 27.60) = 525(11.19) + 525(27.60)$

$\quad\quad = 5874.75 + 14,490$

$\quad\quad = 20,364.75$

$525(11.19 + 27.60) = 525(38.79) = 20,364.75$

25. Dimensions: 3 by $x + 6$

Area $= 3(x + 6)$

26. $3(x + 6) = 3(x) + 3(6) = 3x + 18$

27. a. $\boxed{\text{Total yearly pay}} = \boxed{12} \left(\boxed{\begin{array}{c}\text{Employee 1's}\\\text{monthly salary}\end{array}} + \boxed{\begin{array}{c}\text{Employee 2's}\\\text{monthly salary}\end{array}} + \boxed{\begin{array}{c}\text{Employee 3's}\\\text{monthly salary}\end{array}} \right)$

b. $12(1800 + 1500 + 1300) = 12(1800) + 12(1500) + 12(1300)$

$\quad\quad = 21,600 + 18,000 + 15,600$

$\quad\quad = 55,200$

You pay your employees a total of $55,200 per year.

28. D

29. a. Answers vary.

b. Answers vary.

2.2 GEOMETRY CONNECTION:
Simplifying by Adding Like Terms

ONGOING ASSESSMENT

1. Perimeter: $3x + x + 2 + 5x + x + 2 = 10x + 4$

$x = 1$: $10x + 4 = 10(1) + 4 = 14$

$x = 2$: $10x + 4 = 10(2) + 4 = 24$

$x = 3$: $10x + 4 = 10(3) + 4 = 34$

$x = 4$: $10x + 4 = 10(4) + 4 = 44$

$x = 5$: $10x + 4 = 10(5) + 4 = 54$

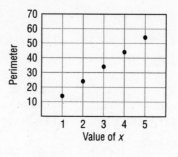

x	1	2	3	4	5
Perimeter, $10x + 4$	14	24	34	44	54

2. Perimeter increases by 10.

EXERCISES

1. Two or more terms in an expression that have the same variables, raised to the same powers; *sample answer:* $5x$ and $2x$

2. *Sample answer:* $2x + 3x = 5x$

x	x	

$+$

x	x	x

$=$

x	x	x	x	x

3. *Sample answer:* Two numbers can be added in any order.

4. When simplifying or evaluating an expression

5. Yes; $3x$ and x are like terms, so they can be added.
$3x + x = 4x$

6. No; not like terms

7. No; not like terms

8. Yes; 5 and 2(8) are like terms, so they can be added.

$5 + 2(x + 8) = 5 + 2(x) + 2(8)$
$= 5 + 2x + 16$
$= 2x + 21$

9. $2a + a = 2a + 1a$
$= (2 + 1)a$
$= 3a$

10. $5b + 7b + 10 = (5 + 7)b + 10$
$= 12b + 10$

11. $3x + 6x + 9 = (3 + 6)x + 9$
$= 9x + 9$

12. $3a + 2b + 5a = 3a + 5a + 2b$
$= (3 + 5)a + 2b$
$= 8a + 2b$

13. $6x + x + 2y = 6x + 1x + 2y$
$$= (6 + 1)x + 2y$$
$$= 7x + 2y$$

14. $5 + r + 2s + 13r = 5 + 1r + 13r + 2s$
$$= 5 + (1 + 13)r + 2s$$
$$= 5 + 14r + 2s$$

15. $p + 9q + 9 + 14p = 1p + 14p + 9q + 9$
$$= (1 + 14)p + 9q + 9$$
$$= 15p + 9q + 9$$

16. $2x + 4y + 3z + 17z = 2x + 4y + (3 + 17)z$
$$= 2x + 4y + 20z$$

17. $a + 2b + 2a + b + 2c = 1a + 2a + 2b + 1b + 2c$
$$= (1 + 2)a + (2 + 1)b + 2c$$
$$= 3a + 3b + 2c$$

18. $b + b^2 + 2b = 1b + 2b + b^2$
$$= (1 + 2)b + b^2$$
$$= 3b + b^2$$

19. $x^2 + x^2 = 1x^2 + 1x^2$
$$= (1 + 1)x^2$$
$$= 2x^2$$

20. $3(x + 3) + 4x = 3x + 3(3) + 4x$
$$= 3x + 9 + 4x$$
$$= 3x + 4x + 9$$
$$= (3 + 4)x + 9$$
$$= 7x + 9$$

21. $8(y + 2) + y + 4 = 8y + 8(2) + 1y + 4$
$$= 8y + 16 + 1y + 4$$
$$= 8y + 1y + 16 + 4$$
$$= (8 + 1)y + 16 + 4$$
$$= 9y + 20$$

22. $3(a + b) + 3(b + a) = 3(a + b) + 3(a + b)$
$$= (3 + 3)(a + b)$$
$$= 6(a + b)$$
$$= 6a + 6b$$

23. $5(x + y) + 2(y + x) = 5(x + y) + 2(x + y)$
$$= (5 + 2)(x + y)$$
$$= 7(x + y)$$
$$= 7x + 7y$$

24. *Sample answer:* $8x + 2x + 5 + 6x$

25. Add like terms first: $2x + 5x = 7x; 7x + 3$

26. $2x + 3x + y = 5x + y$
$$5x + y = 5(2) + (5)$$
$$= 10 + 5$$
$$= 15$$

27. $y + 4y + 8x = 5y + 8x$
$$5y + 8x = 5(5) + 8(2)$$
$$= 25 + 16$$
$$= 41$$

28. $4(x + y) + x = 4x + 4y + x$
$$= 5x + 4y$$
$$5x + 4y = 5(2) + 4(5)$$
$$= 10 + 20$$
$$= 30$$

29. $3y + 2x + 6y = 9y + 2x$

$\qquad 9y + 2x = 9(5) + 2(2)$

$\qquad\qquad\quad = 45 + 4$

$\qquad\qquad\quad = 49$

30. $5x + 2(2x + y) = 5x + 4x + 2y$

$\qquad\qquad\qquad\quad = 9x + 2y$

$\qquad 9x + 2y = 9(2) + 2(5)$

$\qquad\qquad\quad = 18 + 10$

$\qquad\qquad\quad = 28$

31. $6x + 6y + 6x = 12x + 6y$

$\qquad 12x + 6y = 12(2) + 6(5)$

$\qquad\qquad\quad = 24 + 30$

$\qquad\qquad\quad = 54$

32. $(x + y)4 + 7x = 4x + 4y + 7x$

$\qquad\qquad\qquad = 11x + 4y$

$\qquad 11x + 4y = 11(2) + 4(5)$

$\qquad\qquad\quad = 22 + 20$

$\qquad\qquad\quad = 42$

33. $xy + x^2 + xy = x^2 + 2xy$

$\qquad x^2 + 2xy = (2)^2 + 2(2)(5)$

$\qquad\qquad\quad = 4 + 20$

$\qquad\qquad\quad = 24$

34. $6xy + x^2 + x^2 = 2x^2 + 6xy$

$\qquad 2x^2 + 6xy = 2(2^2) + 6(2)(5)$

$\qquad\qquad\quad = 2(4) + 6(10)$

$\qquad\qquad\quad = 8 + 60$

$\qquad\qquad\quad = 68$

35. 1st perimeter: $x + (x + 3) + 2x + (x + 1) = 5x + 4$

2nd perimeter: $(2x + 2) + x + 1 + (3x + 2) = 6x + 5$

The expressions are not equivalent.

If the expressions were equivalent, then the perimeters would be the same for all values of x. But there are no such values.

36. 1st perimeter: $x + (x + 3) + x + (x + 2) + (x + 2) = 5x + 7$

2nd perimeter: $(x + 2) + (2x + 1) + (x + 1) + (x + 1) = 5x + 5$

The expressions are not equivalent.

If the expressions were equivalent, then the perimeters would be the same for all values of x. But there are no such values.

37. Perimeter: $6x + 3x + 6x + 3x = 18x$

$x = 1$: $18x = 18(1) = 18$

$x = 2$: $18x = 18(2) = 36$

$x = 3$: $18x = 18(3) = 54$

$x = 4$: $18x = 18(4) = 72$

$x = 5$: $18x = 18(5) = 90$

x	1	2	3	4	5
Perimeter, $18x$	18	36	54	72	90

Perimeter increases by 18 as x increases by 1.

38. Perimeter: $2x + x + x + 2x + x + x = 8x$

$x = 1$: $8x = 8(1) = 8$

$x = 2$: $8x = 8(2) = 16$

$x = 3$: $8x = 8(3) = 24$

$x = 4$: $8x = 8(4) = 32$

$x = 5$: $8x = 8(5) = 40$

x	1	2	3	4	5
Perimeter, $8x$	8	16	24	32	40

Perimeter increases by 8 as x increases by 1.

39. $\dfrac{5\text{ h}}{\text{day}} \times 4$ days

40. C; $6(x) + 2(x) + x + 1 = 9x + 1$

41. B; $x(6 + 1 + 2 + 4 + 3) = 16x$

42. **a.** $x(3 \times 3 + 9) = 18x$
b. $18(\$3.25) = \$58.50$

2.3 ALGEBRA CONNECTION: Solving Equations

ONGOING ASSESSMENT

1. What number can be added to 655 to get 690?;
$x = 35$

2. $290 + x = 90$
$x = 400$
The increase in sales was $400 million.

EXERCISES

1. *Sample answer:*
$4(x + 2) = 4x + 8$

2. *Sample answer:*
$x + 1 = 3$

3. Substitute the number into the original equation, simplify, and see if you get an identity.

4. B;
$$5x + 7 = 22$$
$$5(3) + 7 \overset{?}{=} 22$$
$$15 + 7 \overset{?}{=} 22$$
$$22 = 22$$

5. C;
$$10 - 2y = 2$$
$$10 - 2(4) \overset{?}{=} 2$$
$$10 - 8 \overset{?}{=} 2$$
$$2 = 2$$

6. D;
$$n^2 - 4 = 21$$
$$(5)^2 - 4 \overset{?}{=} 21$$
$$25 - 4 \overset{?}{=} 21$$
$$21 = 21$$

7. A;
$$\dfrac{20}{x^2} = 5$$
$$\dfrac{20}{2^2} \overset{?}{=} 5$$
$$\dfrac{20}{4} \overset{?}{=} 5$$
$$5 = 5$$

8. What number can be added to 8 to obtain 14?
$z = 6$

9. What number can be multiplied by 7 to obtain 42?
$x = 6$

10. What number can 18 be subtracted from to obtain 16? $y = 34$

11. What number can 9 be divided by to obtain 3?
$x = 3$

12. $33 - x = 24$; 9

13. $7 + x = 19$; 12

14. $8x = 56$; 7

15. $\dfrac{x}{9} = 5$; 45

16.
$$5r = 20$$
$$5(4) \overset{?}{=} 20$$
$$20 = 20$$
Yes, $r = 4$ is a solution.

17.
$$19 - r = 15$$
$$19 - 4 \overset{?}{=} 15$$
$$15 = 15$$
Yes, $r = 4$ is a solution.

18.
$$24 = 8r$$
$$24 \overset{?}{=} 8(4)$$
$$24 \neq 32$$
No, $r = 4$ is not a solution.
$r = 3$ is a solution.

19. $3r + r = 16$

$3(4) + 4 \stackrel{?}{=} 16$

$12 + 4 \stackrel{?}{=} 16$

$16 = 16$

Yes, $r = 4$ is a solution.

20. a. $x - 15 = 8$

$x = 23$

b. $15 - x = 8$

$x = 7$

$23 \neq 7$, so they do not have the same solution.

21. a. $x + 4 = 17$

$x = 13$

b. $4 + x = 17$

$x = 13$

$13 = 13$, so they have the same solution.

22. a. $3x = 12$

$x = 4$

b. $\dfrac{x}{12} = 3$

$x = 36$

$4 \neq 36$, so they do not have the same solution.

23. a. $x \div 3 = 6$

$x = 18$

b. $3 \div x = 6$

$\dfrac{1}{2} = x$

$18 \neq \frac{1}{2}$, so they do not have the same solution.

24. $r = 3$

Check: $r + 11 = 14$

$3 + 11 \stackrel{?}{=} 14$

$14 = 14$

25. $n = 21$

Check: $20 + n = 41$

$20 + 21 \stackrel{?}{=} 41$

$41 = 41$

26. $x = 15$

Check: $x - 13 = 2$

$15 - 13 \stackrel{?}{=} 2$

$2 = 2$

27. $y = 5$

Check: $81 - y = 76$

$81 - 5 \stackrel{?}{=} 76$

$76 = 76$

28. $x = 5$

Check: $11x = 55$

$11(5) \stackrel{?}{=} 55$

$55 = 55$

29. $m = 7$

Check: $21 = 3m$

$21 \stackrel{?}{=} 3(7)$

$21 = 21$

30. $x = 36$

Check: $\dfrac{x}{4} = 9$

$\dfrac{36}{4} \stackrel{?}{=} 9$

$9 = 9$

31. $y = 13$

Check: $\dfrac{26}{y} = 2$

$\dfrac{26}{13} \stackrel{?}{=} 2$

$2 = 2$

32. Identity. True for all values of x.

33. Conditional equation. True only for $x = 10$.

34. Conditional equation. True only for $x = 9$.

35. $209.5 + 780.5 = x$

$x = 990$

The 1994 winner weighed 990 pounds.

36. $990 - 106 = x$

$x = 884$

The 1993 winner weighed 884 pounds.

37. $x + 22 = 990$

$x = 968$

The 1995 winner weighed 968 pounds.

38. B;

2: $2x + 2 + 2x + 2 + 2 + 2 + 2 + 2 = 4x + 12$

4: $2x + 3 + 2x + 3 + 2 + 1 + 2 + 1 = 4x + 12$

39.

$$\boxed{\text{Hours worked}} \times \boxed{\text{Pay per hour}} = \boxed{\text{Money earned}}$$

$4x = 12$

$x = 3$

You earned \$3 per hour.

40. $\boxed{\begin{array}{c}\text{Hours}\\\text{worked}\end{array}} \times \boxed{\begin{array}{c}\text{Pay per}\\\text{hour}\end{array}} = \boxed{\begin{array}{c}\text{Money}\\\text{earned}\end{array}}$

$3x = 12$

$x = 4$

You earned \$4 per hour.

41. Answers vary.

42. Answers vary.

Lab 2.4

Part A

1. Remove 5 from both sides. You should use this step.

2. Remove x from one side and 3 from the other side. You should not use this step because you need to subtract the same number from both sides.

3. You should remove all of the single tiles from the side of the equation containing the x-tile. Then remove the same amount from the other side of the equation.

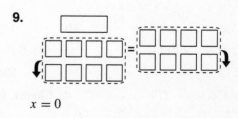

Part B

4. $x + 5 = 11$

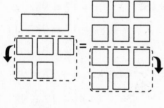

$x = 6$

$6 + 5 \overset{?}{=} 11 \checkmark$

5. $x + 2 = 7$

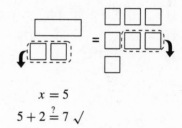

$x = 5$

$5 + 2 \overset{?}{=} 7 \checkmark$

6.

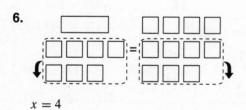

$x = 4$

7.

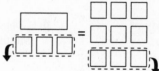

$x = 7$

8.

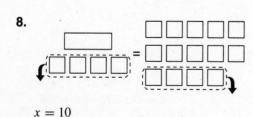

$x = 10$

9.

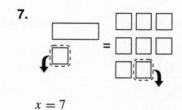

$x = 0$

10. *Sample answer:* $x + 2 = 12$, $x + 5 = 15$

11. *Sample answer:* $x + 5 = 10$, $x + 1 = 6$

12. There is an infinite number of equations.

2.4 Solving Equations: Add or Subtract

ONGOING ASSESSMENT

1. Answers vary.

EXERCISES

1. *Sample answer:* $x = 4$, so $x + 3 = 4 + 3$ and $x + 3 = 7$.

2. $x = 3$, so $x + 5 = 3 + 5$ and $x + 5 = 8$.

3. Subtract 24 from both sides.

4. Add 16 to both sides.

5. Subtract 72 from both sides.

6. Add 68 to both sides.

7. Associative Property of Multiplication

8. Commutative Property of Multiplication

9. Commutative Property of Addition

10. Associative Property of Addition

11.
$$x - 34 = 52$$
$$x - 34 + 34 = 52 + 34$$
$$x = 86$$

12.
$$76 = y - 29$$
$$76 + 29 = y - 29 + 29$$
$$105 = y$$

13.
$$r + 62 = 111$$
$$r + 62 - 62 = 111 - 62$$
$$r = 49$$

14.
$$279 = t + 194$$
$$279 - 194 = t + 194 - 194$$
$$85 = t$$

15.
$$n + 17 = 98$$
$$n + 17 - 17 = 98 - 17$$
$$n = 81$$
Check: $n + 17 = 98$
$$81 + 17 \overset{?}{=} 98$$
$$98 = 98$$

16.
$$m + 39 = 81$$
$$m + 39 - 39 = 81 - 39$$
$$m = 42$$
Check: $m + 39 = 81$
$$42 + 39 \overset{?}{=} 81$$
$$81 = 81$$

17.
$$x - 61 = 78$$
$$x - 61 + 61 = 78 + 61$$
$$x = 139$$
Check: $x - 61 = 78$
$$139 - 61 \overset{?}{=} 78$$
$$78 = 78$$

18.
$$z - 129 = 200$$
$$z - 129 + 129 = 200 + 129$$
$$z = 329$$
Check: $z - 129 = 200$
$$329 - 129 \overset{?}{=} 200$$
$$200 = 200$$

19.
$$356 = y - 219$$
$$356 + 219 = y - 219 + 219$$
$$575 = y$$
Check: $356 = y - 219$
$$356 \overset{?}{=} 575 - 219$$
$$356 = 356$$

20.
$$445 = t - 193$$
$$445 + 193 = t - 193 + 193$$
$$638 = t$$
Check: $445 = t - 193$
$$445 \overset{?}{=} 638 - 193$$
$$445 = 445$$

21.
$$736 = x + 598$$
$$736 - 598 = x + 598 - 598$$
$$138 = x$$
Check: $736 = x + 598$
$$736 \overset{?}{=} 138 + 598$$
$$736 = 736$$

22.
$$907 = s + 316$$
$$907 - 316 = s + 316 - 316$$
$$591 = s$$
Check: $907 = s + 316$
$$907 \stackrel{?}{=} 591 + 316$$
$$907 = 907$$

23.
$$n + 1.7 = 3.9$$
$$n + 1.7 - 1.7 = 3.9 - 1.7$$
$$n = 2.2$$
Check: $n + 1.7 = 3.9$
$$2.2 + 1.7 \stackrel{?}{=} 3.9$$
$$3.9 = 3.9$$

24.
$$11.31 = 5.31 + y$$
$$11.31 - 5.31 = 5.31 + y - 5.31$$
$$6 = y$$
Check: $11.31 = 5.31 + y$
$$11.31 \stackrel{?}{=} 5.31 + 6$$
$$11.31 = 11.31$$

25.
$$7.49 = m - 5.86$$
$$7.49 + 5.86 = m - 5.86 + 5.86$$
$$13.35 = m$$
Check: $7.49 = m - 5.86$
$$7.49 \stackrel{?}{=} 13.35 - 5.86$$
$$7.49 = 7.49$$

26.
$$q - 12.42 = 9$$
$$q - 12.42 + 12.42 = 9 + 12.42$$
$$q = 21.42$$
Check: $q - 12.42 = 9$
$$21.42 - 12.42 \stackrel{?}{=} 9$$
$$9 = 9$$

27. Added 193 to both sides.

28. Subtracted 598 from both sides.

29. $598.07 \boxed{-} 217.46 \boxed{=} 380.61$

30. $952.7 \boxed{-} 420.38 \boxed{=} 532.32$

31. $1.397 \boxed{+} 1.973 \boxed{=} 3.370$

32. $13.01 \boxed{+} 4.85 \boxed{=} 17.86$

33. $9785 \boxed{-} 1024 \boxed{=} 8761$

34. $5826 \boxed{+} 2290 \boxed{=} 8116$

35.
$$x + 49 = 165$$
$$x + 49 - 49 = 165 - 49$$
$$x = 116$$

36.
$$r + 2.4 = 7.2$$
$$r + 2.4 - 2.4 = 7.2 - 2.4$$
$$r = 4.8$$

37.
$$y - 5.8 = 12.2$$
$$y - 5.8 + 5.8 = 12.2 + 5.8$$
$$y = 18$$

38.
$$n - 40 = 38$$
$$n - 40 + 40 = 38 + 40$$
$$n = 78$$

39.
$$189 = n + 137$$
$$189 - 137 = n + 137 - 137$$
$$52 = n$$

40.
$$317 = n - 723$$
$$317 + 723 = n - 723 + 723$$
$$1040 = n$$

41.
$$8200 + x = 11{,}250$$
$$8200 + x - 8200 = 11{,}250 - 8200$$
$$3050 = x$$
The summit is 3050 feet higher than the base.

42. $x = 8200 + 1530$
$x = 9730$
The beginner slope starts at 9730 feet.

43. $y - 89.99 = 5.63$
$y - 89.99 + 89.99 = 5.63 + 89.99$
$y = 95.62$
You had $95.62 before buying the skis.

44. B

45. B; $x + 18 = 56$
$x + 18 - 18 = 56 - 18$
$x = 38$

46. Answers vary.

Mid-Chapter **A S S E S S M E N T**

1. $5(x + 3) = 5(x) + 5(3)$
$= 5x + 15$

2. $2(a + 2b + 4) = 2(a) + 2(2b) + 2(4)$
$= 2a + 4b + 8$

3. Perimeter: $2x + 2y = 2(x + y)$
A   G

4. Perimeter: $23(x + 1) = 6x + 2$
B   F

5. Distributive Property
$6(2.50 + 1.20) = 6(3.70)$
$= 22.20$
$6(2.50) + 6(1.20) = 15.00 + 7.20$
$= 22.20$
Total cost is $22.20.

6. $2a + 10a = (2 + 10)a$
$= 12a$

7. $2x + 8 + x = 2x + 1x + 8$
$= (2 + 1)x + 8$
$= 3x + 8$

8. $7(x + 3) + 2x = 7x + 21 + 2x$
$= 7x + 2x + 21$
$= (7 + 2)x + 21$
$= 9x + 21$

9. $2(3x + 4) + x = 6x + 8 + x$
$= 7x + 8$
$7x + 8 = 7(4) + 8$
$= 28 + 8$
$= 36$

10. $3(2x + 1) + 3x = 6x + 3 + 3x$ (A)
$= 9x + 3$ (C)

11. Perimeter $= 2(x + 2 + 3) = 2(x + 5) = 2x + 10$
Area $= 3(x + 2) = 3x + 6$

12. $3x = 39$
$x = 13$

13. $\frac{n}{4} = 20$
$n = 80$

14. $\frac{1}{2}x = 7$
$x = 14$

15. $x + 13 = 28$
$x + 13 - 13 = 28 - 13$
$x = 15$

16.
$$19 = m - 4$$
$$19 + 4 = m - 4 + 4$$
$$23 = m$$

17.
$$2 + 7 = x$$
$$x = 9$$
9 million people run.

18.
$$6 + x = 17$$
$$x = 11$$
11 million people lift weights.

Lab 2.5

1. Remove 2 groups from both sides. You should not use this step because the groups were not equal. You should remove 2 sets of 3 tiles from the right.

2. Remove a group from both sides. You should not use this step because the groups are not equal. You should remove 4 from the right.

3.
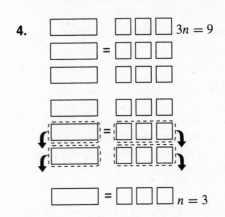

$$2x = 4$$
$$x = 2$$

4.
$$3n = 9$$
$$n = 3$$

5.
$$4y = 12$$

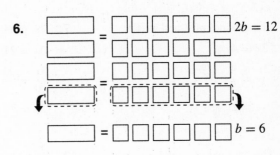

$$y = 3$$

6.
$$2b = 12$$
$$b = 6$$

7. Divide your equation into equal groups so each side of the equation has the same number of groups. Then remove the same number of groups from both sides, leaving one group on each side.

Exercise 1:

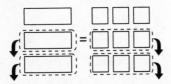

Exercise 2:

2.5 Solving Equations: Multiply or Divide

ONGOING ASSESSMENT

Sample answers:

a. You are driving a truck at 50 mi/h for 3 hours. How far will you get? $50 \times 3 = 150$ mi

b. You are buying 4 lbs of meat at \$2.50 per lb. How much will you spend? $4 \times 2.50 = \$10$

c. Your car gets 28 mi/gal. How far can the car go on 10 gal? $28 \times 10 = 280$ mi

EXERCISES

1. Multiplying both sides of an equation by the same nonzero number or dividing both sides of an equation by the same nonzero number produces an equivalent equation.

2. *Sample answers:* If $\dfrac{n}{3} = 6$, then $3 \cdot \dfrac{n}{3} = 3 \cdot 6$ and $n = 18$. If $3n = 6$, then $\dfrac{3n}{3} = \dfrac{6}{3}$ and $n = 2$.

3. Divide by 6 $\left(\text{or multiply by } \tfrac{1}{6}\right)$.

4. Multiply by 3.

5. Answers vary.

6. The product of 2 and x is 4.

$$2x = 4$$
$$\frac{2x}{2} = \frac{4}{2}$$
$$x = 2$$

7. The product of 3 and x is 21.

$$3x = 21$$
$$\frac{3x}{3} = \frac{21}{3}$$
$$x = 7$$

8. The quotient of b and 2 is 3.

$$\frac{b}{2} = 3$$
$$2 \cdot \frac{b}{2} = 2 \cdot 3$$
$$b = 6$$

9. The quotient of a and 3 is 3.

$$\frac{a}{3} = 3$$
$$3 \cdot \frac{a}{3} = 3 \cdot 3$$
$$a = 9$$

10.
$$4x = 16$$
$$\frac{4x}{4} = \frac{16}{4}$$
$$x = 4$$

Check: $4x = 16$
$$4(4) \stackrel{?}{=} 16$$
$$16 = 16$$

11.
$$12y = 144$$
$$\frac{12y}{12} = \frac{144}{12}$$
$$y = 12$$

Check: $12y = 144$
$$12(12) \stackrel{?}{=} 144$$
$$144 = 144$$

12.
$$56 = 7n$$
$$\frac{56}{7} = \frac{7n}{7}$$
$$8 = n$$

Check: $56 = 7n$
$$56 \stackrel{?}{=} 7(8)$$
$$56 = 56$$

13.
$$6s = 48$$
$$\frac{6s}{6} = \frac{48}{6}$$
$$s = 8$$

Check: $6s = 48$
$$6(8) \stackrel{?}{=} 48$$
$$48 = 48$$

14.
$$2z = 50$$
$$\frac{2z}{2} = \frac{50}{2}$$
$$z = 25$$

Check: $2z = 50$
$$2(25) \stackrel{?}{=} 50$$
$$50 = 50$$

15. $10a = 240$

$$\frac{10a}{10} = \frac{240}{10}$$

$$a = 24$$

Check: $10a = 240$

$$10(24) \overset{?}{=} 240$$

$$240 = 240$$

16. $5x = 625$

$$\frac{5x}{5} = \frac{625}{5}$$

$$x = 125$$

Check: $5x = 625$

$$5(125) \overset{?}{=} 625$$

$$625 = 625$$

17. $5y = 100$

$$\frac{5y}{5} = \frac{100}{5}$$

$$y = 20$$

Check: $5y = 100$

$$5(20) \overset{?}{=} 100$$

$$100 = 100$$

18. $\dfrac{n}{4} = 25$

$$4 \cdot \frac{n}{4} = 4 \cdot 25$$

$$n = 100$$

Check: $\dfrac{n}{4} = 25$

$$\frac{100}{4} \overset{?}{=} 25$$

$$25 = 25$$

19. $\dfrac{m}{3} = 3$

$$3 \cdot \frac{m}{3} = 3 \cdot 3$$

$$m = 9$$

Check: $\dfrac{m}{3} = 3$

$$\frac{9}{3} \overset{?}{=} 3$$

$$3 = 3$$

20. $\dfrac{b}{20} = 2$

$$20 \cdot \frac{b}{20} = 20 \cdot 2$$

$$b = 40$$

Check: $\dfrac{b}{20} = 2$

$$\frac{40}{20} \overset{?}{=} 2$$

$$2 = 2$$

21. $16 = \dfrac{x}{4}$

$$4 \cdot 16 = 4 \cdot \frac{x}{4}$$

$$64 = x$$

Check: $16 = \dfrac{x}{4}$

$$16 \overset{?}{=} \frac{64}{4}$$

$$16 = 16$$

22. $6.3 = 3y$

$$\frac{6.3}{3} = \frac{3y}{3}$$

$$2.1 = y$$

Check: $6.3 = 3y$

$$6.3 \overset{?}{=} 3(2.1)$$

$$6.3 = 6.3$$

23. $5t = 6.5$

$$\frac{5t}{5} = \frac{6.5}{5}$$

$$t = 1.3$$

Check: $5t = 6.5$

$$5(1.3) \overset{?}{=} 6.5$$

$$6.5 = 6.5$$

24. $4.8b = 36$

$$\frac{4.8b}{4.8} = \frac{36}{4.8}$$

$$b = 7.5$$

Check: $4.8b = 36$

$$4.8(7.5) \overset{?}{=} 36$$

$$36 = 36$$

25. $9.6x = 72$

$$\frac{9.6x}{9.6} = \frac{72}{9.6}$$

$$x = 7.5$$

Check: $9.6x = 72$

$$9.6(7.5) \overset{?}{=} 72$$

$$72 = 72$$

26. $\dfrac{z}{3.2} = 8$

$$3.2 \cdot \frac{z}{3.2} = 3.2 \cdot 8$$

$$z = 25.6$$

Check: $\dfrac{z}{3.2} = 8$

$$\frac{25.6}{3.2} \overset{?}{=} 8$$

$$8 = 8$$

27.
$$\frac{t}{7.4} = 6$$
$$7.4 \cdot \frac{t}{7.4} = 7.4 \cdot 6$$
$$t = 44.4$$
Check: $\frac{t}{7.4} = 6$
$$\frac{44.4}{7.4} \stackrel{?}{=} 6$$
$$6 = 6$$

28. $524 = \frac{a}{1}$
$$524 = a$$
Check: $524 = \frac{a}{1}$
$$524 \stackrel{?}{=} \frac{524}{1}$$
$$524 = 524$$

29.
$$\frac{y}{6} = 345$$
$$6 \cdot \frac{y}{6} = 6 \cdot 345$$
$$y = 2070$$
Check: $\frac{y}{6} = 345$
$$\frac{2070}{6} \stackrel{?}{=} 345$$
$$345 = 345$$

30. $\frac{1368}{456} = 3$

31. $\frac{1648}{824} = 2$

32. $\frac{966}{23} = 42$

33. $\frac{3025}{55} = 55$

34. $9 \cdot 1025 = 9225$

35. $8 \cdot 624 = 4992$

36. $136 \cdot 17 = 2312$

37. $189 \cdot 19 = 3591$

38. $3n = 15$
$$\frac{3n}{3} = \frac{15}{3}$$
$$n = 5 \text{ ft}$$

39. $9s = 27$
$$\frac{9s}{9} = \frac{27}{9}$$
$$s = 3 \text{ cm}$$

40. $2x = 38$
$$\frac{2x}{2} = \frac{38}{2}$$
$$x = 19 \text{ m}$$

41. $6w = 48$
$$\frac{6w}{6} = \frac{48}{6}$$
$$w = 8 \text{ km}$$

42. $4f = 28$
$$\frac{4f}{4} = \frac{28}{4}$$
$$f = 7$$

43. $4d = 100$
$$\frac{4d}{4} = \frac{100}{4}$$
$$d = 25$$

44. $\frac{b}{12} = 2$
$$12 \cdot \frac{b}{12} = 12 \cdot 2$$
$$b = 24$$

45. $\frac{t}{6} = 10$
$$6 \cdot \frac{t}{6} = 6 \cdot 10$$
$$t = 60$$

46. a. Area $= l \cdot w$
$$4700 = 50 \cdot x$$

b. $\frac{4700}{50} = \frac{50x}{50}$
$$94 = x$$

The length of a basketball court is 94 feet.

47.
$$\boxed{\text{Points per game}} \times \boxed{\text{Number of games}} = \boxed{\text{Total points scored}}$$

48. $24 \times 15.75 = x$
$$378 = x$$

49. $5x = 20.5$
$$\frac{5x}{5} = \frac{20.5}{5}$$
$$x = 4.1$$

You rollerblade 4.1 miles a day.

50. C; Distance $\div$ Time = Speed
$$3.9 \text{ km} \div 10 \text{ min} = s$$
$$3.9 \text{ km} \times \frac{1}{10 \text{ min}} = 0.39 \frac{\text{km}}{\text{min}}$$
$$= 0.39 \times 60$$
$$= 23.4 \frac{\text{km}}{\text{hr}}$$

51. Answers vary.

1. $3x + 1 = 3(6) + 1$
$= 18 + 1$
$= 19$

2. $\dfrac{x}{3} + 4 = \dfrac{6}{3} + 4$
$= 2 + 4$
$= 6$

4. $\dfrac{x}{2} - 3 = \dfrac{6}{2} - 3$
$= 3 - 3$
$= 0$

5. $(x - 1) \cdot 2 = (6 - 1) \cdot 2$
$= 5 \cdot 2$
$= 10$

6.

$= 4$

7. $\frac{1}{4} \cdot x^2 = \frac{1}{4} \cdot 6^2$
$= \frac{1}{4} \cdot 36$
$= 9$

8. $(x^2 - 12) \div 4 = (6^2 - 12) \div 4$
$= (36 - 12) \div 4$
$= 24 \div 4$
$= 6$

9. $16r + 2 - 12r = 4r + 2$
$4r + 2 = 4(4) + 2$
$= 16 + 2$
$= 18$

10. $2r^2 + r + r^2 = 3r^2 + r$
$3r^2 + r = 3(4^2) + 4$
$= 3(16) + 4$
$= 48 + 4$
$= 52$

11. $4s + 3r + 2s = 6s + 3r$
$6s + 3r = 6(5) + 3(4)$
$= 30 + 12$
$= 42$

12. $3(r + s) - 2r = 3r + 3s - 2r$
$= r + 3s$
$r + 3s = 4 + 3(5)$
$= 4 + 15$
$= 19$

13. $2(r^2 + s) + r^2 = 2r^2 + 2s + r^2$
$= 3r^2 + 2s$
$3r^2 + 2s = 3(4^2) + 2(5)$
$= 3(16) + 10$
$= 48 + 10$
$= 58$

14. $\frac{1}{5} + s + 3s = \frac{1}{5} + 4s$
$= \frac{1}{5} + 4(5)$
$= \frac{1}{5} + 20$
$= 20\frac{1}{5}$

15. $10.00 - 4.99 - 3 \times 1.5 = 10.00 - 4.99 - 4.5$
$= \$.51$

Using a Spreadsheet

1. Answers vary.

2. Answers vary.

Modeling Verbal Expressions

1. Total cost $= 12c + 15d$

$12(5) + 15(0) = \$60$

$12(0) + 15(4) = \$60$

There are 2 different combinations: 5 cassettes and 0 CDs, and 0 cassettes and 4 CDs.

EXERCISES

1. $t - 20°$

2. $s + 5$

3. $0.10m + 1.00$

4. $5n - 10$

5. B

6. D

7. F

8. E

9. A

10. C

11. $\dfrac{r}{23}$

12. $\dfrac{s}{7}$

13. $10y + 9$

14. $1 + 2x$

15. $5n - 4$

16. $8 - 2a$

17. $102n$

18. $11(6 + m)$

19. $\dfrac{x}{2 + y}$

20. $10 - \dfrac{a}{b}$

21. $m + 4$

22. $s + 572$

23. $6m$

24. $3m$

25. $r - 2$

26. $c - 4$

27. $\dfrac{s}{3}$

28. $\dfrac{1}{2}m$

29. $a - 8$

30. $10a$

31. $\dfrac{3}{4}a$

32. a. $1.5c + b$

   b. $1.5(4) + 2 = 8$

   The cost is $8.00.

33. a. $7 + 3h$

   b. $\dfrac{7 + 3h}{4}$ or $\dfrac{1}{4}(7 + 3h)$

   c. If you play for $2\frac{1}{2}$ hours, you play for 3 additional $\frac{1}{2}$ hours after the first hour.

$$\frac{1}{4}[7 + 3(3)] = \frac{1}{4}(7 + 9)$$
$$= \frac{1}{4}(16)$$
$$= 4$$

   Your cost is $4.00.

34. x = Number of U.S. dollars

$1.38x$ = Number of Canadian dollars

U.S. Dollars	$1	$2	$5	$10	$n	$6	$8	$1
Canadian Dollars	$1.38	$2.76	$6.90	$13.80	$1.38n	$8.28	$11.04	$1.38

U.S.: $1.38(5) = 6.90$

$1.38(10) = 13.80$

Canadian: $1.38n = 8.28$

$\dfrac{1.38n}{1.38} = \dfrac{8.28}{1.38}$

$n = 6$

$1.38n = 11.04$

$\dfrac{1.38}{1.38} = \dfrac{11.04}{1.38}$

$n = 8$

35. B; $2 \times \$25 + 3 \times \$14 = \$50 + \$42 = \$92$

36. C; $8(4) - 2(3.5) = 32 - 7 = 25$

37. Answers vary.

2.7 *Real-Life Modeling with Equations*

ONGOING ASSESSMENT

1. *Sample answer:* Driving for 5 h at 65 mi/h, what is the distance traveled?

2. Let d = distance.

$\dfrac{d}{5} = 65$

$65 \cdot 5 = d$

$325 \text{ mi} = d$

EXERCISES

1. Equation

$3 + x = 19$

$3 + x - 3 = 19 - 3$

$x = 16$

2. Expression

$5x - 3x + 6$

$2x + 6$

3. Equation

$2x = 18$

$\dfrac{2x}{2} = \dfrac{18}{2}$

$x = 9$

4. Equation

$\dfrac{x}{3} = 7$

$3 \cdot \dfrac{x}{3} = 3 \cdot 7$

$x = 21$

5. $c - 21 = 84$

Addition Property of Equality

6. $10x = \$75$

Division Property of Equality

7. C **8.** F **9.** A **10.** D **11.** B **12.** E

13.
$$d + 9 = 20$$
$$d + 9 - 9 = 20 - 9$$
$$d = 11$$
Subtraction Property of Equality

14.
$$16 = t - 3$$
$$16 + 3 = t - 3 + 3$$
$$19 = t$$
Addition Property of Equality

15.
$$\frac{p}{12} = 4$$
$$12 \cdot \frac{p}{12} = 12 \cdot 4$$
$$p = 48$$
Multiplication Property of Equality

16.
$$3x = 90.75$$
$$\frac{3x}{3} = \frac{90.75}{3}$$
$$x = 30.25$$
Division Property of Equality

17.
$$\frac{y}{45} = 5$$
$$45 \cdot \frac{y}{45} = 45 \cdot 5$$
$$y = 225$$
Multiplication Property of Equality

18. The sum of a number and 15 is 33.

19. 90 is the difference of a number and 3.

20. The product of 7 and a number is 56.

21. The quotient of a number and 9 is 8.

22. The sum of 11 and a number is 23.

23. 21 is the difference of a number and 18.

24. Verbal model: $\boxed{\text{Missing number}} \times \boxed{38} = \boxed{912}$

Label: Missing number $= n$

Algebraic model: $n \cdot 38 = 912$
$$\frac{n \cdot 38}{38} = \frac{912}{38}$$
$$n = 24$$
The missing number is 24.

25. Verbal model: $\boxed{\text{Larger number}} = \boxed{\text{Smaller number}} + \boxed{251}$

Labels: Larger number $= 420$

Smaller number $= s$

Algebraic model:
$$420 = s + 251$$
$$420 - 251 = s + 251 - 251$$
$$169 = s$$
The smaller number is 169.

26.
$$25 = 2(w + 8)$$
$$25 \overset{?}{=} 2(4.5 + 8)$$
$$25 \overset{?}{=} 2(12.5)$$
$$25 = 25$$
$$w = 4.5 \text{ units}$$

27.
$$24 = w(w + 2)$$
$$24 \overset{?}{=} 4(4 + 2)$$
$$24 \overset{?}{=} 4(6)$$
$$24 = 24$$
$$w = 4 \text{ cm}$$

28. n represents this week's sales.

29. In the graph there are 190 sweaters out of 1000 designs sold, $\frac{190}{1000} = \frac{95}{500}$. So, for every 500 designs sold, you would expect to sell 95 sweaters.

30. a. $\boxed{\text{Total points}} \div \boxed{\text{Number of games}} = \boxed{\text{Average number of points per game}}$

b. $560 \div 16 = n$
$$n = 35 \text{ points}$$

c. $(35 + 4) \times 16 = 640$ points

31. D

32. a. $\dfrac{\text{Number of pages advertising per year}}{\text{Number of monthly issues per year}} = \text{Number of pages advertising per issue}$

Number of pages advertising per year $= 80$

Number of monthly issues per year $= 12$

Number of pages advertising per issue $= x$

$$\frac{80}{12} = x$$

b. 6.67 or about 7 pages

Spiral **R E V I E W**

1. Subtract 2.

2. Divide by 5 or multiply by $\frac{1}{5}$.

3. Multiply by 3.

4. Add 4.

5. $2f + 3f = 5f$

6. $12r - 3r = 9r$

7. $2(g + 3) = 2g + 6$

8. $5(4t + 3) = 20t + 15$

9. $2s + 3s + s = 6s$

10. $8p + 2p - p = 9p$

11. $4 + 3h + 2h = 4 + 5h$

12. $2q + 9 + 12 = 2q + 21$

13. $8n = 32$

$$\frac{8n}{8} = \frac{32}{8}$$

$n = 4$

14. $m - 12 = 20$

$m - 12 + 12 = 20 + 12$

$m = 32$

15. $3n = 2$

$$\frac{3n}{3} = \frac{2}{3}$$

$n = \dfrac{2}{3}$

16. $y + 6 = 10$

$y + 6 - 6 = 10 - 6$

$y = 4$

17. $x - 4 = 6$

$x - 4 + 4 = 6 + 4$

$x = 10$

18. $\dfrac{t}{8} = 2$

$8 \cdot \dfrac{t}{8} = 8 \cdot 2$

$t = 16$

19. $y + 2 = 2$

$y + 2 - 2 = 2 - 2$

$y = 0$

20. $\dfrac{z}{12} = 3$

$12 \cdot \dfrac{z}{12} = 12 \cdot 3$

$z = 36$

21. $\$130 \div 5 = \$26$ per week

Communicating About Mathematics

1. $\boxed{\begin{array}{c}\text{Cost for an order}\\\text{of jeans}\end{array}} = \boxed{\begin{array}{c}\text{Cost to make a}\\\text{pair of jeans}\end{array}} \cdot \boxed{\begin{array}{c}\text{Number of}\\\text{jeans ordered}\end{array}}$

2. $\boxed{\begin{array}{c}\text{Total sales of}\\\text{traditional jeans}\end{array}} = \boxed{\begin{array}{c}\text{Total}\\\text{sales}\end{array}} - \boxed{\begin{array}{c}\text{Total sales of}\\\text{designer jeans}\end{array}} = \boxed{\begin{array}{c}\text{Total}\\\text{sales}\end{array}} - \frac{1}{7} \cdot \boxed{\begin{array}{c}\text{Total}\\\text{sales}\end{array}}$

3. Question 1:

    Labels: Cost for an order of jeans = 144,000 (dollars)
               Cost to make a pair of jeans = 8 (dollars)
               Number of jeans ordered = x (pairs)

    Equation: $144,000 = 8x$

                $18,000 = x$

    The number of jeans that were ordered was 18,000.

4. $45; 65 - 20 = 45$

Question 2:

    Labels: Total sales of traditional jeans = x (billion dollars)
               Total sales = 7 (billion dollars)

    Equation: $x = 7 - \frac{1}{7} \cdot 7$

                $x = 6$

    The total sales of traditional jeans in a year in the U.S. is $6 billion.

5. $70; 65 + p = 135$

               $p = 70$

Retail stores make a profit of $70 per pair of designer jeans.

2.8   *A Problem Solving Plan*

ONGOING ASSESSMENT

1. *Sample answer:* Suppose the cost of a master's degree is $20,000. If you will work 41 years with a bachelor's degree, then you will work $41 - 2 = 39$ years with a master's degree. Then $39(\$48,851) - \$20,000 = \$1,885,189$. Since this is about $173,000 more than someone with a bachelor's degree, this would be a good financial investment.

EXERCISES

1. D, A, F, C, B, E

2. Check your solution. The solution of the equation may not be the answer to the question.

3. $\boxed{\text{Total points needed}} \leq \boxed{\text{Number of points obtained}} + \boxed{\text{Final test score}}$

4. Total points needed = 460
    Number of points obtained $= 89 + 85 + 92 + 97$
                           $= 363$
    Final test score = x (points)

5. $460 \leq 363 + x$

6. $460 \leq 363 + x$
    $460 - 363 \leq 363 + x - 363$
               $97 \leq x$

7. You will need to score a 97 or higher to earn an A.

8. *Sample answer:* Out of 100 points, it is possible to get a 97.

9. Yes, because you only needed a 97 to get an A.

10. $\boxed{\text{Trail length}} = \boxed{\text{Number of miles traveled}} + \boxed{\text{Distance to go}}$

11. Trail length = 29 (miles)
    Number of miles traveled = $8 + 11 = 19$
    Distance to go = x (miles)

12. $29 = 19 + x$

13.
$$29 = 19 + x$$
$$29 - 19 = 19 + x - 19$$
$$10 = x$$

14. You will need to travel 10 mi on day 3.

15. The distance is between 0 and 29.

16. $\boxed{\text{Sales commission}} = \boxed{\text{Commission rate}} \cdot \boxed{\text{Annual sales}}$

17. Sales commission $= x$ (dollars)
Commission rate $= \frac{1}{20}$
Annual sales $= \$150,000$

18. $x = \frac{1}{20} \cdot 150,000$

19. $x = \frac{1}{20} \cdot 150,000$

$x = 7500$

Annual earnings $=$ Base salary $+$ Sales commission

$\qquad\qquad = 16,500 + 7500$

$\qquad\qquad = 24,000$

You made $\$24,000$.

20. 7 days; 7 miles; 2 ways
$7 \cdot 7 \cdot 2 = 98$
She travels 98 miles per week.

21. 17 shirts sold;
each shirt sells for $\$9.50$.
$17(9.50) = 161.5$
You have raised $\$161.50$.

22. B

23. C

24. No, the distance is too far (over 2000 miles) to be driven in 12 hours.

25. No, the area is too big to be a reasonably-sized desktop.

2.9 Exploring Variables and Inequalities

ONGOING ASSESSMENT

1.
$x - 7 < 3$	*Write original inequality.*
$x - 7 + 7 < 3 + 7$	*Add 7 to each side.*
$x < 10$	*Solution*

2.
$2n > 10$	*Write original inequality.*
$\dfrac{2n}{2} > \dfrac{10}{2}$	*Divide each side by 2.*
$n > 5$	*Solution*

3.
$4 < \dfrac{m}{2}$	*Write original inequality.*
$4 \cdot 2 < \dfrac{m}{2} \cdot 2$	*Multiply each side by 2.*
$8 < m$	*Solution*

EXERCISES

1. $<$ is less than.
$\leq$ is less than or equal to.
$>$ is greater than.
$\geq$ is greater than or equal to.

2. True. For example, any number greater than 3 is a solution of $x > 3$.

3. Yes
$$x - 5 < 11$$
$$11 - 5 \overset{?}{<} 11$$
$$6 < 11$$

4. No
$$x - 5 < 11$$
$$16 - 5 \overset{?}{<} 11$$
$$11 \not< 11$$

5. Yes
$$x - 5 < 11$$
$$15 - 5 \overset{?}{<} 11$$
$$10 < 11$$

6. No
$$x - 5 < 11$$
$$30 - 5 \overset{?}{<} 11$$
$$25 \not< 11$$

7.
$$x + 4 \leq 7$$
$$x + 4 - 4 \leq 7 - 4$$
$$x \leq 3$$

8.
$$3x \geq 10$$
$$\frac{3x}{3} \geq \frac{10}{3}$$
$$x \geq \frac{10}{3}, \text{ or } 3\frac{1}{3}$$

9.
$$9 < x - 5$$
$$9 + 5 < x - 5 + 5$$
$$14 < x$$

10. *Sample answer:* No more than 10 people are allowed on the elevator.

11.–16. *Sample answers:*

11. $1, \ 3\frac{1}{2}$

12. $12.35, \ 20$

13. $46, 1000$

14. $100, 6$

15. $2\frac{1}{4}, \ 2$

16. $0, 7$

17.
$$x + 5 < 11$$
$$x + 5 - 5 < 11 - 5$$
$$x < 6$$

18.
$$s - 4 > 9$$
$$s - 4 + 4 > 9 + 4$$
$$s > 13$$

19.
$$7y \leq 42$$
$$\frac{7y}{7} \leq \frac{42}{7}$$
$$y \leq 6$$

20.
$$22 \leq b + 22$$
$$22 - 22 \leq b + 22 - 22$$
$$0 \leq b$$

21.
$$16 \geq s - 3$$
$$16 + 3 \geq s - 3 + 3$$
$$19 \geq s$$

22.
$$56 < 14t$$
$$\frac{56}{14} < \frac{14t}{14}$$
$$4 < t$$

23.
$$45 > 5m$$
$$\frac{45}{5} > \frac{5m}{5}$$
$$9 > m$$

24.
$$n - 34 \leq 16$$
$$n - 34 + 34 \leq 16 + 34$$
$$n \leq 50$$

25.
$$17y \geq 68$$
$$\frac{17y}{17} \geq \frac{68}{17}$$
$$y \geq 4$$

26.
$$x + 3.4 > 5.8$$
$$x + 3.4 - 3.4 > 5.8 - 3.4$$
$$x > 2.4$$

27.
$$y - 13.7 < 5.4$$
$$y - 13.7 + 13.7 < 5.4 + 13.7$$
$$y < 19.1$$

28.
$$8.9k \geq 17.8$$
$$\frac{8.9k}{8.9} \geq \frac{17.8}{8.9}$$
$$k \geq 2$$

29. $\dfrac{x}{8} \geq 11$

$8 \cdot \dfrac{x}{8} \geq 8 \cdot 11$

$x \geq 88$

30. $\dfrac{x}{2} \leq 52$

$2 \cdot \dfrac{x}{2} \leq 2 \cdot 52$

$x \leq 104$

31. $\dfrac{a}{2.5} \leq 4.2$

$2.5 \cdot \dfrac{a}{2.5} \leq 2.5 \cdot 4.2$

$a \leq 10.5$

32. $c + 5 \geq 19.3$

$c + 5 - 5 \geq 19.3 - 5$

$c \geq 14.3$

33. $b - 7 < 24$

$b - 7 + 7 < 24 + 7$

$b < 31$

34. $2x < 42$

$\dfrac{2x}{2} < \dfrac{42}{2}$

$x < 21$

35. $3y > 39$

$\dfrac{3y}{3} > \dfrac{39}{3}$

$y > 13$

36. $20 \geq \dfrac{m}{6}$

$6 \cdot 20 \geq 6 \cdot \dfrac{m}{6}$

$120 \geq m$

37. $15 \leq \dfrac{x}{5}$

$5 \cdot 15 \leq 5 \cdot \dfrac{x}{5}$

$75 \leq x$

38. $x \geq \$320$ and
$x \leq \$4500$

39. The sum of d and 11 is less than 52.

40. The difference of f and 5 is greater than or equal to 29.

41. The product of 3 and h is less than or equal to 60.

42. The quotient of p and 36 is greater than 2.

43. 17 is greater than the difference of c and 31.

44. 23 is less than or equal to the sum of a and 9.

45. a. Hot Wheelers; $69 \text{ min} \times \dfrac{1 \text{ h}}{60 \text{ min}} = \dfrac{69 \text{ h}}{60} = 1.15 \text{ h}$

b. $\boxed{\begin{array}{c}\text{Last place time}\\\text{in minutes}\end{array}} - \boxed{\text{Minutes}} < \boxed{\begin{array}{c}\text{First place time}\\\text{in minutes}\end{array}}$

$85 - m < 69$

$m > 16$

c. $\boxed{\begin{array}{c}\text{Cruisin' Kids' time}\\\text{in minutes}\end{array}} - \boxed{\text{Minutes}} \leq \boxed{\begin{array}{c}\text{Brave Bikers' time}\\\text{in minutes}\end{array}}$

$76 - m \leq 71$

$m \geq 5$

d. $D = r \cdot t$

$20 = 69r$

$\dfrac{20}{69} = \dfrac{69r}{69}$

$r = \dfrac{20 \text{ mi}}{69 \text{ min}} \times \dfrac{60 \text{ min}}{1 \text{ h}} = \dfrac{1200 \text{ mi}}{69 \text{ h}} \approx 17.39 \text{ mi/h}$

46. B

47. Yes.
$4 + 5 > 6$
$4 + 6 > 5$
$5 + 6 > 4$

48. No.
$2 + 3 \not> 6$

49. No.
$4 + 6 \not> 12$

50. Yes.
$8 + 9 > 11$
$8 + 11 > 9$
$9 + 11 > 8$

1. $4(x + 2) = 4x + 8$

2. $3(6z + 1) = 18z + 3$

3. $2(6m + 12) = 12m + 24$

4. $5(a + b) = 5a + 5b$

5. $7(d + f + 2) = 7d + 7f + 14$

6. $2(3a + b + 2c) = 6a + 2b + 4c$

7. $5(g + 2h) = 5g + 10h$

8. $4(5 + y) = 20 + 4y$

9. $8w + 9w = 17w$

10. $3x + 4 + x = 4x + 4$

11. $14 + 7v + v = 14 + 8v$

12. $16 + 5b + 3b + 9 = 25 + 8b$

13. $5 + 6t + 9 + 2a = 14 + 6t + 2a$

14. $2x + 3t + x + 2t = 3x + 5t$

15. 1

16. 22

17. 2

18. 10

19. 3

20. 27

21. 4

22. 12

23. $$m - 54 = 72$$
$$m - 54 + 54 = 72 + 54$$
$$m = 126$$

24. $$n + 13 = 132$$
$$n + 13 - 13 = 132 - 13$$
$$n = 119$$

25. $$t - \quad 6 = 50.11$$
$$\underline{\quad +6 \quad +6 \quad}$$
$$t \quad\quad = 56.11$$

26. $$w + \quad 19.95 = \quad 20$$
$$\underline{\quad -19.95 \quad -19.95}$$
$$w \quad = \quad 0.05$$

27. $$\frac{32k}{32} = \frac{8}{32}$$
$$k = \frac{1}{4}$$

28. $$\frac{25q}{25} = \frac{100}{25}$$
$$q = 4$$

29. $$\frac{r}{0.7} = 1400$$
$$r = 1400 \cdot 0.7$$
$$= 980$$

30. $$\frac{g}{3} = 13$$
$$g = 13 \cdot 3$$
$$= 39$$

31. $s + 10$

32. $5t$

33. $5 + w$

34. $a - 5$

35. $$\text{Area} = x \cdot x$$
$$576 = x \cdot x$$
$$x = 24 \text{ ft}$$
$$2 \cdot \text{perimeter} = \text{distance walked}$$
$$2 \cdot (4x) = \text{distance}$$
$$8x = \text{distance}$$
$$8(24) = 192 \text{ ft}$$

36. $\text{Amount} \times \text{Cost per pound} = \text{Total cost}$
$\text{Amount} = 2\frac{1}{4} \text{ pound}$
$\text{Cost per pound} = \$1.05$
$\text{Total cost} = x$
$2.25 \cdot 1.05 = x$
$\$2.36 = x$

37. $\frac{1}{3} \cdot 900 = 300$ students

38. $$w(10 - 2.5) = 47$$
$$7.5w = 47$$
$$\frac{7.5w}{7.5} = \frac{47}{7.5}$$
$$w = 6.2\overline{6}$$
You will have enough money in 7 weeks.

39. $$p \times \frac{1}{100} = 1200$$
$$p \times \frac{1}{100} \div \frac{1}{100} = 1200 \div \frac{1}{100}$$
$$p = 120,000$$
Your company made a profit of $120,000.

40. $60 + 60 + 40 = 160$ ft

41.
$$y - 13 < 3$$
$$y - 13 + 13 < 3 + 13$$
$$y < 16$$

42.
$$z + 13 \leq 16$$
$$\underline{-13-13}$$
$$z \leq 3$$

43.
$$\frac{6k}{6} \geq \frac{30}{6}$$
$$k \geq 5$$

44.
$$\frac{5g}{5} < \frac{15}{5}$$
$$g < 3$$

45.
$$\frac{1.2}{0.2} \geq \frac{0.2t}{0.2}$$
$$6 \geq t$$

46.
$$\frac{p}{4} < 12$$
$$p < 12 \cdot 4$$
$$p < 48$$

47.
$$2.08 < v + 0.31$$
$$\underline{-0.31 -0.31}$$
$$1.77 < v$$

48.
$$21 < \frac{w}{0.7}$$
$$21 \cdot 0.7 < w$$
$$14.7 < w$$

Chapter **ASSESSMENT**

1. $7(a + 2) = 7(a) + 7(2)$
$$= 7a + 14$$

2. $3(b + 2c + 3) = 3(b) + 3(2c) + 3(3)$
$$= 3b + 6c + 9$$

3. $2d + 12 = 2(d + 6)$

4. $6e + 4d + 2 = 2(3e + 2d + 1)$

5.
$$3x = 15$$
$$\frac{3x}{3} = \frac{15}{3}$$
$$x = 5$$

6.
$$y - 6 = 0$$
$$y - 6 + 6 = 0 + 6$$
$$y = 6$$

7.
$$p + 2 = 9$$
$$p + 2 - 2 = 9 - 2$$
$$p = 7$$

8.
$$\tfrac{1}{4} = 3q$$
$$\tfrac{1}{3} \cdot \tfrac{1}{4} = \tfrac{1}{3} \cdot 3q$$
$$\tfrac{1}{12} = q$$

9.
$$x - 2 > 4$$
$$x - 2 + 2 > 4 + 2$$
$$x > 6$$

10.
$$10 \geq 3 + y$$
$$10 - 3 \geq 3 + y - 3$$
$$7 \geq y$$

11.
$$7 + z < 4$$
$$7 + z - 7 < 4 - 7$$
$$z < -3$$

12.
$$a + 9 \leq 24$$
$$a + 9 - 9 \leq 24 - 9$$
$$a \leq 15$$

13. Perimeter: $2(4) + 2(2 + x) = 8 + 4 + 2x$
$$= 2x + 12$$

Area: $4(2 + x) = 8 + 4x$

14. a. $\boxed{\begin{array}{c}\text{Yearly cost to} \\ \text{operate both stores}\end{array}} = 52 \cdot \left(\boxed{\begin{array}{c}\text{Weekly cost to} \\ \text{operate Store 1}\end{array}} + \boxed{\begin{array}{c}\text{Weekly cost to} \\ \text{operate Store 2}\end{array}} \right)$

b. $52(3500 + 5600) = 52(9100)$
$$= \$473{,}200$$

15. $0.50n$

16. $0.50n = 3.00$

17.
$$0.50n = 3.00$$
$$\frac{0.50n}{0.50} = \frac{3.00}{0.50}$$
$$n = 6$$

18. $3a + 6b + 2a = 5a + 6b$

19. $12p + 4q + 2q + 3p = 15p + 6q$

20. $3x + 5y + 9x + 10z = 12x + 5y + 10z$

21. $n - 14 \geq 36$

$n - 14 + 14 \geq 36 + 14$

$n \geq 50$

22. $12n = 60$

$\dfrac{12n}{12} = \dfrac{60}{12}$

$n = 5$

23. Perimeter $= 2x + x + 3x + x = 7x$

$x = 1$: $7x = 7(1) = 7$

$x = 2$: $7x = 7(2) = 14$

$x = 3$: $7x = 7(3) = 21$

$x = 4$: $7x = 7(4) = 28$

x	1	2	3	4
Perimeter, $7x$	7	14	21	28

24. Perimeter $= 3x + x + x + x + 3x + x + x + x = 12x$

$x = 1$: $12x = 12(1) = 12$

$x = 2$: $12x = 12(2) = 24$

$x = 3$: $12x = 12(3) = 36$

$x = 4$: $12x = 12(4) = 48$

x	1	2	3	4
Perimeter, $12x$	12	24	36	48

Standardized Test Practice

1. C

2. D; $3x + x + 3 + x + 2x = 7x + 3$

3. C

4. D

5. C; $6 - 9 \overset{?}{\leq} 3$ $12 - 9 \overset{?}{\leq} 3$ $13 - 9 \overset{?}{\leq} 3$ $10 - 9 \overset{?}{\leq} 3$

$-3 \leq 3 \checkmark$ $3 \leq 3 \checkmark$ $4 \nleq 3$ $1 \leq 3 \checkmark$

6. D; $y - 4.2 = 5.7$

$y - 4.2 + 4.2 = 5.7 + 4.2$

$y = 9.9$

7. A

8. C; $\dfrac{2 \text{ mi}}{5 \text{ min}} \cdot \dfrac{60 \text{ min}}{1 \text{ h}} = \dfrac{120 \text{ mi}}{5h} = 24 \text{ mi/h}$

9. C

10. C; $p \times 0.25 = 13.75$

$\dfrac{p \times 0.25}{0.25} = \dfrac{13.75}{0.25}$

$p = 55$

Chapter 3
Modeling Integers

3.1 Integers and Absolute Value

ONGOING ASSESSMENT

1. False; *sample answer:* −6 lies to the left of −4 on the number line.

2. True; *sample answer:* −0 = 0

3. False; *sample answer:* −6 ≤ −4 but 6 ≥ 4.

EXERCISES

1. All of them

2. 0, 1, 2, 3, 4

3. 1, 2, 3, 4

4. 1

5. −1

6. 0

7. −4 and 4, −3 and 3, −2 and 2, *or* − 1 and 1

8. 5, −5

9. To the right of zero

10. *Sample answer:* in computing how far below par in golf

11.

12.

13.

14.

15.

16.

17. < **18.** < **19.** > **20.** > **21.** > **22.** >

23. −1, 1

24. 4, 4

25. 3, 3

26. −3, 3

27. −20, 20

28. 32, 32

29. 100, 100

30. −144, 144

31. −250

32. 5050

33. 25

34. 100

35. −17 **36.** 40 **37.** −15 **38.** 6

39. −6, −3, 0, 4, 5 **40.** −10, −6, −4, −1, 1 **41.** −4, −2, −1, 0, 2

42. −11, −9, −7, 1, 11 **43.** −5, −4, −2, 4, 6 **44.** −9, −8, −7, −6, −5

45. |40| = 40 mi **46.** |−60| = 60 mi **47.** |15| + |−60| = 75 mi

48. |−105| = 105 mi **49.** |−105| − |−60| = 105 − 60 = 45 mi **50.** |40| + |−105| = 145 mi

51.–54. *Sample answers:*

51. True; distance cannot be negative.

52. False; |0| = 0

53. True; |−6| $\overset{?}{>}$ |−4|; 6 > 4 ✓

54. False; let $a = -4$ and $b = -6$, $-4 \geq -6$ does not mean that $|-4| \geq |-6|$ or that $4 \geq 6$.

55. C; |−2| = |−2|

56. Answers vary.

Lab 3.2

Part A

1. ⊕⊕⊕⊕⊕ ⊕⊕

7

2. ⊖⊖⊖ ⊖⊖

−5

3. ⊖⊖⊖⊖⊖⊖ ⊖⊖⊖

−9

4. ⊕⊕ ⊕⊕⊕ ⊕⊕

7

5. ⊖ ⊖⊖ ⊖⊖

5

6. ⊖⊖⊖ ⊖⊖⊖ ⊖⊖

8

7. The sum of two positive integers is always positive.

8. The sum of two negative integers is always negative.

Part B

9. ⊖⊖ / ⊕⊕ ⊕⊕

3

10. ⊕⊕⊕⊕ ⊕⊕ / ⊖⊖⊖

2

11. ⊖⊖⊖⊖⊖ ⊖ / ⊕⊕⊕⊕⊕

−1

12. ⊕⊕⊕⊕⊕ / ⊖⊖⊖⊖⊖ ⊖⊖

−2

13. ⊖⊖ / ⊕⊕⊕⊕⊕⊕⊕⊕

6

14. ⊖⊖⊖⊖⊖ / ⊕⊕⊕⊕⊕

0

15. ⊕⊕⊕⊕⊕ ⊕⊕⊕⊕

9

16. ⊖⊖⊖⊖⊖ ⊖⊖⊖

−9

17. ⊖⊖ ⊕⊕⊕⊕⊕

3

18. ⊕⊕⊕ ⊕ ⊕ ⊕ ⊕ ⊖⊖⊖⊖⊖⊖⊖⊖

−1

19. Yes; yes; the sign of a sum will be the same as the sign of the integer with the greater absolute value.

20. Yes; they are opposites.

Adding Two Integers

ONGOING ASSESSMENT

1. *Sample answer:* How much more of the $25 you borrowed from your uncle do you owe if you already paid him back $15?

$$-25 + 15 = -10$$

2. *Sample answer:* How much do you owe your sister if you already owe her $15 and borrow another $15 from her?

$$-15 + (-15) = -30$$

3. *Sample answer:* How much do you owe your mom if you borrowed $40 from her and paid it all back?

$$-40 + 40 = 0$$

EXERCISES

1. $4 + 3 = 7$

2. $2 + (-2) = 0$

3. $7 + (-5) = 2$

4. $-7 + (-5) = -12$

5. $a = -3$, $b = -1$, $c = 0$, $d = 2$
$a + d = -3 + 2 = -1$
$b + c = -1 + 0 = -1$
Solution: a and d or b and c

6. $a = -4$, $b = -3$, $c = 2$, $d = 3$
$a + d = -4 + 3 = -1$
$b + c = -3 + 2 = -1$
Solution: a and d or b and c

7. Rule 1: To add two integers with the same sign, add their absolute values and write the common sign.

Rule 2: To add two integers with opposite signs, subtract the smaller absolute value from the larger absolute value and write the sign of the integer with the greater absolute value.

Since 8 and −11 have opposite signs, Rule 2 should be used to add them.

8. Positive, $|b| > |a|$.
Suppose, for example, that $a = -1$ and $b = 2$; then $a + b = -1 + 2 = 1$ (a positive number) and $|2| > |-1|$.

9. $11 + 15 = 26$

10. $-8 + (-2) = -10$

11. $-13 + (-13) = -26$

12. $10 + 24 = 34$

13. $10 + (-10) = 0$

14. $-8 + 8 = 0$

15. $-13 + 13 = 0$

16. $24 + (-24) = 0$

17. $13 + 0 = 13$

18. $-7 + 0 = -7$

19. $0 + 15 = 15$

20. $0 + (-33) = -33$

21. $2 + (-9) = -7$

22. $39 + (-21) = 18$

23. $-16 + 12 = -4$

24. $-17 + 13 = -4$

25.
$$4 + 2 = 6$$
$$4 + 1 = 5$$
$$4 + 0 = 4$$
$$4 + (-1) = 3$$
Pattern: sums decrease by 1.

26.
$$-2 + (-2) = -4$$
$$-2 + (-1) = -3$$
$$-2 + 0 = -2$$
$$-2 + 1 = -1$$
Pattern: sums increase by 1.

27.
$$3 + (-5) = -2$$
$$3 + (-3) = 0$$
$$3 + (-1) = 2$$
$$3 + 1 = 4$$
Pattern: sums increase by 2.

28.
$$-6 + (-5) = -11$$
$$-6 + (-6) = -12$$
$$-6 + (-7) = -13$$
$$-6 + (-8) = -14$$
Pattern: sums decrease by 1.

29. D; -2; $2 debt

30. A; 2; 2nd floor

31. C; 45; 45 yd line

32. B; 25; 25°F

33. $4 + x = 7$
$x = 3$

34. $6 + n = 5$
$n = -1$

35. $-2 + m = -5$
$m = -3$

36. $-3 + y = 0$
$y = 3$

37. *Sample answer:*
6, 1; 0, 7; 10, -3

38. *Sample answer:*
$-2, 0; -1, -1; 4, -6$

39. *Sample answer:*
$-4, -4; 0, -8; -9, 1$

40. *Sample answer:*
5, 5: 11, -1; 6, 4

41. $-63 + (-122) = -185$
Jurassic Period

42. $-205 + 117 = -88$
Cretaceous Period

43. $-138 + (-72) = -210$
Triassic Period

44. C; $|-10| + (-1) = 10 + (-1) = 9$

45. D; $|5| + |-8| = 5 + 8 = 13$

46. Answers vary.
Jason jumped $15 + (-3) = 12$ ft.
Abdul jumped $15 + 2 = 17$ ft.
Van jumped $15 + 4 = 19$ ft.
Maha jumped $15 + (-1) = 14$ ft.

3.3 *Adding Three or More Integers*

ONGOING ASSESSMENT

1.–3. You can use mental math to add the coefficients.

1. $4x + (-2x) + 3 = 2x + 3$

2. $-6m + (-7m) + m = -12m$

3. $2y + (-y) + z = y + z$

EXERCISES

1.

$4 + 2 + (-6) = 0$

2.

$2 + (-5) + 8 = 5$

3. $-3x, 5x, 7; 2x + 7$

4. Positive; $a + c$ is positive because $|c| > |a|$, and b is positive. Suppose, for example, that $a = -3$ and $c = 4$; then $a + c = -3 + 4 = 1$ (a positive number) and $|4| > |-3|$, while b is between 0 and 4.

5. $4 + (-5) + 6 = -1 + 6 = 5$;
$4 + (-5) + 6 = 5$

6. $3 + (-9) + 13 = -6 + 13 = 7$;
$3 + (-9) + 13 = 7$

7. $-7 + 1 + (-8) = -6 + (-8) = -14$;
$-7 + 1 + (-8) = -14$

8. $-6 + 2 + (-15) = -4 + (-15) = -19$;
$-6 + 2 + (-15) = -19$

9. $-8 + 12 + (-1) = 4 + (-1) = 3$;
$-8 + 12 + (-1) = 3$

10. $-10 + 16 + (-4) = 6 + (-4) = 2$;
$-10 + 16 + (-4) = 2$

11. $-12 + (-4) + (-8) = -16 + (-8) = -24$;
$-12 + (-4) + (-8) = -24$

12. $-11 + (-7) + (-3) = -18 + (-3) = -21$;
$-11 + (-7) + (-3) = -21$

13. $5 + (-6) + (-13) = -1 + (-13) = -14$;
$5 + (-6) + (-13) = -14$

14. $4 + (-8) + 9 + (-2) = -4 + 9 + (-2)$
$= 5 + (-2) = 3$;
$4 + (-8) + 9 + (-2) = 3$

15. $-7 + (-6) + 2 + (-7) = -13 + 2 + (-7)$
$= -11 + (-7) = -18$;
$-7 + (-6) + 2 + (-7) = -18$

16. $-12 + (-4) + 20 = -16 + 20 = 4$;
$-12 + (-4) + 20 = 4$

17. Negative; $|-237| > |122 + 69|$

18. Positive; $|-142| < |127 + 89|$

19. Negative;
$|(-213) + (-97)| > |230|$

20. $-36 + 49 + (-2) + 15 = 26$

21. $-23 + 112 + (-9) + 13 = 93$

22. $19 + (-39) + (-51) = -71$

23. $92 + (-20) + (-101) = -29$

24. $84 + (-89) + (-40) = -45$

25. $111 + 105 + (-99) = 117$

26. Kite: $+5 + (-3) + (-6) + (-2) = 2 + (-6) + (-2)$
$= -4 + (-2)$
$= -6$

Rocca: $(-1) + (-3) + (-2) + 3 = -4 + (-2) + 3$
$= -6 + 3$
$= -3$

Stankowski: $-4 + 2 + (-3) + 2 = -2 + (-3) + 2$
$= -5 + 2$
$= -3$

Watson: $+3 + (-4) + (-3) + 0 = -1 + (-3) + 0$
$= -4$

Woods: $-2 + (-6) + (-7) + (-3) = -8 + (-7) + (-3)$
$= -15 + (-3)$
$= -18$

27. Rocca and Stankowski tied at 3 below par.

28. Woods $= -18$
Kite $= -6$
$|(-18) - (-6)| = |-12| = 12$ strokes

29. $6 + (-3) + (-4) + 8 = 3 + 4 = 7$ and
$7 < 10$; so, no, the team does not earn a first down.

30. $8 + 1 + (-5) + 7 = 9 + 2 = 11$ and
$11 \geq 10$; so, yes, the team does earn a first down.

31.
$$-20 + (-15) + 25 + (-30) + 42 + (-45) + 38 = -35 + 25 + (-30) + 42 + (-45) + 38$$
$$= -10 + (-30) + 42 + (-45) + 38$$
$$= -40 + 42 + (-45) + 38$$
$$= 2 + (-45) + 38$$
$$= -43 + 38$$
$$= -\$5$$

32. $50 + (-5) = \$45$

33. $-x + 4x + 9 = 3x + 9$
$3x + 9 = 3(2) + 9$
$= 6 + 9$
$= 15$

34. $8x + (-6x) + 3 = 2x + 3$
$2x + 3 = 2(2) + 3$
$= 4 + 3$
$= 7$

35. $-2x + 10x + (-7x) = 8x + (-7x)$
$= x$
$x = 2$

36. $9x + 13x + (-10x) = 22x + (-10x)$
$= 12x$
$12x = 12(2)$
$= 24$

37. $13x + (-11x) + x = 2x + x$
$= 3x$
$3x = 3(2)$
$= 6$

38. $9x + (-x) + 2x = 8x + 2x$
$= 10x$
$10x = 10(2)$
$= 20$

39. $-3x + 2x + 26x = -x + 26x$
$= 25x$
$25x = 25(2)$
$= 50$

40. $-4x + 9x + 6x = 5x + 6x$
$= 11x$
$11x = 11(2)$
$= 22$

41. $-7x + 8 + 17x = 10x + 8$
$10x + 8 = 10(2) + 8$
$= 20 + 8$
$= 28$

42. $-8x + 10 + 12x = 4x + 10$
$4x + 10 = 4(2) + 10$
$= 8 + 10$
$= 18$

43. $5x + 3 + (-8) + (-3x) = 2x + (-5)$
$2x + (-5) = 2(2) + (-5)$
$= 4 + (-5)$
$= -1$

44. $9x + 6 + (-18) + (-6x) = 3x + (-12)$
$3x + (-12) = 3(2) + (-12)$
$= 6 + (-12)$
$= -6$

45. D; $|7 - (-6)| = |13| = 13$ degrees

46. Answers vary.
First down: gained 7 yards
Second down: lost 3 yards
Third down: lost 9 yards
Fourth down: gained 15 yards
$7 + (-3) + (-9) + 15 = 10$ yards, so yes, the team gained the yards they needed for a first down.

Spiral R E V I E W

1. $6n - 12 = 6(3) - 12$
$= 18 - 12$
$= 6$

2. $n^2 - 4 = (3)^2 - 4$
$= 9 - 4$
$= 5$

3. $13n + 16 = 13(3) + 16$
$= 39 + 16$
$= 55$

4. $1.2n + 1.5 = 1.2(3) + 1.5$
$= 3.6 + 1.5$
$= 5.1$

5. $6 \times (n - 1) = 6 \times (3 - 1)$
$= 6 \times 2$
$= 12$

6. $\frac{1}{4}(n \times 8) = \frac{1}{4}(3 \times 8)$
$= \frac{1}{4}(24)$
$= 6$

7. $n^2 \div 3 = 3^2 \div 3$
$= 9 \div 3$
$= 3$

8. $14 \times (n + 2) - 15 = 14 \times (3 + 2) - 15$
$= 14 \times 5 - 15$
$= 70 - 15$
$= 55$

9. $\frac{1}{8}(32)$ $\boxed{?}$ $\frac{1}{4}(16)$
$4 = 4$

10. $16 + (-8)$ $\boxed{?}$ $10 + (-3)$
$8 > 7$

11. $-12 + (-2)$ $\boxed{?}$ $-17 + 5$
$-14 < -12$

12. $x - 12 = 4$
$x - 12 + 12 = 4 + 12$
$x = 16$
$x = 17$
No, the solutions are different.

13. $x - 2 = 14$
$x - 2 + 2 = 14 + 2$
$x = 16$
$16 - 2 = 14 \checkmark$

14. $y + 5 = 6$
$y + 5 - 5 = 6 - 5$
$y = 1$
$1 + 5 = 6 \checkmark$

15. $14 + z = 34$
$14 + z - 14 = 34 - 14$
$z = 20$
$14 + 20 = 34 \checkmark$

16. $a - 11 = 22$
$a - 11 + 11 = 22 + 11$
$a = 33$
$33 - 11 = 22 \checkmark$

17. $3b = 6$
$\frac{3b}{3} = \frac{6}{3}$
$b = 2$
$3(2) = 6 \checkmark$

18. $16c = 32$

$\dfrac{16c}{16} = \dfrac{32}{16}$

$c = 2$

$16(2) = 32$ ✓

19. $\dfrac{1}{2}p = 5$

$2 \cdot \dfrac{1}{2}p = 2 \cdot 5$

$p = 10$

$\dfrac{1}{2}(10) = 5$ ✓

20. $10q = \dfrac{1}{2}$

$\dfrac{10q}{10} = \dfrac{1}{2} \div 10$

$q = \dfrac{1}{20}$

$10\left(\dfrac{1}{20}\right) = \dfrac{1}{2}$ ✓

21. $x(9 + 12 + 16) = 37x$

$37(4.5) = \$166.50$

Lab 3.4

Part A

1. 

2

2. 

−1

3. 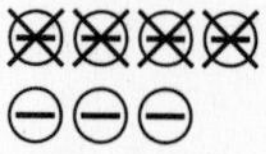

−3

Part B

4. 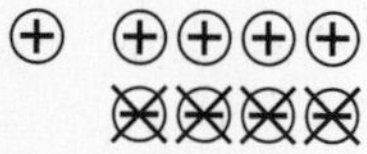

5

5. 

−2

6. 

−7

7. 

1

8. 

2

9. 

−11

10. 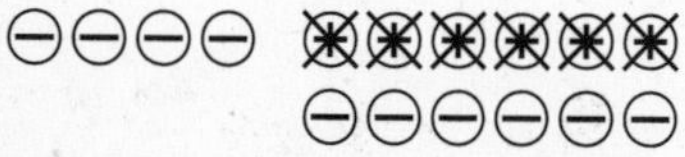

−10

3.4 *Subtracting Integers*

ONGOING ASSESSMENT

1. "The weather is not bad" means "the weather is good." Two negative conditions applied to a noun and two negative conditions applied to a number both result in a positive condition.

EXERCISES

1. To subtract -2 from 5, add the opposite of -2 to 5; the opposite of -2 is 2.
$$5 - (-2) = 5 + 2 = 7$$

2. $r(s - t) = rs - rt$

3. All values of x.
$$5x - 2x - 12 = 5x + (-2x) + (-12)$$
$$3x - 12 = 3x + (-12)$$
Subtracting a quantity gives the same result as adding its opposite.

4. Some values of x.
x can only be 0.

5. No values of x.
$$3(x - 4) = 3x - (-12)$$
$$3x - 12 = 3x + 12$$
The last equation cannot be true for any value of x.

6. Some values of x.
The statement is false when $x \leq 0$.

7. $19 - 17 = 2$

8. $5 - 9 = 5 + (-9) = -4$;
$5 - 9 = -4$

9. $23 - (-8) = 23 + (8) = 31$;
$23 - (-8) = 31$

10. $2 - (-4) = 2 + (4) = 6$;
$2 - (-4) = 6$

11. $-10 - 7 = -10 + (-7) = -17$;
$-10 - 7 = -17$

12. $-3 - 3 = -3 + (-3) = -6$;
$-3 - 3 = -6$

13. $-5 - (-5) = -5 + 5 = 0$;
$-5 - (-5) = 0$

14. $-16 - (-8) = -16 + 8 = -8$;
$-16 - (-8) = -8$

15. $-5 - 5 = -5 + (-5) = -10$;
$-5 - 5 = -10$

16. $-16 - 8 = -16 + (-8) = -24$;
$-16 - 8 = -24$

17. $0 - 27 = 0 + (-27) = -27$;
$0 - 27 = -27$

18. $0 - (-61) = 0 + 61 = 61$;
$0 - (-61) = 61$

19. The $\boxed{+/-}$ key refers to the sign of a number, usually negative; the $\boxed{-}$ key refers to the operation of subtraction and is used between two numbers.

20. Let $a = 5$: $a - 1 = 5 - 1 = 4$;
Let $a = -5$: $a - 1 = -5 - 1 = -5 + (-1) = -6$

21. Let $a = 5$: $1 - a = 1 - 5 = 1 + (-5) = -4$;
Let $a = -5$: $1 - a = 1 - (-5) = 1 + 5 = 6$

22. Let $a = 5$: $a - 6 = 5 - 6 = 5 + (-6) = -1$;
Let $a = -5$: $a - 6 = -5 - 6 = -5 + (-6) = -11$

23. Let $a = 5$: $6 - a = 6 - 5 = 1$;
Let $a = -5$: $6 - a = 6 - (-5) = 6 + 5 = 11$

24. $3x - 2x + 16 = 3x + (-2x) + 16$;
$3x, \ -2x, \ 16$

25. $7x - 9x - 5 = 7x + (-9x) + (-5)$;
$7x, \ -9x, \ -5$

26. $7a - 5b = 7a + (-5b)$;
$7a, \ -5b$

27. $4 - 2n + 4m = 4 + (-2n) + 4m$;
$4, \ -2n, \ 4m$

28. $9x - 6x - 17 = 3x - 17$

29. $18n - 12n + 4 = 6n + 4$

30. $-11y - (-15y) - 2 = -11y + 15y - 2$
$$= 4y - 2$$

31. $-20x - (-30x) + 10 = -20x + 30x + 10$
$$= 10x + 10$$

32. $b - (-2b) = b + 2b$
$$= 3b$$

33. $3x - (-3x) = 3x + 3x$
$$= 6x$$

34. $-2a - 3a - 4 = -2a + (-3a) - 4$
$$= -5a - 4$$

35. $-13x - 13x - 13 = -13x + (-13x) - 13$
$$= -26x - 13$$

36. $4m - 6m + 8 = 4m + (-6m) + 8$
$$= -2m + 8$$

37. $16y - 20y + 24 = 16y + (-20y) + 24$
$$= -4y + 24$$

38. $-14x - (-10x) = -14x + 10x$
$$= -4x$$

39. $-30x - (-19x) = -30x + 19x$
$$= -11x$$

40. $11,049 - (-282) = 11,331$ ft

41. Mercury: $800 - (-280) = 800 + 280 = 1080°$;
Venus: $925 - 721 = 204°$;
Earth: $136 - (-129) = 136 + 129 = 265°$;
Mars: $68 - (-220) = 68 + 220 = 288°$

42. $-129 - (-220) = -129 + 220 = 91°$

43. $800 - 925 = 800 + (-925)$
$$= -125°$$

44. *Sample answer:* $x = 3, \ y = 2$

45. *Sample answer:*
$x = 2, \ y = 3$

46. *Sample answer:*
$x = -3, \ y = -2$

47. *Sample answer:*
$x = -2, \ y = -3$

48. $5 - 3 = 2$

49. $3 - 5 = 3 + (-5) = -2$

50. $-7 - 12 = -7 + (-12) = -19$

51. $12 - (-7) = 12 + 7 = 19$

52. Conjecture: $a - b$ and $b - a$ are opposites.

When $a = 6$ and $b = 4$, $a - b = 6 - 4 = 2$ and $b - a = 4 - 6 = 4 + (-6) = -2$.
When $a = 5$ and $b = 8$, $a - b = 5 - 8 = 5 + (-8) = -3$ and $b - a = 8 - 5 = 3$.
When $a = -1$ and $b = 3$, $a - b = -1 - 3 = -1 + (-3) = -4$ and $b - a = 3 - (-1) = 3 + 1 = 4$.

53. C; $9 - 4 = 5, 5 - 4 = 1, 1 - 4 = -3$

54. Answers vary.

Lab 3.5

Part A

1.

-4

2.

-20

3.

-15

Part B

4.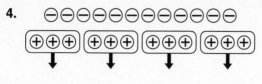

−12

5. (a row of minus signs above three groups of plus signs with downward arrows)

−15

6. (a row of minus signs above six groups of two plus signs with downward arrows)

−12

Part C

7.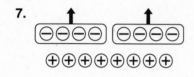

8

8.

3

9.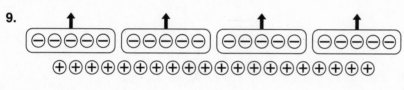

20

10.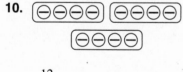

−12

11. (two boxes with minus signs and upward arrows above two plus signs)

2

12. (a long row of minus signs above four groups of four plus signs with downward arrows)

−16

13. (five boxes each with two minus signs and upward arrows, above ten plus signs)

10

14. (four boxes each with three minus signs)

−12

15.

-8

16. It is always negative; no.

17. The product of two negative integers is always positive.

3.5 Multiplying Integers

ONGOING ASSESSMENT

$$C = \tfrac{5}{9}(F - 32)$$

1. $C = \tfrac{5}{9}(-4 - 32)$

$= \tfrac{5}{9}(-36)$

$= -\tfrac{180}{9}$

$= -20°C$

2. $C = \tfrac{5}{9}(140 - 32)$

$= \tfrac{5}{9}(108)$

$= \tfrac{540}{9}$

$= 60°C$

EXERCISES

1. $3(-4); -12$

2. $3(-x); -3x$

3. $4(-8); -32$

4. a and b are both negative, so ab is positive.
a is negative and c is positive, so ac is negative.
b is negative and c is positive, so bc is negative.

5. $(-4)^2; -4^2 = (-4)(4)$

6.

If x is	then x^2 is	then $2x$ is	then $-4x$ is
positive	positive	positive	negative
negative	positive	negative	positive

Answer: x^2

7. $-4 \cdot (-6) = 24$

8. $-10 \cdot (-2) = 20$

9. $5 \cdot (-11) = -55$

10. $-8 \cdot 6 = -48$

11. $(-7)(-9) = 63$

12. $(-10)(3) = -30$

13. $(-1)(54) = -54$

14. $(-20)(0) = 0$

15. Negative. For example:

$(-1)(-1)(-1) = (1)(-1)$

$= -1$

16. Positive. For example:

$(-1)(-1)(-1)(-1) = 1(-1)(-1)$

$= (-1)(-1)$

$= 1$

35. $4z + 6z - 9y - 25 = 10z - 9y - 25$

$10z - 9y - 25 = 10(6) - 9(4) - 25$

$= 60 - 36 - 25$

$= 24 - 25$

$= 24 + (-25)$

$= -1$

36. $-16 + 5x - 3x + y = -16 + 2x + y$

$-16 + 2x + y = -16 + 2(3) + 4$

$= -16 + 6 + 4$

$= -10 + 4$

$= -6$

37. $6(5x - 3x + x) = 6(3x)$

$= 18x$

$18x = 18(3)$

$= 54$

38. $3(2y + y) + 16 = 3(3y) + 16$

$= 9y + 16$

$9y + 16 = 9(4) + 16$

$= 36 + 16$

$= 52$

39. $z(y + 2) + |-y| = zy + 2z + |y|$

$3y + 2z + |y| = (6)(4) + 2(6) + |4|$

$= 24 + 12 + 4$

$= 40$

40. $|-z| + 3(y - 1) = |z| + 3y - 3$

$|z| + 3y - 3 = |6| + 3(4) - 3$

$= 6 + 12 - 3$

$= 15$

41.

42.

43.

44.

45. $D = r \cdot t$

$20 = r \cdot 80$

$0.25 \approx r$

To convert to mi/h:

$$\frac{0.25 \text{ mi}}{\text{min}} \cdot \frac{60 \text{ min}}{1 \text{ hr}} = \frac{15 \text{ mi}}{\text{hr}}$$

You traveled about 15 mi/h.

46. $D = r \cdot t$

$20 = r \cdot 85$

$0.2353 \approx r$

To convert to mi/h:

$$\frac{0.2353 \text{ mi}}{\text{min}} \cdot \frac{60 \text{ min}}{1 \text{ hr}} = \frac{14.11 \text{ mi}}{\text{hr}}$$

Your friend traveled about 14 mi/h.

47.–50.

51. $x + 7 = 16$

$x + 7 - 7 = 16 - 7$

$x = 9$

52. $y + 5 = -6$

$y + 5 - 5 = -6 - 5$

$y = -6 + (-5)$

$y = -11$

53. $z - 8 = -16$

$z - 8 + 8 = -16 + 8$

$z = -8$

54.
$$a - 8 = 13$$
$$a - 8 + 8 = 13 + 8$$
$$a = 21$$

55.
$$10b = 100$$
$$\frac{10b}{10} = \frac{100}{10}$$
$$b = 10$$

56.
$$-9x = 36$$
$$\frac{-9x}{-9} = \frac{36}{-9}$$
$$x = -4$$

57.
$$\frac{y}{-12} = 8$$
$$-12 \cdot \left(\frac{y}{-12}\right) = (-12) \cdot 8$$
$$y = -96$$

58.
$$\frac{m}{4} = 16$$
$$4 \cdot \frac{m}{4} = 4 \cdot 16$$
$$m = 64$$

59.
$$n + 6 < 7$$
$$n + 6 - 6 < 7 - 6$$
$$n < 1$$

60.
$$p + 4 > 12$$
$$p + 4 - 4 > 12 - 4$$
$$p > 8$$

61.
$$x - 2 \geq 5$$
$$x - 2 + 2 \geq 5 + 2$$
$$x \geq 7$$

62.
$$y - 11 \leq 9$$
$$y - 11 + 11 \leq 9 + 11$$
$$y \leq 20$$

63.
$$15c > 30$$
$$\frac{15c}{15} > \frac{30}{15}$$
$$c > 2$$

64.
$$26 > 13t$$
$$\frac{26}{13} > \frac{13t}{13}$$
$$2 > t$$

65.
$$\frac{q}{3} \leq 25$$
$$3 \cdot \frac{q}{3} \leq 3 \cdot 25$$
$$q \leq 75$$

66.
$$40 \leq \frac{s}{9}$$
$$9 \cdot 40 \leq 9 \cdot \frac{s}{9}$$
$$360 \leq s$$

67.
$$-12 = n + 9$$
$$-12 - 9 = n + 9 - 9$$
$$-21 = n$$

68.
$$x - 16 \leq 20$$
$$x - 16 + 16 \leq 20 + 16$$
$$x \leq 36$$

69.
$$7n > 91$$
$$\frac{7n}{7} > \frac{91}{7}$$
$$n > 13$$

70.
$$3 = \frac{n}{4}$$
$$4 \cdot 3 = 4 \cdot \frac{n}{4}$$
$$12 = n$$

71. Green figure: $(1, 2)$, $(1, 4)$, $(-1, 4)$, $(-1, 2)$
Blue figure: $(-1, -1)$, $(-1, 3)$, $(-3, 3)$, $(-3, -1)$
Yellow figure: $(2, -1)$, $(2, 2)$, $(-1, 2)$, $(-1, -1)$
Red figure: $(5, -1)$, $(5, 4)$, $(2, 4)$, $(2, -1)$

Perimeter of green figure: $2 + 2 + 2 + 2 = 8$ units
Perimeter of blue figure: $4 + 2 + 4 + 2 = 12$ units
Perimeter of yellow figure: $3 + 3 + 3 + 3 = 12$ units
Perimeter of red figure: $3 + 5 + 3 + 5 = 16$ units

Area of the entire shaded figure = Area of green figure + Area of blue figure
$$+ \text{ Area of yellow figure} + \text{ Area of red figure}$$
$$= 2^2 + 4(2) + 3^2 + 5(3)$$
$$= 36 \text{ units}^2$$

72. Green figure: $(1, 0)$, $(1, 4)$, $(-1, 4)$, $(-1, 0)$

Blue figure: $(-1, -1)$, $(-1, 2)$, $(-6, 2)$, $(-6, -1)$

Yellow figure: $(-1, -4)$, $(-1, -1)$, $(-5, -1)$, $(-5, -4)$

Red figure: $(4, -3)$, $(4, 0)$, $(-1, 0)$, $(-1, -3)$

Perimeter of green figure: $4 + 2 + 4 + 2 = 12$ units

Perimeter of blue figure: $3 + 5 + 3 + 5 = 16$ units

Perimeter of yellow figure: $3 + 4 + 3 + 4 = 14$ units

Perimeter of red figure: $3 + 5 + 3 + 5 = 16$ units

Area of the entire shaded figure = Area of green figure + Area of blue figure

$$+ \text{ Area of yellow figure} + \text{Area of red figure}$$

$$= 4(2) + 3(5) + 3(4) + 3(5)$$

$$= 50 \text{ units}^2$$

Chapter 4
Exploring the Language of Algebra

Lab 4.1

Part A

1. a. No
   b. Yes; $x = 1$
   c. Yes; $x = 3$

2. One x-tile is isolated on one side of the equation.

3. $2X + 5 = 9$

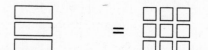

$X = 2$

4. $3M + 4 = 13$

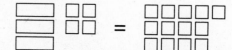

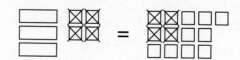

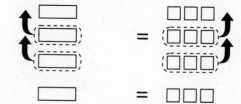

$M = 3$

5. $13 = 5 + 4Y$

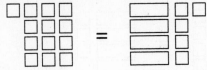

$Y = 2$

Part B

6.

$3x + 2 = 5$	*Write original equation.*
$3x + 2 - 2 = 5 - 2$	*Subtract 2 from each side.*
$3x = 3$	*Simplify.*
$\dfrac{3x}{3} = \dfrac{3}{3}$	*Divide each side by 3.*
$x = 1$	*Simplify.*

7. $3x + 2 = 14$

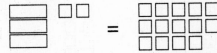

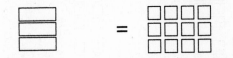

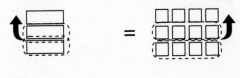

$x = 4$

8. $15 = 2n + 1$

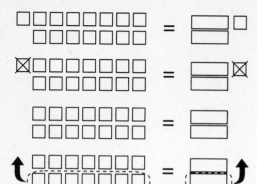

$7 = n$

9. $11 = 3 + 4y$

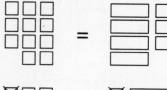
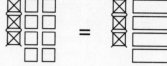
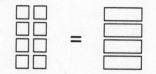
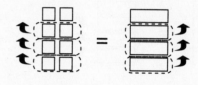

$2 = y$

10. $6m + 3 = 15$

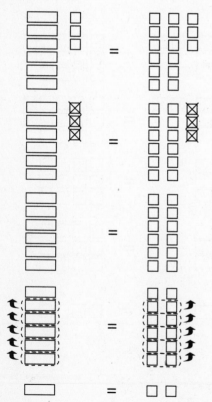

$m = 2$

11. a. You must subtract the 1-tiles before dividing to isolate the x-tile.

b.

4.1 ALGEBRA CONNECTION: Solving Two-Step Equations

ONGOING ASSESSMENT

1.–3. Answers vary.

1.

$5x - 4 = 6$	*Original equation*
$5x - 4 + 4 = 6 + 4$	*Add 4 to each side.*
$5x = 10$	*Simplify.*
$\dfrac{5x}{5} = \dfrac{10}{5}$	*Divide each side by 5.*
$x = 2$	*Simplify.*

2.

$\dfrac{n}{3} + 7 = 9$	*Original equation*
$\dfrac{n}{3} + 7 - 7 = 9 - 7$	*Subtract 7 from each side.*
$\dfrac{n}{3} = 2$	*Simplify.*
$3 \cdot \dfrac{n}{3} = 2 \cdot 3$	*Multiply each side by 3.*
$n = 6$	*Simplify.*

3.

$13 = 3m + 7$	*Original equation*
$13 - 7 = 3m + 7 - 7$	*Subtract 7 from each side.*
$6 = 3m$	*Simplify.*
$\dfrac{6}{3} = \dfrac{3m}{3}$	*Divide each side by 3.*
$2 = m$	*Simplify.*

EXERCISES

1. Add 4 to each side.

2. Subtract 3 from each side.

3. Subtract 2 from each side.

4. 8 was not divided by 3. When dividing each side of an equation by a number, each term must be divided by the number.

5. B; $2x + 8 = 16$
$2x + 8 - 8 = 16 - 8$
$2x = 8$

6. D; $2x - 8 = 16$
$2x - 8 + 8 = 16 + 8$
$2x = 24$

7. A; $2x - 8 = -16$
$2x - 8 + 8 = -16 + 8$
$2x = -8$

8. C; $2x + 8 = -16$
$2x + 8 - 8 = -16 - 8$
$2x = -24$

9.
$$3x + 15 = 24$$
$$3x + 15 - 15 = 24 - 15$$
$$3x = 9$$
$$\frac{3x}{3} = \frac{9}{3}$$
$$x = 3$$

Check:
$$3x + 15 = 24$$
$$3(3) + 15 \overset{?}{=} 24$$
$$9 + 15 \overset{?}{=} 24$$
$$24 = 24$$

10.
$$4x + 11 = 31$$
$$4x + 11 - 11 = 31 - 11$$
$$4x = 20$$
$$\frac{4x}{4} = \frac{20}{4}$$
$$x = 5$$

Check:
$$4x + 11 = 31$$
$$4(5) + 11 \overset{?}{=} 31$$
$$20 + 11 \overset{?}{=} 31$$
$$31 = 31$$

11.
$$6p + 8 = 2$$
$$6p + 8 - 8 = 2 - 8$$
$$6p = -6$$
$$\frac{6p}{6} = \frac{-6}{6}$$
$$p = -1$$

Check:
$$6p + 8 = 2$$
$$6(-1) + 8 \overset{?}{=} 2$$
$$-6 + 8 \overset{?}{=} 2$$
$$2 = 2$$

12.
$$5q + 14 = 4$$
$$5q + 14 - 14 = 4 - 14$$
$$5q = -10$$
$$\frac{5q}{5} = \frac{-10}{5}$$
$$q = -2$$

Check:
$$5q + 14 = 4$$
$$5(-2) + 14 \overset{?}{=} 4$$
$$-10 + 14 \overset{?}{=} 4$$
$$4 = 4$$

13.
$$-2r - 4 = 22$$
$$-2r - 4 + 4 = 22 + 4$$
$$-2r = 26$$
$$\frac{-2r}{-2} = \frac{26}{-2}$$
$$r = -13$$

Check:
$$-2r - 4 = 22$$
$$-2(-13) - 4 \overset{?}{=} 22$$
$$26 - 4 \overset{?}{=} 22$$
$$22 = 22$$

14.
$$-3s - 5 = -20$$
$$-3s - 5 + 5 = -20 + 5$$
$$-3s = -15$$
$$\frac{-3s}{-3} = \frac{-15}{-3}$$
$$s = 5$$

Check:
$$-3s - 5 = -20$$
$$-3(5) - 5 \overset{?}{=} -20$$
$$-15 - 5 \overset{?}{=} -20$$
$$-20 = -20$$

15.
$$\frac{t}{2} + 6 = 10$$
$$\frac{t}{2} + 6 - 6 = 10 - 6$$
$$\frac{t}{2} = 4$$
$$2 \cdot \frac{t}{2} = 2 \cdot 4$$
$$t = 8$$

Check:
$$\frac{t}{2} + 6 = 10$$
$$\frac{8}{2} + 6 \overset{?}{=} 10$$
$$4 + 6 \overset{?}{=} 10$$
$$10 = 10$$

16.
$$\frac{z}{3} + 17 = 21$$
$$\frac{z}{3} + 17 - 17 = 21 - 17$$
$$\frac{z}{3} = 4$$
$$3 \cdot \frac{z}{3} = 3 \cdot 4$$
$$z = 12$$

Check:
$$\frac{z}{3} + 17 = 21$$
$$\frac{12}{3} + 17 \overset{?}{=} 21$$
$$4 + 17 \overset{?}{=} 21$$
$$21 = 21$$

17.
$$\frac{x}{4} - 2 = -7$$
$$\frac{x}{4} - 2 + 2 = -7 + 2$$
$$\frac{x}{4} = -5$$
$$4 \cdot \frac{x}{4} = 4 \cdot -5$$
$$x = -20$$

Check:
$$\frac{x}{4} - 2 = -7$$
$$\frac{-20}{4} - 2 \overset{?}{=} -7$$
$$-5 - 2 \overset{?}{=} -7$$
$$-7 = -7$$

18. $3x + 4 = 7$

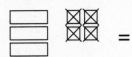

$x = 1$

19.–24. $x = $ the number

19.
$$3x + 7 = 34$$
$$3x + 7 - 7 = 34 - 7$$
$$3x = 27$$
$$\frac{3x}{3} = \frac{27}{3}$$
$$x = 9$$

20.
$$8x + 12 = 100$$
$$8x + 12 - 12 = 100 - 12$$
$$8x = 88$$
$$\frac{8x}{8} = \frac{88}{8}$$
$$x = 11$$

21.
$$\tfrac{1}{4}x - 2 = 5$$
$$\tfrac{1}{4}x - 2 + 2 = 5 + 2$$
$$\tfrac{1}{4}x = 7$$
$$4 \cdot \tfrac{1}{4}x = 4 \cdot 7$$
$$x = 28$$

22.
$$\tfrac{1}{2}x + 13 = 30$$
$$\tfrac{1}{2}x + 13 - 13 = 30 - 13$$
$$\tfrac{1}{2}x = 17$$
$$2 \cdot \tfrac{1}{2}x = 2 \cdot 17$$
$$x = 34$$

23.
$$21 + 7x = -14$$
$$21 + 7x - 21 = -14 - 21$$
$$7x = -35$$
$$\frac{7x}{7} = \frac{-35}{7}$$
$$x = -5$$

24.
$$84 + \frac{x}{2} = -36$$
$$84 + \frac{x}{2} - 84 = -36 - 84$$
$$\frac{x}{2} = -120$$
$$2 \cdot \frac{x}{2} = 2 \cdot -120$$
$$x = -240$$

25.
$$3x + 17 = 38$$
$$3x + 17 - 17 = 38 - 17$$
$$3x = 21$$
$$\frac{3x}{3} = \frac{21}{3}$$
$$x = 7$$

26.
$$4x + 20 = 72$$
$$4x + 20 - 20 = 72 - 20$$
$$4x = 52$$
$$\frac{4x}{4} = \frac{52}{4}$$
$$x = 13$$

27. Answers vary.

28. a.

$$\boxed{\begin{array}{c}\text{Cost of}\\\text{first minute}\end{array}} + \boxed{\begin{array}{c}\text{Cost of each}\\\text{additional minute}\end{array}} \times \boxed{\begin{array}{c}\text{Number of}\\\text{additional minutes}\end{array}} = \boxed{\begin{array}{c}\text{Money}\\\text{you have}\end{array}}$$

Cost of first minute $= 25$ (cents)
Cost of each additional minute $= 15$ (cents)
Number of additional minutes $= n$
Money you have $= 95$ (cents)

$$25 + 15n = 95$$
$$25 + 15n - 25 = 95 - 25$$
$$15n = 70$$
$$\frac{15n}{15} = \frac{70}{15}$$
$$n = 4\tfrac{2}{3}$$

b. Since you would be charged 15 cents for any part of a minute, you can talk only 4 additional minutes. You can talk 1 minute $+$ 4 minutes or 5 minutes.

Check: $25 + 15(4) = 75 < 95$
$25 + 15(5) = 100 > 95$

29. $h =$ number of hours taken to repair the car.

$$22h + 156 = 321$$
$$22h + 156 - 156 = 321 - 156$$
$$22h = 165$$
$$\frac{22h}{22} = \frac{165}{22}$$
$$h = 7.5$$

It took $7\tfrac{1}{2}$ hours to repair the car.

30. A

31. C

32. \$5.00; \$.078760 kW•h

33. Total charges $= x$ kW•h $\times$ rate per kilowatt hour $+$ basic service charge

34. \$43.59

35.
$$0.078760x + 5 = 40$$
$$0.078760x = 40 - 5$$
$$0.078760x = 35$$
$$x = \frac{35}{0.078760}$$
$$x = 444 \text{ kW•h}$$

4.2 Solving Multi-Step Equations

ONGOING ASSESSMENT

1. $3m - (2m + 4)$

$3m - 2m - 4$ *Distribute minus sign.*

$m - 4$

2. $6n - (5n - 2)$

$6n - 5n + 2$ *Distribute minus sign.*

$n + 2$

EXERCISES

1. Combine like terms, subtract 8 from each side, and divide each side by 2.

2. Combine like terms, subtract 7 from each side, $(-1)x = -x$, and divide each side by -1.

3. Combine like terms, subtract 11 from each side, and divide each side by -8.

4. $4(1) - 1 - 5 \stackrel{?}{=} -8$

$\quad -2 \neq -8$, no

$4x - x - 5 = -8$

$3x - 5 = -8$

$3x - 5 + 5 = -8 + 5$

$3x = -3$

$\dfrac{3x}{3} = \dfrac{-3}{3}$

$x = -1$

5. $4(3) - 2(3) - 8 \stackrel{?}{=} 1$

$\quad -2 \neq 1$, no

$4t - 2t - 8 = 1$

$2t - 8 = 1$

$2t - 8 + 8 = 1 + 8$

$2t = 9$

$\dfrac{2t}{2} = \dfrac{9}{2}$

$t = \dfrac{9}{2}$

6. $2 \stackrel{?}{=} 3(3) - 8(3) + 17$

$2 = 2 \; \checkmark$, yes

7. $2a + 3a = 15$

$5a = 15$

$a = 3$

Check:

$2a + 3a = 15$

$2(3) + 3(3) \stackrel{?}{=} 15$

$6 + 9 \stackrel{?}{=} 15$

$15 = 14$

8. $s + 5s - 3s = 21$

$6s - 3s = 21$

$3s = 21$

$s = 7$

Check:

$s + 5s - 3s = 21$

$7 + 5(7) - 3(7) \stackrel{?}{=} 21$

$7 + 35 - 21 \stackrel{?}{=} 21$

$42 - 21 \stackrel{?}{=} 21$

$21 = 21$

9. $22 = 12t + 4t - 5t$

$22 = 16t - 5t$

$22 = 11t$

$2 = t$

Check:

$22 = 12t + 4t - 5t$

$22 \stackrel{?}{=} 12(2) + 4(2) - 5(2)$

$22 \stackrel{?}{=} 24 + 8 - 10$

$22 = 22$

10. $8x + 2x - 4 = 6$

$10x - 4 = 6$

$10x - 4 + 4 = 6 + 4$

$10x = 10$

$\dfrac{10x}{10} = \dfrac{10}{10}$

$x = 1$

Check:

$8x + 2x - 4 = 6$

$8(1) + 2(1) - 4 \stackrel{?}{=} 6$

$8 + 2 - 4 \stackrel{?}{=} 6$

$6 = 6$

11. $6y - 3y + 2 = -16$

$3y + 2 = -16$

$3y + 2 - 2 = -16 - 2$

$3y = -18$

$\dfrac{3y}{3} = \dfrac{-18}{3}$

$y = -6$

Check:

$6y - 3y + 2 = -16$

$6(-6) - 3(-6) + 2 \stackrel{?}{=} -16$

$-36 + 18 + 2 \stackrel{?}{=} -16$

$-16 = -16$

12. $42 = 8a - 2a + 12$

$42 = 6a + 12$

$42 - 12 = 6a + 12 - 12$

$30 = 6a$

$\dfrac{30}{6} = \dfrac{6a}{6}$

$5 = a$

Check:

$42 = 8a - 2a + 12$

$42 \stackrel{?}{=} 8(5) - 2(5) + 12$

$42 \stackrel{?}{=} 40 - 10 + 12$

$42 = 42$

13.
$$6m - 2m - 6 = -60$$
$$4m - 6 = -60$$
$$4m - 6 + 6 = -60 + 6$$
$$4m = -54$$
$$\frac{4m}{4} = \frac{-54}{4}$$
$$m = -13.5$$

Check:
$$6m - 2m - 6 = -60$$
$$6(-13.5) - 2(-13.5) - 6 \stackrel{?}{=} -60$$
$$-81 + 27 - 6 \stackrel{?}{=} -60$$
$$-60 = -60$$

14.
$$5x - 3x + 12 = 8$$
$$2x + 12 = 8$$
$$2x + 12 - 12 = 8 - 12$$
$$2x = -4$$
$$\frac{2x}{2} = \frac{-4}{2}$$
$$x = -2$$

Check:
$$5x - 3x + 12 = 8$$
$$5(-2) - 3(-2) + 12 \stackrel{?}{=} 8$$
$$-10 + 6 + 12 \stackrel{?}{=} 8$$
$$8 = 8$$

15.
$$n - 3n + 8 = -8$$
$$-2n + 8 = -8$$
$$-2n + 8 - 8 = -8 - 8$$
$$-2n = -16$$
$$\frac{-2n}{-2} = \frac{-16}{-2}$$
$$n = 8$$

Check:
$$n - 3n + 8 = -8$$
$$8 - 3(8) + 8 \stackrel{?}{=} -8$$
$$8 - 24 + 8 \stackrel{?}{=} -8$$
$$-8 = -8$$

16.
$$2y - 7y - 4y = 81$$
$$-9y = 81$$
$$\frac{-9y}{-9} = \frac{81}{-9}$$
$$y = -9$$

Check:
$$2y - 7y - 4y = 81$$
$$2(-9) - 7(-9) - 4(-9) \stackrel{?}{=} 81$$
$$-18 + 63 + 36 \stackrel{?}{=} 81$$
$$81 = 81$$

17.
$$\frac{5}{2}x - \frac{1}{2}x - 3 = 5$$
$$2x - 3 = 5$$
$$2x - 3 + 3 = 5 + 3$$
$$2x = 8$$
$$\frac{2x}{2} = \frac{8}{2}$$
$$x = 4$$

Check:
$$\frac{5}{2}x - \frac{1}{2}x - 3 = 5$$
$$\frac{5}{2}(4) - \frac{1}{2}(4) - 3 = 5$$
$$10 - 2 - 3 = 5$$
$$5 = 5$$

18.
$$\frac{3}{2}x - \frac{1}{2}x - 2 = 4$$
$$x - 2 = 4$$
$$x - 2 + 2 = 4 + 2$$
$$x = 6$$

Check:
$$\frac{3}{2}x - \frac{1}{2}x - 2 = 4$$
$$\frac{3}{2}(6) - \frac{1}{2}(6) - 2 \stackrel{?}{=} 4$$
$$9 - 3 - 2 \stackrel{?}{=} 4$$
$$4 = 4$$

19.
$$5 - 3(x + 1) = 5$$
$$5 - 3x - 3 = 5$$
$$-3x + 5 - 3 = 5$$
$$-3x + 2 = 5$$
$$-3x = 5 - 2$$
$$-3x = 3$$
$$x = -1$$

Check:
$$5 - 3(x + 1) = 5$$
$$5 - 3(-1 + 1) \stackrel{?}{=} 5$$
$$5 - 3(0) \stackrel{?}{=} 5$$
$$5 = 5$$

20.
$$4 - (x + 1) = 8$$
$$4 - x - 1 = 8$$
$$-x + 4 - 1 = 8$$
$$-x + 3 = 8$$
$$-x = 8 - 3$$
$$-x = 5$$
$$x = -5$$

Check:
$$4 - (x + 1) = 8$$
$$4 - (-5 + 1) \stackrel{?}{=} 8$$
$$4 - (-4) \stackrel{?}{=} 8$$
$$8 = 8$$

21.
$$3p - (6p + 24) = 0$$
$$3p - 6p - 24 = 0$$
$$-3p - 24 = 0$$
$$-3p = 24$$
$$p = -8$$

Check:
$$3p - (6p + 24) = 0$$
$$3(-8) - (6(-8) + 24) \stackrel{?}{=} 0$$
$$-24 - (-48 + 24) \stackrel{?}{=} 0$$
$$-24 - (24) \stackrel{?}{=} 0$$
$$0 = 0$$

22. $3x + 2x + 7x + 6 = 42$

$12x + 6 = 42$

$12x + 6 - 6 = 42 - 6$

$12x = 36$

$\dfrac{12x}{12} = \dfrac{36}{12}$

$x = 3$

23. $(4y - y) - 5 = -29$

$3y - 5 = -29$

$3y - 5 + 5 = -29 + 5$

$3y = -24$

$\dfrac{3y}{3} = \dfrac{-24}{3}$

$y = -8$

24. $(2x + 8) + (5x - 2) = 90$

$7x + 6 = 90$

$7x + 6 - 6 = 90 - 6$

$7x = 84$

$\dfrac{7x}{7} = \dfrac{84}{7}$

$x = 12$

25. $(5x + 15) + (x + 20) + (4x - 5) = 180$

$10x + 30 = 180$

$10x + 30 - 30 = 180 - 30$

$10x = 150$

$\dfrac{10x}{10} = \dfrac{150}{10}$

$x = 15$

26. $n = $ number of posters that must be sold to make a profit of \$300.

$300 = 5 \cdot n - (275 + 3 \cdot n)$

$300 = 5n - 275 - 3n$

$300 = 2n - 275$

$300 + 275 = 2n - 275 + 275$

$575 = 2n$

$\dfrac{575}{2} = \dfrac{2n}{2}$

$287.5 = n$

Since you can sell only whole posters, you must sell 288 posters to make a profit of \$300.

27. $b = $ number of bottles that must be sold to earn a profit of \$2000.

$2000 = 0.75b - (10{,}000 + 0.3b)$

$2000 = 0.75b - 10{,}000 - 0.3b$

$2000 = 0.45b - 10{,}000$

$2000 + 10{,}000 = 0.45b - 10{,}000 + 10{,}000$

$12{,}000 = 0.45b$

$\dfrac{12{,}000}{0.45} = \dfrac{0.45b}{0.45}$

$26{,}666.\overline{6} = b$

Since you can sell only whole bottles, you must sell 26,667 bottles to make a profit of \$2000.

28. $(1 + 2 + 2 + 1 + 3 + 5)x = 252$

$14x = 252$

$\dfrac{14x}{14} = \dfrac{252}{14}$

$x = 18$

You get paid \$18 per lawn.

29. C

30. B

31. $x + y = 7$

$x = -2:$ $-2 + y = 7$
               $y = 9,$ $(-2, 9)$

$x = -1:$ $-1 + y = 7$
               $y = 8,$ $(-1, 8)$

$x = 0:$ $0 + y = 7$
               $y = 7,$ $(0, 7)$

$x = 1:$ $1 + y = 7$
               $y = 6,$ $(1, 6)$

$x = 2:$ $2 + y = 7$
               $y = 5,$ $(2, 5)$

x	-2	-1	0	1	2
y	9	8	7	6	5

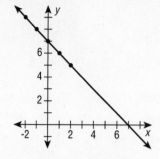

The graph is a straight line.

32. $2x - y = 5$

$x = -2:$ $2(-2) - y = 5$
               $y = -9,$ $(-2, -9)$

$x = -1:$ $2(-1) - y = 5$
               $y = -7,$ $(-1, -7)$

$x = 0:$ $2(0) - y = 5$
               $y = -5,$ $(0, -5)$

$x = 1:$ $2(1) - y = 5$
               $y = -3,$ $(1, -3)$

$x = 2:$ $2(2) - y = 5$
               $y = -1,$ $(2, -1)$

x	-2	-1	0	1	2
y	-9	-7	-5	-3	-1

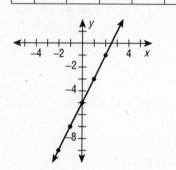

The graph is a straight line.

33. $-2x + y = 1$

$x = -2:$ $-2(-2) + y = 1$
               $y = -3,$ $(-2, -3)$

$x = -1:$ $-2(-1) + y = 1$
               $y = -1,$ $(-1, -1)$

$x = 0:$ $-2(0) + y = 1$
               $y = 1,$ $(0, 1)$

$x = 1:$ $-2(1) + y = 1$
               $y = 3,$ $(1, 3)$

$x = 2:$ $-2(2) + y = 1$
               $y = 5,$ $(2, 5)$

x	-2	-1	0	1	2
y	-3	-1	1	3	5

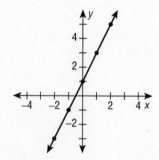

The graph is a straight line.

34. $x + y = 0$

$x = -2$: $\quad -2 + y = 0$
$\qquad\qquad\qquad y = 2, \quad (-2, 2)$

$x = -1$: $\quad -1 + y = 0$
$\qquad\qquad\qquad y = 1, \quad (-1, 1)$

$x = 0$: $\qquad 0 + y = 0$
$\qquad\qquad\qquad y = 0, \quad (0, 0)$

$x = 1$: $\qquad 1 + y = 0$
$\qquad\qquad\qquad y = -1, \quad (1, -1)$

$x = 2$: $\qquad 2 + y = 0$
$\qquad\qquad\qquad y = -2, \quad (2, -2)$

x	-2	-1	0	1	2
y	2	1	0	-1	-2

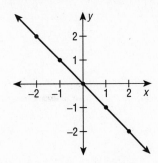

The graph is a straight line.

Spiral **R E V I E W**

1. $6b - 3 = 6(5) - 3$
$\qquad\quad = 30 - 3$
$\qquad\quad = 27$

2. $a - 2b = 4 - 2(5)$
$\qquad\quad = 4 - 10$
$\qquad\quad = -6$

3. $a^2 - 2b - 3 = 4^2 - 2(5) - 3$
$\qquad\qquad\quad = 16 - 10 - 3$
$\qquad\qquad\quad = 3$

4. Add 2 to each side, divide each side by 4.

5.

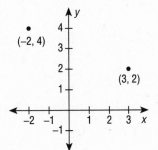

6. $4(3 + 2y) = 4(3) + 4(2y)$
$\qquad\qquad = 12 + 8y$

7. $4(2x - 3) = 4(2x) - 4(3)$
$\qquad\qquad = 8x - 12$

8. $0.25(4m + 8) = 0.25(4m) + 0.25(8)$
$\qquad\qquad\qquad = m + 2$

9. $2y - 14 = 0$
$\quad\; 2y = 14$
$\quad\; \dfrac{2y}{2} = \dfrac{14}{2}$
$\quad\; y = 7$

10. $16a + 14 = 110$
$\qquad 16a = 96$
$\qquad \dfrac{16a}{16} = \dfrac{96}{16}$
$\qquad a = 6$

11. $2.06r + 1.14r = 8.32$
$\qquad\quad 3.2r = 8.32$
$\qquad\quad \dfrac{3.2r}{3.2} = \dfrac{8.32}{3.2}$
$\qquad\quad r = 2.6$

12. $\dfrac{5}{2}x - \dfrac{1}{2}x = -1$
$\qquad 2x = -1$
$\qquad \dfrac{2x}{2} = \dfrac{-1}{2}$
$\qquad x = -\dfrac{1}{2}$

13. $\dfrac{m}{3} + 1 = 7$
$\qquad \dfrac{m}{3} = 6$
$\quad 3 \cdot \dfrac{m}{3} = 3 \cdot 6$
$\qquad m = 18$

14. $2c + 4c - c = 10$
$\qquad\quad 5c = 10$
$\qquad\quad \dfrac{5c}{5} = \dfrac{10}{5}$
$\qquad\quad c = 2$

15. $0.32x = 2.56$
$\quad\; \dfrac{0.32x}{0.32x} = \dfrac{2.56}{0.32}$
$\qquad x = 8$
You sent 8 invitations.

Using a Calculator

1. $2x + 5x - 7 = 9$

$$7x - 7 = 9$$
$$7x - 7 + 7 = 9 + 7$$
$$7x = 16$$
$$\frac{7x}{7} = \frac{16}{7}$$
$$x \approx 2.29$$

Check: $\qquad 2x + 5x - 7 = 9$

$$2(2.29) + 5(2.29) - 7 \overset{?}{=} 9$$
$$4.58 + 11.45 - 7 \overset{?}{=} 9$$
$$9.03 \approx 9$$

No, the answer was approximated.

2. $3y - 7 + 4y = 10$

$$7y - 7 = 10$$
$$7y - 7 + 7 = 10 + 7$$
$$7y = 17$$
$$\frac{7y}{7} = \frac{17}{7}$$
$$y \approx 2.43$$

Check: $\qquad 3y - 7 + 4y = 10$

$$3(2.43) - 7 + 4(2.43) \overset{?}{=} 10$$
$$7.29 - 7 + 9.72 \overset{?}{=} 10$$
$$10.01 \approx 10$$

No, the answer was approximated.

3. $2n + 7n - 13 = -4$

$$9n - 13 = -4$$
$$9n - 13 + 13 = -4 + 13$$
$$9n = 9$$
$$\frac{9n}{9} = \frac{9}{9}$$
$$n = 1$$

Check: $\quad 2n + 7n - 13 = -4$

$$2(1) + 7(1) - 13 \overset{?}{=} -4$$
$$-4 = -4$$

4. $-5a + 17 + 2a = 8$

$$-3a + 17 = 8$$
$$-3a + 17 - 17 = 8 - 17$$
$$-3a = -9$$
$$\frac{-3a}{-3} = \frac{-9}{-3}$$
$$a = 3$$

Check: $\quad -5a + 17 + 2a = 8$

$$-5(3) + 17 + 2(3) \overset{?}{=} 8$$
$$-15 + 17 + 6 \overset{?}{=} 8$$
$$8 = 8$$

5. $\qquad 12 = -2x + 5x - 9$

$$12 = 3x - 9$$
$$12 + 9 = 3x - 9 + 9$$
$$21 = 3x$$
$$\frac{21}{3} = \frac{3x}{3}$$
$$7 = x$$

Check: $12 = -2x + 5x - 9$

$$12 \overset{?}{=} -2(7) + 5(7) - 9$$
$$12 \overset{?}{=} -14 + 35 - 9$$
$$12 = 12$$

6. $\qquad -13 = 4y + 8y + 9$

$$-13 = 12y + 9$$
$$-13 - 9 = 12y + 9 - 9$$
$$-22 = 12y$$
$$\frac{-22}{12} = \frac{12y}{12}$$
$$-1.83 \approx y$$

Check: $-13 = 4y + 8y + 9$

$$-13 \overset{?}{=} 4(-1.83) + 8(-1.83) + 9$$
$$-13 \overset{?}{=} -7.32 - 14.64 + 9$$
$$-13 \approx -12.96$$

No, the answer was approximated.

7. $-4n - 14 - 5n = 11$

$$-9n - 14 = 11$$

$$-9n - 14 + 14 = 11 + 14$$

$$-9n = 25$$

$$\frac{-9n}{-9} = \frac{25}{-9}$$

$$n \approx -2.78$$

Check:

$$-4n - 14 - 5n = 11$$

$$-4(-2.78) - 14 - 5(-2.78) \overset{?}{=} 11$$

$$11.12 - 14 + 13.9 \overset{?}{=} 11$$

$$11.1 \approx 11$$

No, the answer was approximated.

8. $5m + 8m - 14 = 23$

$$13m - 14 = 23$$

$$13m = 37$$

$$\frac{13m}{13} = \frac{37}{13}$$

$$m \approx 2.85$$

Check:

$$5m + 8m - 14 = 23$$

$$5(2.85) + 8(2.85) - 14 \overset{?}{=} 23$$

$$14.25 + 22.8 - 14 \overset{?}{=} 23$$

$$23.05 \approx 23$$

No, the answer was approximated.

9. $5b - 21 - 2b = 10$

$$3b - 21 = 10$$

$$3b + 21 - 21 = 10 + 21$$

$$3b = 31$$

$$\frac{3b}{3} = \frac{31}{3}$$

$$b \approx 10.33$$

Check:

$$5b - 21 - 2b = 10$$

$$5(10.33) - 21 - 2(10.33) \overset{?}{=} 10$$

$$51.65 - 21 - (20.66) \overset{?}{=} 10$$

$$9.99 \approx 10$$

No, the answer was approximated.

4.3 Two-Step Equations and Problem Solving

ONGOING ASSESSMENT

1. Answers vary.

EXERCISES

1. $3 \cdot \frac{1}{3} = 1$, answer: 3

2. $-4 \cdot \left(-\frac{1}{4}\right) = 1$, answer: -4

3. $\left(-\frac{1}{5}\right) \cdot (-5) = 1$, answer: $-\frac{1}{5}$

4. $\boxed{?} \cdot 0 = 1$, answer: not possible

5.
$$7x = -28$$
$$\frac{1}{7} \cdot 7x = \frac{1}{7} \cdot (-28)$$
$$x = -4$$

6.
$$-\frac{1}{4}x = 12$$
$$-4 \cdot \left(-\frac{1}{4}x\right) = -4 \cdot 12$$
$$x = -48$$

7. $6x = 36 + 24$

$6x = 60$

$x = 10$

8. You could solve the problem without algebra by solving

$$\frac{36 + 24}{6} = 10.$$

9. Divide each side by $\frac{1}{3}$, multiply each side by 3.

10. Divide each side by -2, multiply each side by $-\frac{1}{2}$.

11. Divide each side by 9, multiply each side by $\frac{1}{9}$.

12. Divide each side by $-\frac{1}{4}$, multiply each side by -4.

13. $2y - 12 = 4$

$2y = 16$

$\dfrac{2y}{2} = \dfrac{16}{2}$

$y = 8$

14. $5n - 21 = 24$

$5n = 45$

$\dfrac{5n}{5} = \dfrac{45}{5}$

$n = 9$

15. $-\frac{1}{8}x + 14 = 6$

$-\frac{1}{8}x = -8$

$(-8)\left(-\frac{1}{8}x\right) = (-8)(-8)$

$x = 64$

16. $-12t - 7 = -15$

$-12t = -8$

$\dfrac{-12t}{-12} = \dfrac{-8}{-12}$

$t = \dfrac{2}{3}$

17. $21z - 16 = 12$

$21z = 28$

$\dfrac{21z}{21} = \dfrac{28}{21}$

$z = \dfrac{4}{3}$

18. $5r + 15 = 10$

$5r = -5$

$\dfrac{5r}{5} = \dfrac{-5}{5}$

$r = -1$

19. $-\frac{1}{10}m - 11 = 1$

$-\frac{1}{10}m = 12$

$-10 \cdot \left(-\frac{1}{10}m\right) = -10 \cdot 12$

$m = -120$

20. $\frac{1}{5}x - 3 = -2$

$\frac{1}{5}x = 1$

$5 \cdot \frac{1}{5}x = 5 \cdot 1$

$x = 5$

21. $-\frac{1}{3}y + 27 = 39$

$-\frac{1}{3}y = 12$

$-3 \cdot \left(-\frac{1}{3}y\right) = (-3) \cdot 12$

$y = -36$

22. $-\frac{1}{7}b + 2 = 1$

$-\frac{1}{7}b = -1$

$-7 \cdot \left(-\frac{1}{7}b\right) = (-7) \cdot -1$

$b = 7$

23. $\frac{1}{5}p - 3 = 0$

$\frac{1}{5}p = 3$

$5 \cdot \frac{1}{5}p = 5 \cdot 3$

$p = 15$

24. $\frac{2}{3}x - \frac{1}{3}x = 12$

$\frac{1}{3}x = 12$

$3 \cdot \frac{1}{3}x = 3 \cdot 12$

$x = 36$

25. $-11t + 16 = -6$

$-11t = -22$

$\dfrac{-11t}{-11} = \dfrac{-22}{-11}$

$t = 2$

26. $0.2x + 7 = 27$

$0.2x + 7 - 7 = 27 - 7$

$0.2x = 20$

$\dfrac{0.2x}{0.2} = \dfrac{20}{0.2}$

$x = 100$

27. $1.25t + 2 = 6$

$1.25t + 2 - 2 = 6 - 2$

$\dfrac{1.25t}{1.25} = \dfrac{4}{1.25}$

$t = 3.2$

28. a.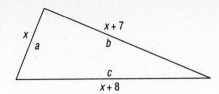

b. $(x + 7) + (x + 8) + x = 30$

$$3x + 15 = 30$$

$$3x = 15$$

$$\frac{3x}{3} = \frac{15}{3}$$

$$x = 5$$

Side a: 5 cm
Side b: $x + 7 = 5 + 7 = 12$ cm
Side c: $x + 8 = 5 + 8 = 13$ cm

29. $2,259,000 = (3A - 169,000) + A$

$$2,259,000 = 4A - 169,000$$

$$\frac{2,428,000}{4} = \frac{4A}{4}$$

$$607,000 = A$$

Population of Alaska: 607,000
Population of Nebraska:

$$3A - 169,000 = 3(607,000) - 169,000$$

$$= 1,652,000$$

30. $C + \left(\frac{1}{2}C + 363,000\right) = 5,274,000$

$$\frac{3}{2}C + 363,000 = 5,274,000$$

$$\frac{3}{2}C = 4,911,000$$

$$\frac{2}{3} \cdot \frac{3}{2}C = 4,911,000 \cdot \frac{2}{3}$$

$$C = 3,274,000$$

Population of Connecticut: 3,274,000
Population of Utah:

$$\frac{1}{2}C + 363,000 = \frac{1}{2}(3,274,000) + 363,000$$

$$= 2,000,000$$

31. C; $\boxed{\text{Dario's age}} + \boxed{\text{Brother's age}} + \boxed{\text{Sister's age}} = \boxed{\text{Uncle's age}}$

$$x + \frac{x}{2} + x + 6 = 31$$

$$\frac{x}{2} + 2x + 6 = 31$$

32. a. Answers vary.
b. Answers vary.

4.4 Solving Equations: The Distributive Property

ONGOING ASSESSMENT

1.

$3x + 3(x - 4) = 12$	*Original equation*
$3x + 3x - 12 = 12$	*Distributive Property*
$6x - 12 = 12$	*Combine like terms.*
$6x - 12 + 12 = 12 + 12$	*Add 12 to each side.*
$6x = 24$	*Simplify.*
$\dfrac{6x}{6} = \dfrac{24}{6}$	*Divide each side by 6.*
$x = 4$	*Simplify.*

2.

$3 = \dfrac{1}{3}(3n - 6)$	*Original equation*
$3 = n - 2$	*Distributive Property*
$3 + 2 = n - 2 + 2$	*Add 2 to each side.*
$5 = n$	*Simplify.*

3. $5p - 2(p - 7) = 21$ *Original equation*

$5p - 2p + 14 = 21$ *Distributive Property*

$3p + 14 = 21$ *Combine like terms.*

$3p + 14 - 14 = 21 - 14$ *Subtract 14 from each side.*

$3p = 7$ *Simplify.*

$\dfrac{3p}{3} = \dfrac{7}{3}$ *Divide each side by 3.*

$p = \dfrac{7}{3}$ *Simplify.*

EXERCISES

1.–3. Answers vary.

4. $6x + 4(x - 3) = 8$ *Original equation*

$6x + 4x - 12 = 8$ *Distributive Property*

$10x - 12 = 8$ *Combine like terms.*

$10x - 12 + 12 = 8 + 12$ *Add 12 to each side.*

$10x = 20$ *Simplify.*

$\dfrac{10x}{10} = \dfrac{20}{10}$ *Divide each side by 10.*

$x = 2$ *Simplify.*

5. $2(x - 2) \neq 2x - 2$

$2(x - 2) = 4$

$2x - 4 = 4$

$2x = 8$

$x = 4$

6. $\dfrac{-2}{-2} \neq -1$

$5x - 7x + 5 = 3$

$-2x + 5 = 3$

$-2x = -2$

$x = 1$

7. $-2x - 4x \neq -2x$

$-2x - 4x + 6 = 10$

$-6x + 6 = 10$

$-6x = 4$

$x = -\dfrac{2}{3}$

8. $x + 4(x + 6) = -1$

$x + 4x + 24 = -1$

$5x + 24 = -1$

$5x = -25$

$x = -5$

Check:

$x + 4(x + 6) = -1$

$-5 + 4(-5 + 6) \stackrel{?}{=} -1$

$-5 + 4(1) \stackrel{?}{=} -1$

$-1 = -1$

9. $1 = y + 3(y - 9)$

$1 = y + 3y - 27$

$1 = 4y - 27$

$28 = 4y$

$7 = y$

Check:

$1 = y + 3(y - 9)$

$1 \stackrel{?}{=} 7 + 3(7 - 9)$

$1 \stackrel{?}{=} 7 + 3(-2)$

$1 = 1$

10. $3x + 2(x + 8) = 21$

$3x + 2x + 16 = 21$

$5x + 16 = 21$

$5x = 5$

$x = 1$

Check:

$3x + 2(x + 8) = 21$

$3(1) + 2(1 + 8) \stackrel{?}{=} 21$

$3 + 2(9) \stackrel{?}{=} 21$

$21 = 21$

11. $3(4 - s) - 5s = 52$

$12 - 3s - 5s = 52$

$12 - 8s = 52$

$-8s = 40$

$s = -5$

Check:

$3(4 - s) - 5s = 52$

$3(4 - (-5)) - 5(-5) \stackrel{?}{=} 52$

$3(9) + 25 \stackrel{?}{=} 52$

$52 = 52$

12. $5(2n + 3) = 65$

$2n + 3 = 13$

$2n = 10$

$n = 5$

Check:

$5(2n + 3) = 65$

$5(2 \cdot 5 + 3) \stackrel{?}{=} 65$

$5(13) \stackrel{?}{=} 65$

$65 = 65$

13. $8(4z - 7) = -56$

$4z - 7 = -7$

$4z = 0$

$z = 0$

Check:

$8(4z - 7) = -56$

$8(4 \cdot 0 - 7) \stackrel{?}{=} -56$

$8(-7) \stackrel{?}{=} -56$

$-56 = -56$

14. $\frac{1}{2}(x + 12) = -8$

$x + 12 = -16$

$x + 12 - 12 = -16 - 12$

$x = -28$

Check:

$\frac{1}{2}(x + 12) = -8$

$\frac{1}{2}(-28 + 12) \stackrel{?}{=} -8$

$\frac{1}{2}(-16) \stackrel{?}{=} -8$

$-8 = -8$

15. $14 = \frac{1}{4}(q - 9)$

$4 \cdot 14 = 4 \cdot \frac{1}{4}(q - 9)$

$56 = q - 9$

$65 = q$

Check:

$14 = \frac{1}{4}(q - 9)$

$14 \stackrel{?}{=} \frac{1}{4}(65 - 9)$

$14 \stackrel{?}{=} \frac{1}{4}(56)$

$14 = 14$

16. $-3(y + 4) = 18$

$y + 4 = -6$

$y = -10$

Check:

$-3(y + 4) = 18$

$-3(-10 + 4) \stackrel{?}{=} 18$

$-3(-6) \stackrel{?}{=} 18$

$18 = 18$

17. $2 = n - (2n + 3)$

$2 = n - 2n - 3$

$2 = -n - 3$

$5 = -n$

$-5 = n$

Check:

$2 = n - (2n + 3)$

$2 = -5 - (2(-5) + 3)$

$2 = -5 - (-7)$

$2 = 2$

18. $5r - 7(1 + r) = 5$

$5r - 7 - 7r = 5$

$-2r - 7 = 5$

$-2r = 12$

$r = -6$

Check:

$5r - 7(1 + r) = 5$

$5(-6) - 7(1 + (-6)) = 5$

$-30 - 7(-5) = 5$

$5 = 5$

19. $6(2n - 5) = 42$

$2n - 5 = 7$

$2n = 12$

$n = 6$

Check:

$6(2n - 5) = 42$

$6(2 \cdot 6 - 5) \stackrel{?}{=} 42$

$6(7) \stackrel{?}{=} 42$

$42 = 42$

20. a. $\frac{1}{3}(x - 6) = 6$

$\frac{1}{3}x - 2 = 6$

$\frac{1}{3}x = 8$

$3 \cdot \frac{1}{3}x = 3 \cdot 8$

$x = 24$

b. $\frac{1}{3}(x - 6) = 6$

$3 \cdot \frac{1}{3}(x - 6) = 3 \cdot 6$

$x - 6 = 18$

$x = 24$

c. Answers vary.

21. $9(x + 3) = 63$

$x + 3 = 7$

$x = 4$

22. $12(x - 5) = 48$

$x - 5 = 4$

$x = 9$

23. $5(2x - 1) = 35$

$2x - 1 = 7$

$2x = 8$

$x = 4$

24. $(x + x) + x + (x + x) + x = 177$

$6x = 177$

$x = 29.5$

25. $(3x - 6) + (5x + 5) + (3x - 6) = 180$

$11x - 7 = 180$

$11x = 187$

$x = 17$

26. a. $480x + 2200(x + 5) - 7500 = 11{,}540$

b. $480x + 2200x + 11{,}000 = 19{,}040$

$2680x + 11{,}000 = 19{,}040$

$2680x + 11{,}000 - 11{,}000 = 19{,}040 - 11{,}000$

$2680x = 8040$

$\dfrac{2680x}{2680} = \dfrac{8040}{2680}$

$x = 3$

You charge $x + 5 = 3 + 5 = 8$ dollars per foot for installing insulation.

27. B; $\quad 510 = 2(3x + 4)$

$510 = 6x + 8$

$510 - 8 = 6x + 8 - 8$

$502 = 6x$

$\dfrac{502}{6} = \dfrac{6x}{6}$

$83\tfrac{2}{3} = x$

28. C; $300 + 0.05(x - 100) = 450$

$300 + 0.05x - 5 = 450$

$295 + 0.05x = 450$

$295 - 295 + 0.05x = 450 - 295$

$0.05x = 155$

$\dfrac{0.05x}{0.05} = \dfrac{155}{0.05}$

$x = 3100$

29. $C = \tfrac{5}{9}(F - 32)$

a. $\quad 6 = \tfrac{5}{9}(F - 32)$

$\tfrac{9}{5} \cdot 6 = \tfrac{9}{5} \cdot \tfrac{5}{9}(F - 32)$

$10.8 = F - 32$

$42.8° = F$

b. 78.8°F; the difference in temperature between the warm water and the cold water must be at least 36°F, so the warm surface water must be at least $42.8° + 36° = 78.8°$.

Mid-Chapter **A S S E S S M E N T**

1.

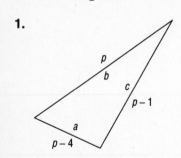

$(p - 4) + (p - 1) + p = 16$

$3p - 5 = 16$

$3p = 27$

$p = 7$

Side *a*: $p - 4 = 7 - 4 = 3$ cm

Side *b*: $p - 1 = 7 - 1 = 6$ cm

Side *c*: 7 cm

2. $3 \cdot \tfrac{1}{3} = 1$; answer: $\tfrac{1}{3}$

3. $-\tfrac{1}{21} \cdot -21 = 1$; answer: -21

4. $-\tfrac{1}{5} \cdot -5 = 1$; answer: -5

5. $2y - 4 = 10$

$\qquad 2y = 14$

$\qquad y = 7$

Check:

$\qquad 2y - 4 = 10$

$\qquad 2(7) - 4 \overset{?}{=} 10$

$\qquad\qquad 10 = 10$

6. $4t + 16 = 0$

$\qquad 4t = -16$

$\qquad t = -4$

Check:

$\qquad 4t + 16 = 0$

$\qquad 4(-4) + 16 \overset{?}{=} 0$

$\qquad\qquad 0 = 0$

7. $8 - 2b = 2$

$\qquad -2b = -6$

$\qquad b = 3$

Check:

$\qquad 8 - 2b = 2$

$\qquad 8 - 2(3) \overset{?}{=} 2$

$\qquad\qquad 2 = 2$

8. $\frac{1}{2}r + 6 = 8$

$\qquad \frac{1}{2}r = 2$

$\qquad 2 \cdot \frac{1}{2}r = 2 \cdot 2$

$\qquad r = 4$

Check:

$\qquad \frac{1}{2}r + 6 = 8$

$\qquad \frac{1}{2}(4) + 6 \overset{?}{=} 8$

$\qquad\qquad 8 = 8$

9. $6m + 5 = -1$

$\qquad 6m = -6$

$\qquad m = -1$

Check:

$\qquad 6m + 5 = -1$

$\qquad 6(-1) + 5 \overset{?}{=} -1$

$\qquad\qquad -1 = -1$

10. $20p - 8 = 32$

$\qquad 20p = 40$

$\qquad p = 2$

Check:

$\qquad 20p - 8 = 32$

$\qquad 20(2) - 8 \overset{?}{=} 32$

$\qquad\qquad 32 = 32$

11. $9s + 6s - 12s = 15$

$\qquad 3s = 15$

$\qquad s = 5$

Check:

$\qquad 9s + 6s - 12s = 15$

$\qquad 9(5) + 6(5) - 12(5) \overset{?}{=} 15$

$\qquad 45 + 30 - 60 \overset{?}{=} 15$

$\qquad\qquad 15 = 15$

12. $10t - 7t + t = -24$

$\qquad 4t = -24$

$\qquad t = -6$

Check:

$\qquad 10t - 7t + t = -24$

$\qquad 10(-6) - 7(-6) + (-6) \overset{?}{=} -24$

$\qquad\qquad -24 = -24$

13. $19 + 12p - 17p = -1$

$\qquad 19 - 5p = -1$

$\qquad -5p = -20$

$\qquad p = 4$

Check:

$\qquad 19 + 12p - 17p = -1$

$\qquad 19 + 12(4) - 17(4) \overset{?}{=} -1$

$\qquad 19 + 48 - 68 \overset{?}{=} -1$

$\qquad\qquad -1 = -1$

14. $3(n + 4) + 1 = 28$

$\qquad 3n + 12 + 1 = 28$

$\qquad 3n + 13 = 28$

$\qquad 3n = 15$

$\qquad n = 5$

Check:

$\qquad 3(n + 4) + 1 = 28$

$\qquad 3(5 + 4) + 1 \overset{?}{=} 28$

$\qquad 3(9) + 1 \overset{?}{=} 28$

$\qquad\qquad 28 = 28$

15. $2x + 3 = 21$

$\qquad 2x = 18$

$\qquad x = 9$

16. $\frac{x}{4} - 3 = 1$

$\qquad \frac{x}{4} = 4$

$\qquad x = 16$

17.
$$2x + x + 5 = 17$$
$$3x + 5 = 17$$
$$3x = 12$$
$$x = 4$$

18. $N =$ number of miles to Nairobi
$$12{,}259 = 4196 + \frac{1}{2}N$$
$$8063 = \frac{1}{2}N$$
$$16{,}000 \text{ km} \approx N$$

19. $A =$ number of miles to Austin, TX
$$2480 = \frac{1}{4}(500 + A)$$
$$2480 = 125 + \frac{A}{4}$$
$$2355 = \frac{A}{4}$$
$$9000 \text{ km} \approx A$$

Lab 4.5

1.
$$3x = x + 6$$
$$3x - x = x - x + 6$$
$$2x = 6$$
$$\frac{2x}{2} = \frac{6}{2}$$
$$x = 3$$

Check:
$$3x = x + 6$$
$$3(3) \overset{?}{=} 3 + 6$$
$$9 + 9$$

2. $4x + 3 = 3x + 5$

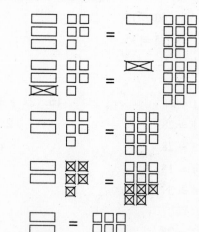

$$x = 2$$

3. $y + 9 = 3y + 3$

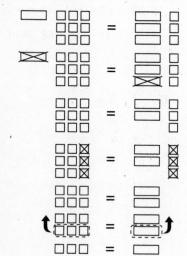

$$3 = y$$

4. $3n + 5 = n + 11$

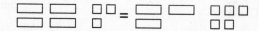

$$n = 3$$

5. $5m + 2 = 2m + 14$

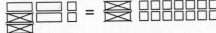

$$m = 4$$

4.5 GEOMETRY CONNECTION:
Solving Equations: Variables on Both Sides

ONGOING ASSESSMENT

1. $x > 3$

2.

x	0	1	2	3	4	5	6
Rectangle's perimeter: $4x + 6$	6	10	14	18	22	26	30
Triangle's perimeter: $3x + 9$	9	12	15	18	21	24	27

EXERCISES

1. Answers vary.

2. The sides of an equilateral triangle are equal in length.

3. Left side; the coefficient of the x-term is greater.

4. Right side; the coefficient of the y-term is greater.

5. Right side; the coefficient of the x-term is greater.

6. Right side; the coefficient of the x-term is greater.

7.
$$7x + 12 = 13x$$
$$7x + 12 - 7x = 13x - 7x$$
$$12 = 6x$$
$$2 = x$$
Check:
$$7x + 12 = 13x$$
$$7(2) + 12 \overset{?}{=} 13(2)$$
$$26 = 26$$

8.
$$10x + 17 = 4x - 1$$
$$10x + 17 - 4x = 4x - 1 - 4x$$
$$6x + 17 = -1$$
$$6x = -18$$
$$x = -3$$
Check:
$$10x + 17 = 4x - 1$$
$$10(-3) + 17 \overset{?}{=} 4(-3) - 1$$
$$-13 = -13$$

9.
$$5x - 8 = -2x + 6$$
$$5x + 2x - 8 = -2x + 2x + 6$$
$$7x - 8 = 6$$
$$7x - 8 + 8 = 6 + 8$$
$$7x = 14$$
$$x = 2$$

10.
$$-5x + 6 = x + 12$$
$$-5x + 6 + 5x = x + 12 + 5x$$
$$6 = 6x + 12$$
$$-6 = 6x$$
$$-1 = x$$
Check:
$$-5x + 6 = x + 12$$
$$-5(-1) + 6 \overset{?}{=} -1 + 12$$
$$11 = 11$$

11.
$$-2x + 6 = -x$$
$$-2x + 6 + 2x = -x + 2x$$
$$6 = x$$
Check:
$$-2x + 6 = -x$$
$$-2(6) + 6 \overset{?}{=} -6$$
$$-6 = -6$$

12.
$$7y = 3(5y - 8)$$
$$7y = 15y - 24$$
$$7y - 7y = 15y - 24 - 7y$$
$$0 = 8y - 24$$
$$24 = 8y$$
$$3 = y$$
Check:
$$7y = 3(5y - 8)$$
$$7(3) \overset{?}{=} 3(5 \cdot 3 - 8)$$
$$21 \overset{?}{=} 3(7)$$
$$21 = 21$$

13.
$$10(2n + 10) = 120n$$
$$2n + 10 = 12n$$
$$2n + 10 - 2n = 12n - 2n$$
$$10 = 10n$$
$$1 = n$$
Check:
$$10(2n + 10) = 120n$$
$$10(2(1) + 10) \overset{?}{=} 120(1)$$
$$10(12) \overset{?}{=} 120$$
$$120 = 120$$

14.
$$4(7 + y) = 16 - 2y$$
$$28 + 4y = 16 - 2y$$
$$28 + 4y + 2y = 16 - 2y + 2y$$
$$28 + 6y = 16$$
$$6y = -12$$
$$y = -2$$
Check:
$$4(7 + y) = 16 - 2y$$
$$4(7 + (-2)) \overset{?}{=} 16 - 2(-2)$$
$$20 = 20$$

15.
$$6(x - 3) = 4(x + 3)$$
$$6x - 18 = 4x + 12$$
$$6x - 18 - 4x = 4x + 12 - 4x$$
$$2x - 18 = 12$$
$$2x = 30$$
$$x = 15$$
Check:
$$6(x - 3) = 4(x + 3)$$
$$6(15 - 3) \overset{?}{=} 4(15 + 3)$$
$$6(12) \overset{?}{=} 4(18)$$
$$72 = 72$$

16.
$$2(x-9) = 3(x-6)$$
$$2x-18 = 3x-18$$
$$2x-18-2x = 3x-18-2x$$
$$-18 = x-18$$
$$0 = x$$

Check:
$$2(x-9) = 3(x-6)$$
$$2(0-9) \stackrel{?}{=} 3(0-6)$$
$$-18 = -18$$

17.
$$\tfrac{7}{2}t + 12 = 6 + \tfrac{5}{2}t$$
$$\tfrac{7}{2}t + 12 - \tfrac{5}{2}t = 6 + \tfrac{5}{2}t - \tfrac{5}{2}t$$
$$t + 12 = 6$$
$$t = -6$$

Check:
$$\tfrac{7}{2}t + 12 = 6 + \tfrac{5}{2}t$$
$$\tfrac{7}{2}(-6) + 12 \stackrel{?}{=} 6 + \tfrac{5}{2}(-6)$$
$$-21 + 12 \stackrel{?}{=} 6 - 15$$
$$-9 = -9$$

18.
$$-13 - \tfrac{1}{12}s = \tfrac{11}{12}s + 2$$
$$-13 - \tfrac{1}{12}s + \tfrac{1}{12}s = \tfrac{11}{12}s + 2 + \tfrac{1}{12}s$$
$$-13 = s + 2$$
$$-15 = s$$

Check:
$$-13 - \tfrac{1}{12}s = \tfrac{11}{12}s + 2$$
$$-13 - \tfrac{1}{12}(-15) \stackrel{?}{=} \tfrac{11}{12}(-15) + 2$$
$$-13 + \tfrac{5}{4} \stackrel{?}{=} -\tfrac{55}{4} + 2$$
$$-\tfrac{47}{4} = -\tfrac{47}{4}$$

19. $x =$ the number
$$3x - 1 = x + 19$$
$$3x - 1 - x = x + 19 - x$$
$$2x - 1 = 19$$
$$2x = 20$$
$$x = 10$$
The number is 10.

20. $x =$ the number
$$4x + 17 = 7x + 2$$
$$17 - 2 = 7x - 4x$$
$$15 = 3x$$
$$5 = x$$
The number is 5.

21.
$$2(x-1) + 2(x+3) = (x+1) + (x+3) + (x+5)$$
$$2x - 2 + 2x + 6 = 3x + 9$$
$$4x + 4 = 3x + 9$$
$$4x + 4 - 3x = 3x + 9 - 3x$$
$$x + 4 = 9$$
$$x = 5$$
$$(x+1) + (x+3) + (x+5) = (5+1) + (5+3) + (5+5)$$
$$= 6 + 8 + 10$$
$$= 24$$

The perimeter is 24.

22.
$$x + 3 = 2x - 4$$
$$x + 3 - x = 2x - 4 - x$$
$$3 = x - 4$$
$$7 = x$$

23.
$$4x + 11 = 8(x-1)$$
$$4x + 11 = 8x - 8$$
$$4x + 11 - 4x = 8x - 8 - 4x$$
$$11 = 4x - 8$$
$$19 = 4x$$
$$4\tfrac{3}{4} = x$$

24. $7x = 350 + 3x$
$$4x = 350$$
$$x = 87.5$$

The answer represents the number of movies you would have to see before buying a VCR and renting movies becomes cheaper.

25. B

26.
$$50t = 0.25t + 1000$$
$$49.75t = 1000$$
$$t = 20.1 \text{ seconds}$$

27. The tortoise; the hare will catch up to the tortoise when the tortoise has run $20.1(0.25) = 5.025$ ft. The tortoise will have crossed the finish line before the hare catches up.

28. C;
$$4t + 9 = 11t - 83$$
$$4t - 4t + 9 = 11t - 4t - 83$$
$$9 = 7t - 83$$
$$9 + 83 = 7t - 83 + 83$$
$$92 = 7t$$
$$\frac{92}{7} = \frac{7t}{t}$$
$$13\tfrac{1}{7} = t$$

29. A;
Left-hand side of equation:
$$20(3(-6) + 6)$$
$$20(-18 + 6)$$
$$20(-12)$$
$$-240$$
Right-hand side of equation
for A: $-246 - (-6) = -240$
for B: $1086 - (-6) = 1092$
for C: $480 - (-6) = 486$
for D: $486 - (-6) = 492$

30. Standard: $0.75 + 0.006x$
Fluorescent: $25 + 0.0016x$

31. About 5511 hours

4.6 Problem Solving Strategies

ONGOING ASSESSMENT

1.

Years	0	1	2	3	4	5	6
Logged land (mi^2)	12	15	18	21	24	27	30
Reforested land (mi^2)	0	5	10	15	20	25	30

$$12 + 3n = 5n$$
$$12 + 3n - 3n = 5n - 3n$$
$$12 = 2n$$
$$6 = n$$

It will take 6 years.

EXERCISES

1. Answers vary.

2. Height of cornstalk now $= 5$ (inches)
Stalk's rate of growth $= 2\tfrac{1}{2}$ (inches per week)
Number of weeks $= n$ (weeks)
Height of weed now $= 11$ (inches)
Weed's rate of growth $= 1$ (inch per week)

3. $5 + 2\frac{1}{2}(n) = 11 + 1(n)$

$5 + \frac{5}{2}n = 11 + n$

$5 + \frac{5}{2}n - n = 11 + n - n$

$5 + \frac{3}{2}n = 11$

$5 - 5 + \frac{3}{2}n = 11 - 5$

$\frac{3}{2}n = 6$

$\frac{2}{3} \cdot \frac{3}{2}n = \frac{2}{3} \cdot 6$

$n = 4$

4. The corn stalk and the weed will be the same height in 4 weeks.

5. a.

Number of CDs	1	2	3	4	5	6	7	8	9	10
Bookstore cost ($)	35	70	105	140	175	210	245	280	315	350
CD club cost ($)	75	100	125	150	175	200	225	250	275	300

b. You have to buy 5 CDs for the costs of both options to be the same.

c. (S)he is if you buy more than 5, otherwise (s)he is not.

d.

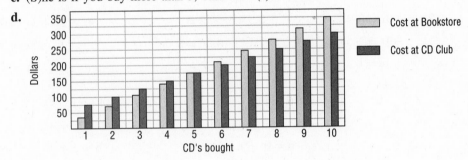

The cost at the CD club is less when you buy more than 5 CD's.

6.

| 3:00 P.M. Santa Fe temperature | − | Santa Fe's rate of decrease | · | Number of hours | = | 3:00 P.M. Minot temperature | + | Minot's rate of increase | · | Number of hours |

7. 3:00 P.M. Santa Fe temperature = 86   (degrees Fahrenheit)
Santa Fe's rate of decrease = 3   (degrees per hour)
Number of hours = h (hours)
3:00 P.M. Minot temperature = 56   (degrees Fahrenheit)
Minot's rate of increase = 2   (degrees per hour)

8. $86 - 3h = 56 + 2h$

9. $86 - 3h = 56 + 2h$

$86 - 3h + 3h = 56 + 2h + 3h$

$86 = 56 + 5h$

$30 = 5h$

$6 = h$

10. The temperatures will be the same in 6 hours.

11. Substitute $h = 6$ into the algebraic model.

12. $h = $ number of hours of lessons that costs the same at both clubs.

$$6h = 30 + 4.5h$$
$$6h - 4.5h = 30 + 4.5h - 4.5h$$
$$1.5h = 30$$
$$h = 20$$

Club 1 is cheaper for taking less than 20 hours of lessons, Club 2 is cheaper for taking more than 20 hours of lessons.

13. $n = $ number sold.

$$1500 + 15n = 32n$$
$$1500 + 15n - 15n = 32n - 15n$$
$$1500 = 17n$$
$$88.235 \approx n$$

You must sell 89 skateboards to break even.

14. C; $3(24) = 72$

15. a. $3(20.45 - 12.32) = \$24.39$ more
$3(12.32 - 8) = \$12.96$ less

b. Answers vary.

Spiral REVIEW

1. $4a = 28$
$a = 7$

2. $6 - 9x = -48$
$-9x = -54$
$x = 6$

3. $4.5r - 2 = 7$
$4.5r = 9$
$r = 2$

4. $12x + 3x = 30$
$15x = 30$
$x = 2$

5. $3a = 2 + 2a$
$3a - 2a = 2 + 2a - 2a$
$a = 2$

6. $14s - 6 = 12s$
$14s - 6 - 12s = 12s - 12s$
$2s - 6 = 0$
$2s = 6$
$s = 3$

7. $z + 2(4 - z) = 4$
$z + 8 - 2z = 4$
$8 - z = 4$
$-z = -4$
$z = 4$

8. $\frac{4}{3}p = \frac{12}{3} + \frac{2}{3}p$
$\frac{4}{3}p - \frac{2}{3}p = \frac{12}{3} + \frac{2}{3}p - \frac{2}{3}p$
$\frac{2}{3}p = \frac{12}{3}$
$\frac{3}{2} \cdot \frac{2}{3}p = \frac{3}{2} \cdot \frac{12}{3}$
$p = 6$

9. $x = $ the number.
$6x = 3$
$x = \frac{1}{2}$

10. $3x + 2 = 8x$
$3x + 2 - 3x = 8x - 3x$
$2 = 5x$
$\frac{2}{5} = x$

11. $5x = 1 - x$
$5x + x = 1 - x + x$
$6x = 1$
$x = \frac{1}{6}$

12. $2(x + 2) = -x$
$2x + 4 = -x$
$2x + 4 - 2x = -x - 2x$
$4 = -3x$
$-\frac{4}{3} = x$

13. $14 + 24 + 20 + 12 + 17 + 22 + 7 + 20 = 136$;
$\frac{136}{8} = 17$

14. $-2.4 + 1.1 + 2.7 + (-1.4) + (-0.5) = -0.5$;
$\frac{-0.5}{5} = -0.1$

15. $2x \geq 1$

$x \geq \frac{1}{2}$

16. $7y < 28$

$y < 4$

17. $48 < 16y$

$3 < y$

18. $3c < 21$

$c < 7$

19. $\frac{r}{4} \geq 6$

$r \geq 24$

20. $0.2p \leq 12$

$p \leq 60$

21. $(21 + 13) - 25 = 34 - 25$

$= 9$ families

Communicating About Mathematics

1. $17,100m = 500,000$

$\dfrac{17,100m}{17,100} = \dfrac{500,000}{17,100}$

$m \approx 29.24$ min

Solving for m tells you how many minutes it takes to pump 500,000 gallons of cold water.

2. $\dfrac{5}{1000} \cdot 17,100 = 85.5$ gallons; answers vary.

3. $5,000,000 \cdot \dfrac{1}{10,000} = 500$ watts; answers vary.

4. *Sample answer:* Cuba, Peru, Brazil, Guinea, Somalia, southern India, the Philipines

4.7 Solving Equations Using Technology

ONGOING ASSESSMENT

1. $5.00 = 1.53 + 0.92t$

$3.47 = 0.92t$

$4 = t$

The total length of the phone call is 4 min.

2. $16.25 = 1.53 + 0.92t$

$14.72 = 0.92t$

$16 = t$

The total length of the phone call is 16 min.

3. $30.00 = 1.53 + 0.92t$

$28.47 = 0.92t$

$31 = t$

The total length of the phone call is 31 min.

EXERCISES

1. A; because it is in decimal form.

2. $0.25(3.2x + 4.1) = 7.2$

$0.8x + 1.025 = 7.2$

$0.8x = 6.175$

$x = 7.71875$

$x \approx 7.72$

3. $x = 2.5$ is an exact answer and $x \approx 2.5$ is an approximate answer.

4. B; a person's weight varies at least a tenth of a pound each day.

5. $1.1(2.5x - 3.5) = 11.2$

$2.75x - 3.85 = 11.2$

$2.75x = 15.05$

$x \approx 5.47$

Rounding was done too early (in 2nd step).

6. $0.26(2.39x - 4.91) = 10.64$

$0.6214x - 1.2766 = 10.64$

$0.6214x = 11.9166$

$x \approx 19.18$

Rounding was done too early (in 2nd step).

7. $3x + 12 = 17$

$3x = 5$

$x \approx 1.67$

8. $13y + 22 = 16$

$13y = -6$

$y \approx -0.46$

9. $29t - 17 = -86$

$29t = -69$

$t \approx -2.38$

10. $15 - 11x = 108$

$-11x = 93$

$x \approx -8.45$

11. $6(4x - 12) = 8x + 9$

$24x - 72 = 8x + 9$

$24x - 72 - 8x = 8x + 9 - 8x$

$16x - 72 = 9$

$16x = 81$

$x \approx 5.06$

12. $13x - 22 = 2(9x + 10)$

$13x - 22 = 18x + 20$

$13x - 22 - 13x = 18x + 20 - 13x$

$-22 = 5x + 20$

$-42 = 5x$

$-8.4 = x$

13. $1.3y + 22.1 = 12.9$

$1.3y = -9.2$

$y \approx -7.08$

14. $-7.4m + 36.4 = 9.5$

$-7.4m = -26.9$

$m \approx 3.64$

15. $0.15(9.85x + 3.70) = 4.65$

$1.4775x + 0.555 = 4.65$

$1.4775x = 4.095$

$x \approx 2.77$

16. $2.16(3.47x - 8.60) = 17.59$

$7.4952x - 18.576 = 17.59$

$7.4952x = 36.166$

$x \approx 4.83$

17. $0.19t - 1.57 = 0.46t$

$0.19t - 1.57 - 0.19t = 0.46t - 0.19t$

$-1.57 = 0.27t$

$-5.81 \approx t$

18. $2.4x + 13.7 = 8.1x - 22.5$

$2.4x + 13.7 - 2.4x = 8.1x - 22.5 - 2.4x$

$13.7 = 5.7x - 22.5$

$36.2 = 5.7x$

$6.35 \approx x$

19. $3.14x + 17.5 = 9.77x + 24.1$

$3.14x + 17.5 - 3.14x = 9.77x + 24.1 - 3.14x$

$17.5 = 6.63x + 24.1$

$-6.6 = 6.63x$

$-1.00 \approx x$

20. $p + 0.06p = 6.35$

$1.06p = 6.35$

$p \approx 5.99$

The price was about $5.99.

21. $p + 0.05p = 2.62$

$1.05p = 2.62$

$p \approx 2.50$

The price was about $2.50.

22.

| Cost of first ounce | + | Cost of each additional ounce | × | Number of additional ounces | = | Total cost |

23.

Additional ounces	1	2	3	4	5	6	7	8	9
Cost ($)	0.55	0.78	1.01	1.24	1.47	1.70	1.93	2.16	2.36

Your letter can weigh a total of 8 ounces.

24. Provider A:

Cost for first five hours	+	Cost of each additional hour	×	Number of additional hours

$$9.95 + 2.95(t - 5)$$

Provider B:

Cost for first hour	+	Cost of each additional hour	×	Number of additional hours

$$4.95 + 2.50(t - 1)$$

25.
$$9.95 + 2.95(t - 5) = 4.95 + 2.50(t - 1)$$
$$9.95 + 2.95t - 14.75 = 4.95 + 2.50t - 2.50$$
$$2.95t - 4.80 = 2.50t + 2.45$$
$$0.45t - 4.80 = 2.45$$
$$0.45t = 7.25$$
$$t \approx 16.11 \text{ hours}$$

Provider B would be less expensive after 16.11 hours.

26. A;
$$0.75x + 3.22 = 6.97$$
$$0.75x + 3.22 - 3.22 = 6.97 - 3.22$$
$$0.75x = 3.75$$
$$\frac{0.75x}{0.75} = \frac{3.75}{0.75}$$
$$x = 5$$

27. C;
$$0.12x - 0.65 = 1.28$$
$$0.12x - 0.65 + 0.65 = 1.28 + 0.65$$
$$0.12x = 1.93$$
$$\frac{0.12x}{0.12} = \frac{1.93}{0.12}$$
$$x \approx 16.08$$

28. *Sample answer:* Company A; Company B is cheaper if you talk less than 12 minutes.

4.8 GEOMETRY CONNECTION: *Formulas and Variables in Geometry*

ONGOING ASSESSMENT

1. Answers vary.

EXERCISES

1. Answers vary.

2. B; the area of a square is the square of a side.

3. C (also B); the perimeter of a rectangle is the sum of twice the length and twice the width.

4. A; the area of a triangle is one-half the product of the base and the height.

5. B; the perimeter of a square is four times a side.

6. C (also B); the area of a rectangle is the product of the base and height.

7. An octagon has 8 sides.

8.
$$P = 8s$$
$$99 = 8s$$
$$12.4 = s$$
Each side is 12.4 inches.

9.
$$P = 8s$$
$$P = 8(10)$$
$$P = 80$$
The perimeter is 80 inches.

10.
$$P = 2l + 2w$$
$$36 = 2(4x - 2) + 2(x)$$
$$36 = 8x - 4 + 2x$$
$$36 = 10x - 4$$
$$40 = 10x$$
$$4 = x$$
Width: $x = 4$ units
Length: $4x - 2 = 4(4) - 2$
$$= 14 \text{ units}$$

11.
$$P = 2l + 2w$$
$$58 = 2(3x + 6) + 2(6x - 4)$$
$$58 = 6x + 12 + 12x - 8$$
$$58 = 18x + 4$$
$$54 = 18x$$
$$3 = x$$
Width: $6x - 4 = 6(3) - 4$
$$= 14 \text{ units}$$
Length: $3x + 6 = 3(3) + 6$
$$= 15 \text{ units}$$

12.
$$P = 4s$$
$$16 = 4(x - 5)$$
$$4 = x - 5$$
$$9 = x$$
Side: $x - 5 = 9 - 5 = 4$ units

13.
$$A = bh$$
$$320 = (3x - 2)16$$
$$20 = 3x - 2$$
$$22 = 3x$$
$$\tfrac{22}{3} = x$$

Height (entire television): 16 in.
Base (entire television): $3x - 2 = 3\left(\tfrac{22}{3}\right) - 2 = 20$ in.
Height (television screen): $16 - 4 = 12$ in.
Base (television screen): $20 - 4 = 16$ in.
Area (television screen): $16(12) = 192$ in.^{2}

14.
$$P = 4x$$
$$360 = 4x$$
$$90 = x$$
The distance between first base and second base is 90 ft.

15.
$$P = 5s$$
$$90 = 5(5x - 7)$$
$$18 = 5x - 7$$
$$25 = 5x$$
$$5 = x$$
Side: $5x - 7 = 5(5) - 7$
$$= 18 \text{ units}$$

16.
$$A = \tfrac{1}{2}bh$$
$$155 = \tfrac{1}{2}(3x + 10)10$$
$$155 = 5(3x + 10)$$
$$31 = 3x + 10$$
$$21 = 3x$$
$$7 = x$$
Base: $3x + 10 = 3(7) + 10$
$$= 31 \text{ units}$$

17.
$$A = lw$$
$$225 = (2x + 9)9$$
$$25 = 2x + 9$$
$$16 = 2x$$
$$8 = x$$
Length: $2x + 9 = 2(8) + 9$
$$= 25 \text{ units}$$

18. *Sample answer:*

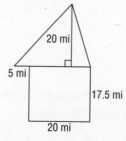

20 mi
5 mi
17.5 mi
20 mi

$$A = \tfrac{1}{2}(25 \times 20) + 20 \times 17.5$$
$$= 250 + 350$$
$$= 600 \text{ mi}^2$$

19. *Sample answer:*

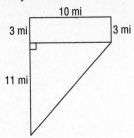

$$A = 3 \times 10 + \tfrac{1}{2}(10 \times 11)$$
$$= 30 + 55$$
$$= 85 \text{ mi}^2$$

20. B;
Area of rectangle $= 2 \times 8 = 16$ inches^2
Area of square $= 16$, so each side is 4 inches.
Perimeter of square $= 4 + 4 + 4 + 4 = 16$ inches

21. D; Area $= \tfrac{1}{2} \times b \times h = 84$ units^2

22. Answers vary.

Chapter R E V I E W

1. $\dfrac{x}{2} + 12 = 20$
$\dfrac{x}{2} = 8$
$x = 16$

2. $5t - 4 = 21$
$5t = 25$
$t = 5$

3. $7 - 5x = -3$
$-5x = -10$
$x = 2$

4. $7n - 2n - 1 = 29$
$5n - 1 = 29$
$5n = 30$
$n = 6$

5. $s + 5s - 3s = 36$
$3s = 36$
$s = 12$

6. $-31 = \tfrac{2}{3}x - 26 + \tfrac{1}{3}x$
$-31 = -26 + x$
$-5 = x$

7. $12 = 3t - t + 4$
$8 = 3t - t$
$8 = 2t$
$4 = t$

8. $2y - 5y + 4 = 10$
$-3y + 4 = 10$
$-3y = 6$
$y = -2$

9. $-12 = g + 9 - 4g$
$-12 = -3g + 9$
$-21 = -3g$
$7 = g$

10. $\tfrac{1}{5}x + 1 = 9$
$\tfrac{1}{5}x = 8$
$x = 40$

11. $-2 = \tfrac{1}{2}x - 5$
$3 = \tfrac{1}{2}x$
$6 = x$

12. $7s + 11 = 53$
$7s = 42$
$s = 6$

13. $5(t - 9) = 55$
$5t - 45 = 55$
$5t = 100$
$t = 20$

14. $-2(x + 1) + x = -8$
$-2x - 2 + x = -8$
$-2 - x = -8$
$-x = -6$
$x = 6$

15. $11(m - 6) - 17 = 38$
$11m - 66 - 17 = 38$
$11m - 83 = 38$
$11m = 121$
$m = 11$

16. $2x - 9 = 5x$
$-9 = 3x$
$-3 = x$

17. $6y + 39 = -7y$

$39 = -13y$

$-3 = y$

18. $\frac{5}{2}x + 4 = \frac{1}{2}x$

$4 = -2x$

$-2 = x$

19. $3(3 - b) = 5(2b + 7)$

$9 - 3b = 10b + 35$

$-26 = 13b$

$-2 = b$

20. $3x - 13 = x + 5$

$2x = 18$

$x = 9$

21.

Time	12:00	1:00	2:00	3:00
First canoe's distance (miles)	4	8	12	16
Your canoe's distance (miles)	0	6	12	18

Your canoe will catch up at 2:00 P.M.

22. $\boxed{\text{Rate of first canoe}} \cdot \boxed{\text{Number of hours traveled by first canoe}} = \boxed{\text{Rate of your canoe}} \cdot \boxed{\text{Number of hours traveled by your canoe}}$

Rate of first canoe = 4 (mi/h)

Number of hours traveled by first canoe = t (hours)

Rate of your canoe = 6 (mi/h)

Number of hours traveled by your canoe = $t - 1$ (hours)

$4t = 6(t - 1)$

$3 = t$

You will catch up to the first canoe after it has been traveling for 3 hours, which is 2:00 P.M.

23. $2.12(4.86y - 3.79) = 19$

$10.3032y - 8.0348 = 19$

$10.3032y = 27.0348$

$y \approx 2.62$

24. $2.50x - 150 = 600$

$2.50x - 150 + 150 = 600 + 150$

$2.50x = 750$

$\dfrac{2.50x}{2.50} = \dfrac{750}{2.50}$

$x = 300$

Your class must sell 300 subs to raise enough money.

25. $120 = 3(2x - 4)$

$120 = 6x - 12$

$132 = 6x$

$22 = x$

Each side: $2x - 4 = 2(22) - 4$

$= 44 - 4$

$= 40$ in.

Chapter ASSESSMENT

1. $4y - 2 = 18$

$4y = 20$

$y = 5$

2. $3 - 3a = 21$

$-3a = 18$

$a = -6$

3. $12(r - 2) = 36$

$r - 2 = 3$

$r = 5$

4. $8x + 4 - 3x = 19$

$\qquad 5x + 4 = 19$

$\qquad 5x = 15$

$\qquad x = 3$

5. $\qquad 7s - 12 = s$

$\qquad 7s - 12 - 7s = s - 7s$

$\qquad -12 = -6s$

$\qquad 2 = s$

6. $\qquad \frac{1}{2}(x + 8) = 4$

$\qquad 2 \cdot \frac{1}{2}(x + 8) = 2 \cdot 4$

$\qquad x + 8 = 8$

$\qquad x = 0$

7. $\qquad 0.7x = 1.3x - 1.2$

$\qquad 0.7x - 1.3x = 1.3x - 1.2 - 1.3x$

$\qquad -0.6x = -1.2$

$\qquad x = 2$

8. $p + 2(p - 1) = 2p$

$\qquad p + 2p - 2 = 2p$

$\qquad 3p - 2 = 2p$

$\qquad 3p - 2 - 3p = 2p - 3p$

$\qquad -2 = -p$

$\qquad 2 = p$

9. $-\frac{1}{2} \cdot (-2) = 1$, answer: -2

10. $10 \cdot \frac{1}{10} = 1$, answer: $\frac{1}{10}$

11. $5(3 + x) - 2x = 17$

$\qquad 15 + 5x - 2x = 17$

$\qquad 15 + 3x = 17$

$\qquad 3x = 2$

$\qquad x \approx 0.67$

12. $\frac{1}{7}(4x - 5) = 152$

$\qquad \frac{4}{7}x - \frac{5}{7} = 152$

$\qquad \frac{4}{7}x = 152.71$

$\qquad x \approx 267.25$

13. $0.11(3.45x - 2.80) = 8.33$

$\qquad 0.3795x - 0.308 = 8.33$

$\qquad 0.3795x = 8.638$

$\qquad x \approx 22.76$

14. $2x + 3 + x = 180$

$\qquad 3x + 3 = 180$

$\qquad 3x = 177$

$\qquad x = 59$

$\qquad 2x + 3 = 2(59) + 3$

$\qquad = 121$

The angle measures are $59°$ and $121°$.

15. $172 = 2(5x + 2) + 2(2x)$

$\qquad 172 = 10x + 4 + 4x$

$\qquad 172 = 14x + 4$

$\qquad 168 = 14x$

$\qquad 12 = x$

16. Length: $5x + 2 - 2(6) = 5(12) + 2 - 2(6)$

$\qquad = 60 + 2 - 12$

$\qquad = 50$

Width: $2x - 2(3) = 2(12) - 2(3)$

$\qquad = 24 - 6$

$\qquad = 18$

The dimensions of the swimming pool are 18 ft $\times$ 50 ft.

17. $A = lw$

$\qquad = (50)(18)$

$\qquad = 900$

The area is 900 ft^2.

18.

Minutes	0	1	2	3	4	5	6	7	8
Number of exercises you have solved	0	2	4	6	8	10	12	14	16
Number of exercises your friend has solved	6	7	8	9	10	11	12	13	14

19. $x = $ number of minutes you will take to catch up.

$$6 + 2x = 3x$$
$$6 = x$$

You will take 6 minutes to catch up to your friend.

20. $2x = 2(6) = 12$

You will have done 12 exercises.

Standardized Test Practice

1. C; $2(7x - 2) + 2(3x + 1) = 38$
$$14x - 4 + 6x + 2 = 38$$
$$20x - 2 = 38$$
$$20x = 40$$
$$x = 2$$

$7x - 2$
$7(2) - 2 = 14 - 2 = 12$

$3x + 1$
$3(2) + 1 = 6 + 1 = 7$

2. C

3. D; $(6x - 1) + (2x + 10) + (4x + 3) = 180$
$$12x + 12 = 180$$
$$12x = 168$$
$$x = 14$$
$\angle 1 = 6x - 1 = 6(14) - 1 = 84 - 1 = 83°$

4. A; $2y - 4(y - 3) = 10$
$$2y - 4y + 12 = 10$$
$$-2y + 12 = 10$$
$$-2y = -2$$
$$y = 1$$

5. C; $55x = 45x + 100$
$$10x = 100$$
$$x = 10$$

6. A; Club A is more expensive after the first 9 months.

7. B; $-2.9n - 4.89 = 1.75(n + 14.5)$
$$-2.9n - 4.89 = 1.75n + 25.375$$
$$-4.89 = 4.65n + 25.375$$
$$-30.265 = 4.65n$$
$$-6.51 \approx n$$

Chapter 5
Exploring Data and Graphs

5.1 | *Exploring Pictographs and Time Lines*

ONGOING ASSESSMENT

1. *Sample answer:* There were about 10 million more air passengers than there were people in the U.S.

2. *Sample answer:* Some people are counted more than once as passengers because they fly more than once a year.

EXERCISES

1. Tokyo, Sydney, London, New York, Toronto, Mexico City

2. $17.58 \div 2.52 \approx 6.97$; about 7 times greater

3. $170 - 45 = 145$ million

4.
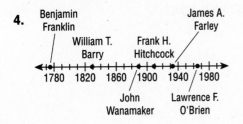

5.

6. 10 million

7. $8(10) = 80$
About 80 million passengers traveled *United*.

8. $8(10) - \left[5(10) + \frac{1}{2}(10)\right] = 80 - (50 + 5)$
$$= 80 - 55$$
$$= 25$$

About 25 million more passengers traveled on *American* than on *USAir*.

9. *Sample answer:* The pictograph would contain half as many planes.

10.

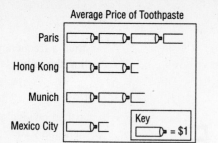

Average Price of Toothpaste

Paris

Hong Kong

Munich

Mexico City

Key ▭◨▭ = $1

11. 10 years

12. About 1838

13. Declared independence from Great Britain

14. First railroad built, Webster Ashburton Treaty

15.

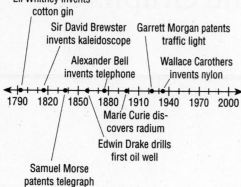

Eli Whitney invents cotton gin

Sir David Brewster invents kaleidoscope

Garrett Morgan patents traffic light

Alexander Bell invents telephone

Wallace Carothers invents nylon

1790 1820 1850 1880 1910 1940 1970 2000

Marie Curie discovers radium

Edwin Drake drills first oil well

Samuel Morse patents telegraph

16. Answers vary.

17. B; $a - b < d$

$$-2 - 4 \overset{?}{<} -4$$

$$-6 < -4$$

18. Answers vary.

5.2 *Exploring Bar Graphs and Histograms*

ONGOING ASSESSMENT

1.

Frequency Distribution

Interval	Tally	Total
54-57.9	III	3
58-61.9	ΗΙΙ IIII	9
62-65.9	ΗΙΙ ΗΙΙ III	13
66-69.9	ΗΙΙ	5

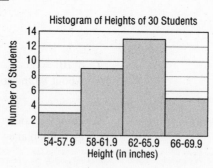

Histogram of Heights of 30 Students

Number of Students

14
12
10
8
6
4
2

54-57.9 58-61.9 62-65.9 66-69.9

Height (in inches)

2. The histogram in the text gives a fairer representation of the data. The more the data is condensed, the less detail is observable. For example, the decrease in frequency from 58–59.9 to 60–61.9 before the final increase from 60–61.9 to 62–63.9 cannot be observed in the more condensed histogram.

EXERCISES

1. You should begin by deciding which intervals will help you see the patterns of the data. Construct a frequency distribution by making tally marks to show the number of items in each interval and then totaling the tally marks.

2. It is used to make a histogram.

3. Most: own a car;
Fewest: become rich

4. Most adults had owning a home as their goal; 109

5. Simple bar graph; *sample answer:* Each category has one piece of data, so a simple bar graph is sufficient.

6.

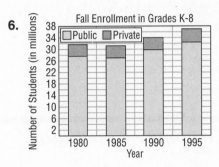

Fall Enrollment in Grades K-8

7.

Frequency Distribution		
Interval	Tally	Total
6-7	II	2
8-9	JHT I	6
10-11	JHT IIII	9
12-13	JHT III	8
14-15	JHT I	6
16-17	JHT	5

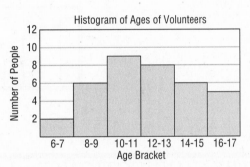

Histogram of Ages of Volunteers

8.

Skill: Word Processing/Typing, Reading, Mathematics, Hand-eye Coordination, Writing, Thinking/reasoning, Analytical problem solving, Speed
Number of Parents

9. Under 5 and 14–17

10. Under 5

11. 14–17

12. About 2 million

13. Answers vary.

14. A

15. D

16. Answers vary.

Spiral REVIEW

1. Triple bar graph

2. Gym shoes

3. About 7%

4.
$$3x + 4 = x$$
$$3x + 4 - 3x = x - 3x$$
$$4 = -2x$$
$$-2 = x$$

5. $2(2x + 1) = 8$
$$2x + 1 = 4$$
$$2x = 3$$
$$x = \frac{3}{2}$$

6. $\frac{1}{3}(6x - 3) = 7$
$$2x - 1 = 7$$
$$2x - 1 + 1 = 7 + 1$$
$$2x = 8$$
$$x = 4$$

7. $4t + 6t = 8t - 13$
$$10t = 8t - 13$$
$$10t - 8t = 8t - 13 - 8t$$
$$2t = -13$$
$$t = -\frac{13}{2}$$

Using a Graphing Calculator

1.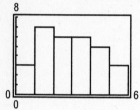

2.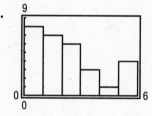

5.3 *GEOMETRY CONNECTION: Exploring Line Graphs*

ONGOING ASSESSMENT

1. 4-sided polygon $= 4 \times 180° = 720°$
5-sided polygon $= 5 \times 180° = 900°$

   $900 - 720 = 180°$

2. It is the same.

EXERCISES

1. 40

2. $47 - 28 = 19$
The number of female representatives increased by about 19 people.

3. $20 - 6 = 14$
The number of Hispanic representatives increased by about 14 people.

4. Horizontal: years
Vertical: price in thousands of dollars

5. Each color represents a different region of the U.S.: Northeast, Midwest, South, and West

6. 1985: $80,000
1995: About $135,000

7. South

8. West from 1990 to 1995

9. $A = \frac{1}{2}bh$

$\frac{1}{2}(2)(2) = 2 \qquad \frac{1}{2}(3)(2) = 3$

$\frac{1}{2}(4)(2) = 4 \qquad \frac{1}{2}(5)(2) = 5$

Base	2	3	4	5
Height	2	2	2	2
Area	2	3	4	5

10.

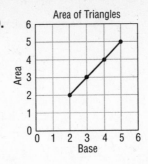

11.

12.

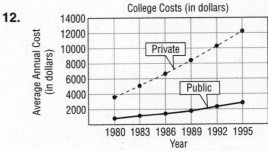

13. Slightly slower; answers vary.

14. Answers vary.

15. B

16.

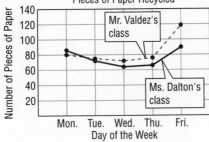

17. Mr. Valdez's class

18. Friday; *sample answer:* Maybe both classes cleaned up on Friday.

Lab 5.4

Part A

1. *Sample answer:*

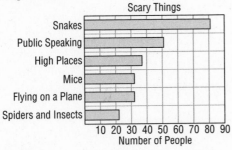

2. *Sample answer:* Choice could be a pictograph, bar graph, or line graph.

3. Line graph; *sample answer:* The categories (scary things) do not have a numerical order, so a line graph does not fit the data.

Part B

4. Line graph:

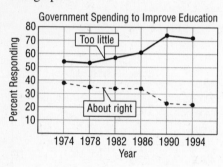

Bar graph:

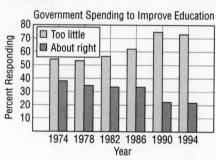

5. *Sample answer:* In the line graph because you can focus on the line that represents the response "about right" and see how it changes over time.

Part C

6. Answers vary.

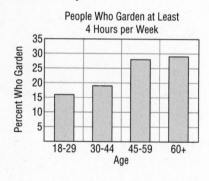

7. *Sample answer:* A bar graph or pictograph will work equally well.

8. Time line

9. *Sample answer:*

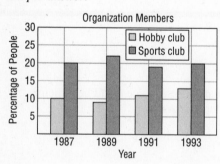

10. *Sample answer:* A line graph would also be appropriate because you can observe how each organization's membership changes over time.

11. *Sample answer:* A histogram would not work because there aren't any intervals to observe.

ONGOING ASSESSMENT

1. *Sample answer:* It might make more of a visual impact.

2. *Sample answer:* It is easier to read numbers more accurately.

EXERCISES

1. 6.8
    − 4.4
    ─────
    2.4 miles

2. $6.8 \div 2 = 3.4$
    Retail salesperson

3. $649 - 223 = 426$

4. Brown; red

5. *Sample answer:* bar graph; pictograph; choose one of these because the data fall into distinct categories.

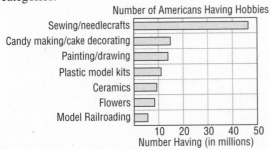

6. *Sample answer:* line graph; choose a line graph to show the change over time.

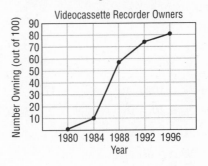

7. *Sample answer:* bar graph, pictograph; the data fall into distinct categories.

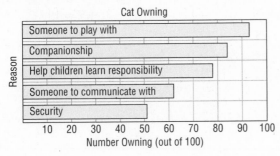

8. A bar graph or pictograph is appropriate.

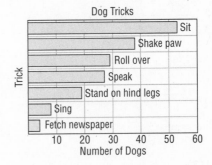

Sample answer: A pictograph makes the data clear and would make an impact.

9.

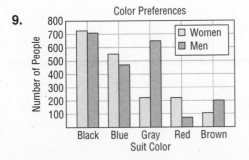

A double bar graph is better for showing differences because it compares men's and women's preferences. A stacked bar graph is better for showing overall color because it compares all those who prefer each color.

10. 1980: about 1.7 million
1985: about 2 million
1995: about 2.6 million

11. The increase was about 2.6 million players.

12. 1955–1960

13. *Sample answer:* It shows clearly how it has changed over the years.

14. A

15. D; $55,000 - 36,000 = 19,000$

16. Answers vary.

Spiral R E V I E W

1. $3 + 6 \times 8 \div 2 = 3 + 48 \div 2 = 3 + 24 = 27$

2. $10 \times 7 - 2 \times 4 = 70 - 8 = 62$

3. $16 - 5 + 2 \times 6 = 16 - 5 + 12 = 23$

4. $12 \div 3 + 3 \times 2 = 4 + 6 = 10$

5. $25 + 45 \div 3^2 = 25 + 45 \div 9 = 25 + 5 = 30$

6. $4 \times 2^3 - 5 = 4 \times 8 - 5 = 32 - 5 = 27$

7. -6
8. -5
9. 10
10. 42
11. 31

12. -2
13. -12
14. -88
15. 30

16.
$$16 + 2k = 10$$
$$16 - 16 + 2k = 10 - 16$$
$$2k = -6$$
$$\frac{2k}{2} = \frac{-6}{2}$$
$$k = -3$$

17.
$$5d + 11 = 76$$
$$5d + 11 - 11 = 76 - 11$$
$$5d = 65$$
$$\frac{5d}{5} = \frac{65}{5}$$
$$d = 13$$

18.
$$22 = 6 - 4w$$
$$22 - 6 = 6 - 6 - 4w$$
$$16 = -4w$$
$$\frac{16}{-4} = \frac{-4w}{-4}$$
$$-4 = w$$

19.
$$\frac{1}{3}a - 5 = 17$$
$$\frac{1}{3}a - 5 + 5 = 17 + 5$$
$$3 \times \frac{1}{3}a = 22 \times 3$$
$$a = 66$$

20.
$$24 = 4(m - 7)$$
$$24 = 4m - 28$$
$$24 + 28 = 4m - 28 + 28$$
$$\frac{52}{4} = \frac{4m}{4}$$
$$13 = m$$

21.
$$3z + 7 = 19$$
$$3z + 7 - 7 = 19 - 7$$
$$\frac{3z}{3} = \frac{12}{3}$$
$$z = 4$$

22.
$$\frac{14w}{14} = \frac{112}{14}$$
$$w = 8$$
You have to save for 8 weeks.

Mid-Chapter A S S E S S M E N T

1. Line graph

2. Apparel

3. Restaurants

4. Movies

5.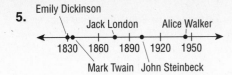

6.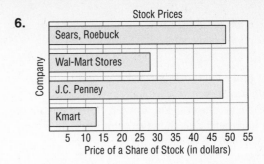

Sample answer: A bar graph because the data fall in distinct categories.

8. Simple bar graph

7.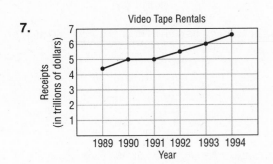

Sample answer: A line graph is appropriate because you want to display changes over time.

9. Talking on the telephone

10. About 75

11. Boredom

5.5 *Problem Solving: Misleading Graphs*

ONGOING ASSESSMENT

1.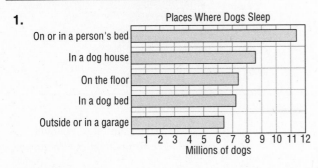

2.

EXERCISES

1. There appears to be four times as many junior high schools with modems in 1995 than in 1992.

2. *Sample answer:* From the scale on the vertical axis, you can tell that the 1995 value is about twice as large as the 1992 value. However, the area of the school building for 1995 is about four times as large as the one for 1992.

3. There are more than twice as many drummers as saxophone players.

4. 3.7 million drummers to 2.5 million saxophonists

5. The broken vertical axis makes it appear that there are about twice as many drummers as saxophone players. You can tell from the scale on the horizontal axis, however, that there are really only about 1.5 as many.

6.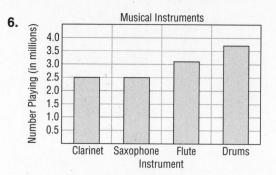

7. The hourly pay in mid-1996 appears to be 3 times as much as the hourly pay in early 1995.

8. The hourly pay in mid-1996 is about $12.80 and the pay in early 1995 is $12.20.

9. The broken vertical scale makes it appear that the hourly pay in mid-1996 is 3 times as much hourly pay instead of about 1.05 times as much pay.

10. The graph on the left; answers vary.

11. The graph on the right; answers vary.

12. The house sizes are different, but each house represents the same amount.

13. Answers vary.

14. C

15. Answers vary.

5.6   *Statistics: Line Plots*

ONGOING ASSESSMENT

1. $\frac{306}{18} = 17$ and $\frac{396}{18} = 22$, so remove an X from above 17 and add an X above 22.

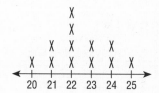

EXERCISES

1. *Sample answer:* Statistics is a type of mathematics that involves organizing data.

2. 6

3. There are more younger squirrels than older squirrels.

4.

```
            X
      X  X  X  X  X
      X  X  X  X  X
   X  X  X  X  X  X  X
   X  X  X  X  X  X  X  X  X  X
  +--+--+--+--+--+--+--+--+--+--+
   0  1  2  3  4  5  6  7  8  9
```

5. Yes; *sample answer:* You could have the ages on the line and then make an X for each person in the category.

6. No; *sample answer:* There are too many cars in each category to represent with a line plot.

7. Each X represents the number of hours one student spent doing homework during one week.

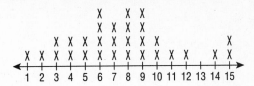

8. Each X represents the number of brothers and/or sisters one student has.

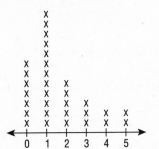

9. a. 4; 6

b. 3, 4, and 7; 347, 374, 437, 473, 734, 743

10. a. 6; 6(5) = 30

b.
$$\frac{6(1) + 3(2) + 8(3) + 7(4) + 6(5)}{30} = \frac{6 + 6 + 24 + 28 + 30}{30}$$
$$= \frac{94}{30}$$
$$= 3\frac{2}{15}$$

The average number of miles jogged per day is $3\frac{2}{15}$ miles.

11. Each X represents one team's number of wins in the 1996 Major League Soccer regular season.

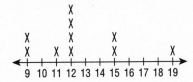

12. a. Each of 3 tan figures: 1; each of 2 red figures: 2; each of 3 green figures: 4; 1 purple figure: 6; 1 blue figure: 8

b. Each X represents one figure's area.

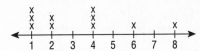

c. 33 units^2

13. C; 82 − 12 = 70

14. Answers vary.

Spiral R E V I E W

1. There appears to be more than two times as much spent by Ford as Chrysler.

2. The vertical scales are different.

3. *Sample answer:* with a line graph having an unbroken vertical scale

4. $5(n - 2) = 0$

$ n - 2 = 0$

$ n = 2$

5. $6r - 2 = 2r$

$6r - 2 - 6r = 2r - 6r$

$-2 = -4r$

$\frac{1}{2} = r$

6. $2r + 6r = 4r - 28$

$8r - 4r = 4r - 28 - 4r$

$4r = -28$

$r = -7$

7. $2(p + 1) = -2(p + 1)$

$2p + 2 = -2p - 2$

$2p + 2 + 2p = -2p - 2 + 2p$

$4p + 2 = -2$

$4p = -4$

$p = -1$

8. $\frac{4}{5}s + 3.2 = -\frac{1}{5}s$

$\frac{4}{5}s + 3.2 - \frac{4}{5}s = -\frac{1}{5}s - \frac{4}{5}s$

$3.2 = -1s$

$-3.2 = s$

9. $\frac{1}{7}(x + 1) = 6$

$7 \cdot \frac{1}{7}(x + 1) = 7 \cdot 6$

$x + 1 = 42$

$x = 41$

10. $18 - 2(2) = 18 - 4 = 14$ in.;

$12 - 2(2) = 12 - 4 = 8$ in.;

14 in. $\times$ 8 in.

11. $14 \times 8 = 112$ in.^{2}

12. Total area: $18 \times 12 = 216$ in.^{2}

Area of picture frame = Total area − area of picture

$216 - 112 = 104$ in.^{2}

Communicating About Mathematics

1. Answers vary.

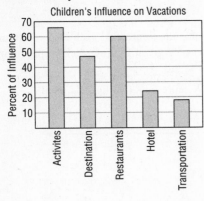

Children's Influence on Vacations

2. No; only 24% of 53 million children, or 12.72 million children, think they influence the family's choice of hotel.

3. 53 million $\times$ 60% = 53 $\times$ 0.6 = 31.8, or 31.8 million

4. 25% $\times$ 100 = 25 adults

5. *Sample answer:* 58% of adults believe that it is okay to advertise candy during children's TV programming.

5.7 | *Statistics: Scatter Plots*

ONGOING ASSESSMENT

1. Positive

2. No

3. Negative

EXERCISES

1. Negative

2. About 3 million

3. *Sample answer:* No; because you can't sell a negative number of televisions.

4. Negative

5. Positive

6. No

7. Positive

8. Negative

9. No

10. Positive

11.

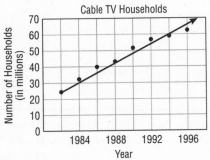

12. Have a positive correlation

13.

About 23.5 lb/in.^{2}

14. About 35 lb/in.^{2}

15. About 12 feet

16. About 59 million

17.

18. About 80 million

19.

$12 = 2(1) + 2(x)$	$12 = 2(2) + 2(x)$	$12 = 2(3) + 2(x)$
$12 = 2 + 2x$	$12 = 4 + 2x$	$12 = 6 + 2x$
$10 = 2x$	$8 = 2x$	$6 = 2x$
$5 = x$	$4 = x$	$3 = x$

Length, l	1	2	3	4	5
Width, w	5	4	3	2	1
Perimeter	12	12	12	12	12

20.

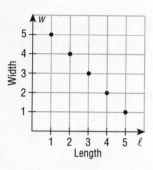

Yes; negative correlation

21. The data in Example 3; the data in Example 2; *sample answer:* The data points in Example 3 are very close to the line of fit, but the data points in Example 2 are more scattered.

22. C

23. Answers vary.

Lab 5.8

Part A

1. No; *sample answer:* There are five possible numbers, so each number has a probability of $\frac{1}{5}$.

2. a.–c. Answers vary.

3. About 20%; there are five possible numbers, so each number has a probability of $\frac{1}{5}$, or 20%.

Part B

4. Answers vary.

5. Answers vary.

6. Answers vary.

7. *Sample answer:* a large set; when we combined our data from other groups, the percent of the time that each number occurred got closer to 20%.

8. *Sample answer:* You could draw numbered pieces of paper from a hat.

9. *Sample answer:* about 100 times; there are ten numbers, so each number should occur about one tenth of the time.

ONGOING ASSESSMENT

1. *Sample answer:* No; the sample of 600 adults does not represent the population of children about which your friend is making predictions.

EXERCISES

1. The probability of 0.5 means that the event is equally likely to occur as not occur.

2. Door B; *sample answer:* The prize is more likely to be behind door B.

3. Yes; 8 out of 10 times it will rain.

4. Divide the number of ways that an event can occur favorably by the total number of trials.

5. $\frac{3}{12} = \frac{1}{4} = 0.25$

6. $\frac{5}{12} \approx 0.42$

7. $\frac{1}{12} \approx 0.083$

8. $\frac{2}{12} = \frac{1}{6} \approx 0.17$

9. $\frac{1}{2}$

10. Answers vary.

11. Answers vary.

12. Answers vary.

13. $\frac{1}{7} \approx 0.14$

14. $\frac{4}{7} \approx 0.57$

15. Answers vary.

16. Answers vary.

17.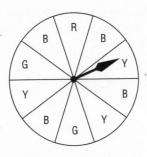

18. Yes; *sample answer:*

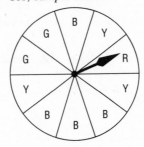

19. a. $\frac{76}{200} = 0.38$

    b. $\frac{4}{200} = 0.02$

    c. $\frac{68 + 12}{200} = \frac{80}{200} = 0.4$

20. $\frac{76 + 68 + 18 + 6}{200} = \frac{168}{200}$
$$= 0.84$$

21. *Sample answer:* No; the sample of people on one street does not accurately represent the entire population that will vote.

22. B; $0.25 \times 8 = 4$

23. Answers vary.

Chapter **R E V I E W**

1. About 37.5 lb

2.

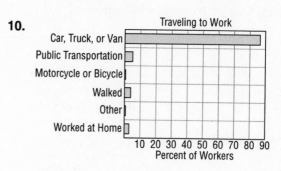

3. Simple bar graph; *sample answer:* Each type of animal is a distinct category that can be represented by a bar.

4. 1–3, 10–12, and 13–15 have the smallest number of people.

5. 4–6

6. Gross income

7. About $8 billion

8. 1998

9.

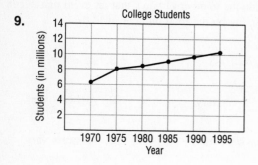

10.

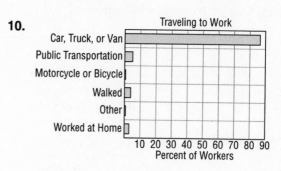

Sample answer: A bar graph is good for these data since they fall in distinct categories and you want to compare totals.

11.

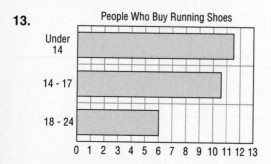

Sample answer: A line graph is good for these data because you can trace changes over time.

12. Because the horizontal scale is broken.

13.

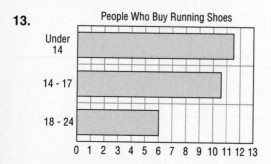

14. Most: 2
Least: 5

15.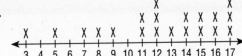

16.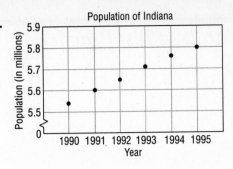

1997: about 5.91 million

17. $\frac{2}{8} = \frac{1}{4} = 0.25$

18. $\frac{3}{8} = 0.375$

19. $\frac{3}{8} = 0.375$

Chapter ASSESSMENT

1. Pictograph

2. Magazines

3. About 95 billion; $5(17) + 2.5(4) = 85 + 10 = 95$

4. Line graph

5. The 1990 average hourly wage appears to be over 3 times as much as the 1980 average hourly wage.

6. The vertical scale is broken.

7.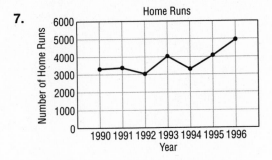

Sample answer: A line graph helps you follow the changes over time.

8.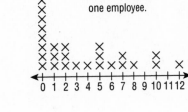

Each × represents one employee.

9. 10

10.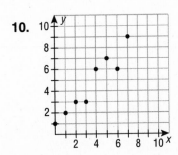

11. Yes; positive correlation

12. $\frac{3}{12} = \frac{1}{4}$

Standardized Test Practice

1. D

2. C; $150 + 250 + 325 + 275 = 1000$

3. D

4. C; $\frac{4}{10} = 0.4$

5. B

Chapter 6
Exploring Number Theory

6.1 GEOMETRY CONNECTION: Divisibility Tests

ONGOING ASSESSMENT

1. 1, 2, 3, 5, 6, 10, 15, 30   **2.** 1, 31   **3.** 1, 2, 4, 8, 16, 32

Sample answer: For each exercise, I found pairs of numbers whose product is the given number. Each factor has a partner because none of the numbers is a perfect square.

EXERCISES

1. If one natural number divides evenly into another natural number, then the second number is said to be divisible by the first.

2. Divisible by

2: no; 4485 is not even.
3: yes; $4 + 4 + 8 + 5 = 21$, $21 \div 3 = 7$
4: no; 4485 is not even.
5: yes; the last digit is 5.

6: no; 4485 is not even.
8: no; 4485 is not even.
9: no; $4 + 4 + 8 + 5 = 21$, $21 \div 9 \neq$ natural number
10: no; the last digit is not 0.

3. 36: 36×1, 18×2, 12×3, 9×4, 6×6;

1, 2, 3, 4, 6, 9, 12, 18, 36

4. The side lengths are the factors.

5. False; 6 is divisible by 3, but is not divisible by 9.

6. True; $10 = 2 \times 5$

7. True; $6 \times 12 = 72$

8. False; The factors of 9 are 1, 3, and 9.

9. Divisible by

2: yes; 2160 is even.
3: yes; $2 + 1 + 6 + 0 = 9$, $9 \div 3 = 3$
4: yes; $60 \div 4 = 15$
5: yes; the last digit is 0.

6: yes; 2160 is even and divisible by 3.
8: yes; $160 \div 8 = 20$
9: yes; $2 + 1 + 6 + 0 = 9$, $9 \div 9 = 1$
10: yes; the last digit is 0.

10. Divisible by

2: yes; 25,920 is even.
3: yes; $2 + 5 + 9 + 2 + 0 = 18$; $18 \div 3 = 6$
4: yes; $20 \div 4 = 5$
5: yes; the last digit is 0.

6: yes; 25,920 is even and divisible by 3.
8: yes; $920 \div 8 = 115$
9: yes; $2 + 5 + 9 + 2 + 0 = 18$, $18 \div 9 = 2$
10: yes; the last digit is 0.

11. Divisible by

2: yes; 192 is even.
3: yes; $1 + 9 + 2 = 12$, $12 \div 3 = 4$
4: yes; $92 \div 4 = 23$
5: no; the last digit is not 0 or 5.

6: yes; 192 is even and divisible by 3.
8: yes; $192 \div 8 = 24$
9: no; $1 + 9 + 2 = 12$, $12 \div 9 \neq$ natural number
10: no; the last digit is not 0.

12. Divisible by

2: yes; 9756 is even.
3: yes; $9 + 7 + 5 + 6 = 27$, $27 \div 3 = 9$
4: yes; $56 \div 4 = 14$
5: no; the last digit is not 0 or 5.

6: yes; 9756 is even and divisible by 3.
8: no; $756 \div 8 \neq$ natural number
9: yes; $9 + 7 + 5 + 6 = 27$, $27 \div 9 = 3$
10: no; the last digit is not 0.

13. Divisible by

2: yes; 1234 is even.
3: no; $1 + 2 + 3 + 4 = 10$, $10 \div 3 \neq$ natural number
4: no; $34 \div 4 \neq$ natural number
5: no; the last digit is not 0 or 5.

6: no; 1234 is not divisible by 3.
8: no; 1234 is not divisible by 4.
9: no; 1234 is not divisible by 3.
10: no; the last digit is not 0.

14. Divisible by

2: no; 3725 is not even.
3: no; $3 + 7 + 2 + 5 = 17$, $17 \div 3 \neq$ natural number
4: no; $25 \div 4 \neq$ natural number
5: yes; the last digit is 5.

6: no; 3725 is not even.
8: no; 3725 is not even.
9: no; 3725 is not divisible by 3.
10: no; the last digit is not 0.

15. Divisible by

2: no; 6859 is not even.
3: no; $6 + 8 + 5 + 9 = 28$, $28 \div 3 \neq$ natural number
4: no; 6859 is not even.
5: no; the last digit is not 0 or 5.

6: no; 6859 is not even.
8: no; 6859 is not even.
9: no; 6859 is not divisible by 3.
10: no; the last digit is not 0.

16. Divisible by

2: no; 2401 is not even.
3: no; $2 + 4 + 0 + 1 = 7$, $7 \div 3 \neq$ natural number
4: no; 2401 is not even.
5: no; the last digit is not 0 or 5.

6: no; 2401 is not even.
8: no; 2401 is not even.
9: no; 2401 is not divisible by 3.
10: no; the last digit is not 0.

17. $34?21 \rightarrow 3 + 4 + 2 + 1 + ? = 10 + ?$

2: $10 + 2 = 12$, $12 \div 3 = 4$
5: $10 + 5 = 15$, $15 \div 3 = 5$
8: $10 + 8 = 18$, $18 \div 3 = 6$

18. $39,9?8 \rightarrow 3 + 9 + 9 + 8 + ? = 29 + ?$

7: $29 + 7 = 36$, $36 \div 9 = 4$

19. $5,43?,216,789 \rightarrow 5 + 4 + 3 + 2 + 1 + 6 + 7 + 8 + 9 + ? = 45 + ?$

0: $45 + 0 = 45$, $45 \div 9 = 5$
9: $45 + 9 = 54$, $54 \div 9 = 6$

20. $12,?51 \rightarrow 1 + 2 + 5 + 1 + ? = 9 + ?$

0: $9 + 0 = 9$, $9 \div 9 = 1$
9: $9 + 9 = 18$, $18 \div 9 = 2$

21. $2,546,?24 \rightarrow 2 + 5 + 4 + 6 + 2 + 4 + ? = 23 + ?$

4: $23 + 4 = 27$, $27 \div 9 = 3$

22. $3 \times 4 \times 5 = 60$ so, the numbers less than 200 divisible by 3, 4, and 5 are multiples of 60: 60, 120, 180.

23. $2 \times 2 \times 2$ is divisible by 2, 4, and 8. 2×3 is divisible by 2, 3, and 6. 3×3 is divisible by 3 and 9. 5 is divisible by 5. So $2 \times 2 \times 2 \times 3 \times 3 \times 5$ is divisible by 2, 3, 4, 5, 6, 8, and 9. $2 \times 2 \times 2 \times 3 \times 3 \times 5 = 360$; answers vary.

24. 18: 1×18, 2×9, 3×6;
1, 2, 3, 6, 9, 18

25. 36: 1×36, 2×18, 3×12, 4×9, 6×6;
1, 2, 3, 4, 6, 9, 12, 18, 36

26. 42: 1×42, 2×21, 3×14, 6×7;
1, 2, 3, 6, 7, 14, 21, 42

27. 45: 1×45, 3×15, 5×9;
1, 3, 5, 9, 15, 45

28. 50: 1×50, 2×25, 5×10;
1, 2, 5, 10, 25, 50

29. 100: 1×100, 2×50, 4×25, 5×20, 10×20;
1, 2, 4, 5, 10, 20, 25, 50, 100

30. 72: 1×72, 2×36, 3×24, 4×18, 6×12, 8×9;
1, 2, 3, 4, 6, 8, 9, 12, 18, 36, 72

31. 96: 1×96, 2×48, 3×32, 4×24, 6×16, 8×12;
1, 2, 3, 4, 6, 8, 12, 16, 24, 32, 48, 96

32. $A = lw$
$64 = lw$;
1×64, 2×32, 4×16, or 8×8

33. 4 or 5 ways; 80 times $1, 16 times $5, 8 times $10, 4 times $20, and possibly 40 times $2

34. 1 ft $\times$ 1600 ft, 2 ft $\times$ 800 ft, 4 ft $\times$ 400 ft, 5 ft $\times$ 320 ft, 8 ft $\times$ 200 ft, 10 ft $\times$ 160 ft, 16 ft $\times$ 100 ft, 20 ft $\times$ 80 ft, 25 ft $\times$ 64 ft, 32 ft $\times$ 50 ft, and 40 ft $\times$ 40 ft

35. 40 ft by 40 ft

36. No; $15 = 3 \times 5$ and 3 is not a factor of 350.

37. Because 3 is not divisible by 9.

38. Because 8 is divisible by 4.

39. **a.** In a natural number, the digits in the places beyond the tens' place represent multiples of 100 (such as 300, 9000, or 70,000), which are all multiples of 4 ($300 = 3 \times 4 \times 25$, $9000 = 9 \times 4 \times 250$, $70,000 = 7 \times 4 \times 2500$). So, if the number represented by the last two digits is divisible by 4, then the natural number is divisible by 4.

b. In a natural number, the digits in the places beyond the hundreds' place represent multiples of 1000 (such as 4000, 100,000, or 70,000), which are all multiples of 8 ($4000 = 4 \times 8 \times 125$, $100,000 = 100 \times 8 \times 125$, $70,000 \times 8 \times 125$). So, if the number represented by the last three digits is divisible by 8, then the natural number is divisible by 8.

40.–43. Let $a = 3x$ and $b = 3y$, and let x and y be integers.

40. $a + b = 3x + 3y = 3(x + y)$; divisible by 3

41. $a - b = 3x - 3y = 3(x - y)$; divisible by 3

42. $ab = 3x(3y)$; divisible by 3

43. $\dfrac{a}{b} = \dfrac{3x}{3y} = \dfrac{x}{y}$; $\dfrac{x}{y}$ may be a fraction or an integer that is not divisible by 3.

44. D; 60 is divisible by 4 so 360 is also. 360 ends in 0 so it is divisible by 5. $3 + 6 + 0 = 9$ is divisible by 9 so 360 is also.

45. Yes; 45 is divisible by 3, so you will fit all the beats in 15 measures.

Lab 6.2

Part A

1. 2, 3, 5, 7, 11, 13, 17, 19, 23, 29; prime numbers

2. Move to the next number that is not crossed out, 7. Keep it and cross out every multiple of 7 after 7.
All the other multiples of 7 (14, 21, 28) have already been crossed out.

3. 31 ~~32~~ ~~33~~ ~~34~~ ~~35~~ ~~36~~ 37 ~~38~~
~~39~~ ~~40~~ 41 ~~42~~ 43 ~~44~~ ~~45~~ ~~46~~
47 ~~48~~ ~~49~~ ~~50~~ ~~51~~ ~~52~~ 53 ~~54~~
~~55~~ ~~56~~ ~~57~~ ~~58~~ 59 ~~60~~

31, 37, 41, 43, 47, 53, 59; prime numbers

Part B

5. Rows 2, 4, and 6
Prime number(s): 2
There is one prime number.

6. Rows 3 and 6
Prime number(s): 3
This is one prime number.

7.

1	⑦	⑬	⑲	25	㉛	㊲	㊸	49	55	(61)	(67)	(73)	(79)	85	91
②	8	14	20	26	32	38	44	50	56	62	68	74	80	86	92
③	9	15	21	27	33	39	45	51	57	63	69	75	81	87	93
4	10	16	22	28	34	40	46	52	58	64	70	76	82	88	94
⑤	⑪	⑰	㉓	㉙	35	㊶	㊼	(53)	(59)	65	(71)	77	(83)	(89)	95
6	12	18	24	30	36	42	48	54	60	66	72	78	84	90	96

Rows 2, 3, 4, and 6 do not contain any prime numbers except 2 and 3. Rows 1 and 5 contain many prime numbers.

8. No, because one of the numbers would be an even number so it would be divisible by 2 and therefore it would not be prime.

9. Yes; 3 and 5, 5 and 7, 11 and 13, 17 and 19

10. Yes, 211 is prime because it is not divisible by any numbers except 1 and 211.

6.2 *Factors and Primes*

ONGOING ASSESSMENT

1.

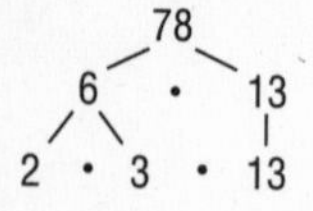

78
6 · 13
2 · 3 · 13

$78 = 2 \cdot 3 \cdot 13$

2.

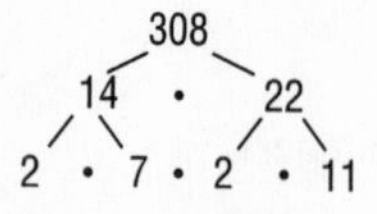

308
14 · 22
2 · 7 · 2 · 11

$308 = 2^2 \cdot 7 \cdot 11$

3.

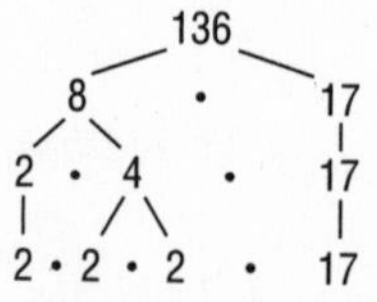

136
8 · 17
2 · 4 · 17
2 · 2 · 2 · 17

$136 = 2^3 \cdot 17$

EXERCISES

1.

$$18 = 2 \cdot 3^2$$

2.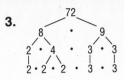

$$24 = 2^3 \cdot 3$$

3.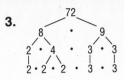

$$72 = 2^3 \cdot 3^2$$

4.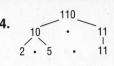

$$110 = 2 \cdot 5 \cdot 11$$

5. True

6. True

7. True

8. False;
$56 = 2 \cdot 2 \cdot 2 \cdot 7 = 2^3 \cdot 7$

9. 17 is prime; it is divisible only by itself and 1.

10. 9 is composite; $9 = 3^2$

11. 35 is composite; $35 = 5 \cdot 7$

12. 27 is composite; $27 = 3^3$

13. $12 = 2 \cdot 2 \cdot 3 = 2^2 \cdot 3$

14. $18 = 2 \cdot 3 \cdot 3 = 2 \cdot 3^2$

15. $60 = 2 \cdot 2 \cdot 3 \cdot 5 = 2^2 \cdot 3 \cdot 5$

16. $36 = 2 \cdot 2 \cdot 3 \cdot 3 = 2^2 \cdot 3^2$

17.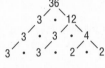

$$36 = 2^2 \cdot 3^2$$

18.

$$63 = 3^2 \cdot 7$$

19.

$$84 = 2^2 \cdot 3 \cdot 7$$

20.

$$100 = 2^2 \cdot 5^2$$

21.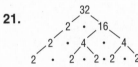

$$32 = 2^5$$

22.

$$64 = 2^6$$

23.

$$72 = 2^3 \cdot 3^2$$

24.

$$90 = 2 \cdot 3^2 \cdot 5$$

25. $-27 = (-1) \cdot 3 \cdot 3 \cdot 3$
$ = (-1) \cdot 3^3$

26. $-28 = (-1) \cdot 2 \cdot 2 \cdot 7$
$ = (-1) \cdot 2^2 \cdot 7$

27. $9x^3 = 3 \cdot 3 \cdot x \cdot x \cdot x$
$ = 3^2 \cdot x^3$

28. $125y^4 = 5 \cdot 5 \cdot 5 \cdot y \cdot y \cdot y \cdot y$
$ = 5^3 \cdot y^4$

29. $8a^3b^2 = 2 \cdot 2 \cdot 2 \cdot a \cdot a \cdot a \cdot b \cdot b$
$ = 2^3 \cdot a^3 \cdot b^2$

30. $12p^4q = 2 \cdot 2 \cdot 3 \cdot p \cdot p \cdot p \cdot p \cdot q$
$ = 2^2 \cdot 3 \cdot p^4 \cdot q$

31. $-45mn^3 = (-1) \cdot 3 \cdot 3 \cdot 5 \cdot m \cdot n \cdot n \cdot n$
$ = (-1) \cdot 3^2 \cdot 5 \cdot m \cdot n^3$

32. $-50s^2t^5 = (-1) \cdot 2 \cdot 5 \cdot 5 \cdot s \cdot s \cdot t \cdot t \cdot t \cdot t \cdot t$
$ = (-1) \cdot 2 \cdot 5^2 \cdot s^2 \cdot t^5$

33. $2^3 \cdot 3 \cdot 5 = 8 \cdot 15$
$ = 120$

34. $3^2 \cdot 2 \cdot 13 = 9 \cdot 26$
$ = 234$

35. $-1 \cdot 3^2 \cdot 5 \cdot 13 = -9 \cdot 65$
$ = -585$

36. $-1 \cdot 2^3 \cdot 3 \cdot 7 = -8 \cdot 21$
$= -168$

37. $8:\ 1 \times 8, 2 \times 4;$
$1, 2, 4, 8$

38. $16:\ 1 \times 16, 2 \times 8, 4 \times 4;$
$1, 2, 4, 8, 16$

39. $32:\ 1 \times 32, 2 \times 16, 4 \times 8;$
$1, 2, 4, 8, 16, 32$

40. $64:\ 1 \times 64, 2 \times 32, 4 \times 16, 8 \times 8;$
$1, 2, 4, 8, 16, 32, 64$

41. Yes; no; *samples:* 15 (4 factors; 1, 3, 5, 15) and 30 (8 factors: 1, 2, 3, 5, 6, 10, 15, 30), 22 (4 factors: 1, 2, 11, 22) and 44 (6 factors: 1, 2, 4, 11, 22, 44)

42. *Sample answer:*

$20 = 3 + 17$	$26 = 3 + 23$	$32 = 3 + 29$	$38 = 7 + 31$
$22 = 3 + 19$	$28 = 5 + 23$	$34 = 3 + 31$	$40 = 3 + 37$
$24 = 5 + 19$	$30 = 7 + 23$	$36 = 5 + 31$	

43. 17 and 19, 29 and 31, 41 and 43, 59 and 61, 71 and 73

44. No. Let x equal the smallest integer; then the perimeter $= x + (x+1) + (x+2) = 3x + 3 = 3(x+1)$, which is divisible by 3.

45. No; because each group consists of more than one student, the number of students in the class would be equal to the product of two numbers (the number of groups and the number of students in each group), neither of which is 1.

46. $1: neither;
$2: prime;
$5: prime;
$10: composite, $10 = 2 \cdot 5$;
$20: composite, $20 = 2 \cdot 2 \cdot 5 = 2^2 \cdot 5$;
$50: composite, $50 = 2 \cdot 5 \cdot 5 = 2 \cdot 5^2$;
$100: composite, $100 = 2 \cdot 2 \cdot 5 \cdot 5 = 2^2 \cdot 5^2$

47. $500 = 2 \cdot 2 \cdot 5 \cdot 5 \cdot 5 = 2^2 \cdot 5^3$;
$1000 = 2 \cdot 2 \cdot 2 \cdot 5 \cdot 5 \cdot 5 = 2^3 \cdot 5^3$;
$5000 = 2 \cdot 2 \cdot 2 \cdot 5 \cdot 5 \cdot 5 \cdot 5 = 2^3 \cdot 5^4$;
$10,000 = 2 \cdot 2 \cdot 2 \cdot 2 \cdot 5 \cdot 5 \cdot 5 \cdot 5 = 2^4 \cdot 5^4$;
$100,000 = 2 \cdot 2 \cdot 2 \cdot 2 \cdot 2 \cdot 5 \cdot 5 \cdot 5 \cdot 5 \cdot 5$
$= 2^5 \cdot 5^5$

48. D

49.

✕	18	8	35
42	3/6	2	7
60	6/3	4	5
72	9	8	1

50.

✕	36	30	56
35	1	5	7
24	4	3/6	8
18	9	6/3	2

Spiral R E V I E W

1. Divisible by

2: yes; 612 is even.
3: yes; $6 + 1 + 2 = 9$, $9 \div 3 = 3$
4: yes; $12 \div 4 = 3$
5: no; the last digit is not 0 or 5.

6: yes; 612 is even and divisible by 3.
8: no; $612 \div 8 \neq$ natural number
9: yes; $6 + 1 + 2 = 9$, $9 \div 9 = 1$
10: no; the last digit is not 0.

2. Divisible by

11: no; $612 \div 11 \neq$ natural number
12: yes; $612 \div 12 = 51$
13: no; $612 \div 13 \neq$ natural number
14: no; $612 \div 14 \neq$ natural number
15: no; $612 \div 15 \neq$ natural number

16: no; $612 \div 16 \neq$ natural number
17: yes; $612 \div 17 = 36$
18: yes; $612 \div 18 = 34$
19: no; $612 \div 19 \neq$ natural number
20: no; $612 \div 20 \neq$ natural number

3. $\frac{1}{12}$

4. $\frac{5}{12}$

5. $\frac{2}{12} = \frac{1}{6}$

6. $\frac{7}{12}$

7.
$$\underset{3 \quad \cdot \quad 29}{\overset{87}{\diagup \diagdown}}$$
$$87 = 3 \cdot 29$$

8.
$$98 = 2 \cdot 7 \cdot 7$$
$$= 2 \cdot 7^2$$

9.
$$76 = 2 \cdot 2 \cdot 19$$
$$= 2^2 \cdot 19$$

10.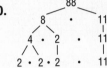
$$88 = 2 \cdot 2 \cdot 2 \cdot 11$$
$$= 2^3 \cdot 11$$

11.
$$\frac{1}{2}(x + 2) = 4$$
$$2 \cdot \frac{1}{2}(x + 2) = 2 \cdot 4$$
$$x + 2 = 8$$
$$x + 2 - 2 = 8 - 2$$
$$x = 6$$

12.
$$\frac{1}{4}(r - 1) = 0$$
$$4 \cdot \frac{1}{4}(r - 1) = 4 \cdot 0$$
$$r - 1 = 0$$
$$r - 1 + 1 = 0 + 1$$
$$r = 1$$

13.
$$7(y + 2) = 5y$$
$$7y + 14 = 5y$$
$$7y + 14 - 7y = 5y - 7y$$
$$14 = -2y$$
$$\frac{14}{-2} = \frac{-2y}{-2}$$
$$-7 = y$$

14.
$$3.2 + 1.2s = -0.4s$$
$$3.2 + 1.2s - 1.2s = -0.4s - 1.2s$$
$$3.2 = -1.6s$$
$$\frac{3.2}{-1.6} = \frac{-1.6s}{-1.6}$$
$$-2 = s$$

15. $-3 + (-2) = 5$
Your score is 5 under par.

Lab 6.3

1. 1-by-1: yes
2-by-2: yes
3-by-3: no
4-by-4: yes
5-by-5: no
6-by-6: no

2. No; answers vary.

3. 1-by-1 tiles   2-by-2 tiles   3-by-3 tiles

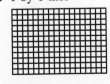   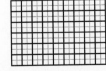

Yes   No   Yes

4.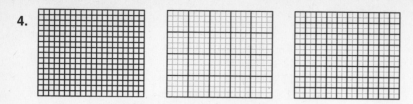

1, 2, and 4 are the common factors. 4 is the greatest common factor.

5.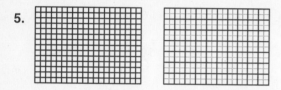

1 and 2 are the common factors. 2 is the greatest common factor.

6.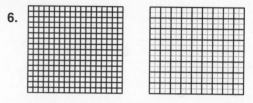

1 and 2 are the common factors. 2 is the greatest common factor.

6.3 | *Greatest Common Factor*

ONGOING ASSESSMENT

1. Factors of 135: 1, 3, 5, 9, 15, 27, 45, 135
Factors of 224: 1, 2, 4, 7, 8, 14, 16, 28, 32, 56, 112, 224
The greatest common factor is 1.
Yes, they are relatively prime.

2. Factors of 135: 1, 3, 5, 9, 15, 27, 45, 135
Factors of 225: 1, 3, 5, 9, 15, 25, 45, 75, 225
The greatest common factor is 45.
No, they are not relatively prime.

3. Factors of 134: 1, 2, 67, 134
Factors of 224: 1, 2, 4, 7, 8, 14, 16, 28, 32, 56, 112, 224
The greatest common factor is 2.
No, they are not relatively prime.

EXERCISES

1. The common factors of 12 and 18 are 1, 2, 3, and 6. The greatest common factor is 6.

2. The common factors of 24 and 16 are 1, 2, 4, and 8. The greatest common factor is 8.

3. The common factors of 20 and 35 are 1 and 5. The greatest common factor is 5.

4. The common factor of 39 and 25 is 1. The greatest common factor is 1.

5. 1

6. Factors of 160: 1, 2, 4, 5, 8, 10, 16, 20, 32, 40, 80, 160
Factors of 189: 1, 3, 7, 9, 21, 27, 63, 189
Yes, they are relatively prime. The greatest common factor is 1.

7. Factors of 20: 1, 2, 4, 5, 10, 20
Factors of 32: 1, 2, 4, 8, 16, 32
The greatest common factor is 4.

8. Factors of 36: 1, 2, 3, 4, 6, 9, 12, 18, 36
Factors of 54: 1, 2, 3, 6, 9, 18, 27, 54
The greatest common factor is 18.

9.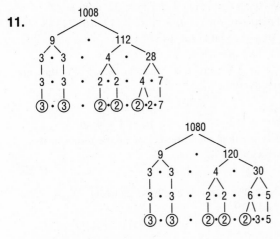

$2 \cdot 3 \cdot 5 = 30$
The greatest common factor is 30.

10.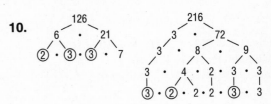

$2 \cdot 3 \cdot 3 = 18$
The greatest common factor is 18.

11.

$2 \cdot 2 \cdot 2 \cdot 3 \cdot 3 = 72$
The greatest common factor is 72.

12.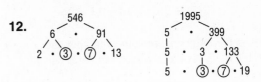

The greatest common factor is $3 \cdot 7 = 21$.

13.

$128 = 128$
$256 = 2 \cdot 128$
The greatest common factor is 128.

14.

The greatest common factor is 1.

15.–18. *Sample answers:*

15. 16 and 20;
16 and 28

16. 18 and 24;
18 and 30

17. 21 and 42;
21 and 63

18. 36 and 54;
54 and 72

19. 384 is divisible by 3 ($3+8+4 = 15$ and $15 \div 3 = 5$) and 945 is divisible by 3 ($9 + 4 + 5 = 18$ and $18 \div 3 = 6$). So, they are not relatively prime.

20. Prime factorization of 80: $2 \cdot 2 \cdot 2 \cdot 2 \cdot 5$
Prime factorization of 189: $3 \cdot 3 \cdot 3 \cdot 7$
Greatest common factor: 1
They are relatively prime.

21. 120 and 336 are each divisible by 2. (They are both even numbers.) So, they are not relatively prime.

22. 220 is divisible by 5 (its last digit is 0) and 315 is divisible by 5 (its last digit is 5). So, they are not relatively prime.

23. Perimeter $= 2(3) + 2(5) = 6 + 10 = 16$
Factors of 16: 1, 2, 4, 8, 16
Area $= (3)(5) = 15$
Factors of 15: 1, 3, 5, 15
Because the greatest common factor is 1, they are relatively prime.

24. Perimeter $= 2(10) + 2(12) = 20 + 24 = 44$
Area $= (10)(12) = 120$
Because the numbers are both even, they are divisible by 2. Therefore, they are not relatively prime.

25. Perimeter $= 2(7) + 2(6) = 14 + 12 = 26$
Area $= (7)(6) = 42$
Because the numbers are both even, they are divisible by 2. Therefore, they are not relatively prime.

26. Perimeter $= 2(11) + 2(13) = 22 + 26 = 48$
Factors of 48: 1, 2, 3, 4, 6, 8, 12, 16, 24, 48
Area $= (11)(13) = 143$
Factors of 143: 1, 11, 13, 143
Because the greatest common factor is 1, they are relatively prime.

27. $6 = 6 \times 1$, $12 = 6 \times 2$, $18 = 6 \times 3$, etc.
The greatest common factor of the terms in the sequence is 6.

28. $8 = 4 \times 2$, $12 = 4 \times 3$, $16 = 4 \times 4$, etc.
The greatest common factor of the terms in the sequence is 4.

29. Prime factorization of 39: $3 \cdot 13$
Prime factorization of 52: $2 \cdot 2 \cdot 13$
Prime factorization of 65: $5 \cdot 13$
Greatest common factor: 13
The strings should be cut into 13 cm pieces.

30. False; the greatest common factor is $2 \cdot 3 \cdot 19$.

31. True; the only factors of a prime are 1 and itself.

32. $2y^2z = 2 \cdot y \cdot y \cdot z$
$8yz^2 = 2 \cdot 2 \cdot 2 \cdot y \cdot z \cdot z$
The greatest common factor is $2yz$.

33. $3x^2y^2 = 3 \cdot x \cdot x \cdot y \cdot y$
$15x^2y = 3 \cdot 5 \cdot x \cdot x \cdot y$
The greatest common factor is $3x^2y$.

34. $9r^2z = 3 \cdot 3 \cdot r \cdot r \cdot z$
$21rz = 3 \cdot 7 \cdot r \cdot z$
The greatest common factor is $3rz$.

35. $42s^3t^4 = 2 \cdot 3 \cdot 7 \cdot s \cdot s \cdot s \cdot t \cdot t \cdot t \cdot t$
$70s^4t^3 = 2 \cdot 5 \cdot 7 \cdot s \cdot s \cdot s \cdot s \cdot t \cdot t \cdot t$
The greatest common factor is $14s^3t^3$.

36. B; $84x^2y = 2 \cdot 2 \cdot 3 \cdot 7 \cdot x \cdot x \cdot y$
$96xy^2 = 2 \cdot 2 \cdot 2 \cdot 2 \cdot 2 \cdot 3 \cdot x \cdot y \cdot y$
GCF: $2 \cdot 2 \cdot 3 \cdot x \cdot y = 12xy$

37. D: $9 = 3 \cdot 3$
$56 = 2 \cdot 2 \cdot 2 \cdot 7$

38. No; they fit in an area of 72 inches by 60 inches, where 30 albums fit.

39. 6×6: no
9×9: yes; $72 = 9 \times 8$, $63 = 9 \times 7$
5×5: no

6.4 | *GEOMETRY CONNECTION: Least Common Multiple*

ONGOING ASSESSMENT

1. $8 = 2 \cdot 2 \cdot 2$;

$12 = 2 \cdot 2 \cdot 3$;

Least common multiple:

$2 \cdot 2 \cdot 2 \cdot 3 = 24$

2. $15 = 3 \cdot 5$;

$24 = 2 \cdot 2 \cdot 2 \cdot 3$;

Least common multiple:

$2 \cdot 2 \cdot 2 \cdot 3 \cdot 5 = 120$

3. $9m = 3 \cdot 3 \cdot m$;

$6mn = 2 \cdot 3 \cdot m \cdot n$;

Least common multiple:

$2 \cdot 3 \cdot 3 \cdot m \cdot n = 18mn$

EXERCISES

1. 4, 12, 24

2. 12, 24, 36

3. Multiples of 4: 4, 8, 12

Multiples of 6: 6, 12

Least common multiple: 12

4. First way: With two small numbers, you can find their least common multiple by listing multiples of each number. The smallest duplicate in the two lists is the least common multiple. Use the first way to find the least common multiple of 10 and 16.

Second way: With two larger numbers, you can find their least common multiple by writing their prime factorizations. The highest power of each prime number that is a factor of either number must be a factor of the least common multiple. For example, if the prime factors of the numbers are $a^2 \cdot b^2 \cdot c$ and $a^3 \cdot b$, respectively, then the least common multiple is $a^3 \cdot b^2 \cdot c$. Use the second way to find the least common multiple of 112 and 204.

5. C; $2^3 \cdot 5^2 = 8 \cdot 25 = 200$

6. B; $2 \cdot 3^2 \cdot 5 = 2 \cdot 9 \cdot 5 = 90$

7. A; $2^2 \cdot 3 \cdot 5^2 = 4 \cdot 3 \cdot 25$

$= 300$

5.–7. The least common multiple of 200, 90, and 300 is $2^3 \cdot 3^2 \cdot 5^2 = 8 \cdot 9 \cdot 25 = 1800$.

8. $2a^2b^3 = 2 \cdot a \cdot a \cdot b \cdot b \cdot b$

$4ab^4 = 2 \cdot 2 \cdot a \cdot b \cdot b \cdot b \cdot b$

The least common multiple is $2^2 \cdot a^2 \cdot b^4 = 4a^2b^4$.

9. Multiples of 3: 3, 6, 9, 12, 15, 18, 21

Multiples of 7: 7, 14, 21

The least common multiple is 21.

10. Multiples of 7: 7, 14, 21, 28, 35, 42, 49, 56

Multiples of 8: 8, 16, 24, 32, 40, 48, 56

The least common multiple is 56.

11. Multiples of 6: 6, 12, 18, 24

Multiples of 8: 8, 16, 24

The least common multiple is 24.

12. Multiples of 3: 3, 6, 9

Multiples of 9: 9

The least common multiple is 9.

13. Multiples of 8: 8, 16, 24, 32, 40

Multiples of 10: 10, 20, 30, 40

The least common multiple is 40.

14. Multiples of 10: 10, 20, 30

Multiples of 15: 15, 30

The least common multiple is 30.

15. Multiples of 10: 10, 20, 30, 40, 50, 60, 70, 80, 90, 100, 110, 120, 130

Multiples of 26: 26, 52, 78, 104, 130

The least common multiple is 130.

16. Multiples of 4: 4, 8, 12, 16, 20, 24, 28, 32, 36, 40, 44

Multiples of 22: 22, 44

The least common multiple is 44.

17. Multiples of 3: 3, 6, 9, 12, 15, 18, 21, 24, 27, 30, 33, 36

Multiples of 4: 4, 8, 12, 16, 20, 24, 28, 32, 36

Multiples of 18: 18, 36

The least common multiple is 36.

18. Multiples of 3: 3, 6, 9, 12, 15, 18

Multiples of 6: 6, 12, 18

Multiples of 9: 9, 18

The least common multiple is 18.

19. Multiples of 5: 5, 10, 15, 20

Multiples of 10: 10, 20

Multiples of 20: 20

The least common multiple is 20.

20. Multiples of 6: 6, 12, 18

Multiples of 9: 9, 18

Multiples of 18: 18

The least common multiple is 18.

21.

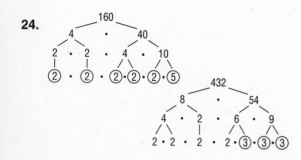

$90 = 2 \cdot 3 \cdot 3 \cdot 5 = 2 \cdot 3^2 \cdot 5$

$108 = 2 \cdot 2 \cdot \cdot 3 \cdot 3 \cdot 3 = 2^2 \cdot 3^3$

The least common multiple is $2^2 \cdot 3^3 \cdot 5 = 4 \cdot 27 \cdot 5$
$$= 540.$$

22.

$7 = 7$

$8 = 2 \cdot 2 \cdot 2 = 2^3$

The least common multiple is $2^3 \cdot 7 = 8 \cdot 7 = 56.$

23.

$125 = 5 \cdot 5 \cdot 5 = 5^3$

$500 = 2 \cdot 2 \cdot 5 \cdot 5 \cdot 5 = 2^2 \cdot 5^3$

The least common multiple is $2^2 \cdot 5^3 = 4 \cdot 125 = 500.$

24.

$160 = 2 \cdot 2 \cdot 2 \cdot 2 \cdot 2 \cdot 5 = 2^5 \cdot 5$

$432 = 2 \cdot 2 \cdot 2 \cdot 2 \cdot 3 \cdot 3 \cdot 3 = 2^4 \cdot 3^3$

The least common multiple is $2^5 \cdot 3^3 \cdot 5 = 32 \cdot 27 \cdot 5$
$$= 4320.$$

25.

$135 = 3 \cdot 3 \cdot 3 \cdot 5 = 3^3 \cdot 5$

$375 = 3 \cdot 5 \cdot 5 \cdot 5 = 3 \cdot 5^3$

The least common multiple is $3^3 \cdot 5^3 = 27 \cdot 125 = 3375.$

26.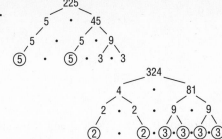

$$225 = 3 \cdot 3 \cdot 5 \cdot 5 = 3^2 \cdot 5^2$$
$$324 = 2 \cdot 2 \cdot 3 \cdot 3 \cdot 3 \cdot 3 = 2^2 \cdot 3^4$$

The least common multiple is $2^2 \cdot 3^4 \cdot 5^2 = 4 \cdot 81 \cdot 25$
$$= 8100.$$

27.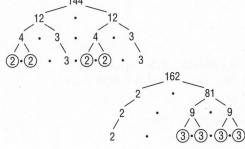

$$144 = 2 \cdot 2 \cdot 2 \cdot 2 \cdot 3 \cdot 3 = 2^4 \cdot 3^2$$
$$162 = 2 \cdot 3 \cdot 3 \cdot 3 \cdot 3 = 2 \cdot 3^4$$

The least common multiple is $2^4 \cdot 3^4 = 16 \cdot 81$
$$= 1296.$$

28. $16x = 2 \cdot 2 \cdot 2 \cdot 2 \cdot x = 2^4 \cdot x$
$32x^4 = 2 \cdot 2 \cdot 2 \cdot 2 \cdot 2 \cdot x \cdot x \cdot x \cdot x$
$$= 2^5 \cdot x^4$$

The least common multiple is $2^5 \cdot x^4 = 32x^4$.

29. $7s^2t = 7 \cdot s \cdot s \cdot t = 7 \cdot s^2 \cdot t$
$49st^2 = 7 \cdot 7 \cdot s \cdot t \cdot t = 7^2 \cdot s \cdot t^2$

The least common multiple is $7^2 \cdot s^2 \cdot t^2 = 49s^2t^2$.

30. $2x^3y = 2 \cdot x \cdot x \cdot x \cdot y = 2 \cdot x^3 \cdot y$
$3xy^5 = 3 \cdot x \cdot y \cdot y \cdot y \cdot y \cdot y$
$$= 3 \cdot x \cdot y^5$$

The least common multiple is $2 \cdot 3 \cdot x^3 \cdot y^5 = 6x^3y^5$.

31. $3m^4n^4 = 3 \cdot m \cdot m \cdot m \cdot m \cdot n \cdot n \cdot n \cdot n$
$$= 3 \cdot m^4 \cdot n^4$$
$7m^6n^2 = 7 \cdot m \cdot m \cdot m \cdot m \cdot m \cdot m \cdot n \cdot n$
$$= 7 \cdot m^6 \cdot n^2$$

The least common multiple is $3 \cdot 7 \cdot m^6 \cdot n^4 = 21m^6n^4$.

32. $4a^6b^3 = 2 \cdot 2 \cdot a \cdot a \cdot a \cdot a \cdot a \cdot a \cdot b \cdot b \cdot b$
$$= 2^2 \cdot a^6 \cdot b^3$$
$8a^7b^5 = 2 \cdot 2 \cdot 2 \cdot a \cdot a \cdot a \cdot a \cdot a \cdot a \cdot a \cdot b \cdot b \cdot b \cdot b \cdot b$
$$= 2^3 \cdot a^7 \cdot b^5$$

The least common multiple is $2^3 \cdot a^7 \cdot b^5 = 8a^7b^5$.

33. The product of the 2 numbers.
Sample answer:
12, 7: LCM = 84;
3, 11: LCM = 33

34. The number that is the multiple.
Sample answer:
12, 4: LCM = 12;
44, 11: LCM = 44

35. 3 and 8 are relatively prime, therefore, the least common multiple is $3 \cdot 8 = 24$.

36. 8 and 9 are relatively prime, therefore, the least common multiple is $8 \cdot 9 = 72$.

37. 6 is a multiple of 3; therefore, the least common multiple is 6.

38. 24 is a multiple of 8; therefore, the least common multiple is 24.

39. 5 and 7

40. 4 and 16; 8 and 16; 16 and 16

41. 1 and 36; 4 and 9; 4 and 36; 9 and 36; 36 and 36

42. 2 and 12; 4 and 6; 4 and 12; 6 and 12; 12 and 12

43.

14 in.   14 in.

4 in.
4 in.
4 in.
4 in. } 7(4) = 28
4 in.
4 in.
4 in.

2(14) = 28

14 tiles;

Multiples of 4: 4, 8, 12, 16, 20, 24, 28, ...

Multiples of 14: 14, 28, ...

The LCM of 4 and 14 is 28, so each side of the square region is 28 in. Then two 14's and seven 4's are needed for the sides of the square region; $2 \times 7 = 14$.

44. The large gear with 46 teeth and the small gear with 27 teeth are relatively prime. The LCM is the product of the two numbers.

$$LCM = 46 \times 27 = 1242$$

The gears align at the starting position after each rotates for 1242 teeth. So the large gear makes 27 complete revolutions and the small gear makes 46 complete revolutions.

45. The 1st stoplight turns red when these numbers of minutes have passed: 6, 12, 18, 24, 30, ... The 2nd stoplight turns red when these numbers of minutes have passed: 8, 16, 24, 32, 40, ... The 3rd stoplight turns red when these numbers of minutes have passed: 10, 20, 30, 40, 50, ... So all three stoplights will turn red when a number of minutes equal to the LCM of 6, 8, and 10 have passed.
$6 = 2 \cdot 3$, $8 = 2 \cdot 2 \cdot 2$, and $10 = 2 \cdot 5$
LCM of 6, 8, and 10: $2 \cdot 2 \cdot 2 \cdot 3 \cdot 5 = 120$
When 120 minutes or 2 hours have passed, all three stoplights will turn red. So the next time is 4:00 P.M.

46. B;
$20 = 2 \cdot 2 \cdot 5$
$30 = 3 \cdot 2 \cdot 5$
$LCM = 2 \cdot 2 \cdot 3 \cdot 5 = 60$

47. B;
$4x^2y = 2 \cdot 2 \cdot x \cdot x \cdot y$
$6xy^2 = 2 \cdot 3 \cdot x \cdot y \cdot y$
$LCM = 2 \cdot 2 \cdot 3 \cdot x \cdot x \cdot y \cdot y$
$= 12x^2y^2$

48. Every fourth beat

6.5 *Simplifying and Comparing Fractions*

ONGOING ASSESSMENT

1.

$\frac{1}{2}$ $\frac{9}{16}$ $\frac{11}{16}$ $\frac{3}{4}$ $\frac{7}{8}$

0 $\frac{1}{16}$ $\frac{2}{16}$ $\frac{3}{16}$ $\frac{4}{16}$ $\frac{5}{16}$ $\frac{6}{16}$ $\frac{7}{16}$ $\frac{8}{16}$ $\frac{9}{16}$ $\frac{10}{16}$ $\frac{11}{16}$ $\frac{12}{16}$ $\frac{13}{16}$ $\frac{14}{16}$ $\frac{15}{16}$ 1

2. $\frac{1}{2}, \frac{9}{16}, \frac{11}{16}, \frac{3}{4}, \frac{7}{8}$

EXERCISES

1. $\frac{3}{9} = \frac{1}{3}$

2. $\frac{5}{8}$

3. $\frac{6}{12} = \frac{1}{2}$

4. $\frac{10}{24} = \frac{5}{12}$

5. $\frac{2}{3}$; $\frac{2}{3} \times \frac{4}{4} = \frac{8}{12}$

$\frac{3}{4}$; $\frac{3}{4} \times \frac{3}{3} = \frac{9}{12}$

$\frac{3}{4}$ is larger.

6. $\frac{4}{6}$; $\frac{4}{6} \times \frac{4}{4} = \frac{16}{24}$

$\frac{5}{8}$; $\frac{5}{8} \times \frac{3}{3} = \frac{15}{24}$

$\frac{4}{6}$ is larger.

7. Factors of 14: 1, 2, 7, 14
Factors of 20: 1, 2, 4, 5, 10, 20
The GCF if 2.
$$\frac{14 \div 2}{20 \div 2} = \frac{7}{10}$$

8. Factors of 16: 1, 2, 4, 8, 16
Factors of 36: 1, 2, 3, 4, 6, 9, 12, 18, 36
The GCF is 4.
$$\frac{16 \div 4}{36 \div 4} = \frac{4}{9}$$

9. Factors of 9: 1, 3, 9
Factors of 42: 1, 2, 3, 6, 7, 14, 21, 42
The GCF is 3.
$$\frac{9 \div 3}{42 \div 3} = \frac{3}{14}$$

10. Factors of 63: 1, 3, 7, 9, 21, 63
Factors of 105: 1, 3, 5, 7, 15, 21, 35, 105
The GCF is 21.
$$\frac{63 \div 21}{105 \div 21} = \frac{3}{5}$$

11. Factors of 10: 1, 2, 5, 10
Factors of 75: 1, 3, 5, 15, 25, 75
The GCF is 5.
$$\frac{10 \div 5}{75 \div 5} = \frac{2}{15}$$

12. Factors of 8: 1, 2, 4, 8
Factors of 28: 1, 2, 4, 7, 14, 28
The GCF is 4.
$$\frac{8 \div 4}{28 \div 4} = \frac{2}{7}$$

13. Factors of 36: 1, 2, 3, 4, 6, 9, 12, 18, 36
Factors of 54: 1, 2, 3, 6, 9, 18, 27, 54
The GCF is 18.
$$\frac{36 \div 18}{54 \div 18} = \frac{2}{3}$$

14.

117: 9 · 13; 9 = 3 · 3, 13

143: 11 · 13

The GCF is 13.
$$\frac{117 \div 13}{143 \div 13} = \frac{9}{11}$$

15. $\dfrac{2ab}{8b^2} = \dfrac{2 \cdot a \cdot b}{2 \cdot 2 \cdot 2 \cdot b \cdot b} = \dfrac{a}{4b}$

16. $\dfrac{3x^2y}{9y} = \dfrac{3 \cdot x \cdot x \cdot y}{3 \cdot 3 \cdot y} = \dfrac{x^2}{3}$

17. $\dfrac{25z^2}{150z^3} = \dfrac{5 \cdot 5 \cdot z \cdot z}{3 \cdot 2 \cdot 5 \cdot 5 \cdot z \cdot z \cdot z} = \dfrac{1}{6z}$

18. $\dfrac{22s^3t}{55s^3t^2} = \dfrac{2 \cdot 11 \cdot s \cdot s \cdot s \cdot t}{5 \cdot 11 \cdot s \cdot s \cdot s \cdot t \cdot t} = \dfrac{2}{5t}$

19. $\dfrac{6yz}{8y} = \dfrac{2 \cdot 3 \cdot y \cdot z}{2 \cdot 2 \cdot 2 \cdot y} = \dfrac{3z}{4}$

20. $\dfrac{15x}{21x^2} = \dfrac{3 \cdot 5 \cdot x}{3 \cdot 7 \cdot x \cdot x} = \dfrac{5}{7x}$

21. $\dfrac{28p^2q^2}{42p^3q^3} = \dfrac{2 \cdot 2 \cdot 7 \cdot p \cdot p \cdot q \cdot q}{2 \cdot 3 \cdot 7 \cdot p \cdot p \cdot p \cdot q \cdot q \cdot q} = \dfrac{2}{3pq}$

22. $\dfrac{34m^2}{68mn} = \dfrac{2 \cdot 17 \cdot m \cdot m}{2 \cdot 2 \cdot 17 \cdot m \cdot n} = \dfrac{m}{2n}$

23. A fraction is in simplest form if the only common factor of the numerator and denominator is 1.

24.–27. *Sample answers:*

24. $\frac{1}{2} = \frac{1}{2} \times \frac{2}{2} = \frac{2}{4}$; $\frac{1}{2} = \frac{1}{2} \times \frac{3}{3} = \frac{3}{6}$; $\frac{1}{2} = \frac{1}{2} \times \frac{4}{4} = \frac{4}{8}$

25. $\frac{2}{5} = \frac{2}{5} \times \frac{2}{2} = \frac{4}{10}$; $\frac{2}{5} = \frac{2}{5} \times \frac{3}{3} = \frac{6}{15}$;
$\frac{2}{5} = \frac{2}{5} \times \frac{4}{4} = \frac{8}{20}$

26. $\frac{10}{22} = \frac{10}{22} \times \frac{2}{2} = \frac{20}{44}$; $\frac{10 \div 2}{22 \div 2} = \frac{5}{11}$; $\frac{5}{11} \times \frac{3}{3} = \frac{15}{33}$

27. $\frac{8}{18} = \frac{8}{18} \times \frac{2}{2} = \frac{16}{36}$; $\frac{8 \div 2}{18 \div 2} = \frac{4}{9}$; $\frac{4}{9} \times \frac{3}{3} = \frac{12}{27}$

28.
$\frac{1}{7} \boxed{?} \frac{1}{6}$

$\frac{6}{6} \cdot \frac{1}{7} \boxed{?} \frac{7}{7} \cdot \frac{1}{6}$

$\frac{6}{42} \boxed{<} \frac{7}{42}$

29.
$\frac{18}{38} \boxed{?} \frac{27}{57}$

$\frac{2 \cdot 9}{2 \cdot 19} \boxed{?} \frac{3 \cdot 9}{3 \cdot 19}$

$\frac{9}{19} \boxed{=} \frac{9}{19}$

30.
$\frac{1}{12} \boxed{?} \frac{1}{13}$

$\frac{13}{13} \cdot \frac{1}{12} \boxed{?} \frac{12}{12} \cdot \frac{1}{13}$

$\frac{13}{156} \boxed{>} \frac{12}{156}$

31.
$\frac{8}{14} \boxed{?} \frac{6}{13}$

$\frac{2 \cdot 4}{2 \cdot 7} \boxed{?} \frac{6}{13}$

$\frac{4}{7} \boxed{?} \frac{6}{13}$

$\frac{13}{13} \cdot \frac{4}{7} \boxed{?} \frac{7}{7} \cdot \frac{6}{13}$

$\frac{52}{91} \boxed{>} \frac{42}{91}$

32.
$\frac{7}{8} \boxed{?} \frac{8}{9}$

$\frac{9}{9} \cdot \frac{7}{8} \boxed{?} \frac{8}{8} \cdot \frac{8}{9}$

$\frac{63}{72} \boxed{<} \frac{64}{72}$

33.
$\frac{0}{2} \boxed{?} \frac{0}{100}$

$0 \boxed{=} 0$

34.
$\frac{15}{39} \boxed{?} \frac{5}{13}$

$\frac{3 \cdot 5}{3 \cdot 13} \boxed{?} \frac{5}{13}$

$\frac{5}{13} \boxed{=} \frac{5}{13}$

35.
$\frac{26}{50} \boxed{?} \frac{27}{51}$

$\frac{2 \cdot 13}{2 \cdot 25} \boxed{?} \frac{3 \cdot 9}{3 \cdot 17}$

$\frac{13}{25} \boxed{?} \frac{9}{17}$

$\frac{17}{17} \cdot \frac{13}{25} \boxed{?} \frac{25}{25} \cdot \frac{9}{17}$

$\frac{221}{425} \boxed{<} \frac{225}{425}$

36. $\frac{1}{125}$; to decrease the shutter speed means to leave it open for a longer period of time, so the fraction would have to be larger than $\frac{1}{250}$;
$\frac{1}{125} \times \frac{2}{2} = \frac{2}{250} > \frac{1}{250}$.

37. $\frac{3}{21} = \frac{1}{7}$

38. $\frac{12}{21} = \frac{4}{7}$

39. $\frac{7}{21} = \frac{1}{3}$;
your friend is correct.

40. $\frac{6}{21} = \frac{2}{7}$;
your friend is incorrect.

41. B

42. B

43. C

44. $\frac{90}{90}, \frac{96}{90}, \frac{108}{90}, \frac{120}{90}, \frac{135}{90}, \frac{144}{90}, \frac{160}{90}, \frac{180}{90}$; answers vary.

45. Pay Scale A:

Rate $\times$ Time $=$ Amount paid

Rate $= r$ (dollars per hour)

Time $= \frac{1}{2}$ (hours)

Amount paid $= 4$ (dollars)

$r \times \frac{1}{2} = 4$

$r = 8$

Pay Scale A pays $8.00 per hour.

Prefer Pay Scale A because it pays $.50 more per hour.

Pay Scale B:

Rate $\times$ Time $=$ Amount paid

Rate $= R$ (dollars per hour)

Time $= \frac{2}{3}$ (hours)

Amount paid $= 5$ (dollars)

$R \times \frac{2}{3} = 5$

$R = 7.5$

Pay Scale B pays $7.50 per hour.

Spiral **R E V I E W**

1. $m + 11$

$7 + 11 = 18$

2. $22 - m$

$22 - 7 = 15$

3. $84 \div m$

$84 \div 7 = 12$

4. $6 \times m$

$6 \times 7 = 42$

5. $13 > x - 14$

$13 + 14 > x - 14 + 14$

$27 > x$

6. $19 + n \le 24$

$19 - 19 + n \le 24 - 19$

$n \le 5$

7. $7y \ge 105$

$\dfrac{7y}{7} \ge \dfrac{105}{7}$

$y \ge 15$

8.–10.

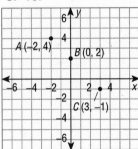

8. Quadrant 2

9. None

10. Quadrant 4

11. *Sample answer:* $(-3, 5), (-1, 3), (1, 1), (2, 0),$ $(4, -2)$

12. Both club offers contain 15 cassettes or compact discs, so calculate the cost to buy the required cassettes or compact discs.

Club 1: $7(13.98) = \$97.86$

Club 2: $6(15.99) = \$95.94$

13. Club 1: $97.86 + 13.98d$
Club 2: $95.94 + 15.99d$

14. $97.86 + 13.98d = 95.94 + 15.99d$

$$1.92 = 2.01d$$

$$.96 = d$$

Club 1: $\$97.86 + \$13.98(.96) = \$111.28$
Club 2: $\$95.94 + \$15.99(.96) = \$111.29$

Club 1 is less expensive if you plan to get more than 15 cassettes.

Mid-Chapter ASSESSMENT

1. Divisible by

2: yes, 510 is even.
3: yes, $5 + 1 + 0 = 6$; $6 \div 3 = 2$
4: no, $10 \div 4 \neq$ natural number
5: yes, the last digit is 0.

6: yes, 510 is even and divisible by 3.
8: no, 510 is not divisible by 4.
9: no, $5 + 1 = 6$; $6 \div 9 \neq$ natural number
10: yes, the last digit is 0.

2. Divisible by

2: yes, 1360 is even.
3: no, $1 + 3 + 6 + 0 = 10$; $10 \div 3 \neq$ natural number
4: yes, $60 \div 4 = 15$
5: yes, the last digit is 0.

6: no, 1360 is not divisible by 3.
8: yes, $360 \div 8 = 45$
9: no, 1360 is not divisible by 3.
10: yes, the last digit is 0.

3. Divisible by

11: no, $816 \div 11 \neq$ natural number
12: yes, $816 \div 12 = 68$
13: no, $816 \div 13 \neq$ natural number
14: no, $816 \div 14 \neq$ natural number
15: no $816 \div 15 \neq$ natural number

16: yes, $816 \div 16 = 51$
17: yes, $816 \div 17 = 48$
18: no, $816 \div 18 \neq$ natural number
19: no, $816 \div 19 \neq$ natural number
20: no, $816 \div 20 \neq$ natural number

4. $56 = 1 \times 56$; 2×28; 4×14; 7×8

1, 2, 4, 7, 8, 14, 28, 56

5.

```
        80
      /    \
     4  ·   20
    / \    / \
   2 · 2  4 · 5
  /   /  / \
 2 · 2 · 2 · 2 · 5
```

$80 = 2 \cdot 2 \cdot 2 \cdot 2 \cdot 5 = 2^4 \cdot 5$

6.

```
      44
     /  \
    4  · 11
   / \
  2 · 2 · 11
```

$44 = 2 \cdot 2 \cdot 11 = 2^2 \cdot 11$

7.

```
       105
      /   \
     5  ·  21
    /     /  \
   5  :  3 · 7
```

$105 = 3 \cdot 5 \cdot 7$

8. $12 = 12$

$60 = 5 \cdot 12$

The greatest common factor is 12.

9. Factors of 15: 1, 3, 5, 15
Factors of 36: 1, 2, 3, 4, 6, 9, 12, 18, 36
The greatest common factor is 3.

10.

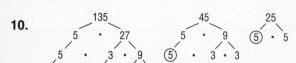

The greatest common factor is 5.

11. 5 and 13 are prime numbers.
The least common multiple is $5 \cdot 13 = 65$.

12. Multiples of 14: 14, 28, 42
Multiples of 21: 21, 42
The least common multiple is 42.

13. $6x = 2 \cdot 3 \cdot x$
$9x^2 = 3 \cdot 3 \cdot x \cdot x = 3^2 \cdot x^2$
The least common multiple is $2 \cdot 3^2 \cdot x^2 = 18x^2$.

14. $\dfrac{5}{25} = \dfrac{5 \div 5}{25 \div 5} = \dfrac{1}{5}$

15.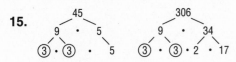

The GCF is $3 \cdot 3 = 9$.
$\dfrac{45}{306} = \dfrac{45 \div 9}{306 \div 9} = \dfrac{5}{34}$

16. $\dfrac{8y^2}{24y} = \dfrac{2 \cdot 2 \cdot 2 \cdot y \cdot y}{2 \cdot 2 \cdot 2 \cdot 3 \cdot y} = \dfrac{y}{3}$

17. The sides of the tile are 3 and 6. 6 is a multiple of 3, so the number of tiles is $6 \div 3 = 2$.

18. The sides of the tile are 4 and 7. 4 and 7 are relatively prime, so the number of tiles is $4 \times 7 = 28$.

17.–18. The length of the square's side is the LCM of the lengths of the tile's sides.

19. Multiples of 6: 6, 12, 18, 24, 30, 36, 42
Multiples of 14: 14, 28, 42
The least common multiple of 6 and 14 is 42.
6 in.: $42 \div 6 = 7$
14 in.: $42 \div 14 = 3$

20. Least common multiple

6.6 *Rational Numbers and Decimals*

ONGOING ASSESSMENT

1. $0.375 = \dfrac{375}{1000}$ *Write as 375 thousandths.*

$= \dfrac{3 \cdot 125}{8 \cdot 125}$ *Factor.*

$= \dfrac{3}{8}$ *Simplify.*

2. $x = 1.6666\ldots$ *Let x represent the number.*

$100x = 166.6666\ldots$ *Multiply each side by 100.*

$99x = 165$ *Subtract first equation from second.*

$x = \frac{165}{99}$ *Divide each side by 99.*

$x = \frac{5}{3}$ *Simplify.*

3.

$$x = 0.8383\ldots \qquad \textit{Let } x \textit{ represent the number.}$$

$$100x = 83.8383\ldots \qquad \textit{Multiply each side by 100.}$$

$$99x = 93 \qquad \textit{Subtract first equation from second.}$$

$$x = \frac{83}{99} \qquad \textit{Divide each side by 99.}$$

4.

$$x = 0.0454545\ldots \qquad \textit{Let } x \textit{ represent the number.}$$

$$100x = 4.5454545\ldots \qquad \textit{Multiply each side by 100.}$$

$$99x = 4.5 \qquad \textit{Subtract first equation from second.}$$

$$x = \frac{4.5}{99} \qquad \textit{Divide each side by 99.}$$

$$x = \frac{1}{22} \qquad \textit{Simplify.}$$

EXERCISES

1. Rational; $-\frac{3}{1}$

2. Irrational

3. Rational; $\frac{13}{5}$

4. Rational; $\frac{7}{1}$

5. Rational; $\frac{4}{10} = \frac{2}{5}$

6. $36(0.01) = 0.36;\ \dfrac{36}{100} = \dfrac{9 \cdot \cancel{4}}{25 \cdot \cancel{4}} = \dfrac{9}{25}$

7. $75(0.01) = 0.75;\ \dfrac{75}{100} = \dfrac{3 \cdot \cancel{25}}{4 \cdot \cancel{25}} = \dfrac{3}{4}$

8. $64(0.01) = 0.64;\ \dfrac{64}{100} = \dfrac{16 \cdot \cancel{4}}{25 \cdot \cancel{4}} = \dfrac{16}{25}$

9. $5(0.01) = 0.05,\ \dfrac{5}{100} = \dfrac{\cancel{5} \cdot 1}{\cancel{5} \cdot 20} = \dfrac{1}{20}$

10. Write the whole number as a fraction with the same denominator as the fraction, then add.

11. $5 = \dfrac{5}{1}$

12. $0.75 = \dfrac{75}{100} = \dfrac{3 \cdot \cancel{25}}{4 \cdot \cancel{25}} = \dfrac{3}{4}$

13. $0.25 = \dfrac{25}{100} = \dfrac{\cancel{25} \cdot 1}{\cancel{25} \cdot 4} = \dfrac{1}{4}$

14. $-9 = \dfrac{-9}{1} = -\dfrac{9}{1}$

15. $1\frac{1}{6} = \dfrac{6}{6} + \dfrac{1}{6} = \dfrac{7}{6}$

16. $2\frac{2}{9} = \dfrac{18}{9} + \dfrac{2}{9} = \dfrac{20}{9}$

17. $-1\frac{5}{8} = -\left(\dfrac{8}{8} + \dfrac{5}{8}\right) = -\dfrac{13}{8}$

18. $-2\frac{4}{5} = -\left(\dfrac{10}{5} + \dfrac{4}{5}\right) = -\dfrac{14}{5}$

19. $\frac{3}{5}$ is rational; $3 \div 5 = 0.6$; it is terminating.

20. $\frac{9}{11}$ is rational; $9 \div 11 = 0.\overline{81}$; it is repeating.

21. $\sqrt{8}$ is irrational; $\sqrt{8} = 2.8284\ldots$; it is nonrepeating.

22. $\sqrt{9}$ is rational; $\sqrt{9} = 3$; it is terminating.

23. $\frac{8}{15}$ is rational; $8 \div 15 = 0.5\overline{3}$; it is repeating.

24. $\frac{7}{10}$ is rational; $7 \div 10 = 0.7$; it is terminating.

25. $\frac{7}{2}$ is rational; $7 \div 2 = 3.5$; it is terminating.

26. $\frac{13}{12}$ is rational; $13 \div 12 = 1.08\overline{3}$; it is repeating.

27. $0.8 = \dfrac{8}{10} = \dfrac{\cancel{2} \cdot 4}{\cancel{2} \cdot 5} = \dfrac{4}{5}$

28. $0.35 = \dfrac{35}{100} = \dfrac{\cancel{5} \cdot 7}{\cancel{5} \cdot 20} = \dfrac{7}{20}$

29. $0.84 = \dfrac{84}{100} = \dfrac{\cancel{4} \cdot 21}{\cancel{4} \cdot 25} = \dfrac{21}{25}$

30. $0.64 = \dfrac{64}{100} = \dfrac{\cancel{4} \cdot 16}{\cancel{4} \cdot 25} = \dfrac{16}{25}$

31. $x = 0.454545\ldots$

$100x = 45.4545\ldots$

$99x = 45$

$x = \dfrac{45}{99} = \dfrac{9 \cdot 5}{9 \cdot 11} = \dfrac{5}{11}$

32. $x = 0.868686\ldots$

$100x = 86.8686\ldots$

$99x = 86$

$x = \dfrac{86}{99}$

33. $x = 2.333\ldots$

$10x = 23.33\ldots$

$9x = 21$

$x = \dfrac{21}{9} = \dfrac{\cancel{3} \cdot 7}{\cancel{3} \cdot 3} = \dfrac{7}{3}$

34. $x = 1.135135135\ldots$

$1000x = 1135.135135\ldots$

$999x = 1134$

$x = \dfrac{1134}{999} = \dfrac{27 \cdot 42}{27 \cdot 37} = \dfrac{42}{37}$

35. E; $\dfrac{10}{120} = 0.08\overline{3}$

36. A; $\dfrac{6}{15} = 0.4$

37. C;

$\dfrac{75}{25} + \dfrac{3}{25} = \dfrac{78}{25}$

$\quad = 3.12$

38. D;

$\dfrac{5}{18} = 0.27\overline{7}$

39. F;

$\dfrac{8}{27} = 0.\overline{296}$

40. B;

$\dfrac{225}{75} + \dfrac{6}{75} = \dfrac{231}{75}$

$\quad = 3.08$

41. $\dfrac{1}{11} = 0.\overline{09}$ $\dfrac{4}{11} = 0.\overline{36}$

$\dfrac{2}{11} = 0.\overline{18}$ $\dfrac{5}{11} = 0.\overline{45}$

$\dfrac{3}{11} = 0.\overline{27}$ $\dfrac{6}{11} = 0.\overline{54}$

Pattern: Each term, after the first, is $\dfrac{1}{11}$ or $0.\overline{09}$ more than the preceding term.

42. $\dfrac{1}{2} = 0.5$ $\dfrac{7}{8} = 0.875$

$\dfrac{3}{4} = 0.75$ $\dfrac{9}{10} = 0.9$

$\dfrac{5}{6} = 0.8\overline{3}$ $\dfrac{11}{12} = 0.91\overline{6}$

Pattern: Each term, after the first, has a numerator and denominator that are 2 more than the numerator and denominator of the preceding term.

43. $\dfrac{2}{3} - \dfrac{1}{2} = 0.\overline{66} - 0.5 = 0.1\overline{66}$;

$x = 0.166\ldots$

$100x = 16.66\ldots$

$\dfrac{99x}{99} = \dfrac{16.50}{99}$

$x = \dfrac{16.5}{99} = \dfrac{1}{6}$

44. $\dfrac{2}{3} + \dfrac{1}{9} = 0.\overline{66} + 0.\overline{11} = 0.\overline{77}$;

$x = 0.77\ldots$

$100x = 77.77\ldots$

$\dfrac{99x}{99} = \dfrac{77}{99}$

$x = \dfrac{77}{99} = \dfrac{7}{9}$

45. $P = 2\left(1\frac{1}{5}\right) + 2\left(\frac{3}{5}\right)$

$= 2\left(\frac{6}{5}\right) + 2\left(\frac{3}{5}\right)$

$= \dfrac{12}{5} + \dfrac{6}{5}$

$= \dfrac{18}{5}$

$\dfrac{18}{5}$ in., $3\frac{3}{5}$ in., 3.6 in.

46. $P = \dfrac{3}{11} + \dfrac{5}{11} + \dfrac{6}{11}$

$= \dfrac{14}{11}$

$\dfrac{14}{11}$ in., $1\frac{3}{11}$ in., $1.\overline{27}$ in.

47. $P = 2\left(1\frac{1}{3}\right) + 2\left(1\frac{2}{3}\right) + \dfrac{2}{3}$

$= 2\left(\frac{4}{3}\right) + 2\left(\frac{5}{3}\right) + \dfrac{2}{3}$

$= \dfrac{8}{3} + \dfrac{10}{3} + \dfrac{2}{3}$

$= \dfrac{20}{3}$

$\dfrac{20}{3}$ in., $6\frac{2}{3}$ in., $6.\overline{6}$ in.

48. a. Orange: $\dfrac{21}{50} = 0.42$

Banana: $\dfrac{13}{25} = 0.52$

Pear: $\dfrac{41}{100} = 0.41$

Strawberry: $\dfrac{9}{20} = 0.45$

Apple: $\dfrac{41}{50} = 0.82$

b. Apple, banana, strawberry, orange, pear

49. D

50. a. $5\frac{6}{60}, 4\frac{20}{60}, 5\frac{45}{60}, 4\frac{42}{60}$

b. 5.1, $4.\overline{3}$, 5.75, 4.7

c. Yes; total time = $5.1 + 4.33 + 5.75 + 4.7$

$= 19.88$ min

6.7 Powers and Exponents

ONGOING ASSESSMENT

1. $5^3 \cdot 5^4 = 5^{3+4} = 5^7$
   $5^3 \cdot 5^4 = (5 \cdot 5 \cdot 5) \cdot (5 \cdot 5 \cdot 5 \cdot 5) = 5^7$

2. $5^3 \cdot 5^{-4} = 5^{3+(-4)} = 5^{-1}$;
   $5^3 \cdot 5^{-4} = \dfrac{\cancel{5} \cdot \cancel{5} \cdot \cancel{5}}{\cancel{5} \cdot \cancel{5} \cdot \cancel{5} \cdot 5} = \dfrac{1}{5}$

3. $\dfrac{5^4}{5^2} = 5^{4-2} = 5^2$;
   $\dfrac{5^4}{5^2} = \dfrac{\cancel{5} \cdot \cancel{5} \cdot 5 \cdot 5}{\cancel{5} \cdot \cancel{5}} = 5^2$

4. $\dfrac{5^3}{5} = 5^{3-1} = 5^2$;
   $\dfrac{5^3}{5} = \dfrac{\cancel{5} \cdot 5 \cdot 5}{\cancel{5}} = 5^2$

EXERCISES

1. *Sample answer:* Let n be a positive integer and let a be a nonzero number.
   $a^{-n} = \dfrac{1}{a^n}$ and $a^0 = 1$

2. $4^{-1} = \dfrac{1}{4^1} = \dfrac{1}{4}$

3. $5^{-2} = \dfrac{1}{5^2}$ or $\dfrac{1}{25}$

4. $100^0 = 1$

5. $x^{-3} = \dfrac{1}{x^3}$

6. *Sample answer:* To multiply two powers with the same base, add their exponents. To divide two powers with the same base, subtract the exponent of the denominator from the exponent of the numerator.

7. $p^5 \cdot p^2 = p^{5+2} = p^7$

8. $r^2 \cdot s^3 = r^2 s^3$

9. $\dfrac{m^6}{n^4}$

10. $\dfrac{x^4}{x^2} = x^{4-2} = x^2$

11. $3^{-2} = \dfrac{1}{3^2} = \dfrac{1}{9}$

12. $-10^{-3} = -\dfrac{1}{10^3} = -\dfrac{1}{1000}$

13. $16^0 = 1$

14. $(-9)^2 = 81$

15. $t^{-4} = \dfrac{1}{t^4}$

16. $2x^{-3} = 2 \cdot \dfrac{1}{x^3} = \dfrac{2}{x^3}$

17. $3s^{-2} = 3 \cdot \dfrac{1}{s^2} = \dfrac{3}{s^2}$

18. $r^0 = 1$

19. $(-6)^{-3} \cdot (-6)^5 = (-6)^{-3+5}$
    $= (-6)^2$
    $= 36$

20. $8^0 \cdot 8^4 = 8^{0+4}$
    $= 8^4$
    $= 4096$

21. $x^{25} \cdot x^{-10} = x^{25+(-10)}$
    $= x^{15}$

22. $y^{-6} \cdot y^4 = y^{-6+4}$
$= y^{-2}$
$= \dfrac{1}{y^2}$

23. $\dfrac{7^5}{7^4} = 7^{5-4}$
$= 7^1$
$= 7$

24. $\dfrac{-9^2}{-9^4} = \dfrac{9^2}{9^4}$
$= 9^{2-4}$
$= 9^{-2}$
$= \dfrac{1}{9^2}$
$= \dfrac{1}{81}$

25. $\dfrac{a^{12}}{a^0} = a^{12-0}$
$= a^{12}$

26. $\dfrac{b^7}{b^{10}} = b^{7-10}$
$= b^{-3}$
$= \dfrac{1}{b^3}$

27. $2.5^{-4} \approx 0.026$

28. $5.5^{-2} \approx 0.033$

29. $5.5^3 \cdot 5.5^2 = 5.5^{3+2}$
$= 5.5^5$
≈ 5032.844

30. $\dfrac{0.5^3}{0.5^6} = 0.5^{3-6}$
$= 0.5^{-3}$
$= 8$

31. $\dfrac{2^5}{2^2} = 2n$
$5 - 2 = n$
$3 = n$

32. $\left(\frac{1}{2}\right)^n = 1$
$n = 0$

33. $3^{-3} \cdot 3^n = 3^3$
$-3 + n = 3$
$n = 6$

34. $4^{-5} = \dfrac{1}{4^n}$
$4^{-5} = 4^{-n}$
$5 = n$

35. $n = 15$: $2^{15} = 32{,}768 < 100{,}000$
$n = 16$: $2^{16} = 65{,}536 < 100{,}000$
$n = 17$: $2^{17} = 131{,}072 > 100{,}000$
The largest value of n is 16.

36. $n = 9$: $3^{-9} \approx 0.0000508 > 0.00001$
$n = 10$: $3^{-10} \approx 0.0000169 > 0.00001$
$n = 11$: $3^{-11} \approx 0.0000056 < 0.00001$
The largest value of n is 10.

37. 3^{10} ⬚?⬚ $3 \cdot 3^9$
3^{10} ⬚?⬚ 3^{1+9}
$3^{10} = 3^{10}$

38. 2^{-5} ⬚?⬚ 5^{-2}
$\dfrac{1}{2^5}$ ⬚?⬚ $\dfrac{1}{5^2}$
$\dfrac{1}{32} < \dfrac{1}{25}$

39. $\dfrac{4^3}{4^2}$ ⬚?⬚ $\dfrac{4^2}{4^3}$
4^{3-2} ⬚?⬚ 4^{2-3}
$4^1 > 4^{-1}$

40. $\dfrac{4^{14}}{4^3}$ ⬚?⬚ 4^{10}
4^{14-3} ⬚?⬚ 4^{10}
$4^{11} > 4^{10}$

41. $10^0, 10^1, 10^2, 10^3, 10^4, 10^5, 10^6$

42. $10^0, 10^{-1}, 10^{-2}, 10^{-3}, 10^{-4}, 10^{-5}, 10^{-6}, 10^{-7}$

43. Rubik's Cube: $4^3 = 64$ cubes
Rubik's Cubes in stack: $4^3 = 64$ Rubik's cubes
There are $4^3 \cdot 4^3 = 4^6 = 4096$ small cubes in the stack.

44. $\dfrac{1.7(10^{10}) \text{ lb}}{2.6(10^8) \text{ people}} \approx 0.654(10^{10-8})$
$= 0.654(10^2)$
$= 0.654(100)$
$= 65.4 \text{ lb}$

45. $10 \cdot 10^{-6} = 10^{1+(-6)}$
$= 10^{-5}$

46. $0.05^2 = \left(\frac{5}{100}\right)^2$
$= \left(\frac{1}{20}\right)^2$
$= \frac{1}{400}$

47. C; $270,000,000 = 2.7(10^8)$

48. The red cube contains the most money; the yellow cube has $3^3 \cdot 20 = 27 \cdot 20 = \$540$; the red cube has $4^3 \cdot 10 = 64 \cdot 10 = \$640$; and the blue cube has $5^3 \cdot 5 = 125 \cdot 5 = \$625$.

6.8 | *Scientific Notation*

ONGOING ASSESSMENT

1. No;
$12.4 \times 10^{-3} = 1.24 \times 10^1 \times 10^{-3}$
$= 1.24 \times 10^{-2}$

2. Yes

3. No;
$0.05 \times 10^4 = 5 \times 10^{-2} \times 10^4$
$= 5 \times 10^2$

EXERCISES

1. B

2. $350,000 = 3.5 \times 10^5$

3. $0.00943 = 9.43 \times 10^{-3}$

4. $6.25 \times 10^5 = 625,000$

5. $8.7 \times 10^{-6} = 0.0000087$

6. **A.** 2.9×10^7: Canada
B. 1.2×10^9: China
China has more people and $9 > 7$.

7. $5000 = 5 \times 10^3$

8. $643,000 = 6.43 \times 10^5$

9. $0.00041 = 4.1 \times 10^{-4}$

10. $0.18 = 1.8 \times 10^{-1}$

11. $32,610,000 = 3.261 \times 10^7$

12. $5,730,000,000 = 5.73 \times 10^9$

13. $0.000000012 = 1.2 \times 10^{-8}$

14. $0.000008 = 8 \times 10^{-6}$

15. $5.7 \times 10^{-3} = 0.0057$

16. $3.41 \times 10^{-6} = 0.00000341$

17. $2.50 \times 10^4 = 25,000$

18. $2.4 \times 10^9 = 2,400,000,000$

19. $6.2 \times 10^{10} = 62,000,000,000$

20. $8.59 \times 10^5 = 859,000$

21. $3.63 \times 10^{-7} = 0.000000363$

22. $5.99 \times 10^{-1} = 0.599$

23. Yes

24. No;
$0.392 \times 10^6 = 3.92 \times 10^{-1} \times 10^6$
$= 3.92 \times 10^5$

25. No;
$25.6 \times 10^8 = 2.56 \times 10^1 \times 10^8$
$= 2.56 \times 10^9$

26. Yes

27. No;
$791 \times 10^{-4} = 7.91 \times 10^2 \times 10^{-4}$
$= 7.91 \times 10^{-2}$

28. No;

$$68.8 \times 10^3 = 6.88 \times 10^1 \times 10^3$$
$$= 6.88 \times 10^4$$

29. $(6.2 \times 10^2)(8 \times 10^3) = (6.2 \times 8)(10^2 \times 10^3)$
$$= 49.6 \times 10^5$$
$$= 4.96 \times 10^6$$
$$= 4,960,000$$

30. $(4.5 \times 10^{-3})(3.4 \times 10^5) = (4.5 \times 3.4)(10^{-3} \times 10^5)$
$$= 15.3 \times 10^2$$
$$= 1.53 \times 10^3$$
$$= 1530$$

31. $(0.3 \times 10^{-4})(0.6 \times 10^{-1}) = (0.3 \times 0.6)(10^{-4} \times 10^{-1})$
$$= 0.18 \times 10^{-5}$$
$$= 1.8 \times 10^{-6}$$
$$= 0.0000018$$

32. $(9.7 \times 10^4)(2.4 \times 10^2) = (9.7 \times 2.4)(10^4 \times 10^2)$
$$= 23.28 \times 10^6$$
$$= 2.328 \times 10^7$$
$$= 23,280,000$$

33. $1 \times 10^9 > 9 \times 10^8$; $9 > 8$

34. $5 \times 10^{-5} < 1 \times 10^{-4}$; $-4 > -5$

35. $(5.88 \times 10^{12})(8 \times 10^4) = 4.704 \times 10^{17}$

36. $6,000,000,000,000 = 6 \times 10^{12}$

37. $100,000,000,000,000 = 1 \times 10^{14}$

38. Piano: $2.06 \times 10^7 = 20,600,000$
Guitar: $1.89 \times 10^7 = 18,900,000$
Organ: $6.3 \times 10^6 = 6,300,000$
Flute: $4 \times 10^6 = 4,000,000$
Clarinet: $4 \times 10^6 = 4,000,000$
Drums: $3 \times 10^6 = 3,000,000$

Instrument	Piano	Guitar	Organ	Flute	Clarinet	Drums
Number	20,600,000	18,900,000	6,300,000	4,000,000	4,000,000	3,000,000

39. Chlorine: $0.00295 = 2.95 \times 10^{-3}$
Helium: $0.0001664 = 1.664 \times 10^{-4}$
Hydrogen: $0.00008375 = 8.375 \times 10^{-5}$
Nitrogen: $0.001165 = 1.165 \times 10^{-3}$
Oxygen: $0.001332 = 1.332 \times 10^{-3}$
Ordered from lightest to heaviest: hydrogen, helium, nitrogen, oxygen, chlorine

40. B; $(8.4 \times 10^3)(4.2 \times 10^2) = 8.4 \times 4.2 \times 10^{3+2}$
$$= 35.28 \times 10^5$$
$$= 3.528 \times 10^6 \text{ cm}^2$$

41. $2.0 \times 10^4 = 20,000$

42. $\frac{3}{8} = 0.375 = 3.75 \times 10^{-1}$

Using a Calculator

1. $(3.6 \times 10^4)(6.3 \times 10^2) = 2.268 \times 10^7$

2. $(9.83 \times 10^{10})(5.2 \times 10^8) = 5.1116 \times 10^{19}$

3. $(1.35 \times 10^{-3})(8.2 \times 10^{-9}) = 1.107 \times 10^{-11}$

4. $(4.7 \times 10^{-7})(2.65 \times 10^{-5}) = 1.2455 \times 10^{-11}$

5. $(422,000)(135,000) = 5.697 \times 10^{10}$

6. $(9,364,000)(2150) = 2.01326 \times 10^{10}$

7. $(0.014) \div (560,000) = 2.5 \times 10^{-8}$

8. $(9.12 \times 10^{-3}) \div (2.4 \times 10) = 3.8 \times 10^{-4}$

9. Exercise 8: 3.8×10^{-2}
The answer to Exercise 8 is different. The power key followed order of operations and evaluated $((9.12 \times 10^{-3}) \div 2.4) \times 10$. The EE button, unlike the power key, is designed to compute using scientific notation.

Communicating About Mathematics

1. $\dfrac{4,000,000 \text{ monarchs}}{1 \text{ acre}} \cdot \dfrac{1 \text{ acre}}{43,560 \text{ ft}^2} \approx 92$ monarchs per foot^2

2. 4th: Yes; they fly to Mexico for the winter.
5th: No; they spend time in Texas and Louisiana and the Great Lakes region.
6th: No; they spend time in the Great Lakes region and the Appalachian Mountains.
7th: Yes; they fly to Mexico for the winter.

3. 1st, 4th, 7th, 10th, and so on

4. 3rd, 6th, 9th, 12th, and so on

6.9 ALGEBRA CONNECTION: Exploring Patterns

ONGOING ASSESSMENT

1. 9th: $92 + 25 = 117$ or 9th $= \frac{1}{2} \cdot 9 \cdot (3 \cdot 9 - 1) = \frac{1}{2} \cdot 9 \cdot 26 = 117$;
10th: $117 + 28 = 145$ or 10th $= \frac{1}{2} \cdot 10 \cdot (3 \cdot 10 - 1) = \frac{1}{2} \cdot 10 \cdot 29 = 145$

EXERCISES

1.

n	1	2	3	4	5	6
$2n^2 + 1$	3	9	19	33	51	73

$n = 1: 2(1)^2 + 1 = 2 + 1 = 3$

$n = 4: 2(4)^2 + 1 = 2(16) + 1 = 32 + 1 = 33$

$n = 2: 2(2)^2 + 1 = 2(4) + 1 = 8 + 1 = 9$

$n = 5: 2(5)^2 + 1 = 2(25) + 1 = 50 + 1 = 51$

$n = 3: 2(3)^2 + 1 = 2(9) + 1 = 18 + 1 = 19$

$n = 6: 2(6)^2 + 1 = 2(36) + 1 = 72 + 1 = 73$

2.

15   21

3. $3 - 1 = 2$

$6 - 3 = 3$

$10 - 6 = 4$

$15 - 10 = 5$

$21 - 15 = 6$

Pattern: To get the next number, add 2, add 3, add 4, add 5, and so on, to the preceding number.

$21 + 7 = 28; 28 + 8 = 36$

4. $\frac{1}{2} \cdot 7(7 + 1) = \frac{1}{2} \cdot 7 \cdot 8 = 28;$

$\frac{1}{2} \cdot 8(8 + 1) = \frac{1}{2} \cdot 8 \cdot 9 = 36$

5.

n	1	2	3	4	5	6
$n^2 + 1$	2	5	10	17	26	37

$n = 1: 1^2 + 1 = 1 + 1 = 2$ $n = 4: 4^2 + 1 = 16 + 1 = 17$

$n = 2: 2^2 + 1 = 4 + 1 = 5$ $n = 5: 5^2 + 1 = 25 + 1 = 26$

$n = 3: 3^2 + 1 = 9 + 1 = 10$ $n = 6: 6^2 + 1 = 36 + 1 = 37$

6.

n	1	2	3	4	5	6
$n^2 + n$	2	6	12	20	30	42

$n = 1: 1^2 + 1 = 1 + 1 = 2$ $n = 4: 4^2 + 4 = 16 + 4 = 20$

$n = 2: 2^2 + 2 = 4 + 2 = 6$ $n = 5: 5^2 + 5 = 25 + 5 = 30$

$n = 3: 3^2 + 3 = 9 + 3 = 12$ $n = 6: 6^2 + 6 = 36 + 6 = 42$

7.

n	1	2	3	4	5	6
2^{n-1}	1	2	4	8	16	32

$n = 1: 2^{1-1} = 2^0 = 1$ $n = 4: 2^{4-1} = 2^3 = 8$

$n = 2: 2^{2-1} = 2^1 = 2$ $n = 5: 2^{5-1} = 2^4 = 16$

$n = 3: 2^{3-1} = 2^2 = 4$ $n = 6: 2^{6-1} = 2^5 = 32$

8.

n	1	2	3	4	5	6
2^{1-n}	1	$\frac{1}{2}$	$\frac{1}{4}$	$\frac{1}{8}$	$\frac{1}{16}$	$\frac{1}{32}$

$n = 1: 2^{1-1} = 2^0 = 1$ $n = 4: 2^{1-4} = 2^{-3} = \frac{1}{8}$

$n = 2: 2^{1-2} = 2^{-1} = \frac{1}{2}$ $n = 5: 2^{1-5} = 2^{-4} = \frac{1}{16}$

$n = 3: 2^{1-3} = 2^{-2} = \frac{1}{4}$ $n = 6: 2^{1-6} = 2^{-5} = \frac{1}{32}$

9.–12. *Sample answers:*

9. Pattern: Each difference between adjacent numbers is 1 more than the previous difference.

$11 + 5 = 16$

$16 + 6 = 22$

$22 + 7 = 29$

16, 22, 29

10. Pattern: To get the next number, square the position number of the number and subtract 1.

$6^2 - 1 = 35$

$7^2 - 1 = 48$

$8^2 - 1 = 63$

35, 48, 63

11. Pattern: Each difference between adjacent numbers is 3 more than the previous difference.

$-15 - 3(5) = -30$

$-30 - 3(6) = -48$

$-48 - 3(7) = -69$

−30, −48, −69

12. Pattern: To get the next number, multiply the preceding number by 2, by 3, by 4, and so on.

$240 \cdot 6 = 1440$

$1440 \cdot 7 = 10{,}080$

$10{,}080 \cdot 8 = 80{,}640$

1440, 10,080, 80,640

13. $4\frac{1}{8}, 4\frac{2}{8}, 4\frac{3}{8}$

Thursday: $4\frac{4}{8} = 4\frac{1}{2}$

14. Pattern: To get the next number, square the position number; or add 3, add 5, add 7, add 9, and so on, to the preceding number.

Prediction: $5^2 = 25$; $6^2 = 36$

 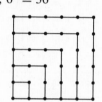

15. Pattern: To get the next number, add 5, add 9, add 13, add 17, and so on, to the preceding number.

Prediction: $28 + 17 = 45$; $45 + 21 = 66$

16. 28: 1, 2, 4, 7, 14, 28

$1 + 2 + 4 + 7 + 14 = 28$

17. 10: 1, 2, 5, 10

$1 + 2 + 5 = 8 \neq 10$

12: 1, 2, 3, 4, 6, 12

$1 + 2 + 3 + 4 + 6 = 16 \neq 12$

18.–19.

p	2^{p-1}	$2^p - 1$	$2^{p-1}(2^p - 1)$
5	16	31	496

$2^{5-1} = 2^4 = 16$

$2^5 - 1 = 32 - 1 = 31$; yes

$16(31) = 496$

20. 496: 1×496, 2×248, 4×124, 8×62, 16×31

1, 2, 4, 8, 16, 31, 62, 124, 248, 496

$1 + 2 + 4 + 8 + 16 + 31 + 62 + 124 + 248 = 496$

21. Pattern: To get the next number, after the first three, add the preceding three numbers.

$7 + 13 + 24 = 44$

$13 + 24 + 44 = 81$

$24 + 44 + 81 = 149$

44, 81, 149

22. *Sample answer:* 1, 1, 3, 5, 9, 17, 31, ...

23. B; $\frac{1}{2} \cdot 20(20 + 1) = \frac{1}{2} \cdot 20 \cdot 21 = 210$

24. 2, 1, 1 occurs four times.

25. *Sample answer:* Pattern: The first three positions of the notes are followed by the same three positions in reverse order, then that 6-position sequence is repeated one position higher.

Chapter **R E V I E W**

1. 180 divisible by

2: yes; 180 is even.

3: yes; $1 + 8 + 0 = 9$, $9 \div 3 = 3$

4: yes; $80 \div 4 = 20$

5: yes; last digit is 0.

6: yes; 180 is even and $180 \div 3 = 60$.

8: no; $180 \div 4 = 45$, which is odd.

9: yes; $1 + 8 + 0 = 9$, $9 \div 9 = 1$

10: yes; last digit is 0.

2. 184 divisible by

2: yes; 184 is even.

3: no; $1 + 8 + 4 = 13$

4: yes; $184 \div 4 = 46$

5: no; last digit is not 0 or 5.

6: no; not divisible by 3

8: yes; $184 \div 4 = 46$, which is even.

9: no; $1 + 8 + 4 = 13$

10: no; last digit is not 0.

3. 235 divisible by

2: no; not even

3: no; $2 + 3 + 5 = 10$

4: no; not even

5: yes; last digit is 5.

6: no; not divisible by 2 or 3

8: no; not even

9: no; $2 + 3 + 5 = 10$

10: no; last digit is not 0.

4. 336 divisible by

2: yes; 336 is even.

3: yes; $3 + 3 + 6 = 12$, $12 \div 3 = 4$

4: yes; $336 \div 4 = 84$

5: no; last digit is not 5 or 0.

6: yes; 336 is even and $336 \div 3 = 112$

8: yes; $336 \div 4 = 84$, which is even.

9: no; $3 + 3 + 6 = 12$ which is not divisible by 9.

10: no; last digit is not 0.

5. Yes, 101 is prime.

6. $27x^2 = 3 \cdot 3 \cdot 3 \cdot x \cdot x$ *(Expanded form)*

$\quad\quad = 3^3 x^2$ *(Exponent form)*

7. $45 = 3 \cdot 3 \cdot 5$
$30 = 2 \cdot 3 \cdot 5$
$\text{GCF} = 3 \cdot 5 = 15$

8. $84 = 2 \cdot 2 \cdot 3 \cdot 7$
$28 = 2 \cdot 2 \cdot 7$
$\text{GCF} = 28$

9. $15 = 3 \cdot 5$
$29 = 1 \cdot 29$
$\text{GCF} = 1$

10. $160 = 2 \cdot 2 \cdot 2 \cdot 2 \cdot 2 \cdot 5$
$195 = 5 \cdot 39$
$\text{GCF} = 5$

11. $68 = 2 \cdot 2 \cdot 17$
$34 = 2 \cdot 17$
$\text{LCM} = 2 \cdot 2 \cdot 17 = 68$

12. $90 = 2 \cdot 3 \cdot 3 \cdot 5$
$100 = 2 \cdot 2 \cdot 5 \cdot 5$
$\text{LCM} = 2 \cdot 2 \cdot 3 \cdot 3 \cdot 5 \cdot 5$
$\qquad = 900$

13. $13 = 1 \cdot 13$
$52 = 2 \cdot 2 \cdot 13$
$\text{LCM} = 2 \cdot 2 \cdot 13 = 52$

14. $12 = 3 \cdot 2 \cdot 2$
$15 = 3 \cdot 5$
$\text{LCM} = 5 \cdot 3 \cdot 2 \cdot 2 = 60$

15. $\frac{32}{6} = \frac{16}{3}$

16. $\frac{65}{20} = \frac{13}{4}$

17. $\frac{200x^2}{14x} = \frac{100x}{7}$

18. $\frac{48m}{64m^3} = \frac{3}{4m^2}$

19. $\frac{7}{11} = 0.\overline{63}$

20. $2.\overline{6} = 2.6666\ldots$
$x = 2.6666\ldots$
$10x = 26.6666\ldots$
$9x = 24$
$x = \frac{24}{9} = \frac{8}{3}$

21. $4x^{-4} = \frac{4}{x^4}$

22. $\frac{x^4}{x^{10}} = x^{4-10}$
$\qquad = x^{-6}$
$\qquad = \frac{1}{x^6}$

23. $5y^2 \cdot 3y^4 = 15y^{2+4}$
$\qquad\qquad = 15y^6$

24. $\frac{15^3}{15^2} = 15^{3-2} = 15$

25. $743{,}000 = 7.43 \times 10^5$

26. $0.00012 = 1.2 \times 10^{-4}$

27. $1{,}203{,}000 = 1.203 \times 10^6$

28. $0.0407 = 4.07 \times 10^{-2}$

29. $26, 37, 50;$
$17 + 9 = 26,$
$26 + 11 = 37,$
$37 + 13 = 50$

30. $14, 18, 22;$
$10 + 4 = 14,$
$14 + 4 = 18,$
$18 + 4 = 22$

31. $0, -5, -11;$
$4 - 4 = 0,$
$0 - 5 = -5,$
$-5 - 6 = -11$

32. $1250; 6250; 31{,}250;$
$250 \times 5 = 1250,$
$1250 \times 5 = 6250,$
$6250 \times 5 = 31{,}250$

Chapter ASSESSMENT

1. Divisible by

   2: yes; 1224 is even.

   3: yes; $1 + 2 + 2 + 4 = 9; 9 \div 3 = 3$

   4: yes; $24 \div 4 = 6$

   5: no; the last digit is not 5 or 0.

   6: yes; 1224 is even and divisible by 3.

   8: yes; $224 \div 8 = 28$

   9: yes; $1 + 2 + 2 + 4 = 9; 9 \div 9 = 1$

   10: no; the last digit is not 0.

2. Divisible by

   11: no; $1224 \div 11 \neq$ natural number

   12: yes; $1224 \div 12 = 102$

   13: no; $1224 \div 13 \neq$ natural number

   14: no; $1224 \div 14 \neq$ natural number

   15: no; $1224 \div 15 \neq$ natural number

   16: no; $1224 \div 16 \neq$ natural number

   17: yes; $1224 \div 17 = 72$

   18: yes; $1224 \div 18 = 68$

   19: no; $1224 \div 19 \neq$ natural number

   20: no; $1224 \div 20 \neq$ natural number

3.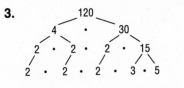

   $120 = 2 \cdot 2 \cdot 2 \cdot 3 \cdot 5 = 2^3 \cdot 3 \cdot 5$

4.

   $125 = 5 \cdot 5 \cdot 5 = 5^3$

5. $99ab = 3^2 \cdot 11 \cdot a \cdot b$

6. $121x^2 = 11^2 \cdot x^2$

7. Factors of 48: 1, 2, 3, 4, 6, 8, 12, 16, 24, 48

   Factors of 36: 1, 2, 3, 4, 6, 9, 12, 18, 36

   The GCF is 12.

8. Factors of 56: 1, 2, 4, 7, 8, 14, 28, 56

   Factors of 98: 1, 2, 7, 14, 49, 98

   The GCF is 14.

9. $10 = 2 \cdot 5$

   $35 = 5 \cdot 7$

   The LCM is $2 \cdot 5 \cdot 7 = 70$.

10. $5 = 5$

    $18 = 2 \cdot 3 \cdot 3 = 2 \cdot 3^2$

    The LCM is $2 \cdot 3^2 \cdot 5 = 90$.

11. $7 = 7$

    $10 = 2 \cdot 5$

    $14 = 2 \cdot 7$

    The LCM is $2 \cdot 5 \cdot 7 = 70$.

12. $\dfrac{20}{800} = \dfrac{20}{20 \cdot 40} = \dfrac{1}{40}$

13. $\dfrac{3}{11} \times \dfrac{2}{2} = \dfrac{6}{22}$;

    $\dfrac{3}{11}$ is larger than $\dfrac{5}{22}$.

14. $0.65 = \dfrac{65}{100} = \dfrac{5 \cdot 13}{5 \cdot 20} = \dfrac{13}{20}$

15. $x^9 \cdot x^{-4} = x^{9+(-4)} = x^5$

16. D; $1.6 \cdot 10^4 = 16,000$

17. A; $1.6 \times 10^{-4} = 0.00016$

18. B; $1.6 \times 10^{-2} = 0.016$

19. C; $1.6 \times 10^2 = 160$

20. Pattern: Each difference between adjacent numbers is 1 more than the previous difference.

    14, 19, 25

21. Pattern: Each difference between adjacent numbers is 4 more than the previous difference.

    8, −12, −36

22. Pattern: To get the next number, multiply the preceding number by 3.

567, 1701, 5103

23. Pattern: To get the next number, multiply the preceding number by 3.

405, 1215, 3645

24. $300,000 = 3 \times 10^5$ kilometers per second

25. $500 = 5 \times 10^2$ seconds

26. Distance $= \left(300,000\dfrac{\text{kilometers}}{\text{second}}\right)(500 \text{ seconds})$

$= (3 \times 10^5)(5 \times 10^2)$

$= (3 \times 5)(10^5 \times 10^2)$

$= 15 \times 10^7$

$= 1.5 \times 10^8$ kilometers

Standardized Test Practice

1. D; $6 + 5 + 4 = 15 \div 9 \neq$ natural number

2. D

3. C; $126 = 2 \cdot 3 \cdot 3 \cdot 7$

4. B; the GCF is 4.

5. C; $12 = 2 \cdot 2 \cdot 3$

$18 = 2 \cdot 3 \cdot 3$

$GCF = 2 \cdot 3 = 6$

6. C; 20: 40

8: 16, 24, 32, 40

7. D; $\dfrac{3}{12} = \dfrac{6}{24} \neq \dfrac{15}{24}$

8. B; $5x^{-4} = \dfrac{5}{x^4}$

9. B; $150,000 = 1.5 \times 10^5$

10. C; $5 \times 3.6 \times 10^{-7+4} = 18 \times 10^{-3}$

$= 1.8 \times 10^{-2}$

11. B; $1^4, 2^4, 3^4, 4^4, 5^4$

$5^4 = 625$

Cumulative REVIEW

1. Pattern: To get the next number, add 7 to the preceding number.

35, 42, 49

2. Pattern: To get the next number, add 2 to the preceding number.

13, 15, 17

3. Pattern: To get the next letter, skip 1 letter.

I, K, M

4. Pattern: To get the next letter, skip 2 letters backward.

N, K, H

5. $2 \cdot 5 = 10$

6. $3 \cdot 9 = 27$

7. $5^7 = 78,125$

8. $\left(\frac{4}{9}\right)^4 \approx 0.04$

9. $\sqrt{84} \approx 9.17$

10. $(5^4 - 20) \div 11 + 9 = 64$

11. $\sqrt{\frac{5}{12}} \approx 0.65$

12. $(6.3)^6 \approx 62{,}523.50$

13. $\sqrt{17.82} \approx 4.22$

14. $2^5 + (24 - 6) \cdot 3 = 86$

15. $|-8| + 17 - 13 - 5 = 8 + 17 - 13 - 5 = 7$

16. $|-6| - 9 - 4 + 21 = 6 - 9 - 4 + 21 = 14$

17. $(-5)(3)(-6)(-2) = -180$

18. $\dfrac{-625}{-5} = 125$

19. $43 + (7 - 2)^2 \div 5 = 43 + (5)^2 \div 5$
$= 43 + 25 \div 5$
$= 43 + 5$
$= 48$

20. $32 - (7 - 4)^3 \cdot 3 = 32 - (3)^3 \cdot 3$
$= 32 - (27) \cdot 3$
$= 32 - 81$
$= -49$

21. $x + 5 = 21$
$x = 16$

22. $17 - y = 8$
$y = 9$

23. $4z = 32$
$z = 8$

24. $\dfrac{w}{3} = 7$
$w = 21$

25. $\boxed{\begin{array}{c}\text{Cost of}\\\text{palette}\end{array}} + \boxed{\begin{array}{c}\text{Number of}\\\text{tubes of}\\\text{paint}\end{array}} \cdot \boxed{\begin{array}{c}\text{Cost of}\\\text{tube of}\\\text{paint}\end{array}} = \boxed{\begin{array}{c}\text{Total}\\\text{cost}\end{array}}$

26. Cost of palette $= 5.70$ (dollars)
Number of tubes of paint $= 8$ (tubes)
Cost of a tube of paint $= 2.70$ (dollars)
Total cost $= x$ (dollars)

27. $5.70 + 8 \cdot 2.70 = x$

28. $5.70 + 21.60 = x$
$\$27.30 = x$

29. $5.70 + 8 \cdot 2.70 = 27.30$

30. $n + 16 = 3$
$n = -13$

31. $-8y = -104$
$\dfrac{-8y}{-8} = \dfrac{-104}{-8}$
$y = 13$

32. $\dfrac{x}{5} \geq 25$
$x \geq 25 \cdot 5$
$x \geq 125$

33. $-18 = x - 9$
$-9 = x$

34. $z + 9 < -5$
$z < -14$

35. $7m > 147$
$\dfrac{7m}{7} > \dfrac{147}{7}$
$m > 21$

36. Yes; $+1 + (-4) + 2 + 3 + (-1) = (-3) + 2 + 3 + (-1)$
$= 1 + 3 + (-1)$
$= 4 + (-1)$
$= 3$ miles over goal

37. Mon: $7 + 1 = 8$; Tue: 0;
Wed: $7 - 4 = 3$; Thur: $7 + 2 = 9$;
Fri: $7 + 3 = 10$; Sat: $7 - 1 = 6$;
Sun: 0

38. $8 + 0 + 3 + 9 + 10 + 6 + 0 = 11 + 9 + 10 + 6$
$= 20 + 10 + 6$
$= 30 + 6$
$= 36$ miles

39. $5(x + y + z) = 5x + 5y + 5z$

$5x + 5y + 5z = 5(-2) + 5(4) + 5(5)$

$= -10 + 20 + 25$

$= 35$

40. $-4(x - y + 2z) = -4x + 4y - 8z$

$-4x + 4y - 8z = -4(-2) + 4(4) - 8(5)$

$= 8 + 16 - 40$

$= 24 - 40$

$= -16$

41. $3y - 6x + 3z - 5y = -2y - 6x + 3z$

$-2y - 6x + 3z = -2(4) - 6(-2) + 3(5)$

$= -8 + 12 + 15$

$= 19$

42. $-2(4x + 3x + y) = -2(7x + y)$

$= -14x - 2y$

$-14x - 2y = -14(-2) - 2(4)$

$= 28 - 8$

$= 20$

43. $-7 + x(z + y) = -7 + xz + xy$

$-7 + xz + xy = -7 + (-2)(5) + (-2)(4)$

$= -7 - 10 - 8$

$= -25$

44. $2(3z - z) - |-y| = 2(2z) - |y|$

$= 4z - |y|$

$4z - |y| = 4(5) - |4|$

$= 20 - 4$

$= 16$

45. $4 + (0) = 4$

$4 + (-1) = 3$

$4 + (-2) = 2$

$4 + (-3) = 1;$

Pattern: To get the next solution, subtract 1 from the preceding solution.

46. $5 - (-6) = 11$

$6 - (-6) = 12$

$7 - (-6) = 13$

$8 - (-6) = 14;$

Pattern: To get the next solution, add 1 to the preceding solution.

47. $7 \times 21 = 147$

$7 \times 18 = 126$

$7 \times 15 = 105$

$7 \times 12 = 84;$

Pattern: To get the next solution, subtract 21 from the preceding solution.

48. $6 \div 3 = 2$

$12 \div 3 = 4$

$24 \div 3 = 8$

$48 \div 3 = 16;$

Pattern: To get the next solution, double the preceding solution.

49. Perimeter $= 4(2) = 8$ units
Area $= (2)(2) = 4$ units^2

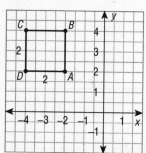

50. Perimeter $= 2(5) + 2(3) = 16$ units
Area $= (3)(5) = 15$ units^2

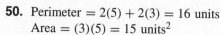
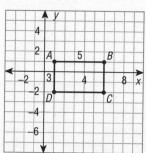

51. Perimeter = 4(3) = 12 units
Area = (3)(3) = 9 units^2

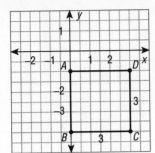

52. Perimeter = 2(4) + 2(3) = 14 units
Area = (4)(3) = 12 units^2

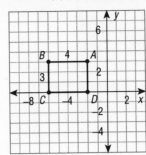

Note to teachers: The checks for the solutions to Exercises 53–64 will not be shown, but students should continue to check their work.

53. $6x - 17 = 7$
$6x = 24$
$x = 4$

54. $4y + 13 = -19$
$4y = -32$
$y = -8$

55. $-\dfrac{n}{7} + 9 = 5$
$-\dfrac{n}{7} = -4$
$(-7) \cdot \left(-\dfrac{n}{7}\right) = (-7) \cdot -4$
$n = 28$

56. $8m + 3m - 2 = 9$
$11m - 2 = 9$
$11m = 11$
$m = 1$

57. $\frac{3}{4}z - \frac{1}{4}z + 6 = 12$
$\frac{2}{4}z + 6 = 12$
$\frac{1}{2}z = 6$
$2 \cdot \frac{1}{2}z = 2 \cdot 6$
$z = 12$

58. $15t + 14 - 7t = 30$
$8t + 14 = 30$
$8t = 16$
$t = 2$

59. $10y - 27 = y$
$-27 = -9y$
$3 = y$

60. $13x - 80 = 60 - 7x$
$20x - 80 = 60$
$20x = 140$
$x = 7$

61. $3(4t + 3) = 2t$
$12t + 9 = 2t$
$9 = -10t$
$-\dfrac{9}{10} = t$

62. $b + 6 = 2(b - 2)$
$b + 6 = 2b - 4$
$6 = b - 4$
$10 = b$

63. $2\left(4n + \frac{1}{2}\right) = 10n$
$4n + \frac{1}{2} = 5n$
$\frac{1}{2} = n$

64. $3(y - 2) + 2 = -y$
$3y - 6 + 2 = -y$
$3y - 4 = -y$
$-4 = -4y$
$1 = y$

65. $15x - 21 = -42x + 89.2$
$57x - 21 = 89.2$
$57x = 110.2$
$x \approx 1.9$

66. $14.1(2.37y + 5.6) = 0.71y - 29.3$
$33.417y + 78.96 = 0.71y - 29.3$
$32.707y + 78.96 = -29.3$
$32.707y = -108.26$
$y \approx -3.3$

67. $-7.3 + 6p = -32p + 23.8$
$-7.3 + 38p = 23.8$
$38p = 31.1$
$p \approx 0.8$

68. $4.62s - 18.5 = 7.23(9.78s + 3.6)$

$\, 4.62s - 18.5 = 70.71s + 26.028$

$\, -18.5 = 66.09s + 26.028$

$\, -44.528 = 66.09s$

$\, -0.7 \approx s$

69.

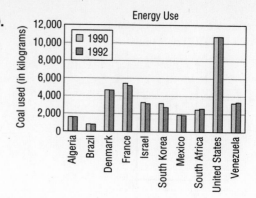

70.

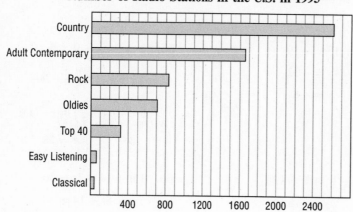

Number of Radio Stations in the U.S. in 1995

71.

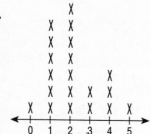

72.

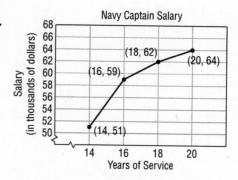

73. Salary increases with years of service.

74.

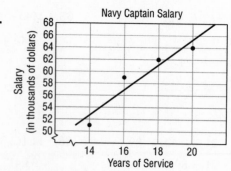

About $68,000

75. $\frac{1}{16}$

76. $\frac{3}{16}$

77. $\frac{8}{16} = \frac{1}{2}$

78. $\frac{4}{16} = \frac{1}{4}$

79. 12,985 divisible by

2: no; not even
3: no; $1 + 2 + 9 + 8 + 5 = 25$
4: no; not divisible by 2
5: yes; ends in 5

6: no; not divisible by 2 or 3
8: no; not divisible by 2
9: no; not divisible by 3
10: no; does not end in 0

80. 567 divisible by

2: no; not even
3: yes; $5 + 6 + 7 = 18 = 3(6)$
4: no; not divisible by 2
5: no; does not end in 5 or 0

6: no; not divisible by 2
8: no; not divisible by 2
9: yes; $5 + 6 + 7 = 18 = 9(2)$
10: no; does not end in 0

81. 1893 divisible by

2: no; not even
3: yes; $1 + 8 + 9 + 3 = 21 = 3(7)$
4: no; not divisible by 2
5: no; does not end in 0 or 5

6: no; not divisible by 2 or 3
8: no; not divisible by 2
9: no; not divisible by 3
10: no; does not end in 0

82. 4556 divisible by

2: yes; even
3: no; $4 + 5 + 5 + 6 = 20$
4: yes; $56 \div 4 = 14$
5: no; does not end in 0 or 5

6: no; not divisible by 3 or 2
8: no; $4556 \div 4 = 1339$; not even
9: no; not divisible by 3
10: no; does not end in 0

83. 711 divisible by

2: no; not even
3: yes; $7 + 1 + 1 = 9 = 3(3)$
4: no; not even
5: no; does not end in 0 or 5

6: no; not even
8: no; not even
9: yes; $7 + 1 + 1 = 9 = 9(1)$
10: no; does not end in 0

84. 16,543 divisible by

2: no; not even
3: no; $1 + 6 + 5 + 4 + 3 = 19$
4: no; not even
5: no; does not end in 0 or 5

6: no; not even
8: no; not even
9: no; not divisible by 3
10: no; does not end in 0

85. 810 divisible by

2: yes; even
3: yes; $8 + 1 + 0 = 9 = 3(3)$
4: no; not divisible by 4
5: yes; ends in 0

6: yes; divisible by 3 and 2
8: no; not divisible by 4
9: yes; $8 + 1 + 0 = 9 = 9(1)$
10: yes; ends in 0

86. 7232 divisible by

2: yes; even

3: no; $7 + 2 + 3 + 2 = 14$

4: yes; 32 is divisible by 4

5: no; does not end in 0 or 5

6: no; not divisible by 3

8: yes; $7232 \div 4 = 1808$; even

9: no; not divisible by 3

10: no; does not end in 0

87. $7 = 7$;

$49 = 7 \cdot 7 = 7^2$;

LCM: $7^2 = 49$

88. $4 = 2 \cdot 2 = 2^2$;

$18 = 2 \cdot 3 \cdot 3 = 2 \cdot 3^2$;

LCM: $2^2 \cdot 3^2 = 36$

89.

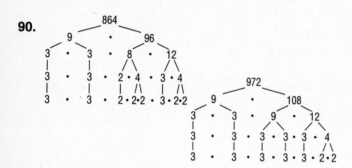

$270 = 2 \cdot 3^3 \cdot 5$; $450 = 2 \cdot 3^2 \cdot 5^2$

LCM: $2 \cdot 3 \cdot 3 \cdot 3 \cdot 5 \cdot 5 = 2 \cdot 3^3 \cdot 5^2 = 1350$

90.

$864 = 2^5 \cdot 3^2$; $972 = 2^2 \cdot 3^5$

LCM: $2 \cdot 2 \cdot 2 \cdot 2 \cdot 2 \cdot 3 \cdot 3 \cdot 3 \cdot 3 \cdot 3 = 2^5 \cdot 3^5 = 7776$

91. $6x^2y = 2 \cdot 3 \cdot x^2 \cdot y$;

$8xy^3 = 2^3 \cdot x \cdot y^3$;

LCM: $2^3 \cdot 3 \cdot x^2 \cdot y^3 = 24x^2y^3$

92. $9a^2b = 3^2 \cdot a^2 \cdot b$;

$12ab^4 = 2^2 \cdot 3 \cdot a \cdot b^4$;

LCM: $2^2 \cdot 3^2 \cdot a^2 \cdot b^4 = 36a^2b^4$

93. $\dfrac{6}{48} = \dfrac{\cancel{6} \cdot 1}{\cancel{6} \cdot 8}$

$= \dfrac{1}{8}$

94. $\dfrac{25}{45} = \dfrac{\cancel{5} \cdot 5}{\cancel{5} \cdot 9}$

$= \dfrac{5}{9}$

95. $\dfrac{10}{15} = \dfrac{\cancel{5} \cdot 2}{\cancel{5} \cdot 3}$

$= \dfrac{2}{3}$

96. $\dfrac{52}{54} = \dfrac{\cancel{2} \cdot 26}{\cancel{2} \cdot 27}$

$= \dfrac{26}{27}$

97. $5^0 = 1$

98. $3^{-2} = \dfrac{1}{3^2}$

$= \dfrac{1}{9}$

99. $a^{-4} = \dfrac{1}{a^4}$

100. $\dfrac{x}{x^3} = x^{1-3}$

$= x^{-2}$

$= \dfrac{1}{x^2}$

101. $\dfrac{8a}{10a^2} = \dfrac{4 \cdot \cancel{2} \cdot \cancel{a}}{5 \cdot \cancel{2} \cdot \cancel{a} \cdot a}$

$\qquad = \dfrac{4}{5a}$

102. $4^2 \cdot 4^{-2} = 4^{2+(-2)}$

$\qquad\qquad = 4^0$

$\qquad\qquad = 1$

103. $\dfrac{3^4}{3^5} = 3^{4-5}$

$\qquad = 3^{-1}$

$\qquad = \dfrac{1}{3}$

104. $\dfrac{10^0}{10^4} = \dfrac{1}{10^4}$

$\qquad = \dfrac{1}{10{,}000}$

Chapter 7
Rational Numbers and Percents

| **7.1** | *ALGEBRA CONNECTION:*
Addition and Subtraction of Like Fractions |

ONGOING ASSESSMENT

1. $\dfrac{5}{6} + \dfrac{2}{6}$ *Write original equation.*

$\qquad = \dfrac{(5+2)}{6}$ *Add numerators.*

$\qquad = \dfrac{7}{6}$ *Simplify.*

2. $\dfrac{5}{12} - \dfrac{1}{12}$ *Write original equation.*

$\qquad = \dfrac{(5-1)}{12}$ *Subtract numerators.*

$\qquad = \dfrac{4}{12}$ *Simplify.*

$\qquad = \dfrac{4 \cdot 1}{4 \cdot 3}$ *Factor numerator and denominator.*

$\qquad = \dfrac{1}{3}$ *Simplify.*

3. $\dfrac{2}{5} + \dfrac{3}{5}$ *Write original equation.*

$\qquad = \dfrac{(2+3)}{5}$ *Add numerators.*

$\qquad = \dfrac{5}{5}$ *Simplify.*

$\qquad = 1$ *Simplify.*

EXERCISES

1. $\dfrac{5}{6} - \dfrac{3}{6} = \dfrac{2}{6} = \dfrac{1}{3}$ **2.** $\dfrac{1}{4} + \dfrac{2}{4} = \dfrac{3}{4}$

3. To add like fractions, add the numerators and write the sum over the denominator. For example, see answer to Exercise 2.

To subtract like fractions, subtract the numerators and write the difference over the denominator. For example, see answer to Exercise 1.

4. $\dfrac{2}{6} + \dfrac{3}{6} = \dfrac{2+3}{6}$

$\qquad\qquad = \dfrac{5}{6}$

5. $\dfrac{8}{12} - \dfrac{4}{12} = \dfrac{8-4}{12}$

$\qquad\qquad = \dfrac{4}{12}$

$\qquad\qquad = \dfrac{1}{3}$

6. $\dfrac{-8}{15} - \dfrac{7}{15} = \dfrac{-8-7}{15}$

$\qquad\qquad = \dfrac{-15}{15}$

$\qquad\qquad = -1$

7. $\dfrac{-3}{8} + \dfrac{-7}{8} = \dfrac{-3+(-7)}{8}$

$\qquad\qquad = \dfrac{-10}{8}$

$\qquad\qquad = \dfrac{\cancel{2}\cdot(-5)}{\cancel{2}\cdot 4}$

$\qquad\qquad = -\dfrac{5}{4}$

8. $\dfrac{-a}{5} - \dfrac{4a}{5} = \dfrac{-a-4a}{5}$

$\qquad\qquad = \dfrac{-5a}{5}$

$\qquad\qquad = -a$

9. $\dfrac{12y}{10} - \dfrac{4y}{10} = \dfrac{12y-4y}{10}$

$\qquad\qquad = \dfrac{8y}{10}$

$\qquad\qquad = \dfrac{\cancel{2}\cdot 4\cdot y}{\cancel{2}\cdot 5}$

$\qquad\qquad = \dfrac{4y}{5}$

10. $3\dfrac{1}{2} + 1\dfrac{1}{2} = \dfrac{7}{2} + \dfrac{3}{2}$

$\qquad\qquad = \dfrac{7+3}{2}$

$\qquad\qquad = \dfrac{10}{2}$

$\qquad\qquad = 5$

11. $3\dfrac{2}{3} - 4\dfrac{1}{3} = \dfrac{11}{3} - \dfrac{13}{3}$

$\qquad\qquad = \dfrac{11-13}{3}$

$\qquad\qquad = -\dfrac{2}{3}$

12. $\dfrac{1}{z} + \dfrac{6}{z} = \dfrac{1+6}{z}$

$\qquad\qquad = \dfrac{7}{z}$

13. $\dfrac{2}{4t} - \dfrac{9}{4t} = \dfrac{2-9}{4t}$

$\qquad\qquad = \dfrac{-7}{4t}$

14. $\dfrac{4}{5b} - \dfrac{1}{5b} = \dfrac{4-1}{5b}$

$\qquad\qquad = \dfrac{3}{5b}$

15. $\dfrac{1}{8x} + \dfrac{3}{8x} - \dfrac{7}{8x} = \dfrac{1+3-7}{8x}$

$\qquad\qquad\qquad = -\dfrac{3}{8x}$

16. $x + \dfrac{2}{3} = \dfrac{4}{3}$

$x + \dfrac{2}{3} - \dfrac{2}{3} = \dfrac{4}{3} - \dfrac{2}{3}$

$x = \dfrac{4-2}{3}$

$x = \dfrac{2}{3}$

17. $y - \dfrac{6}{8} = \dfrac{5}{8}$

$y - \dfrac{6}{8} + \dfrac{6}{8} = \dfrac{5}{8} + \dfrac{6}{8}$

$y = \dfrac{5+6}{8}$

$y = \dfrac{11}{8}$

18. $m + \dfrac{19}{5} = \dfrac{4}{5}$

$m + \dfrac{19}{5} - \dfrac{19}{5} = \dfrac{4}{5} - \dfrac{19}{5}$

$m = \dfrac{4-19}{5}$

$m = \dfrac{-15}{5}$

$m = -3$

19. $n - \dfrac{1}{6} = \dfrac{-9}{6}$

$n - \dfrac{1}{6} + \dfrac{1}{6} = \dfrac{-9}{6} + \dfrac{1}{6}$

$n = \dfrac{-9+1}{6}$

$n = \dfrac{-8}{6}$

$n = \dfrac{\cancel{2}\cdot(-4)}{\cancel{2}\cdot(3)}$

$n = -\dfrac{4}{3}$

20. $s + \dfrac{5}{4} = \dfrac{-9}{4}$

$s + \dfrac{5}{4} - \dfrac{5}{4} = \dfrac{-9}{4} - \dfrac{5}{4}$

$s = \dfrac{-9-5}{4}$

$s = \dfrac{-14}{4}$

$s = \dfrac{\cancel{2}\cdot(-7)}{\cancel{2}\cdot 2}$

$s = -\dfrac{7}{2}$

21. $t - \dfrac{8}{11} = \dfrac{-6}{11}$

$t - \dfrac{8}{11} + \dfrac{8}{11} = \dfrac{-6}{11} + \dfrac{8}{11}$

$t = \dfrac{-6+8}{11}$

$t = \dfrac{2}{11}$

22.
$$3x + \frac{1}{2} = \frac{5}{2}$$
$$3x + \frac{1}{2} - \frac{1}{2} = \frac{5}{2} - \frac{1}{2}$$
$$3x = \frac{5-1}{2}$$
$$3x = \frac{4}{2}$$
$$3x = 2$$
$$x = \frac{2}{3}$$

23.
$$2z - \frac{8}{7} = \frac{6}{7}$$
$$2z - \frac{8}{7} + \frac{8}{7} = \frac{6}{7} + \frac{8}{7}$$
$$2z = \frac{14}{7}$$
$$2z = 2$$
$$z = 1$$

24. $\frac{1}{7} + \frac{3}{7} \approx 0.57$

25. $\frac{7}{6} - \frac{3}{6} \approx 0.67$

26. $\frac{5}{9} - \frac{8}{9} \approx -0.33$

27. $\frac{5}{16} - \frac{11}{16} \approx -0.38$

28.
$$\frac{1}{8} + \frac{2}{8} = \frac{1+2}{8} = \frac{3}{8}$$
$$\frac{3}{8} + \frac{4}{8} = \frac{3+4}{8} = \frac{7}{8}$$
$$\frac{5}{8} + \frac{6}{8} = \frac{5+6}{8} = \frac{11}{8}$$
$$\frac{7}{8} + \frac{8}{8} = \frac{7+8}{8} = \frac{15}{8}$$

Pattern: Every fraction, after the first, is $\frac{4}{8}$ greater than the preceding fraction.
$$\frac{9}{8} + \frac{10}{8} = \frac{9+10}{8} = \frac{19}{8}$$
$$\frac{11}{8} + \frac{12}{8} = \frac{11+12}{8} = \frac{23}{8}$$
$$\frac{13}{8} + \frac{14}{8} = \frac{13+14}{8} = \frac{27}{8}$$

Solution: $\frac{19}{8}, \frac{23}{8}, \frac{27}{8}$

29.
$$\frac{10}{2} - \frac{1}{2} = \frac{10-1}{2} = \frac{9}{2}$$
$$\frac{-9}{2} - \frac{2}{2} = \frac{-9-2}{2} = -\frac{11}{2}$$
$$\frac{8}{2} - \frac{3}{2} = \frac{8-3}{2} = \frac{5}{2}$$
$$\frac{-7}{2} - \frac{4}{2} = \frac{-7-4}{2} = -\frac{11}{2}$$

Pattern: Every fraction, in every odd-numbered position after the first, is $\frac{4}{2}$ less than the preceding fraction in an odd-numbered position. Every fraction in an even-numbered position is $-\frac{11}{2}$.
$$\frac{6}{2} - \frac{5}{2} = \frac{6-5}{2} = \frac{1}{2}$$
$$\frac{4}{2} - \frac{7}{2} = \frac{4-7}{2} = -\frac{3}{2}$$

Solution: $\frac{1}{2}, -\frac{11}{2}, -\frac{3}{2}$

30. In the first step, only the numerators should be added;
$$\frac{2}{5} + \frac{1}{5} = \frac{2+1}{5}$$
$$= \frac{3}{5}$$

31. The student added the fractional parts incorrectly;
$$\frac{1}{3} + \frac{1}{3} = \frac{2}{3}, \text{ so } 3 + \frac{2}{3} = 3\frac{2}{3}$$

32. $\frac{1}{4} + \frac{2}{4} = \frac{3}{4}$

33. $\frac{6}{8} - \frac{5}{8} = \frac{1}{8}$

34. mashed ripe banana: $\frac{1}{2} + \frac{1}{2} = \frac{2}{2} = 1$ cup
instant nonfat milk powder: $\frac{1}{4}$ cup
frozen orange juice: $\frac{3}{4} + \frac{2}{4} = \frac{5}{4} = 1\frac{1}{4}$ cup
frozen pineapple juice: $\frac{1}{4}$ cup
crushed ice: $\frac{1}{3} + \frac{1}{3} = \frac{2}{3}$ cup
sparkling water: $\frac{1}{4} + \frac{1}{4} = \frac{2}{4} = \frac{1}{2}$ cup

35. B; $1\frac{9}{10} - 1\frac{7}{10} = \frac{2}{10} = \frac{1}{5}$ meter

36.

$$x + \frac{2}{8} = \frac{10}{16} \qquad \frac{10}{16} = \frac{\cancel{2} \cdot 5}{\cancel{2} \cdot 8}$$

$$x + \frac{2}{8} = \frac{5}{8} \qquad\qquad = \frac{5}{8}$$

$$x + \frac{2}{8} - \frac{2}{8} = \frac{5}{8} - \frac{2}{8}$$

$$x = \frac{5 - 2}{8}$$

$$x = \frac{3}{8}$$

Lab 7.2

Part A

1.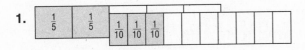

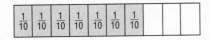

$\frac{2}{5} + \frac{3}{10} = \frac{7}{10}$

2.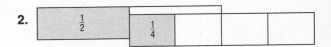

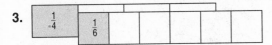

$\frac{1}{2} + \frac{1}{4} = \frac{3}{4}$

3.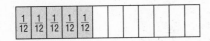

$\frac{1}{4} + \frac{1}{6} = \frac{5}{12}$

4.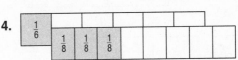

$\frac{1}{24}$

$\frac{1}{6} + \frac{3}{8} = \frac{13}{24}$

5.

Fractions	Sum	Denominators	Least Common Multiple of Denominators
$\frac{2}{5} + \frac{3}{10}$	$\frac{7}{10}$	5, 10	10
$\frac{1}{2} + \frac{1}{4}$	$\frac{3}{4}$	2, 4	4
$\frac{1}{4} + \frac{1}{6}$	$\frac{5}{12}$	4, 6	12
$\frac{1}{6} + \frac{3}{8}$	$\frac{13}{24}$	6, 8	24

Sample answer: The denominator of the sum is the same as the least common multiple of the fractions' denominators.

Part B

6.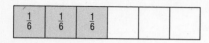

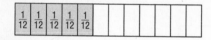

$\frac{2}{3} - \frac{1}{6} = \frac{3}{6} = \frac{1}{2}$

7.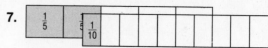

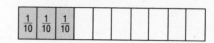

$\frac{2}{5} - \frac{1}{10} = \frac{3}{10}$

8.

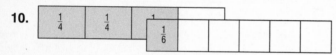

$\frac{2}{3} - \frac{1}{4} = \frac{5}{12}$

9.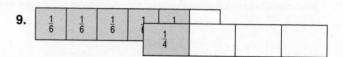

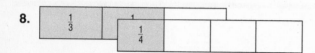

$\frac{5}{6} - \frac{1}{4} = \frac{7}{12}$

10.

$\frac{3}{4} - \frac{1}{6} = \frac{7}{12}$

11. *Sample answer:* The denominator of the difference is the same as the least common multiple of the fractions' denominators.

12.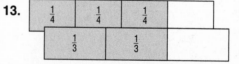

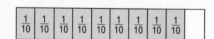

$\frac{2}{5} + \frac{1}{2} = \frac{9}{10}$

13.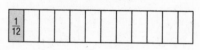

$\frac{3}{4} - \frac{2}{3} = \frac{1}{12}$

14. a. 10
   b. $\frac{4}{10}$; $\frac{5}{10}$
   c. $\frac{4}{10} + \frac{5}{10} = \frac{9}{10}$; yes

d. (a) 12
   (b) $\frac{9}{12}$; $\frac{8}{12}$
   (c) $\frac{9}{12} - \frac{8}{12} = \frac{1}{12}$; yes

7.2 Addition and Subtraction of Unlike Fractions

ONGOING ASSESSMENT

1. $\dfrac{5}{6} + \dfrac{2}{3}$ *Write original equation.*

$= \dfrac{5}{6} + \dfrac{4}{6}$ *Write fractions with common denominators.*

$= \dfrac{5+4}{6}$ *Add numerators.*

$= \dfrac{9}{6}$ *Simplify.*

$= \dfrac{3}{2}$ *Simplify.*

2. $\dfrac{5}{12} - \dfrac{1}{6}$ *Write original equation.*

$= \dfrac{5}{12} - \dfrac{2}{12}$ *Write fractions with common denominators.*

$= \dfrac{5-2}{12}$ *Subtract numerators.*

$= \dfrac{3}{12}$ *Simplify.*

$= \dfrac{1}{4}$ *Simplify.*

3. $\dfrac{2}{5} + \dfrac{3}{4}$ *Write original equation.*

$= \dfrac{8}{20} + \dfrac{15}{20}$ *Write fractions with common denominators.*

$= \dfrac{8+15}{20}$ *Add numerators.*

$= \dfrac{23}{20}$ *Simplify.*

EXERCISES

1. Fraction for left green region: $\dfrac{2}{3}$

Fraction for right green region: $\dfrac{1}{2}$

$\dfrac{2}{3} + \dfrac{1}{2} = \dfrac{2}{3} \cdot \dfrac{2}{2} + \dfrac{1}{2} \cdot \dfrac{3}{3}$

$= \dfrac{4}{6} + \dfrac{3}{6}$

$= \dfrac{7}{6}$

2. Fraction for left green region: $\dfrac{5}{8}$

Fraction for right green region: $\dfrac{1}{2}$

$\dfrac{5}{8} + \dfrac{1}{2} = \dfrac{5}{8} + \dfrac{1}{2} \cdot \dfrac{4}{4}$

$= \dfrac{5}{8} + \dfrac{4}{8}$

$= \dfrac{9}{8}$

3. $\dfrac{2}{5} + \dfrac{1}{3} = \dfrac{2}{5} \cdot \dfrac{3}{3} + \dfrac{1}{3} \cdot \dfrac{5}{5}$ *Least common denominator is 15.*

$= \dfrac{6}{15} + \dfrac{5}{15}$ *Rewrite as like fractions.*

$= \dfrac{11}{15}$ *Add like fractions.*

4. $\frac{4}{5} - \frac{3}{10} = \frac{4}{5} \cdot \frac{2}{2} - \frac{3}{10}$ *Least common denominator is 10.*

           $= \frac{8}{10} - \frac{3}{10}$ *Rewrite as like fractions.*

           $= \frac{5}{10}$ *Subtract like fractions.*

           $= \frac{1}{2}$ *Simplify fraction.*

5. $\frac{a}{2} - \frac{a}{3} = \frac{a}{2} \cdot \frac{3}{3} - \frac{a}{3} \cdot \frac{2}{2}$ *Least common denominator is 6.*

           $= \frac{3a}{6} - \frac{2a}{6}$ *Rewrite as like fractions.*

           $= \frac{a}{6}$ *Subtract like fractions.*

6. $\frac{4}{t} + \frac{2}{2t} = \frac{4}{t} \cdot \frac{2}{2} + \frac{2}{2t}$ *Least common denominator is 2t.*

           $= \frac{8}{2t} + \frac{2}{2t}$ *Rewrite as like fractions.*

           $= \frac{10}{2t}$ *Add like fractions.*

           $= \frac{5}{t}$ *Simplify.*

7. $\frac{1}{6} + \frac{7}{12} = \frac{1}{6} \cdot \frac{2}{2} + \frac{7}{12}$

           $= \frac{2}{12} + \frac{7}{12}$

           $= \frac{9}{12}$

           $= \frac{3}{4}$

8. $\frac{2}{3} - \frac{3}{8} = \frac{2}{3} \cdot \frac{8}{8} - \frac{3}{8} \cdot \frac{3}{3}$

           $= \frac{16}{24} - \frac{9}{24}$

           $= \frac{7}{24}$

9. $\frac{-1}{2} + \frac{-7}{12} = \frac{-1}{2} \cdot \frac{6}{6} + \frac{-7}{12}$

           $= \frac{-6}{12} + \frac{-7}{12}$

           $= -\frac{13}{12}$

10. $\frac{7}{9} - \frac{4}{5} = \frac{7}{9} \cdot \frac{5}{5} - \frac{4}{5} \cdot \frac{9}{9}$

           $= \frac{35}{45} - \frac{36}{45}$

           $= -\frac{1}{45}$

11. $\frac{-11}{15} + \frac{2}{5} = \frac{-11}{15} + \frac{2}{5} \cdot \frac{3}{3}$

           $= \frac{-11}{15} + \frac{6}{15}$

           $= -\frac{5}{15}$

           $= -\frac{1}{3}$

12. $\frac{-3}{7} - \frac{1}{3} = \frac{-3}{7} \cdot \frac{3}{3} - \frac{1}{3} \cdot \frac{7}{7}$

           $= \frac{-9}{21} - \frac{7}{21}$

           $= -\frac{16}{21}$

13. $\frac{-3}{10} + \frac{7}{8} = \frac{-3}{10} \cdot \frac{4}{4} + \frac{7}{8} \cdot \frac{5}{5}$

           $= \frac{-12}{40} + \frac{35}{40}$

           $= \frac{23}{40}$

14. $\frac{1}{2} + \frac{5}{6} - \frac{7}{9} = \frac{1}{2} \cdot \frac{9}{9} + \frac{5}{6} \cdot \frac{3}{3} - \frac{7}{9} \cdot \frac{2}{2}$

           $= \frac{9}{18} + \frac{15}{18} - \frac{14}{18}$

           $= \frac{10}{18}$

           $= \frac{5}{9}$

15. $\dfrac{x}{3} + \dfrac{x}{6} = \dfrac{x}{3} \cdot \dfrac{2}{2} + \dfrac{x}{6}$

$\qquad = \dfrac{2x}{6} + \dfrac{x}{6}$

$\qquad = \dfrac{3x}{6}$

$\qquad = \dfrac{x}{2}$

16. $\dfrac{a}{8} - \dfrac{a}{12} = \dfrac{a}{8} \cdot \dfrac{3}{3} - \dfrac{a}{12} \cdot \dfrac{2}{2}$

$\qquad = \dfrac{3a}{24} - \dfrac{2a}{24}$

$\qquad = \dfrac{a}{24}$

17. $\dfrac{2}{x} + \dfrac{9}{10} = \dfrac{2}{x} \cdot \dfrac{10}{10} + \dfrac{9}{10} \cdot \dfrac{x}{x}$

$\qquad = \dfrac{20}{10x} + \dfrac{9x}{10x}$

$\qquad = \dfrac{20 + 9x}{10x}$

18. $\dfrac{4}{a} + \dfrac{11}{15} = \dfrac{4}{a} \cdot \dfrac{15}{15} + \dfrac{11}{15} \cdot \dfrac{a}{a}$

$\qquad = \dfrac{60}{15a} + \dfrac{11a}{15a}$

$\qquad = \dfrac{60 + 11a}{15a}$

19. $\dfrac{-2}{3t} - \dfrac{4}{9t} = \dfrac{-2}{3t} \cdot \dfrac{3}{3} - \dfrac{4}{9t}$

$\qquad = \dfrac{-6}{9t} - \dfrac{4}{9t}$

$\qquad = -\dfrac{10}{9t}$

20. $\dfrac{-7}{s} + \dfrac{4}{2s} = \dfrac{-7}{s} \cdot \dfrac{2}{2} + \dfrac{4}{2s}$

$\qquad = \dfrac{-14}{2s} + \dfrac{4}{2s}$

$\qquad = \dfrac{-10}{2s}$

$\qquad = \dfrac{-5}{s}$

21. $\dfrac{2}{n} - \dfrac{1}{3n} = \dfrac{2}{n} \cdot \dfrac{3}{3} - \dfrac{1}{3n}$

$\qquad = \dfrac{6}{3n} - \dfrac{1}{3n}$

$\qquad = \dfrac{5}{3n}$

22. $1\frac{2}{3} + 1\frac{3}{4} = \frac{5}{3} + \frac{7}{4}$

$\qquad = \frac{5}{3} \cdot \frac{4}{4} + \frac{7}{4} \cdot \frac{3}{3}$

$\qquad = \frac{20}{12} + \frac{21}{12}$

$\qquad = \frac{41}{12}$ or $3\frac{5}{12}$

23. To get the next fraction, add 1 to the absolute values of both the numerator and denominator and change the sign of the fraction to its opposite.

24. $\frac{5}{6}; -\frac{6}{7}$

25. $\frac{1}{2} + \left(-\frac{2}{3}\right) + \frac{3}{4} = \frac{1}{2} - \frac{2}{3} + \frac{3}{4}$

$\qquad = \frac{1}{2} \cdot \frac{6}{6} - \frac{2}{3} \cdot \frac{4}{4} + \frac{3}{4} \cdot \frac{3}{3}$

$\qquad = \frac{6}{12} - \frac{8}{12} + \frac{9}{12}$

$\qquad = \frac{7}{12}$

26. $\frac{1}{2} + \left(-\frac{2}{3}\right) + \frac{3}{4} + \left(-\frac{4}{5}\right) + \frac{5}{6} = \frac{1}{2} - \frac{2}{3} + \frac{3}{4} - \frac{4}{5} + \frac{5}{6}$

$\qquad = \frac{1}{2} \cdot \frac{30}{30} - \frac{2}{3} \cdot \frac{20}{20} + \frac{3}{4} \cdot \frac{15}{15} - \frac{4}{5} \cdot \frac{12}{12} + \frac{5}{6} \cdot \frac{10}{10}$

$\qquad = \frac{30}{60} - \frac{40}{60} + \frac{45}{60} - \frac{48}{60} + \frac{50}{60}$

$\qquad = \frac{37}{60}$

27. $1\frac{1}{2} + 1\frac{3}{4} + 2\frac{2}{3} + 1\frac{3}{4} = \frac{3}{2} + \frac{7}{4} + \frac{8}{3} + \frac{7}{4}$

$\qquad = \frac{3}{2} \cdot \frac{6}{6} + \frac{7}{4} \cdot \frac{3}{3} + \frac{8}{3} \cdot \frac{4}{4} + \frac{7}{4} \cdot \frac{3}{3}$

$\qquad = \frac{18}{12} + \frac{21}{12} + \frac{32}{12} + \frac{21}{12}$

$\qquad = \frac{92}{12}$

$\qquad = \frac{23}{3}$ or $7\frac{2}{3}$

28. $4\frac{2}{3} + 2\frac{1}{8} + 3\frac{3}{4} = \frac{14}{3} + \frac{17}{8} + \frac{15}{4}$

$$= \frac{14}{3} \cdot \frac{8}{8} + \frac{17}{8} \cdot \frac{3}{3} + \frac{15}{4} \cdot \frac{6}{6}$$

$$= \frac{112}{24} + \frac{51}{24} + \frac{90}{24}$$

$$= \frac{253}{24} \text{ or } 10\frac{13}{24}$$

29. $\frac{7}{25} + \frac{9}{50} = \frac{7}{25} \cdot \frac{2}{2} + \frac{9}{50}$

$$= \frac{14}{50} + \frac{9}{50}$$

$$= \frac{23}{50}$$

30. $\frac{3}{20} - \frac{11}{100} = \frac{3}{20} \cdot \frac{5}{5} - \frac{11}{100}$

$$= \frac{15}{100} - \frac{11}{100}$$

$$= \frac{4}{100}$$

$$= \frac{1}{25}$$

31. $\frac{11}{100} + \frac{7}{25} + \frac{7}{25} + \frac{9}{50} + \frac{3}{20} = \frac{11}{100} + \frac{7}{25} \cdot \frac{4}{4} + \frac{7}{25} \cdot \frac{4}{4} + \frac{9}{50} \cdot \frac{2}{2} + \frac{3}{20} \cdot \frac{5}{5}$

$$= \frac{11}{100} + \frac{28}{100} + \frac{28}{100} + \frac{18}{100} + \frac{15}{100}$$

$$= \frac{100}{100}$$

$$= 1$$

32. a. $P = 4\frac{1}{2} + 4\frac{1}{2} + 6\frac{1}{8} + 6\frac{1}{8}$

$$= \frac{9}{2} + \frac{9}{2} + \frac{49}{8} + \frac{49}{8}$$

$$= \frac{36}{8} + \frac{36}{8} + \frac{49}{8} + \frac{49}{8}$$

$$= \frac{170}{8}$$

$$= 21\frac{2}{8}$$

$$= 21\frac{1}{4} \text{ in.}$$

b. $4\frac{1}{2} - \left(1\frac{1}{4} + 1\frac{1}{4}\right) = 4\frac{1}{2} - 2\frac{2}{4}$

$$= 4\frac{1}{2} - 2\frac{1}{2}$$

$$= 2 \text{ in.}$$

$6\frac{1}{8} - \left(1\frac{1}{4} + 1\frac{1}{4}\right) = 6\frac{1}{8} - 2\frac{2}{4}$

$$= 6\frac{1}{8} - 2\frac{4}{8}$$

$$= \frac{49}{8} - \frac{20}{8}$$

$$= \frac{29}{8}$$

$$= 3\frac{5}{8} \text{ in.}$$

The dimensions are 2 inches by $3\frac{5}{8}$ inches.

33. C; $10\frac{3}{8} - 2\frac{1}{2} - 4\frac{1}{8} = 10\frac{3}{8} - 2\frac{4}{8} - 4\frac{1}{8}$

$$= \frac{83}{8} - \frac{20}{8} - \frac{33}{8}$$

$$= \frac{30}{8}$$

$$= 3\frac{6}{8}$$

$$= 3\frac{3}{4} \text{ cm}$$

34. C; $15\frac{4}{7} + 27\frac{6}{11} = \frac{109}{7} + \frac{303}{11}$

$$= \frac{1199}{77} + \frac{2121}{77}$$

$$= \frac{3320}{77}$$

$$= 43\frac{9}{77}$$

35.–40. *Sample answers:*

35. $\frac{1}{12}$

36. $\frac{1}{3}$

37. $\frac{1}{3}$

38. $\frac{1}{12}$

39. $\frac{1}{24}$

40. $\frac{3}{24}$

7.3 Exploring Fractions and Decimals

ONGOING ASSESSMENT

1. $\frac{3}{7} + \frac{5}{16} \approx 0.429 + 0.3125 \approx 0.74$

2. $\frac{12}{13} - \frac{5}{7} \approx 0.923 - 0.714 \approx 0.21$

EXERCISES

1. $\frac{7}{9} + \frac{11}{19} \approx 0.778 + 0.579$ *Write as decimals rounded to 3 decimal places.*

$= 1.357$ *Add decimals.*

≈ 1.36 *Round to 2 decimal places.*

2. $x + \left(\frac{2}{5} + \frac{1}{12} + \frac{11}{60}\right) = 1$

$x + 0.\overline{6} = 1$

$x \approx 0.33;$

Sample answer: I chose decimals so I could use a calculator.

3. 0.67 is greater.

$0.67 - \frac{2}{3} = \frac{67}{100} - \frac{2}{3}$

$= \frac{67}{100} \cdot \frac{3}{3} - \frac{2}{3} \cdot \frac{100}{100}$

$= \frac{201}{300} - \frac{200}{300}$

$= \frac{1}{300}$

$= 0.00\overline{3}$

It is $0.00\overline{3}$ greater.

4. $\frac{2}{5} - \frac{10}{13} \approx -0.37$

5.
$$\begin{array}{r} 0.31 \\ + 0.55 \\ \hline 0.86 \end{array}$$

6.
$$\begin{array}{r} 1.823 \\ + 0.021 \\ \hline 1.844 \end{array}$$

7.
$$\begin{array}{r} 3.73 \\ - 2.09 \\ \hline 1.64 \end{array}$$

8.
$$\begin{array}{r} 2.009 \\ - 1.793 \\ \hline 0.216 \end{array}$$

9. $\frac{17}{36} + \frac{14}{25} \approx 0.472 + 0.56$

$= 1.032$

$\approx 1.03,$ or $\frac{929}{900}$

10. $\frac{7}{12} + \frac{5}{9} \approx 0.583 + 0.556$

$= 1.139$

$\approx 1.14,$ or $\frac{41}{36}$

11. *Sample answer:*

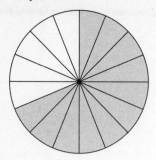

12. *Sample answer:*

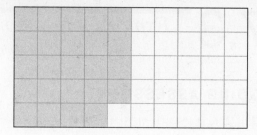

13. *Sample answer:*

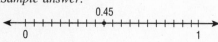

14. *Sample answer:*

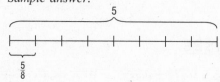

Note: $\frac{5}{8} = 0.625$

15. $\frac{73}{111} + \frac{54}{109} + \frac{82}{89} - \frac{76}{127} \approx 0.658 + 0.495 + 0.9213 - 0.5984$

$$= 1.475$$
$$\approx 1.48$$

16. $2y - \left(\frac{21}{56}y + \frac{32}{99}y + \frac{3}{25}y\right) \approx 2y - (0.375y + 0.323y + 0.12y)$

$$= 2y - 0.818y$$
$$= 1.182y$$
$$\approx 1.18y$$

17. $6.50 \div 4\frac{1}{3} = 6.50 \div \frac{13}{3}$

$$= 6.50 \times \frac{3}{13}$$
$$= \frac{19.50}{13}$$
$$= \$1.50$$

18. $\frac{12}{25} + \frac{1}{20} + \frac{4}{25} + \frac{3}{20} = 0.48 + 0.05 + 0.16 + 0.15$

$$= 0.84$$

19. $1 - 0.84 = 0.16$

20. $\frac{3}{20} + \frac{1}{20} = 0.15 + 0.05 = 0.20$

21. $2\frac{1}{2} + \frac{3}{4} + 3 = \frac{5}{2} + \frac{3}{4} + 3$

$$= \frac{10}{4} + \frac{3}{4} + \frac{12}{4}$$
$$= \frac{25}{4}$$

$10 - \frac{25}{4} = \frac{40}{4} - \frac{25}{4}$

$$= \frac{15}{4}$$
$$= 3\frac{3}{4} \text{ min}$$

22. B

23. D; $\frac{-9}{11} \overset{?}{>} -0.9$

$-0.82 > -0.9$

24. $\frac{1}{10} = 0.1$

25. $\frac{5}{12} = 0.41\overline{6}$

26. $\frac{3}{8} = 0.375$

7.4

GEOMETRY CONNECTION:
Multiplication of Rational Numbers

ONGOING ASSESSMENT

1. $\frac{3}{5} \cdot \frac{10}{3} = \frac{30}{15}$ *Multiply numerators and multiply denominators.*

     $= 2$ *Simplify.*

2. $\frac{5}{4} \cdot \frac{1}{2} = \frac{5}{8}$ *Multiply numerators and multiply denominators.*

3. $\frac{6}{7} \cdot 14 = \frac{84}{7}$ *Multiply.*

     $= 12$ *Simplify.*

EXERCISES

1. To multiply fractions, multiply the numerators and multiply the denominators.

2. $\frac{4}{7} \cdot \frac{3}{5} = \frac{4 \cdot 3}{7 \cdot 5}$

     $= \frac{12}{35}$

3. $\frac{4}{7} \cdot \frac{7}{4} = \frac{4 \cdot 7}{7 \cdot 4}$

     $= \frac{1}{1}$

     $= 1$

4. $\frac{5x}{9} \cdot \frac{2}{4} = \frac{5x \cdot 2}{9 \cdot 4}$

     $= \frac{5 \cdot x \cdot 2}{9 \cdot 2 \cdot 2}$

     $= \frac{5x}{18}$

5. $1\frac{3}{5} \cdot 2\frac{1}{2} = \frac{8}{5} \cdot \frac{5}{2}$

     $= \frac{8 \cdot 5}{5 \cdot 2}$

     $= \frac{4 \cdot 2 \cdot 5}{5 \cdot 2}$

     $= 4$

6. $\frac{2}{3}$ unit by $\frac{4}{5}$ unit;

     $A = \frac{2}{3} \cdot \frac{4}{5}$

     $= \frac{2 \cdot 4}{3 \cdot 5}$

     $= \frac{8}{15}$ units^2

7. $\frac{6}{7}$ unit by $\frac{3}{6}$ unit

     $A = \frac{6}{7} \cdot \frac{3}{6}$

     $= \frac{6 \cdot 3}{7 \cdot 6}$

     $= \frac{3}{7}$ units^2

8. $\frac{3}{4}$ unit by $\frac{5}{6}$ unit

     $A = \frac{3}{4} \cdot \frac{5}{6}$

     $= \frac{3 \cdot 5}{4 \cdot 6}$

     $= \frac{3 \cdot 5}{4 \cdot 2 \cdot 3}$

     $= \frac{5}{8}$ units^2

9. $\frac{7}{8}$ unit by $\frac{3}{4}$ unit

     $A = \frac{7}{8} \cdot \frac{3}{4}$

     $= \frac{7 \cdot 3}{8 \cdot 4}$

     $= \frac{21}{32}$ units^2

10. $\frac{1}{4} \cdot \frac{4}{5} = \frac{1 \cdot 4}{4 \cdot 5}$

     $= \frac{1}{5}$

11. $\dfrac{-2}{3} \cdot \dfrac{8}{9} = \dfrac{-2 \cdot 8}{3 \cdot 9}$

$= -\dfrac{16}{27}$

12. $\dfrac{-5}{6} \cdot \dfrac{-3}{4} = \dfrac{-5 \cdot (-3)}{6 \cdot 4}$

$= \dfrac{-5 \cdot (-1) \cdot \not{3}}{2 \cdot \not{3} \cdot 4}$

$= \dfrac{5}{8}$

13. $1\dfrac{2}{5} \cdot 2\dfrac{2}{7} = \dfrac{7}{5} \cdot \dfrac{16}{7}$

$= \dfrac{7 \cdot 16}{5 \cdot 7}$

$= \dfrac{16}{5}$

14. $1\dfrac{1}{5} \cdot \left(-6\dfrac{2}{3}\right) = \dfrac{6}{5} \cdot \dfrac{-20}{3}$

$= \dfrac{6 \cdot (-20)}{5 \cdot 3}$

$= \dfrac{\not{3} \cdot 2 \cdot (-4) \cdot \not{5}}{\not{5} \cdot \not{3}}$

$= -8$

15. $-4\dfrac{1}{2} \cdot \left(-2\dfrac{5}{9}\right) = -\dfrac{9}{2} \cdot \left(-\dfrac{23}{9}\right)$

$= \dfrac{-9 \cdot (-23)}{2 \cdot 9}$

$= \dfrac{\not{9} \cdot (-1) \cdot (-23)}{2 \cdot \not{9}}$

$= \dfrac{23}{2}$

16. $\dfrac{2}{3} \cdot \dfrac{-4}{7} \cdot \dfrac{4}{5} = \dfrac{2 \cdot (-4) \cdot 4}{3 \cdot 7 \cdot 5}$

$= -\dfrac{32}{105}$

17. $\dfrac{-4}{9} \cdot \dfrac{2}{3} \cdot \dfrac{-3}{8} = \dfrac{-4 \cdot 2 \cdot (-3)}{9 \cdot 3 \cdot 8}$

$= \dfrac{\not{2} \cdot 2 \cdot (-1) \cdot \not{2} \cdot \not{3} \cdot (-1)}{3 \cdot 3 \cdot \not{3} \cdot \not{2} \cdot \not{2} \cdot \not{2}}$

$= \dfrac{1}{9}$

18. $\dfrac{5x}{6} \cdot 12 = \dfrac{5x}{6} \cdot \dfrac{12}{1}$

$= \dfrac{5x \cdot 12}{6 \cdot 1}$

$= \dfrac{5x \cdot \not{6} \cdot 2}{\not{6} \cdot 1}$

$= 10x$

19. $7 \cdot \dfrac{8y}{3} = \dfrac{7}{1} \cdot \dfrac{8y}{3}$

$= \dfrac{7 \cdot 8y}{1 \cdot 3}$

$= \dfrac{56y}{3}$

20. $\dfrac{-13t}{20} \cdot \dfrac{-1}{2} = \dfrac{-13t \cdot (-1)}{20 \cdot 2}$

$= \dfrac{13t}{40}$

21. $\dfrac{-5}{6} \cdot \dfrac{-6a}{15} = \dfrac{-5 \cdot (-6a)}{6 \cdot 15}$

$= \dfrac{\not{5} \cdot (-1) \cdot \not{6} \cdot (-a)}{\not{6} \cdot \not{5} \cdot 3}$

$= \dfrac{a}{3}$

22. $A = 5\dfrac{1}{3} \cdot 2\dfrac{5}{8}$

$= \dfrac{16}{3} \cdot \dfrac{21}{8}$

$= \dfrac{16 \cdot 21}{3 \cdot 8}$

$= \dfrac{2 \cdot \not{8} \cdot \not{3} \cdot 7}{\not{3} \cdot \not{8}}$

$= 14 \text{ yd}^2$

23. $A = \dfrac{1}{2} \cdot \left(1\dfrac{5}{9}\right) \cdot \left(2\dfrac{4}{7}\right)$

$= \dfrac{1}{2} \cdot \dfrac{14}{9} \cdot \dfrac{18}{7}$

$= \dfrac{1 \cdot 14 \cdot 18}{2 \cdot 9 \cdot 7}$

$= \dfrac{1 \cdot 2 \cdot \not{7} \cdot 2 \cdot \not{9}}{2 \cdot \not{9} \cdot \not{7}}$

$= 2 \text{ in.}^2$

24. $A = 3\dfrac{2}{3} \cdot 2\dfrac{1}{8}$

$= \dfrac{11}{3} \cdot \dfrac{17}{8}$

$= \dfrac{11 \cdot 17}{3 \cdot 8}$

$= \dfrac{187}{24}$

$= 7\dfrac{19}{24} \text{ ft}^2$

25. $\dfrac{9}{16} \cdot \dfrac{6}{13} \approx 0.260$

26. $\dfrac{17}{25} \cdot 2\dfrac{3}{4} = \dfrac{17}{25} \cdot \dfrac{11}{4}$

$= 1.87$

27. $\dfrac{23}{48} \cdot (-7) \approx -3.354$

28. $\dfrac{-21}{32} \cdot \dfrac{2}{5} \approx -0.263$

29.
$$0.25 = \frac{25}{100}$$
$$= \frac{1}{4}$$

$$x = 0.\overline{6}$$
$$10x = 6.\overline{6}$$
$$9x = 6$$
$$x = \frac{2}{3}$$

$$\frac{1}{4} \cdot \frac{2}{3} = \frac{1 \cdot 2}{4 \cdot 3}$$
$$= \frac{1 \cdot \cancel{2}}{\cancel{2} \cdot 2 \cdot 3}$$
$$= \frac{1}{6}$$

30.
$$x = 0.\overline{3}$$
$$10x = 3.\overline{3}$$
$$9x = 3$$
$$x = \frac{1}{3}$$
$$0.75 = \frac{75}{100}$$
$$= \frac{3}{4}$$
$$\frac{1}{3} \cdot \frac{3}{4} = \frac{1 \cdot \cancel{3}}{\cancel{3} \cdot 4}$$
$$= \frac{1}{4}$$

31.
$$0.2 = \frac{2}{10}$$
$$= \frac{1}{5}$$
$$0.625 = \frac{625}{1000}$$
$$= \frac{\cancel{125} \cdot 5}{\cancel{125} \cdot 8}$$
$$= \frac{5}{8}$$
$$\frac{1}{5} \cdot \frac{5}{8} = \frac{1 \cdot \cancel{5}}{\cancel{5} \cdot 8}$$
$$= \frac{1}{8}$$

32.
$$0.375 = \frac{375}{1000}$$
$$= \frac{\cancel{125} \cdot 3}{\cancel{125} \cdot 8}$$
$$= \frac{3}{8}$$
$$0.7 = \frac{7}{10}$$
$$\frac{3}{8} \cdot \frac{7}{10} = \frac{3 \cdot 7}{8 \cdot 10}$$
$$= \frac{21}{80}$$

33. Length of Allosaurus $= \dfrac{1}{3} \cdot 90$
$$= \frac{1}{3} \cdot \frac{90}{1}$$
$$= \frac{1 \cdot 90}{3 \cdot 1}$$
$$= \frac{1 \cdot \cancel{3} \cdot 30}{\cancel{3} \cdot 1}$$
$$= 30 \text{ feet}$$

34. See Exercise 33.
Stegosaurus $= \dfrac{2}{3} \cdot 30$
$$= \frac{2}{3} \cdot \frac{30}{1}$$
$$= \frac{2 \cdot 30}{3 \cdot 1}$$
$$= \frac{2 \cdot \cancel{3} \cdot 10}{\cancel{3} \cdot 1}$$
$$= 20 \text{ feet}$$

35. See Exercise 34.
Ankylosaurus $= \dfrac{3}{4} \cdot 20$
$$= \frac{3}{4} \cdot \frac{20}{1}$$
$$= \frac{3 \cdot 20}{4 \cdot 1}$$
$$= \frac{3 \cdot \cancel{4} \cdot 5}{\cancel{4} \cdot 1}$$
$$= 15 \text{ feet}$$

36. See Exercise 35.
Tyrannosaurus $= 2\dfrac{2}{3} \cdot 15$
$$= \frac{8}{3} \cdot 15$$
$$= \frac{8}{3} \cdot \frac{15}{1}$$
$$= \frac{8 \cdot 15}{3 \cdot 1}$$
$$= \frac{8 \cdot \cancel{3} \cdot 5}{\cancel{3} \cdot 1}$$
$$= 40 \text{ feet}$$

37. $\dfrac{1}{100} + \dfrac{1}{100} + \dfrac{10}{100} = \dfrac{12}{100}$
$$= \frac{3}{25}$$

38. $\dfrac{10}{100} + \dfrac{1}{100} + \dfrac{25}{100} = \dfrac{36}{100}$
$$= \frac{9}{25}$$

39. $\dfrac{10}{100} + \dfrac{10}{100} + \dfrac{5}{100} + \dfrac{5}{100} = \dfrac{30}{100}$
$$= \frac{3}{10}$$

40. A; $8 \times 6\frac{3}{4} = 8 \times \frac{27}{4}$

$\qquad = \frac{216}{4}$

$\qquad = 54 \text{ ft}^2$

41. Answers vary.

Spiral REVIEW

1. ÷

2. +

3. ÷

4. −

5. ×

6. ÷

7. $a + \frac{2}{3} = \frac{4}{3}$

$a + \frac{2}{3} - \frac{2}{3} = \frac{4}{3} - \frac{2}{3}$

$a = \frac{2}{3}$

8. $y + \frac{1}{4} = \frac{3}{4}$

$y + \frac{1}{4} - \frac{1}{4} = \frac{3}{4} - \frac{1}{4}$

$y = \frac{2}{4}$

$y = \frac{1}{2}$

9. $\frac{14}{9} = b - \frac{13}{9}$

$\frac{14}{9} + \frac{13}{9} = b - \frac{13}{9} + \frac{13}{9}$

$\frac{27}{9} = b$

$3 = b$

10. $x - \frac{3}{10} = \frac{-9}{10}$

$x - \frac{3}{10} + \frac{3}{10} = \frac{-9}{10} + \frac{3}{10}$

$x = \frac{-6}{10}$

$x = \frac{-3}{5}$

11. Multiples of 2: 2, 4, 6, 8, 10, 12, 14, . . .

Multiples of 7: 7, 14, . . .

The LCM is 14.

12. $10 = 2 \cdot 5$

$16 = 2^4$

The LCM is $2^4 \cdot 5 = 80$.

13. $3 = 3$

$4 = 2^2$

$5 = 5$

The LCM is $2^2 \cdot 3 \cdot 5 = 60$.

14. $4 = 2^2$

$5 = 5$

$6 = 2 \cdot 3$

The LCM is $2^2 \cdot 3 \cdot 5 = 60$.

15. $\frac{1}{20} + \frac{1}{4} = \frac{1}{20} + \frac{1}{4} \cdot \frac{5}{5}$

$\qquad = \frac{1}{20} + \frac{5}{20}$

$\qquad = \frac{6}{20}$

$\qquad = \frac{3}{10}$

16. $\frac{2}{3} - \frac{1}{5} = \frac{2}{3} \cdot \frac{5}{5} - \frac{1}{5} \cdot \frac{3}{3}$

$\qquad = \frac{10}{15} - \frac{3}{15}$

$\qquad = \frac{7}{15}$

17. $\frac{99}{100} - \frac{6}{25} = \frac{99}{100} - \frac{6}{25} \cdot \frac{4}{4}$

$\qquad = \frac{99}{100} - \frac{24}{100}$

$\qquad = \frac{75}{100}$

$\qquad = \frac{3}{4}$

18. $\frac{4}{5} + \frac{6}{25} = \frac{4}{5} \cdot \frac{5}{5} + \frac{6}{25}$

$\qquad = \frac{20}{25} + \frac{6}{25}$

$\qquad = \frac{26}{25}$

19. $\dfrac{\text{Number of A's}}{\text{Number of Letters}} = \frac{3}{7}$

Mid-Chapter ASSESSMENT

1. $\frac{1}{11} + \frac{3}{11} = \frac{1+3}{11}$

$\qquad = \frac{4}{11}$

2. $\frac{5}{6} - \frac{1}{6} = \frac{5-1}{6}$

$\qquad = \frac{4}{6}$

$\qquad = \frac{2 \cdot 2}{2 \cdot 3}$

$\qquad = \frac{2}{3}$

3. $\dfrac{7}{10} - \dfrac{4}{25} = \dfrac{7}{10} \cdot \dfrac{5}{5} - \dfrac{4}{25} \cdot \dfrac{2}{2}$

$\phantom{\dfrac{7}{10} - \dfrac{4}{25}} = \dfrac{35}{50} - \dfrac{8}{50}$

$\phantom{\dfrac{7}{10} - \dfrac{4}{25}} = \dfrac{35 - 8}{50}$

$\phantom{\dfrac{7}{10} - \dfrac{4}{25}} = \dfrac{27}{50}$

4. $\dfrac{9}{10} - \dfrac{1}{2} = \dfrac{9}{10} - \dfrac{1}{2} \cdot \dfrac{5}{5}$

$\phantom{\dfrac{9}{10} - \dfrac{1}{2}} = \dfrac{9}{10} - \dfrac{5}{10}$

$\phantom{\dfrac{9}{10} - \dfrac{1}{2}} = \dfrac{9 - 5}{10}$

$\phantom{\dfrac{9}{10} - \dfrac{1}{2}} = \dfrac{4}{10}$

$\phantom{\dfrac{9}{10} - \dfrac{1}{2}} = \dfrac{\cancel{2} \cdot 2}{\cancel{2} \cdot 5}$

$\phantom{\dfrac{9}{10} - \dfrac{1}{2}} = \dfrac{2}{5}$

5. $-\dfrac{4}{7} \cdot \dfrac{7}{8} = \dfrac{-4 \cdot 7}{7 \cdot 8}$

$\phantom{-\dfrac{4}{7} \cdot \dfrac{7}{8}} = \dfrac{-1 \cdot \cancel{4} \cdot \cancel{7}}{\cancel{7} \cdot \cancel{4} \cdot 2}$

$\phantom{-\dfrac{4}{7} \cdot \dfrac{7}{8}} = -\dfrac{1}{2}$

6. $\dfrac{2}{3} \cdot \dfrac{3}{4} \cdot \dfrac{4}{5} = \dfrac{2 \cdot \cancel{3} \cdot \cancel{4}}{\cancel{3} \cdot \cancel{4} \cdot 5}$

$\phantom{\dfrac{2}{3} \cdot \dfrac{3}{4} \cdot \dfrac{4}{5}} = \dfrac{2}{5}$

7. $\dfrac{7}{10} \cdot 2 = \dfrac{7 \cdot 2}{10}$

$\phantom{\dfrac{7}{10} \cdot 2} = \dfrac{14}{10}$

$\phantom{\dfrac{7}{10} \cdot 2} = \dfrac{7}{5}$

8. $\dfrac{2}{5} \cdot \left(-\dfrac{6}{5}\right) = \dfrac{2 \cdot (-6)}{5 \cdot 5}$

$\phantom{\dfrac{2}{5} \cdot \left(-\dfrac{6}{5}\right)} = -\dfrac{12}{25}$

9. $\dfrac{3}{8} + \dfrac{9}{17} \approx 0.375 + 0.529$

$\phantom{\dfrac{3}{8} + \dfrac{9}{17}} \approx 0.90$

10. $\dfrac{18}{29}x + \dfrac{35}{48}x \approx 0.621x + 0.729x$

$\phantom{\dfrac{18}{29}x + \dfrac{35}{48}x} \approx 1.35x$

11. $\dfrac{7}{9}y - \dfrac{7}{11}y \approx 0.778y - 0.636y$

$\phantom{\dfrac{7}{9}y - \dfrac{7}{11}y} \approx 0.14y$

12. $\dfrac{27}{31} - \dfrac{11}{50} \approx 0.871 - 0.22$

$\phantom{\dfrac{27}{31} - \dfrac{11}{50}} \approx 0.65$

13. $P = 2\left(5\dfrac{1}{3}\right) + 2\left(2\dfrac{2}{5}\right)$

$ = 2\left(\dfrac{16}{3}\right) + 2\left(\dfrac{12}{5}\right)$

$ = \dfrac{2}{1} \cdot \dfrac{16}{3} + \dfrac{2}{1} \cdot \dfrac{12}{5}$

$ = \dfrac{2 \cdot 16}{1 \cdot 3} + \dfrac{2 \cdot 12}{1 \cdot 5}$

$ = \dfrac{32}{3} + \dfrac{24}{5}$

$ = \dfrac{32}{3} \cdot \dfrac{5}{5} + \dfrac{24}{5} \cdot \dfrac{3}{3}$

$ = \dfrac{160}{15} + \dfrac{72}{15}$

$ = \dfrac{232}{15}$

$ = 15\dfrac{7}{15}$ in.

$A = \left(5\dfrac{1}{3}\right)\left(2\dfrac{2}{5}\right)$

$ = \dfrac{16}{3} \cdot \dfrac{12}{5}$

$ = \dfrac{16 \cdot 12}{3 \cdot 5}$

$ = \dfrac{16 \cdot \cancel{3} \cdot 4}{\cancel{3} \cdot 5}$

$ = \dfrac{64}{5}$

$ = 12\dfrac{4}{5}$ in.^{2}

14. $A = \dfrac{7}{8} \cdot \dfrac{1}{2}$

$ = \dfrac{7 \cdot 1}{8 \cdot 2}$

$ = \dfrac{7}{16}$ units^2

15. $30 \cdot \frac{1}{3} = \frac{30}{1} \cdot \frac{1}{3}$

$= \frac{30}{3}$

$= \$10$

16. $30 \cdot \frac{1}{2} = \frac{30}{1} \cdot \frac{1}{2}$

$= \frac{30}{2}$

$= 15$

$30 - 15 = 15$

The least you could expect to pay is $15.

17. $\frac{8}{11}$ is larger.

$\frac{8}{11} - 0.72 = \frac{8}{11} - \frac{72}{100}$

$= \frac{8}{11} - \frac{18}{25}$

$= \frac{8}{11} \cdot \frac{25}{25} - \frac{18}{25} \cdot \frac{11}{11}$

$= \frac{200}{275} - \frac{198}{275}$

$= \frac{2}{275}$

$= 0.00\overline{72}$

It is $0.00\overline{72}$ larger.

18. A. $2.85 \cdot \frac{1}{5} = \frac{2.85}{1} \cdot \frac{1}{5} = \frac{2.85}{5} = 0.57$

B. $2.85 \cdot \frac{1}{4} = \frac{2.85}{1} \cdot \frac{1}{4} = \frac{2.85}{4} = 0.7125$

C. $2.85 \cdot \frac{1}{3} = \frac{2.85}{1} \cdot \frac{1}{3} = \frac{2.85}{3} = 0.95$

Choice B, one-fourth of $2.85 cannot be represented exactly with U.S. coins.

7.5 *Division of Rational Numbers*

ONGOING ASSESSMENT

1.–2. Answers vary.

1. dollars

2. hours

EXERCISES

1. $\frac{5}{1} = 5$

2. $-\frac{3}{2}$

3. $\frac{1}{7}$

4. $\frac{t}{4}$

5. The reciprocal of 3 is $\frac{1}{3}$, not $\frac{3}{1}$.

$\frac{5}{6} \div 3 = \frac{5}{6} \cdot \frac{1}{3}$

$= \frac{5 \cdot 1}{6 \cdot 3}$

$= \frac{5}{18}$

6. Multiply the denominators also, not just the numerators.

$-\frac{4}{3} \div \frac{3}{2} = \frac{-4}{3} \cdot \frac{2}{3}$

$= \frac{-4 \cdot 2}{3 \cdot 3}$

$= -\frac{8}{9}$

7. $\frac{1}{2} \div \frac{5}{6} = \frac{1}{2} \cdot \frac{6}{5}$

$= \frac{1 \cdot 6}{2 \cdot 5}$

$= \frac{1 \cdot \cancel{2} \cdot 3}{\cancel{2} \cdot 5}$

$= \frac{3}{5}$

8. $6 \div \dfrac{4}{9} = \dfrac{6}{1} \cdot \dfrac{9}{4}$

$= \dfrac{6 \cdot 9}{1 \cdot 4}$

$= \dfrac{\cancel{2} \cdot 3 \cdot 9}{1 \cdot \cancel{2} \cdot 2}$

$= \dfrac{27}{2}$

9. $\dfrac{n}{3} \div \dfrac{3}{2} = \dfrac{n}{3} \cdot \dfrac{2}{3}$

$= \dfrac{n \cdot 2}{3 \cdot 3}$

$= \dfrac{2n}{9}$

10. $3\dfrac{1}{2} \div \dfrac{4}{x} = \dfrac{7}{2} \cdot \dfrac{x}{4}$

$= \dfrac{7 \cdot x}{2 \cdot 4}$

$= \dfrac{7x}{8}$

11. 4

12. $\dfrac{x}{3}$

13. $\dfrac{5}{7a}$

14. $-2\dfrac{2}{3} = -\dfrac{8}{3}$

Reciprocal: $-\dfrac{3}{8}$

15. Multiply by the reciprocal of $\frac{3}{5}$, not by the reciprocal of $-\frac{3}{2}$.

$-\dfrac{3}{2} \div \dfrac{3}{5} = -\dfrac{3}{2} \cdot \dfrac{5}{3}$

$= \dfrac{-3 \cdot 5}{2 \cdot 3}$

$= \dfrac{-1 \cdot \cancel{3} \cdot 5}{2 \cdot \cancel{3}}$

$= -\dfrac{5}{2}$

16. The reciprocal of $2\frac{1}{2}$ is $\frac{2}{5}$, not $\frac{5}{2}$.

$8 \div 2\dfrac{1}{2} = 8 \div \dfrac{5}{2}$

$= \dfrac{8}{1} \cdot \dfrac{2}{5}$

$= \dfrac{8 \cdot 2}{1 \cdot 5}$

$= \dfrac{16}{5}$

17. Multiply by the reciprocal of $\frac{1}{3}$, not by $\frac{1}{3}$.

$\dfrac{1}{3} \div \dfrac{1}{3} = \dfrac{1}{3} \cdot \dfrac{3}{1}$

$= \dfrac{1 \cdot \cancel{3}}{\cancel{3} \cdot 1}$

$= 1$

18. $\dfrac{3}{2} \div \dfrac{1}{2} = \dfrac{3}{2} \cdot \dfrac{2}{1}$

$= \dfrac{3 \cdot \cancel{2}}{\cancel{2} \cdot 1}$

$= 3$

19. $\dfrac{3}{2} \div \dfrac{1}{3} = \dfrac{3}{2} \cdot \dfrac{3}{1}$

$= \dfrac{3 \cdot 3}{2 \cdot 1}$

$= \dfrac{9}{2}$

20. $\dfrac{3}{2} \div \dfrac{1}{4} = \dfrac{3}{2} \cdot \dfrac{4}{1}$

$= \dfrac{3 \cdot 4}{2 \cdot 1}$

$= \dfrac{3 \cdot \cancel{2} \cdot 2}{\cancel{2} \cdot 1}$

$= 6$

21. $\dfrac{3}{2} \div \dfrac{1}{5} = \dfrac{3}{2} \cdot \dfrac{5}{1}$

$= \dfrac{3 \cdot 5}{2 \cdot 1}$

$= \dfrac{15}{2}$

22. $\dfrac{3}{4} \div 2 = \dfrac{3}{4} \cdot \dfrac{1}{2}$

$= \dfrac{3 \cdot 1}{4 \cdot 2}$

$= \dfrac{3}{8}$

23. $3 \div \dfrac{-5}{6} = \dfrac{3}{1} \cdot \dfrac{6}{-5}$

$= \dfrac{3 \cdot 6}{1 \cdot (-5)}$

$= -\dfrac{18}{5}$

24. $\dfrac{-1}{2} \div \dfrac{1}{3} = \dfrac{-1}{2} \cdot \dfrac{3}{1}$

$= \dfrac{-1 \cdot 3}{2 \cdot 1}$

$= \dfrac{-3}{2}$

25. $\dfrac{7}{4} \div \dfrac{1}{-4} = \dfrac{7}{4} \cdot \dfrac{-4}{1}$

$= \dfrac{7 \cdot (-4)}{4 \cdot 1}$

$= \dfrac{7 \cdot (-1) \cdot \cancel{4}}{\cancel{4} \cdot 1}$

$= -7$

26. $3\dfrac{1}{2} \div \dfrac{3}{4} = \dfrac{7}{2} \cdot \dfrac{4}{3}$

$= \dfrac{7 \cdot 4}{2 \cdot 3}$

$= \dfrac{7 \cdot \cancel{2} \cdot 2}{\cancel{2} \cdot 3}$

$= \dfrac{14}{3}$

27. $\dfrac{4}{5} \div 1\dfrac{1}{2} = \dfrac{4}{5} \div \dfrac{3}{2}$

$= \dfrac{4}{5} \cdot \dfrac{2}{3}$

$= \dfrac{4 \cdot 2}{5 \cdot 3}$

$= \dfrac{8}{15}$

28. $\dfrac{x}{2} \div (-4) = \dfrac{x}{2} \cdot \dfrac{1}{-4}$

$= \dfrac{x \cdot 1}{2 \cdot (-4)}$

$= -\dfrac{x}{8}$

29. $\dfrac{-3}{5} \div \dfrac{9}{x} = \dfrac{-3}{5} \cdot \dfrac{x}{9}$

$= \dfrac{-3 \cdot x}{5 \cdot 9}$

$= \dfrac{-1 \cdot \cancel{3} \cdot x}{5 \cdot \cancel{3} \cdot 3}$

$= -\dfrac{x}{15}$

30. $6\dfrac{2}{3} \div a = \dfrac{20}{3} \cdot \dfrac{1}{a}$

$= \dfrac{20 \cdot 1}{3 \cdot a}$

$= \dfrac{20}{3a}$

31. $n \div 1\dfrac{1}{4} = n \div \dfrac{5}{4}$

$= \dfrac{n}{1} \cdot \dfrac{4}{5}$

$= \dfrac{n \cdot 4}{1 \cdot 5}$

$= \dfrac{4n}{5}$

32. $\dfrac{1}{y} \div \dfrac{4}{y} = \dfrac{1}{y} \cdot \dfrac{y}{4}$

$= \dfrac{1 \cdot \cancel{y}}{\cancel{y} \cdot 4}$

$= \dfrac{1}{4}$

33. $\dfrac{3b}{2} \div \dfrac{9b}{5} = \dfrac{3b}{2} \cdot \dfrac{5}{9b}$

$= \dfrac{3b \cdot 5}{2 \cdot 9b}$

$= \dfrac{\cancel{3b} \cdot 5}{2 \cdot 3 \cdot \cancel{3b}}$

$= \dfrac{5}{6}$

34. $\dfrac{1}{4} \div 2 = \dfrac{1}{4} \cdot \dfrac{1}{2}$

$= \dfrac{1 \cdot 1}{4 \cdot 2}$

$= \dfrac{1}{8}$

35. $\dfrac{1}{4} \div 3 = \dfrac{1}{4} \cdot \dfrac{1}{3}$

$= \dfrac{1 \cdot 1}{4 \cdot 3}$

$= \dfrac{1}{12}$

36. $\dfrac{1}{4} \div 4 = \dfrac{1}{4} \cdot \dfrac{1}{4}$

$= \dfrac{1 \cdot 1}{4 \cdot 4}$

$= \dfrac{1}{16}$

37. $\dfrac{1}{4} \div 5 = \dfrac{1}{4} \cdot \dfrac{1}{5}$

$= \dfrac{1 \cdot 1}{4 \cdot 5}$

$= \dfrac{1}{20}$

38. 0.13; 0.08; 0.06; 0.05
Pattern: Each denominator, after the first, is 4 more than the preceding denominator. The result gets smaller and smaller.

39. $11 \div 2\dfrac{3}{4} = 11 \div \dfrac{11}{4}$

$= 11 \cdot \dfrac{4}{11}$

$= \dfrac{\cancel{11} \cdot 4}{\cancel{11}}$

$= 4$

You will ride the trail in 4 segments, so you will stop and rest 3 times.

40. $12 \div 3\dfrac{3}{4} = 12 \div \dfrac{15}{4}$

$= \dfrac{12}{1} \cdot \dfrac{4}{15}$

$= \dfrac{12 \cdot 4}{1 \cdot 15}$

$= \dfrac{\cancel{3} \cdot 4 \cdot 4}{1 \cdot \cancel{3} \cdot 5}$

$= \dfrac{16}{5}$

$= 3\dfrac{1}{5}$

$= \$3.20$ per hour

To check your answer, multiply the answer by $3\dfrac{3}{4}$.

41. $3 \div \dfrac{3}{8} = \dfrac{3}{1} \cdot \dfrac{8}{3}$

$\qquad = \dfrac{\cancel{3} \cdot 8}{1 \cdot \cancel{3}}$

$\qquad = 8$

You can feed 8 people.

42. $\dfrac{3}{4} \div \dfrac{1}{16} = \dfrac{3}{4} \cdot \dfrac{16}{1}$

$\qquad = \dfrac{3 \cdot 16}{4 \cdot 1}$

$\qquad = \dfrac{3 \cdot \cancel{4} \cdot 4}{\cancel{4} \cdot 1}$

$\qquad = 12$

You can fill 12 glasses.

43. $\dfrac{2}{5}x = \dfrac{7}{15}$

$\dfrac{2}{5}x \div \dfrac{2}{5} = \dfrac{7}{15} \div \dfrac{2}{5}$

$x = \dfrac{7}{15} \div \dfrac{5}{2}$

$x = \dfrac{7 \cdot 5}{15 \cdot 2}$

$x = \dfrac{7 \cdot \cancel{5}}{3 \cdot \cancel{5} \cdot 2}$

$x = \dfrac{7}{6}$

44. $3\dfrac{1}{2}x = \dfrac{63}{4}$

$\dfrac{7}{2}x = \dfrac{63}{4}$

$\dfrac{7}{2}x \div \dfrac{7}{2} = \dfrac{63}{4} \div \dfrac{7}{2}$

$x = \dfrac{63}{4} \cdot \dfrac{2}{7}$

$x = \dfrac{63 \cdot 2}{4 \cdot 7}$

$x = \dfrac{\cancel{7} \cdot 9 \cdot \cancel{2}}{2 \cdot \cancel{2} \cdot \cancel{7}}$

$x = \dfrac{9}{2}$

45. $\dfrac{1}{2}\left(2\dfrac{1}{4}x\right) = \dfrac{9}{8}$

$\dfrac{1}{2}\left(\dfrac{9}{4}x\right) = \dfrac{9}{8}$

$\dfrac{9}{8}x = \dfrac{9}{8}$

$\dfrac{9}{8}x \div \dfrac{9}{8} = \dfrac{9}{8} \div \dfrac{9}{8}$

$x = \dfrac{9}{8} \cdot \dfrac{8}{9}$

$x = \dfrac{\cancel{9} \cdot \cancel{8}}{\cancel{8} \cdot \cancel{9}}$

$x = 1$

46. $\dfrac{3}{8}x = \dfrac{3}{40}$

$\dfrac{3}{8}x \div \dfrac{3}{8} = \dfrac{3}{40} \div \dfrac{3}{8}$

$x = \dfrac{3}{40} \cdot \dfrac{8}{3}$

$x = \dfrac{3 \cdot 8}{40 \cdot 3}$

$x = \dfrac{\cancel{3} \cdot \cancel{8}}{\cancel{8} \cdot 5 \cdot \cancel{3}}$

$x = \dfrac{1}{5}$

47. D; $\dfrac{b}{3} \div 6 = \dfrac{1}{18}$, $\dfrac{b}{3} = \dfrac{6}{18}$, $b = 1$

48. a. Iron from cereal: $\dfrac{12 \text{ mg}}{3\frac{1}{2} \, \cancel{oz}} \cdot 5 \, \cancel{oz} = \dfrac{60}{3\frac{1}{2}} = 60 \div 3\dfrac{1}{2} = 60 \div \dfrac{7}{2} = 60 \cdot \dfrac{2}{7} = \dfrac{120}{7} = 17\dfrac{1}{7} \text{ mg}$

Calcium from milk: $\dfrac{70 \text{ mg}}{3\frac{1}{2} \, \cancel{oz}} \cdot 4 \, \cancel{oz} = \dfrac{280}{3\frac{1}{2}} = 280 \div 3\dfrac{1}{2} = 280 \div \dfrac{7}{2} = 280 \cdot \dfrac{2}{7} = \dfrac{560}{7} = 80 \text{ mg}$

Calcium from orange juice: $\dfrac{131 \text{ mg}}{3\frac{1}{2} \, \cancel{oz}} \cdot 6 \, \cancel{oz} = \dfrac{786}{3\frac{1}{2}} = 786 \div 3\dfrac{1}{2} = 786 \div \dfrac{7}{2} = 786 \cdot \dfrac{2}{7} = \dfrac{1572}{7} = 224\dfrac{4}{7} \text{ mg}$

b. Total Calcium: $80 + 224\dfrac{4}{7} = 304\dfrac{4}{7} = 304\dfrac{4}{7} \text{ mg}$

$304\dfrac{4}{7} \div 1200 = \dfrac{2132}{7} \cdot \dfrac{1}{1200} = \dfrac{2132}{8400} \approx \dfrac{1}{4}$

c. Total Iron: $17\dfrac{1}{7} \text{ mg}$

$17\dfrac{1}{7} \div 15 = \dfrac{120}{7} \cdot \dfrac{1}{15} = \dfrac{\cancel{15} \cdot 8}{7 \cdot \cancel{15}} = \dfrac{8}{7} = 1\dfrac{1}{7}$

Spiral REVIEW

1. $4(x + 4) = 48$
$4x + 16 = 48$
$4x = 32$
$x = 8;$
$8 + 4 = 12$
12 units by 12 units

2. $2(3x + 5) + 2(4x - 1) = 50$
$6x + 10 + 8x - 2 = 50$
$14x + 8 = 50$
$14x = 42$
$x = 3;$
$3(3) + 5 = 14$
$4(3) - 1 = 11$
11 units by 14 units

3. $2x + x + 2x - 6 = 51$
$5x - 6 = 51$
$5x = 57$
$x = 11\frac{2}{5};$
$2\left(11\frac{2}{5}\right) = 22\frac{4}{5}$
$2\left(11\frac{2}{5}\right) - 6 = 16\frac{4}{5}$
$11\frac{2}{5}$ units by $16\frac{4}{5}$ units
by $22\frac{4}{5}$ units

4. $\frac{5}{6} - \frac{1}{4} = \frac{10}{12} - \frac{3}{12}$
$= \frac{7}{12}$

5. $\frac{1}{2} + \frac{5}{9} = \frac{9}{18} + \frac{10}{18}$
$= \frac{19}{18}$
$= 1\frac{1}{18}$

6. $\frac{-2}{3} + \frac{4}{15} = \frac{-10}{15} + \frac{4}{15}$
$= \frac{-6}{15}$
$= \frac{-2}{5}$

7. $\frac{-3}{10} - \frac{1}{8} = \frac{-12}{40} - \frac{5}{40}$
$= \frac{-17}{40}$

8. $-2\frac{1}{4} \cdot 1\frac{5}{6} = \frac{-9}{4} \cdot \frac{11}{6}$
$= \frac{-3 \cdot \cancel{3} \cdot 11}{4 \cdot \cancel{3} \cdot 2}$
$= \frac{-33}{8}$
$= -4\frac{1}{8}$

9. $\frac{-5}{9} \cdot \frac{-3}{5} = \frac{-1 \cdot \cancel{5} \cdot -1 \cdot \cancel{3}}{\cancel{3} \cdot 3 \cdot \cancel{5}}$
$= \frac{1}{3}$

10. $2 \div \frac{-3}{8} = 2 \cdot \frac{-8}{3}$
$= \frac{-16}{3}$
$= -5\frac{1}{3}$

11. $3\frac{1}{3} \div 5 = \frac{10}{3} \div 5$
$= \frac{10}{3} \cdot \frac{1}{5}$
$= \frac{2 \cdot \cancel{5}}{3 \cdot \cancel{5}}$
$= \frac{2}{3}$

12. $38 \div 9.5 = 4$ lawns

Lab 7.6

Part A

1. $\frac{25}{100} = \frac{1}{4}$

2. $\frac{20}{100} = \frac{1}{5}$

3. $\frac{45}{100} = \frac{\cancel{5} \cdot 9}{\cancel{5} \cdot 20} = \frac{9}{20}$

4.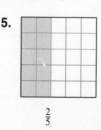
$\frac{1}{5}$

5.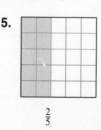
$\frac{2}{5}$

6.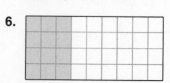

7.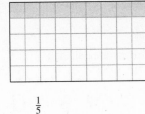

$\frac{1}{5}$

8.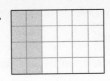

7.6 ALGEBRA CONNECTION: Exploring Percents

ONGOING ASSESSMENT

1. *Sample answer:*

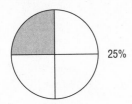

25%

2. *Sample answer:*

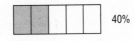 40%

3. *Sample answer:*

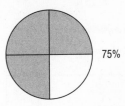

75%

EXERCISES

1.

Fraction Form	Percent Symbol Form	Verbal Form
$\frac{24}{100}$	24%	24 percent
$\frac{83}{100}$	83%	83 percent
$\frac{49}{100}$	49%	49 percent

2. $\frac{4}{8} = \frac{1}{2} = \frac{1}{2} \cdot \frac{50}{50} = \frac{50}{100} = 50\%$

3. $\frac{9}{20} = \frac{9}{20} \cdot \frac{5}{5} = \frac{45}{100} = 45\%$

4. *Sample answer:*

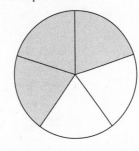 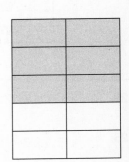

5. $\frac{9}{25} \cdot \frac{4}{4} = \frac{36}{100}$
$= 36\%$

6. $\frac{48}{100} = 48\%$

7. $\frac{8.5}{25} = \frac{8.5}{25} \cdot \frac{4}{4}$
$= \frac{34}{100}$
$= 34\%$

8. $\frac{14}{100} = 14\%$

9. A. $\frac{6}{8} = \frac{3}{4} = \frac{3}{4} \cdot \frac{25}{25} = \frac{75}{100} = 75\%$ **B.** $\frac{18}{25} = \frac{18}{25} \cdot \frac{4}{4} = \frac{72}{100} = 72\%$

C. $\frac{7}{10} = \frac{7}{10} \cdot \frac{10}{10} = \frac{70}{100} = 70\%$ **D.** $\frac{4}{8} = \frac{1}{2} = \frac{1}{2} \cdot \frac{50}{50} = \frac{50}{100} = 50\%$

Therefore, **D** has the least percent of its area shaded and **A** has the greatest percent of its area shaded.

10. $\frac{1}{10} = \frac{1}{10} \cdot \frac{10}{10}$

$= \frac{10}{100}$

$= 10\%$

11. $\frac{1}{20} = \frac{1}{20} \cdot \frac{5}{5}$

$= \frac{5}{100}$

$= 5\%$

12. $\frac{31}{50} = \frac{31}{50} \cdot \frac{2}{2}$

$= \frac{62}{100}$

$= 62\%$

13. $\frac{7}{25} = \frac{7}{25} \cdot \frac{4}{4}$

$= \frac{28}{100}$

$= 28\%$

14. $\frac{24}{32} = \frac{3 \cdot \cancel{8}}{4 \cdot \cancel{8}}$

$= \frac{3}{4} \cdot \frac{25}{25}$

$= \frac{75}{100}$

$= 75\%$

15. $\frac{18}{40} = \frac{\cancel{2} \cdot 9}{\cancel{2} \cdot 20}$

$= \frac{9}{20} \cdot \frac{5}{5}$

$= \frac{45}{100}$

$= 45\%$

16. $\frac{45}{150} = \frac{\cancel{15} \cdot 3}{\cancel{15} \cdot 5 \cdot 2}$

$= \frac{3}{10} \cdot \frac{10}{10}$

$= \frac{30}{100}$

$= 30\%$

17. $\frac{180}{300} = \frac{\cancel{3} \cdot 60}{\cancel{3} \cdot 100}$

$= \frac{60}{100}$

$= 60\%$

18. *Sample answer:*

$25\% = \frac{25}{100} = \frac{1}{4}$

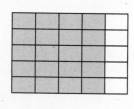

19. *Sample answer:*

$20\% = \frac{20}{100} = \frac{1}{5}$

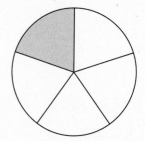

20. *Sample answer:*

$80\% = \frac{80}{100} = \frac{\cancel{20} \cdot 4}{\cancel{20} \cdot 5} = \frac{4}{5}$

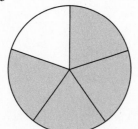

21. *Sample answer:*

$100\% = \frac{100}{100} = 1$

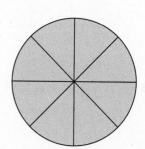

22. $\frac{5}{9} \approx 0.556 = 55.6\%$

23. $\frac{3}{6} = \frac{1}{2} \cdot \frac{50}{50} = \frac{50}{100} = 50\%$

24. $\frac{6}{12} = \frac{1}{2} \cdot \frac{50}{50} = \frac{50}{100} = 50\%$

25. $\frac{2}{4} \cdot \frac{25}{25} = \frac{50}{100} = 50\%$

26. $\frac{41}{66} \approx 62\%$

27. The full region is 100%.

$100\% - 62\% = 38\%$

28. D; $\frac{2}{10} = 20\%$

29. 3–5 servings; $\frac{3}{15} = 20\%$

30. 6–11 servings; $\frac{6}{15} = 40\%$

7.7 Percents, Decimals, and Fractions

ONGOING ASSESSMENT

1.–2. *Sample answer:* Subtract the percent green from the whole (100%) to get the percent orange.

1. $100\% - (30\% + 20\% + 10\% + 25\%) = 100\% - 85\%$
$$= 15\%$$

2. $100\% - (17\% + 23\% + 3\% + 12\%) = 100\% - 55\%$
$$= 45\%$$

EXERCISES

1. 0.60

2. 0.50

3. 0.667

4. 0.167

5. $\frac{36}{100} = 0.36 = 36\%$

6. $\frac{44}{100} = 0.44 = 44\%$

7. $\frac{12}{100} = 0.12 = 12\%$

8. $\frac{30}{100} = 0.30 = 30\%$

9. *Sample answer:* To rewrite a percent as a decimal, remove the percent sign and then divide by 100.
$48\% = \frac{48}{100} = 0.48$

10. *Sample answer:* To rewrite a fraction as a percent, rewrite the fraction in decimal form and then multiply the decimal by 100%.
$\frac{5}{16} = 0.3125 = 0.3125(100\%) = 31.25\%$

11. *Sample answer:* To rewrite a decimal as a percent, multiply the decimal by 100%.
$0.045 = 0.045(100\%) = 4.5\%$

12. *Sample answer:* A 150% increase in the price of some jewelry.

13. $36\% = \frac{36}{100} = 0.36$

14. $1.44\% = \frac{1.44}{100} = 0.0144$

15. $115\% = \frac{115}{100} = 1.15$

16. $14\frac{2}{3}\% \approx 14.7\%$
$$= \frac{14.7}{100}$$
$$= 0.147$$

17. $0.25 = 0.25(100\%)$
$$= 25\%$$

18. $0.826 = 0.826(100\%)$
$$= 82.6\%$$

19. $0.7 = 0.7(100\%)$
$$= 70\%$$

20. $1.4 = 1.4(100\%)$
$$= 140\%$$

21. $52\% = \frac{52}{100}$
$$= \frac{\cancel{4} \cdot 13}{\cancel{4} \cdot 25}$$
$$= \frac{13}{25}$$

22. $75\% = \frac{75}{100}$
$$= \frac{\cancel{25} \cdot 3}{\cancel{25} \cdot 4}$$
$$= \frac{3}{4}$$

23. $6\% = \dfrac{6}{100}$

$= \dfrac{\cancel{2} \cdot 3}{\cancel{2} \cdot 50}$

$= \dfrac{3}{50}$

24. $8\% = \dfrac{8}{100}$

$= \dfrac{\cancel{4} \cdot 2}{\cancel{4} \cdot 25}$

$= \dfrac{2}{25}$

25. $160\% = \dfrac{160}{100}$

$= \dfrac{\cancel{20} \cdot 8}{\cancel{20} \cdot 5}$

$= \dfrac{8}{5}$

26. $248\% = \dfrac{248}{100}$

$= \dfrac{\cancel{4} \cdot 62}{\cancel{4} \cdot 25}$

$= \dfrac{62}{25}$

27. $102\% = \dfrac{102}{100}$

$= \dfrac{\cancel{2} \cdot 51}{\cancel{2} \cdot 50}$

$= \dfrac{51}{50}$

28. $95\% = \dfrac{95}{100}$

$= \dfrac{\cancel{5} \cdot 19}{\cancel{5} \cdot 20}$

$= \dfrac{19}{20}$

29. $\dfrac{13}{208} = 0.0625$

$= 0.0625(100\%)$

$= 6.25\%$

30. $\dfrac{52}{650} = 0.08$

$= 0.08(100\%)$

$= 8\%$

31. $\dfrac{78}{99} \approx 0.7879$

$= 0.7879(100\%)$

$= 78.79\%$

32. $\dfrac{375}{450} \approx 0.8333$

$= 0.8333(100\%)$

$= 83.33\%$

33. $\dfrac{104}{64} = 1.625$

$= 1.625(100\%)$

$= 162.5\%$

34. $\dfrac{429}{286} = 1.5$

$= 1.5(100\%)$

$= 150\%$

35. $\dfrac{180}{54} \approx 3.3333$

$= 3.3333(100\%)$

$= 333.33\%$

36. $\dfrac{357}{252} \approx 1.417$

$= 1.417(100\%)$

$= 141.7\%$

37. $\dfrac{3}{8}$ $\boxed{?}$ 3.75%

$\dfrac{3}{8} = 0.375$

$= 0.375(100\%)$

$= 37.5\%$

$\dfrac{3}{8}$ $\boxed{>}$ 3.75%

38. $\dfrac{7}{16}$ $\boxed{?}$ 43.75%

$\dfrac{7}{16} = 0.4375$

$= 0.4375(100\%)$

$= 43.75\%$

$\dfrac{7}{16}$ $\boxed{=}$ 43.75%

39. $\dfrac{1}{25}$ $\boxed{?}$ 4%

$\dfrac{1}{25} = 0.04$

$= 0.04(100\%)$

$= 4\%$

$\dfrac{1}{25}$ $\boxed{=}$ 4%

40. $\dfrac{3}{50}$ $\boxed{?}$ 0.6%

$\dfrac{3}{50} = 0.06$

$= 0.06(100\%)$

$= 6\%$

$\dfrac{3}{50}$ $\boxed{>}$ 0.6%

41. B

42. C

43. D

44. A

45.

	Percent	Fraction	Decimal
Television	91%	$\dfrac{91}{100}$	0.91
Radio	83%	$\dfrac{83}{100}$	0.83
Newspapers	82%	$\dfrac{82}{100} = \dfrac{41}{50}$	0.82
Internet	9%	$\dfrac{9}{100}$	0.09

46. 91% is about 10 times larger than 9%.

47. Some people use more than one source of media.

48. $250 \times 0.09 = 22.5$

About 23 people access the Internet; answers vary.

49. D; $\dfrac{3}{9} = \dfrac{1}{3} = 33\dfrac{1}{3}\%$

50. $B = D \approx \frac{1}{4} = 0.25 = 0.25(100\%) = 25\%$

$A \approx \frac{1}{4} + \left(\frac{1}{4} \div 2\right)$

$\quad = \frac{1}{4} + \left(\frac{1}{4} \cdot \frac{1}{2}\right)$

$\quad = \frac{1}{4} + \frac{1}{8}$

$\quad = \left(\frac{1}{4} \cdot \frac{2}{2}\right) + \frac{1}{8}$

$\quad = \frac{2}{8} + \frac{1}{8}$

$\quad = \frac{3}{8}$

$\quad = 0.375$

$\quad = 0.375(100\%)$

$\quad = 37.5\%$

$\quad\quad A \approx C + D$

$37.5\% \approx C + 25\%$

$12.5\% \approx C$

B and D; each is about $\frac{1}{4}$ of the circle graph.

52. $E + D + C \approx \frac{1}{4} = 0.25 = 0.25(100\%) = 25\%$

$E = D = C = \frac{1}{3} \cdot \frac{1}{4} = \frac{1}{12} \approx 0.08 = 0.08(100\%) = 8\%$

$A \approx 8\%$

$B = 100\% - (8\% + 8\% + 8\% + 8\%)$

$\quad = 100\% - 32\%$

$\quad = 68\%$

A, C, D, E; three parts together are about $\frac{1}{4}$ of the circle graph and one part is about $\frac{1}{3}$ of $\frac{1}{4}$ of the circle graph.

51. $C \approx \frac{1}{4} = 0.25 = 0.25(100\%) = 25\%$

$D \approx 3\%$

$A + B + C + D \approx \frac{1}{2} = 0.50 = 0.50(100\%) = 50\%$

$A + B + 25\% + 3\% \approx 50\%$

$\quad\quad A + B + 28\% \approx 50\%$

$\quad\quad\quad\quad A + B \approx 22\%$

$A = B \approx 11\%$

$E + F \approx \frac{1}{2} = 0.50 = 0.50(100\%) = 50\%$

$F \approx 20\%$

$E \approx 50\% - 20\% = 30\%$

C; it is about $\frac{1}{4}$ of the circle graph.

7.8 | *Finding a Percent of a Number*

ONGOING ASSESSMENT

1. $100 - 37.4 - 43.0 - 18.9 = 0.7\% = 0.007$

$0.007 \times 104{,}000{,}000 = 728{,}000$ people

EXERCISES

1. *Sample answer:* To find the percent of a number, multiply the decimal form of the percent by the number.

2. 45% of $380 = 0.45 \times 380 = 171$

3. a. 10% of $48 = \frac{1}{10}$ of $48 = 4.8$

b. $33\frac{1}{3}\%$ of $96 = \frac{1}{3}$ of $96 = 32$

c. 50% of $64 = \frac{1}{2}$ of $64 = 32$

d. 200% of $23 = 2 \times 23 = 46$

4. $16\% = 0.16$
$0.16 \times 50 = 8$

5. $80\% = 0.8$
$0.8 \times 285 = 228$

6. $76\% = 0.76$
$0.76 \times 375 = 285$

7. $340\% = 3.4$
$3.4 \times 5 = 17$

8. $120\% = 1.2$
$1.2 \times 35 = 42$

9. $250\% = 2.5$
$2.5 \times 46 = 115$

10. $0.8\% = 0.008$
$0.008 \times 500 = 4$

11. $6.5\% = 0.065$
$0.065 \times 800 = 52$

12. $25\% = \dfrac{25}{100} = \dfrac{25 \cdot 1}{25 \cdot 4} = \dfrac{1}{4} \Rightarrow \dfrac{1}{4}$ of $120 \Rightarrow$ D

$\dfrac{1}{4}$ of $120 = 30$

13. $60\% = \dfrac{60}{100} = \dfrac{20 \cdot 3}{20 \cdot 5} = \dfrac{3}{5} \Rightarrow \dfrac{3}{5}$ of $120 \Rightarrow$ C

$\dfrac{1}{5}$ of $120 = 24$, so $\dfrac{3}{5}$ of $120 = 3 \cdot 24 = 72$.

14. $12.5\% = \dfrac{12.5}{100} = \dfrac{125}{1000} = \dfrac{125 \cdot 1}{125 \cdot 8} = \dfrac{1}{8} \Rightarrow \dfrac{1}{8}$ of $120 \Rightarrow$ A

$\dfrac{1}{8}$ of $120 = 15$

15. $33\frac{1}{3}\% = \dfrac{1}{3} \Rightarrow \dfrac{1}{3}$ of $120 \Rightarrow$ B

$\dfrac{1}{3}$ of $120 = 40$

16.

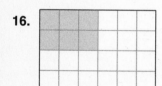

$25\% = \frac{1}{4}$

17.

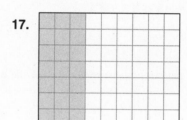

$33\frac{1}{3}\% = \frac{1}{3}$

18.

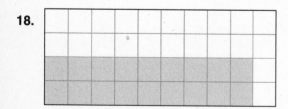

$4 \times 10 = 40$

45% of $40 = 0.45 \times 40$

$\qquad\qquad = 18$

19. 96% of $25 = 24$

20. 185% of $40 = 74$

21. 624% of $50 = 312$

22. 1.5% of $800 = 12$

23. a. 35% of $40 = 0.35 \times 40 = 14$. The discount is $\$14$.

b. $40 - 14 = 26$. You have to pay $\$26$ for the sweater.

24.

Physical Fitness

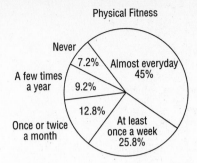

Never 7.2%
A few times a year 9.2%
Once or twice a month 12.8%
Almost everyday 45%
At least once a week 25.8%

25. 3% of 326 = 0.03 × 326 = 9.78

There are 9.78 million cubic miles of fresh water on Earth.

26. See Exercise 25.

326 − 9.78 = 316.22

There are 316.22 million cubic miles of salt water on Earth.

27. 9.78 million = 9,780,000 = 9.78×10^6

$(9.78 \times 10^6)(9.5 \times 10^{11}) = (9.78 \times 9.5)(10^6 \times 10^{11})$

$= 92.91 \times 10^{17}$

$= 9.291 \times 10^{18}$ gallons

28. A; $\frac{750}{2500} = \frac{3}{10} = 30\%$

29. D; $\frac{1}{8} \cdot 56 = 7$

30. Answers vary.

Using a Computer

1.

Year	Interest	Balance
1	0.07 · 120 = $8.40	120.00 + 8.40 = $128.40
2	0.07 · 128.40 = $8.99	128.40 + 8.99 = $137.39
3	0.07 · 137.39 = $9.62	137.39 + 9.62 = $147.01
4	0.07 · 147.01 = $10.29	147.01 + 10.29 = $157.30

2. $A = P(1 + r)^n$

$= 80(1 + 0.07)^8$

$= \$137.45$

3. $A = P(1 + r)^n$

$= 500(1 + 0.06)^{20}$

$= \$1603.57$

4. $A = P(1 + r)^n$

$= 500(1 + 0.08)^{10}$

$= \$1079.46$

5. $A = P(1 + r)^n$

$= 1000(1 + 0.08)^5$

$= \$1469.33$

Communicating About Mathematics

1. 0.2 + 0.9 + 0.5 + 2.5 + 0.5 + 1.7 + 2.2 + 4.9 = 13.4

$\frac{13.4}{16.5}$; $\frac{13.4}{16.5} \approx 81.2\%$

2. Nevada, New Mexico, Wyoming, Mexico, Utah, Arizona, Colorado, California

Least: Nevada

Most: California

Answers vary.

3.

Region	Acre–Feet of Water (millions)	Gallons of Water (millions)
NV	$1.8\% \times 16.5 \approx 0.3$	$0.3 \times 325{,}850 \approx 98{,}000$
UT	$10.3\% \times 16.5 \approx 1.7$	$1.7 \times 325{,}850 \approx 550{,}000$
WY	$6.4\% \times 16.5 \approx 1.1$	$1.1 \times 325{,}850 \approx 360{,}000$
CO	$23.5\% \times 16.5 \approx 3.9$	$3.9 \times 325{,}850 \approx 1{,}300{,}000$
NM	$5.2\% \times 16.5 \approx 0.9$	$0.9 \times 325{,}850 \approx 290{,}000$
AZ	$17.0\% \times 16.5 \approx 2.8$	$2.8 \times 325{,}850 \approx 910{,}000$
CA	$26.7\% \times 16.5 \approx 4.4$	$4.4 \times 325{,}850 \approx 1{,}400{,}000$
Mexico	$9.1\% \times 16.5 \approx 1.5$	$1.5 \times 325{,}850 \approx 490{,}000$
Total	≈ 16.6 million	$\approx 5{,}398{,}000$ million

No; some states use less than they were assigned, while others use more.

4. *Sample answer:*

California: Assigned $26.7\% \times 16.5 \approx 4.4$

Used 4.9:

$$\frac{4.9}{4.4} \approx 1.11 \text{ or } 111\%$$

7.9 Problem Solving with Percents

ONGOING ASSESSMENT

a.–f. Multiply the percents of those who answered true to each question by 400.

1. a. 328; 82% of $400 = 0.82 \times 400 = 328$

   b. 349; 87.2% of $400 = 0.872 \times 400 = 348.8 \approx 349$

   c. 384; 96% of $400 = 0.96 \times 400 = 384$

   d. 301; 75.2% of $400 = 0.752 \times 400 = 300.8 \approx 301$

   e. 152; 38% of $400 = 0.38 \times 400 = 152$

   f. 229; 57.2% of $400 = 0.572 \times 400 = 228.8 \approx 229$

EXERCISES

1. $19.79 \times 5.75\% = 19.79 \times 0.0575$
$$\approx \$1.14$$
$19.79 + 1.14 = \$20.93$

2. $27.53 \times 5.75\% = 27.53 \times 0.0575$
$$\approx \$1.58$$
$27.53 + 1.58 = \$29.11$

3. See Exercise 2.
$29.11 \times 15\% = 29.11 \times 0.15 \approx \$4.37$

4. $\frac{104}{175} \approx 0.594 \approx 59\%$

5. $4.65 \times 4\% = 4.65 \times 0.04 \approx \$0.19$
$4.65 + 0.19 = \$4.84$

6. $10.39 \times 4\% = 10.39 \times 0.04 \approx \$0.42$
$10.39 + 0.42 = \$10.81$

7. $50 \times 4\% = 50 \times 0.04 = \$2$
$50 + 2 = \$52$

8. $463.87 \times 4\% = 463.87 \times 0.04 \approx \$18.55$
$463.87 + 18.55 = \$482.42$

9. $\dfrac{58 \text{ million}}{250 \text{ million}} = 0.232 = 23.2\%$

10. $\dfrac{39 \text{ million}}{250 \text{ million}} = 0.156 = 15.6\%$

11. $\dfrac{33 \text{ million}}{250 \text{ million}} = 0.132 = 13.2\%$

12. $\dfrac{24 \text{ million}}{250 \text{ million}} = 0.096 = 9.6\%$

13. $\dfrac{15 \text{ million}}{250 \text{ million}} = 0.06 = 6\%$

14. $\dfrac{12 \text{ million}}{250 \text{ million}} = 0.048 = 4.8\%$

15. $\dfrac{10 \text{ million}}{250 \text{ million}} = 0.04 = 4\%$

16. $\dfrac{9 \text{ million}}{250 \text{ million}} = 0.036 = 3.6\%$

17. $\dfrac{9 \text{ million}}{250 \text{ million}} = 0.036 = 3.6\%$

18. $\dfrac{6 \text{ million}}{250 \text{ million}} = 0.024 = 2.4\%$

19. $\dfrac{6 \text{ million}}{250 \text{ million}} = 0.024 = 2.4\%$

20. $\dfrac{5 \text{ million}}{250 \text{ million}} = 0.02 = 2\%$

21. $\dfrac{5 \text{ million}}{250 \text{ million}} = 0.02 = 2\%$

22. $\dfrac{4 \text{ million}}{250 \text{ million}} = 0.016 = 1.6\%$

23. $350 \times 5.75\% = 350 \times 0.0575 \approx \$20.13$
$350 + 20.13 = \$370.13$

24. $476,000 \times 17\% = 476,000 \times 0.17 = \$80,920$
$476,000 - 80,920 = \$395,080$
No; $\$395,080 < \$397,000$

25. $650 \times 18.1\% = 650 \times 0.181 = \$117.65$

26. $650 \times 2.8\% = 650 \times 0.028 = \$18.20$

27. $650 \times 6.2\% = 650 \times 0.062 = \$40.30$

28. $650 \times 1\% = 650 \times 0.01 = \$6.50$

29. $650 \times 1.5\% = 650 \times 0.015 = \$9.75$

30. See Exercises 25–29.
$650 - (117.65 + 18.20 + 40.30 + 6.50 + 9.75) = 650 - 192.40$
$= \$457.60$

31. About 37,700; $\dfrac{31,500}{60,200} \times 72,000 \approx 37,700;$
Answers vary.

32. C; $\dfrac{620}{4886} \approx 12.5\%$

33. C; $\dfrac{1028}{4886} \approx 21\%$

34. $\dfrac{66,000 - 16,000}{66,000} = \dfrac{50,000}{66,000} \approx 75.8\%$

Chapter REVIEW

1. $\dfrac{3}{6} + \dfrac{1}{6} = \dfrac{3+1}{6} = \dfrac{4}{6} = \dfrac{2}{3}$

2. $\dfrac{4}{8} + \dfrac{4}{8} = \dfrac{4+4}{8} = \dfrac{8}{8} = 1$

3. $\dfrac{7}{9} + \dfrac{8}{9} = \dfrac{7+8}{9} = \dfrac{15}{9} = \dfrac{5}{3}$

4. $\dfrac{24}{25} - \dfrac{19}{25} = \dfrac{24-19}{25} = \dfrac{5}{25} = \dfrac{1}{5}$

5. $\dfrac{2w}{6} - \dfrac{w}{6} = \dfrac{2w-w}{6} = \dfrac{w}{6}$

6. $\dfrac{12y}{7} - \dfrac{10y}{7} = \dfrac{12y-10y}{7} = \dfrac{2y}{7}$

7. $1\frac{2}{3} - \frac{1}{3} = \frac{5}{3} - \frac{1}{3} = \frac{5-1}{3} = \frac{4}{3} = 1\frac{1}{3}$

8. $\frac{2}{5t} + \frac{3}{5t} = \frac{2+3}{5t} = \frac{5}{5t} = \frac{1}{t}$

9. $\frac{1}{6} + \frac{4}{9} = \frac{3}{18} + \frac{8}{18} = \frac{11}{18}$

10. $\frac{2}{8} + \frac{4}{5} = \frac{10}{40} + \frac{32}{40} = \frac{42}{40} = \frac{21}{20}$

11. $\frac{3}{2} + \frac{w}{3} = \frac{9}{6} + \frac{2w}{6} = \frac{9+2w}{6}$

12. $\frac{7}{8} - \frac{7}{9} = \frac{63}{72} - \frac{56}{72} = \frac{7}{72}$

13. $2\frac{1}{4} - 1\frac{1}{2} = \frac{9}{4} - \frac{3}{2} = \frac{9}{4} - \frac{6}{4} = \frac{3}{4}$

14. $\frac{4}{9} - \frac{2}{c} = \frac{4c}{9c} - \frac{18}{9c} = \frac{4c-18}{9c}$

15. $\frac{a}{25} - \frac{a}{5} = \frac{a}{25} - \frac{5a}{25} = \frac{a-5a}{25} = \frac{-4a}{25}$

16. $\frac{m}{3} - \frac{m}{7} = \frac{7m-3m}{21} = \frac{4m}{21}$

17. $\frac{7}{100} + \frac{11}{100} = \frac{18}{100}$
$$= \frac{2 \cdot 9}{2 \cdot 50}$$
$$= \frac{9}{50}$$

18. $\frac{16}{25} - \frac{9}{50} = \frac{16}{25} \cdot \frac{2}{2} - \frac{9}{50}$
$$= \frac{32}{50} - \frac{9}{50}$$
$$= \frac{23}{50}$$

19. $\frac{63}{163} + \frac{32}{123} \approx 0.3865 + 0.2602 \approx 0.65$

20. $\frac{12y}{17} + \frac{11y}{13} \approx 0.7059y + 0.8461y \approx 1.55y$

21. $\frac{12}{29} + \frac{29}{24} \approx 0.4138 + 1.2083 \approx 1.62$

22. $\frac{45}{76} - \frac{51}{121} \approx 0.5921 - 0.4214 \approx 0.17$

23. $\frac{187}{768} - \frac{5}{900} \approx 0.2435 - 0.0056 \approx 0.24$

24. $\frac{k}{325} + \frac{78k}{957} \approx 0.0031k + 0.0815k \approx 0.09k$

25. $\frac{1}{9} \cdot \frac{3}{4} = \frac{3}{36} = \frac{1}{12}$

26. $2\frac{2}{5} \cdot 3\frac{1}{2} = \frac{12}{5} \cdot \frac{7}{2} = \frac{84}{10} = \frac{42}{5} = 8\frac{2}{5}$

27. $\frac{11}{121} \cdot \frac{22}{33} = \frac{242}{3993} = \frac{(121)2}{(121)33} = \frac{2}{33}$

28. $\frac{4x}{5} \cdot 10 = \frac{40x}{5} = 8x$

29. $\frac{2}{13} \cdot \frac{2}{3} = \frac{4}{39}$

30. $\frac{12h}{15} \cdot \frac{5}{3} = \frac{60h}{45} = \frac{4h(15)}{3(15)} = \frac{4h}{3}$

31. $\frac{6}{7} \div \frac{1}{14} = \frac{6}{7} \cdot \frac{14}{1} = \frac{6 \cdot 2 \cdot 7}{7} = 12$

32. $\frac{5}{6} \div \frac{5}{3} = \frac{5}{6} \times \frac{3}{5} = \frac{15}{30} = \frac{1}{2}$

33. $\frac{8}{9} \div \frac{2}{3} = \frac{8}{9} \times \frac{3}{2} = \frac{24}{18} = \frac{4}{3}$

34. $4\frac{1}{2} \div 2\frac{1}{4} = \frac{9}{2} \div \frac{9}{4} = \frac{9}{2} \times \frac{4}{9} = \frac{36}{18} = 2$

35. $\frac{6n}{5} \div \frac{2}{3} = \frac{6n}{5} \times \frac{3}{2} = \frac{18n}{10} = \frac{9n}{5}$

36. $2\frac{2}{5} \div \frac{5}{6} = \frac{12}{5} \times \frac{6}{5} = \frac{72}{25} = 2\frac{22}{25}$

37. $\frac{7}{20} = 0.35 = 35\%$

38. $\frac{3}{20} = 0.15 = 15\%$

39. $\frac{6}{30} = 0.20 = 20\%$

40. $\frac{8}{20} = 0.4 = 40\%$

41. $6\% = \frac{6}{100} = 0.06$

42. $25\% = \frac{25}{100} = \frac{1}{4}$

43. $\frac{8}{9} \approx 0.889 = 88.9\%$

44. $0.231 \times 100 = 23.1\%$

45. $0.30 \times 120 = 36$

46. $7\frac{3}{4}\%$ of $19{,}500 = \frac{31}{4}\% \times 19{,}500$

$\qquad\qquad\qquad = 7.75\% \times 19{,}500$

$\qquad\qquad\qquad = 0.0775 \times 19{,}500$

$\qquad\qquad\qquad = 1511.25$

47. $0.333 \times 162 \approx 54$

48. 10% of $1500 = 0.10 \times 1500 = 150$

49. California: $0.06 \times 47.50 = 2.85$ sales tax

$\qquad\qquad 47.50 + 2.85 = \$50.35;$ No

Rhode Island: $0.07 \times 47.50 = 3.33$ sales tax

$\qquad\qquad 47.50 + 3.33 = \$50.83;$ No

Utah: $0.04875 \times 47.50 = 2.33$ sales tax

$\qquad\qquad 47.50 + 2.33 = \$49.82;$ Yes

Ohio: $0.05 \times 47.50 = 2.38$ sales tax

$\qquad\qquad 47.50 + 2.38 = \$49.88;$ Yes

Texas: $0.0625 \times 47.50 = 2.97$ sales tax

$\qquad\qquad 47.50 + 2.97 = \$50.47;$ No

Wyoming: $0.04 \times 47.50 = 1.90$ sales tax

$\qquad\qquad 47.50 + 1.90 = \$49.40;$ Yes

Chapter **ASSESSMENT**

1. $\dfrac{1}{5} + \dfrac{3}{5} = \dfrac{1+3}{5}$

$\qquad\quad = \dfrac{4}{5}$

2. $\dfrac{11}{12}x - \dfrac{7}{12}x = \dfrac{11x - 7x}{12}$

$\qquad\qquad\quad = \dfrac{4x}{12}$

$\qquad\qquad\quad = \dfrac{4 \cdot x}{4 \cdot 3}$

$\qquad\qquad\quad = \dfrac{x}{3}$

3. $\dfrac{4}{5} + \dfrac{1}{10} = \dfrac{4}{5} \cdot \dfrac{2}{2} + \dfrac{1}{10}$

$\qquad\qquad = \dfrac{8}{10} + \dfrac{1}{10}$

$\qquad\qquad = \dfrac{8+1}{10}$

$\qquad\qquad = \dfrac{9}{10}$

4. $\dfrac{11}{18} - \dfrac{2}{3} = \dfrac{11}{18} - \dfrac{2}{3} \cdot \dfrac{6}{6}$

$\qquad\qquad = \dfrac{11}{18} - \dfrac{12}{18}$

$\qquad\qquad = \dfrac{11 - 12}{18}$

$\qquad\qquad = -\dfrac{1}{18}$

5. $\dfrac{4}{5} \cdot \dfrac{1}{2} = \dfrac{4 \cdot 1}{5 \cdot 2}$

$\qquad\quad = \dfrac{2 \cdot 2 \cdot 1}{5 \cdot 2}$

$\qquad\quad = \dfrac{2}{5}$

6. $\dfrac{4}{5} \div \dfrac{1}{2} = \dfrac{4}{5} \cdot \dfrac{2}{1}$

$\qquad\quad = \dfrac{4 \cdot 2}{5 \cdot 1}$

$\qquad\quad = \dfrac{8}{5}$

7. $1\dfrac{1}{3} \times 1\dfrac{1}{2} = \dfrac{4}{3} \times \dfrac{3}{2}$

$\qquad\qquad = \dfrac{4 \cdot 3}{3 \cdot 2}$

$\qquad\qquad = \dfrac{2 \cdot 2 \cdot 3}{3 \cdot 2}$

$\qquad\qquad = 2$

8. $\dfrac{5s}{6} \div \dfrac{3s}{5} = \dfrac{5s}{6} \cdot \dfrac{5}{3s}$

$\qquad\qquad = \dfrac{5s \cdot 5}{6 \cdot 3s}$

$\qquad\qquad = \dfrac{5 \cdot 5 \cdot s}{6 \cdot 3 \cdot s}$

$\qquad\qquad = \dfrac{25}{18}$

9. Total area $= \left(\dfrac{6}{5} + \dfrac{4}{5}\right) \cdot \left(\dfrac{2}{3} + \dfrac{7}{3}\right)$

$= \dfrac{10}{5} \cdot \dfrac{9}{3}$

$= 2 \cdot 3$

$= 6 \text{ m}^2$

Red area $= \dfrac{4}{5} \cdot \dfrac{2}{3}$

$= \dfrac{4 \cdot 2}{5 \cdot 3}$

$= \dfrac{8}{15} \text{ m}^2$

Percent red $= \dfrac{8}{15} \div 6$

$= \dfrac{8}{15} \cdot \dfrac{1}{6}$

$= \dfrac{8 \cdot 1}{15 \cdot 6}$

$= \dfrac{4 \cdot \cancel{2} \cdot 1}{15 \cdot \cancel{2} \cdot 3}$

$= \dfrac{4}{45}$

≈ 0.089

$\approx 8.9\%$

Blue area $= \dfrac{6}{5} \cdot \dfrac{2}{3}$

$= \dfrac{6 \cdot 2}{5 \cdot 3}$

$= \dfrac{\cancel{3} \cdot 2 \cdot 2}{5 \cdot \cancel{3}}$

$= \dfrac{4}{5} \text{ m}^2$

Percent blue $= \dfrac{4}{5} \div 6$

$= \dfrac{4}{5} \cdot \dfrac{1}{6}$

$= \dfrac{4 \cdot 1}{5 \cdot 6}$

$= \dfrac{2 \cdot 2 \cdot 1}{5 \cdot 3 \cdot \cancel{2}}$

$= \dfrac{2}{15}$

≈ 0.133

$\approx 13.3\%$

Yellow area $= \dfrac{7}{3} \cdot \left(\dfrac{4}{5} + \dfrac{6}{5}\right)$

$= \dfrac{7}{3} \cdot \dfrac{10}{5}$

$= \dfrac{7 \cdot 10}{3 \cdot 5}$

$= \dfrac{7 \cdot \cancel{5} \cdot 2}{3 \cdot \cancel{5}}$

$= \dfrac{14}{3} \text{ m}^2$

Percent yellow $= \dfrac{14}{3} \div 6$

$= \dfrac{14}{3} \cdot \dfrac{1}{6}$

$= \dfrac{14 \cdot 1}{3 \cdot 6}$

$= \dfrac{\cancel{2} \cdot 7 \cdot 1}{3 \cdot 3 \cdot \cancel{2}}$

$= \dfrac{7}{9}$

≈ 0.778

$\approx 77.8\%$

10. $59\% \times 2546 = 0.59 \times 2546 = 1502.14$

1502 would be fiction.

You would expect to sell about 1502 fiction books.

11. $\dfrac{10}{25} = \dfrac{10}{25} \cdot \dfrac{4}{4} = \dfrac{40}{100} = 40\%$

12. $0.365 \times 100\% = 36.5\%$

13. $\dfrac{24.5\%}{100\%} = 0.245$

14. $32\% = \dfrac{32}{100} = \dfrac{\cancel{4} \cdot 8}{\cancel{4} \cdot 25} = \dfrac{8}{25}$

15. $\dfrac{18}{65} \approx 0.277$

$0.277 \times 100\% = 27.7\%$

16. $\dfrac{5}{18} \approx 0.278$

$0.278 \times 100\% = 27.8\%$

17.

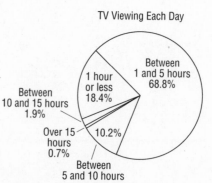

TV Viewing Each Day

Between 1 and 5 hours 68.8%

1 hour or less 18.4%

Between 10 and 15 hours 1.9%

Over 15 hours 0.7%

10.2%

Between 5 and 10 hours

18. $18.4\% \times 415 = 0.184 \times 415 = 76.36;$

76 adults

Standardized Test Practice

1. D; $1\frac{1}{6} + \frac{3}{4} + \frac{3}{4} + 1\frac{1}{2} = \frac{7}{6} + \frac{3}{4} + \frac{3}{4} + \frac{3}{2}$

$$= \frac{14}{12} + \frac{9}{12} + \frac{9}{12} + \frac{18}{12}$$

$$= \frac{50}{12}$$

$$= 4\frac{2}{12}$$

$$= 4\frac{1}{6}$$

2. C; 35 people represent the yellow region.

3. C; $\frac{3}{10} \times l = \frac{1}{2}$

$$l = \frac{1}{2} \div \frac{3}{10}$$

$$l = \frac{1}{2} \times \frac{10}{3}$$

$$l = \frac{10}{6}$$

$$l = 1\frac{2}{3}$$

4. B; $\qquad y + \frac{3}{5} = \frac{-12}{5}$

$$y + \frac{3}{5} - \frac{3}{5} = \frac{-12}{5} - \frac{3}{5}$$

$$y = \frac{-15}{3}$$

$$y = -3$$

5. C; $\frac{9}{15} = 0.60 = 60\%$

6. B; $50 \times 0.1 = 5$ people

7. B; $0.4 \times 50 = 20$

Chapter 8
Proportion, Percent, and Probability

8.1 *Exploring Rates and Ratios*

ONGOING ASSESSMENT

1. The quotient is a rate because the units are different.

$$\frac{10{,}000 \text{ people}}{4 \text{ years}} = \frac{\cancel{4} \cdot 2500}{\cancel{4} \cdot 1}$$

$$= 2500 \text{ people per year}$$

2. The quotient is a ratio because the units are the same.

$$\frac{10{,}000 \text{ \cancel{people}}}{4000 \text{ \cancel{people}}} = \frac{\cancel{2000} \cdot 5}{\cancel{2000} \cdot 2} = \frac{5}{2} = 2.5$$

EXERCISES

1. $\frac{a}{b}$ is a rate, read "*a* per *b*," if *a* and *b* have different units of measure; *sample answer:* 50 miles per hour;

   $\frac{a}{b}$ is a ratio, read "*a* to *b*," if *a* and *b* have the same units of measure; *sample answer:* 20 feet to 1 foot

2. Rate; $\frac{100 \text{ mi}}{4 \text{ hr}} = 25$ mph

3. Ratio; $\frac{10 \text{\cancel{in.}}}{4 \text{\cancel{in.}}} = \frac{\cancel{2} \cdot 5}{\cancel{2} \cdot 2} = \frac{5}{2} = 5$ to 2

4. Ratio; $\frac{8 \text{ \cancel{balloons}}}{24 \text{ \cancel{balloons}}} = \frac{1}{3} = 1$ to 3

5. Rate; $\frac{\$27.99}{3 \text{ lb}} = \$9.33$ per lb

6. $\frac{\$60}{12 \text{ hr}} = \$5$ per hr

7. $\frac{4}{5}, \frac{5}{4}, \frac{4}{9}, \frac{9}{4}, \frac{5}{9}, \frac{9}{5}$

8. C

9. Ratio; $\frac{16 \text{ \cancel{students}}}{18 \text{ \cancel{students}}} = \frac{8 \cdot \cancel{2}}{9 \cdot \cancel{2}} = \frac{8}{9} = 8$ to 9

10. Rate; $\frac{120 \text{ m}}{15 \text{ sec}} = 8$ meters per second

11. Rate; $\frac{88 \text{ points}}{4 \text{ games}} = 22$ points per game

12. Ratio; $\frac{3 \text{ \cancel{cars}}}{5 \text{ \cancel{cars}}} = \frac{3}{5} = 3$ to 5

13. $\frac{4 \text{ doctors}}{5 \text{ doctors}}$; it is a ratio because the units are the same.

14. $\frac{9 \text{ inspectors}}{10 \text{ inspectors}}$; it is a ratio because the units are the same.

15. $\dfrac{1600 \text{ miles}}{3 \text{ days}}$; it is a rate because the units are different.

16. $\dfrac{40 \text{ questions}}{60 \text{ minutes}}$; it is a rate because the units are different.

17. $\dfrac{2 \text{ ft}}{18 \text{ in.}} = \dfrac{2(12 \text{ in.})}{18 \text{ in.}} = \dfrac{24 \text{ in.}}{18 \text{ in.}}$
$= \dfrac{\cancel{6} \cdot 4}{\cancel{6} \cdot 3} = \dfrac{4}{3}$

18. $\dfrac{2640 \text{ ft}}{1 \text{ mi}} = \dfrac{2640 \text{ ft}}{5280 \text{ ft}} = \dfrac{1}{2}$

19. $\dfrac{2 \text{ min}}{300 \text{ s}} = \dfrac{2(60 \text{ s})}{300 \text{ s}} = \dfrac{120 \text{ s}}{300 \text{ s}}$
$= \dfrac{\cancel{60} \cdot 2}{\cancel{60} \cdot 5} = \dfrac{2}{5}$

20. $\dfrac{1 \text{ h}}{3600 \text{ s}} = \dfrac{60 \text{ min}}{3600 \text{ s}} = \dfrac{60(60 \text{ s})}{3600 \text{ s}}$
$= \dfrac{3600 \text{ s}}{3600 \text{ s}} = \dfrac{1}{1}$

21. $\dfrac{640¢}{\$4} = \dfrac{640¢}{4(100¢)} = \dfrac{640¢}{400¢} = \dfrac{8 \cdot \cancel{80}}{5 \cdot \cancel{80}} = \dfrac{8}{5}$

22. $\dfrac{2 \text{ gal}}{10 \text{ qt}} = \dfrac{2(4 \text{ qt})}{10 \text{ qt}} = \dfrac{8 \text{ qt}}{10 \text{ qt}} = \dfrac{\cancel{2} \cdot 4}{\cancel{2} \cdot 5} = \dfrac{4}{5}$

23. $\dfrac{200 \text{ cm}}{3 \text{ m}} = \dfrac{200 \text{ cm}}{3(100 \text{ cm})} = \dfrac{200 \text{ cm}}{300 \text{ cm}}$
$= \dfrac{\cancel{100} \cdot 2}{\cancel{100} \cdot 3} = \dfrac{2}{3}$

24. $\dfrac{2 \text{ L}}{50 \text{ mL}} = \dfrac{2(1000 \text{ mL})}{50 \text{ mL}} = \dfrac{2000 \text{ mL}}{50 \text{ mL}} = \dfrac{40}{1}$

25. $\dfrac{9000 \text{ tickets}}{6 \text{ hours}} = 1500 \text{ tickets per hour}$

26. $\dfrac{78 \text{ in.}}{24 \text{ h}} = \dfrac{\cancel{6} \cdot 13 \text{ in.}}{\cancel{6} \cdot 4 \text{ h}} = \dfrac{13}{4} \text{ in. per h}$
$= 3\dfrac{1}{4} \text{ in. per h}$

27. $\dfrac{\$1.18}{6 \text{ apples}} \approx \$.197 \text{ per apple}$

$\dfrac{\$1.79}{10 \text{ apples}} = \$.179 \text{ per apple}$

10 apples is a better buy;
17.9¢ per apple < 19.7¢ per apple

28. $\dfrac{\$2.69}{12 \text{ ounces}} \approx \$.224 \text{ per ounce}$

$\dfrac{\$3.99}{18 \text{ ounces}} \approx \$.222 \text{ per ounce}$

18 oz box is a better buy;
22.2¢ per ounce < 22.4¢ per ounce

29. $\dfrac{\$7.89}{2 \text{ lb } 4 \text{ oz}} = \dfrac{\$7.89}{2(16 \text{ oz}) + 4 \text{ oz}} = \dfrac{\$7.89}{36 \text{ oz}} \approx \$.219 \text{ per oz}$

$\dfrac{\$18.89}{5 \text{ lb } 2 \text{ oz}} = \dfrac{\$18.89}{5(16 \text{ oz}) + 2 \text{ oz}} = \dfrac{\$18.89}{82 \text{ oz}} \approx \$.230 \text{ per oz}$

2 lb, 4 oz is a better buy; 21.9¢ per ounce < 23.0¢ per ounce

30. $\dfrac{\$2.69}{6(12 \text{ oz})} = \dfrac{\$2.69}{72 \text{ oz}} \approx \$.037 \text{ per oz}$

$\dfrac{\$4.59}{\frac{1}{2} \text{ gal}} = \dfrac{\$4.59}{64 \text{ oz}} \approx \$.072 \text{ per oz}$

six 12 oz cans is a better buy; 3.7¢ per ounce < 7.2¢ per ounce

31. $\dfrac{3543 \text{ miles}}{86 \text{ hours}} \approx 41.2 \text{ mi/h}$

32. $\dfrac{50 \text{ ft}}{3.75 \text{ in.}} = \dfrac{50(12 \text{ in.})}{3.75 \text{ in.}} = \dfrac{600 \text{ in.}}{3.75 \text{ in.}}$
$= \dfrac{160}{1}$

33. Green perimeter $= 32$

Yellow perimeter $= 18$

$\dfrac{32}{18} = \dfrac{\cancel{2} \cdot 16}{\cancel{2} \cdot 9} = \dfrac{16}{9}$

Green area $= 15$

Yellow area $= 20$

$\dfrac{15}{20} = \dfrac{3 \cdot \cancel{5}}{4 \cdot \cancel{5}} = \dfrac{3}{4}$

$\dfrac{16}{9} > \dfrac{3}{4}$; so the ratio of perimeters is greater.

34. Green perimeter $= 20$

Yellow perimeter $= 18$

$\dfrac{20}{18} = \dfrac{10 \cdot \cancel{2}}{9 \cdot \cancel{2}} = \dfrac{10}{9}$

Green area $= 3 \cdot 7 = 21$

Yellow area $= 2 \cdot 7 = 14$

$\dfrac{21}{14} = \dfrac{\cancel{7} \cdot 3}{\cancel{7} \cdot 2} = \dfrac{3}{2}$

Since $\dfrac{10}{9} \approx 1.111$ and $\dfrac{3}{2} = 1.5$, $\dfrac{3}{2} > \dfrac{10}{9}$; so the ratio of areas is greater.

35. Green perimeter $= 4 + 3 + 5 = 12$

Yellow perimeter $= 4 + \dfrac{5}{2} + 5 + \left(3 + \dfrac{5}{2}\right) = 4 + \dfrac{5}{2} + 5 + 3 + \dfrac{5}{2}$

$\qquad\qquad = 12 + \dfrac{10}{2} = 17$

$\dfrac{12}{17}$

Green area $= \dfrac{1}{2}(4)(3) = 6$

Total area $= \left(3 + \dfrac{5}{2}\right) \cdot 4 = \left(\dfrac{3}{1} \cdot \dfrac{2}{2} + \dfrac{5}{2}\right) \cdot 4$

$\qquad\quad = \left(\dfrac{6}{2} + \dfrac{5}{2}\right) \cdot 4 = \dfrac{11}{2} \cdot 4 = 22$

Yellow area $= 22 - 6 = 16$

$\dfrac{6}{16} = \dfrac{\cancel{2} \cdot 3}{\cancel{2} \cdot 8} = \dfrac{3}{8}$

Since $\dfrac{12}{17} \approx 0.706$ and $\dfrac{3}{8} = 0.375$, $\dfrac{12}{17} > \dfrac{3}{8}$; so the ratio of perimeters is greater.

36. Green perimeter $= \left(\dfrac{2}{3} + \dfrac{1}{3}\right) + \left(\dfrac{2}{3} + \dfrac{1}{3}\right) + \dfrac{2}{3} + \dfrac{1}{3} + \dfrac{2}{3} + \dfrac{1}{3}$

$\qquad\qquad = 1 + 1 + 1 + 1 = 4$

Yellow perimeter $= 4\left(\dfrac{1}{3}\right) = \dfrac{4}{3}$

$\dfrac{4}{\frac{4}{3}} = 4 \div \dfrac{4}{3} = 4 \cdot \dfrac{3}{4} = \dfrac{\cancel{4} \cdot 3}{1 \cdot \cancel{4}} = \dfrac{3}{1}$

Yellow area $= \dfrac{1}{3} \cdot \dfrac{1}{3} = \dfrac{1}{9}$

Total area $= \left(\dfrac{2}{3} + \dfrac{1}{3}\right) \cdot \left(\dfrac{2}{3} + \dfrac{1}{3}\right) = 1 \cdot 1 = 1$

Green area $= 1 - \dfrac{1}{9} = \dfrac{1}{1} \cdot \dfrac{9}{9} - \dfrac{1}{9} = \dfrac{9}{9} - \dfrac{1}{9} = \dfrac{8}{9}$

$\dfrac{\frac{8}{9}}{\frac{1}{9}} = \dfrac{8}{9} \div \dfrac{1}{9} = \dfrac{8}{9} \cdot \dfrac{9}{1} = \dfrac{8 \cdot \cancel{9}}{\cancel{9} \cdot 1} = \dfrac{8}{1}$

$\dfrac{8}{1} > \dfrac{3}{1}$; so the ratio of areas is greater.

37. B; 20 to 8 or 5 to 2

38. Formalwear shop: $\dfrac{\$5.50}{2 \text{ days}} = \$2.75$ per day;

Costume supplier: $\dfrac{\$10.50}{5 \text{ days}} = \$2.10$ per day;

Sample answer: Choose the costume supplier, because it was the cheaper rate per day.

Lab 8.2

Part A

1. $\dfrac{2}{1}$; $\dfrac{3}{2}$; $\dfrac{5}{3}$; $\dfrac{8}{5}$; $\dfrac{13}{8}$

2. Pattern: Each length, after the first, is the sum of the preceding length and width, and each width, after the first, is the same as the preceding length; or each length, after the first two, is the sum of the two preceding lengths and each width, after the first two, is the sum of the two preceding widths.

Lengths: 21, 34, 55
Widths: 13, 21, 34

3.

Length	2	3	5	8	13	21	34	55
Width	1	2	3	5	8	13	21	34
Ratio	$\dfrac{2}{1} = 2$	$\dfrac{3}{2} = 1.5$	$\dfrac{5}{3} = 1.\overline{6}$	$\dfrac{8}{5} = 1.6$	$\dfrac{13}{8} = 1.625$	$\dfrac{21}{13} \approx 1.615$	$\dfrac{34}{21} \approx 1.619$	$\dfrac{55}{34} \approx 1.618$

4. $\dfrac{\sqrt{5}+1}{2} \approx 1.618$

Each succeeding ratio in the table is closer to 1.618 than the previous one.

Part B

5.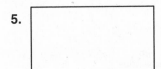

6.

This rectangle is also a golden rectangle.

7. $\dfrac{2}{3} = \dfrac{4}{6}$; $2 \times 6 = 12$; $3 \times 4 = 12$

8. $\dfrac{5}{2} = \dfrac{20}{8}$; $5 \times 8 = 20$; $2 \times 20 = 40$

9. $\dfrac{6}{21} = \dfrac{2}{7}$; $6 \times 7 = 42$; $21 \times 2 = 42$

10. The cross products of two equivalent fractions are equal.

11. *Sample answer:* Yes; the ratios are approximately the same.

8.2 GEOMETRY CONNECTION: Solving Proportions

ONGOING ASSESSMENT

1. Solution 1:

$$\frac{x}{5} = \frac{3}{30}$$

$$5 \cdot \frac{x}{5} = 5 \cdot \frac{3}{30}$$

$$x = \frac{1}{2}$$

Solution 2:

$$\frac{x}{5} = \frac{3}{30}$$

$$15 = 30x$$

$$\frac{1}{2} = x$$

2. Solution 1:

$$\frac{4}{n} = \frac{2}{15}$$

$$\frac{n}{4} = \frac{15}{2}$$

$$4 \cdot \frac{n}{4} = 4 \cdot \frac{15}{2}$$

$$n = 30$$

Solution 2:

$$\frac{4}{n} = \frac{2}{15}$$

$$2n = 60$$

$$n = 30$$

3. Solution 1:

$$\frac{5}{3} = \frac{m}{5}$$

$$5 \cdot \frac{5}{3} = 5 \cdot \frac{m}{5}$$

$$\frac{25}{3} = m$$

Solution 2:

$$\frac{5}{3} = \frac{m}{5}$$

$$3m = 25$$

$$m = \frac{25}{3}$$

4. Solution 1:

$$\frac{4}{7} = \frac{6}{y}$$

$$\frac{7}{4} = \frac{y}{6}$$

$$6 \cdot \frac{7}{4} = 6 \cdot \frac{y}{6}$$

$$\frac{21}{2} = y$$

Solution 2:

$$\frac{4}{7} = \frac{6}{y}$$

$$42 = 4y$$

$$\frac{42}{4} = y$$

$$\frac{21}{2} = y$$

EXERCISES

1. $\dfrac{2000}{80,000} = \dfrac{\cancel{2000}}{\cancel{2000} \cdot 40} = \dfrac{1}{40} = 0.025$

$\dfrac{3000}{100,000} = \dfrac{\cancel{1000} \cdot 3}{\cancel{1000} \cdot 100} = \dfrac{3}{100} = 0.03$

No; $\dfrac{2000}{80,000} \neq \dfrac{3000}{100,000}$

2. *Sample answer:* batting averages, cost per unit

3–6. To check your answer, substitute the answer for the variable and simplify where possible.

3. $\dfrac{b}{3} = \dfrac{4}{12}$

$3 \cdot \dfrac{b}{3} = 3 \cdot \dfrac{4}{12}$

$b = 1$

4. $\dfrac{9}{x} = \dfrac{3}{5}$

$\dfrac{x}{9} = \dfrac{5}{3}$

$9 \cdot \dfrac{x}{9} = 9 \cdot \dfrac{5}{3}$

$x = 15$

5. $\dfrac{2}{3} = \dfrac{m}{36}$

$36 \cdot \dfrac{2}{3} = 36 \cdot \dfrac{m}{36}$

$24 = m$

6. $\dfrac{7}{18} = \dfrac{21}{y}$

$\dfrac{18}{7} = \dfrac{y}{21}$

$21 \cdot \dfrac{18}{7} = 21 \cdot \dfrac{y}{21}$

$54 = y$

7. Because the angles have the same measure, the triangles are similar.

$$\frac{a}{d} = \frac{b}{e}, \ \frac{a}{d} = \frac{c}{f}, \ \frac{b}{e} = \frac{c}{f}$$

8. Because the angles do not have the same measure, the triangles are not similar.

9. True;

$$\frac{1}{4} \overset{?}{=} \frac{3}{12}$$

$$\frac{1}{4} = \frac{1}{4}$$

10. False;

$$\frac{6}{16} \overset{?}{=} \frac{3}{7}$$

$$\frac{\cancel{2} \cdot 3}{\cancel{2} \cdot 8} \overset{?}{=} \frac{3}{7}$$

$$\frac{3}{8} \neq \frac{3}{7}$$

11. True;

$$\frac{4}{9} \overset{?}{=} \frac{16}{36}$$

$$\frac{4}{9} \overset{?}{=} \frac{\cancel{4} \cdot 4}{\cancel{4} \cdot 9}$$

$$\frac{4}{9} = \frac{4}{9}$$

12. False;

$$\frac{9}{7} \overset{?}{=} \frac{18}{15}$$

$$\frac{9}{7} \overset{?}{=} \frac{\cancel{3} \cdot 6}{\cancel{3} \cdot 5}$$

$$\frac{9}{7} \neq \frac{6}{5}$$

13.

$$\frac{x}{3} = \frac{4}{9}$$

$$3 \cdot \frac{x}{3} = 3 \cdot \frac{4}{9}$$

$$x = \frac{4}{3}$$

14.

$$\frac{y}{5} = \frac{8}{5}$$

$$y = 8$$

15.

$$\frac{5}{7} = \frac{z}{2}$$

$$2 \cdot \frac{5}{7} = 2 \cdot \frac{z}{2}$$

$$\frac{10}{7} = z$$

16.

$$\frac{5}{12} = \frac{t}{2}$$

$$2 \cdot \frac{5}{12} = 2 \cdot \frac{t}{2}$$

$$\frac{5}{6} = t$$

17.

$$\frac{8}{m} = \frac{2}{5}$$

$$\frac{m}{8} = \frac{5}{2}$$

$$8 \cdot \frac{m}{8} = 8 \cdot \frac{5}{2}$$

$$m = 20$$

18.

$$\frac{9}{x} = \frac{15}{2}$$

$$\frac{x}{9} = \frac{2}{15}$$

$$9 \cdot \frac{x}{9} = 9 \cdot \frac{2}{15}$$

$$x = \frac{6}{5}$$

19.

$$\frac{2}{3} = \frac{12}{b}$$

$$\frac{3}{2} = \frac{b}{12}$$

$$12 \cdot \frac{3}{2} = 12 \cdot \frac{b}{12}$$

$$18 = b$$

20.

$$\frac{2.8}{y} = \frac{11}{2.5}$$

$$\frac{y}{2.8} = \frac{2.5}{11}$$

$$2.8 \cdot \frac{y}{2.8} = 2.8 \cdot \frac{2.5}{11}$$

$$y = \frac{7}{11}$$

21.

$$\frac{x}{6} = \frac{8}{9}$$

$$6 \cdot \frac{x}{6} = 6 \cdot \frac{8}{9}$$

$$x = \frac{16}{3}$$

22.

$$\frac{y}{5} = \frac{6}{17}$$

$$5 \cdot \frac{y}{5} = 5 \cdot \frac{6}{17}$$

$$y = \frac{30}{17}$$

23.

$$\frac{3}{8} = \frac{m}{24}$$

$$24 \cdot \frac{3}{8} = 24 \cdot \frac{m}{24}$$

$$9 = m$$

24.

$$\frac{2}{5} = \frac{10}{n}$$

$$\frac{5}{2} = \frac{n}{10}$$

$$10 \cdot \frac{5}{2} = 10 \cdot \frac{n}{10}$$

$$25 = n$$

25.

$$\frac{5}{6} = \frac{12}{s}$$

$$\frac{6}{5} = \frac{s}{12}$$

$$12 \cdot \frac{6}{5} = 12 \cdot \frac{s}{12}$$

$$\frac{72}{5} = s$$

26.

$$\frac{2}{t} = \frac{4}{13}$$

$$\frac{t}{2} = \frac{13}{4}$$

$$2 \cdot \frac{t}{2} = 2 \cdot \frac{13}{4}$$

$$t = \frac{13}{2}$$

27. $\dfrac{14}{15} = \dfrac{x}{25}$

$14 \times 25 \div 15 = 23.33$

28. $\dfrac{y}{32} = \dfrac{16}{27}$

$16 \times 32 \div 27 = 18.96$

29. $\dfrac{p}{21} = \dfrac{8}{42}$

$8 \times 21 \div 42 = 4$

30. $\dfrac{14}{15} = \dfrac{x}{36}$

$14 \times 36 \div 15 = 33.6$

31. a. x = number of minutes Canoe 1 takes to complete the race.

$$\frac{20 \text{ mi}}{4 \text{ mi}} = \frac{x \text{ min}}{25 \text{ min}}$$

$$5 = \frac{x}{25}$$

$$25 \cdot 5 = 25 \cdot \frac{x}{25}$$

$$125 = x$$

Canoe 1 takes 125 minutes to complete the race.

y = number of minutes Canoe 2 takes to complete the race.

$$\frac{20 \text{ mi}}{3 \text{ mi}} = \frac{y \text{ min}}{20 \text{ min}}$$

$$\frac{20}{3} = \frac{y}{20}$$

$$20 \cdot \frac{20}{3} = 20 \cdot \frac{y}{20}$$

$$\frac{400}{3} = y$$

$$133\frac{1}{3} = y$$

Canoe 2 takes $133\frac{1}{3}$ minutes to complete the race.

Canoe 1: $125 \text{ min} \times \dfrac{1 \text{ hr}}{60 \text{ min}} = \dfrac{125}{60}$ hr

$$= \frac{25 \cdot \cancel{5}}{12 \cdot \cancel{5}} = \frac{25}{12} = 2\frac{1}{12} \text{ hr}$$

Canoe 2: $133\dfrac{1}{3} \text{ min} \times \dfrac{1 \text{ hr}}{60 \text{ min}} = \dfrac{\frac{400}{3}}{60}$ hr

$$= \frac{400}{3} \div 60 = \frac{400}{3} \cdot \frac{1}{60} = \frac{400 \cdot 1}{3 \cdot 60}$$

$$= \frac{\cancel{20} \cdot 20}{3 \cdot \cancel{20} \cdot 3} = \frac{20}{9} = 2\frac{2}{9} \text{ hr}$$

b. Canoe 1: $\dfrac{20 \text{ mi}}{2\frac{1}{12} \text{ hr}} = \dfrac{20}{\frac{25}{12}} = 20 \div \dfrac{25}{12} = 20 \cdot \dfrac{12}{25} = \dfrac{48}{5} = 9\dfrac{3}{5}$ mph

Canoe 2: $\dfrac{20 \text{ mi}}{2\frac{2}{9} \text{ hr}} = \dfrac{20}{\frac{20}{9}} = 20 \div \dfrac{20}{9} = 20 \cdot \dfrac{9}{20} = 9$ mph

c. Canoe 1 won the race because it took Canoe 1 125 minutes to complete the race, while it took Canoe 2 $133\frac{1}{3}$ minutes to complete the race.

32.

$$\frac{e}{b} = \frac{f}{c} \qquad \frac{e}{b} = \frac{d}{a}$$

$$\frac{8}{4} = \frac{f}{5} \qquad \frac{8}{4} = \frac{d}{6}$$

$$2 = \frac{f}{5} \qquad 2 = \frac{d}{6}$$

$$5 \cdot 2 = 5 \cdot \frac{f}{5} \qquad 6 \cdot 2 = 6 \cdot \frac{d}{6}$$

$$10 = f \qquad 12 = d$$

33.

$$\frac{e}{b} = \frac{f}{c} \qquad \frac{e}{b} = \frac{d}{a}$$

$$\frac{3}{9} = \frac{f}{15} \qquad \frac{3}{9} = \frac{d}{12}$$

$$\frac{1}{3} = \frac{f}{15} \qquad \frac{1}{3} = \frac{d}{12}$$

$$15 \cdot \frac{1}{3} = 15 \cdot \frac{f}{15} \qquad 12 \cdot \frac{1}{3} = 12 \cdot \frac{d}{12}$$

$$5 = f \qquad 4 = d$$

34.

$$\frac{f}{c} = \frac{e}{b}$$

$$\frac{1}{2} = \frac{e}{3\frac{1}{2}}$$

$$\frac{1}{2} = \frac{e}{\frac{7}{2}}$$

$$\frac{1}{2} = e \div \frac{7}{2}$$

$$\frac{1}{2} = e \cdot \frac{2}{7}$$

$$\frac{7}{2} \cdot \frac{1}{2} = \frac{7}{2} \cdot \frac{2}{7}e$$

$$\frac{7}{4} = e$$

$$\frac{f}{c} = \frac{d}{a}$$

$$\frac{1}{2} = \frac{d}{3\frac{1}{2}}$$

$$\frac{1}{2} = \frac{d}{\frac{7}{2}}$$

$$\frac{1}{2} = d \div \frac{7}{2}$$

$$\frac{1}{2} = d \cdot \frac{2}{7}$$

$$\frac{1}{2} \cdot \frac{7}{2} = d \cdot \frac{2}{7} \cdot \frac{7}{2}$$

$$\frac{7}{4} = d$$

35.

$$\frac{e}{b} = \frac{d}{a}$$

$$\frac{1}{2} = \frac{d}{2\frac{1}{5}}$$

$$\frac{1}{2} = \frac{d}{\frac{11}{5}}$$

$$\frac{1}{2} = d \div \frac{11}{5}$$

$$\frac{1}{2} = d \cdot \frac{5}{11}$$

$$\frac{11}{5} \cdot \frac{1}{2} = \frac{11}{5} \cdot \frac{5}{11}d$$

$$\frac{11}{10} = d$$

$$\frac{e}{b} = \frac{f}{c}$$

$$\frac{1}{2} = \frac{f}{1}$$

$$\frac{1}{2} = f$$

36. x = number of cones sold on a given day.

$$\frac{12 \text{ hr}}{3 \text{ hr}} = \frac{x \text{ cones}}{170 \text{ cones}}$$

$$4 = \frac{x}{170}$$

$$170 \cdot 4 = 170 \cdot \frac{x}{170}$$

$$680 = x$$

680 cones

37. B; $1040 \text{ words} \times \dfrac{1 \text{ minutes}}{26 \text{ words}} = 40 \text{ minutes}$

38.

$$\frac{24}{56} = \frac{36}{56 + x}$$

$$2016 = 24(56 + x)$$

$$2016 = 1344 + 24x$$

$$672 = 24x$$

$$28 = x$$

You need to add 28 inches to the length.

8.3 Problem Solving Using Proportions

ONGOING ASSESSMENT

1. $\dfrac{\$16}{3h} = \dfrac{\$12}{2h}$

$16 \times 2 = 32;\ 3 \times 12 = 36$

No; it is not fair.

EXERCISES

1.

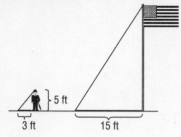

5 ft

3 ft   15 ft

2. B

3. $\dfrac{h}{5} = \dfrac{15}{3}$

4.

$$\dfrac{h}{5} = \dfrac{15}{3}$$

$$5 \cdot \dfrac{h}{5} = 5 \cdot 5$$

$$h = 25$$

The height of the flagpole is 25 feet.

5. x = number of beats in 10 seconds.

1 min = 60 sec

$$\dfrac{x \text{ beats}}{72 \text{ beats}} = \dfrac{10 \text{ sec}}{60 \text{ sec}}$$

$$\dfrac{x}{72} = \dfrac{1}{6}$$

$$72 \cdot \dfrac{x}{72} = 72 \cdot \dfrac{1}{6}$$

$$x = 12$$

You would feel 12 beats.

6. x = number of beats in 1 minute.

1 min = 60 sec

$$\dfrac{x \text{ beats}}{11 \text{ beats}} = \dfrac{60 \text{ sec}}{6 \text{ sec}}$$

$$\dfrac{x}{11} = 10$$

$$11 \cdot \dfrac{x}{11} = 11 \cdot 10$$

$$x = 110$$

Your heartbeat rate is 110 beats per minute.

7. x = number of beats in 1 minute.

1 min = 60 sec

$$\dfrac{x \text{ beats}}{40 \text{ beats}} = \dfrac{60 \text{ sec}}{15 \text{ sec}}$$

$$40 \cdot \dfrac{x}{40} = 4 \cdot 40$$

$$x = 160$$

Your heartbeat rate is 160 beats per minute.

8. $\dfrac{x \text{ Americans}}{317{,}600 \text{ Americans}} = \dfrac{1 \text{ day}}{30 \text{ days}}$

$$30x = 317{,}600$$

$$x \approx 10{,}600$$

About 10,600 Americans a day became teenagers in 1995.

9. $\dfrac{317{,}600 \text{ Americans}}{x \text{ Americans}} = \dfrac{1 \text{ month}}{12 \text{ months}}$

$$x = 317{,}600 \cdot 12$$

$$x = 4{,}000{,}000$$

About 4 million Americans became teenagers in 1995.

10. x = number of hours slept by age 30.

$$\dfrac{x \text{ hours}}{220{,}000 \text{ hours}} = \dfrac{30 \text{ years}}{70 \text{ years}}$$

$$\dfrac{x}{220{,}000} = \dfrac{3}{7}$$

$$220{,}000 \cdot \dfrac{x}{220{,}000} = 220{,}000 \cdot \dfrac{3}{7}$$

$$x \approx 94{,}000$$

You will have slept about 94,000 hours by the time you were 30 years old.

11. x = property tax in dollars for $110,000 house.

$$\frac{x \text{ dollars}}{1500 \text{ dollars}} = \frac{110,000 \text{ dollars}}{90,000 \text{ dollars}}$$

$$\frac{x}{1500} = \frac{11}{9}$$

$$1500 \cdot \frac{x}{1500} = 1500 \cdot \frac{11}{9}$$

$$x \approx 2000$$

You would expect to pay about $2000 property tax on a $110,000 house.

12. A

13. Photo amoeba width = 25 millimeters

Actual amoeba width = a millimeters

$$\frac{25}{a} = \frac{100}{1}$$

14.

$$\frac{25}{a} = \frac{100}{1}$$

$$\frac{a}{25} = \frac{1}{100}$$

$$25 \cdot \frac{a}{25} = 25 \cdot \frac{1}{100}$$

$$a = \frac{25}{100} \text{ or } 0.25$$

The width of the actual amoeba is 0.25 millimeters.

15.

$$768 \cdot \frac{832}{624} = \frac{x}{768} \cdot 768$$

$$\frac{638,976}{624} = x$$

$$1024 = x$$

16. B; $\dfrac{1 \text{ ft}}{\frac{1}{4} \text{ in.}} = \dfrac{x \text{ ft}}{16 \text{ in.}}$

$$16 = \tfrac{1}{4}x$$

$$4 \cdot 16 = 4 \cdot \tfrac{1}{4}x$$

$$64 = x$$

17. 24 ft; 6 ft by 3 ft

8.4 *ALGEBRA CONNECTION: Solving Percent Equations*

ONGOING ASSESSMENT

1. Yes

EXERCISES

1. $\dfrac{a}{160} = \dfrac{65}{100}$ *Write the percent equation.*

$\dfrac{a}{160} = 0.65$ *Divide to obtain decimal form.*

$a = 104$ *Multiply each side by 160.*

2. $\dfrac{50}{40} = \dfrac{P}{100}$ *Write the percent equation.*

$1.25 = \dfrac{P}{100}$ *Divide to obtain decimal form.*

$125 = P$ *Multiply each side by 100.*

3. 25 is the base.

$$\frac{20}{25} = \frac{p}{100}$$

$$\frac{4}{5} = \frac{p}{100}$$

$$100 \cdot \frac{4}{5} = p$$

$$80 = p$$

20 is 80% of 25.

4. 50 is the base.

$$\frac{a}{50} = \frac{16}{100}$$

$$\frac{a}{50} = 0.16$$

$$a = 50 \cdot 0.16$$

$$a = 8$$

8 is 16% of 50.

5. The base is unknown.

$$\frac{90}{b} = \frac{75}{100}$$

$$\frac{b}{90} = \frac{100}{75}$$

$$\frac{b}{90} = \frac{25 \cdot 4}{25 \cdot 3}$$

$$b = 90 \cdot \frac{4}{3}$$

$$b = 120$$

90 is 75% of 120.

6. Yes; $\dfrac{15}{6} = \dfrac{250}{100}$

7.

$$\frac{13}{25} = \frac{p}{100}$$

$$100 \cdot \frac{13}{25} = p$$

$$52 = p$$

8.

$$\frac{a}{20} = \frac{85}{100}$$

$$\frac{a}{20} = \frac{17}{20}$$

$$a = 17$$

9.

$$\frac{3}{b} = \frac{60}{100}$$

$$\frac{3}{b} = \frac{3}{5}$$

$$b = 5$$

10.

$$\frac{22}{30} = \frac{p}{100}$$

$$\frac{11}{15} = \frac{p}{100}$$

$$100 \cdot \frac{11}{15} = p$$

$$73.33 \approx p$$

22 is 73.33% of 30.

11.

$$\frac{a}{165} = \frac{33}{100}$$

$$\frac{a}{165} = 0.33$$

$$a = 165 \cdot 0.33$$

$$a = 54.45$$

54.45 is 33% of 165.

12.

$$\frac{a}{360} = \frac{2}{100}$$

$$\frac{a}{360} = 0.02$$

$$a = 360 \cdot 0.02$$

$$a = 7.2$$

7.2 is 2% of 360.

13.

$$\frac{66}{b} = \frac{120}{100}$$

$$\frac{b}{66} = \frac{100}{120}$$

$$\frac{b}{66} = \frac{20 \cdot 5}{20 \cdot 6}$$

$$b = 66 \cdot \frac{5}{6}$$

$$b = 55$$

66 is 120% of 55.

14.

$$\frac{34}{b} = \frac{50}{100}$$

$$\frac{b}{34} = \frac{100}{50}$$

$$\frac{b}{34} = 2$$

$$b = 34 \cdot 2$$

$$b = 68$$

34 is 50% of 68.

15.

$$\frac{45}{20} = \frac{p}{100}$$

$$\frac{9}{4} = \frac{p}{100}$$

$$100 \cdot \frac{9}{4} = p$$

$$225 = p$$

45 is 225% of 20.

16.

$$\frac{a}{110} = \frac{110}{100}$$

$$\frac{a}{110} = 1.1$$

$$a = 110 \cdot 1.1$$

$$a = 121$$

121 is 110% of 110.

17.

$$\frac{6.06}{b} = \frac{20.2}{100}$$

$$\frac{b}{6.06} = \frac{100}{20.2}$$

$$b = 6.06 \cdot \frac{100}{20.2}$$

$$b = \frac{606}{20.2}$$

$$b = 30$$

6.06 is 20.2% of 30.

18.
$$\frac{71.5}{90} = \frac{p}{100}$$
$$100 \cdot \frac{71.5}{90} = p$$
$$\frac{7150}{90} = p$$
$$79.44 \approx p$$

71.5 is 79.44% of 90.

19.
$$\frac{a}{270} = \frac{25.5}{100}$$
$$\frac{a}{270} = 0.255$$
$$a = 270 \cdot 0.255$$
$$a = 68.85$$

68.85 is 25.5% of 270.

20.
$$\frac{100}{b} = \frac{200}{100}$$
$$b = 50$$

100 is 200% of 50.

21.
$$\frac{a}{200} = \frac{50}{100}$$
$$a = 100$$

100 is 50% of 200.

22.
$$\frac{100}{b} = \frac{100}{100}$$
$$b = 100$$

100 is 100% of 100.

23.
$$\frac{5}{15} = \frac{p}{100}$$
$$\frac{1}{3} = \frac{p}{100}$$
$$100 \cdot \frac{1}{3} = p$$
$$33\frac{1}{3} = p$$

5 is $33\frac{1}{3}$% of 15.

24.
$$\frac{45}{150} = \frac{p}{100}$$

25.
$$\frac{a}{50} = \frac{24}{100}$$

26.
$$\frac{31}{35} = \frac{p}{100}$$
$$100 \cdot \frac{31}{35} = p$$
$$89 \approx p$$

No; $\frac{31}{35} \approx 89\% < 90\%$.

27.
$$\frac{2.75}{54.99} = \frac{p}{100}$$
$$100 \cdot \frac{2.75}{54.99} = p$$
$$\frac{275}{54.99} = p$$
$$5.00 \approx p$$

There is a 5% sales tax.

28.
$$\frac{24}{b} = \frac{75}{100}$$
$$\frac{b}{24} = \frac{100}{75}$$
$$\frac{b}{24} = \frac{\cancel{25} \cdot 4}{\cancel{25} \cdot 3}$$
$$b = 24 \cdot \frac{4}{3}$$
$$b = 32$$

He attempted 32 field goals.

29.
$$\frac{28}{81} = \frac{p}{100}$$
$$100 \cdot \frac{28}{81} = p$$
$$\frac{2800}{81} = p$$
$$34.6 \approx p$$

The number of awards given in 1958 is about 35% of the number of awards given in 1993.

30.
$$\frac{81}{28} = \frac{p}{100}$$
$$100 \cdot \frac{81}{28} = p$$
$$\frac{8100}{28} = p$$
$$289.3 \approx p$$

The number of awards given in 1993 is about 290% of the number of awards given in 1958.

31. B; $\dfrac{4 \times 4}{8 \times 8} = \dfrac{16}{64} = 0.25 = 25\%$ **32.** C; $\dfrac{64 - 16}{16} = \dfrac{p}{100}$

$$\dfrac{48}{16} = \dfrac{p}{100}$$

$$p = 300$$

33. $350 \times 0.05 = 17.5 \approx 18$

$350 - 18 = 332$ tickets

Spiral R E V I E W

Note to teachers: The checks for the solutions to Exercises 1–9 will not be shown, but students should continue to check their work.

1. $4(x + 2) = 12$

    $x + 2 = 3$

        $x = 1$

2. $3y = 4y - 7$

    $y = -7$

    $y = 7$

3. $a + \frac{5}{3} = 2a - \frac{1}{3}$

    $\frac{5}{3} = a - \frac{1}{3}$

    $\frac{6}{3} = a$

    $2 = a$

4. $\frac{1}{12}p - \frac{1}{12} = \frac{5}{12}$

    $\frac{1}{12}p = \frac{1}{2}$

  $12 \cdot \frac{1}{12}P = 12 \cdot \frac{1}{2}$

      $P = 6$

5. $5 + 2(q - 3) = 0$

    $5 + 2q - 6 = 0$

       $2q - 1 = 0$

          $2q = 1$

           $q = \frac{1}{2}$

6. $0.2s - 5.4 = 0$

    $0.2s = 5.4$

      $s = 27$

7. $1 = \frac{1}{2}(p - 1)$

  $2 \cdot 1 = 2 \cdot \frac{1}{2}(p - 1)$

     $2 = p - 1$

     $3 = p$

8. $\frac{1}{4}x + \frac{1}{4}x = 3$

      $\frac{1}{2}x = 3$

  $2 \cdot \frac{1}{2}x = 2 \cdot 3$

       $x = 6$

9. $\frac{1}{3}p - 2 = 2$

    $\frac{1}{3}p = 4$

  $3 \cdot \frac{1}{3}p = 3 \cdot 4$

     $p = 12$

10. $52\% = \frac{52}{100} = 0.52$

11. $83\% = \frac{83}{100} = 0.83$

12. $146\% = \frac{146}{100} = 1.46$

13. $206\% = \frac{206}{100} = 2.06$

14. Rate; $\dfrac{16 \text{ yards}}{2 \text{ jumps}} = 8$ yards per jump

15. Rate; $\dfrac{28 \text{ points}}{4 \text{ quarters}} = 7$ points per quarter

16. Ratio; $\dfrac{2 \text{ animals}}{20 \text{ animals}} = \dfrac{1}{10}$

17. Rate; $\dfrac{4 \text{ feet}}{10 \text{ seconds}} = \dfrac{2 \cdot 2}{2 \cdot 5}$

                   $= \dfrac{2}{5}$ feet per second

                   $= 2$ feet per 5 seconds

18. $\dfrac{1}{6} = \dfrac{3}{18}$

    $\dfrac{2}{9} = \dfrac{4}{18}$

Your cousin ate more.

$\dfrac{4}{18} - \dfrac{3}{18} = \dfrac{1}{18}$

He ate $\dfrac{1}{18}$ more.

Mid-Chapter **A S S E S S M E N T**

1. Rate; $\dfrac{100 \text{ meters}}{18 \text{ seconds}} = 50$ meters per 9 seconds

2. Rate; $\dfrac{18 \text{ lures}}{6 \text{ fisherman}} = 3$ lures per fisherman

3. Ratio; $\dfrac{42 \text{ pounds}}{3 \text{ pounds}} = \dfrac{14}{1}$

4. Rate; $\dfrac{5 \text{ days}}{1 \text{ week}} = 5$ days per week

5. The angles have the same measure; therefore, the triangles are similar.

$$\dfrac{a}{d} = \dfrac{b}{e}; \ \dfrac{a}{d} = \dfrac{c}{f}; \ \dfrac{b}{e} = \dfrac{c}{f}$$

6. The angles do not have the same measure; therefore, the triangles are not similar.

7. True;

$$\dfrac{2}{11} \overset{?}{=} \dfrac{10}{55}$$

$$\dfrac{2}{11} \overset{?}{=} \dfrac{2 \cdot \cancel{5}}{\cancel{5} \cdot 11}$$

$$\dfrac{2}{11} = \dfrac{2}{11}$$

8. False;

$$\dfrac{250}{350} \overset{?}{=} \dfrac{2}{3}$$

$$\dfrac{\cancel{50} \cdot 5}{\cancel{50} \cdot 7} \overset{?}{=} \dfrac{2}{3}$$

$$\dfrac{5}{7} \neq \dfrac{2}{3}$$

9. True;

$$\dfrac{5}{7} \overset{?}{=} \dfrac{25}{35}$$

$$\dfrac{5}{7} \overset{?}{=} \dfrac{\cancel{5} \cdot 5}{\cancel{5} \cdot 7}$$

$$\dfrac{5}{7} = \dfrac{5}{7}$$

Note to teachers: The checks for the solutions to Exercises 10–13 will not be shown, but students should continue to check their work.

10. $\dfrac{x}{4} = \dfrac{8}{2}$

$\dfrac{x}{4} = 4$

$x = 16$

11. $\dfrac{3}{7} = \dfrac{a}{9}$

$9 \cdot \dfrac{3}{7} = 9 \cdot \dfrac{a}{9}$

$\dfrac{27}{7} = a$

12. $\dfrac{18}{b} = \dfrac{25}{36}$

$\dfrac{b}{18} = \dfrac{36}{25}$

$18 \cdot \dfrac{b}{18} = 18 \cdot \dfrac{36}{25}$

$b = \dfrac{648}{25}$

$b = 25.92$

13. $\dfrac{y}{3} = \dfrac{10}{2}$

$3 \cdot \dfrac{y}{3} = 3 \cdot 5$

$y = 15$

14. $\dfrac{a}{18} = \dfrac{35}{100}$

$\dfrac{a}{18} = 0.35$

$a = 18 \cdot 0.35$

$a = 6.3$

6.3 is 35% of 18.

15. $\dfrac{18}{b} = \dfrac{150}{100}$

$\dfrac{b}{18} = \dfrac{100}{150}$

$\dfrac{b}{18} = \dfrac{2}{3}$

$b = 18 \cdot \dfrac{2}{3}$

$b = 12$

18 is 150% of 12.

16. $\dfrac{36}{150} = \dfrac{p}{100}$

$\dfrac{6}{25} = \dfrac{p}{100}$

$100 \cdot \dfrac{6}{25} = p$

$24 = p$

36 is 24% of 150.

17. x = height in feet of the Gateway Arch.

$$\frac{60}{\frac{1}{2}} = \frac{x}{5\frac{1}{4}}$$

$$\frac{60}{\frac{1}{2}} = \frac{x}{\frac{21}{4}}$$

$$60 \div \frac{1}{2} = x \div \frac{21}{4}$$

$$60 \cdot 2 = x \cdot \frac{4}{21}$$

$$120 = \frac{4}{21}x$$

$$\frac{21}{4} \cdot 120 = \frac{21}{4} \cdot \frac{4}{21}x$$

$$630 = x$$

The Gateway Arch is 630 feet tall.

18., 19.

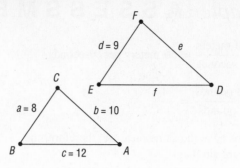

18. f is the longest side.

$$\frac{d}{a} = \frac{f}{c}$$

$$\frac{9}{8} = \frac{f}{12}$$

$$12 \cdot \frac{9}{8} = f$$

$$\frac{27}{2} \text{ or } 13\frac{1}{2} = f$$

19. e is the third side.

$$\frac{d}{a} = \frac{e}{b}$$

$$\frac{9}{8} = \frac{e}{10}$$

$$10 \cdot \frac{9}{8} = e$$

$$\frac{45}{4} \text{ or } 11\frac{1}{4} = e$$

8.5 *Problem Solving Using Percents*

ONGOING ASSESSMENT

1. Applying $10 off first: $50 - 10 = 40$
$40 \times 0.20 = 8$
$40 - 8 = 32$
The shoes would cost you $32.

Applying 20% off first: $50 \times 0.20 = 10$
$50 - 10 = 40$
$40 - 10 = 30$
The shoes would cost you $30.

You save more money if you take 20% off then take $10 off.

EXERCISES

1. a. $38.15 + 16.35 = \$54.50$

b. $\dfrac{16.35}{54.50} = \dfrac{p}{100}$

$0.3 = \dfrac{p}{100}$

$30 = p$

The discount is 30%.

2. $29.99 is 75% of the original price.

Solve $\dfrac{29.99}{b} = \dfrac{75}{100}$.

3. $\dfrac{9}{b} = \dfrac{20}{100}$

$\dfrac{b}{9} = \dfrac{100}{20}$

$\dfrac{b}{9} = 5$

$b = 45$

45 students were surveyed.

4. See Exercise 3.

a. $\dfrac{a}{45} = \dfrac{40}{100}$

$\dfrac{a}{45} = 0.4$

$a = 45 \cdot 0.4$

$a = 18$

18 students said that pop was their favorite.

b. $\dfrac{a}{45} = \dfrac{31}{100}$

$\dfrac{a}{45} = 0.31$

$a = 45 \cdot 0.31$

$a \approx 14$

About 14 students said that rhythm and blues was their favorite.

c. $\dfrac{a}{45} = \dfrac{9}{100}$

$\dfrac{a}{45} = 0.09$

$a = 45 \cdot 0.09$

$a \approx 4$

About 4 students said that easy listening was their favorite.

5. $\dfrac{410{,}000}{b} = \dfrac{41}{100}$

$\dfrac{b}{410{,}000} = \dfrac{100}{41}$

$b = 410{,}000 \cdot \dfrac{100}{41}$

$b = 1{,}000{,}000$

1,000,000 Americans took a language course.

6. $\dfrac{a}{1{,}000{,}000} = \dfrac{27.4}{100}$

$a = \dfrac{27.4}{100} \cdot 1{,}000{,}000$

$a = 274{,}000$

274,000 Americans took a course in French.

7. $1(470) + 0.035(470) = 1.035(470)$

8. $1.035(470) = \$486.45, \ 486.45(1.035) \approx \$503.48$

9. $172.3 + 63.3 + 46.2 + 14.7 + 13.3 + 33.2 = 343$

Americans own 343 million radios.

10. $\dfrac{172.3}{343} = \dfrac{p}{100}$

$100 \cdot \dfrac{172.3}{343} = p$

$\dfrac{1723}{343} = p$

$50.2 \approx p$

About 50.2% of Americans' radios are in bedrooms.

11. $\dfrac{63.3}{343} = \dfrac{p}{100}$

$100 \cdot \dfrac{63.3}{343} = p$

$\dfrac{6330}{343} = p$

$18.5 \approx p$

About 18.5% of Americans' radios are in living rooms.

12. $\dfrac{46.2}{343} = \dfrac{p}{100}$

$100 \cdot \dfrac{46.2}{343} = p$

$\dfrac{4620}{343} = p$

$13.5 \approx p$

About 13.5% of Americans' radios are in kitchens.

13. $\dfrac{21.40}{b} = \dfrac{25}{100}$

$\dfrac{b}{21.40} = \dfrac{100}{25}$

$\dfrac{b}{21.40} = 4$

$b = 4 \cdot 21.40$

$b = 85.6$

The regular price was $85.60.

14. $\dfrac{1050}{b} = \dfrac{35}{100}$

$\dfrac{b}{1050} = \dfrac{100}{35}$

$b = \dfrac{100}{35} \cdot 1050$

$b = \$3000$

15. Add the total income for all categories.

16. a. $\dfrac{1170}{3000} = \dfrac{p}{100}$

$\dfrac{39}{100} = \dfrac{p}{100}$

$39 = p$

Calling and credit cards make up 39% of the yearly income.

b. $\dfrac{488}{3000} = \dfrac{p}{100}$

$100 \cdot \dfrac{488}{3000} \approx p$

$16 \approx p$

Collect calls make up about 16% of the yearly income.

c. $\dfrac{292}{3000} = \dfrac{p}{100}$

$100 \cdot \dfrac{292}{3000} = p$

$10 \approx p$

Third-party calls make up about 10% of the yearly income.

17. C; $\dfrac{50}{x} = \dfrac{75}{100}$

$75x = 5000$

$x = 66\frac{2}{3}$ cm^2

18. $5p = 5 - 3.50$

$5p = 1.50$

$p = 0.30$

Percent discount is 30%.

8.6 *Exploring Percent of Increase or Decrease*

ONGOING ASSESSMENT

1. $0.28 - 0.25 = 0.03$; $\dfrac{0.03}{0.28} \approx 0.107 = 10.7\%$ decrease

2. $0.28 - 0.25 = 0.03$; $\dfrac{0.03}{0.25} = 0.12 = 12\%$ increase

3. *Sample answer:* The percents are different even though the change in cost are the same.

EXERCISES

1. $\dfrac{0.48 - 0.28}{0.48} = \dfrac{0.20}{0.48}$

≈ 0.417

$\approx 41.7\%$

2. $\dfrac{0.31 - 0.28}{0.28} = \dfrac{0.03}{0.28}$

≈ 0.107

$\approx 10.7\%$

3. Increase;

$\dfrac{18.21 - 16.35}{16.35} = \dfrac{1.86}{16.35}$

≈ 0.114

$\approx 11.4\%$

4. Decrease;

$\dfrac{1056 - 972}{1056} = \dfrac{84}{1056}$

≈ 0.080

$\approx 8.0\%$

5. Increase;

$\dfrac{12 - 10}{10} = \dfrac{2}{10}$

$= 0.2$

$= 20\%$

6. Decrease;

$\dfrac{15 - 12}{15} = \dfrac{3}{15}$

$= 0.2$

$= 20\%$

7. Decrease;

$\dfrac{75 - 60}{75} = \dfrac{15}{75}$

$= 0.2$

$= 20\%$

8. Increase;

$\dfrac{143 - 110}{110} = \dfrac{33}{110}$

$= 0.3$

$= 30\%$

9. Increase;

$\dfrac{200 - 90}{90} = \dfrac{110}{90}$

≈ 1.222

$\approx 122.2\%$

10. Decrease;

$$\frac{260 - 160}{260} = \frac{100}{260}$$
$$\approx 0.385$$
$$\approx 38.5\%$$

11. Increase;

$$\frac{201.59 - 171.33}{171.33} = \frac{30.26}{171.33}$$
$$\approx 0.177$$
$$\approx 17.7\%$$

12. Decrease;

$$\frac{31.99 - 22.39}{31.99} = \frac{9.6}{31.99}$$
$$\approx 0.300$$
$$\approx 30.0\%$$

13. Decrease;

$$\frac{521.43 - 413.68}{521.43} = \frac{107.75}{521.43}$$
$$\approx 0.207$$
$$\approx 20.7\%$$

14. Increase;

$$\frac{19.17 - 18.77}{18.77} = \frac{0.4}{18.77}$$
$$\approx 0.021$$
$$\approx 2.1\%$$

15. $2 \times 1 = 2$, $2 \times 2 = 4$, $2 \times 4 = 8$

Pattern: Each number, after the first, is 2 times or 200% of the preceding number.

$2 \times 8 = 16$, $2 \times 16 = 32$, $2 \times 32 = 64$

16. $\frac{1}{4} \cdot 4096 = 1024$, $\frac{1}{4} \cdot 1024 = 256$, $\frac{1}{4} \cdot 256 = 64$

Pattern: Each number, after the first, is $\frac{1}{4}$ of or 25% of the preceding number.

$\frac{1}{4} \cdot 64 = 16$, $\frac{1}{4} \cdot 16 = 4$, $\frac{1}{4} \cdot 4 = 1$

17. $\frac{1}{5} \cdot 15625 = 3125$, $\frac{1}{5} \cdot 3125 = 625$, $\frac{1}{5} \cdot 625 = 125$

Pattern: Each number, after the first, is $\frac{1}{5}$ of or 20% of the preceding number.

$\frac{1}{5} \cdot 125 = 25$, $\frac{1}{5} \cdot 25 = 5$, $\frac{1}{5} \cdot 5 = 1$

18. $3 \times 1 = 3$, $3 \times 3 = 9$, $3 \times 9 = 27$

Pattern: Each number, after the first, is 3 times or 300% of the preceding number.

$3 \times 27 = 81$, $3 \times 81 = 243$, $3 \times 243 = 729$

19. Answers vary.

20. Answers vary.

21.

Original Number	New Number	Percent Change
45	72	60% Increase
45	18	60% Decrease
400	500	25% Increase
400	300	25% Decrease

$$\frac{72 - 45}{45} = \frac{27}{45}$$
$$= \frac{3}{5} = 60\% \text{ Increase}$$
$$\frac{45 - 18}{45} = \frac{27}{45}$$
$$= \frac{3}{5} = 60\% \text{ Decrease}$$

$n =$ new number

$$\frac{n - 400}{400} = 0.25$$
$$400 \cdot \frac{n - 400}{400} = 400 \cdot 0.25$$
$$n - 400 = 100$$
$$n = 500$$

$n =$ new number

$$\frac{400 - n}{400} = 0.25$$
$$400 \cdot \frac{400 - n}{400} = 400 \cdot 0.25$$
$$400 - n = 100$$
$$-n = -300$$
$$n = 300$$

22. 90–91: $\dfrac{235 - 177}{177} = \dfrac{58}{177} \approx 0.328 \approx 32.8\%$ increase

91–92: $\dfrac{235 - 232}{235} = \dfrac{3}{235} \approx 0.013 \approx 1.3\%$ decrease

92–93: $\dfrac{232 - 231}{232} = \dfrac{1}{232} \approx 0.004 \approx 0.4\%$ decrease

93–94: $\dfrac{255 - 231}{231} = \dfrac{24}{231} \approx 0.104 \approx 10.4\%$ increase

94–95: $\dfrac{255 - 210}{255} = \dfrac{45}{255} \approx 0.176 \approx 17.6\%$ decrease

95–96: $\dfrac{210 - 139}{210} = \dfrac{71}{210} \approx 0.338 \approx 33.8\%$ decrease

23. True; $2n = n + n(100\%) \Rightarrow 2n = n + n$

24. True; $\frac{1}{2}n = n - n(50\%) \Rightarrow \frac{1}{2}n = n - \frac{1}{2}n$

25. False; $80 - 80(20\%) = 80 - 80(0.20)$
$$= 80 - 16 = 64 \neq 60$$

26. True; $100 + 100(25\%) = 100 + 100(0.25)$
$$= 100 + 25 = 125$$

27. $\dfrac{32{,}562 - 28{,}894}{32{,}562} = \dfrac{3668}{32{,}562}$
$$\approx 0.1126$$
$$\approx 11.3\%$$

28. Year 1: $24{,}000 \times 0.04 = 960$
$24{,}000 + 960 = \$24{,}960$;
Year 2: $24{,}960 \times 0.04 = 998.40$
$24{,}960 + 998.40 = \$25{,}958.40$;
Year 3: $25{,}958.40 \times 0.04 = 1038.3$
$25{,}958.40 + 1038.3 = \$26{,}996.70$;
Year 4: $26{,}996.70 \times 0.04 = 1079.8$
$26{,}996.70 + 1079.8 = \$28{,}076.50$;
Year 5: $28{,}076.50 \times 0.04 = 1123.00$
$28{,}076.50 + 1123.00 = \$29{,}199.50$

29. 1–2: $\dfrac{25{,}000 - 24{,}000}{24{,}000} = \dfrac{1000}{24{,}000} \approx 0.0416 \approx 4.2\%$

2–3: $\dfrac{26{,}000 - 25{,}000}{25{,}000} = \dfrac{1000}{25{,}000} = 0.04 = 4\%$

3–4: $\dfrac{27{,}000 - 26{,}000}{26{,}000} = \dfrac{1000}{26{,}000} \approx 0.038 \approx 3.8\%$

4–5: $\dfrac{28{,}000 - 27{,}000}{27{,}000} = \dfrac{1000}{27{,}000} \approx 0.037 \approx 3.7\%$

5–6: $\dfrac{29{,}000 - 28{,}000}{28{,}000} = \dfrac{1000}{28{,}000} \approx 0.036 \approx 3.6\%$

The percent of increase gets smaller every year in Job 2.

30. *Sample answer:* Job 1; Job 2 pays more during the first four years, but Job 1 pays more from the fifth year on.

31. D; $\dfrac{15 - 12}{12} = \dfrac{3}{12} = 0.25 = 25\%$

32. A; $\dfrac{12{,}000 - 10{,}800}{12{,}000} = \dfrac{1200}{12{,}000} = 0.1 = 10\%$

33. a. Percent increase in attendence $= \dfrac{(220 + 30) - (180 + 70)}{(220 + 30)} = 0\%$

b. Percent increase in revenue $= \dfrac{(180 \times 3.5 + 70 \times 5) - (220 \times 3.5 + 30 \times 5)}{(220 \times 3.5 + 30 \times 5)}$

$$= \dfrac{980 - 920}{920} = \dfrac{60}{920} \approx 0.065 \approx 6.5\%$$

1. $\frac{3}{8}$

2. $\frac{2}{8} = \frac{1}{4}$

3. $\frac{2}{8} = \frac{1}{4}$

4. $\frac{1}{8}$

5. $|ab| = |(-8)(2)|$
$\quad = |-16|$
$\quad = 16$

6. $|a^2| = |(-8)^2|$
$\quad = |64|$
$\quad = 64$

7. $|a| - |b| = |-8| - |2|$
$\quad = 8 - 2$
$\quad = 6$

8. $|a - b| = |-8 - 2|$
$\quad = |-10|$
$\quad = 10$

9.

10. $\frac{1}{2} = 0.5 \qquad \frac{3}{7} \approx 0.4286$

$\quad \frac{1}{3} = 0.\overline{3} \qquad \frac{4}{9} = 0.\overline{4}$

$\quad \frac{5}{8} = 0.625$

Ordered from least to greatest: $\frac{1}{3}, \frac{3}{7}, \frac{4}{9}, \frac{1}{2}, \frac{5}{8}$

11. $\dfrac{-1.02 + (-0.98) + (-1.01) + (-1) + (-1.04)}{5} = \dfrac{-5.05}{5} = -1.01$

12. $3x + 2y + x = 4x + 2y$
$\quad 4x + 2y = 4(5) + 2(-4)$
$\qquad\quad = 20 - 8$
$\qquad\quad = 12$

13. $4x - 5y$ cannot be simplified.
$\quad 4x - 5y = 4(5) - 5(-4)$
$\qquad\quad = 20 + 20$
$\qquad\quad = 40$

14. $xy - 2y$ cannot be simplified.
$\quad xy - 2y = (5)(-4) - 2(-4)$
$\qquad\quad = -20 + 8$
$\qquad\quad = -12$

15. $10x + 20y + 2x = 12x + 20y$
$\quad 12x + 20y = 12(5) + 20(-4)$
$\qquad\quad = 60 - 80$
$\qquad\quad = -20$

16. $\dfrac{a}{80} = \dfrac{35}{100}$

$\quad \dfrac{a}{80} = 0.35$

$\quad a = 80 \cdot 0.35$

$\quad a = 28$

28 is 35% of 80.

17. $\dfrac{32}{b} = \dfrac{45}{100}$

$\quad \dfrac{b}{32} = \dfrac{100}{45}$

$\quad \dfrac{b}{32} = \dfrac{20}{9}$

$\quad b = 32 \cdot \dfrac{20}{9}$

$\quad b = \dfrac{640}{9}$

$\quad b = 71\frac{1}{9}$

32 is 45% of $71\frac{1}{9}$.

18. $\dfrac{190}{310} = \dfrac{p}{100}$

$\quad \dfrac{19}{31} = \dfrac{p}{100}$

$\quad 100 \cdot \dfrac{19}{31} = p$

$\quad \dfrac{1900}{31} = p$

$\quad 61.3 \approx p$

190 is about 61.3% of 310.

19. $\dfrac{a}{92} = \dfrac{116}{100}$

$\dfrac{a}{92} = 1.16$

$a = 92 \cdot 1.16$

$a = 106.72$

106.72 is 116% of 92.

20. Sales tax: $\$89.99 \times 0.07 = \$6.30$

Total price: $\$89.99 + 6.30 = \$96.29$

Lab 8.7

Part A

1.

1 + 8	8 + 28	28 + 56	56 + 70	70 + 56	56 + 28	28 + 8	8 + 1

1   9   36   84   126   126   84   36   9   1

2.

1 + 9	9 + 36	36 + 84	84 + 126	126 + 126	126 + 84	84 + 36	36 + 9	9 + 1

1   10   45   120   210   252   210   120   45   10   1

3. 0th Row = 1

1st Row = $1 + 1 = 2$

2nd Row = $1 + 2 + 1 = 4$

3rd Row = $1 + 3 + 3 + 1 = 8$

4th Row = $1 + 4 + 6 + 4 + 1 = 16$

5th Row = $1 + 5 + 10 + 10 + 5 + 1 = 32$

6th Row = $1 + 6 + 15 + 20 + 15 + 6 + 1 = 64$

7th Row = $1 + 7 + 21 + 35 + 35 + 21 + 7 + 1 = 128$

Row	0	1	2	3	4	5	6	7
Sum	1	2	4	8	16	32	64	128

4. Pattern: Each sum, after the first, is twice the preceding sum.

Solution: 256

$128 \times 2 = 256$

8.7 *The Counting Principle*

ONGOING ASSESSMENT

1. Let a, b, c, d, e, f represent 6 people.

15 choices

2. Row 6 $\Rightarrow$ 1 6 15 20 15 6 1

⟵ Choose 2 people from 6.

15 choices

EXERCISES

1. $2 \cdot 4 = 8$

2.

3 <0,5 6 <0,5 9 <0,5 from 1; and 3 <0,5 6 <0,5 9 <0,5 from 7

There are 12 possible numbers.

3. $3 \times 4 \times 6 = 72$ ways

4. 21; go to the 7th row and count in 2 places from 1.

Row 7 ⇒ 1 7 21 35 35 21 7 1
         ↑
      Choose 2
      sweaters from 7.

5. $4 \cdot 5 = 20$

Check:

w = white rice, r = rice pilaf, b = baked potato, m = mashed potatoes, h = home fries

C = cole slaw, G= green beans, V = mixed vegetables, S = salad

wC, wG, wV, wS, rC, rG, rV, rS, bC, bG, bV, bS, mC, mG, mV, mS, hC, hG, hV, hS

6. a. $3 \times 6 = 18$

b.
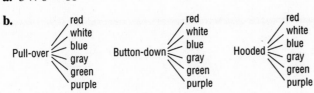

Pull-over — red, white, blue, gray, green, purple Button-down — red, white, blue, gray, green, purple Hooded — red, white, blue, gray, green, purple

7. A; there are 2 ways to answer each question, so the Counting Principle is used.

8. $3 \times 6 \times 10 = 180$ outfits

9. Row 7 ⇒ 1 7 21 35 35 21 7 1
              ↑
           Choose 3
           books from 7.

10. Row 8 ⇒ 1 8 28 56 70 56 28 8 1
                    ↑
                 Choose 4
                 pencils from 8.

11. Row 6 ⇒ 1 6 15 20 15 6 1
                    ↑
                 Choose 5
                 CDs from 6.

12. Row 9 ⇒ 1 9 36 84 126 126 84 36 9 1
                    ↑
                 Choose 3
                 photos from 9.

13. C

14. a. Row 10 ⇒ 1   10   45   120   210   252   210   120   45   10   1

↑
Choose 3
groups from 10.

b. $10 \times 9 \times 8 = 720$

Communicating About Mathematics

1. Let w = weight the beetle carries on its back. Then $\dfrac{w}{0.1 \text{ oz}} = \dfrac{30}{1}$. $w = 30(0.1) = 3$ oz;

the weight the beetle carries is to its own weight as 30 is to 1.

2. $850 \times \dfrac{1}{10}$ oz $= 85$ oz;

$\dfrac{10}{85} \approx 0.118 \approx 11.8\%$

3. The beetle can lift 100 times its weight, so a 150 lb person could lift $100 \times 150 = 15,000$ pounds.

4. The beetle can lift 30 times its weight without stress, so a 150 lb person could lift $30 \times 150 = 4500$ pounds.

Using a Computer

1. $1000 \times 100 = 100,000$

2. $1(1) + 1(3) + 2(4) + 3(5) + 8(6) + 5(7)$
$+ 10(8) + 13(9) + 12(10) + 11(11) + 11(12)$
$+ 9(13) + 5(14) + 7(15) + 1(17) + 1(18)$
$= 1 + 3 + 8 + 15 + 48 + 35 + 80 + 117 + 120$
$+ 121 + 132 + 117 + 70 + 105 + 17 + 18$
$= 1007$

3. $\dfrac{1007}{100,000} = 0.01007 = 1.007\%$

8.8 | *Probability and Simulations*

ONGOING ASSESSMENT

1. a. Multiples of 3: 3, 6, 9
Number of digits: 3
$\dfrac{1}{3 \cdot 3} = \dfrac{1}{27}$

b. $\dfrac{1}{3 \cdot 2 \cdot 1} = \dfrac{1}{6}$

2. b

EXERCISES

1. Row 5 $\Rightarrow$ 1 5   10   10   5   1

   $\uparrow$

   Choose 2 officers
   from 5.

   There are 10 committees possible.

2. $3 \cdot 2 = 6$

   $\frac{6}{10} = \frac{3}{5}$, or 0.6

3. $\frac{3}{10}$, or 0.3

4. $\frac{1}{10}$, or 0.1

5. $\frac{1}{2} \cdot \frac{1}{2} = \frac{1}{4}$, or 0.25

6. $\frac{1}{2} \cdot \frac{1}{2} = \frac{1}{4}$, or 0.25

7. Answers vary.

8. There are 5 even numbers: 0, 2, 4, 6, 8

   $\frac{1}{5} \cdot \frac{1}{5} = \frac{1}{25}$ or 0.04

9. $\frac{1}{5} \cdot \frac{1}{4} = \frac{1}{20}$, or 0.05

10. Answers vary.

11. $\frac{1}{10} \cdot \frac{1}{10} = \frac{1}{100}$, or 0.01

12. $\frac{1}{26} \cdot \frac{1}{26} = \frac{1}{676}$, or 0.0015

13. $\frac{21}{26} \cdot \frac{5}{26} = \frac{105}{676}$, or 0.155

14. Exercise 12: $\frac{1}{24} \cdot \frac{1}{24} = \frac{1}{576}$, or 0.0017

   Exercise 13: $\frac{21}{24} \cdot \frac{3}{24} = \frac{63}{576} = \frac{7}{64}$, or 0.109

15. Answers vary.

16. $\frac{1}{5} \cdot \frac{1}{8} = \frac{1}{40}$, or 0.025

17. $\frac{1}{5} \cdot \frac{1}{8} = \frac{1}{40}$, or 0.025

18. $\frac{2}{5} \cdot \frac{1}{8} = \frac{2}{40} = \frac{1}{20}$, or 0.05

19. $\frac{2}{5} \cdot \frac{4}{8} = \frac{8}{40} = \frac{1}{5}$, or 0.2

20. $\frac{3}{5} \cdot \frac{1}{8} = \frac{3}{40}$, or 0.075

21. $\frac{3}{5} \cdot \frac{4}{8} = \frac{12}{40} = \frac{3}{10}$, or 0.03

22. A; $\frac{1}{4} \cdot \frac{1}{5} \cdot \frac{1}{6} = \frac{1}{120}$

23. Named species $= 12{,}000 - 10{,}300 = 1700$

   Probability fo choosing the same $= \frac{1}{1700}$, or 0.0006

Chapter **R E V I E W**

1. $\dfrac{1500 \text{ miles}}{2 \text{ days}}$; rate

2. $\dfrac{3 \text{ feet}}{24 \text{ inches}} = \dfrac{3 \text{ feet}}{2 \text{ feet}} = \dfrac{3}{2} = 1.5$

3. Ground beef: $\dfrac{\$3.98}{2 \text{ lb}} = \$1.99/\text{lb}$

   Ground turkey: $\dfrac{\$6.25}{5 \text{ lb}} = \$1.25/\text{lb}$

   Ground turkey is a better buy.

4. $\dfrac{x}{4} = \dfrac{5}{8}$

   $20 = 8x$

   $\dfrac{20}{8} = x$

   $2\dfrac{4}{8} = x$

   $2\dfrac{1}{2} = x$

5. $\dfrac{10}{3} = \dfrac{12}{t}$

   $\dfrac{3}{10} = \dfrac{t}{12}$

   $12 \cdot \dfrac{3}{10} = t$

   $\dfrac{18}{5} = t$

6.
$$\frac{14}{s} = \frac{56}{9}$$
$$\frac{s}{14} = \frac{9}{56}$$
$$14 \cdot \frac{s}{14} = \frac{9}{56} \cdot 14$$
$$s = \frac{9}{4}, \text{ or } 2.25$$

7. $16 \cdot \frac{5}{7} = \frac{m}{16} \cdot 16$
$$\frac{80}{7} = m$$

8.
$$\frac{5}{7.5} = \frac{2}{y}$$
$$5 \cdot y = 2 \cdot 7.5$$
$$5y = 15$$
$$y = 3$$

9.
$$\frac{6}{8} = \frac{7.5}{z}$$
$$6 \cdot z = 8 \cdot 7.5$$
$$6z = 60$$
$$z = 10$$

10. Use answer for Exercise 8.
$$\frac{6}{8} = \frac{3}{w}$$
$$8 \cdot 3 = 6 \cdot w$$
$$24 = 6w$$
$$4 = w$$

11.
$$\frac{35}{40} = \frac{p}{100}$$
$$\frac{7}{8} = \frac{p}{100}$$
$$100 \cdot \frac{7}{8} = p$$
$$87.5 = p$$
35 is 87.5% of 40.

12.
$$\frac{a}{22} = \frac{68}{100}$$
$$\frac{a}{22} = 0.68$$
$$a = 22 \cdot 0.68$$
$$a = 14.96$$
14.96 is 68% of 22.

13.
$$\frac{44}{b} = \frac{25}{100}$$
$$\frac{b}{44} = \frac{100}{25}$$
$$\frac{b}{44} = 4$$
$$b = 44 \cdot 4$$
$$b = 176$$
44 is 25% of 176.

14.
$$\frac{55}{25} = \frac{p}{100}$$
$$\frac{11}{5} = \frac{p}{100}$$
$$100 \cdot \frac{11}{5} = p$$
$$220 = p$$
55 is 220% of 25.

15.
$$\frac{a}{15} = \frac{45}{100}$$
$$\frac{a}{15} = 0.45$$
$$a = 15 \cdot 0.45$$
$$a = 6.75$$
$$15 - 6.75 = \$68.25$$
The sale price of the hat is $8.25.

16.
$$\frac{9.36}{b} = \frac{45}{100}$$
$$\frac{b}{9.36} = \frac{100}{45}$$
$$\frac{b}{9.36} = \frac{5 \cdot 20}{5 \cdot 9}$$
$$b = 9.36 \cdot \frac{20}{9}$$
$$b = 20.8$$
The original price of the hat is $20.80.

17. Increase; $\dfrac{777.21 - 740.20}{740.20} = \dfrac{37.01}{740.20} = 0.05 = 5\%$

18. Decrease; $\dfrac{65.50 - 45.85}{65.50} = \dfrac{19.65}{65.50} = 0.3 = 30\%$

19.

short-haired — black, brown, white

long-haired — black, brown, white

6 choices

No; you have a choice of six different types of rabbits and there are only five rabbits in the pet store.

20. $\frac{1}{26} \cdot \frac{1}{10} = \frac{1}{260}$, or 0.004

21. $\frac{1}{26} \cdot \frac{1}{26} = \frac{1}{676}$, or 0.001

Chapter **A S S E S S M E N T**

1. $\dfrac{3}{4.5} = \dfrac{\cancel{1.5} \cdot 2}{\cancel{1.5} \cdot 3}$

$\qquad = \dfrac{2}{3}$

2. $\dfrac{2}{3} = \dfrac{5}{f}$

$\quad \dfrac{3}{2} = \dfrac{f}{5}$

$5 \cdot \dfrac{3}{2} = 5 \cdot \dfrac{f}{5}$

$\quad \dfrac{15}{2} = f$

$\quad 7.5 = f$

3. $\dfrac{2}{3} = \dfrac{4}{e}$

$\quad \dfrac{3}{2} = \dfrac{e}{4}$

$4 \cdot \dfrac{3}{2} = 4 \cdot \dfrac{e}{4}$

$\qquad 6 = e$

4. $\dfrac{4}{6} = \dfrac{2}{3}$

5. $\dfrac{95 - 76}{76} = \dfrac{19}{76} = 0.25 = 25\%$ increase

6. $\dfrac{15.00 - 9.00}{15.00} = \dfrac{6}{15} = 0.4 = 40\%$ decrease

7. $\dfrac{195 \text{ dollars}}{5 \text{ days}} = \$39$ per day

8. $\dfrac{a}{115} = \dfrac{82}{100}$

$\quad \dfrac{a}{115} = 0.82$

$\qquad a = 115 \cdot 0.82$

$\qquad a = 94.3$

94.3 is 82% of 115.

9. $\dfrac{56}{70} = \dfrac{p}{100}$

$\quad \dfrac{4}{5} = \dfrac{p}{100}$

$100 \cdot \dfrac{4}{5} = p$

$\qquad 80 = p$

56 is 80% of 70.

10. $\frac{9}{24} = \frac{3}{8} = 0.375 = 0.375 \cdot 100\% = 37.5\%$

11. $\frac{2}{24} = \frac{1}{12} \approx 0.0833 = 0.0833 \cdot 100\% \approx 8.3\%$

12. $\frac{5}{24}$, or 0.2083

13. $\frac{15}{24} = \frac{5}{8}$, or 0.625

14.

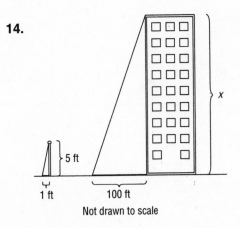

5 ft

1 ft

100 ft

Not drawn to scale

15. $\dfrac{100}{1} = \dfrac{x}{5}$

16. $\dfrac{100}{1} = \dfrac{x}{5}$

$5 \cdot \dfrac{100}{1} = 5 \cdot \dfrac{x}{5}$

$500 = x$

The building is 500 feet tall.

17. 7th-graders: A, B, C

8th-graders: X, Y, Z

Committees: AX, AY, AZ, BX, BY, BZ, CX, CY, CZ

18. $3 \times 3 = 9$

19. $\dfrac{217}{10{,}500} \approx \dfrac{210}{10{,}500} = \dfrac{1}{50}$, or 0.02

20. $\dfrac{5}{10{,}500} = \dfrac{1}{2100}$, or 0.0005

Standardized Test Practice

1. A; $\dfrac{1.99}{5} \overset{?}{=} \dfrac{3.89}{10}$

$1.99 \times 10 \overset{?}{=} 5 \times 3.89$

$19.9 \neq 19.45$

2. C; $\dfrac{9}{6} = \dfrac{a}{8}$

$6a = 72$

$a = 12$

3. C; $\dfrac{1}{484} = \dfrac{9}{x}$

$x = 4356 \text{ in.} \times \dfrac{1 \text{ ft}}{12 \text{ in.}} = 363 \text{ ft}$

4. C

5. A; $\dfrac{225 - 180}{225} = 0.20 = 20\%$ decrease

6. C; $\dfrac{50}{x} = \dfrac{20}{100}$

$20x = 5000$

$x = 250$ people were surveyed

$0.28 \times 250 = 70$

$0.18 \times 250 = 45$

$70 - 45 = 25$ people

7. D; $5 \times 2 \times 4 = 40$

8. A; $\dfrac{1}{10} \times \dfrac{1}{10} = \dfrac{1}{100}$

Chapter 9
Real Numbers and Inequalities

9.1 · *Exploring Square Roots*

ONGOING ASSESSMENT

1. $16t^2 = 20$

$\dfrac{16t^2}{16} = \dfrac{20}{16}$

$t^2 = \dfrac{5}{4}$

$t = \sqrt{\dfrac{5}{4}}$

$t \approx 1.12$ s

2. $16t^2 = 40$

$\dfrac{16t^2}{16} = \dfrac{40}{16}$

$t^2 = \dfrac{5}{2}$

$t = \sqrt{\dfrac{5}{2}}$

$t \approx 1.58$ s

3. $16t^2 = 80$

$\dfrac{16t^2}{16} = \dfrac{80}{16}$

$t^2 = 5$

$t = \sqrt{5}$

$t \approx 2.24$ s

4. No

EXERCISES

1. $r^2 = 4$ has 2 solutions because $2^2 = 4$ and $(-2)^2 = 4$.

2. $7, -7$

3. $\sqrt{5}, -\sqrt{5}$

4. $0.5, -0.5$

5. $\dfrac{5}{2}, -\dfrac{5}{2}$

6. $2x^2 = 228$

$x^2 = 114$

$x = \sqrt{114} \approx 10.68$

$x = -\sqrt{114} \approx -10.68$

7. $\sqrt{14}, -\sqrt{14}$

8. $\sqrt{22}, -\sqrt{22}$

9. $8, -8$

10. $13, -13$

11. $16, -16$

12. $40, -40$

13. $0.6, -0.6$

14. $\dfrac{8}{3}, -\dfrac{8}{3}$

15. $t^2 = 9$

$t = \sqrt{9} = 3$

$t = -\sqrt{9} = -3$

16. $x^2 = 100$

$x = \sqrt{100} = 10$

$x = -\sqrt{100} = -10$

17. $p^2 = 22$

$p = \sqrt{22} \approx 4.69$

$p = -\sqrt{22} \approx -4.69$

18. $r^2 = 17$

$r = \sqrt{17} \approx 4.123$

$r = -\sqrt{17} \approx -4.123$

19. $b^2 + 2 = 27$

$b^2 + 2 - 2 = 27 - 2$

$b^2 = 25$

$b = \sqrt{25} = 5$

$b = -\sqrt{25} = -5$

20. $y^2 - 6 = 30$

$y^2 - 6 + 6 = 30 + 6$

$y^2 = 36$

$y = \sqrt{36} = 6$

$y = -\sqrt{36} = -6$

21. $3a^2 = 243$

$\dfrac{3a^2}{3} = \dfrac{243}{3}$

$a^2 = 81$

$a = \sqrt{81} = 9$

$a = -\sqrt{81} = -9$

22. $4s^2 = 49$

$\dfrac{4s^2}{4} = \dfrac{49}{4}$

$s^2 = \dfrac{49}{4}$

$s = \sqrt{\dfrac{49}{4}} = \dfrac{\sqrt{49}}{\sqrt{4}} = \dfrac{7}{2}$

$s = -\sqrt{\dfrac{49}{4}} = -\dfrac{\sqrt{49}}{\sqrt{4}} = -\dfrac{7}{2}$

23. 4.5; Check: $\sqrt{20} \approx 4.5$

24. 7.5; Check: $\sqrt{56} \approx 7.5$

25. 5.6; Check: $\sqrt{31} \approx 5.6$

26. 6.2; Check: $\sqrt{39} \approx 6.2$

27. $\sqrt{25} = x$

$5 = x$

28. $3r^2 = 27$

$\dfrac{3r^2}{3} = \dfrac{27}{3}$

$r^2 = 9$

$r = \sqrt{9} = 3$

$r = -\sqrt{9} = -3$

29. $a^2 + 6 = 15$

$a^2 + 6 - 6 = 15 - 6$

$a^2 = 9$

$a = \sqrt{9} = 3$

$a = -\sqrt{9} = -3$

30. $y^2 = 47$

$y = \sqrt{47}$

$y = -\sqrt{47}$

31. $-16t^2 + s = 0$

$-16t^2 + 20 = 0$

$-16t^2 + 20 - 20 = 0 - 20$

$-16t^2 = -20$

$\dfrac{-16t^2}{-16} = \dfrac{-20}{-16}$

$t^2 = 1.25$

$t = \sqrt{1.25} \approx 1.1$

It takes the ball about 1.1 seconds to fall 20 feet.

32. $d^2 = \dfrac{3}{2}h$

$d^2 = \dfrac{3}{2}(10)$

$d^2 = 15$

$d = \sqrt{15} \approx 3.87$

You can see for about 3.87 miles.

33. $d^2 = \dfrac{3}{2}h$

$d^2 = \dfrac{3}{2}(30)$

$d^2 = 45$

$d = \sqrt{45} \approx 6.71$

You can see for about 6.71 miles.

34. $6(x^2) = 216$

$\dfrac{6x^2}{6} = \dfrac{216}{6}$

$x^2 = 36$

$x = \sqrt{36} = 6$

Each edge is 6 cm long.

35. C

36. C; $\sqrt{8100} = 90$ ft

37.

Height, h	25	50	75	100	125	150
$64h$	1600	3200	4800	6400	8000	9600
Speed $\approx \sqrt{64h}$	40	57	69	80	89	98

a. No

b. Answers vary.

9.2 The Real Number System

ONGOING ASSESSMENT

1. No; $-\sqrt{\dfrac{1}{2}} \approx -0.07$

$-\dfrac{1}{2} = -0.05$

$-0.07 < -0.05$

2.
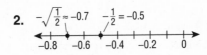

EXERCISES

1. *Sample answer:* A rational number is a number that can be written as the quotient (or ratio) of two integers.

2. The decimal form of a rational number either terminates or repeats, while the decimal form of an irrational number does not terminate and does not repeat.

3. a. Rational; the decimal terminates.
 b. Rational; the decimal repeats.
 c. Irrational; the decimal neither terminates nor repeats.

4. $\dfrac{8}{2} = 4$; rational

5. $\sqrt{5} \approx 2.23606797\ldots$; irrational

6. $\sqrt{9} = 3$; rational

7. $-\sqrt{\dfrac{16}{9}} = -\dfrac{\sqrt{16}}{\sqrt{9}} = -\dfrac{4}{3} = -1.\overline{3}$; rational

8. $-\dfrac{5}{3} = -1.\overline{6}$, $-\sqrt{4} = -2$, $\sqrt{6} \approx 2.45$, $-\sqrt{8} = -2.83$

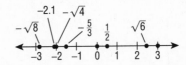

9. $\frac{11}{5}$; it is rational because it is the quotient of two integers.

10. $-\frac{21}{16}$; it is rational because it is the quotient of two integers.

11. $\sqrt{10} \approx 3.162\ldots$; it is irrational because its decimal form neither terminates nor repeats.

12. $-\sqrt{15} \approx -3.872\ldots$; it is irrational because its decimal form neither terminates nor repeats.

13. $\sqrt{1.44} = 1.2$; it is rational because its decimal form terminates.

14. $-\sqrt{\dfrac{100}{36}} = -\dfrac{\sqrt{100}}{\sqrt{36}} = -\dfrac{10}{6}$; it is rational because it is the quotient of two integers.

15. $-\sqrt{\dfrac{3}{2}} \approx -1.224\ldots$; it is irrational because its decimal form neither terminates nor repeats.

16. $\sqrt{\dfrac{9}{6}} \approx 1.224\ldots$; it is irrational because its decimal form neither terminates nor repeats.

17. A real number is *sometimes* a rational number. Real numbers consist of rational numbers and irrational numbers.

18. An irrational number is *always* a real number. Real numbers consist of rational numbers and irrational numbers.

19. A negative integer is *never* an irrational number. All integers are rational numbers.

20. A square root of a number is *sometimes* an irrational number. $\sqrt{9}$ is rational and $\sqrt{10}$ is irrational.

21. $\sqrt{a} + \sqrt{b} = \sqrt{2} + \sqrt{4} = \sqrt{2} + 2 \approx 3.414\ldots$
No; the decimal neither terminates nor repeats.

22. $\sqrt{b} - \sqrt{c} = \sqrt{4} - \sqrt{9} = 2 - 3 = -1$
Yes; it can be represented as the quotient of two integers.

23. $\sqrt{c} \cdot \sqrt{b} = \sqrt{9} \cdot \sqrt{4} = 3 \cdot 2 = 6$
Yes; it can be represented as the quotient of two integers.

24. $\sqrt{c} \div \sqrt{b} = \sqrt{9} \div \sqrt{4} \approx 3 \div 2 = \frac{3}{2}$
Yes; it can be represented as the quotient of two integers.

25. E; $\sqrt{8} \approx 2.83$

26. A; $-\sqrt{15} \approx -3.87$

27. C; 0.49

28. D; $\sqrt{3.8} \approx 1.95$

29. B; $-\sqrt{\dfrac{25}{16}} = -\dfrac{5}{4} = -1.25$

30. $\sqrt{0.16}\ \boxed{?}\ 0.16$
$0.4\ \boxed{>}\ 0.16$

31. $-7\ \boxed{?}\ -\sqrt{7}$
$-7\ \boxed{<}\ \approx -2.646$

32. $\sqrt{2.25}\ \boxed{?}\ \dfrac{3.6}{2.4}$
$1.5\ \boxed{=}\ 1.5$

33. $\sqrt{3}\ \boxed{?}\ \dfrac{23}{13}$
$\approx 1.732\ \boxed{<}\ \approx 1.769$

34. $-\dfrac{3}{4}, -\dfrac{1}{2}, -\dfrac{1}{8}$

35. $-2\dfrac{1}{4}, -1\dfrac{1}{2}, -\dfrac{7}{8}$

36. $-3.5, -2, -0.5$

37. $-1.3, -0.75, -0.5$

38. 35%, 45%, 125%

39. 25%, $\dfrac{1}{2}$, 0.75

40. No. The area of the shaded square is half the area of the larger square, or 50. So each side length of the shaded square is $\sqrt{50}$. $\sqrt{50}$ is an irrational number, so its decimal form neither terminates nor repeats.

41. Answers vary.

42. B

43.

	Natural	Whole	Integers	Rational	Irrational	Real
-5			✓	✓		✓
$\frac{15}{12}$				✓		✓
$\sqrt{7}$					✓	✓
11	✓	✓	✓	✓		✓
0		✓	✓	✓		✓

$\frac{15}{12} = 1.25$

$\sqrt{7} \approx 2.64575133\ldots$

Lab 9.3

Part A

1. $3 \times 3 = 9$ units^2;
$4 \times 4 = 16$ units^2;
$5 \times 5 = 25$ units^2;
$9 + 16 = 25$

2. $a^2 + b^2 = c^2$

Part B

3.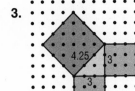

$3^2 + 3^2 \overset{?}{\approx} 4.25^2$

$9 + 9 \overset{?}{\approx} 18.0625$

$18 \approx 18.0625$

4.

$2^2 + 4^2 \overset{?}{\approx} 4.5^2$

$4 + 16 \overset{?}{\approx} 20.25$

$20 \approx 20.25$

5. Answers vary.

6. $4^2 + 5^2 = 16 + 25$
$\quad\quad = 41$ units^2

7. $c^2 = 41$
$\quad c = \sqrt{41}$
$\quad c \approx 6.4$

8. Answers vary.

ONGOING ASSESSMENT

1. *Sample answer:* 3, 4, 5; 5, 12, 13; 8, 15, 17; 7, 24, 25

EXERCISES

1.

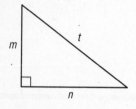

$m^2 + n^2 = t^2$

2. No; $180° - 90° = 90°$, so the sum of the two remaining angles must be 90°. The measure of each angle will be less than 90°.

3. $a^2 + b^2 = c^2$
$6^2 + 7^2 = c^2$
$36 + 49 = c^2$
$85 = c^2$
$\sqrt{85} = c$
$9.2 \approx c$

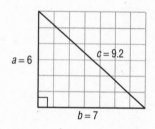

4. $a^2 + b^2 = c^2$
$3^2 + b^2 = 5^2$
$9 + b^2 = 25$
$9 + b^2 - 9 = 25 - 9$
$b^2 = 16$
$b = \sqrt{16}$
$b = 4$

5. Never

6. Always

7. Sometimes

8. Sometimes

9.–14. $a^2 + b^2 = c^2$

9. $7^2 + 11^2 = c^2$
$49 + 121 = c^2$
$170 = c^2$
$\sqrt{170} = c$
$13.04 \approx c$

10. $16^2 + b^2 = 34^2$
$256 + b^2 = 1156$
$256 + b^2 - 256 = 1156 - 256$
$b^2 = 900$
$b = \sqrt{900}$
$b = 30$

11. $a^2 + 12^2 = 15^2$
$a^2 + 144 = 225$
$a^2 + 144 - 144 = 225 - 144$
$a^2 = 81$
$a = \sqrt{81}$
$a = 9$

12.
$$6^2 + b^2 = 16.16^2$$
$$36 + b^2 = 261.1456$$
$$36 + b^2 - 36 = 261.1456 - 36$$
$$b^2 = 225.1456$$
$$b = \sqrt{225.1456}$$
$$b \approx 15.00$$

13.
$$a^2 + 42^2 = 43.17^2$$
$$a^2 + 1764 = 1863.6489$$
$$a^2 + 1764 - 1764 = 1863.6489 - 1764$$
$$a^2 = 99.6489$$
$$a = \sqrt{99.6489}$$
$$a \approx 9.98$$

14.
$$18^2 + 28^2 = c^2$$
$$324 + 784 = c^2$$
$$1108 = c^2$$
$$\sqrt{1108} = c$$
$$33.29 \approx c$$

15.
$$8^2 + 15^2 \overset{?}{=} 17^2$$
$$64 + 225 \overset{?}{=} 289$$
$$289 = 289$$

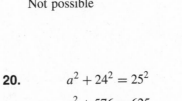

16.
$$5^2 + 12^2 \overset{?}{=} 13^2$$
$$25 + 144 \overset{?}{=} 169$$
$$169 = 169$$

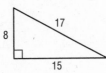

17.
$$9^2 + 38^2 \overset{?}{=} 41^2$$
$$81 + 1444 \overset{?}{=} 1681$$
$$1525 \neq 1681$$
Not possible

18.
$$13^2 + 36^2 \overset{?}{=} 40^2$$
$$169 + 1296 \overset{?}{=} 1600$$
$$1465 \neq 1600$$
Not possible

19.–22. $a^2 + b^2 = c^2$

19.
$$6^2 + 6^2 = c^2$$
$$36 + 36 = c^2$$
$$72 = c^2$$
$$\sqrt{72} = c$$
$$8.49 \approx c$$

20.
$$a^2 + 24^2 = 25^2$$
$$a^2 + 576 = 625$$
$$a^2 + 576 - 576 = 625 - 576$$
$$a^2 = 49$$
$$a = \sqrt{49}$$
$$a = 7$$

21.
$$15^2 + b^2 = 39^2$$
$$225 + b^2 = 1521$$
$$225 + b^2 - 225 = 1521 - 225$$
$$b^2 = 1296$$
$$b = \sqrt{1296}$$
$$b = 36$$

22.
$$5^2 + 9^2 = c^2$$
$$25 + 81 = c^2$$
$$106 = c^2$$
$$\sqrt{106} = c$$
$$10.30 \approx c$$

23. l = length of each piece of rope.
$$4^2 + 8^2 = l^2$$
$$16 + 64 = l^2$$
$$80 = l^2$$
$$\sqrt{80} = l$$
$$8.944 \approx l$$

Each piece of rope is about 8.9 ft or 8 ft 11 in. long.

24. $4(8.944) = 35.776 \approx 36$

You need about 36 ft of rope.

25. c = distance in ft between stakes A and B.

$$4^2 + 4^2 = c^2$$
$$16 + 16 = c^2$$
$$32 = c^2$$
$$\sqrt{32} = c$$
$$5.66 \approx c$$

The distance between stakes A and B is about 5.7 ft or 5 ft 8 in.

26. c = distance in miles traveled through town.

$$7^2 + 6^2 = c^2 \qquad (7 + 6) - 9.22 = 13 - 9.22$$
$$49 + 36 = c^2 \qquad\qquad\qquad = 3.78 \text{ or about } 3.8$$
$$85 = c^2$$
$$\sqrt{85} = c$$
$$9.22 \approx c$$

You would have saved about 3.8 mi.

27.

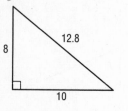

$$8^2 + 10^2 = c^2 \qquad\qquad a^2 + 8^2 = 10^2$$
$$64 + 100 = c^2 \qquad\qquad a^2 + 64 = 100$$
$$164 = c^2 \qquad a^2 + 64 - 64 = 100 - 64$$
$$\sqrt{164} = c \qquad\qquad\qquad a^2 = 36$$
$$12.8 \approx c \qquad\qquad\qquad a = \sqrt{36}$$
$$a = 6$$

28.

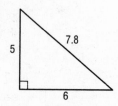

$$5^2 + 6^2 = c^2 \qquad\qquad 5^2 + b^2 = 6^2$$
$$25 + 36 = c^2 \qquad\qquad 25 + b^2 = 36$$
$$61 = c^2 \qquad 25 + b^2 - 25 = 36 - 25$$
$$\sqrt{61} = c \qquad\qquad\qquad b^2 = 11$$
$$7.8 \approx c \qquad\qquad\qquad b = \sqrt{11}$$
$$b \approx 3.3$$

29. C; $x^2 + 24^2 = 26^2$

$$x^2 + 576 = 676$$
$$x^2 = 100$$
$$x = \sqrt{100}$$
$$x = 10 \text{ cm}$$

30. a. $12^2 + 10^2 = c^2$

$$144 + 100 = c^2$$
$$244 = c^2$$
$$15.62 \approx c$$

The length of the track is approximately 15.6 ft or 15 ft 7 in.

b. Answers vary.

Spiral **R E V I E W**

1. $3^2 + 4^2 = m^2$

$$9 + 16 = m^2$$
$$25 = m^2$$
$$\sqrt{25} = m$$
$$5 = m$$

2. $8^2 + n^2 = 12^2$

$$64 + n^2 = 144$$
$$64 + n^2 - 64 = 144 - 64$$
$$n^2 = 80$$
$$n = \sqrt{80}$$
$$n \approx 8.94$$

3. $x^2 + x^2 = 141^2$

$$2x^2 = 19{,}881$$
$$\frac{2x^2}{2} = \frac{19{,}881}{2}$$
$$x^2 = 9940.5$$
$$x = \sqrt{9940.5}$$
$$x \approx 99.70$$

4.
$$p^2 + 9^2 = 15^2$$
$$p^2 + 81 = 225$$
$$p^2 + 81 - 81 = 225 - 81$$
$$p^2 = 144$$
$$p = \sqrt{144}$$
$$p = 12$$

5.
$$x + 2 \geq 9$$
$$x + 2 - 2 \geq 9 - 2$$
$$x \geq 7$$

6.
$$2p < 14$$
$$\frac{2p}{2} < \frac{14}{2}$$
$$p < 7$$

7.
$$5n > 8$$
$$\frac{5n}{5} > \frac{8}{5}$$
$$n > \frac{8}{5}$$

8.
$$y - 7 \leq 4$$
$$y - 7 + 7 \leq 4 + 7$$
$$y \leq 11$$

9.
$$24 = 2 \cdot 2 \cdot 2 \cdot 3$$
$$39 = 3 \cdot 13$$
The GCF is 3.

10.
$$88 = 2 \cdot 2 \cdot 2 \cdot 11$$
$$60 = 2 \cdot 2 \cdot 3 \cdot 5$$
The GCF is $2 \cdot 2 = 4$.

11.
$$100x = 2 \cdot 2 \cdot 5 \cdot 5 \cdot x$$
$$222y = 2 \cdot 3 \cdot 37 \cdot y$$
The GCF is 2.

12.
$$9 = 3 \cdot 3$$
$$12 = 2 \cdot 2 \cdot 3$$
$$15 = 3 \cdot 5$$
The GCF is 3.

13.
$$2.5 \times 130 - 400 = 325 - 400$$
$$= -75$$
Your class did not make a profit.

Lab 9.4

1.
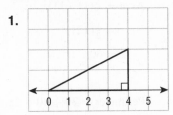

2.
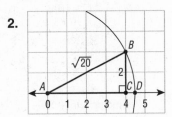

3.
$$6^2 + 4^2 = c^2$$
$$36 + 16 = c^2$$
$$52 = c^2$$
$$\sqrt{52} = c;$$
$$\sqrt{52} \approx 7.2$$

4.
$$8^2 + 3^2 = c^2$$
$$64 + 9 = c^2$$
$$73 = c^2$$
$$\sqrt{73} = c;$$
$$\sqrt{73} \approx 8.5$$

5.
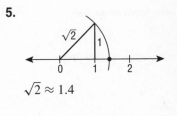
$$\sqrt{2} \approx 1.4$$

6.
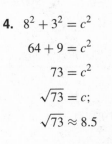
$$\sqrt{5} \approx 2.2$$

7.
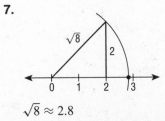
$$\sqrt{8} \approx 2.8$$

8.
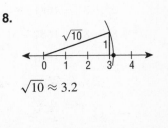
$$\sqrt{10} \approx 3.2$$

9.4 Problem Solving Using the Pythagorean Theorem

ONGOING ASSESSMENT

1. Answers vary.

2. Use the Pythagorean Theorem; answers vary.

3. Answers vary.

EXERCISES

1. Answers vary.

2. No, use the Pythagorean Theorem to find the length of the other leg.

$$45^2 + b^2 = 75^2$$
$$2025 + b^2 = 5625$$
$$2025 + b^2 - 2025 = 5625 - 2025$$
$$b^2 = 3600$$
$$b = \sqrt{3600}$$
$$b = 60$$

Perimeter $= 45 + 60 + 75$
$= 180$ m

Area $= \frac{1}{2}(45 \cdot 60)$
$= \frac{1}{2}(2700)$
$= 1350$ m^2

3.
$$7^2 + 10^2 = c^2$$
$$49 + 100 = c^2$$
$$149 = c^2$$
$$\sqrt{149} = c$$
$$12.21 \approx c$$

Perimeter $= 10 + 7 + 12.21$
$= 29.21$ m

Area $= \frac{1}{2}(7 \cdot 10)$
$= \frac{1}{2}(70)$
$= 35$ m^2

4.
$$11^2 + 11^2 = c^2$$
$$121 + 121 = c^2$$
$$242 = c^2$$
$$\sqrt{242} = c$$
$$15.56 \approx c$$

Perimeter $= 11 + 11 + 15.56$
$= 37.56$ ft

Area $= \frac{1}{2}(11 \cdot 11)$
$= \frac{1}{2}(121)$
$= 60.5$ ft^2

5.
$$6^2 + b^2 = 24^2$$
$$36 + b^2 = 576$$
$$b^2 = 540$$
$$b = \sqrt{540}$$
$$b \approx 23.24$$

Perimeter $= 6 + 24 + 23.24$
$= 53.24$ in.

Area $= \frac{1}{2}(6 \cdot 23.24)$
$= \frac{1}{2}(139.44)$
$= 69.72$ in.^{2}

6.
$$30^2 + b^2 = 40^2$$
$$900 + b^2 = 1600$$
$$b^2 = 700$$
$$b = \sqrt{700}$$
$$b \approx 26.46$$

Perimeter $= 30 + 40 + 26.46$
$= 96.46$ cm

Area $= \frac{1}{2}(30 \cdot 26.46)$
$= \frac{1}{2}(793.8)$
$= 396.9$ cm^2

7.
$$a^2 + 9^2 = 41^2$$
$$a^2 + 81 = 1681$$
$$a^2 + 81 - 81 = 1681 - 81$$
$$a^2 = 1600$$
$$a = \sqrt{1600}$$
$$a = 40$$

Perimeter $= 40 + 9 + 41$
$= 90$ mi

Area $= \frac{1}{2}(9 \cdot 40)$
$= \frac{1}{2}(360)$
$= 180$ mi^2

8.
$$16^2 + b^2 = 20^2$$
$$256 + b^2 = 400$$
$$256 + b^2 - 256 = 400 - 256$$
$$b^2 = 144$$
$$b = \sqrt{144}$$
$$b = 12$$

Perimeter $= 2(16) + 2(12)$
$$= 32 + 24$$
$$= 56 \text{ km}$$
Area $= 12 \cdot 16$
$$= 192 \text{ km}^2$$

9.
$$s^2 + s^2 = \left(\sqrt{8}\right)^2$$
$$2s^2 = \sqrt{8} \cdot \sqrt{8}$$
$$2s^2 = 8$$
$$\frac{2s^2}{2} = \frac{8}{2}$$
$$s^2 = 4$$
$$s = \sqrt{4}$$
$$s = 2$$

Perimeter $= 4(2) = 8$ ft
Area $= 2^2 = 4$ ft^2

10.
$$2^2 + 4^2 = c^2$$
$$4 + 16 = c^2$$
$$20 = c^2$$
$$\sqrt{20} = c$$
$$4.47 \approx c$$

Perimeter $= 2(4.47) + 2 + 2$
$$= 8.94 + 4$$
$$= 12.94 \text{ m}$$
Area $= \frac{1}{2}(4)(4)$
$$= \frac{1}{2}(16)$$
$$= 8 \text{ m}^2$$

11. $h =$ height in feet of the tent.
$$\left(\tfrac{1}{2} \cdot 16\right)^2 + h^2 = 10^2$$
$$8^2 + h^2 = 10^2$$
$$64 + h^2 = 100$$
$$64 + h^2 - 64 = 100 - 64$$
$$h^2 = 36$$
$$h = \sqrt{36}$$
$$h = 6$$

The tent is 6 ft high, so a person 6 ft tall could stand inside the tent.

12.
$$9^2 + b^2 = 15^2$$
$$81 + b^2 = 225$$
$$b^2 = 144$$
$$b = \sqrt{144}$$
$$b = 12$$

$$\frac{10}{15} = \frac{a}{12}$$
$$12 \cdot 10 = 15a$$
$$120 = 15a$$
$$8 = a$$

13. $h =$ height in ft of the kite.
$$135^2 + h^2 = 200^2$$
$$18{,}225 + h^2 = 40{,}000$$
$$18{,}225 + h^2 - 18{,}225 = 40{,}000 - 18{,}225$$
$$h^2 = 21{,}775$$
$$h = \sqrt{21{,}775}$$
$$h \approx 147.56$$
The kite is about 147.56 ft high.

14.
$$a^2 + 60^2 = 175^2$$
$$a^2 + 3600 = 30{,}625$$
$$a^2 = 27{,}025$$
$$a = \sqrt{27{,}025}$$
$$a \approx 164.39$$

Flying distance: $164.39 + 25 = 189.39$ mi
Driving distance: $175 + 60 + 25 = 260$ mi
Miles saved: $260 - 189.39 = 70.61$ mi

15. C; $9^2 + 12^2 \stackrel{?}{=} 15^2$

$81 + 144 \stackrel{?}{=} 225$

$225 = 225$

16. B; $4^2 + 20^2 = c^2$

$16 + 400 = c^2$

$416 = c^2$

$\sqrt{416} = c$

$20.4 \approx c$

17. *Sample answer:* The number of spaces must form a Pythagorean triple.

18. A. $4^2 + 5^2 \stackrel{?}{=} 6^2$

$16 + 25 \stackrel{?}{=} 36$

$41 \neq 36$

No, not a right triangle.

B. $5^2 + 12^2 \stackrel{?}{=} 13^2$

$25 + 144 \stackrel{?}{=} 169$

$169 = 169$

Yes, is a right triangle.

C. $6^2 + 8^2 \stackrel{?}{=} 10^2$

$36 + 64 \stackrel{?}{=} 100$

$100 = 100$

Yes, is a right triangle.

D. $5^2 + 7^2 \stackrel{?}{=} 9^2$

$25 + 49 \stackrel{?}{=} 81$

$74 \neq 81$

No, not a right triangle.

Using a Calculator

1. $39^2 + 104^2 = f^2$ $13^2 + 104^2 = e^2$

$1521 + 10{,}816 = f^2$ $169 + 10{,}816 = e^2$

$12{,}337 = f^2$ $10{,}985 = e^2$

$\sqrt{12{,}337} = f$ $\sqrt{10{,}985} = e$

$111.1 \approx f$ $104.8 \approx e$

Length of cable $= 111.1 + 104.8 = 215.9$ ft

2. *Sample answer:* Use more than two triangles.

Mid-Chapter **ASSESSMENT**

1. $4, -4$

2. $11, -11$

3. $0.7, -0.7$

4. $0.6, -0.6$

5. 5.74 cm

6. 11 in.

7. $\sqrt{7}, -\sqrt{7}$

8. $7, -7$

9. $s^2 + 3 = 4$

$s^2 = 1$

$s^2 = \sqrt{1}$

$s = 1, -1$

10. $3k^2 = 39$

$k^2 = 13$

$k = \sqrt{13}, -\sqrt{13}$

11. $\sqrt{250} = 15.811388\ldots$; it is irrational because its decimal form neither terminates nor repeats.

12. $\sqrt{25} = 5$; it is rational because it is an integer.

13. $\sqrt{2.5} = 1.5811388\ldots$; it is irrational because its decimal form neither terminates nor repeats.

14. $\sqrt{0.25} = 0.5$; it is rational because its decimal form terminates.

15.
$$12^2 + 3^2 = h^2$$
$$144 + 9 = h^2$$
$$153 = h^2$$
$$\sqrt{153} = h$$
$$12.37 \approx h$$

16.
$$12^2 + r^2 = 13^2$$
$$144 + r^2 = 169$$
$$144 + r^2 - 144 = 169 - 144$$
$$r^2 = 25$$
$$r = \sqrt{25}$$
$$r = 5$$

17.
$$q^2 + q^2 = 128^2$$
$$2q^2 = 16{,}384$$
$$\frac{2q^2}{2} = \frac{16{,}384}{2}$$
$$q^2 = 8192$$
$$q = \sqrt{8192}$$
$$q \approx 90.51$$

18.
$$s^2 + s^2 = 50^2$$
$$2s^2 = 2500$$
$$\frac{2s^2}{2} = \frac{2500}{2}$$
$$s^2 = 1250$$
$$s = \sqrt{1250}$$
$$s \approx 35.36$$

19.
$$20^2 + l^2 = 29^2$$
$$400 + l^2 = 841$$
$$400 + l^2 - 400 = 841 - 400$$
$$l^2 = 441$$
$$l = \sqrt{441}$$
$$l = 21 \text{ in.}$$

20. $20 + 21 + 29 = 70$ in.

21.
$$\tfrac{1}{2}(20 \cdot 21) = \tfrac{1}{2}(420)$$
$$= 210 \text{ in.}^2$$

22. False; $\sqrt{5}$ is irrational.

9.5   *Graphing Inequalities*

1.
$3 + b \geq 5$	*Write original inequality.*
$3 - 3 + b \geq 5 - 3$	*Subtract 3 from each side.*
$b \geq 2$	*Solution: b is by itself.*

2.
$-3 \geq x + 2$	*Write original inequality.*
$-3 - 2 \geq x + 2 - 2$	*Subtract 2 from each side.*
$-5 \geq x$	*Solution: x is by itself.*

3.
$y - 4 < -8$	*Write original inequality.*
$y - 4 + 4 < -8 + 4$	*Add 4 to each side.*
$y < -4$	*Solution: y is by itself.*

EXERCISES

1. C   **2.** D   **3.** B   **4.** A

5. $x < 15;\ 15 > x$ **6.** $x \geq 0;\ 0 \leq x$ **7.** $x > -3;\ -3 < x$ **8.** $x \leq -11;\ -11 \geq x$

9. $x + 5 < -2$

$x + 5 - 5 < -2 - 5$

$x < -7$

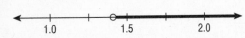

10. $x - 5 \geq -2$

$x - 5 + 5 \geq -2 + 5$

$x \geq 3$

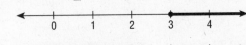

11.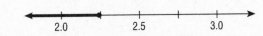

12.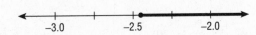

13.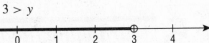

14.

15. $x \geq -5$ **16.** $x < 4$

17. $x \leq -1$ **18.** $x \geq 2$

19. $x > \sqrt{2}; \sqrt{2} \approx 1.41$

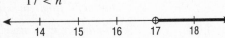

20. $x \leq \sqrt{5}; \sqrt{5} \approx 2.24$

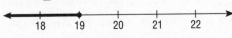

21. $x < -\sqrt{3}; -\sqrt{3} \approx -1.73$

22. $x \geq -\sqrt{6}; -\sqrt{6} \approx -2.45$

23. $x + 3 \geq 2$

$x + 3 - 3 \geq 2 - 3$

$x \geq -1$

24. $5 > y + 2$

$5 - 2 > y + 2 - 2$

$3 > y$

25. $13 < n - 4$

$13 + 4 < n - 4 + 4$

$17 < n$

26. $t - 1 \leq 7$

$t - 1 + 1 \leq 7 + 1$

$t \leq 8$

27. $z + 7 > -2$

$z + 7 - 7 > -2 - 7$

$z > -9$

28. $15 \geq w - 4$

$15 + 4 \geq w - 4 + 4$

$19 \geq w$

29. $x \leq -20$

$-20 \geq x$

The set of all real numbers less than or equal to -20.

30. $y > -3$

$-3 < y$

The set of all real numbers greater than -3.

31. $s < 17$

$17 > s$

The set of all real numbers less than 17.

32. $m \geq 13$

$13 \leq m$

The set of all real numbers greater than or equal to 13.

33. D; 0 mi/h and 48.71 mi/h were both attained by the Sunraycer.

34. $d \geq 93,000,000$ mi

35. $T \geq -459.7°F$

36. $w \leq 300; 300 \geq w$

37. B; a number of students must be a whole number.

38. A; a number of degrees can be any real number.

39. D

40. a. Speed at Y: $16\sqrt{\frac{64}{3}} \approx 73.90$ ft/s

Speed at Z: $8\sqrt{\frac{64}{3}} \approx 36.95$ ft/s

b. 36.95 ft/s $< x <$ 73.90 ft/s or between 36.95 ft/s and 73.90 ft/s

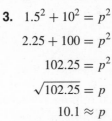

c. Answers vary.

Spiral **R E V I E W**

1.
$$\frac{x}{10} = \frac{60}{1.5}$$
$$\frac{x}{10} = 40$$
$$10 \cdot \frac{x}{10} = 10 \cdot 40$$
$$x = 400$$

The height of the building is 400 feet.

2.
$$60^2 + 400^2 = y^2$$
$$3600 + 160{,}000 = y^2$$
$$163{,}600 = y^2$$
$$\sqrt{163{,}600} = y$$
$$404.5 \approx y$$

The distance from the top of the building to the end of the building's shadow is about 404.5 feet.

3.
$$1.5^2 + 10^2 = p^2$$
$$2.25 + 100 = p^2$$
$$102.25 = p^2$$
$$\sqrt{102.25} = p$$
$$10.1 \approx p$$

The distance from the top of the pole to the end of its shadow is 10.1 feet.

4.
$$x + 2 > 12$$
$$x + 2 - 2 > 12 - 2$$
$$x > 10$$

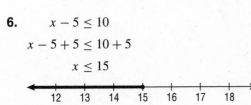

5.
$$0 > x - 2$$
$$0 + 2 > x - 2 + 2$$
$$2 > x$$

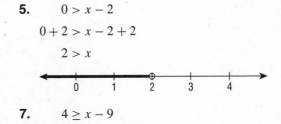

6.
$$x - 5 \leq 10$$
$$x - 5 + 5 \leq 10 + 5$$
$$x \leq 15$$

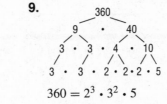

7.
$$4 \geq x - 9$$
$$4 + 9 \geq x - 9 + 9$$
$$13 \geq x$$

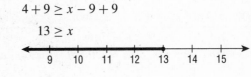

8.

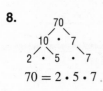

$70 = 2 \cdot 5 \cdot 7$

9.

360
9 • 40
3 • 3 • 4 • 10
3 • 3 • 2 • 2 • 2 • 5

$360 = 2^3 \cdot 3^2 \cdot 5$

10.

270
9 • 30
3 • 3 • 3 • 10
3 • 3 • 3 • 2 • 5

$270 = 2 \cdot 3^3 \cdot 5$

11.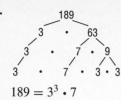

$$189 = 3^3 \cdot 7$$

12.

$$369 = 3^2 \cdot 41$$

13.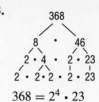

$$368 = 2^4 \cdot 23$$

14. $350 \cdot 0.36 = 126$ students

Communicating About Mathematics

1.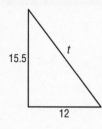

$$15.5^2 + 12^2 = t^2$$
$$240.25 + 144 = t^2$$
$$384.25 = t^2$$
$$\sqrt{384.25} = t$$
$$19.6 = t$$

About 20 ft of track is covered during a $15\frac{1}{2}$ ft drop.

2. $v^2 = 64h$

$$= 64 \cdot 155$$
$$= 9920$$
$$v = \sqrt{9920}$$
$$\approx 99.6 \text{ ft/s} \times \frac{1 \text{ mi}}{5280 \text{ ft}} \times \frac{60 \text{ s}}{1 \text{ min}} \times \frac{60 \text{ min}}{1 \text{ h}}$$
$$\approx 67.9 \text{ mi/h}$$

3. $v^2 = 64h$

$$= 64 \cdot 124$$
$$= 7936$$
$$v = \sqrt{7936}$$
$$\approx 89.1 \text{ ft/s}$$
$$\approx 60.75 \text{ mi/h;}$$

Answers vary.

4. $\dfrac{5427 \text{ ft}}{2\frac{3}{4} \text{ min}} \approx 1973.5 \text{ ft/min} \times \dfrac{1 \text{ mi}}{5280 \text{ ft}} \times \dfrac{60 \text{ min}}{1 \text{ h}}$

$$\approx 22.4 \text{ mi/h}$$

5. $\dfrac{1600 \text{ passengers}}{1 \text{ h}} \cdot \dfrac{1 \text{ h}}{60 \text{ min}} \cdot \dfrac{2\frac{3}{4} \text{ min}}{\text{ride}} \approx 73.3 \dfrac{\text{passengers}}{\text{ride}}$

Yes; *sample answer:* The Mean Streak has more than 1 train in motion at a time because $28 \cdot 2 = 56 < 73$.

9.6 | *Solving Inequalities: Multiplying and Dividing*

ONGOING ASSESSMENT

1. *Sample answer:* Substitute several numbers into the original inequality. If the substituted number makes the answer true, then the simplified original inequality should also be true.

To check an equation, you only need to substitute one number.

EXERCISES

1. $4 > -x$

$$\frac{4}{-1} < \frac{-x}{-1}$$

$$-4 < x$$

2. $-3 \geq -t$

$$\frac{-3}{-1} \leq \frac{-t}{-1}$$

$$3 \leq t$$

3. $3y > 15$

$$\frac{3y}{3} > \frac{15}{3}$$

$$y > 5$$

4. $-2 \geq -\frac{1}{2}a$

$$-2 \cdot (-2) \leq (-2) \cdot \left(-\frac{1}{2}a\right)$$

$$4 \leq a$$

5. Yes

6. No

7. No

8. Yes

9. $4b > 24$

$$\frac{46}{4} > \frac{24}{4}$$

$$b > 6$$

10. $-\frac{1}{4}x \leq 14$

$$-4 \cdot \left(-\frac{1}{4}x\right) \geq -4 \cdot 14$$

$$x \geq -56$$

11. $-5 < 0.2h$

$$\frac{-5}{0.2} < \frac{0.2h}{0.2}$$

$$-25 < h$$

12. $36 \geq -\frac{1}{2}f$

$$(-2) \cdot 36 \leq -2 \cdot \left(-\frac{1}{2}f\right)$$

$$-72 \leq f$$

13. The left side was not divided by -0.4, as it should have been.

14. The direction of the inequality symbol was reversed, but it should not have been.

15. The direction of the inequality symbol was not reversed, as it should have been.

16. C; $0.7x \leq 1.4$

$$\frac{0.7x}{0.7} \leq \frac{1.4}{0.7}$$

$$x \leq 2$$

17. B; $-1 > -\frac{1}{2}x$

$$(-2) \cdot -1 < (-2) \cdot \left(-\frac{1}{2}x\right)$$

$$2 < x$$

18. D; $\frac{1}{8} \leq \frac{1}{16}x$

$$16 \cdot \frac{1}{8} \leq 16 \cdot \frac{1}{16}x$$

$$2 \leq x$$

19. A; $-3x > -6$

$$\frac{-3x}{-3} < \frac{-6}{-3}$$

$$x < 2$$

20. $3m < 4$

$$\frac{3m}{3} < \frac{4}{3}$$

$$m < \frac{4}{3}$$

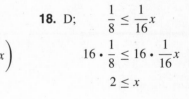

21. $2n \geq 5$

$$\frac{2n}{2} \geq \frac{5}{2}$$

$$n \geq \frac{5}{2}$$

22. $\frac{x}{2} \leq 8$

$$2 \cdot \frac{x}{2} \leq 2 \cdot 8$$

$$x \leq 16$$

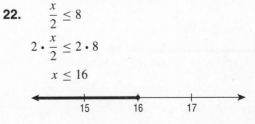

23. $\dfrac{y}{9} > 4$

$9 \cdot \dfrac{y}{9} > 9 \cdot 4$

$y > 36$

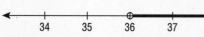

24. $35 \geq -5b$

$\dfrac{35}{-5} \leq \dfrac{-5b}{-5}$

$-7 \leq b$

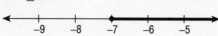

25. $\dfrac{1}{2} < -2a$

$\dfrac{1}{2} \div (-2) > \dfrac{-2a}{-2}$

$\dfrac{1}{2} \cdot \left(-\dfrac{1}{2}\right) > a$

$-\dfrac{1}{4} > a$

26. $-\dfrac{1}{2}z > 5$

$-2 \cdot \left(-\dfrac{1}{2}z\right) < -2 \cdot 5$

$z < -10$

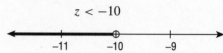

27. $-\dfrac{1}{5}p \leq 2$

$-5 \cdot \left(-\dfrac{1}{5}p\right) \geq -5 \cdot 2$

$p \geq -10$

28. $-3a \leq -6$

$-\dfrac{1}{3} \cdot (-3a) \geq -\dfrac{1}{3} \cdot (-6)$

$a \geq 2$

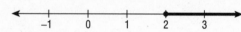

29. $-1.2x \geq -3.6$

$\dfrac{-1.2x}{-1.2} \leq \dfrac{-3.6}{-1.2}$

$x \leq 3$

30. $4 < 0.8r$

$\dfrac{4}{0.8} < \dfrac{0.8r}{0.8}$

$5 < r$

31. $-1.4m \geq -5.6$

$\dfrac{-1.4m}{-1.4} \leq \dfrac{-5.6}{-1.4}$

$m \leq 4$

32. $\dfrac{a}{6} > -2$

$6 \cdot \dfrac{a}{6} > 6 \cdot (-2)$

$a > -12$

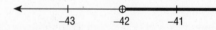

33. $\dfrac{3}{5}y \leq -6$

$\dfrac{5}{3} \cdot \left(\dfrac{3}{5}y\right) \leq \dfrac{5}{3} \cdot (-6)$

$y \leq -\dfrac{30}{3}$

$y \leq -10$

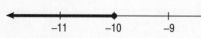

34. $14 > -\dfrac{1}{3}n$

$-3 \cdot 14 < -3 \cdot \left(-\dfrac{1}{3}\right)n$

$-42 < n$

35.
$$-\frac{3}{2} < -\frac{1}{4}x$$
$$-4 \cdot \left(-\frac{3}{2}\right) > -4 \cdot \left(-\frac{1}{4}x\right)$$
$$\frac{12}{2} > x$$
$$6 > x$$

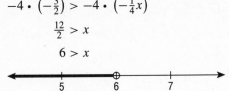

36. $3b \leq 60$
$b \leq 20$
The border can be at most 20 ft.

37. s = number of sandwiches that must be sold.
$$0.75s \geq 300$$
$$\frac{0.75s}{0.75} \geq \frac{300}{0.75}$$
$$s \geq 400$$
You need to sell at least 400 sandwiches.

38. h = number of hours that you need to baby-sit.
$$3h \geq 26.95$$
$$\frac{3h}{3} \geq \frac{26.95}{3}$$
$$h \geq 8.98\overline{3}$$
You need to babysit at least 9 hours.

39. d = distance traveled in km
$$d \leq 40 \cdot 3$$
$$d \leq 120$$
You can go at most 120 km.

40. B; $x \cdot 0.05 \geq 100$
$$\frac{x \cdot 0.05}{0.05} \geq \frac{100}{0.05}$$
$$x \geq 2000$$

41. A;
$$\frac{45}{75} \leq \frac{n}{120}$$
$$\frac{45}{75} \cdot 120 \leq \frac{n}{120} \cdot 120$$
$$72 \leq n$$

42. a.
$$140 \geq \frac{4}{3}h$$
$$140 \cdot 3 \geq 4h$$
$$420 \geq 4h$$
$$105 \geq h$$

b. Answers vary.

9.7 ALGEBRA CONNECTION: Solving Multi-Step Inequalities

ONGOING ASSESSMENT

1.

$2x + 6 > 12$	Write original inequality.
$2x + 6 - 6 > 12 - 6$	Subtract 6 from each side.
$2x > 6$	Simplify.
$\dfrac{2x}{2} > \dfrac{6}{2}$	Divide each side by 2.
$x > 3$	Solution: x is by itself.

2.

$-n - 5 \geq 11$	Write original inequality.
$-n - 5 + 5 \geq 11 + 5$	Add 5 to each side.
$-n \geq 16$	Simplify.
$(-1)(-n) \leq 16(-1)$	Multiply each side by -1 and reverse the inequality.
$n \leq -16$	Solution: n is by itself.

3.

$6 < 8 - 2p$	Write original inequality.
$6 - 8 < 8 - 8 - 2p$	Subtract 8 from each side.
$-2 < -2p$	Simplify.
$\dfrac{-2}{-2} > \dfrac{-2p}{-2}$	Divide each side by -2 and reverse the inequality.
$1 > p$	Solution: p is by itself.

EXERCISES

1.

$3x - 2 \leq 13$ *Write original inequality.*

$3x - 2 + 2 \leq 13 + 2$ *Add 2 to each side.*

$3x \leq 15$ *Simplify.*

$\dfrac{3x}{3} \leq \dfrac{15}{3}$ *Divide each side by 3.*

$x \leq 5$ *Solution: x is by itself.*

2.

$4 < -\frac{1}{5}y + 2$ *Write original inequality.*

$4 - 2 < -\frac{1}{5}y + 2 - 2$ *Subtract 2 from each side.*

$2 < -\frac{1}{5}y$ *Simplify.*

$-5 \cdot 2 > -5 \cdot \left(-\frac{1}{5}y\right)$ *Multiply each side by –5 and reverse the inequality.*

$-10 > y$ *Solution: y is by itself.*

3. When you multiply or divide each side of the inequality by a negative number

4.

$4y - 1 > -3$

$4y - 1 + 1 > -3 + 1$

$4y > -2$

$\dfrac{4y}{4} > \dfrac{-2}{4}$

$y > -\dfrac{1}{2}$

5.

$-18 + 10y \geq 12$

$-18 + 18 + 10y \geq 12 + 18$

$10y \geq 30$

$\dfrac{10y}{10} \geq \dfrac{30}{10}$

$y \geq 3$

6. The direction of the inequality symbol was not reversed, as it should have been.

$-4x + 7 \geq -5$

$-4x + 7 - 7 \geq -5 - 7$

$-4x \geq -12$

$\dfrac{-4x}{-4} \leq \dfrac{-12}{-4}$

$x \leq 3$

7. The direction of the inequality symbol was reversed, but it should not have been.

$3(2y - 1) < -7$

$6y - 3 < -7$

$6y - 3 + 3 < -7 + 3$

$6y < -4$

$\left(\frac{1}{6}\right)(6y) < \left(\frac{1}{6}\right)(-4)$

$y < -\dfrac{2}{3}$

8. The left side becomes $-\frac{1}{4}x$, not $\frac{1}{4}x$; so each side should be multiplied by -4, not 4.

$\frac{1}{2}x \leq \frac{3}{4}x + \frac{1}{4}$

$\frac{1}{2}x - \frac{3}{4}x \leq \frac{3}{4}x + \frac{1}{4} - \frac{3}{4}x$

$-\frac{1}{4}x \leq \frac{1}{4}$

$-4 \cdot \left(-\frac{1}{4}x\right) \geq -4 \cdot \left(\frac{1}{4}\right)$

$x \geq -1$

9. Never;

$-5x + 9 \leq -11$

$-5x + 9 - 9 \leq -11 - 9$

$-5x \leq -20$

$\dfrac{-5x}{-5} \geq \dfrac{-20}{-5}$

$x \geq 4$

10. Sometimes;

$5y - 20 \geq 15$

$5y - 20 + 20 \geq 15 + 20$

$5y \geq 35$

$\dfrac{5y}{5} \geq \dfrac{35}{5}$

$y \geq 7$

11. Always;

$-15b - 12 > -3$

$-15b - 12 + 12 > -3 + 12$

$-15b > 9$

$\dfrac{-15b}{-15} < \dfrac{9}{-15}$

$b < -\dfrac{9}{15}$, or $b < -\dfrac{3}{5}$

12. Sometimes;

$$4(2a - 1) < 8$$

$$\frac{1}{4} \cdot 4(2a - 1) < \frac{1}{4} \cdot 8$$

$$2a - 1 < 2$$

$$2a - 1 + 1 < 2 + 1$$

$$2a < 3$$

$$\frac{2a}{2} < \frac{3}{2}$$

$$a < \frac{3}{2}$$

13. C;

$$2x + 13 > 9$$

$$2x + 13 - 13 > 9 - 13$$

$$2x > -4$$

$$\frac{2x}{2} > \frac{-4}{2}$$

$$x > -2$$

14. A;

$$-2x - 8 > -4$$

$$-2x - 8 + 8 > -4 + 8$$

$$-2x > 4$$

$$\frac{-2x}{-2} < \frac{4}{-2}$$

$$x < -2$$

15. B;

$$6 < 18 - 6x$$

$$6 - 18 < 18 - 18 - 6x$$

$$-12 < -6x$$

$$\frac{-12}{-6} > \frac{-6x}{-6}$$

$$2 > x$$

16. D;

$$16 - 10x < 4 - 4x$$

$$16 - 10x + 10x < 4 - 4x + 10x$$

$$16 < 4 + 6x$$

$$16 - 4 < 4 + 6x - 4$$

$$12 < 6x$$

$$\frac{12}{6} < \frac{6x}{6}$$

$$2 < x$$

17.

$$-11x + 3 < -30$$

$$-11x + 3 - 3 < -30 - 3$$

$$-11x < -33$$

$$\frac{-11x}{-11} > \frac{-33}{-11}$$

$$x > 3$$

18.

$$\frac{1}{5}y + 12 \le 8$$

$$\frac{1}{5}y + 12 - 12 \le 8 - 12$$

$$\frac{1}{5}y \le -4$$

$$5 \cdot \frac{1}{5}y \le 5 \cdot (-4)$$

$$y \le -20$$

19.

$$5a + 6 \ge -9$$

$$5a + 6 - 6 \ge -9 - 6$$

$$5a \ge -15$$

$$\frac{5a}{5} \ge \frac{-15}{5}$$

$$a \ge -3$$

20.

$$-9 < 2b - 13$$

$$-9 + 13 < 2b - 13 + 13$$

$$4 < 2b$$

$$\frac{4}{2} < \frac{2b}{2}$$

$$2 < b$$

21.

$$\frac{3}{4}m \le \frac{1}{4}m + 2$$

$$\frac{3}{4}m - \frac{1}{4}m \le \frac{1}{4}m + 2 - \frac{1}{4}m$$

$$\frac{1}{2}m \le 2$$

$$2 \cdot \frac{1}{2}m \le 2 \cdot 2$$

$$m \le 4$$

22.

$$-\frac{1}{5}x > \frac{4}{5}x + 3$$

$$-\frac{1}{5}x - \frac{4}{5}x > \frac{4}{5}x + 3 - \frac{4}{5}x$$

$$-x > 3$$

$$\frac{-x}{-1} < \frac{3}{-1}$$

$$x < -3$$

23.
$$2(x + 1) \geq -2$$
$$2x + 2 \geq -2$$
$$2x + 2 - 2 \geq -2 - 2$$
$$2x \geq -4$$
$$\frac{2x}{2} \geq \frac{-4}{2}$$
$$x \geq -2$$

24.
$$4x + 1 \leq 2(x + 2)$$
$$4x + 1 \leq 2x + 4$$
$$4x + 1 - 2x \leq 2x + 4 - 2x$$
$$2x + 1 \leq 4$$
$$2x + 1 - 1 \leq 4 - 1$$
$$2x \leq 3$$
$$\frac{2x}{2} \leq \frac{3}{2}$$
$$x \leq \frac{3}{2}$$

25.
$$-4x + 3 \geq -5x$$
$$-4x + 3 + 4x \geq -5x + 4x$$
$$3 \geq -x$$
$$\frac{3}{-1} \leq \frac{-x}{-1}$$
$$-3 \leq x$$

26.
$$n + n + 1 \leq 7$$
$$2n + 1 \leq 7$$
$$2n + 1 - 1 \leq 7 - 1$$
$$2n \leq 6$$
$$\frac{2n}{2} \leq \frac{6}{2}$$
$$n \leq 3$$

27.
$$n + n + 1 + n + 2 > 18$$
$$3n + 3 > 18$$
$$3n + 3 - 3 > 18 - 3$$
$$3n > 15$$
$$\frac{3n}{3} > \frac{15}{3}$$
$$n > 5$$

28.
$$n + n + 1 + n + 2 < 20$$
$$3n + 3 < 20$$
$$3n + 3 - 3 < 20 - 3$$
$$3n < 17$$
$$\frac{3n}{3} < \frac{17}{3}$$
$$n < \frac{17}{3} \text{ or } 5\frac{2}{3}$$

29.
$$4(-x + 3) \geq 28$$
$$\frac{1}{4} \cdot 4(-x + 3) \geq \frac{1}{4} \cdot 28$$
$$-x + 3 \geq 7$$
$$-x + 3 - 3 \geq 7 - 3$$
$$-x \geq 4$$
$$\frac{-x}{-1} \leq \frac{4}{-1}$$
$$x \leq -4$$

30.
$$(15 - x) + (4x - 3) + (33 - 6x) \leq 36$$
$$-3x + 45 \leq 36$$
$$-3x + 45 - 45 \leq 36 - 45$$
$$-3x \leq -9$$
$$\frac{-3x}{-3} \geq \frac{-9}{-3}$$
$$x \geq 3$$

Also $x < 5\frac{1}{2}$, so that the length of the base is positive.

31. $x =$ serving size
$$20 \leq 6 + 2x$$
$$20 - 6 \leq 6 - 6 + 2x$$
$$\frac{14}{2} \leq \frac{2x}{2}$$
$$7 \leq x$$

You should plan to serve at least 7 oz of macaroni and cheese.

32. $t =$ number of tickets you can buy.
$$10 + 0.25t \leq 20$$
$$10 + 0.25t - 10 \leq 20 - 10$$
$$0.25t \leq 10$$
$$\frac{0.25t}{0.25} \leq \frac{10}{0.25}$$
$$t \leq 40$$

You can buy at most 40 tickets.

33.

Number of tickets bought	4	8	12	16	20	24	28	32	36	40
Total cost in dollars	11	12	13	14	15	16	17	18	19	20

34. h = number of hours you will ride your bike.

$$15h > 12$$

$$\frac{15h}{15} > \frac{12}{15}$$

$$h > \frac{4}{5}$$

You will ride your bike for more than $\frac{4}{5}$ of an hour.

35. D; $4(3) - 5(-1) \overset{?}{\leq} 21$ $\qquad$ $3 + (-1) \overset{?}{>} 0$ $\qquad$ $-2(3) + 4(-1) \overset{?}{\leq} -10$ $\qquad$ $3(3) - (-1) \overset{?}{<} 10$

$\qquad\qquad 12 + 5 \overset{?}{\leq} 21$ $\qquad\qquad\quad 2 > 0 \checkmark$ $\qquad\qquad\quad -6 + (-4) \overset{?}{\leq} -10$ $\qquad\qquad 9 + 1 \overset{?}{<} 10$

$\qquad\qquad\quad 17 \leq 21 \checkmark$ $\qquad\qquad\qquad\qquad\qquad\qquad\quad -10 \leq -10 \checkmark$ $\qquad\qquad\quad 10 < 10 \checkmark$

36.

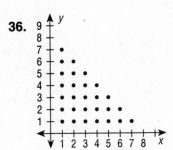

9.8 *The Triangle Inequality*

ONGOING ASSESSMENT

1. Not a triangle; $50 + 10 \not> 71$

2. Triangle

3. Not a triangle; $53 + 85 \not> 138$

EXERCISES

1. A and C; by the Triangle Inequality

2. Yes;

3. No;

4. Yes;

5.–7. x = measure of third side

5. $x + 3 > 5$ $\qquad$ $3 + 5 > x$

$\qquad x > 2$ $\qquad\quad$ $8 > x$

Greater than 2, less than 8

6. $x + 9 > 11$ $\qquad$ $9 + 11 > x$

$\qquad x > 2$ $\qquad\quad$ $20 > x$

Greater than 2, less than 20

7. $x + 16 > 20$ $\qquad$ $16 + 20 > x$

$\qquad x > 4$ $\qquad\qquad$ $36 > x$

Greater than 4, less than 36

8. No; $1 + 3 \not> 5$ **9.** No; $8 + 5 \not> 13$ **10.** Yes; $6 + 8 > 10$,

$$6 + 10 > 8,$$
$$8 + 10 > 6$$

11. Yes; $5 + 5 > 5$

12.

Measure of Side 1	Measure of Side 2	Measure of Side 3 is greater than	Measure of Side 3 is less than
3 cm	8 cm	$8 - 3 = 5$ cm	$8 + 3 = 11$ cm
9 in.	16 in.	$16 - 9 = 7$ in.	$16 + 9 = 25$ in.
10 ft	21 ft	$21 - 10 = 11$ ft	$21 + 10 = 31$ ft
30 m	45 m	$45 - 30 = 15$ m	$45 + 30 = 75$ m
100 cm	225 cm	$225 - 100 = 125$ cm	$225 + 100 = 325$ cm

13. Yes; $\frac{5}{2} + \frac{7}{2} = \frac{12}{2} > \frac{9}{2}$,

$\frac{5}{2} + \frac{9}{2} = \frac{14}{2} > \frac{7}{2}$,

$\frac{7}{2} + \frac{9}{2} = \frac{16}{2} > \frac{5}{2}$

14. $\sqrt{2} \approx 1.41$

$\sqrt{3} \approx 1.73$

$\sqrt{10} \approx 3.16$

No; $1.41 + 1.73 = 3.14 \not> 3.16$

15. No; $3.25 + 6.79 = 10.04 \not> 10.1$

16. No; $\frac{1}{8} + \frac{1}{4} = \frac{1}{8} + \frac{2}{8} = \frac{3}{8} \not> \frac{4}{8} = \frac{1}{2}$

17. Yes; the sum of the two shorter lengths is greater than the longest length.

18. No; the sum of the two shorter lengths is not greater than the longest length.

19. $b + d > \boxed{e}$ **20.** $a + b + \boxed{c} > e$ **21.** $a < d + \boxed{c}$ **22.** $b + \boxed{a} + e > c$

23. $3.75 + 3.75 > x$

$7.5 > x$

The tips can be less than 7.5 in. apart by the Triangle Inequality.

24. For each right triangle with side lengths of 6 and 10, the third side must be 8 by the Pythagorean Theorem.

$$6^2 + b^2 = 10^2$$
$$36 + b^2 = 100$$
$$36 + b^2 - 36 = 100 - 36$$
$$b^2 = 64$$
$$b = \sqrt{64}$$
$$b = 8$$

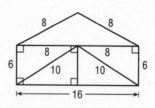

Then the top triangle has sides of 8, 8, and $8 + 8$ or 16, which is impossible by the Triangle Inequality. So, if the 6's and 10's are correct, the 8's are incorrect.

25. $11 + 14 = 25$ $11 + 14 + 25 = 50$

$14 - 11 = 3$ $11 + 14 + 3 = 28$

The perimeter, in centimeters, must be between 28 and 50.

26. B; $9 + 15 > x > 15 - 9$

$24 > x > 6$

27. D; $8 + 6 > x > 8 - 6$

$14 > x > 2$

28.

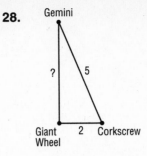

$5 + 2 > x > 5 - 2$

$7 > x > 3$

It takes between 3 and 7 minutes.

Chapter **R E V I E W**

1. $y^2 = 169$

$y = \sqrt{169}, -\sqrt{169}$

$y = 13, -13$

2. $5m^2 = 605$

$\dfrac{5m^2}{5} = \dfrac{605}{5}$

$m^2 = 121$

$m = \sqrt{121}, -\sqrt{121}$

$m = 11, -11$

3. $s^2 + 5 + 14$

$s^2 + 5 - 5 = 14 - 5$

$s^2 = 9$

$s = \sqrt{9}$

$s = 3, -3$

4. $3 + r^2 = 10$

$3 - 3 + r^2 = 10 - 3$

$r^2 = 7$

$r = \sqrt{7}, -\sqrt{7}$

5. $\frac{7}{4}$ is rational; $\sqrt{12} = 3.46410\ldots$ is irrational; $\frac{5}{2}$ is rational;

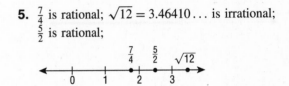

6. $\frac{3}{5}$ is rational; 1.2 is rational; $\sqrt{3} = 1.7320\ldots$ is irrational;

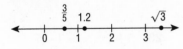

7. $\sqrt{5} = 2.2360\ldots$ is irrational; $\frac{4}{3}$ is rational; -2.2 is rational;

8. 1 is rational; $\sqrt{6} = 2.449\ldots$ is irrational; $-\sqrt{2} = -1.4142\ldots$ is irrational;

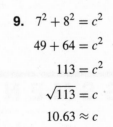

9. $7^2 + 8^2 = c^2$

$49 + 64 = c^2$

$113 = c^2$

$\sqrt{113} = c$

$10.63 \approx c$

10. $4^2 + b^2 = 10^2$

$16 + b^2 = 100$

$b^2 = 84$

$b = \sqrt{84}$

$b \approx 9.17$

11. $7^2 + 3^2 = c^2$

$49 + 9 = c^2$

$58 = c^2$

$\sqrt{58} = c$

$7.62 \approx c$

12. $12^2 + b^2 = 14^2$

$144 + b^2 = 196$

$b^2 = 52$

$b \approx 7.21$

13.
$8^2 + b^2 = 9^2$

$64 + b^2 = 81$

$b^2 = 17$

$b = \sqrt{17}$

$b \approx 4$ ft

14. $x \leq 4$

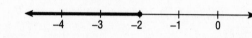

15. $x > -3$

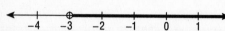

16.
$-4x - 5 \geq 3$

$-4x - 5 + 5 \geq 3 + 5$

$-4x \geq 8$

$\dfrac{-4x}{-4} \leq \dfrac{8}{-4}$

$x \leq -2$

17.
$-\dfrac{1}{4} < \dfrac{1}{10}x$

$-\dfrac{1}{4} \cdot 10 < \dfrac{1}{10}x \cdot 10$

$-\dfrac{10}{4} < x$

$-\dfrac{5}{2} < x$

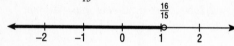

18.
$6x + 7 \leq 4$

$6x + 7 - 7 \leq 4 - 7$

$6x \leq -3$

$x \leq -\dfrac{1}{2}$

19.
$-\dfrac{5}{8}x > -\dfrac{2}{3}$

$-\dfrac{8}{5} \cdot -\dfrac{5}{8}x < -\dfrac{2}{3} \cdot -\dfrac{8}{5}$

$x < \dfrac{16}{15}$

20. No; $2 + 3 \not> 12$

21. Yes; $5 + 6 > 9$,

$5 + 9 > 6$,

$6 + 9 > 5$

22. Yes; $17 + 7 > 21$,

$17 + 21 > 7$,

$21 + 7 > 17$

23. $5 + 7 > x > 7 - 5$

$12 > x > 2$

It is between 2 in. and 12 in.

Chapter **ASSESSMENT**

1. $15, -15$

2.
$a^2 + 3 = 39$

$a^2 + 3 - 3 = 39 - 3$

$a^2 = 36$

$a = \sqrt{36} = 6$

$a = -\sqrt{36} = -6$

3.
$8 - s^2 = -6$

$8 - 8 - s^2 = -6 - 8$

$-s^2 = -14$

$s^2 = 14$

$s = \sqrt{14}, -\sqrt{14}$

4. $s^2 = 65.61$

$s = \sqrt{65.61}$

$s = 8.1$ in.

5. $12 - 3 < x < 12 + 3$

$9 < x < 15$

It is between 9 in. and 15 in.

6. $22 - 3 < x < 22 + 3$

$19 < x < 25$

It is between 19 ft and 25 ft.

7. $15 - 8 < x < 15 + 8$

$7 < x < 23$

It is between 7 m and 23 m.

8. C; $\frac{9}{5} = 1.8$

9. D; $\frac{9}{4} = 2.25$

10. B; $\sqrt{3} \approx 1.73$

11. A; $\sqrt{0.2} \approx 0.45$

12. $4^2 + 9^2 = c^2$

$16 + 81 = c^2$

$97 = c^2$

$\sqrt{97} = c$

$9.85 \approx c$

The diagonal cut is 9.85 in.

13. $10^2 + 8^2 = a^2$

$100 + 64 = a^2$

$164 = a^2$

$\sqrt{164} = a$

$12.81 \approx a$

14. $7^2 + b^2 = 7.6^2$

$49 + b^2 = 57.76$

$49 + b^2 - 49 = 57.76 - 49$

$b^2 = 8.76$

$b = \sqrt{8.76}$

$b \approx 2.96$

15. $7^2 + c^2 = 9.9^2$

$49 + c^2 = 98.01$

$49 + c^2 - 49 = 98.01 - 49$

$c^2 = 49.01$

$c = \sqrt{49.01}$

$c \approx 7.00$

16. $-x < 2$

$\dfrac{-x}{-1} > \dfrac{2}{-1}$

$x > -2$

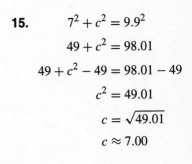

17. $-8r + 16 \leq 8$

$-8r + 16 - 16 \leq 8 - 16$

$-8r \leq -8$

$\dfrac{-8r}{-8} \geq \dfrac{-8}{-8}$

$r \geq 1$

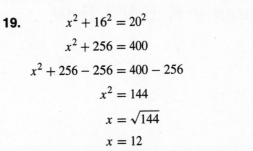

18. $-2p \geq 5$

$\dfrac{-2p}{-2} \leq \dfrac{5}{-2}$

$p \leq -\dfrac{5}{2}$

19. $x^2 + 16^2 = 20^2$

$x^2 + 256 = 400$

$x^2 + 256 - 256 = 400 - 256$

$x^2 = 144$

$x = \sqrt{144}$

$x = 12$

You need to put the bottom of the ladder 12 ft away from the house.

20.
$$x^2 + (16 + 3)^2 = 20^2$$
$$x^2 + 19^2 = 20^2$$
$$x^2 + 361 = 400$$
$$x^2 + 361 - 361 = 400 - 361$$
$$x^2 = 39$$
$$x = \sqrt{39}$$
$$x \approx 6.24$$

You need to put the ladder about 6.24 feet away from the house.

21. h = height of top of ladder.
$$5^2 + h^2 = 20^2$$
$$25 + h^2 = 400$$
$$25 + h^2 - 25 = 400 - 25$$
$$h^2 = 375$$
$$h = \sqrt{375}$$
$$h \approx 19.36$$

The highest you can get the ladder is about 19.36 feet.

Standardized Test Practice

1. C

2. B;
$$4^2 + 2^2 = c^2$$
$$16 + 4 = c^2$$
$$20 = c^2$$
$$\sqrt{20} = c$$
$$4.5 \approx c$$

3. D; $4.5 + 5.5 > x > 5.5 - 4.5$
$$10 > x > 1$$

4. C;
$$5^2 + b^2 = 13^2$$
$$25 + b^2 = 169$$
$$25 - 25 + b^2 = 169 - 25$$
$$b^2 = 144$$
$$b = \sqrt{144}$$
$$b = 12$$

5. D

6. B;
$$-3(x - 1) \geq -9$$
$$-3x + 3 \geq -9$$
$$-3x + 3 - 3 \geq -9 - 3$$
$$-3x \geq -12$$
$$\frac{-3x}{-3} \leq \frac{-12}{-3}$$
$$x \leq 4$$

7. B; $\sqrt{16} = 4$ ft

8. C

Cumulative REVIEW

1.
$$\frac{2}{7} + \frac{4}{7} = \frac{2 + 4}{7}$$
$$= \frac{6}{7}$$

2.
$$\frac{16x}{4} - \frac{14x}{4} = \frac{16x - 14x}{4}$$
$$= \frac{2x}{4}$$
$$= \frac{2 \cdot x}{2 \cdot 2} = \frac{x}{2}$$

3.
$$\frac{1}{4} + \frac{1}{6} = \frac{1}{4} \cdot \frac{3}{3} + \frac{1}{6} \cdot \frac{2}{2}$$
$$= \frac{3}{12} + \frac{2}{12}$$
$$= \frac{5}{12}$$

4.
$$\frac{5}{8} - \frac{17}{32} = \frac{5}{8} \cdot \frac{4}{4} - \frac{17}{32}$$
$$= \frac{20}{32} - \frac{17}{32}$$
$$= \frac{3}{32}$$

5. $\frac{64}{71} + \frac{57}{90} \approx 1.53$

6.
$$\frac{4}{5}x - \frac{2}{7}x = 0.8x - 0.2857x$$
$$= 0.51x$$

7. $2 - \left(\frac{3}{2} + \frac{7}{3}\right) = 2 - (1.5 + 2.33)$
$= 2 - (3.83)$
$= -1.83$

8. $\frac{26}{9}t + \frac{85}{200}t \approx 3.31t$

9. $\frac{5}{12} \cdot \frac{10}{3} = \frac{5 \cdot 10}{12 \cdot 3}$
$= \frac{5 \cdot 5 \cdot \cancel{2}}{6 \cdot \cancel{2} \cdot 3}$
$= \frac{25}{18}$

10. $\frac{5}{2} \div \frac{1}{5} = \frac{5}{2} \cdot \frac{5}{1}$
$= \frac{25}{2}$

11. $\frac{7n}{4} \cdot 16 = \frac{16 \cdot 7n}{4}$
$= \frac{\cancel{4} \cdot 4 \cdot 7n}{\cancel{4}}$
$= 28n$

12. $-\frac{6}{10} \div \frac{z}{5} = \frac{-6}{10} \cdot \frac{5}{z}$
$= \frac{-1 \cdot 3 \cdot \cancel{2} \cdot \cancel{5}}{2 \cdot \cancel{5} \cdot z}$
$= -\frac{3}{z}$

13. $4\frac{1}{9} = \frac{37}{9}; \ 5\frac{5}{6} = \frac{35}{6}$

$P = 2\left(\frac{37}{9}\right) + 2\left(\frac{35}{6}\right)$
$= \frac{74}{9} + \frac{35}{3}$
$= \frac{74}{9} + \frac{35}{3} \cdot \frac{3}{3}$
$= \frac{74}{9} + \frac{105}{9}$
$= \frac{179}{9}$
$= 19\frac{8}{9}$ ft or 19.8 ft

$A = \frac{37}{9} \cdot \frac{35}{6}$
$= \frac{37 \cdot 35}{9 \cdot 6}$
$= \frac{1295}{54}$
$= 23\frac{53}{54}$ ft^2 or 23.98 ft^2

14. $6\frac{7}{8} = \frac{55}{8}$

$P = 4\left(\frac{55}{8}\right)$
$= \frac{55}{2}$
$= 27\frac{1}{2}$ in. or 27.5 in.

$A = \left(\frac{55}{8}\right)^2$
$= \frac{3025}{64}$
$= 47\frac{17}{64}$ in.^{2}
or 47.27 in.^{2}

15. Perimeter $= 2(3.5) + 2(10)$
$= 7 + 20$
$= 27$ m

Area $= 3.5 \times 10$
$= 35$ m^2

16. $\frac{3}{10} = 0.3$
$= 0.3 \times 100\%$
$= 30\%$

17. $\frac{18}{25} = 0.72$
$= 0.72 \times 100\%$
$= 72\%$

18. $\frac{140}{175} = 0.8$
$= 0.8 \times 100\%$
$= 80\%$

19. $\frac{300}{250} = 1.2$
$= 1.2 \times 100\%$
$= 120\%$

20. $\frac{6}{15} = \frac{\cancel{3} \cdot 2}{\cancel{3} \cdot 5} = \frac{2}{5}$
$= 0.4 = 0.4 \times 100\%$
$= 40\%$

21. $632 \times 1.0482 = \$662.46$

22. Rate; $\frac{84 \text{ cups}}{3 \text{ min}} = 28$ cups/min

23. Ratio; $\frac{5 \text{ cars}}{3 \text{ cars}} = \frac{5}{3}$

24. Ratio; $\frac{16 \text{ feet}}{24 \text{ inches}} = \frac{16 \text{ feet}}{2(12 \text{ inches})} = \frac{16 \text{ feet}}{2 \text{ feet}} = \frac{8}{1}$

25. Rate; $\frac{63 \text{ meters}}{1.5 \text{ seconds}} = 42$ meters per second

26.
$$\frac{3}{18} = \frac{t}{30}$$
$$\frac{1}{6} = \frac{t}{30}$$
$$30 \cdot \frac{1}{6} = 30 \cdot \frac{t}{30}$$
$$5 = t$$

27.
$$\frac{12}{16} = \frac{27}{n}$$
$$\frac{16}{12} = \frac{n}{27}$$
$$\frac{4}{3} = \frac{n}{27}$$
$$27 \cdot \frac{4}{3} = 27 \cdot \frac{n}{27}$$
$$36 = n$$

28.
$$\frac{1}{m} = \frac{1.5}{6}$$
$$m = \frac{6}{1.5}$$
$$m = 4$$

29.
$$\frac{x}{55} = \frac{5}{8}$$
$$55 \cdot \frac{x}{55} = 55 \cdot \frac{5}{8}$$
$$x = \frac{275}{8}$$
$$x = 34\frac{3}{8}$$

30. $x =$ property tax you would pay for a \$140,000 house.
$$\frac{x}{2100} = \frac{140,000}{105,000}$$
$$\frac{x}{2100} = \frac{35,000 \cdot 4}{35,000 \cdot 3}$$
$$\frac{x}{2100} = \frac{4}{3}$$
$$2100 \cdot \frac{x}{2100} = 2100 \cdot \frac{4}{3}$$
$$x = 2800$$
You would pay \$2800 tax.

31.
$$\frac{63}{90} = \frac{p}{100}$$
$$\frac{\cancel{9} \cdot 7}{\cancel{9} \cdot 10} = \frac{p}{100}$$
$$100 \cdot \frac{7}{10} = p$$
$$70 = p$$
63 is 70% of 90.

32.
$$\frac{a}{40} = \frac{85}{100}$$
$$\frac{a}{40} = 0.85$$
$$a = 40 \cdot 0.85$$
$$a = 34$$
34 is 85% of 40.

33.
$$\frac{a}{320} = \frac{62.5}{100}$$
$$\frac{a}{320} = 0.625$$
$$a = 320 \cdot 0.625$$
$$a = 200$$
200 is 62.5% of 320.

34.
$$\frac{105}{b} = \frac{150}{100}$$
$$\frac{b}{105} = \frac{100}{150}$$
$$\frac{b}{105} = \frac{\cancel{50} \cdot 2}{\cancel{50} \cdot 3}$$
$$105 \cdot \frac{b}{105} = 105 \cdot \frac{2}{3}$$
$$b = 70$$
105 is 150% of 70.

35.
$$\frac{18}{b} = \frac{12}{100}$$
$$\frac{b}{18} = \frac{100}{12}$$
$$18 \cdot \frac{b}{18} = 18 \cdot \frac{100}{12}$$
$$b = 150$$
150 people were surveyed.

36.
$$\frac{a}{150} = \frac{40}{100}$$
$$\frac{a}{150} = 0.4$$
$$b = 150 \cdot 0.4$$
$$b = 60$$
60 people said drama was their favorite.

37.
$$\frac{a}{150} = \frac{34}{100}$$
$$\frac{a}{150} = 0.34$$
$$a = 150 \cdot 0.34$$
$$a = 51$$
51 people said comedy was their favorite.

38.
$$\frac{a}{150} = \frac{8}{100}$$
$$\frac{a}{150} = 0.08$$
$$a = 150 \cdot 0.08 = 12$$
12 people said western was their favorite.

39.
$$\frac{a}{150} = \frac{6}{100}$$
$$\frac{a}{150} = 0.06$$
$$a = 150 \cdot 0.06 = 9$$
9 people said horror was their favorite.

40. Increase;

$$\frac{215{,}025 - 207{,}100}{207{,}100} = \frac{7925}{207{,}100}$$
$$\approx 0.0383$$
$$= 0.0383 \times 100\%$$
$$= 3.83\%$$

41. Decrease;

$$\frac{39.99 - 25.99}{39.99} = \frac{14}{39.99}$$
$$\approx 0.3501$$
$$= 0.3501 \times 100\%$$
$$= 35.01\%$$

42. 20

43. $10 \cdot 20 = 200$

44. $10 \cdot 20 \cdot 10 = 2000$

45. $\frac{12}{15} = 0.8$; $-\sqrt{3} \approx -1.73$; $-\sqrt{\frac{81}{121}} \approx -0.82$;

$\sqrt{17} = 4.123$; $-\frac{14}{29} \approx -0.48$; $\sqrt{5.76} = 2.4$

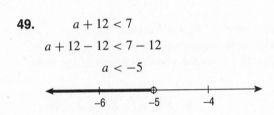

46.

$$60^2 + b^2 = 61^2$$
$$3600 + b^2 = 3721$$
$$3600 + b^2 - 3600 = 3721 - 3600$$
$$b^2 = 121$$
$$b = \sqrt{121}$$
$$b = 11$$

47.

$$9^2 + 15^2 = c^2$$
$$81 + 225 = c^2$$
$$306 = c^2$$
$$\sqrt{306} = c$$
$$17.49 \approx c$$

48.

$$a^2 + 10^2 = 13^2$$
$$a^2 + 100 = 169$$
$$a^2 + 100 - 100 = 169 - 100$$
$$a^2 = 69$$
$$a = \sqrt{69}$$
$$a \approx 8.31$$

49.

$$a + 12 < 7$$
$$a + 12 - 12 < 7 - 12$$
$$a < -5$$

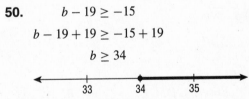

50.

$$b - 19 \geq -15$$
$$b - 19 + 19 \geq -15 + 19$$
$$b \geq 34$$

51. $-4 \geq -6m$

$$\frac{-4}{-6} \leq \frac{-6m}{-6}$$
$$\frac{2}{3} \leq m$$

52.

$$\frac{-n}{8} > \frac{2}{3}$$
$$-8 \cdot \left(\frac{-n}{8}\right) < (-8) \cdot \frac{2}{3}$$
$$n < -\frac{16}{3}$$

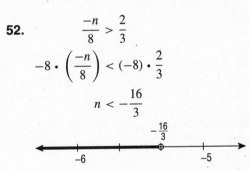

53. Yes; $5 + 9 > 13$,

$5 + 13 > 9$,

$13 + 9 > 5$

54. No; $\frac{1}{16} + \frac{1}{4} \not> \frac{3}{8}$

55. No; $4 + 7 \not> \sqrt{7}$

Chapter 10
Geometry Concepts and Spatial Thinking

10.1 Exploring Points, Lines, and Planes

ONGOING ASSESSMENT

1. *Sample answer:* $\overleftrightarrow{PH}, \overleftrightarrow{HM}, \overrightarrow{PM}$

2. Infinitely many

EXERCISES

1. B

2. A

3. D

4. C

5. $\overrightarrow{RS}; \overline{AB}; \overleftrightarrow{PQ}$

6. *Sample answer:* In a rectangular classroom, parallel lines include opposite edges of the room; intersecting lines meet in the corners of the room.

7. *Sample answer:* $\overleftrightarrow{CD}, \overleftrightarrow{CE}, \overleftrightarrow{DE}, \overleftrightarrow{DF}$

8. $\overline{AC}, \overline{AG}, \overline{CG}$

9. $\overrightarrow{EB}, \overrightarrow{EF}, \overrightarrow{EC}, \overrightarrow{EJ}, \overrightarrow{EH}$

10. $\overleftrightarrow{AG}$ and $\overleftrightarrow{BH}$

11. *Sample answer:* $\overleftrightarrow{AG}$ and $\overleftrightarrow{CF}$; $\overleftrightarrow{BH}$ and $\overleftrightarrow{CF}$

12. No; they extend in opposite directions.

13. Yes; they have the same endpoints.

14. Yes; they refer to the same segment.

15. $3\frac{1}{2}$

16. 5

17. $\overline{AB}, \overline{AC}, \overline{AD}, \overline{AE}, \overline{BC}, \overline{CD}, \overline{DE}, \overline{BE}$

18. A, B, C, D, E

19. B, C, D, E

20. $\overleftrightarrow{CB}$ is parallel to $\overleftrightarrow{DE}$; $\overleftrightarrow{BE}$ is parallel to $\overleftrightarrow{CD}$.

21. *Sample answer:* $\overrightarrow{AE}, \overrightarrow{AB}, \overrightarrow{AC}, \overrightarrow{AD}$

22.

3 parallel lines

23.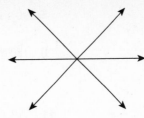

24.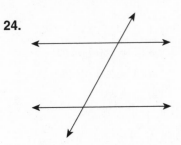

2 parallel lines and 1 line that intersects them

25.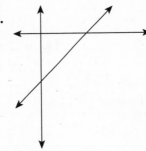

26. All of the windows on each wall lie in the same plane.

27. $BD = 3 + 10 + 3 + 10 + 3 + 10 + 3 = 42$ ft
$DF = 3 + 10 + 3 + 10 + 3 + 10 + 3 = 42$ ft

28. $CD = 3 + 7 + 3 + 7 + 3 + 7 + 3 + 7 + 3 + 7 + 3 = 53$ ft

29. No; the base of a window on the side of the building is not parallel to the base of a window on the front of the building because parallel lines must be in the same plane.

30. $\text{Area}_{\text{front}} = 42 \times 53$
$= 2226 \text{ ft}^2$

$\text{Area}_{\text{glass}} = 14(10 \times 7)$
$= 14(70)$
$= 980 \text{ ft}^2$

$\text{Percent}_{\text{front glass}} = \dfrac{980}{2226}$
≈ 0.44
$0.44 \times 100\% = 44\%$

31. C

32. B

33. $48 + 20 + 73 + 21 + 47 + 59 + 48 + 57 = 373$ mi

10.2 ALGEBRA CONNECTION: Naming, Measuring, and Drawing Angles

ONGOING ASSESSMENT

1. Answers vary.

2. Answers vary.

3. Answers vary.

EXERCISES

1. X

2. $\overrightarrow{XW}, \overrightarrow{XZ}$

3. $\angle X, \angle WXY, \angle ZXW, \angle YXW$

4. $\angle WYZ$

5. 90°; right

6. 115°; obtuse

7. 70°; acute

8. 180°; straight

9. 7; $\angle A$, $\angle B$, $\angle ECD$, $\angle EDC$, $\angle BCD$, $\angle ADE$, $\angle BDC$

10. 2; $\angle ADC$, $\angle EDB$

11. $m\angle AED + m\angle DEC = 180°$
$m\angle AED + 90° = 180°$
$m\angle AED = 90°$

12. 3; $\angle AED$, $\angle DEC$, $\angle BCA$

13. Vertex: D
Sides: $\overrightarrow{DC}$ and $\overrightarrow{DE}$
You can't simply name the angle as $\angle D$ because there are 6 angles with the vertex D.

14. $m\angle 2 = 180 - m\angle 1$
$m\angle 2 = 180 - 45$
$m\angle 2 = 135°$

15. $m\angle 3 = 180 - m\angle 2$
$m\angle 3 = 180 - 135$
$m\angle 3 = 45°$

16. $m\angle 4 = 180 - m\angle 1$
$m\angle 4 = 180 - 45$
$m\angle 4 = 135°$

17. $\angle 1$ and $\angle 4$ are supplementary angles.

18.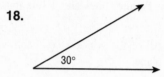

19.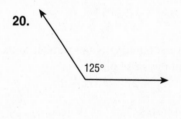

20.

21.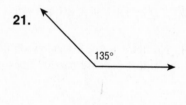

22. 35°

23. 100°

24. 160°

25. 75°

26. If two angles are congruent, then they have the same measure.

27. Straight angle

28. Right angle

29. Obtuse angle

30. Acute angle

31. A

32. B; $8x - 10 + 3x + 25 = 180$
$11x + 15 = 180$
$11x = 165$
$x = 15$
$m\angle A = 8x - 10 = 8(15) - 10 = 120 - 10 = 110°$
$m\angle B = 3x + 25 = 3(15) + 25 = 45 + 25 = 70°$

33. Answers vary.

Spiral REVIEW

1.–4.

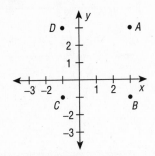

5. $\overleftrightarrow{AB}$ and $\overleftrightarrow{DC}$; $\overleftrightarrow{AD}$ and $\overleftrightarrow{BC}$

6. $\overleftrightarrow{AB}$ and $\overleftrightarrow{BC}$; $\overleftrightarrow{BC}$ and $\overleftrightarrow{CD}$; $\overleftrightarrow{CD}$ and $\overleftrightarrow{DA}$; $\overleftrightarrow{DA}$ and $\overleftrightarrow{AB}$; $\overleftrightarrow{BD}$ and $\overleftrightarrow{AC}$

7. $CD = AD = 4$

$$(CD)^2 + (AD)^2 = (AC)^2$$
$$4^2 + 4^2 = AC^2$$
$$16 + 16 = AC^2$$
$$32 = AC^2$$
$$\sqrt{32} = AC$$
$$5.66 \approx AC$$

8. C

9. D

10. B

11. A

12. $\dfrac{5}{6} + \dfrac{-1}{6} = \dfrac{5-1}{6}$

$$= \dfrac{4}{6}$$
$$= \dfrac{\cancel{2}(2)}{\cancel{2}(3)}$$
$$= \dfrac{2}{3}$$

13. $\dfrac{2}{3} + \dfrac{3}{6} = \dfrac{2 \cdot 2}{3 \cdot 2} + \dfrac{3}{6}$

$$= \dfrac{4}{6} + \dfrac{3}{6}$$
$$= \dfrac{4+3}{6}$$
$$= \dfrac{7}{6}$$

14. $\dfrac{-3}{5} - \dfrac{1}{3} = \dfrac{-3 \cdot 3}{5 \cdot 3} - \dfrac{1 \cdot 5}{3 \cdot 5}$

$$= \dfrac{-9}{15} - \dfrac{5}{15}$$
$$= \dfrac{-9-5}{15}$$
$$= -\dfrac{14}{15}$$

15. $4\dfrac{1}{2} + 1\dfrac{1}{2} = \dfrac{9}{2} + \dfrac{3}{2}$

$$= \dfrac{9+3}{2}$$
$$= \dfrac{12}{2}$$
$$= 6$$

16. $\dfrac{x}{6} + \dfrac{x}{6} = \dfrac{x+x}{6}$

$$= \dfrac{2x}{6}$$
$$= \dfrac{\cancel{(2)}x}{\cancel{(2)}3}$$
$$= \dfrac{x}{3}$$

17. $\dfrac{2}{y} - \dfrac{2}{5} = \dfrac{2 \cdot 5}{y \cdot 5} - \dfrac{2 \cdot y}{5 \cdot y}$

$$= \dfrac{10}{5y} - \dfrac{2y}{5y}$$
$$= \dfrac{10 - 2y}{5y}$$

18. $\dfrac{3}{z} - \dfrac{2}{z} = \dfrac{3-2}{z}$

$$= \dfrac{1}{z}$$

19. $\dfrac{a}{5} - \dfrac{a}{10} = \dfrac{2 \cdot a}{2 \cdot 5} - \dfrac{a}{10}$

$$= \dfrac{2a}{10} - \dfrac{a}{10}$$
$$= \dfrac{2a - a}{10}$$
$$= \dfrac{a}{10}$$

20. $\dfrac{1.5(10^{10}) \text{ dollars}}{2.6(10^8) \text{ Americans}} \approx 57.69$

Each American spent about $57.69 on music.

Lab 10.3

1. Yes; opposite angles are congruent. You can tell by measuring them.

2. There are 8 angles.

3.

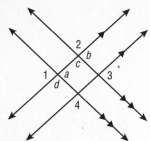

10.3 *Exploring Parallel Lines*

ONGOING ASSESSMENT

1.

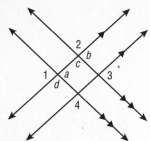

$\angle 1 \cong \angle a$, $\angle a \cong \angle b$, and $\angle b \cong \angle 3$; so $\angle 1 \cong \angle 3$.

$\angle 2 \cong \angle c$, $\angle c \cong \angle d$, and $\angle d \cong \angle 4$; so $\angle 2 \cong \angle 4$.

$\angle 1 \cong \angle a$, $\angle a \cong \angle b$, and $m\angle b + m\angle 2 = 180°$; so $m\angle 1 + m\angle 2 = 180°$. Then, since $m\angle 2 = 84°$, $m\angle 1 + 84° = 180°$ and $m\angle 1 = 96°$.

Because $\angle 1 \cong \angle 3$, $m\angle 3 = 96°$.

Because $\angle 2 \cong \angle 4$, $m\angle 4 = 84°$.

EXERCISES

1. Lines *m* and *n* are parallel.

2. $\angle 1$ and $\angle 3$; $\angle 2$ and $\angle 4$; $\angle 5$ and $\angle 7$; $\angle 6$ and $\angle 8$

3. $\angle 1$ and $\angle 5$; $\angle 2$ and $\angle 6$; $\angle 3$ and $\angle 7$; $\angle 4$ and $\angle 8$

4. $m\angle 2 = 55°$. When two parallel lines are intersected by a third line, the corresponding angles are congruent; so $\angle 6 \cong \angle 2$.

5. $m\angle 4 = 55°$. Vertical angles are congruent; so $\angle 2 \cong \angle 4$.

6. $m\angle 8 = 55°$. Vertical angles are congruent; so $\angle 6 \cong \angle 8$.

7.

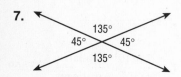

$180° - 45° = 135°$
$45°, 135°, 135°$;
Vertical angles are congruent and the sum of the measures of pairs of angles is 180°.

8.

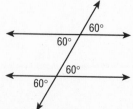

Four of the angles have measures of 60°.

9. $\angle 4 \not\cong \angle 8$ because lines k and m are not parallel.

10. $\angle 1, \angle 4, \angle 9, \angle 12$

11. $\angle 5, \angle 8$

12. $m\angle 1 + m\angle 2 = 180° \Rightarrow 65° + m\angle 2$
$\qquad\qquad = 180° \Rightarrow m\angle 2$
$\qquad\qquad = 115°$
$\angle 2, \angle 3, \angle 10, \angle 11$

13. $m\angle 5 + m\angle 6 = 180° \Rightarrow 75° + m\angle 6$
$\qquad\qquad = 180° \Rightarrow m\angle 6$
$\qquad\qquad = 105°$
$\angle 6, \angle 7$

14. $\angle 1$ and $\angle 5$; $\angle 2$ and $\angle 6$; $\angle 3$ and $\angle 7$; $\angle 4$ and $\angle 8$; $\angle 5$ and $\angle 9$; $\angle 6$ and $\angle 10$; $\angle 7$ and $\angle 11$; $\angle 8$ and $\angle 12$

15. $\angle 1$ and $\angle 9$; $\angle 2$ and $\angle 10$; $\angle 3$ and $\angle 11$; $\angle 4$ and $\angle 12$

16. $\angle 1 \cong \angle 2$, $\angle 2 \cong \angle 3$, and $\angle 3 \cong \angle 4$; so $\angle 1 \cong \angle 4$.

17. $\angle 1 \cong \angle 2$, $\angle 2 \cong \angle 3$, and $\angle 3 \cong \angle 4$; so $\angle 1 \cong \angle 4$.

18. $\overleftrightarrow{AB}, \overleftrightarrow{CD}, \overleftrightarrow{EJ}, \overleftrightarrow{KL}$, and $\overleftrightarrow{MN}$; $\overleftrightarrow{AE}, \overleftrightarrow{CF}, \overleftrightarrow{BM}, \overleftrightarrow{HL}$, and $\overleftrightarrow{JN}$; $\overleftrightarrow{BJ}, \overleftrightarrow{DH}, \overleftrightarrow{AN}, \overleftrightarrow{FK}$, and $\overleftrightarrow{EM}$

19. $\overleftrightarrow{LM}, \overleftrightarrow{NQ}, \overleftrightarrow{RU}$, and $\overleftrightarrow{VZ}$; $\overleftrightarrow{KV}, \overleftrightarrow{MW}, \overleftrightarrow{QX}$, and $\overleftrightarrow{UY}$

20. 10 triangles: $\triangle ABC, \triangle ADF, \triangle AGJ, \triangle AKO, \triangle OJN, \triangle OFM, \triangle OCL, \triangle FIJ, \triangle CEF$, and $\triangle CHJ$

21.

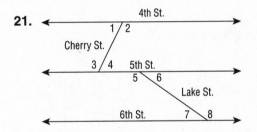

22. $\angle 2 \cong \angle 3$, $\angle 1 \cong \angle 4$, $\angle 6 \cong \angle 7$, $\angle 5 \cong \angle 8$

23. Given that the measure of one of the angles from 4th Street onto Cherry Street is $117°$ and that $\angle 1$ is acute, $m\angle 2 = 117°$. Given that the measure of one of the angles from Lake Street onto 6th Street is $34°$ and that $\angle 8$ is obtuse, $m\angle 7 = 34°$. By measuring, the measures of the other angles are as follows: $m\angle 1 = m\angle 4 = 63°$, $m\angle 3 = 117°$, $m\angle 5 = m\angle 8 = 146°$, $m\angle 6 = 34°$.

24. Yes

25. 6 angle measures; the angle measures are $25°, 65°, 90°, 115°, 155°$, and $180°$.

26. C

27.

a, b, and c are parallel; d and e are parallel.

10.4 *Symmetry*

ONGOING ASSESSMENT

1. *Sample answer:* Z0609Z

2. *Sample answer:* A8008A

3. *Sample answer:* C3803D

EXERCISES

1. *Sample answer:* books, backs of chairs, light fixtures

2. Vertical symmetry

3. Horizontal, vertical, and 180° rotational symmetry

4. Rotational symmetry at 72° and 144° in both directions

5. Horizontal symmetry

6. Vertical symmetry

7. Horizontal, vertical, and 180° rotational symmetry

8. Rotational symmetry at 45°, 90°, and 180° in both directions

9. No symmetry

10.–13. *Sample answers:*

10.

11.

12.

13.

14. Line

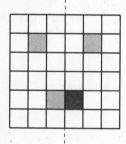

15. Rotational

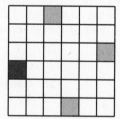

16. Rotational

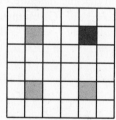

17. Line

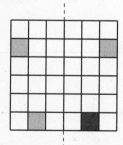

18. No; it will have symmetry by rotating 180°.

19. Yes; *Sample answer:*

20. The bridge with the bridge's reflection has a horizontal line of symmetry.

21. The butterfly has a vertical line of symmetry.

22. The flower has rotational symmetry at 120° in either direction and vertical symmetry.

23. BOX

24. DECK

25. OHIO

26. *Sample answer:* BOOK, DICE; HE DIED.

27. A

28. Answers vary.

10.5 *Exploring Triangles*

ONGOING ASSESSMENT

1. a. Isosceles triangle
  b. Scalene triangle
  c. Equilateral triangle

EXERCISES

1. C; all sides have different lengths.
  D; one angle is obtuse.

2. A; at least two sides have the same length.
  B; all three angles have the same measure.
  E; all three sides have the same length.
  G; all three angles are acute.

3. C; all sides have different lengths.
  G; all three angles are acute.

4. A; at least two sides have the same length.
  F; one angle is right.

5.–10. Answers vary.

5.

6.

7.

8.

9.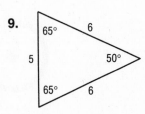

10.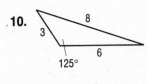

11. Right scalene

12. Acute scalene

13. Obtuse isosceles

14. Equiangular, equilateral, isosceles, acute

15. Obtuse scalene

16. Right isosceles

17. Acute scalene

18. Acute isosceles

19. Equiangular, equilateral, isosceles, acute

20.

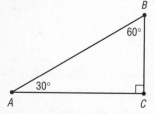

Equiangular, equilateral, acute, isosceles

21.

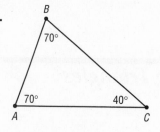

Acute isosceles

22.

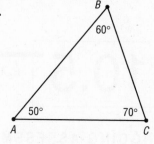

Acute scalene

23.

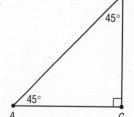

Right scalene

24.

Right isosceles

25.

Obtuse scalene

26. Right isosceles

27. Right scalene

28. Acute isosceles

29. Obtuse scalene

30. No; the side opposite the right angle must be longer than the other two sides. Because an equilateral triangle is equiangular, all of the angle measures are the same, 60°.

31. No; the measure of each angle is 60°.

32. The triangle is rigid. You can adjust the rectangle's sticks to form a different shape of quadrilateral.

33.

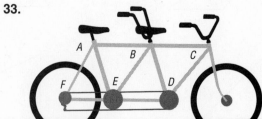

△AEF; △EAB; △BDE; △DBC

34. The triangles keep the frame from collapsing.

35. B

36. Answers vary.

1. Vertical line symmetry

2. Rotational symmetry at 120° in either direction

3. Vertical and horizontal line symmetry; rotational symmetry at 180° in either direction

4. $2b - 2 = -2b$
$4b - 2 = 0$
$4b = 2$
$b = \dfrac{1}{2}$

5. $62p - 203 = 111 - 38p$
$100p - 203 = 111$
$100p = 314$
$p = 3.14$

6. $2a + 4.04 = 16.08$
$2a = 12.04$
$a = 6.02$

7. $\dfrac{1}{4}(3r - 1) = \dfrac{1}{4}$
$4 \cdot \dfrac{1}{4}(3r - 1) = 4 \cdot \dfrac{1}{4}$
$3r - 1 = 1$
$3r = 2$
$r = \dfrac{2}{3}$

8. $p^2 + 4 = 40$
$p^2 = 36$
$p = \sqrt{36} = 6$
$p = -\sqrt{36} = -6$

9. $q - \dfrac{1}{2} = \dfrac{1}{3}$
$q - \dfrac{1}{2} + \dfrac{1}{2} = \dfrac{1}{3} + \dfrac{1}{2}$
$q = \dfrac{1}{3} \cdot \dfrac{2}{2} + \dfrac{1}{2} \cdot \dfrac{3}{3}$
$q = \dfrac{2}{6} + \dfrac{3}{6}$
$q = \dfrac{5}{6}$

10. $2100 = 2.1 \times 10^3$

11. $0.00092 = 9.2 \times 10^{-4}$

12. $16{,}000{,}000 = 1.6 \times 10^7$

13. $0.00000046 = 4.6 \times 10^{-7}$

14. $92.4 \times 10^{18} = 9.24 \times 10^{19}$

15. $0.0704 = 7.04 \times 10^{-2}$

16. $\dfrac{1}{5} + \dfrac{2}{5} = \dfrac{1+2}{5}$
$= \dfrac{3}{5}$

17. $\dfrac{4}{9} - \dfrac{2}{9} = \dfrac{4-2}{9}$
$= \dfrac{2}{9}$

18. $\dfrac{4}{9} + \dfrac{1}{3} = \dfrac{4}{9} + \dfrac{1}{3} \cdot \dfrac{3}{3}$
$= \dfrac{4}{9} + \dfrac{3}{9}$
$= \dfrac{7}{9}$

19. $\dfrac{4}{5} - \dfrac{3}{4} = \dfrac{4}{5} \cdot \dfrac{4}{4} - \dfrac{3}{4} \cdot \dfrac{5}{5}$
$= \dfrac{16}{20} - \dfrac{15}{20}$
$= \dfrac{1}{20}$

20. $\dfrac{3}{8} \times \dfrac{1}{2} = \dfrac{3}{16}$

21. $\dfrac{3}{10} \div \dfrac{9}{2} = \dfrac{3}{10} \cdot \dfrac{2}{9}$
$= \dfrac{\cancel{3} \cdot \cancel{2}}{\cancel{2} \cdot 5 \cdot \cancel{3} \cdot 3}$
$= \dfrac{1}{15}$

22. $7 \div 1.5 = 4\dfrac{2}{3}$
You can play 4 games.

Mid-Chapter ASSESSMENT

1. Q

2. Any two of $\overleftrightarrow{PQ}$, $\overleftrightarrow{KL}$, and $\overleftrightarrow{MN}$

3. P

4. Up

5. $\angle CFA$ and $\angle CFE$

6. $\angle BFA$, $\angle BFC$, $\angle CFD$, and $\angle DFE$

7. $\angle AFD$ and $\angle BFE$

8. $\angle AFE$

9. Vertical

10. Corresponding

11. Corresponding

12. $m\angle 5 + m\angle 6 = 180° \Rightarrow m\angle 5 + 62° = 180°$
$$m\angle 5 = 118°$$
$m\angle 5 = m\angle 3 = m\angle 1 = m\angle 7 = 118°$
$m\angle 6 = m\angle 4 = m\angle 2 = m\angle 8 = 62°$

13. Rotational symmetry, vertical symmetry, and horizontal symmetry

14. Vertical line symmetry

15. Horizontal line symmetry

16. Obtuse scalene

17. Equiangular, equilateral, acute, isosceles

18. Right scalene

19. Acute isosceles

20. No. *Sample answer:*

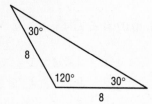

10.6 *Exploring Quadrilaterals*

ONGOING ASSESSMENT

1. *Sample answer:* Every square is a rhombus. Every rectangle is a parallelogram. Every isosceles trapezoid is a trapezoid.

EXERCISES

1. a. Parallelograms that include rectangles, squares, and rhombuses
   b. Kites and some scalene quadrilaterals
   c. Trapezoids that include isosceles trapezoids
   d. Rhombuses that include squares

e. Scalene quadrilaterals that include some trapezoids that are not isosceles

f. Kites, isosceles trapezoids, and parallelograms that include rectangles, squares, and rhombuses

2. Answers vary.

3. A rhombus is a parallelogram and a kite is not.

4. A square is a rectangle with sides of equal length.

5. Trapezoid

6. Kite

7. Square

8. Parallelogram

9. Rhombus

10. Isosceles trapezoid

11. Scalene quadrilateral

12. Rectangle

13. Sometimes; a parallelogram is only one type of quadrilateral.

14. Sometimes; a square is the only type of rectangle that is also a rhombus.

15. Sometimes; a square is only one type of rhombus.

16. Always; a segment joining any two interior points lies completely within a trapezoid.

17. $x = 5$ m, $y = 11$ m;
A kite is not a parallelogram but it has two pair of sides of equal length.

18. $x = y = 10$ cm;
The sides of a square have the same length.

19. $x = 6$ ft, $y = 3$ ft;
The opposite sides of a rectangle have the same length.

20. $x = 6$ in.;
The nonparallel sides of an isosceles trapezoid have the same length.

21. F

22. C, F

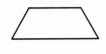

23. E, F

24. B

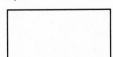

25. A

26. C, F

27. B

28. A

29.–30.

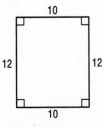

Top: rectangle

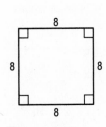

Base: square

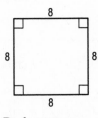

Back: square

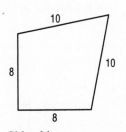

Side: kite

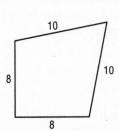

Side: kite

31. D

32. Answers vary.

ONGOING ASSESSMENT

1. Answers vary.

EXERCISES

1. Two polygons are congruent if they are exactly the same size and shape.

2. An equilateral triangle; square

3. A and D

4. A. Hexagon; yes
   B. Hexagon; no
   C. Hexagon; no
   D. Hexagon; yes

5. B

6. C

7. A

8. D

9. A. Equiangular, equilateral, regular
   B. Equiangular, equilateral, regular
   C. Congruent to *D*
   D. Congruent to *C*

10. 120°

11. 3

12. $3 \times 6 = 18$

13. $120° \times 6 = 720°$

14. A polygon is regular if it is equilateral and equiangular. No, see figure for Exercise 4C on page 490 of the textbook.

15. No; no

16. You can use regular triangles, quadrilaterals, and hexagons to tile a floor; you cannot tile with regular pentagons, heptagons, and octagons; only regular polygons with 3, 4, or 6 sides can be used to tile a floor.

17. Area $= 30 + 6 + 8 + 9 + 3 + 9 + 4 + 12$
    $= 81$ units^2
    $s =$ length of side of square.
    $s^2 = 81$
    $s = \sqrt{81} = 9$
    9 units by 9 units

18. Equilateral: square;
    Equiangular: square, rectangle

19.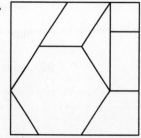

20. B; $75 \div 5 = 15$ mm

21. Answers vary.

Lab 10.8

Part A

1.

Number of sides	Number of triangles	Sum of angle measures	Sketch of figure
3	1	$1(180°) = 180°$	
4	2	$2(180°) = 360°$	
5	3	$3(180°) = 540°$	
6	4	$4(180°) = 720°$	
7	5	$5(180°) = 900°$	
8	6	$6(180°) = 1080°$	
9	7	$7(180°) = 1260°$	
10	8	$8(180°) = 1440°$	
n	$n - 2$	$(n - 2)(180°)$	

2. You subtract 2 from the number of sides, and then multiply this result by $180°$.

3.
$$(4 - 2)180 = 2 \cdot 180$$
$$= 360$$
$$m\angle 4 = 360 - (90° + 70° + 60°)$$
$$= 360 - 220°$$
$$= 140°$$

Part B

4. Equilateral triangle: $\dfrac{180°}{3} = 60°$;

Square: $\dfrac{360°}{4} = 90°$;

Regular pentagon: $\dfrac{540°}{5} = 108°$;

Regular hexagon: $\dfrac{720°}{6} = 120°$;

Regular heptagon: $\dfrac{900°}{7} = 128\tfrac{4}{7}°$;

Regular octagon: $\dfrac{1080°}{8} = 135°$

5. Regular nonagon:
$$\dfrac{1260°}{9} = 140°$$

6.

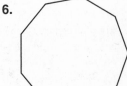

Use a protractor to measure $140°$ for each angle.

7. Regular decagon: $\dfrac{1440°}{10} = 144°$

8.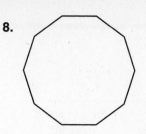

Use a protractor to measure 144° for each angle.

10.8 | *ALGEBRA CONNECTION: Angles of Polygons*

ONGOING ASSESSMENT

1. Because the nut is a regular hexagon, each interior angle measure is:

Angle measure $= \dfrac{(6-2)(180)°}{6} = \dfrac{4(180)°}{6} = 120°$

EXERCISES

1.

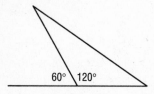

2.

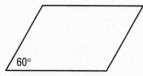

3. $m\angle 1 = 180° - 60° = 120°;$
$m\angle 2 = 120°$ (Symmetrical to 120° angle);
$m\angle 3 = 180° - 90° = 90°;$
$m\angle 4 = 180° - 150° = 30°;$
$m\angle 5 = 180° - m\angle 2 = 180° - 120° = 60°$

4. $m\angle 1 = \dfrac{180°(n-2)}{n}$

$= \dfrac{180°(6-2)}{6}$

$= \dfrac{180°(4)}{6} = 120°;$

$m\angle 2 = m\angle 1 = 120°$ (Hexagon is regular.);
$m\angle 3 = 180° - 120° = 60°;$
$m\angle 4 = 180° - 120° = 60°$

5. $\angle ABC, \angle BCD, \angle CDE, \angle DEA, \angle EAB;$
Sum $= (n-2)(180°)$

$= (5-2)(180°)$

$= 3(180°)$

$= 540°$

6. Sum $= 360°$

7. $m\angle ABC = 180° - m\angle ABG$

$= 180° - 45°$

$= 135°$

8. $m\angle 1 = 180° - 100° = 80°$
$m\angle 2 = 180° - (80° + 55°) = 180° - 135° = 45°$
$m\angle 3 = 180° - m\angle 2 = 180° - 45° = 135°$
$m\angle 4 = 180° - 55° = 125°$

9. $m\angle 1 = 180° - 90° = 90°$

$m\angle 4 = 180° - 65° = 115°$

$m\angle 5 = 180° - 90° = 90°$

$(n - 2)(180°) = (4 - 2)(180°) = 2(180°) = 360°$

$m\angle 3 = 360° - (90° + 90° + 65°)$

$\qquad = 360° - 245°$

$\qquad = 115°$

$m\angle 2 = 180° - m\angle 3 = 180° - 115° = 65°$

10. $m\angle 1 = 180° - 90° = 90°$

$m\angle 2 = 180° - 120° = 60°$

$m\angle 6 = 180° - 80° = 100°$

$m\angle 5 = 180° - 145° = 35°$

$(n - 2)(180°) = (5 - 2)(180°) = 3(180°) = 540°$

$m\angle 4 = 540° - (145° + 120° + m\angle 1 + m\angle 6)$

$\qquad = 540° - (145° + 120° + 90° + 100°)$

$\qquad = 540° - 455°$

$\qquad = 85°$

$m\angle 3 = 180° - m\angle 4 = 180° - 85° = 95°$

11. Measure of interior $\angle = \dfrac{(n - 2)(180°)}{n}$

$\qquad = \dfrac{(8 - 2)(180°)}{8}$

$\qquad = \dfrac{6(180°)}{8}$

$\qquad = \dfrac{1080°}{8}$

$\qquad = 135°$

Measure of exterior $\angle = \dfrac{360°}{n} = \dfrac{360°}{8} = 45°$

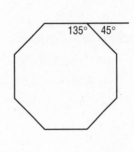

12. Measure of interior $\angle = \dfrac{(n - 2)(180°)}{n}$

$\qquad = \dfrac{(10 - 2)(180°)}{10}$

$\qquad = \dfrac{8(180°)}{10}$

$\qquad = \dfrac{1440°}{10}$

$\qquad = 144°$

Measure of exterior angle $= \dfrac{360°}{n} = \dfrac{360°}{10} = 36°$

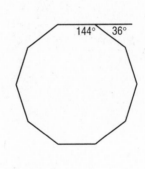

13. Measure of interior $\angle = \dfrac{(n - 2)(180°)}{n}$

$\qquad = \dfrac{(12 - 2)(180°)}{12}$

$\qquad = \dfrac{10(180°)}{12}$

$\qquad = \dfrac{1800°}{12}$

$\qquad = 150°$

Measure of exterior $\angle = \dfrac{360°}{12} = 30°$

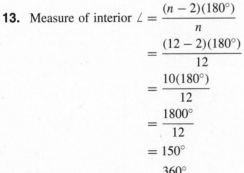

14. $6x + x + 2x = 180°$

$\qquad 9x = 180°$

$\qquad\quad x = 20°$

$6x = 6(20°) = 120°$

$2x = 2(20°) = 40°$

$20°, 40°, 120°$

15. Sum of interior angle measures $= (n - 2)(180°)$

$\qquad\qquad\qquad\qquad\quad = (4 - 2)(180°)$

$\qquad\qquad\qquad\qquad\quad = 2(180°)$

$\qquad\qquad\qquad\qquad\quad = 360°$

$x + x + 2x + (x + 5°) = 360°$

$\qquad\qquad\quad 5x + 5° = 360$

$\qquad\qquad\qquad\quad 5x = 355°$

$\qquad\qquad\qquad\quad\; x = 71°$

$2x = 2 \cdot 71° = 142°$

$x + 5° = 71° + 5° = 76°$

$71°, 71°, 76°, 142°$

16. Sum of interior angle measures $= (n - 2)(180°)$

$\qquad\qquad\qquad\qquad\quad = (5 - 2)(180°)$

$\qquad\qquad\qquad\qquad\quad = 3(180)°$

$\qquad\qquad\qquad\qquad\quad = 540°$

$3x + 4x + 4x + 2x + 2x = 540°$

$\qquad\qquad\qquad\qquad 15x = 540°$

$\qquad\qquad\qquad\qquad\quad x = 36°$

$2x = 2 \cdot 36° = 72°$

$3x = 3 \cdot 36° = 108°$

$4x = 4 \cdot 36° = 144°$

$72°, 72°, 108°, 144°, 144°$

17. Sum of interior angle measures $= (n - 2)(180°)$

$\qquad\qquad\qquad\qquad\quad = (6 - 2)(180°)$

$\qquad\qquad\qquad\qquad\quad = 4(180°)$

$\qquad\qquad\qquad\qquad\quad = 720°$

$2x + 3x + 3x + 2x + 3x + (2x + 45°) = 720°$

$\qquad\qquad\qquad\qquad\qquad 15x + 45° = 720°$

$\qquad\qquad\qquad\qquad\qquad\qquad 15x = 675°$

$\qquad\qquad\qquad\qquad\qquad\qquad\;\; x = 45°$

$2x = 2 \cdot 45° = 90°$

$3x = 3 \cdot 45° = 135°$

$2x + 45 = 2 \cdot 45° + 45° = 90° + 45° = 135°$

$90°, 90°, 135°, 135°, 135°, 135°$

18.

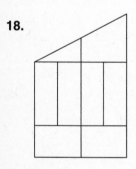

6 rectangles, 1 right triangle, and 1 trapezoid

19. The 4 tall rectangles appear congruent, the 2 bottom rectangles appear congruent, the 2 trapezoids appear congruent, and the 2 triangles appear congruent.

20. $117° - 90° = 27°$

$180° - (27° + 90°) = 180° - 117° = 63°$

$27°, 63°, 90°$

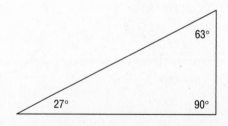

21. Sum of interior angle measures $= (n - 2)(180°)$

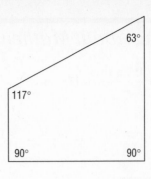

$$= (4 - 2)(180°)$$
$$= 2(180°)$$
$$= 360°$$

The upper right angles of the trapezoid and the triangle are corresponding congruent angles.

$$360° - (90° + 90° + 63°) = 360° - 243°$$
$$= 117°$$

$63°, 90°, 90°, 117°$

22. If the polygon has a vertical line of symmetry and exactly one of the angle measures is incorrect, then the measure of the top angle must be incorrect.

Sum of interior angle measures $= (n - 2)(180°)$

$$= (7 - 2)(180°)$$
$$= 5(180°)$$
$$= 900°$$

$$900° - (110° + 110° + 140° + 140° + 130° + 130°) = 900° - 760°$$
$$= 140°$$

Therefore, the top angle's measure is $140°$.

23. A;

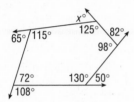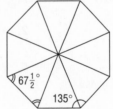

$$180° - 82° = 98°$$
$$180° - 50° = 130°$$
$$180° - 108° = 72°$$
$$180° - 65° = 115°$$
$$98° + 130° + 72° + 115° + n = (5 - 2)180°$$
$$415° + n = 540°$$
$$n = 125°$$
$$180° - 125° = 55°$$

24. a. Because the hexagon is divided into 6 equal triangles with $60°$ for the center angles

b.

$$135° \div 2 = 67\tfrac{1}{2}°$$
$$67\tfrac{1}{2}° + 67\tfrac{1}{2}° + x = 180°$$
$$135° + x = 180°$$
$$x = 45°$$

Place the mirrors $45°$ apart.

Communicating About Mathematics

1. $\dfrac{3696 \text{ ft}}{4} = 924$ ft, or $\dfrac{0.7 \text{ mi}}{4} = 0.175$ mi

2. Macy's = 11 sides = 11-gon
Nordstrom = 7 sides = heptagon
Sears = 5 sides = pentagon
Bloomingdales = 9 sides = nonagon

No, none are congruent.

3.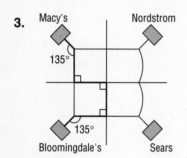

No, this is not the shortest path.

4.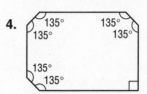

Sum of interior angles = $(7 - 2)(180°) = 900°$
$900° - 90° = 810°$
$810° \div 6 = 135°$

5. $\dfrac{7 \text{ acres}}{75 \text{ acres}} = 0.093 = 9.3\%$

Using a Computer Drawing Program

1. Answers vary.

2. Answers vary.

3. 360°; answers vary.

4. No; three of the angles changed; sum did not change.

5. Yes

6. The sum should equal $(5 - 2)(180°) = 540°$.

7. The sum should equal $(6 - 2)(180°) = 720°$.

8. The sum should equal $(8 - 2)(180°) = 1080°$.

10.9 Angle and Side Relationships

ONGOING ASSESSMENT

1.–3. In Exercise 2, no two sides are the same length; so no two angles have the same measure; so A matches with Exercise 2. The longest side in Exercise 1 is more than 70% longer than the shorter sides, while the longest side in Exercise 3 is less than 33% longer than the shorter sides; so the largest angle in Exercise 1 is larger than the largest angle in Exercise 3; so C matches with Exercise 1. Then B matches with Exercise 3.

1. C

2. A

3. B

EXERCISES

1. **a.** The longest side is opposite the largest angle and the shortest side is opposite the smallest angle.
    b. The angles opposite the sides of the same lengths have equal measures.
    c. All three angles are congruent and all the sides are congruent.

2. An isosceles right triangle has a 90° angle and two angles of equal measure.

    $180° - 90° = 90°, \dfrac{90°}{2} = 45°$

3. Smallest angle: $\angle B$
    Largest angle: $\angle C$
    Shortest side: $\overline{AC}$
    Longest side: $\overline{AB}$

4. $m\angle W = 180° - (90° + 38°)$
    $\qquad = 180° - 128°$
    $\qquad = 52°$
    Smallest angle: $\angle Y$;
    Largest angle: $\angle X$
    Shortest side: $\overline{WX}$;
    Longest side: $\overline{WY}$

5. Smallest angle: $\angle F$
    Largest angle: $\angle D$
    Shortest side: $\overline{DE}$
    Longest side: $\overline{EF}$

6. $3^2 + q^2 = 5^2$
    $9 + q^2 = 25$
    $q^2 + 16$
    $q = \sqrt{16}$
    $q = 4$
    Smallest angle: $\angle R$;
    Largest angle: $\angle P$
    Shortest side: $\overline{PQ}$;
    Longest side: $\overline{RQ}$

7. Shortest side: $\overline{EF}$
    Longest side: $\overline{DE}$

8. Shortest side: $\overline{KL}$
    Longest side: $\overline{JK}$

9. $\angle R = 180° - (36° + 42°)$
    $\qquad = 180° - 78°$
    $\qquad = 102°$
    Shortest side: $\overline{QR}$; longest side: $\overline{PQ}$

10. $\angle Z = 180° - (50° + 90°)$
    $\qquad = 180° - 140°$
    $\qquad = 40°$
    Shortest side: $\overline{XY}$; longest side: $\overline{XZ}$

11.–14. The smallest angle is opposite the shortest side.

11. $a^2 + 10^2 = 12.81^2$
    $a^2 + 100 = 164.0961$
    $a^2 = 64.0961$
    $a = \sqrt{64.0961}$
    $a \approx 8$

    Since $\overline{BC}$ is the shortest side, $\angle A$ is the smallest angle.

12. $6^2 + b^2 = 8.49^2$
    $36 + b^2 = 72.0801$
    $b^2 = 36.0801$
    $b = \sqrt{36.0801}$
    $b \approx 6$

    Since $\overline{BC}$ and $\overline{AC}$ are the same length, $\angle A$ and $\angle B$ are the smallest angles.

13. $a^2 + 5^2 = 7.81^2$

$a^2 + 25 = 60.9961$

$a^2 = 35.9961$

$a = \sqrt{35.9961}$

$a \approx 6$

Since $\overline{AC}$ is the shortest side, $\angle B$ is the smallest angle.

14. $22^2 + b^2 = 29.07^2$

$484 + b^2 = 845.0649$

$b^2 = 361.0649$

$b = \sqrt{361.0649}$

$b \approx 19$

Since $\overline{AC}$ is the shortest side, $\angle B$ is the smallest angle.

15.–18. The shortest side is opposite the smallest angle and the longest side is opposite the largest angle.

15. $\angle ABC = 180° - 108° = 72°$

$\angle A = 180° - (72° + 48°)$

$= 180° - 120°$

$= 60°$

Since $\angle C$ is the smallest angle, $\overline{AB}$ is the shortest side. Since $\angle ABC$ is the largest angle, $\overline{CA}$ is the longest side.

16. $m\angle DEF = 180° - 120° = 60°$

$m\angle F = 180° - (70° + 60°)$

$= 180° - 130°$

$= 50°$

Since $\angle F$ is the smallest angle, $\overline{DE}$ is the shortest side. Since $\angle D$ is the largest angle, $\overline{EF}$ is the longest side.

17. $\angle HGC = 180° - 100° = 80°$

$\angle GHC = 180° - 135° = 45°$

$\angle C = 180° - (80° + 45°)$

$= 180° - 125°$

$= 55°$

Since $\angle GHC$ is the smallest angle, $\overline{GC}$ is the shortest side. Since $\angle HGC$ is the largest angle, $\overline{HC}$ is the longest side.

18. $m\angle QPR = 180° - 135° = 45°$

$m\angle PRQ = 180° - 135° = 45°$

$m\angle Q = 180° - 45° - 45° = 90°$

Since $\angle QPR$ and $\angle PRQ$ are the same measure, there is not a shortest side. Since $\angle PQR$ is the largest angle, $\overline{PR}$ is the longest side.

19. The hypotenuse; it is opposite the largest angle.

20.–23. If a triangle has three sides of the same length, then it has three angles of the same measure; so Exercise 20 matches with C. If no two sides of a triangle have the same length, then no two angles have the same measure; so Exercise 22 matches with B. If a triangle has a shortest side and no longest side, then it has a smallest angle and no largest angle; so Exercise 23 matches with A. Then Exercise 21 matches with D.

20. C   **21.** D   **22.** B   **23.** A

24. $180° - (55° + 62°) = 180° - 117° = 63°$

25. You; the longer side is opposite the larger angle.

26. D

27. $2(12x + 5°) + 10x = 180°$ $m\angle P = m\angle Q$ Smallest angle: $\angle R$

$24x + 10° + 10x = 180°$ $= 12x + 5°$ Largest angle: None

$34x + 10° = 180°$ $= 12(5°) + 5°$ Shortest side: $\overline{PQ}$

$34x = 170°$ $= 65°$ Longest side: None

$x = 5°$ $m\angle R = 10(5°) = 50°$

28. $(5x - 3°) + (3x - 9°) = 180°$

$\quad\quad\quad 8x - 12° = 180°$

$\quad\quad\quad\quad\quad 8x = 192°$

$\quad\quad\quad\quad\quad\quad x = 24°$

$m\angle A = 2x + 13° = 2(24°) + 13° = 61°$

$m\angle ABC = 3x - 9° = 3(24°) - 9° = 63°$

$m\angle C = 180° - (61° + 63°)$

$\quad\quad\quad = 180° - 124°$

$\quad\quad\quad = 56°$

Smallest angle: $\angle C$

Largest angle: $\angle ABC$

Shortest side: $\overline{AB}$

Longest side: $\overline{AC}$

29. $(7x - 6°) + (17x - 6°) = 180°$

$\quad\quad\quad 24x - 12° = 180°$

$\quad\quad\quad\quad\quad 24x = 192°$

$\quad\quad\quad\quad\quad\quad x = 8°$

$m\angle E = 90°$

$m\angle DFE = 7x - 6° = 7(8°) - 6° = 50°$

$m\angle D = 180° - (90° + 50°)$

$\quad\quad\quad = 180° - 140°$

$\quad\quad\quad = 40°$

Smallest angle: $\angle D$

Largest angle: $\angle E$

Shortest side: $\overline{EF}$

Longest side: $\overline{DF}$

Chapter R E V I E W

1. $\overleftrightarrow{AE}, \overleftrightarrow{AG}$

2. $\overline{ED}, \overline{FD}, \overline{BD}, \overline{CD}, \overline{HD}$

3. 140°; obtuse

4. 20°; acute

5. $\angle 2, \angle 4, \angle 8, \angle 6$

6. $m\angle 7 = 180° - 60° = 120°$;

$\angle 2 \cong \angle 6$ by the corresponding angles property of parallel lines, $180° = m\angle 6 + m\angle 7$ by the straight angle definition.

7. Vertical line symmetry; rotational symmetry at 72° and 144° in both directions

8. No symmetry

9. Horizontal and vertical line symmetry; rotational symmetry at 90° and 180° in either direction

$\dfrac{360°}{4} = 90°,\ 2(90°) = 180°$

10. Equiangular, equilateral, acute, isosceles

11. Acute isosceles

12. Obtuse isosceles

13. Right scalene

14. Acute scalene

15. Obtuse scalene

16. Parallelogram

17. Trapezoid

18.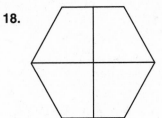

19.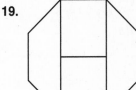

20. Interior angle:
$$\frac{(n-2)(180°)}{n} = \frac{(8-2)(180°)}{8}$$
$$= \frac{6(180°)}{8}$$
$$= \frac{1080°}{8}$$
$$= 135°$$

Exterior angle: $180° - 135° = 45°$

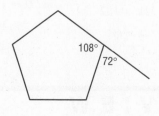

21. Interior angle:
$$\frac{(n-2)(180°)}{n} = \frac{(5-2)(180°)}{5}$$
$$= \frac{3(180°)}{5}$$
$$= \frac{540°}{5}$$
$$= 108°$$

Exterior angle: $180° - 108° = 72°$

22. $\overline{AC}, \overline{AB}, \overline{BC}$

23. $\overline{AB}, \overline{BC}, \overline{AC}$

Chapter ASSESSMENT

1. Right isosceles

2. Obtuse scalene

3. Acute isosceles

4. True; both figures have the same properties (its sides have the same length and its angles have the same measure).

5. False; a kite is not a parallelogram.

6. B

7. C

8. A

9. *Sample answers:* $\overleftrightarrow{MS}, \overleftrightarrow{MK}, \overleftrightarrow{KP}, \overleftrightarrow{KS}, \overleftrightarrow{PS}$

10. $\overrightarrow{PR}, \overrightarrow{PS}, \overrightarrow{PN}, \overrightarrow{PM}$

11. *Sample answers:* $\angle KML$ and $\angle NMP$, $\angle KMN$ and $\angle LMP$, $\angle MPN$ and $\angle RPS$, $\angle MPR$ and $\angle NPS$

12. Yes; when two parallel lines are intersected by a third one, the corresponding angles are congruent.

13. $45°$

14.
$$\frac{(n-2)180}{n} = \frac{(5-2)(180)}{5}$$
$$= \frac{3(180)}{5}$$
$$= \frac{540}{5}$$
$$= 108°$$

Vertical symmetry; rotational symmetry at 72° and 144° in either direction

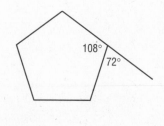

15. $\dfrac{(n-2)180}{n} = \dfrac{(6-2)(180)}{6}$

$= \dfrac{4(180)}{6}$

$= \dfrac{720}{6}$

$= 120°$

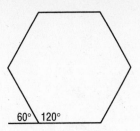

Vertical and horizontal symmetry; there are six lines of symmetry, so there is rotational symmetry of $\frac{360°}{6} = 60°$, 120°, or 180° in either direction.

16. They are parallel.

17. 1 right angle is formed by each color of laser beam.

18. 3 mirrors are parallel.

Standardized Test Practice

1. D   **2.** C   **3.** C   **4.** D   **5.** D

6. B   **7.** D   **8.** A; $180° - 92° = 88°$

$88° \div 2 = 44°$

$44°, 44°, 92°$

Chapter 11
Congruence, Similarity, and Transformations

11.1 | *Area and Perimeter*

ONGOING ASSESSMENT

1.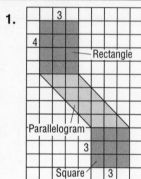

Square area $= bh = 3 \cdot 3 = 9$ ft^2

Parallelogram area $= bh = 3 \cdot 4 = 12$ ft^2

Rectangle area $= bh = 3 \cdot 4 = 12$ ft^2

Total area $= 9 + 12 + 12 = 33$ ft^2

Answer agrees with Example 2.

EXERCISES

1. $A = \frac{1}{2}bh = \frac{1}{2}(8)(6) = 24$ units^2

Each non-horizontal side of the triangle is the hypotenuse of a right triangle.

$2^2 + 6^2 = c^2 \qquad 6^2 + 6^2 = c^2$

$4 + 36 = c^2 \qquad 36 + 36 = c^2$

$\qquad 40 = c^2 \qquad \qquad 72 = c^2$

$\quad \sqrt{40} = c \qquad \qquad \sqrt{72} = c$

$\quad 6.3 \approx c \qquad \qquad 8.5 \approx c$

$P \approx 8 + 6.3 + 8.5 \approx 22.8$ units

2. $A = \frac{1}{2}(b_1 + b_2)h$

$\quad = \frac{1}{2}(6 + 5)5$

$\quad = \frac{1}{2}(11)(5)$

$\quad = \frac{55}{2} = 27.5$ units^2

One side of the trapezoid is the hypotenuse of a right triangle.

$1^2 + 5^2 = c^2$

$1 + 25 = c^2$

$\quad 26 = c^2$

$\sqrt{26} = c$

$\quad 5.1 \approx c$

$P \approx 6 + 5.1 + 5 + 5 \approx 21.1$ units

3. $A = bh = 5(6) = 30$ units^2

Each non-horizontal side of the parallelogram is the hypotenuse of a right triangle.

$2^2 + 6^2 = c^2$

$4 + 36 = c^2$

$40 = c^2$

$\sqrt{40} = c$

$6.3 \approx c$

$P \approx 2(5) + 2(6.3) \approx 10 + 12.6 \approx 22.6$ units

4. Parallelogram:

$A = bh = 8(4) = 32$ units^2

$P = 2(8) + 2(5) = 16 + 10 = 26$ units

Rectangle:

$A = lw = 8(4) = 32$ units^2

$P = 2(8) + 2(4) = 16 + 8 = 24$ units

No, rearranging does not change the area.

Yes, rearranging does change the perimeter.

5. $A = \frac{1}{2}bh = \frac{1}{2}(18)(8) = 9(8) = 72$ units^2

$A = bh = 18(8) = 144$ units^2 or

$A = 2(72) = 144$ units^2

6. $A = \frac{1}{2}bh = \frac{1}{2}(6)(3\sqrt{3}) = 9\sqrt{3} \approx 15.6$ units^2

$A = \frac{1}{2}(b_1 + b_2)h$

$\quad = \frac{1}{2}(6 + 12)(3\sqrt{3})$

$\quad = \frac{1}{2}(18)(3\sqrt{3})$

$\quad = 27\sqrt{3} \approx 46.8$ units or

$A = 3(9\sqrt{3}) \approx 3(15.6) = 46.8$ units^2

7. Area$_{\text{trapezoid}} = \frac{1}{2}(b_1 + b_2)h$

$\quad = \frac{1}{2}(13 + 23)(12)$

$\quad = \frac{1}{2}(36)(12) = 216$ units^2

Area$_{\text{hexagon}} = 2(216) = 432$ units^2

Perimeter$_{\text{trapezoid}} = 3(13) + 23$

$\quad = 39 + 23 = 62$ units

Perimeter$_{\text{hexagon}} = 6(13) = 78$ units

8. Area$_{\text{triangle}} = \frac{1}{2}bh \approx \frac{1}{2}(10)(13.08) = 65.4$ units^2

Area$_{\text{octagon}} \approx 8(65.4) = 523.2$ units^2

Perimeter$_{\text{triangle}} = 2(14) + 10 = 28 + 10 = 38$ units

Perimeter$_{\text{octagon}} = 8(10) = 80$ units

9. a. Area$_{\text{each shorter side}} = \frac{1}{2}(b_1 + b_2)h$

$\quad = \frac{1}{2}(5 + 7)(1)$

$\quad = \frac{1}{2}(12) = 6$ in.^{2}

Area$_{\text{each longer side}} = \frac{1}{2}(7 + 9)(1)$

$\quad = \frac{1}{2}(16) = 8$ in.^{2}

b.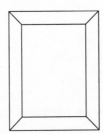

c. Area $= 2(6) + 2(8)$

$\quad = 12 + 16 = 28$ in.^{2}

10. A: Trapezoid; B: Triangle; C: Triangle; D: Trapezoid; E: Parallelogram; F: Square; G: Rectangle; H: Rectangle; J: Triangle; K: Trapezoid; L: Triangle

11. A: $A = \frac{1}{2}(5 + 2)(3) = \frac{1}{2}(7)(3) = 10.5$ units^2

B: $\frac{1}{2}(4)(4) = \frac{1}{2}(16) = 8$ units^2

C: $\frac{1}{2}(3)(4) = 6$ units^2

D: $\frac{1}{2}(4 + 3)(4) = \frac{1}{2}(7)(4) = 14$ units^2

E: $5(3) = 15$ units^2

F: $3(3) = 9$ units^2

G: $1(4) = 4$ units^2

H: $2(4) = 8$ units^2

J: $\frac{1}{2}(6)(3) = 9$ units^2

K: $\frac{1}{2}(1 + 7)(3) = \frac{1}{2}(8)(3) = 12$ units^2

L: $\frac{1}{2}(3)(3) = 4.5$ units^2

12. Add up the areas of the smaller figures:

$$10.5 + 8 + 6 + 14 + 15 + 9 + 4 + 8 + 9 + 12 + 4.5 = 100 \text{ units}^2,$$

or find the area of a square with side length 10:

$$10 \times 10 = 100 \text{ units}^2.$$

13.–16. *Sample answers:*

13. 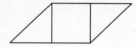 **14.**  **15.** 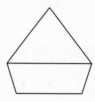 **16.**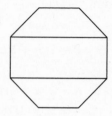

17. B; $5 + 6 + 5 + 12 = 28$ m

18. B; $\frac{1}{2}(12 + 6)(4) = \frac{1}{2}(18)(4)$
$$= \frac{1}{2}(52)$$
$$= 36 \text{ m}^2$$

19. a. $\frac{1}{2}(15.8 + 25)(19.2) = \frac{1}{2}(40.8)(19.2)$
$$= 391.7 \text{ in.}^2$$

b. $(391.7)(6) = 2350 \text{ in.}^2$

11.2 *Exploring Congruence*

ONGOING ASSESSMENT

1. Correct; corresponding angles and sides are congruent: $\angle H \cong \angle M$, $\angle K \cong \angle Q$, $\angle J \cong \angle Z$, $\overline{HK} \cong \overline{MQ}$, $\overline{KJ} \cong \overline{QZ}$, and $\overline{JH} \cong \overline{ZM}$.

2. Incorrect. The corresponding vertices are not in the same order.

3. Correct. Corresponding angles and sides are congruent: $\angle K \cong \angle Q$, $\angle J \cong \angle Z$, $\angle H \cong \angle M$, $\overline{KJ} \cong \overline{QZ}$, $\overline{JH} \cong \overline{ZM}$, and $\overline{HK} \cong \overline{MQ}$.

EXERCISES

1. Two figures are congruent if corresponding sides are congruent and corresponding angles are congruent; answers vary.

2. Triangle ABC is congruent to triangle DGH.

3. Segment AB is congruent to segment DG.

4. Angle C is congruent to angle H.

5. $\angle Y$ **6.** $\overline{YX}$ **7.** $\angle R$ **8.** $\overline{RT}$ **9.** $\angle Z$ **10.** $\overline{ZY}$

11. $\triangle YXZ$; corresponding angles and sides are congruent: $\angle S \cong \angle Y$, $\angle R \cong \angle X$, $\angle T \cong \angle Z$, $\overline{SR} \cong \overline{YX}$, $\overline{RT} \cong \overline{XZ}$, and $\overline{ST} \cong \overline{YZ}$.

12. Yes; the line segments are the same length.

13. Yes; the angles have the same measure.

14. No; the triangles are not the same size.

15. No; the rectangles are not the same size.

16. $\angle K$ **17.** $\overline{MK}$ **18.** $\overline{RQ}$ **19.** $\angle M$ **20.** $\angle Q$ **21.** $\overline{QB}$

22. *Sample answer:* $\angle F \cong \angle M$, $\angle G \cong \angle N$, $\angle H \cong \angle P$, $\overline{FG} \cong \overline{MN}$, $\overline{GH} \cong \overline{NP}$, $\overline{FH} \cong \overline{MP}$

23. B and D; C and E

24.–27. *Sample answers:*

24.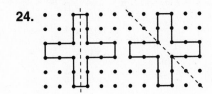

25.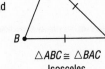

26.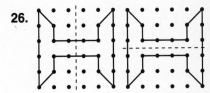

27.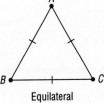

28. A and C; *sample answer:* Three prints were made from the same negative, then one of the prints was retouched to remove a roof window.

29. $(1, -3)$ **30.** $(-2, -1)$ **31.** $(2, 5)$ **32.** Answers vary.   **33.** B

34. Yes; an equilateral triangle.

35. C

A

and

A

$\Rightarrow$

A

$\triangle ABC \cong \triangle ACB$
Isosceles

$\triangle ABC \cong \triangle BAC$
Isosceles

Equilateral

36. *Sample answer:* $\triangle CBD \cong \triangle JHF$; $\triangle DEG \cong \triangle GFD$

Spiral **R E V I E W**

1.–3. Use $A = \frac{1}{2}(b_1 + b_2)h$.

1.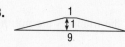

$$\text{Area} = \frac{1}{2}(6 + 12)(2)$$
$$= \frac{1}{2}(18)(2)$$
$$= 18 \text{ units}^2$$

2.

$$\text{Area} = \frac{1}{2}(7 + 8)4$$
$$= \frac{1}{2}(15)4$$
$$= 30 \text{ units}^2$$

3.

$$\text{Area} = \frac{1}{2}(1 + 9)1$$
$$= \frac{1}{2}(10)$$
$$= 5 \text{ units}^2$$

4.
$$x = 0.\overline{1}$$
$$10x = 1.\overline{1}$$
$$9x = 1$$
$$x = \frac{1}{9}$$

5.
$$x = 0.\overline{2}$$
$$10x = 2.\overline{2}$$
$$9x = 2$$
$$x = \frac{2}{9}$$

6.
$$x = 0.\overline{3}$$
$$10x = 3.\overline{3}$$
$$9x = 3$$
$$x = \frac{3}{9} = \frac{1}{3}$$

7.
$$x = 0.\overline{4}$$
$$10x = 4.\overline{4}$$
$$9x = 4$$
$$x = \frac{4}{9}$$

8. $0.\overline{n}$

9.
$$\frac{42.12 - 40.18}{42.12} = \frac{1.94}{42.12}$$
$$\approx 0.046$$
$$= 0.046 \times 100\%$$
$$\approx 4.6\% \text{ decrease}$$

10.
$$\frac{7.6 - 3.6}{3.6} = \frac{4}{3.6}$$
$$\approx 1.111$$
$$= 1.111 \times 100\%$$
$$\approx 111.1\% \text{ increase}$$

11.
$$\frac{77.18 - 66.1}{77.18} = \frac{11.08}{77.18}$$
$$\approx 0.144$$
$$= 0.144 \times 100\%$$
$$\approx 14.4\% \text{ decrease}$$

12.
$$\frac{6.3 - 4.4}{4.4} = \frac{1.9}{4.4}$$
$$\approx 0.432$$
$$= 0.432 \times 100\%$$
$$\approx 43.2\% \text{ increase}$$

13. $2(2.89) + 3(2.50) + 81.75 = 5.78 + 7.50 + 18.75 = \$32.03$

Lab 1.3

1. Answers vary.

2. *Sample answer:* The crease in the paper divides each line segment into two equal halves.

3. *Sample answer:* Yes; the crease in the paper divides each line segment into two equal halves.

4. *Sample answer:* Yes; all pairs of corresponding angles are congruent and all pairs of corresponding sides are congruent.

ONGOING ASSESSMENT

1.

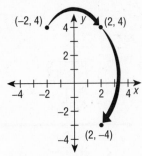

Reflection in the *x*-axis: $(2, -4)$;
Reflection in the *y*-axis: $(-2, 4)$

2.

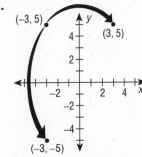

Reflection in the *x*-axis: $(-3, -5)$;
Reflection in the *y*-axis: $(3, 5)$

3.

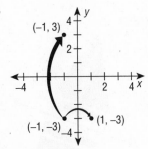

Reflection in the *x*-axis: $(-1, 3)$;
Reflection in the *y*-axis: $(1, -3)$

4.

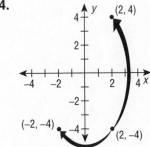

Reflection in the *x*-axis: $(2, 4)$;
Reflection in the *y*-axis: $(-2, -4)$

EXERCISES

1.

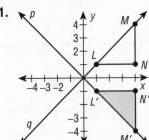

2.

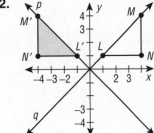

3.

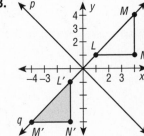

4.

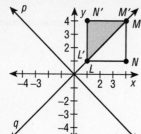

5. a. True
b. False
c. False

6. $\triangle GHJ$

7.

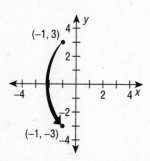

Reflection in the x-axis

8.

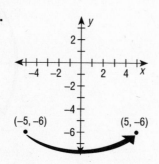

Reflection in the y-axis

9. No;

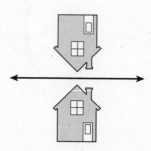

10. Yes

11. Yes

12. No;

13. No; *sample answer:* A photo does not reflect the image.

14.

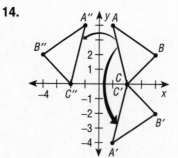

15.

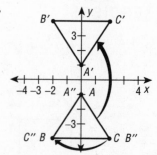

16. Vertical line: A, H, I, M, O, T, U, V, W, X;
Horizontal line: B, C, D, E, H, I, K, O, X

17. The line of reflection is the line $x = 4$.

18. The line of reflection does not change.

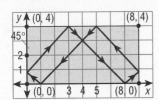

19.

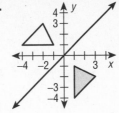

20.

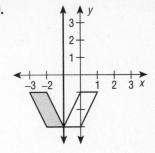

21.

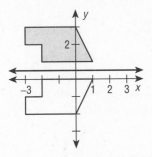

22. C

23. Answers vary.

11.4 Rotations

ONGOING ASSESSMENT

1. $(x, y) \rightarrow (y, -x)$

EXERCISES

1.–4. cl = clockwise and cc = counterclockwise.

1. About 115° cc

2. About 80° cl

3. About 100° cc

4. About 60° cl

5. Rotational symmetry is a special case of a rotation in which the figure fits back on itself.

6. 180°

7. 90°

8. 90°

9. About 90° counterclockwise

10. About 135° counterclockwise

11. About 60° counterclockwise

12. About 110° clockwise

13. $A'(1, 5)$; $B'(3, 1)$; $C'(1, 1)$

14. C; $A(5, -1) \rightarrow A'(1, 5)$;
$B(1, -3) \rightarrow B'(3, 1)$;
$C(1, -1) \rightarrow C'(1, 1)$

15. *Sample answer:* $\triangle ABC \cong \triangle A'B'C'$ because rotations do not change the size or shape of an object.

16.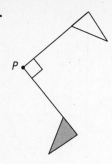

17.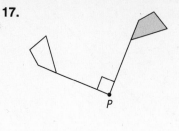

18.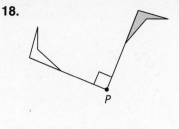

19. $180° \div 14 \text{ days} \approx 13°$ per day

20. B

21. $\overline{CF}$

22. $\triangle BEC$

23. $\overline{FC}$

24. C

25. a. United Kingdom: $180°$; Switzerland: $90°$

    b. Answers vary.

11.5 *Translations*

ONGOING ASSESSMENT

1. $(x, y) \rightarrow (x + 2, y + 2)$

2. $(x, y) \rightarrow (x + 3, y + 2)$

EXERCISES

1. Slide the figure 4 units to the left and 2 units down.

2. Slide the figure 1 unit to the left and 5 units up.

3. Slide the figure 4 units to the right and 5 units down.

4. Reflect the figure in the y-axis.

5. Rotate the figure $90°$ clockwise about the origin.

6. Slide the figure 4 units to the right and 2 units down.

7. C; slide the figure 2 units to the right.

8. B; slide the figure 5 units to the right and 4 units down.

9. A; slide the figure 2 units to the left and 3 units up.

10. a.

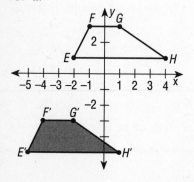

b.

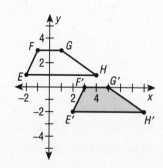

c.

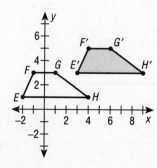

11. $A = \frac{1}{2}(6+2)(2)$

$= \frac{1}{2}(8)(2)$

$= \frac{1}{2}(16)$

$= 8$ units^2;

All of the translated trapezoids also have an area of 8 square units.

12.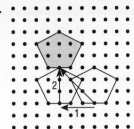

Yes; slide the figure 3 units to the left and 3 units up.

13.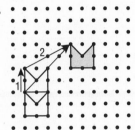

Yes; slide the figure 4 units to the left and 4 units down.

14.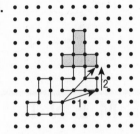

Yes; slide the figure 3 units to the right and 4 units up.

15.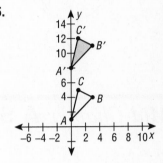

$(x, y+7)$

$A' = (0, 1+7) = (0, 8)$

$B' = (3, 4+7) = (3, 11)$

$C' = (1, 5+7) = (1, 12)$

Slide the figure 7 units up.

16.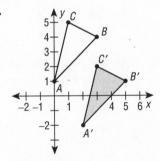

$(x+2, y-3)$

$A' = (0+2, 1-3) = (2, -2)$

$B' = (3+2, 4-3) = (5, 1)$

$C' = (1+2, 5-3) = (3, 2)$

Slide the figure 2 units to the right and 3 units down.

17.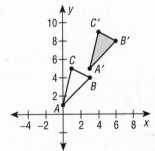

$(x+3, y+4)$

$A' = (0+3, 1+4) = (3, 5)$

$B' = (3+3, 4+4) = (6, 8)$

$C' = (1+3, 5+4) = (4, 9)$

Slide the figure 3 units to the right and 4 units up.

18. Tuscaloosa

19. *Sample answer:* Drive 70 miles west and about 200 miles south.

20. B; $(-2, 0) \rightarrow (1, 5)$

$(-4, -1) \rightarrow (-1, 4)$

$(-1, -2) \rightarrow (2, 3)$

$(-3, -3) \rightarrow (0, 2)$

21. Answers vary.

Communicating About Mathematics

1. *Sample answer:* Yes; congruence simplifies design, and the arrays appear to be congruent.

2. Rotation

3. Yes;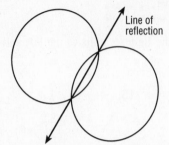

4. Yes;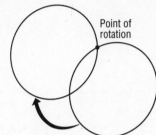

5. *Sample answer:* Too much light might get in the lenses, damaging the telescope.

Mid-Chapter **ASSESSMENT**

1. $\angle A \cong \angle D$

2. $\angle F \cong \angle C$

3. $\overline{AB} \cong \overline{DE}$

4. $\overline{AC} \cong \overline{DF}$

5. Clockwise rotation of 180°

6. Slide the figure 5 units to the right and 2 units down.

7. Reflection in the *y*-axis

8. Counterclockwise rotation of 90°

9. Reflection in the *x*-axis

10. Slide the figure 4 units to the left.

11. B

12. C

13. A

14. D

15. $\dfrac{360°}{8} = 45°$

The angle of rotation from car to car is 45°. There is one car between the red car and the orange car, so $(45°)2 = 90°$.

16. There are 2 cars between the red and yellow cars, so $3(45°) = 135°$.

17. There are 3 cars between the red and blue cars, so $4(45) = 180°$.

11.6 *Exploring Similarity*

ONGOING ASSESSMENT

1.
$$\frac{6 \text{ in.}}{24 \text{ in.}} = \frac{7 \text{ in.}}{w}$$
$$7 \cdot 24 = 6w$$
$$168 = 6w$$
$$28 = w$$

2.
$$\frac{8 \text{ in.}}{24 \text{ in.}} = \frac{3 \text{ in.}}{w}$$
$$8 \cdot w = 24 \cdot 3$$
$$8w = 72$$
$$w = 9 \text{ in.}$$

EXERCISES

1. *Sample answer:* It means that they have the same shape, though they don't have to be the same size or have the same orientation.

2. *Sample answer:* The shapes of books are often close to similar. Anything that is square or circular is similar to any other thing that is square or circular.

3. A and C

4. B and C

5. $\dfrac{HJ}{KL} = \dfrac{HG}{KM}$; $\dfrac{HJ}{KL} = \dfrac{GJ}{ML}$; $\dfrac{HG}{KM} = \dfrac{GJ}{ML}$

6. $\dfrac{HG}{KM} = \dfrac{12}{9} = \dfrac{4}{3}$

7.
$$\dfrac{KL}{HJ} = \dfrac{KM}{HG}$$
$$\dfrac{KL}{18} = \dfrac{9}{12}$$
$$\dfrac{KL}{18} = \dfrac{3}{4}$$
$$18 \cdot \dfrac{KL}{18} = 18 \cdot \dfrac{3}{4}$$
$$KL = 13\dfrac{1}{2}$$

$$\dfrac{GJ}{ML} = \dfrac{HG}{KM}$$
$$\dfrac{GJ}{18} = \dfrac{12}{9}$$
$$\dfrac{GJ}{18} = \dfrac{4}{3}$$
$$18 \cdot \dfrac{GJ}{18} = 18 \cdot \dfrac{4}{3}$$
$$GJ = 24$$

8. $m\angle H = m\angle K$

9. $\dfrac{QR}{WX} = \dfrac{RS}{XY} = \dfrac{ST}{YZ} = \dfrac{QT}{WZ}$

10. $\dfrac{QR}{WX} = \dfrac{10}{6} = \dfrac{5}{3}$

11. $m\angle T = m\angle Z$

12. **a.**
$$\dfrac{QT}{WZ} = \dfrac{QR}{WX}$$
$$\dfrac{QT}{9} = \dfrac{10}{6}$$
$$\dfrac{QT}{9} = \dfrac{5}{3}$$
$$9 \cdot \dfrac{QT}{9} = 9 \cdot \dfrac{5}{3}$$
$$QT = 15$$

b.
$$\dfrac{ST}{YZ} = \dfrac{QR}{WX}$$
$$\dfrac{QT}{8.4} = \dfrac{10}{6}$$
$$\dfrac{QT}{8.4} = \dfrac{5}{3}$$
$$8.4 \cdot \dfrac{QT}{8.4} = 8.4 \cdot \dfrac{5}{3}$$
$$ST = 14$$

c.
$$\dfrac{XY}{RS} = \dfrac{WX}{QR}$$
$$\dfrac{XY}{6} = \dfrac{6}{10}$$
$$\dfrac{XY}{6} = \dfrac{3}{5}$$
$$6 \cdot \dfrac{XY}{6} = 6 \cdot \dfrac{3}{5}$$
$$XY = 3\dfrac{3}{5}$$

13.
$$\dfrac{8}{20} = \dfrac{x}{30}$$
$$8 \cdot 30 = 20 \cdot x$$
$$240 = 20 \cdot x$$
$$12 = x$$

14.
$$\dfrac{4}{16} = \dfrac{2}{x}$$
$$4 \cdot x = 16 \cdot 2$$
$$4x = 32$$
$$x = 8$$

15.
$$\dfrac{75}{60} = \dfrac{x}{36}$$
$$75 \cdot 36 = 60 \cdot x$$
$$2700 = 60x$$
$$45 = x$$

16. *Sample answer:*

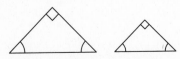

Yes; corresponding angles have the same measure and the ratios of corresponding sides are equal.

17. *Sample answer:* because the triangles formed by their shadows are similar

18.
$$\dfrac{x}{5} = \dfrac{240}{3}$$
$$5 \cdot \dfrac{x}{5} = \dfrac{240}{3} \cdot 5$$
$$x = 400 \text{ ft}$$

19.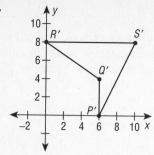

$R' = (2 \cdot 0, 2 \cdot 4) = (0, 8)$

$S' = (5 \cdot 2, 5 \cdot 2) = (10, 10)$

$Q' = (2 \cdot 3, 2 \cdot 2) = (6, 4)$

$P' = (3 \cdot 2, 0 \cdot 2) = (6, 0)$

Scale factor: $\dfrac{2x}{x} = 2$

20.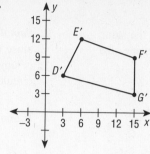

$E' = (2 \cdot 3, 4 \cdot 3) = (6, 12)$

$F' = (5 \cdot 3, 3 \cdot 3) = (15, 9)$

$G' = (5 \cdot 3, 1 \cdot 3) = (15, 3)$

$D' = (1 \cdot 3, 2 \cdot 3) = (3, 6)$

Scale factor: $\dfrac{3x}{x} = 3$

21.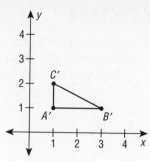

$C' = \left(2 \cdot \tfrac{1}{2}, 4 \cdot \tfrac{1}{2}\right) = (1, 2)$

$B' = \left(6 \cdot \tfrac{1}{2}, 2 \cdot \tfrac{1}{2}\right) = (3, 1)$

$A' = \left(2 \cdot \tfrac{1}{2}, 2 \cdot \tfrac{1}{2}\right) = (1, 1)$

Scale factor: $= \dfrac{\frac{1}{2}x}{x} = \dfrac{1}{2}$

22. C

23. a. A1: $\dfrac{84 \text{ cm}}{\sqrt{2}} = 59.5$ cm by $\dfrac{118.9 \text{ cm}}{\sqrt{2}} = 84.1$ cm

     A2: $\dfrac{59.5 \text{ cm}}{\sqrt{2}} = 42.1$ cm by $\dfrac{84.1 \text{ cm}}{\sqrt{2}} = 59.5$ cm

     A3: $\dfrac{42.1 \text{ cm}}{\sqrt{2}} = 29.7$ cm by $\dfrac{59.5 \text{ cm}}{\sqrt{2}} = 42.1$ cm

     A4: $\dfrac{29.7 \text{ cm}}{\sqrt{2}} = 21.0$ cm by $\dfrac{42.1 \text{ cm}}{\sqrt{2}} = 29.7$ cm

     A5: $\dfrac{21.0 \text{ cm}}{\sqrt{2}} = 14.9$ cm by $\dfrac{29.7 \text{ cm}}{\sqrt{2}} = 21.0$ cm

b. $8.5 \text{ in.} \times \dfrac{2.54 \text{ cm}}{1 \text{ in.}} = 21.59$ cm

    $11 \text{ in.} \times \dfrac{2.54 \text{ cm}}{1 \text{ in.}} = 27.94$ cm

    A4 is closest to 21.59 cm by 27.94 cm.

c. Answers vary.

Lab 11.7

Part A

1.   8 in. $= 2.6$ in. $+ x + 0.4$ in. $+ x + 0.4$ in. $+ x + 1.0$ in.

    8 in. $= 4.4$ in. $+ 3x$

  3.6 in. $= 3x$

  1.2 in. $= x$

2.   10 in. $= 1.0$ in. $+ x + 0.4$ in. $+ x + 0.4$ in. $+ x + 0.4$ in. $+ x + 1.8$ in.

    10 in. $= 4.0$ in. $+ 4x$

    6 in. $= 4x$

  1.5 in. $= x$

3. Scale factor for original: $\dfrac{7}{5} = 1.4$

    Scale factor for small photo: $\dfrac{1.5}{1.2} = 1.25$

    The photos are not similar.

4. B; $\dfrac{5}{4} = 1.25$

Part B

5. $\dfrac{1.2}{5} = \dfrac{1.5}{x}$

$1.2x = 1.5 \cdot 5$

$1.2x = 7.5$

$x = 6.25$ in.

6. $\dfrac{1.5}{7} = \dfrac{1.2}{x}$

$1.5x = 1.2 \cdot 7$

$1.5x = 8.4$

$x = 5.6$ in.

7.

5 in. by $6\frac{1}{4}$ in.

8. Because the width is still the same we can solve as follows.

$\dfrac{1.2}{5} = \dfrac{x}{7}$

$x = 1.68$ in.

9. $\dfrac{1.5}{7} = \dfrac{x}{5}$

$1.5 \cdot 5 = 7 \cdot x$

$7.5 = 7 \cdot x$

$1.07 = x$

10. Answers vary.

11.7 *Problem Solving Using Similar Figures*

ONGOING ASSESSMENT

1. $\dfrac{40}{2} = 20$ in.; $\dfrac{20}{2} = 10$ in.

Area of sketch: $20 \times 10 = 200$ in.^{2}

Ratio: $\dfrac{800 \text{ in.}^2}{200 \text{ in.}^2} = 4$

2. $\dfrac{40}{3} \approx 13.33$ in.; $\dfrac{20}{3} \approx 6.66$ in.

Area of sketch: $13.33 \times 6.66 \approx 88.89$ in.^{2}

Ratio: $\dfrac{800 \text{ in.}^2}{88.89 \text{ in.}^2} \approx 9$

3. $\dfrac{40}{5} = 8$ in.; $\dfrac{20}{5} = 4$ in.

Area of sketch: $8 \times 4 = 32$ in.^{2}

Ratio: $\dfrac{800 \text{ in.}^2}{32 \text{ in.}^2} = 25$

4. The ratio is the scale factor squared. This result agrees with Example 3.

EXERCISES

1. $x = $ height of model's license plate in inches

$\dfrac{x}{6} = \dfrac{1}{12}$

$6 \cdot \dfrac{x}{6} = 6 \cdot \dfrac{1}{12}$

$x = \dfrac{1}{2}$

The height of the model's license plate is $\frac{1}{2}$ in.

2. Scale factor: $\dfrac{12}{1} = 12$

3. Perimeter$_{\text{car plate}}$ $= 2(12) + 2(6) = 24 + 12 = 36$ in.

Perimeter$_{\text{model plate}}$ $= 2(1) + 2\left(\frac{1}{2}\right) = 2 + 1 = 3$ in.

Area$_{\text{car plate}}$ $= 6(12) = 72$ in.^{2}

Area$_{\text{model plate}}$ $= 1\left(\frac{1}{2}\right) = \frac{1}{2}$ in.^{2}

4. $\frac{36}{3} = 12$

It is the same as the scale factor.

5. $\dfrac{72}{\frac{1}{2}} = 72 \div \frac{1}{2} = 72 \cdot 2 = 144$

It is equal to the square of the scale factor.

$12^2 = 144$

6. $w = $ width of actual painting in inches

Width of reduction: $1\frac{3}{4}$ in.

Height of reduction: $1\frac{1}{8}$ in.

$\dfrac{w}{1\frac{3}{4}} = \dfrac{26}{1\frac{1}{8}}$

$\dfrac{w}{\frac{7}{4}} = \dfrac{26}{\frac{9}{8}}$

$\dfrac{w}{\frac{7}{4}} = 26 \div \dfrac{9}{8}$

$\dfrac{w}{\frac{7}{4}} = 26 \cdot \dfrac{8}{9}$

$\dfrac{w}{\frac{7}{4}} = \dfrac{208}{9}$

$w = \dfrac{7}{4} \cdot \dfrac{208}{9} \approx 40.4$

The width of the actual painting is about 40 in.

7. $x = $ length of baby lizard in centimeters

$\dfrac{1}{12} = \dfrac{x}{90}$

$90 \cdot \dfrac{1}{12} = \dfrac{x}{90} \cdot 90$

$\dfrac{90}{12} = x$

$7.5 = x$

The baby lizard is 7.5 cm long.

8. $h = $ height of Kentucky in miles

Width of map: $2\frac{1}{8}$ in.

Height of map: $\frac{15}{16}$ in.

$\dfrac{\frac{15}{16} \text{ in.}}{\frac{17}{8} \text{ in.}} = \dfrac{h \text{ mi}}{420 \text{ mi}}$

$\dfrac{\frac{15}{16}}{\frac{17}{8}} = \dfrac{h}{420}$

$\dfrac{15}{16} \div \dfrac{17}{8} = \dfrac{h}{420}$

$\dfrac{15}{16} \cdot \dfrac{8}{17} = \dfrac{h}{420}$

$\dfrac{120}{272} = \dfrac{h}{420}$

$420 \cdot \dfrac{120}{272} = \dfrac{h}{420} \cdot 420$

$185.3 \text{ mi} \approx h$

The height is about 185 miles.

9. x = length of room in inches

Length of room in blueprint: $2\frac{1}{8}$ in.

Width of room in blueprint: 1 in.

$$\frac{16 \text{ ft}}{1 \text{ in.}} = \frac{x}{2\frac{1}{8}\text{in.}}$$

$$\frac{192 \text{ in.}}{1 \text{ in.}} = \frac{x}{\frac{17}{8} \text{ in.}}$$

$$192 = \frac{x}{\frac{17}{8}}$$

$$\frac{17}{8} \cdot 192 = \frac{x}{\frac{17}{8}} \cdot \frac{17}{8}$$

$$408 \text{ in.} = x$$

$$408 \text{ in.} \cdot \frac{1 \text{ ft}}{12 \text{ in.}} = 34 \text{ ft}$$

y = width of room in inches

$$\frac{16 \text{ ft}}{1 \text{ in.}} = \frac{y}{1 \text{ in.}}$$

$$\frac{192 \text{ in.}}{1 \text{ in.}} = \frac{y}{1 \text{ in.}}$$

$$192 \text{ in.} = y$$

$$192 \text{ in.} \cdot \frac{1 \text{ ft}}{12 \text{ in.}} = 16 \text{ ft}$$

Perimeter$_{actual}$ = $2(34) + 2(16) = 100$ ft

Area$_{actual}$ = $34(16) = 544$ ft

10. Height: 2.5 in.; width: 2 in.

11. Scale factor: $\frac{16}{2} = 8$

12. h = height of actual painting in inches

Width of photo: 2 in.

Height of photo: 2.5 in.

$$\frac{h}{2.5} = \frac{16}{2}$$

$$\frac{h}{2.5} = 8$$

$$h = 8 \cdot 2.5$$

$$h = 20$$

The height of the actual painting is 20 in.

13. Perimeter$_{painting}$ = $2(16) + 2(20)$

$\qquad = 32 + 40 = 72$ in.

Area$_{painting}$ = $16(20) = 320$ in.^{2}

Perimeter$_{photo}$ = $2(2) + 2(2.5)$

$\qquad = 4 + 5$

$\qquad = 9$ in.

Area$_{photo}$ = $2(2.5)$

$\qquad = 5$ in.^{2}

14. $\frac{72}{9} = 8$

It equals the scale factor.

15. $\frac{320}{5} = 64$

It equals the square of the scale factor.

16. D; $\frac{10}{15} = \frac{x}{12}$

$12 \cdot \frac{10}{15} = \frac{x}{12} \cdot 12$

$8 = x$

17. C; $\frac{6}{4} = \frac{h}{6}$

$36 = 4h$

$h = 9$;

$\frac{6}{4} = \frac{b}{8}$

$48 = 4b$

$b = 12$

Area = $\frac{1}{2}(12 + 6)(9)$

$= \frac{1}{2}(18)(9)$

$= 81$ cm^2

18. a. $105 \cdot 15 = 1575$ ft^2

b. No; $6300 > 3150$

$(15 \cdot 2) \cdot (105 \cdot 2) = 30 \cdot 210$

$= 6300$ ft^2

Area of 2 solar panels = $2 \cdot 1575$

$= 3150$ ft^2

c. Answers vary.

ONGOING ASSESSMENT

1. $\sin 48° = \dfrac{\text{opp.}}{\text{hyp.}} = \dfrac{10}{13.45} \approx 0.74$

$\cos 48° = \dfrac{\text{adj.}}{\text{hyp.}} = \dfrac{9}{13.45} \approx 0.67$

2. $\sin 48° = \cos 42°$, $\cos 48° = \sin 42°$

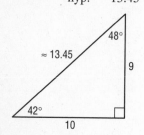

EXERCISES

1. B

2. C

3. A

4.–5. Answers vary.

4.

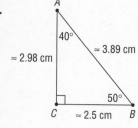

$\sin 40° = \dfrac{2.5}{3.89} \approx 0.643$

$\cos 40° = \dfrac{2.98}{3.89} \approx 0.766$

$\tan 40° = \dfrac{2.5}{2.98} \approx 0.839$

5.

$\sin 40° = \dfrac{5}{7.78} \approx 0.643$

$\cos 40° = \dfrac{5.96}{7.78} \approx 0.766$

$\tan 40° = \dfrac{5}{5.96} \approx 0.839$

Yes, you get the same results as Exercise 4.

6. $\sin X = \frac{12}{13} \approx 0.923$

7. $\cos X = \frac{5}{13} \approx 0.385$

8. $\tan X = \frac{12}{5} = 2.4$

9. $\sin Y = \frac{5}{13} \approx 0.385$

10. $\cos Y = \frac{12}{13} \approx 0.923$

11. $\tan Y = \frac{5}{12} \approx 0.417$

12. $\sin D = \dfrac{6}{\sqrt{45}} \approx 0.894$

13. $\cos D = \dfrac{3}{\sqrt{45}} \approx 0.447$

14. $\tan D = \dfrac{6}{3} = 2$

15. $\sin E = \dfrac{3}{\sqrt{45}} \approx 0.447$ **16.** $\cos E = \dfrac{6}{\sqrt{45}} \approx 0.894$ **17.** $\tan E = \dfrac{3}{6} = 0.5$

18. $180° - (90° + 60°) = 180° - 150° = 30°$

$$5^2 + (\sqrt{75})^2 = c^2 \qquad \sin 60° = \dfrac{\sqrt{75}}{10} \approx 0.866 \qquad \sin 30° = \dfrac{5}{10} = 0.5$$

$$25 + 75 = c^2 \qquad \cos 60° = \dfrac{5}{10} = 0.5 \qquad \cos 30° = \dfrac{\sqrt{75}}{10} \approx 0.866$$

$$100 = c^2$$

$$\sqrt{100} = c \qquad \tan 60° = \dfrac{\sqrt{75}}{5} \approx 1.732 \qquad \tan 30° = \dfrac{5}{\sqrt{75}} \approx 0.577$$

$$10 = c$$

19. $180° - (90° + 60°) = 180° - 150° = 30°$

$$1^2 + b^2 = 2^2 \qquad \sin 60° = \dfrac{\sqrt{3}}{2} \approx 0.866 \qquad \sin 30° = \dfrac{1}{2} = 0.5$$

$$1 + b^2 = 4$$

$$b^2 = 3 \qquad \cos 60° = \dfrac{1}{2} = 0.5 \qquad \cos 30° = \dfrac{\sqrt{3}}{2} \approx 0.866$$

$$b = \sqrt{3} \qquad \tan 60° = \dfrac{\sqrt{3}}{1} = \sqrt{3} \approx 1.732 \qquad \tan 30° = \dfrac{1}{\sqrt{3}} \approx 0.577$$

20. $180° - (90° + 50.2°) = 180° - 140.2° = 39.8°$

$$5^2 + 6^2 = c^2 \qquad \sin 50.2° = \dfrac{6}{\sqrt{61}} \approx 0.768 \qquad \sin 39.8° = \dfrac{5}{\sqrt{61}} \approx 0.640$$

$$25 + 36 = c^2$$

$$61 = c^2 \qquad \cos 50.2° = \dfrac{5}{\sqrt{61}} \approx 0.640 \qquad \cos 39.8° = \dfrac{6}{\sqrt{61}} \approx 0.768$$

$$\sqrt{61} = c \qquad \tan 50.2° = \dfrac{6}{5} = 1.2 \qquad \tan 39.8° = \dfrac{5}{6} \approx 0.833$$

21. $180° - (90° + 63.4°) = 180° - 153.4° = 26.6°$

$$1^2 + 2^2 = c^2 \qquad \sin 63.4° = \dfrac{2}{\sqrt{5}} \approx 0.894 \qquad \sin 26.6° = \dfrac{1}{\sqrt{5}} \approx 0.447$$

$$1 + 4 = c^2$$

$$5 = c^2 \qquad \cos 63.4° = \dfrac{1}{\sqrt{5}} \approx 0.447 \qquad \cos 26.6° = \dfrac{2}{\sqrt{5}} \approx 0.894$$

$$\sqrt{5} = c \qquad \tan 63.4° = \dfrac{2}{1} = 2 \qquad \tan 26.6° = \dfrac{1}{2} = 0.5$$

22.

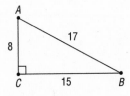

23.

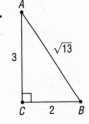

24. $\cos 10° = \dfrac{10}{10.15} \approx 0.985$ $\cos 50° = \dfrac{8.39}{13.05} \approx 0.643$

$\cos 20° = \dfrac{10}{10.64} \approx 0.940$ $\cos 60° = \dfrac{5.77}{11.55} \approx 0.500$

$\cos 30° = \dfrac{10}{11.55} \approx 0.866$ $\cos 70° = \dfrac{3.64}{10.64} \approx 0.342$

$\cos 40° = \dfrac{10}{13.05} \approx 0.766$ $\cos 80° = \dfrac{1.76}{10.15} \approx 0.173$

x	10°	20°	30°	40°	50°	60°	70°	80°
$\sin x$	≈ 0.173	≈ 0.342	≈ 0.500	≈ 0.643	≈ 0.766	≈ 0.866	≈ 0.940	≈ 0.985
$\cos x$	≈ 0.985	≈ 0.940	≈ 0.866	≈ 0.766	≈ 0.643	≈ 0.500	≈ 0.342	≈ 0.173

25. $\sin x = \cos(90° - x)$ and $\cos x = \sin(90° - x)$

26. 45°; $\sin 45° = \cos(90° - 45°) = \cos 45°$

$\sin 45° = \dfrac{a}{c} = \dfrac{b}{c}$

$\cos 45° = \dfrac{a}{c} = \dfrac{b}{c}$

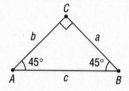

27. When height is 20 meters, $\tan A = \frac{20}{20} = 1$.
When height is 40 meters, $\tan A = \frac{40}{20} = 2$.

28. Increases; only the numerator increases.

29. $x =$ height of balloon in meters

$\tan A = \dfrac{1}{2} = \dfrac{x}{20} \rightarrow x = 10$

The height of the balloon is 10 meters.

30. D; $\tan 30° = \dfrac{\text{opp.}}{\text{adj.}} = \dfrac{4}{\sqrt{48}}$

31.
$\dfrac{25}{13.05} = \dfrac{x}{8.39}$

$8.39 \cdot \dfrac{25}{13.05} = 8.39 \cdot \dfrac{x}{8.39}$

$\dfrac{209.75}{13.05} = x$

$16.07 \approx x$

32.
$\dfrac{14}{10} = \dfrac{x}{5.77}$

$5.77 \cdot \dfrac{14}{10} = 5.77 \cdot \dfrac{x}{5.77}$

$\dfrac{80.78}{10} = x$

$8.08 \approx x$

33.
$\dfrac{15}{13.05} = \dfrac{x}{10}$

$10 \cdot \dfrac{15}{13.05} = 10 \cdot \dfrac{x}{10}$

$\dfrac{150}{13.05} = x$

$11.49 \approx x$

34.
$\dfrac{22}{3.64} = \dfrac{x}{10}$

$10 \cdot \dfrac{22}{3.64} = 10 \cdot \dfrac{x}{10}$

$\dfrac{220}{3.64} = x$

$60.44 \approx x$

Spiral R E V I E W

1. $9^2 + 8^2 = x^2$

$81 + 64 = x^2$

$145 = x^2$

$\sqrt{145} = x$

$x \approx 12.04$

2. $x^2 + x^2 = 128^2$

$2x^2 = 128^2$

$2x^2 = 16{,}384$

$\dfrac{2x^2}{2} = \dfrac{16{,}384}{2}$

$x^2 = 8192$

$x = \sqrt{8192} \approx 90.51$

3. $x^2 + 12^2 = 18.06^2$

$x^2 + 144 = 326.1636$

$x^2 = 182.1636$

$x = \sqrt{182.1636} \approx 13.50$

4. $x^2 + 11^2 = 12^2$

$x^2 + 121 = 144$

$x^2 = 23$

$x = \sqrt{23} \approx 4.80$

5. $\angle A$ is the smallest angle because $\overline{BC}$ is the shortest side.

$\angle C$ is the largest angle because $\overline{AB}$ is the longest side.

6.–9. $22 + 20 + 14 = 56$

6. $\dfrac{22}{56} = \dfrac{11}{28}$

7. $\dfrac{20}{56} = \dfrac{5}{14}$

8. $\dfrac{14}{56} = \dfrac{1}{4}$

9. $\dfrac{20 + 14}{56} = \dfrac{34}{56} = \dfrac{17}{28}$

10. $\boxed{\text{Total number of cars}} \times \boxed{\text{Price per car}} = \boxed{\text{Total amount of money raised}}$

$(78 + 85 + 124)5 = 287 \times 5 = \$1435$

Using a Calculator

1. $\sin 60° \approx 0.866$

$\cos 60° = 0.5$

$\tan 60° \approx 1.732$

2. $\sin 60° = \dfrac{\text{opp.}}{\text{hyp.}} = \dfrac{\sqrt{3}}{2} \approx 0.866$

$\cos 60° = \dfrac{\text{adj.}}{\text{hyp.}} = \dfrac{1}{2} = 0.5$

$\tan 60° = \dfrac{\text{opp.}}{\text{adj.}} = \dfrac{\sqrt{3}}{1} \approx 1.732$

3. Angles vary.

A	$\sin A$	$(\sin A)^2$	$\cos A$	$(\cos A)^2$	$(\sin A)^2 + (\cos A)^2$
30	0.5	0.25	≈ 0.866	0.75	$0.25 + 0.75 = 1$
45	≈ 0.707	0.5	≈ 0.707	0.5	$0.5 + 0.5 = 1$
60	≈ 0.866	0.75	0.5	0.25	$0.75 + 0.25 = 1$

$(\sin A)^2 + (\cos A)^2 = 1$

11.9 ALGEBRA CONNECTION: Problem Solving Using Trigonometric Ratios

ONGOING ASSESSMENT

1.

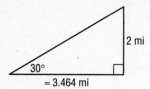

$\tan 30° \approx 0.5774$

$\tan 60° \approx 1.732$

$\tan 30°$ is not half of $\tan 60°$.

No; the shuttle is not at half the height.

EXERCISES

1. $\tan 41° = \dfrac{b}{4}$

$4 \cdot \tan 41° = b$

$3.48 \approx b$

2. $\sin 41° = \dfrac{b}{5.3}$

$5.3 \cdot \sin 41° = b$

$3.48 \approx b$

3. $4^2 + b^2 = (5.3)^2$

$16 + b^2 = 28.09$

$b^2 = 12.09$

$b = \sqrt{12.09}$

$b \approx 3.48$

4. Answers vary.

5. $\cos 33° \approx 0.839$

6. $\tan 74° \approx 3.487$

7. $\sin 44° \approx 0.695$

8. $\cos 80° \approx 0.174$

9. $x =$ height of flagpole in feet

$\tan 40° = \dfrac{x}{50}$

$50 \cdot \tan 40° = x$

$41.95 \approx x$

The height of the flagpole is about 41.95 feet.

10. $\cos 38° = \dfrac{m}{9}$

$9 \cdot \cos 38° = m$

$7.09 \approx m$

11. $\tan 66° = \dfrac{p}{5}$

$5 \cdot \tan 66° = p$

$11.23 \approx p$

12. $\cos 24° = \dfrac{t}{10}$

$10 \cdot \cos 24° = t$

$9.14 \approx t$

13. $\sin 45° = \dfrac{6}{d}$

$\dfrac{1}{\sin 45°} = \dfrac{d}{6}$

$6 \cdot \dfrac{1}{\sin 45°} = d$

$8.49 \approx d$

14. $\sin 45° = \dfrac{a}{6}$

$6 \cdot \sin 45° = a$

$4.24 \approx a$

$\cos 45° = \dfrac{b}{6}$

$6 \cdot \cos 45° = b$

$4.24 \approx b$

$m\angle B = 180° - (90° + 45°)$

$= 180° - 135°$

$= 45°$

15.

$$\sin 20° = \frac{h}{15} \qquad \cos 20° = \frac{g}{15} \qquad m\angle G = 180° - (90° + 20°)$$

$$15 \cdot \sin 20° = h \qquad 15 \cdot \cos 20° = g \qquad \qquad = 180° - 110°$$

$$5.13 \approx h \qquad \qquad 14.10 \approx g \qquad \qquad \qquad = 70°$$

16.

$$\sin 52° = \frac{k}{40} \qquad \cos 52° = \frac{m}{40} \qquad m\angle M = 180° - (90° + 52°)$$

$$40 \cdot \sin 52° = k \qquad 40 \cdot \cos 52° = m \qquad \qquad = 180° - 142°$$

$$31.52 \approx k \qquad \qquad 24.63 \approx m \qquad \qquad \qquad = 38°$$

17.

$$\cos 67° = \frac{8}{f} \qquad \tan 67° = \frac{d}{8} \qquad m\angle E = 180° - (90° + 67°)$$

$$\frac{1}{\cos 67°} = \frac{f}{8} \qquad 8 \cdot \tan 67° = d \qquad \qquad = 180° - 157°$$

$$8 \cdot \frac{1}{\cos 67°} = f \qquad 18.85 \approx d \qquad \qquad = 23°$$

$$20.47 \approx f$$

18. $h =$ height of loading dock in ft

$$\sin 8° = \frac{h}{21.5}$$

$$21.5 \cdot \sin 8° = h$$

$$2.99 \approx h$$

The height of the loading dock is about 2.99 ft.

19. $m =$ mother's height in m

$$\tan 11° = \frac{m}{22}$$

$$22 \cdot \tan 11° = m$$

$$4.276 \approx m$$

The mother is about 4.3 m tall.

20. $b =$ baby's height in m

$$\tan 5° = \frac{b}{22}$$

$$22 \cdot \tan 5° = b$$

$$1.925 \approx b$$

The baby is about 1.9 m tall.

21. The difference in heights is
$4.276 - 1.925 \approx 2.4$ m.

22. D

23. a. *Sample answer:*

x	0°	15°	30°	45°	60°	75°	90°
P	0	8.0	15.5	21.9	26.8	29.9	31

b. 70°

Chapter **REVIEW**

1. $90 \times 50 = 4500$ ft^2

2. $\frac{1}{2}(80 + 60)(40) = \frac{1}{2}(140)(40) = 2800$ ft^2

3. $\frac{1}{2}(120 + 90)(40) = \frac{1}{2}(210)(40) = 4200$ ft^2

4. Exercise 1: $4500(2.4¢) = 10,800¢ = \$108.00$
Exercise 2: $2800(2.4¢) = 6720¢ = \$67.20$
Exercise 3: $4200(2.4¢) = 10,080¢ = \$100.80$

5. $\angle B \cong \angle X$　　　　**6.** $\overline{XV} \cong \overline{BC}$　　　　**7.** $\overline{XN} \cong \overline{CA}$　　　　**8.** $\angle V \cong \angle C$　　　　**9.** $\angle N \cong \angle A$

10. $\overline{AB} \cong \overline{NX}$　　　　**11.** False　　　　**12.** False　　　　**13.** False　　　　**14.** True

15.

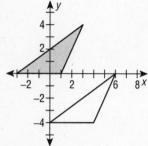

Slide the figure 3 units to the left and 4 units up.

16.

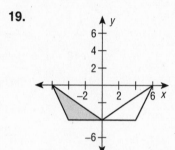

The scale factor of image to original is $\frac{1}{2}$.

17.

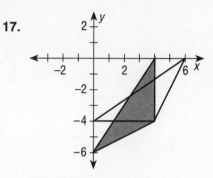

Figure is reflected in the line $y = -x$.

18.

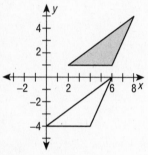

Slide the figure 2 units to the right and 5 units up.

19.

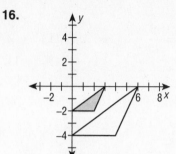

The figure is reflected in the y-axis.

20. $\frac{30}{10} = 3$
The scale factor is 3.

21. $\dfrac{30}{10} = \dfrac{UW}{6}$

$30 \cdot 6 = 10 \cdot UW$

$180 = 10 \cdot UW$

$18 = UW$

22. $\dfrac{30}{10} = \dfrac{21}{YZ}$

$21 \cdot 10 = 30 \cdot YZ$

$210 = 30 \cdot YZ$

$7 = YZ$

23. $\dfrac{6}{4} = \dfrac{18}{W}$

$18 \cdot 4 = 6 \cdot W$

$72 = 6 \cdot W$

$12 \text{ in.} = W$

24. $\sin A = \dfrac{4}{\sqrt{52}} \approx 0.555$

$\cos A = \dfrac{6}{\sqrt{52}} \approx 0.832$

$\tan A = \dfrac{4}{6} \approx 0.667$

25. $\sin B = \dfrac{6}{\sqrt{52}} \approx 0.832$

$\cos B = \dfrac{4}{\sqrt{52}} \approx 0.555$

$\tan B = \dfrac{6}{4} \approx 1.5$

26. $\sin 62° = \dfrac{x}{20}$

$x = \sin 62° \cdot 20$

≈ 17.66

27. $\sin 25° = \dfrac{x}{10}$

$x = 10 \cdot \sin 25° \approx 4.23$

28. $\cos 52° = \dfrac{7}{x}$

$x = \dfrac{7}{\cos 52°} \approx 11.37$

Chapter ASSESSMENT

1. Area $= bh = 6(3) = 18$ units^2

Perimeter $= 2(4) + 2(6) = 8 + 12 = 20$ units

2. Area $= \frac{1}{2}(b_1 + b_2)h$

$\qquad = \frac{1}{2}(6 + 24)(12) = \frac{1}{2}(30)(12)$

$\qquad = 15(12) = 180$ units^2

Perimeter $= 15 + 6 + 15 + 24 = 60$ units

3. $3^2 + 4^2 = c^2$

$\quad 9 + 16 = c^2$

$\qquad 25 = c^2$

$\quad \sqrt{25} = c$

$\qquad 5 = c$

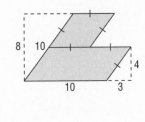

Perimeter $= 5 + 5 + 5 + 5 + 10 + 10 = 40$ units

Area $= 10(4) + 5(8 - 4) = 40 + 20 = 60$ units^2

4.

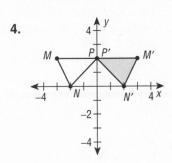

$M'(3, 2), \quad N'(2, 0), \quad P'(0, 2)$

5.

$M'(2, 3), \quad N'(0, 2), \quad P'(2, 0)$

6.

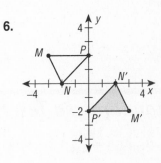

$M'(3, -2), \; N'(2, 0),$
$P'(0, -2)$

7.

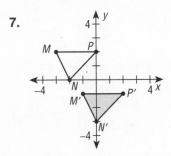

$M'(-1, -1), \; N'(0, -3),$
$P'(2, -1)$

8. Reflection over the line

9. Rotation 45° clockwise

10. Translation 2 units to the right and 3 units down

11. $h =$ height of bird in feet

$\tan 60° = \dfrac{h}{15}$

$15 \cdot \tan 60° = h$

$h \approx 25.98$

The bird is about 26 feet high.

12. d = distance between bird and point P in feet

$$\cos 60° = \frac{15}{d}$$

$$\frac{1}{\cos 60°} = \frac{d}{15}$$

$$15 \cdot \frac{1}{\cos 60°} = d$$

$$30 = d$$

The distance between the bird and point P is 30 feet.

13.
$$\frac{6}{78} = \frac{x}{24}$$

$$\frac{1}{13} = \frac{x}{24}$$

$$24 \cdot \frac{1}{13} = x$$

$$1.85 \approx x$$

The model should be about 1.85 inches wide.

14. Scale factor $= \dfrac{78 \text{ in.}}{6 \text{ in.}}$

$$= 13$$

15. $\tan 35° \approx 0.700$

16.
$$0.700 \approx \frac{AC}{16}$$

$$16 \cdot 0.700 \approx AC$$

$$11.20 \text{ cm} \approx AC$$

17. $\cos 35° \approx 0.819$

18.
$$0.819 \approx \frac{EF}{21}$$

$$21 \cdot 0.819 \approx EF$$

$$17.20 \text{ cm} \approx EF$$

19. No; *sample answer:* They are similar, the corresponding angles are congruent, and $CB \neq EF$.

Standardized Test Practice

1. C; Area $= \frac{1}{2}(5+2)4 = 14$

2. D;
$$4^2 + 3^2 = c^2$$
$$16 + 9 = c^2$$
$$25 = c^2$$
$$5 = c$$
$$5 + 2 + 4 + 5 = 16$$

3. C;

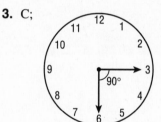

4. C

5. D

6. A; $(1, 0) \rightarrow (2, 3)$
$(3, -2) \rightarrow (4, 1)$
$(-2, -3) \rightarrow (-1, 0)$
$(x, y) \rightarrow (x + 1, y + 3)$

7. C

Chapter 12
Measurements in Geometry

Lab 12.1

Part A

1. $\dfrac{\text{Circumference}}{\text{Diameter}} \approx 3.14$

2. Answers should approximate $\pi \approx 3.14$.

3. The experimental value should approximate $\pi \approx 3.14$.

Part B

4. The ratio is the same for all circles; no; yes

5. $C = 3.14d$ or $C = \pi d$

6. a. $C = 3.14(12) = 37.68$ in.
  b. $C = 3.14(3) = 9.42$ ft
  c. $C = 3.14(2) = 6.28$ cm

7.

d	1	2	3	4	5
C	3.14	6.28	9.42	12.56	15.70

8.

Pattern: Each point increases by 3.14 in C.

9. Yes; *Sample answer:* If you substitute $2d$ for d in the formula $C = \pi d$, the circumference doubles.

GEOMETRY CONNECTION: *Circle Relationships*

ONGOING ASSESSMENT

1. $A = \dfrac{\pi r^2}{4}$

$\approx \dfrac{3.14 \cdot (2)^2}{4}$

$= \dfrac{12.56}{4}$

$\approx 3.1 \text{ in.}^2$

2. $A = \dfrac{\pi r^2}{6}$

$\approx \dfrac{3.14 \cdot (2)^2}{6}$

$= \dfrac{12.56}{6}$

$\approx 2.1 \text{ in.}^2$

EXERCISES

1. $\overline{BC}$

2. $\overline{AB}$ or $\overline{AC}$

3. Circumference $= 2\pi r$

$\approx 2(3.14)(7)$

$= 14\pi$

$\approx 44 \text{ cm}$

4. Area $= \pi r^2$

$\approx 3.14(7)^2$

$\approx 154 \text{ cm}^2$

5. Diameter $= 2(4000)$

$= 8000 \text{ mi}$

Circumference $= \pi(8000)$

$\approx 3.14(8000)$

$\approx 25{,}120 \text{ mi}$

6. $C = \pi d$

$\approx (3.14)(5.8)$

$\approx 18.2 \text{ cm}$

$A = \pi \left(\dfrac{d}{2}\right)^2$

$\approx (3.14)\left(\dfrac{5.8}{2}\right)^2$

$\approx 26.4 \text{ cm}^2$

7. $C = \pi d$

$\approx (3.14)(12.8)$

$\approx 40.2 \text{ in.}$

$A = \pi \left(\dfrac{d}{2}\right)^2$

$\approx (3.14)\left(\dfrac{12.8}{2}\right)^2$

$\approx 128.6 \text{ in.}^2$

8. $C = 2\pi r$

$\approx 2(3.14)(3)$

$\approx 18.8 \text{ cm}$

$A = \pi r^2$

$\approx (3.14)(3)^2$

$\approx 28.3 \text{ cm}^2$

9. $C = 2\pi r$

$\approx 2(3.14)(2)$

$\approx 12.6 \text{ in.}$

$A = \pi r^2$

$\approx (3.14)(2)^2$

$\approx 12.6 \text{ in.}^2$

10.
$$C = \pi d$$
$$11 \approx (3.14)d$$
$$\frac{11}{3.14} = d$$
$$3.503 \approx d$$
$$3.5 \text{ in.} \approx d$$
$$r = \frac{d}{2}$$
$$r \approx \frac{3.503}{2} \approx 1.751 \approx 1.8 \text{ in.}$$

11.
$$A = \pi r^2$$
$$109 \approx (3.14)r^2$$
$$\frac{109}{3.14} = r^2$$
$$\sqrt{\frac{109}{3.14}} = r$$
$$5.8918 \approx r$$
$$5.9 \text{ in.} \approx r$$
$$d = 2r$$
$$d \approx 2(5.8918) \approx 11.7836 \approx 11.8 \text{ in.}$$

12.
$$A = \pi r^2$$
$$113.10 \approx (3.14)r^2$$
$$\frac{113.10}{3.14} = r^2$$
$$\sqrt{\frac{113.10}{3.14}} = r$$
$$6.0016 \approx r$$
$$6.0 \text{ cm} \approx r$$
$$d = 2r$$
$$d \approx 2(6.0016) \approx 12.0032 \approx 12.0 \text{ cm}$$

13.
$$C = \pi d$$
$$20 \approx (3.14)d$$
$$\frac{20}{3.14} = d$$
$$6.3694 \approx d$$
$$6.4 \text{ in.} \approx d$$
$$r = \frac{d}{2}$$
$$r \approx \frac{6.3694}{2} \approx 3.1847 \approx 3.2 \text{ in.}$$

14.
$$
\begin{aligned}
A &= s^2 & A &= \pi r^2 \\
&= 8^2 & &\approx (3.14)(4)^2 \\
&= 64 & &= 50.24
\end{aligned}
$$
$$A = 64 - 50.24 = 13.8 \text{ mm}^2$$

15.
$$
\begin{aligned}
A &= \pi r^2 & A &= \pi r^2 \\
&\approx (3.14)(2)^2 & &\approx (3.14)(1)^2 \\
&= 12.56 & &= 3.14
\end{aligned}
$$
$$A = 12.56 - 3.14 = 9.4 \text{ ft}^2$$

16.
$$
\begin{aligned}
A &= \pi r^2 & A &= s^2 \\
&\approx (3.14)(2)^2 & &= (2.83)^2 \\
&= 12.56 & &\approx 8
\end{aligned}
$$
$$A = 12.56 - 8 = 4.56 \text{ m}^3$$

17.
$$
\begin{aligned}
A &= \pi r^2 & A &= \tfrac{1}{2}bh \\
&\approx (3.14)(4)^2 & &= \tfrac{1}{2}(6.93)(6) \\
&= 50.24 & &= 20.79
\end{aligned}
$$
$$A = 50.24 - 20.79 = 29.45 \text{ in.}^2$$

18. Use $C = 2\pi r$.

Radius	1	2	3	4	5	6
Circumference	6.28	12.56	18.84	25.12	31.40	37.68

$C \approx 2(3.14)(1) = 6.28$ $C \approx 2(3.14)(2) = 12.56$

$C \approx 2(3.14)(3) = 18.84$ $C \approx 2(3.14)(4) = 25.12$

$C \approx 2(3.14)(5) = 31.40$ $C \approx 2(3.14)(6) = 37.68$

19. Use $A = \pi r^2$.

Radius	1	2	3	4	5	6
Area	3.14	12.56	28.26	50.24	78.50	113.04

$A \approx (3.14)(1)^2 = 3.14$ $\qquad A \approx (3.14)(2)^2 = 12.56$

$A \approx (3.14)(3)^2 = 28.26$ $\qquad A \approx (3.14)(4)^2 = 50.24$

$A \approx (3.14)(5)^2 = 78.50$ $\qquad A \approx (3.14)(6)^2 = 113.04$

20. $C_1 = \pi d, \ C_2 = \pi(2d) = 2(\pi d)$
Yes; the circumference doubles. When the
diameter is doubled, the radius is also doubled.
$A_1 = \pi r^2, \ A_2 = \pi(2r)^2 = \pi(4r^2) = 4(\pi r^2)$
No; the area quadruples.

21. $A = \pi \left(\dfrac{d}{2}\right)^2$

$\qquad \approx (3.14) \left(\dfrac{12}{2}\right)^2$

$\qquad = (3.14)(6)^2$

$\qquad = (3.14)(36)$

$\qquad = 113.04 \ \text{in.}^2$

22. $\dfrac{113.04}{14.14} \approx 8$
The pizza is cut into 8 pieces.

23. $\dfrac{113.04}{6} = 18.84 \ \text{in.}^2$

24. $C = \pi d$
$\qquad \approx (3.14)(20)$
$\qquad = 62.8 \ \text{mi}$

25. $A = \pi \left(\dfrac{d}{2}\right)^2$

$\qquad \approx (3.14) \left(\dfrac{20}{2}\right)^2$

$\qquad = (3.14)(10)^2$

$\qquad = 3.14(100)$

$\qquad = 314 \ \text{mi}^2$

26. Washington is almost a square with a side length
of 27 mm. The Beltway is like a circle with
a diameter of about 49 mm. So the area of
Washington, D.C. is about $\dfrac{27^2}{\pi\left(\frac{49}{2}\right)^2}$ of the area of
the region inside the Beltway.

$\qquad \dfrac{27^2}{\pi\left(\frac{49}{2}\right)^2} = \dfrac{729}{\pi(600.25)}$

$\qquad\qquad \approx 0.387$

$\qquad\qquad \approx 0.387 \times 100\%$

$\qquad\qquad \approx 39\%$

27. C; $C = \pi d$
$\qquad \approx 3.14(5)$
$\qquad = 15.7 \ \text{in.}$

28. B; $A = \pi r^2$
$\qquad \approx 3.14\left(\frac{5}{2}\right)^2$
$\qquad = 19.625 \ \text{in.}^2$

29. Yes;

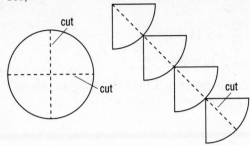

Using a Calculator

Note: From now on, when computing the circumference or area of a circle, the calculator key for π will be used.

1. $C = 2\pi r$
$= 2\pi(1.7)$
≈ 10.68 cm
$A = \pi r^2$
$= \pi(1.7)^2$
≈ 9.08 cm^2

2. $C = 2\pi r$
$= 2\pi(5.5)$
≈ 34.56 ft
$A = \pi r^2$
$= \pi(5.5)^2$
≈ 95.03 ft^2

3. $C = \pi d$
$= \pi(3.9)$
≈ 12.25 in.
$A = \pi\left(\dfrac{d}{2}\right)^2$
$= \pi\left(\dfrac{3.9}{2}\right)^2$
≈ 11.95 in.^{2}

4. $C = \pi d$
$= \pi(10.4)$
≈ 32.67 m
$A = \pi\left(\dfrac{d}{2}\right)^2$
$= \pi\left(\dfrac{10.4}{2}\right)^2$
≈ 84.95 m^2

5. $C = \pi d$
$10 = \pi d$
$\dfrac{10}{\pi} = d$
$3.1831 \approx d$
3.18 in. $\approx d$
$r = \dfrac{d}{2}$
$r \approx \dfrac{3.1831}{2}$
$r \approx 1.5916$
$r \approx 1.59$ in.

6. $A = \pi r^2$
$6 = \pi r^2$
$\dfrac{6}{\pi} = r^2$
$\sqrt{\dfrac{6}{\pi}} = r$
$1.3820 \approx r$
1.38 m $\approx r$
$d = 2r$
$d \approx 2(1.3820)$
$d \approx 2.7640$
$d \approx 2.76$ m

7. $A = \pi r^2 \cdot \dfrac{3}{4}$
$= \pi(3)^2 \cdot \dfrac{3}{4}$
≈ 21.21 units^2

8. $A = \pi r^2 \cdot \dfrac{5}{6}$
$= \pi(3)^2 \cdot \dfrac{5}{6}$
≈ 23.56 units^2

9. $A = \pi r^2 \cdot \dfrac{1}{2}$
$= \dfrac{\pi(3)^2}{2}$
≈ 14.14 units^2

10. $A = \pi r^2 \cdot \dfrac{1}{4}$

$ = \dfrac{\pi (3)^2}{4}$

$ \approx 7.07 \text{ units}^2$

11. $\dfrac{22}{7} \approx 3.14285714$

$\dfrac{355}{113} \approx 3.1415929$

$\pi = 3.14159265$

D; it is closer to 3.14159265 than the others.

Lab 12.2

1. Answers vary.

2. Cube

3. Yes; opposite faces of rectangular prisms must be congruent.

12.2 | *Polyhedrons and Other Solids*

ONGOING ASSESSMENT

1. Front view:

Side view:

Top view:

The front view and the side views are the same.

EXERCISES

1. B

2. A

3. D

4. C

5. a: lateral surface
b: base

6. a: edge
b: vertex
c: face
d: edge
e: vertex

7. a: face
b: vertex
c: edge
d: face
e: edge

8. a: lateral surface
b: base

9. Prism (with pentagons as bases)

10. Cone

11. Pyramid (with a triangle as base)

12. Cylinder

13. Pyramid (with a hexagon as base)

14. Prism (with triangles as bases)

15. No

16. No

17. Yes

18. Yes

19.

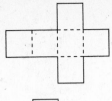 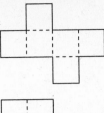 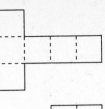

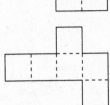 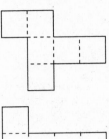 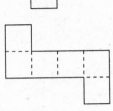

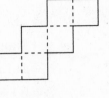 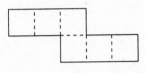

11 different nets are possible.

20. They both have 2 congruent bases.

21. They both have 1 base and come to a point.

22. Front view: ◯

Side view: ◯

Top view: ◯

23. Front view: △

Side view: △

Top view: ◯

24. Front view: △

Side view: △

Top view: ▢

25. Front view: ▢▢

Side view: ▢▢▢

Top view: ⌐

26. A

27. C

28. a. Box car: prism; yes
Gondola car: prism; yes
Tank car: cylinder; no
Passenger car: prism; yes

b. Answers vary.

c. Answers vary.

12.3 *Surface Area of Prisms and Cylinders*

ONGOING ASSESSMENT

1. $B = 6^2 = 36$ units^2

$P = 4(6) = 24$ units

$S = 2B + Ph$

$\quad = 2(36) + 24(6)$

$\quad = 72 + 144$

$\quad = 216$ units^2

The cube (1) has the least surface area.

2. $B = 3(6) = 18$ units^2

$P = 2(3) + 2(6) = 6 + 12 = 18$ units

$S = 2B + Ph$

$\quad = 2(18) + 18(12)$

$\quad = 36 + 216$

$\quad = 252$ units^2

EXERCISES

1. **A.** Prism (with rectangles as bases)
B. Prism (with triangles as bases)
C. Cylinder

2. $B = 5(8)$
$\quad = 40 \text{ units}^2$
$P = 2(5) + 2(8)$
$\quad = 10 + 16$
$\quad = 26 \text{ units}$
$S = 2B + Ph$
$\quad = 2(40) + 26(10)$
$\quad = 80 + 260$
$\quad = 340 \text{ units}^2$

3. $B = \frac{1}{2}bh$
$\quad = \frac{1}{2}(6)(8)$
$\quad = 24 \text{ units}^2$
$P = 6 + 8 + 10$
$\quad = 24 \text{ units}$
$S = 2B + Ph$
$\quad = 2(24) + 24(4)$
$\quad = 48 + 96$
$\quad = 144 \text{ units}^2$

4. $B = \pi r^2$
$\quad = \pi(6)^2$
$\quad = 36\pi \text{ units}^2$
$C = 2\pi r$
$\quad = 2\pi(6)$
$\quad = 12\pi \text{ units}$
$S = 2B + Ch$
$\quad = 2(36\pi) + 12\pi(4.5)$
$\quad = 126\pi$
$\quad \approx 395.8 \text{ units}^2$

5. $B = 12(16)$
$\quad = 192 \text{ units}^2$
$P = 2(12) + 2(16)$
$\quad = 24 + 32$
$\quad = 56 \text{ units}$
$S = 2B + Ph$
$\quad = 2(192) + 56(5)$
$\quad = 384 + 280$
$\quad = 664 \text{ units}^2$

6. $B = 7(3)$
$\quad = 21 \text{ units}^2$
$P = 2(3) + 2(7)$
$\quad = 6 + 14$
$\quad = 20 \text{ units}$
$S = 2B + Ph$
$\quad = 2(21) + 20(15)$
$\quad = 42 + 300$
$\quad = 342 \text{ units}^2$

7. $B = 2^2$
$\quad = 4 \text{ units}^2$
$P = 4(2)$
$\quad = 8 \text{ units}$
$S = 2B + Ph$
$\quad = 2(4) + 8(4)$
$\quad = 8 + 32$
$\quad = 40 \text{ units}^2$

8. $B = \frac{1}{2}Bh$
$\quad = \frac{1}{2}(6)(6)$
$\quad = 18 \text{ units}^2$
$P = 6 + 6 + 8.5$
$\quad = 20.5 \text{ units}$
$S = 2B + Ph$
$\quad = 2(18) + 20.5(3)$
$\quad = 36 + 61.5$
$\quad = 97.5 \text{ units}^2$

9. $5^2 + 12^2 = c^2$
$\quad 25 + 144 = c^2$
$\quad\quad\quad 169 = c^2$
$\quad\quad\quad\; 13 = c$
$B = \frac{1}{2}bh$
$\quad = \frac{1}{2}(12)(5)$
$\quad = 30 \text{ units}^2$
$P = 5 + 12 + 13$
$\quad = 30 \text{ units}$
$S = 2B + Ph$
$\quad = 2(30) + 30(14)$
$\quad = 60 + 420$
$\quad = 480 \text{ units}^2$

10. $B = \pi r^2$
$\quad = \pi(10)^2$
$\quad = 100\pi \text{ units}^2$
$C = 2\pi r$
$\quad = 2\pi(10)$
$\quad = 20\pi \text{ units}$
$S = 2B + Ch$
$\quad = 2(100\pi) + 20\pi(30)$
$\quad = 800\pi$
$\quad \approx 2513.3 \text{ units}^2$

11. $B = \pi r^2$

$\quad = \pi(20)^2$

$\quad = 400\pi \text{ units}^2$

$C = 2\pi r$

$\quad = 2\pi(20)$

$\quad = 40\pi \text{ units}$

$S = 2B + Ch$

$\quad = 2(400\pi) + 40\pi(8)$

$\quad = 1120\pi$

$\quad \approx 3518.6 \text{ units}^2$

12. $B = \frac{1}{2}bh$

$\quad = \frac{1}{2}(3)(4)$

$\quad = 6 \text{ units}^2$

$3^2 + 4^2 = c^2$

$9 + 16 = c^2$

$25 = c^2$

$5 = c$

$P = 3 + 4 + 5$

$\quad = 12 \text{ units}$

$S = 2B + Ph$

$\quad = 2(6) + 12(5)$

$\quad = 12 + 60$

$\quad = 72 \text{ units}^2$

13. $B = 4^2 = 16 \text{ in.}^2$

$P = 4(4) = 16 \text{ in.}$

$S = 2B + Ph$

$\quad = 2(16) + 16(4)$

$\quad = 32 + 64$

$\quad = 96 \text{ in.}^2$

4 in.   4 in.   4 in.

14. *Sample answer:*

2 units × 2 units × 5.5 units

15. $B = 2^2 = 4 \text{ in.}^2$

$P = 4(2) = 8 \text{ in.}$

$S = 2B + Ph$

$\quad = 2(4) + 8(2)$

$\quad = 8 + 16$

$\quad = 24 \text{ in.}^2$

16. $B = 1^2 = 1 \text{ in.}^2$

$P = 4(1) = 4 \text{ in.}$

$S = 2B + Ph$

$\quad = 2(1) + 4(1)$

$\quad = 2 + 4$

$\quad = 6 \text{ in.}^2$

Total surface area $= 6 \text{ in.}^2 \times 8$

$\quad = 48 \text{ in.}^2$

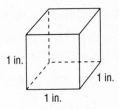

1 in.   1 in.   1 in.

17.

6 cm

27 cm

45 cm

$B = 45(27) = 1215 \text{ cm}^2$

$P = 2(45) + 2(27) = 90 + 54 = 144 \text{ cm}$

$S = 2B + Ph$

$\quad = 2(1215) + 144(6)$

$\quad = 2430 + 864$

$\quad = 3294 \text{ cm}^2$

The surface area of the box is 3294 cm².

A. $A = 50(67)$

$\quad = 3350 \text{ cm}^2$

B. $A = 52(66)$

$\quad = 3432 \text{ cm}^2$

C. $A = (32)(102)$

$\quad = 3264 \text{ cm}^2$

In C, the area of the paper is too small to cover the box; also, the paper is not wide enough: it needs to be (27 + 6) cm wide. In A, the paper is not wide enough: it needs to be (45 + 6) cm wide. So, you should choose B.

18.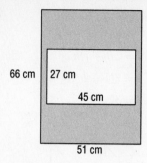

51 cm

33 cm 27 cm 45 cm

102 cm

Width: $\frac{1}{2}(6) + 27 + \frac{1}{2}(6) = 33$ cm
Length: $6 + 45 + 6 + 45 = 102$ cm

Width: $\frac{1}{2}(6) + 45 + \frac{1}{2}(6) = 51$ cm
Length: $6 + 27 + 6 + 27 = 66$ cm

66 cm × 51 cm and 102 cm × 33 cm; the paper's area is 72 cm² more than the box's surface area.

$102 \times 33 = 66 \times 51 = 3366$
$3366 - 3294 = 72$ cm²

19. $B = \pi \left(\dfrac{d}{2}\right)^2 = \pi \left(\dfrac{4}{2}\right)^2 = 4\pi$ ft²

$C = \pi d = \pi \cdot 4 = 4\pi$ ft

$S = 2B + Ch$

$\quad = 2(4\pi) + 4\pi(22)$

$\quad = 96\pi$

$\quad \approx 301.6$ ft²

20. *Sample answer:* Answer could be *less than* if a large amount is cut away and the surface is not highly irregular. Otherwise, the answer would be *greater than.*

21. A

22. C; $B = 10.75(8.5) = 91.375$ in.²

$\quad P = 2(10.75) + 2(8.5) = 38.5$ in.

$\quad S = 2B + Ph$

$\quad\quad = 2(91.375) + 38.5(1.25)$

$\quad\quad = 230.875$ in.²

$\quad\quad \approx 220$ in.²

23. A; $B = \frac{1}{2}bh = \frac{1}{2}(5)(12) = 30$ cm²

$\quad P = 5 + 12 + 13 = 30$ cm

$\quad S = 2B + Ph$

$\quad\quad = 2(30) + 30(6)$

$\quad\quad = 60 + 180$

$\quad\quad = 240$ cm²

24. *Sample answer:*

Box car:

$\quad B = 15.75 \times 2.5 = 39.375$

$\quad P = 2(15.75) + 2(2.5)$

$\quad\quad = 31.5 + 5$

$\quad\quad = 36.5$

$\quad S = 2B + Ph$

$\quad\quad = 2(39.375) + (36.5)(3)$

$\quad\quad = 78.75 + 109.5$

$\quad\quad = 188.25$ in.²

Gondola car:

$\quad B = 12 \times 2.5 = 30$

$\quad P = 2(12) + 2(2.5) = 24 + 5 = 29$

$\quad S = 2B + Ph$

$\quad\quad = 2(30) + 29(2.75)$

$\quad\quad = 60 + 79.75$

$\quad\quad = 139.75$ in.²

–CONTINUED–

24. –CONTINUED–

Tank car:

$B = \pi r^2 = \pi \left(\frac{2.75}{2}\right)^2 = 1.89\pi$

$C = \pi d = 2.75\pi$

$S = 2B + Ch$

$\quad = 2(1.89\pi) + 2.75\pi(10)$

$\quad = 3.78\pi + 27.5\pi$

$\quad = 31.28\pi$

$\quad \approx 98.22 \text{ in.}^2$

Hopper car:

$B = \frac{1}{2} \cdot 3.8(14.3 + 11.3)$

$\quad = \frac{1}{2} \cdot 3.8(25.6)$

$\quad = 48.64$

$P = 14.3 + 11.3 + 4 + 4 = 33.6$

$S = 2B + Ph$

$\quad = 2(48.64) + 33.6(2.6)$

$\quad = 184.64 \text{ in.}^2$

12.4 ALGEBRA CONNECTION: Exploring Volumes of Prisms

ONGOING ASSESSMENT

1. *Sample answer:* 60 ft × 60 ft × 10 ft high; this room has less height, but more floor space.

2. Increasing the height decreases the floor space.

EXERCISES

1. Use $V = lwh$.

A. $V = 5(4)(2) = 40 \text{ units}^3$
B. $V = 6(3)(2) = 36 \text{ units}^3$
C. $V = 4(3)(3) = 36 \text{ units}^3$
D. $V = 8(2)(2) = 32 \text{ units}^3$

B and C have the same volume.

2. Volume = length × width × height

3. Yes, it has 2 bases.

$B = \frac{1}{2}bh$

$\quad = \frac{1}{2}(10)(8.66)$

$\quad = 43.3 \text{ in.}^2$

$V = Bh$

$\quad = 43.3(12)$

$\quad = 519.6 \text{ in.}^3$

4. Yes, it has 2 bases.

$B = \frac{1}{2}bh$

$\quad = \frac{1}{2}(6)(8)$

$\quad = 24 \text{ cm}^2$

$V = Bh$

$\quad = 24(14)$

$\quad = 336 \text{ cm}^3$

5. No, it does not have 2 bases.

6. Yes, it has 2 bases.

$B = \frac{1}{2}bh$

$\quad = \frac{1}{2}(3)(4)$

$\quad = 6 \text{ cm}^2$

$V = Bh$

$\quad = 6(2)$

$\quad = 12 \text{ cm}^3$

7. Is a prism.

$V = lwh$

$27 = x^3$

$\sqrt[3]{27} = x$

$3 \text{ ft} = x$

8. Is a prism.

$V = lwh$

$16 = 4(2)(x)$

$16 = 8x$

$2 \text{ ft} = x$

9. Is a prism.

$V = lwh$

$396 = 12(3)(x)$

$396 = 36x$

$11 \text{ ft} = x$

10. Not a prism.

11.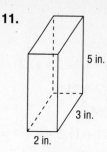

5 in.

3 in.

2 in.

$V = lwh = 2(3)(5) = 30$ in.^{3}

12.

6 in.

4 in.

5 in.

$V = lwh = 5(4)(6) = 120$ in.^{3}

13. $V = lwh$

$= 6(2)(10) = 120$ in.^{3}

14. $V = lwh$

$= 10(5)(4) = 200$ in.^{3}

15. $V = lwh$

$= 7(7)(7) = 343$ cm^3

16. $B = \frac{1}{2}(b_1 + b_2)h$

$= \frac{1}{2}(2 + 3)(1)$

$= \frac{5}{2}$

$= 2.5$ cm^2

$V = Bh = 2.5(7) = 17.5$ cm^3

17. $V = Bh$

$24 = 8x$

3 in. $= x$

18. $B = \frac{1}{2}bh$

$= \frac{1}{2}(2)(4)$

$= 4$ cm^2

$V = Bh$

$32 = 4x$

8 cm $= x$

19. $B = \frac{1}{2}bh = \frac{1}{2}(4)(x) = 2x$

$V = Bh$

$120 = 2x(6)$

$120 = 12x$

10 cm $= x$

20.

$V = Bh$

$50 = 13.75x$

$50 = 13\frac{75}{100}x$

$50 = \frac{1375}{100}x$

$50 \div \frac{1375}{100} = x$

$50 \cdot \frac{100}{1375} = x$

$\frac{40}{11} = x$

$3\frac{7}{11}$ ft $= x$

21. 1 by 1 by 36; 1 by 2 by 18;
1 by 3 by 12; 1 by 4 by 9;
1 by 6 by 6; 2 by 2 by 9;
2 by 3 by 6; 3 by 3 by 4

1 by 1 by 36 has the greatest
surface area.

22.

4

3

2

$B = l \cdot w = 2(3) = 6$ units^2

$P = 2l + 2w = 2(2) + 2(3) = 4 + 6 = 10$ units

$S = 2B + Ph = 2(6) + 10(4) = 12 + 40 = 52$ units^2

$V = l \cdot w \cdot h = 2(3)(4) = 24$ units^3

a. Let the prism be 2 by 3 by 8.
The surface area of 4 of the
faces doubles while the surface
area of 2 of the faces remains
the same.

$V = lwh = 2(3)(8) = 48$ units^3

$\frac{48}{24} = 2$

The volume doubles.

b. Let the prism be 2 by 6 by 8.
The surface area of 4 of the
faces doubles while the surface
area of 2 of the faces quadruples.

$V = lwh = 2(6)(8) = 96$ units^3

$\frac{96}{24} = 4$

The volume quadruples.

c. Let the prism be 4 by 6 by 8.
The surface area quadruples.

$V = lwh = 4(6)(8) = 192$ units^3

$\frac{192}{24} = 8$

The volume is multiplied by 8.

23. $B = \frac{1}{2}bh = \frac{1}{2}(12)(10) = 60 \text{ ft}^2$

$$10^2 + 6^2 = c^2$$

$$136 = c^2$$

$$11.66 \approx c$$

$$11.66 \times 9 = 104.94 \text{ ft}^2$$

$$2(60) + 2(104.94) \approx 330 \text{ ft}^2$$

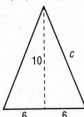

24. $V = \frac{1}{2} \cdot 10 \cdot 12 \cdot 9 = 540 \text{ ft}^3$

25. A. $B = \frac{1}{2}(b_1 + b_2)h = \frac{1}{2}(20 + 30)(6) = 3(50) = 150 \text{ units}^2$

$V = Bh = 150(20) = 3000 \text{ units}^3$

B. $V = l \cdot w \cdot h = 30(20)(5) = 3000 \text{ units}^3$

C. $B = \frac{1}{2}(b_1 + b_2)h = \frac{1}{2}(10 + 30)(10) = 5(40) = 20 \text{ units}^2$

$V = Bh = 20(18) = 3600 \text{ units}^3$

A and B hold the same amount of water.

26. B; $\quad V = lwh$

$$4608 = 16(16)h$$

$$4608 = 256h$$

$$18 = h$$

27. D; $V = lwh$

$$= 7(7)(7)$$

$$= 343 \text{ in.}^3$$

28.

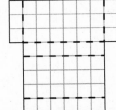

$B = 6(3) = 18 \text{ units}^2$

$P = 2(6) + 2(3) = 12 + 6 = 18 \text{ units}$

$S = 2B + Ph = 2(18) + 18(1) = 36 + 18 = 54 \text{ units}^2$

$V = l \cdot w \cdot h = 6(3)(1) = 18 \text{ units}^3$

29.

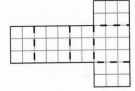

$B = 3(3) = 9 \text{ units}^2$

$P = 4(3) = 12 \text{ units}$

$S = 2B + Ph = 2(9) + 12(2) = 18 + 24 = 42 \text{ units}^2$

$V = l \cdot w \cdot h = 3(3)(2) = 18 \text{ units}^3$

30.

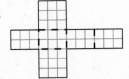

$B = 3(2) = 6 \text{ units}^2$

$P = 2(3) + 2(2) = 6 + 4 = 10 \text{ units}$

$S = 2B + Ph = 2(6) + 10(3) = 12 + 30 = 42 \text{ units}^2$

$V = l \cdot w \cdot h = 3(2)(3) = 18 \text{ units}^3$

31. Box car: $15.75 \times 3 \times 2.5 = 118.125$ in.^{3}

Gondola car: $12 \times 2.75 \times 2.5 = 82.5$ in.^{3}

Hopper car: $B = \frac{1}{2} \cdot 3.8(14.3 + 11.3) = \frac{1}{2} \cdot 3.8(25.6) = 48.64$

$V = Bh = 48.64(2.6) = 126.5$ in.^{3}

Spiral R E V I E W

1. $B = 30 \times 12 = 360$

$P = 2(30) + 2(12) = 60 + 24 = 84$

$S = 2B + Ph$

$\quad = 2(360) + 84(15)$

$\quad = 720 + 1260$

$\quad = 1980$ cm^2

2. $B = \frac{1}{2}(12)(9) = 54$ m^2

$a^2 + b^2 = c^2$

$12^2 + 9^2 = c^2$

$144 + 81 = c^2$

$225 = c^2$

$15 = c$

$P = 9 + 12 + 15 = 36$

$S = 2B + Ph$

$\quad = 2(54) + 36(18)$

$\quad = 108 + 648$

$\quad = 756$ m^2

3. $B = l \cdot w = 30(15) = 450$ ft^2

$P = 2\pi r = 2\pi(12) = 24\pi$ in.

$S = 2B + Ph$

$\quad = 2(144\pi) + (24\pi)(18)$

$\quad = 720\pi \approx 2262$ in.^{2}

4. Select 3

6th row:

1 6 15 <u>20</u> 15 6 1

5. Select 4

5th row:

1 5 10 10 <u>5</u> 1

6. Select 3

7th row: 1 7 21 <u>35</u> 35 21 7 1

7. Select 2

5th row: 1 5 <u>10</u> 10 5 1

8. $4x + 3 = 2$

$4x = -1$

$x = -\frac{1}{4}$

9. $2b + 5 = 7 - 5b$

$7b + 5 = 7$

$7b = 2$

$b = \frac{2}{7}$

10. $\frac{3}{8}r + 2 = \frac{7}{8}r$

$\frac{3}{8}r + 2 - \frac{3}{8}r = \frac{7}{8}r - \frac{3}{8}r$

$2 = \frac{4}{8}r$

$2 = \frac{1}{2}r$

$4 = r$

11. $6 + 2y = 5y$

$6 = 3y$

$2 = y$

12. $5s - 4 = \frac{3}{2}s$

$5s - \frac{3}{2}s = 4$

$\left(\frac{10}{2} - \frac{3}{2}\right)s = 4$

$\frac{2}{7} \cdot \frac{7}{2}s = 4 \cdot \frac{2}{7}$

$s = \frac{8}{7}$

13. $42 + 3m = 4m$

$42 = m$

14. $24 \le -2y$

$\frac{24}{-2} \ge \frac{-2y}{-2}$

$-12 \ge y$

15. $13z + 26 > 0$

$\quad\quad 13z > -26$

$\quad\quad\quad z > -2$

16. $7 - 6t > 4t$

$\quad\quad 7 > 10t$

$\quad\quad \frac{7}{10} > t$

17. $2r - 5 < 5$

$\quad\quad 2r < 10$

$\quad\quad\; r < 5$

18. $-\frac{1}{2}p \geq \frac{11}{2}$

$\left(-\frac{2}{1}\right)\left(-\frac{1}{2}p\right) \leq \left(\frac{11}{2}\right)\left(-\frac{2}{1}\right)$

$\quad\quad\quad\quad p \leq -11$

19. $\frac{1}{8}p \leq -\frac{33}{4}$

$\frac{8}{1} \cdot \frac{1}{8}p \leq \frac{8}{1} \cdot \left(-\frac{33}{4}\right)$

$\quad\quad p \leq \frac{\cancel{4} \cdot 2 \cdot (-3) \cdot 11}{\cancel{1} \cdot \cancel{4}}$

$\quad\quad p \leq -66$

20. $\frac{1}{4} = \frac{x}{92}$

$\quad\;\; \frac{92}{4} = x$

$\quad\;\; 23 = x$

Mid-Chapter ASSESSMENT

1. $C = 2\pi r$ $\quad\quad A = \pi r^2$

$\quad\;\; = 2(\pi)(3)$ $\quad\; = \pi(3)^2$

$\quad\;\; = 6\pi$ $\quad\quad\;\; = 9\pi$

$\quad\;\; \approx 18.8$ cm $\quad \approx 28.3$ cm^2

2. $C = \pi d$ $\quad\quad A = \pi\left(\frac{d}{2}\right)^2$

$\quad\;\; = \pi(5)$

$\quad\;\; \approx 15.7$ in. $\quad = \pi\left(\frac{5}{2}\right)^2$

$\quad\quad\quad\quad\quad\quad = \pi(2.5)^2$

$\quad\quad\quad\quad\quad\quad = 6.25\pi$

$\quad\quad\quad\quad\quad\quad \approx 19.6$ in.^{2}

3. Area of square $= 8^2 = 64$ ft^2

Area of circle $= \pi r^2 = \pi(4)^2 = 16\pi \approx 50.27$ ft^2

Area of blue $= 64 - 50.27 \approx 13.7$ ft^2

4. Area of circle $= \pi r^2$

$\quad\quad\quad\quad\quad\;\; = \pi(5)^2 = 25\pi \approx 78.54$ yd^2

$\quad 10^2 = 8^2 + b^2$

$\quad 100 = 64 + b^2$

$\quad\;\; 36 = b^2$

$\quad\quad 6 = b$

Area of rectangle $= 8 \times 6 = 48$ yd^2

Area of blue $= 78.54 - 48 = 30.5$ yd^2

5. D $\quad\quad$ **6.** C $\quad\quad$ **7.** E $\quad\quad$ **8.** B $\quad\quad$ **9.** A

10. $B = \pi\left(\frac{d}{2}\right)^2 = \pi\left(\frac{24}{2}\right)^2 = \pi(12)^2 = 144\pi$ mm^2

$C = \pi d = \pi \cdot 24 = 24\pi$ mm

$S = 2B + Ch$

$\quad = 2(144\pi) + 24\pi(2)$

$\quad = 336\pi$

$\quad \approx 1055.6$ mm^2

11. $B = \pi\left(\frac{d}{2}\right)^2 = \pi\left(\frac{14}{2}\right)^2 = \pi(7)^2 = 49\pi$ mm^2

$C = \pi d = \pi \cdot 14 = 14\pi$ mm

$S = 2B + Ch$

$\quad = 2(49\pi) + 14\pi(49)$

$\quad = 784\pi$

$\quad \approx 2463.0$ mm^2

12. $B = 5 \times 2.5 = 12.5$

$P = 2(5) = 2(2.5) = 10 + 5 = 15$

$S = 2B + Ph$

$\quad = 2(12.5) + 15(0.5)$

$\quad = 25 + 7.5$

$\quad = 32.5 \text{ cm}^2$

13. $B = \frac{113}{32} \times \frac{59}{16} \approx 13.02$

$P = 2\left(\frac{113}{32}\right) + 2\left(\frac{59}{16}\right) = \frac{113}{16} + \frac{59}{8} \approx 14.44$

$S = 2B + Ph$

$\quad = 2(13.02) + (14.44)(0.125)$

$\quad = 26.04 + 1.805$

$\quad = 27.85 \text{ in.}^2$

14. $V = l \cdot w \cdot h = 5(4)(6) = 120 \text{ in.}^3$

15. $B = \frac{1}{2}bh = \frac{1}{2}(5)(8) = 20 \text{ cm}^2$

$V = Bh = 20(13) = 260 \text{ cm}^3$

16. $V = l \cdot w \cdot h = 20(12)(2) = 480 \text{ m}^3$

17. $B = \frac{1}{2}bh = \frac{1}{2}(15)(4) = 30 \text{ in.}^2$

$V = Bh = 30(14) = 420 \text{ in.}^3$

18. $C = \pi d$

$\quad = \pi(5.41)$

$\quad \approx 17.00 \text{ mi}$

19. $A = \pi \left(\frac{d}{2}\right)^2$

$\quad = \pi \left(\frac{5.41}{2}\right)^2$

$\quad = \pi(2.705)^2$

$\quad = \pi(7.317025)$

$\quad \approx 22.99 \text{ mi}^2$

20. $C = 2\pi r$

$\quad = 2\pi(1.91)$

$\quad = 3.82\pi$

$\quad \approx 12.00 \text{ ft}$

12.5 *Exploring Volumes of Cylinders*

ONGOING ASSESSMENT

A 12-ounce can of soda pop is about 4.5 in. high and has a diameter of about 2.5 in. So, its radius is about $4.5 \div 2 = 1.25$ in. and its volume is $Bh = \pi r^2 h \approx \pi(1.25)^2 \cdot 4.5 \approx 22.08932$ in.^{3}. Since 12 fluid ounces ≈ 22.08932 in.^{3}.

1. 1 fluid ounce $\approx 22.08932 \div 12$

$\quad \approx 1.8408$ in.^{3}

2. 1 cubic inch $\approx 12 \div 22.08932$

$\quad \approx 0.5432$ fl oz

3. Since $1.8408 \cdot 0.5432 \approx 1.000$, they are reciprocals.

EXERCISES

1. $B = \pi r^2$

$\quad = \pi(3)^2$

$\quad = 9\pi$

$\quad \approx 28.27 \text{ units}^2$

2. $h = 5$ units

3. $V = Bh$

4. $V = Bh$

$\quad = (9\pi)5$

$\quad = 45\pi$

$\quad \approx 141.37 \text{ units}^3$

5. $B = \pi \left(\dfrac{d}{2}\right)^2$

$\quad = \pi \left(\dfrac{3}{2}\right)^2$

$\quad = \pi (1.5)^2$

$\quad = 2.25\pi$

$\quad \approx 7.07 \text{ in.}^2$

6. $V = Bh$

$\quad = 2.25\pi(1)$

$\quad = 2.25\pi$

$\quad \approx 7.07 \text{ in.}^3$

7. $B = \pi \left(\dfrac{14}{2}\right)^2$

$\quad = \pi(7)^2$

$\quad \approx 49\pi$

$V = Bh$

$\quad = 49\pi(6.5)$

$\quad \approx 1000.60 \text{ in.}^3$

8. $B = \pi r^2$

$\quad = \pi \left(\dfrac{20}{2}\right)^2$

$\quad = \pi(10)^2$

$\quad = 100\pi$

$V = Bh$

$\quad = 100\pi(24)$

$\quad = 2400\pi$

$\quad \approx 7539.82 \text{ in.}^3$

9. $B = \pi r^2$

$\quad = \pi \left(\dfrac{28}{2}\right)^2$

$\quad = \pi(14)^2$

$\quad = 196\pi$

$V = Bh$

$\quad = 196\pi(14)$

$\quad = 2744\pi$

$\quad \approx 8620.53 \text{ in.}^3$

10. $B = \pi r^2$

$\quad = \pi \left(\dfrac{18}{2}\right)^2$

$\quad = \pi(9)^2$

$\quad = 81\pi$

$V = Bh$

$\quad = 81\pi(24)$

$\quad = 1944\pi$

$\quad \approx 6107.26 \text{ in.}^3$

11. $B = \pi r^2$

$\quad = \pi(2)^2$

$\quad = 4\pi \text{ in.}^2$

$\quad\quad V = Bh$

$\quad 37.7 = 4\pi h$

$\quad \dfrac{37.7}{4\pi} = h$

$\quad 3.00 \text{ in.} \approx h$

12. $B = \pi r^2$

$\quad = \pi(3)^2$

$\quad = 9\pi \text{ m}^2$

$\quad\quad V = Bh$

$\quad 197.9 = 9\pi h$

$\quad \dfrac{197.9}{9\pi} = h$

$\quad 7.00 \text{ m} \approx h$

13.

$\quad\quad V = Bh$

$\quad 290.5 = B(8)$

$\quad \dfrac{290.5}{8} = B$

$\quad 36.3125 \text{ cm}^2 = B$

$\quad\quad B = \pi r^2$

$\quad 36.3125 = \pi r^2$

$\quad \dfrac{36.3125}{\pi} = r^2$

$\quad \sqrt{\dfrac{36.3125}{\pi}} = r$

$\quad 3.40 \text{ cm} \approx r$

14.

$\quad\quad B = \pi r^2$

$\quad 564.1 = B(4)$

$\quad \dfrac{564.1}{4} = B$

$\quad 141.025 \text{ ft}^2 = B$

$\quad\quad B = \pi r^2$

$\quad 141.025 = \pi r^2$

$\quad \dfrac{141.025}{\pi} = r^2$

$\quad \sqrt{\dfrac{141.025}{\pi}} = r$

$\quad 6.70 \text{ ft} \approx r$

15. Greater than; though both volumes involve the numbers 4 and 6, half the larger of the two numbers is squared for Cylinder A.

16.

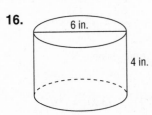

6 in.

4 in.

$B = \pi \left(\dfrac{d}{2}\right)^2 = \pi \left(\dfrac{6}{2}\right)^2 = \pi(3)^2 = 9\pi \text{ in.}^2$

$V = Bh = 9\pi(4) = 36\pi \approx 113.10 \text{ in.}^3$

17.

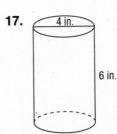

4 in.

6 in.

$B = \pi \left(\dfrac{d}{2}\right)^2 = \pi \left(\dfrac{4}{2}\right)^2 = \pi(2)^2 = 4\pi \text{ in.}^2$

$V = Bh = 4\pi(6) = 24\pi \approx 75.40 \text{ in.}^3$

18. $B = \pi \left(\dfrac{d}{2}\right)^2 = \pi \left(\dfrac{6}{2}\right)^2 = 9\pi$ in.^{2} 　　　$B = \pi \left(\dfrac{d}{2}\right)^2 = \pi \left(\dfrac{4}{2}\right)^2 = 4\pi$ in.^{2}

$C = \pi d = \pi \cdot 6 = 6\pi$ in. 　　　　　$C = \pi d = \pi \cdot 4 = 4\pi$ in.

$S_{\text{cyl A}} = 2B + Ch$ 　　　　　　　$S_{\text{cyl B}} = 2B + Ch$

$\quad = 2(9\pi) + 6\pi(4)$ 　　　　　　　$\quad = 2(4\pi) + 4\pi(6)$

$\quad = 18\pi + 24\pi$ 　　　　　　　　　$\quad = 8\pi + 24\pi$

$\quad = 42\pi$ in.^{2} 　　　　　　　　　　$\quad = 32\pi$ in.^{2}

Yes

19. $B = \pi \left(\dfrac{d}{2}\right)^2$ 　　　　**20.** $B = \pi \left(\dfrac{d}{2}\right)^2$ 　　　　**21.** $577.33 - 280.45 \approx 296.9$ cm^3

$\quad = \pi \left(\dfrac{11.5}{2}\right)^2$ 　　　　　$\quad = \pi \left(\dfrac{16.5}{2}\right)^2$

$\quad = \pi (5.75)^2$ 　　　　　　$\quad = \pi (8.25)^2$

$\quad = 33.0625\pi$ cm^2 　　　$\quad = 68.0625\pi$ cm^2

$V = Bh$ 　　　　　　　　$V = Bh$

$\quad = 33.0625\pi(2.7)$ 　　　$\quad = 68.0625\pi(2.7)$

$\quad = 89.26875\pi$ 　　　　　$\quad = 183.76875\pi$

$\quad \approx 280.45$ cm^3 　　　　$\quad \approx 577.33$ cm^3

22. $B = \pi \left(\dfrac{d}{2}\right)^2 = \pi \left(\dfrac{4}{2}\right)^2 = \pi(2)^2 = 4\pi$ in.^{2} 　　　**23.** $V = Bh = 4\pi(0.42) = 1.68\pi \approx 5.278$ in.^{3}

$V = Bh = 4\pi(3.42) = 13.68\pi \approx 42.977$ in.^{3}

24. $(42.977 - 5.278)(8) = 37.699(8) \approx 301.59$ in.^{3} 　　　**25.** 301.59 in.$^3 \times \dfrac{1 \text{ liter}}{61.02 \text{ in.}^3} \approx 4.94$ liters

26. C 　　　　　　　　　　　　　　　　　**27.** Tank car;

$B = \pi \left(\dfrac{2.75}{2}\right)^2 = \pi(1.375)^2 = 1.891\pi$

$V = Bh = 1.891\pi(10) \approx 59.41$ in.^{3}

Lab 12.6

Part A

1. *Sample answer:* $h = 2.4$ in.; 　　**2.** *Sample answer:* 　　　　**3.** *Sample answer:*
$r = 3.2$ in.

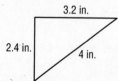

3.2 in.

2.4 in.　　4 in.

The hypotenuse has a length of
4 because it is the radius of the
circle that makes the cone.

$h^2 + r^2 = 4^2$

$(2.4)^2 + (3.2)^2 = 16$

$5.76 + 10.24 = 16$

$16 = 16$

Part B

4.–5. Answers vary.

6. *Sample answer:* The cone with a radius of $2\frac{3}{4}$ in.

7. *Sample answer:* Yes; $4 = 3\frac{1}{4}$ in.

8. *Sample answer:* Make the cone as narrow as possible.

12.6 *Exploring Volumes of Pyramids and Cones*

ONGOING ASSESSMENT

1. The volume calculated is greater than the actual volume because the cone is cut off at the top.

2. *Sample answer:* $6.5 \times 9 \times 8 = 468$ ft^3

EXERCISES

1. The cylinder has two bases.

2. The cylinder has 3 times the volume of the cone.

3. $B = l \cdot w = 12(8) = 96$ in.^{2}
$V = \frac{1}{3}Bh = \frac{1}{3}(96)(10) = 320$ in.^{3}

4. $B = \pi r^2 = \pi(3)^2 = 9\pi$ cm^2
$V = \frac{1}{3}Bh = \frac{1}{3}(9\pi)(10) = 30\pi \approx 94.25$ cm^3

5. $r = 10$ units

6. $h = 10$

7. $B = \pi r^2 = \pi(10)^2 = 100\pi$
$V = \frac{1}{3}Bh = \frac{1}{3}(100\pi)(10) = \frac{1000}{3}\pi \approx 1047$ units^3

8. Substitute $2h$ for h in the formula for volume;
$V = \frac{1}{3}Bh$
$ = \frac{1}{3}(2h) = \frac{1}{3}(1000\pi)(2 \cdot 10) \approx 2094$ units^3

9. $B = l \cdot w = 15(12) = 180$ cm^2
$V = \frac{1}{3}Bh = \frac{1}{3}(180)(20) = 1200$ cm^3

10. $B = \frac{1}{2}bh = \frac{1}{2}(3)(4) = 6$ in.^{2}
$V = \frac{1}{3}Bh = \frac{1}{3}(6)(5) = 10$ in.^{3}

11. $B = s^2 = 30^2 = 900$ ft^2
$V = \frac{1}{3}Bh = \frac{1}{3}(900)(28) = 8400$ ft^3

12. $B = l \cdot w = 6(7) = 42$ m^2
$V = \frac{1}{3}Bh = \frac{1}{3}(42)(10) = 140$ m^3

13. $B = \pi r^2 = \pi(10)^2 = 100\pi$ m^2
$V == \frac{1}{3}Bh = \frac{1}{3}(100\pi)(24) = 800\pi \approx 2513.27$ m^3

14. $B = \pi r^2 = \pi(12)^2 = 144\pi$ ft^2
$V = \frac{1}{3}Bh = \frac{1}{3}(144\pi)(12) = 576\pi \approx 1809.56$ ft^3

15. $B = \pi r^2 = \pi(14)^2 = 196\pi$ in.^{2}
$V = \frac{1}{3}Bh = \frac{1}{3}(196\pi)(26) = \frac{5096}{3}\pi \approx 5336.52$ in.^{3}

16. $B = \pi r^2 = \pi(6)^2 = 36\pi$ cm^2
$h =$ height of cone in centimeters
$6^2 + h^2 = 10^2$
$36 + h^2 = 100$
$h^2 = 64$
$h = 8$
$V = \frac{1}{3}Bh = \frac{1}{3}(36\pi)(8) = 96\pi \approx 301.59$ cm^3

17.–18. Answers vary.

19. $V_{cube} = lwh = 12^3 = 1728$ in.^{3}

$V_{pyramid} = \frac{1}{3}lwh$

$\quad = \frac{1}{3}(12 \cdot 12 \cdot 9)$

$\quad = \frac{1}{3}(1296) = 432$ in.^{3}

$V_{blue} = 1728 + 432$

$\quad = 2160$ in.^{3}

20. $V_{rectangle} = 17 \cdot 9 \cdot 5 = 765$ m^3

$V_{triangle} = \frac{1}{2}bh = \frac{1}{2}(9)(4)$

$\quad = 18 \times h = 18 \times 17$

$\quad = 306$ m^3

$V_{blue} = 765 + 306$

$\quad = 1071$ m^3

21. $V_{cylinder} = \pi r^2 h = \pi(12^2)(15) = 2160\pi$ cm^3

$V_{cone} = \frac{1}{3}\pi r^2 h = \frac{1}{3}\pi(12^2)(10) = 480\pi$ cm^3

$V_{blue} = 2160\pi + 480\pi$

$\quad = 2640\pi$

$\quad \approx 8294$ cm^3

22. A; $\tan 27° = \dfrac{h}{40}$

$h = 40\tan 27°$

$\quad = 20.38$ m

23. Doubling the radius has a greater effect. The radius is squared, while the height is not.

24. C; $V_{cone} = \frac{1}{3}Bh = \frac{1}{3} \cdot \pi \cdot 6^2 \cdot 6 \approx 226.08$ cm^3

$V_{pyramid} = \frac{1}{3}Bh = \frac{1}{3} \cdot 6^2 \cdot 6 = 72$ cm^3

$V_{cylinder} = Bh = \pi \cdot 6^2 \cdot 6 \approx 678.24$ cm^3

$V_{cube} = lwh = 6^3 = 216$ cm^3

25. Answers vary.

26. $h \approx 1$ cm

$V = \frac{1}{3}\pi(1^2)(1) = \frac{1}{3}\pi \approx 1$ cm^3

12.7   *Exploring Volumes of Spheres*

ONGOING ASSESSMENT

1. In Example 2, a radius of 18 ft produced a volume of 24,429 ft^3. Try a radius of 19 ft.

$V = \frac{4}{3}\pi r^3 = \frac{4}{3}\pi \cdot 19^3 \approx 28{,}730.91$ ft$^3 \approx 30{,}000$ ft^3

EXERCISES

1. $\overline{AB}$ or $\overline{AC}$ or $\overline{AD}$

2. Yes; it is a segment from the center to the surface.

3. $\overline{BC}$;

$d = 2r = 2(2) = 4$ ft

4. Hemisphere

5. $V = \frac{4}{3}\pi r^3$

$\quad = \frac{4}{3}\pi(2)^3$

$\quad = \frac{4}{3}\pi(8)$

$\quad = \frac{32}{3}\pi$

$\quad \approx 33.51$ ft^3

6. $V = \frac{4}{3}\pi r^3$

$\quad = \frac{4}{3}\pi(1.5)^3$

$\quad = \frac{4}{3}\pi(3.375)$

$\quad = 4.5\pi$

$\quad \approx 14.14$ in.^{3}

7. $V = \frac{4}{3}\pi r^3$

$\quad = \frac{4}{3}\pi(12)^3$

$\quad = \frac{4}{3}\pi(1728)$

$\quad = 2304\pi$

$\quad \approx 7238.23$ cm^3

8. $V = \dfrac{4}{3}\pi \left(\dfrac{d}{2}\right)^3$

$\quad = \dfrac{4}{3}\pi \left(\dfrac{8.6}{2}\right)^3$

$\quad = \dfrac{4}{3}\pi (4.3)^3$

$\quad = \dfrac{4}{3}\pi (79.507)$

$\quad = \dfrac{318.028}{3}\pi$

$\quad \approx 333.04 \text{ in.}^3$

9. $V = \dfrac{4}{3}\pi \left(\dfrac{d}{2}\right)^3$

$\quad = \dfrac{4}{3}\pi \left(\dfrac{1.68}{2}\right)^3$

$\quad = \dfrac{4}{3}\pi (0.84)^3$

$\quad = \dfrac{4}{3}\pi (0.592704)$

$\quad = 0.790272\pi$

$\quad \approx 2.48 \text{ in.}^3$

10. $V = \dfrac{4}{3}\pi \left(\dfrac{d}{2}\right)^3$

$\quad = \dfrac{4}{3}\pi \left(\dfrac{0.5}{2}\right)^3$

$\quad = \dfrac{4}{3}\pi (0.25)^3$

$\quad = \dfrac{4}{3}\pi (0.15625)$

$\quad = 0.02083\pi$

$\quad \approx 0.07 \text{ in.}^3$

11. $V = \dfrac{4}{3}\pi r^3$

$\quad = \dfrac{4}{3}\pi (11)^3$

$\quad = \dfrac{4}{3}\pi (1331)$

$\quad = \dfrac{5324}{3}\pi$

$\quad \approx 5575.28 \text{ cm}^3$

12. $V = \dfrac{4}{3}\pi \left(\dfrac{d}{2}\right)^3$

$\quad = \dfrac{4}{3}\pi \left(\dfrac{8.25}{2}\right)^3$

$\quad = \dfrac{4}{3}\pi (4.125)^3$

$\quad = 93.5859375\pi$

$\quad \approx 294.01 \text{ in.}^3$

13. $V = \dfrac{4}{3}\pi r^3$

$\quad = \dfrac{4}{3}\pi (1.25)^3$

$\quad = \dfrac{4}{3}\pi (1.953125)$

$\quad = \dfrac{7.8125}{3}\pi$

$\quad \approx 8.18 \text{ in.}^3$

14. $V_{\text{prism}} = l \cdot w \cdot h = 8^3 = 512 \text{ units}^3$

$\quad V_{\text{sphere}} = \dfrac{4}{3}\pi r^3 = \dfrac{4}{3}\pi (4)^3 = \dfrac{4}{3}\pi (64) = \dfrac{256}{3}\pi \approx 268.08 \text{ units}^3$

$\quad V_{\text{orange}} \approx 512 - 268.08 \approx 243.92 \text{ units}^3$

15. $V_{\text{larger}} = \dfrac{4}{3}\pi r^3 = \dfrac{4}{3}\pi (4.5)^3 = \dfrac{4}{3}\pi (91.125) = 121.5\pi \approx 381.70 \text{ units}^3$

$\quad V_{\text{smaller}} = \dfrac{4}{3}\pi \left(\dfrac{d}{2}\right)^3 = \dfrac{4}{3}\pi \left(\dfrac{4.5}{2}\right)^2 = \dfrac{4}{3}\pi (2.25)^3 = 15.1875 \approx 47.71 \text{ units}^3$

$\quad V_{\text{orange}} \approx 381.70 - 47.71 \approx 333.99 \text{ units}^3$

16. $B = \pi \left(\dfrac{d}{2}\right)^2 = \pi \left(\dfrac{3}{2}\right)^2 = \pi (1.5)^2 = 2.25\pi \text{ units}$

$\quad V_{\text{cyl}} = Bh = 2.25\pi (9) = 20.25\pi \approx 63.617 \text{ units}^3$

$\quad V_{\text{each sphere}} = \dfrac{4}{3}\pi r^3 = \dfrac{4}{3}\pi (1.5)^3 = \dfrac{4}{3}\pi (3.375) = 4.5\pi \approx 14.137 \text{ units}^3$

$\quad V_{\text{orange}} \approx 63.617 - 3(14.137) \approx 63.617 - 42.411 \approx 21.21 \text{ units}^3$

17. $B = \pi r^2 = \pi (6)^2 = 36\pi \text{ units}$

$\quad V_{\text{cone}} = \dfrac{1}{3}Bh = \dfrac{1}{3}(36\pi)(20) = 240\pi \approx 753.98 \text{ units}^3$

$\quad V_{\text{sphere}} = \dfrac{4}{3}\pi r^3 = \dfrac{4}{3}\pi (6)^3 = \dfrac{4}{3}\pi (216) = 288\pi \approx 904.78 \text{ units}^3$

$\quad V_{\text{orange}} \approx 753.98 - \dfrac{904.78}{2} \approx 753.98 - 452.39 \approx 301.59 \text{ units}^3$

18. $h = 9$ units

$C = \pi d = 3\pi$ units

$3\pi > 9$

Circumference is larger.

19. $\frac{4}{3}\pi r^3 = V$

$\frac{4}{3}\pi (8)^3 \approx 2144.66$

$\frac{4}{3}\pi (7)^3 \approx 1436.76$

The radius of the sphere is about 7 cm.

20. $\frac{4}{3}\pi r^3 = V$

$\frac{4}{3}\pi (5)^3 \approx 523.60$

$\frac{4}{3}\pi (6)^3 \approx 904.78$

$\frac{4}{3}\pi (5.5)^3 \approx 696.91$

$\frac{4}{3}\pi (5.4)^3 \approx 659.58$

The radius of the sphere is about 5.4 ft.

21. $\frac{4}{3}\pi r^3 = V$

$\frac{4}{3}\pi (3)^3 = 36\pi$

$\frac{4}{3}\pi (2.5)^3 \approx 20.83\pi$

$\frac{4}{3}\pi (2.9)^3 \approx 32.52\pi$

The radius of the sphere is about 2.9 cm.

22. $\frac{4}{3}\pi r^3 = V$

$\frac{4}{3}\pi (12)^3 = 2304\pi$

$\frac{4}{3}\pi (13)^3 \approx 2929.33\pi$

The radius of the sphere is about 13 in.

23. $V = \frac{4}{3}\pi r^3$

$= \frac{4}{3}\pi \left(\frac{16}{2}\right)^3$

$= \frac{4}{3}\pi (8^3)$

$= \frac{4}{3}\pi (512)$

$\approx 2145 \text{ ft}^3$

24. $\left(\frac{3}{4}\right)(2145) \approx 1609 \text{ ft}^3$

25. $V = \frac{4}{3}\pi r^3$

$V = \frac{4}{3}\pi (2)^3 = \frac{32}{3}\pi$

$V = \frac{4}{3}\pi (4)^3 = \frac{256}{3}\pi$

$V = \frac{4}{3}\pi (6)^3 = \frac{864}{3}\pi$

$V = \frac{4}{3}\pi (8)^3 = \frac{2048}{3}\pi$

$\frac{256}{3}\pi \div \frac{32}{3}\pi = \frac{256\not{\pi}}{\not{3}} \cdot \frac{\not{3}}{32\not{\pi}} = 8$

$\frac{864}{3}\pi \div \frac{32}{3}\pi = \frac{864\not{\pi}}{\not{3}} \cdot \frac{\not{3}}{32\not{\pi}} = 27$

$\frac{2048}{3}\pi \div \frac{32}{3}\pi = \frac{2048\not{\pi}}{\not{3}} \cdot \frac{\not{3}}{32\not{\pi}} = 64$

When the radius doubles, the volume is 8 times as much. When the radius triples, the volume is 27 times as much. When the radius quadruples, the volume is 64 times as much.

Pattern: When the radius is x times as much, the volume is x^3 times as much.

26. C

27. c; The area is approximately equal to the sum of the areas of 4 congruent circles.

28. $S = 4\pi \left(\frac{d}{2}\right)^2$

$= 4\pi \left(\frac{3}{2}\right)^2$

$= 4\pi (1.5)^2$

$= 4\pi (2.25)$

$= 9\pi$

$\approx 28.27 \text{ in.}^2$

Spiral **R E V I E W**

1. They are noncongruent corresponding angles.

2. $\angle CDA$; they are vertical angles.

3. $\overrightarrow{DA}$ is a ray.

4. $\overleftrightarrow{BE}, \overleftrightarrow{EH}$

5. Obtuse

6. $\angle CDG = 60°$; they are vertical angles.

7. $m\angle ADC = 180° - m\angle ADE$
$= 180° - 60°$
$= 120°$

8. $V = \frac{4}{3}\pi r^3$
$= \frac{4}{3}\pi \left(\frac{89}{2}\right)^3$
$\approx 369,121 \text{ ft}^3$

9. $A = \pi r^2$
$= \pi(8)^2$
$= 64\pi$
$\approx 201.1 \text{ units}^2$

10. $A = \pi r^2$
$= \pi(13)^2$
$= 169\pi$
$\approx 530.9 \text{ units}^2$

11. $A = \pi \left(\frac{d}{2}\right)^2$
$= \pi \left(\frac{8}{2}\right)^2$
$= \pi(4)^2$
$= 16\pi$
$\approx 50.3 \text{ units}^2$

12. $A = \pi \left(\frac{d}{2}\right)^2$
$= \pi \left(\frac{13}{2}\right)^2$
$= \pi(6.5)^2$
$= 42.25\pi$
$\approx 132.7 \text{ units}^2$

13. $x^2 = 16$
$x = \sqrt{16}, -\sqrt{16}$
$x = 4, -4$

14. $169 = y^2$
$\sqrt{169}, -\sqrt{169} = y$
$13, -13 = y$

15. $121 = p^2$
$\sqrt{121}, -\sqrt{121} = p$
$11, -11 = p$

16. $m^2 = \frac{25}{9}$
$m = \sqrt{\frac{25}{9}}, -\sqrt{\frac{25}{9}}$
$m = \frac{5}{3}, -\frac{5}{3}$

Communicating About Mathematics

1. $V = 9 \cdot 9 \cdot \frac{1}{2} \cdot \frac{4}{3}\pi r^3$
$= 9 \cdot 9 \cdot \frac{1}{2} \cdot \frac{4}{3}\pi \left(\frac{3}{4}\right)^3$
$\approx 71.6 \text{ in.}^3$

2. $71.6 \text{ in.}^3 \cdot \dfrac{\frac{1}{231} \text{ gallon}}{1 \text{ in.}^3} \cdot \dfrac{\$4500}{1 \text{ gallon}} \approx \$1394.81$

3.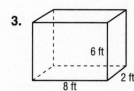

$B = 8(2) = 16 \text{ ft}^2$
$P = 2(8) + 2(2) = 16 + 4 = 20 \text{ ft}$
$S = 2B + Ph = 2(16) + 20(6) = 32 + 120 = 152 \text{ ft}^2$
The answer is in square feet.

4. *Sample answer:* They are both rectangular prisms with the same height and depth; 12 feet long, 6 feet high, and 2 feet deep.

5. $V = lwh = 12(6)(2) = 144 \text{ ft}^3$

$$144 \, \cancel{\text{ft}^3} \cdot \frac{12 \text{ in.}^3}{\cancel{\text{ft}^3}} \cdot \frac{\frac{1}{231} \, \cancel{\text{gallon}}}{1 \, \cancel{\text{in.}^3}} \cdot \frac{\$4500}{1 \, \cancel{\text{gallon}}} = \$33{,}662.34$$

$\$33{,}662.34 + 30{,}000 = \$63{,}662.34$

The cost is about \$63,662.34.

12.8 | *Exploring Similar Solids*

ONGOING ASSESSMENT

1. You can multiply each dimension of the model by 8 to find the dimensions of the actual room in feet (16 ft by 16 ft by 8 ft), then use the dimensions of the actual room to find the surface area and volume of the room. Or you can find the surface area (16 in.^{2}) of the model and multiply by 8^2 to find the surface area of the actual room in square feet, and you can find the volume (4 in.^{3}) of the model and multiply by 8^3 to find the volume of the actual room in cubic feet.

EXERCISES

1. Yes; they have the same shape and their corresponding lengths are proportional $\left(\frac{9}{6} = \frac{6}{4} = \frac{12}{8}\right)$.

2. No; their corresponding lengths are not proportional. $\left(\frac{18}{9} \neq \frac{9}{4}\right)$.

3. Yes; they have the same shape and their corresponding lengths are proportional $\left(\frac{36}{12} = \frac{15}{5}\right)$.

4. Scale factor: $\frac{60}{10} = 6$

5. $B = l \cdot w = 8(10) = 80 \text{ units}^2$

$P = 2l + 2w = 2(8) + 2(10) = 16 + 20 = 36 \text{ units}$

$S = 2B + Ph$

$\quad = 2(80) + 36 \cdot 12$

$\quad = 160 + 432 = 592 \text{ units}^2$

6. $\dfrac{S}{592} = \left(\dfrac{6}{1}\right)^2$

$\dfrac{S}{592} = 36$

$S = 592 \cdot 36$

$S = 21{,}312 \text{ units}^2$

Check: $S = 2B + Ph$

$\quad = 2(72 \cdot 60) + (2 \cdot 72 + 2 \cdot 60)48$

$\quad = 8640 + (264)48$

$\quad = 8640 + 12{,}672$

$\quad = 21{,}312 \text{ units}^2$

7. Volume of Prism $A = 6^3 \cdot$ Volume of Prism B

---

8. A

A. $\frac{6}{12} = \frac{9}{18} = \frac{7}{14}$

B. $\frac{6}{9} \neq \frac{9}{7}$

C. $\frac{6}{16} \neq \frac{7}{16}$

9. C

A. $\frac{40}{24} \neq \frac{16}{10}$

B. $\frac{40}{20} \neq \frac{16}{6}$

C. $\frac{40}{30} = \frac{16}{12}$

10.

$$30^2 + x^2 = (32.5)^2$$
$$900 + x^2 = 1056.25$$
$$x^2 = 156.25$$
$$x = 12.5 \text{ cm}$$
$$\frac{12}{30} = \frac{y}{12.5}$$
$$\frac{2}{5} = \frac{y}{12.5}$$
$$12.5 \cdot \frac{2}{5} = y$$
$$5 \text{ cm} = y$$

11.

$$\frac{y}{8} = \frac{30}{10}$$
$$\frac{y}{8} = 3$$
$$y = 24 \text{ in.}$$
$$\frac{x}{5} = \frac{10}{30}$$
$$\frac{x}{5} = \frac{1}{3}$$
$$x = 5 \cdot \frac{1}{3}$$
$$x = 1\frac{2}{3} \text{ in.}$$

12.

Scale Factor	Solid A Length	Solid A Surface Area	Solid A Volume	Solid B Length	Solid B Surface Area	Solid B Volume
3	15 ft	400 ft^2	300 ft^2	5 ft	$44\frac{4}{9}$ ft^2	$11\frac{1}{9}$ ft^3
7.5	22.5 cm	11,137.5 cm^2	68,343.75 cm^3	3 cm	198 cm^2	162 cm^3

Row 1:

$$\frac{15}{L_B} = 3 \qquad \frac{400}{S_B} = 3^2 \qquad \frac{300}{V_B} = 3^3$$

$$\frac{L_B}{15} = \frac{1}{3} \qquad \frac{400}{S_B} = 9 \qquad \frac{300}{V_B} = 27$$

$$L_B = 15 \cdot \frac{1}{3} \qquad \frac{S_B}{400} = \frac{1}{9} \qquad \frac{V_B}{300} = \frac{1}{27}$$

$$L_B = 5 \text{ ft} \qquad S_B = 400 \cdot \frac{1}{9} \qquad V_B = 300 \cdot \frac{1}{27}$$

$$S_B = 44\frac{4}{9} \text{ ft}^2 \qquad V_B = 11\frac{1}{9} \text{ ft}^3$$

Row 2:

$$\frac{L_A}{3} = 7.5 \qquad \frac{V_A}{162} = 7.5^3 \qquad \frac{11,137.5}{S_B} = 7.5^2$$

$$L_A = 3 \cdot 7.5 \qquad \frac{V_A}{162} = 421.875 \qquad \frac{11,137.5}{S_B} = 56.25$$

$$L_A = 22.5 \text{ cm} \qquad V_A = 162 \cdot 421.875 \qquad \frac{S_B}{11,137.5} = \frac{1}{56.25}$$

$$V_A = 68,343.75 \text{ cm}^3 \qquad S_B = 11,137.5 \cdot \frac{1}{56.25}$$

$$S_B = 198 \text{ cm}^2$$

13. $\dfrac{1 \text{ ft}}{\frac{1}{12} \text{ in.}} = \dfrac{12 \text{ in.}}{\frac{1}{12} \text{ in.}} = 12 \div \dfrac{1}{12} = 12 \cdot 12 = 144$

14. $144^3 = 2{,}985{,}984$

15. Always

16. Never

17. Sometimes

18. Always

19. A; $B = 3^2 = 9$

$P = 3 + 3 + 3 + 3 = 12$

$S = 2B + Ph = 2(9) + 12(3) = 54;$

$B = 9^2 = 81$

$P = 4 \cdot 9 = 36$

$S = 2B + Ph$

$\quad = 2(81) + 36(9) = 486; \ \frac{54}{486} = \frac{1}{9}$

20. a. $\dfrac{10 \cancel{\text{ft}}}{2.5 \text{ in.}} \times \dfrac{12 \text{ in.}}{1 \cancel{\text{ft}}} = \dfrac{120}{2.5} = 48$

Actual length:

$\quad 15.75 \text{ in.} \times 48 = 756 \text{ in.} \times \dfrac{1 \text{ ft}}{12 \text{ in.}} = 63 \text{ ft}$

Actual height:

$\quad 3 \text{ in.} \times 48 = 144 \text{ in.} \times \dfrac{1 \text{ ft}}{12 \text{ in.}} = 12 \text{ ft}$

Actual width: 10 ft

b. $B = lw = 63 \times 10 = 630 \text{ ft}^2$

$P = 2(63) + 2(10) = 126 + 20 = 146 \text{ ft}$

$S = 2B + Ph = 2(630) + 146(12) = 3012 \text{ ft}^2;$

$V = lwh = 63 \times 12 \times 10 = 7560 \text{ ft}^3$

c. No; $\dfrac{3012 \text{ ft}^2}{188.25 \text{ in.}^2} \times \dfrac{12^2 \text{ in.}^2}{1 \text{ ft}^2} = 2304 = 48^2 \neq 48$

Chapter **R E V I E W**

1. $C = \pi d = \pi(14) \approx 43.98 \text{ in.}$

$A = \pi \left(\dfrac{d}{2} \right)^2$

$\quad = \pi \left(\dfrac{14}{2} \right)^2$

$\quad = \pi (7)^2$

$\quad \approx 153.94 \text{ in.}^2$

2. $C = 2\pi r$

$\quad = 2\pi(12) \approx 75.40 \text{ cm}$

$A = \pi r^2$

$\quad = \pi(12)^2 \approx 452.39 \text{ cm}^2$

3. $C = \pi d = \pi(11.2) \approx 35.2 \text{ m};$

$A = \pi r^2 = \pi \left(\dfrac{11.2}{2} \right)^2$

$\quad = \pi(5.6)^2$

$\quad \approx 98.5 \text{ m}^2$

4. Trigangular prism; 5 faces, 6 vertices, 9 edges

5. Hexagonal prism; 8 faces, 12 vertices, 18 edges

6. Cube; 6 faces, 8 vertices, 12 edges

7. $B = \frac{1}{2}bh = \frac{1}{2}(10)(12) = 60 \text{ cm}^2$

$10^2 + 12^2 = c^2$

$100 + 144 = c^2$

$244 = c^2$

$\sqrt{244} = c$

$P = \sqrt{244} + 10 + 12 = \left(22 + \sqrt{244} \right) \text{ cm}$

$S = 2B + Ph = 2(60) + \left(22 + \sqrt{244} \right)18 = 120 + 396 + 18\sqrt{244} = 516 + 18\sqrt{244} \approx 797.17 \text{ cm}^2$

8. $B = \pi r^2 = \pi(8)^2 = 64\pi$ mm^2
$C = 2\pi r = 2\pi(8) = 16\pi$ mm
$S = 2B + Ch$
$\quad = 2(64\pi) + 16\pi(10)$
$\quad = 128\pi + 160\pi$
$\quad = 288\pi$
$\quad \approx 904.78$ mm^2

9. $B = lw = 8(6) = 48$ in.^{2}
$P = 2(8) + 2(6)$
$\quad = 16 + 12 = 28$ in.
$S = 2B + Ph$
$\quad = 2(48) + 28(10)$
$\quad = 96 + 280$
$\quad = 376$ in.^{2}

10. $V = l \cdot w \cdot h$
$\quad = 14(4)(12)$
$\quad = 672$ yd^3

11. $B = \frac{1}{2}(6)(8) = 24$ m^2
$V = Bh$
$\quad = 24(7)$
$\quad = 168$ m^3

12. $B = \frac{1}{2}(3)(4) = 6$ cm^3
$V = 6(9) = 54$ cm^3

13. $B = l \cdot w$
$\quad = 24(8) = 192$ mm^2
$V = \frac{1}{3}Bh$
$\quad = \frac{1}{3}(192)(8)$
$\quad = 512$ mm^3

14. $B = 6(6) = 36$ ft^2
$V = \frac{1}{3}Bh$
$\quad = \frac{1}{3}(36)(6)$
$\quad = 72$ ft^3

15. $B = 7.5(5) = 37.5$ m^2
$V = \frac{1}{3}Bh$
$\quad = \frac{1}{3}(37.5)(10)$
$\quad = 125$ m^3

16. $B = \pi r^2$
$\quad = \pi(4)^2 = 16\pi$ in.^{2}
$V = Bh = 16\pi(1)$
$\quad = 16\pi \approx 50.27$ in.^{3}

17. $B = \pi r^2 = \pi(3)^2 = 9\pi$ m^2
$V = Bh = 9\pi(7) \approx 197.92$ m^3

18. $B = \pi r^2$
$\quad = \pi(2.5)^2$
$\quad = 6.25\pi$ cm^2
$V = Bh$
$\quad = 6.25\pi(10)$
$\quad \approx 196.35$ cm^3

19. $V = \frac{1}{3}Bh$
$\quad = \frac{1}{3}\pi(20)^2(45)$
$\quad \approx 18{,}849.56$ in.^{3}

20. $V = \frac{1}{3}\pi r^2 h$
$\quad = \frac{1}{3}\pi(5^2)(10)$
$\quad \approx 261.80$ cm^3

21. $V = \frac{1}{3}\pi r^2 h$
$\quad = \frac{1}{3}\pi\left(\frac{17}{2}\right)^2(30.1)$
$\quad = \frac{1}{3}\pi(8.5)^2(30.1)$
$\quad \approx 2277.37$ m^3

22. $V = \left(\frac{4}{3}\right)\pi r^3$
$\quad = \left(\frac{4}{3}\right)\pi(2)^3$
$\quad \approx 33.51$ in.^{3}

23. $V = \left(\frac{4}{3}\right)\pi r^3$
$\quad = \left(\frac{4}{3}\right)\pi(8)^3$
$\quad \approx 2144.66$ cm^3

24. $V = \frac{4}{3}\pi r^3$
$\quad = \frac{4}{3}\pi\left(\frac{9.5}{2}\right)^3$
$\quad = \frac{4}{3}\pi(4.75)^3$
$\quad \approx 448.92$ m^3

25. $\frac{54}{9} = 6$

26. $r =$ radius of small cylinder in centimeters
$\frac{r}{18} = \frac{1}{6}$
$r = 18 \cdot \frac{1}{6}$
$r = 3$ cm

Chapter ASSESSMENT

1. 5

2. 6

3. 9

4. $C = 2\pi r = 2\pi(2) = 4\pi \approx 12.57$ ft

5. $B = \pi r^2 = \pi(2)^2 = 4\pi \approx 12.57$ ft^2

6. $S = 2B + Ch$
$= 2(4\pi) + 4\pi(9)$
$= 8\pi + 36\pi$
$= 44\pi \approx 138.23$ ft^2

7. $V = Bh$
$= 4\pi(9)$
$= 36\pi \approx 113.10$ ft^3

8. $B = 3(4) = 12$ cm^2
$V = \frac{1}{3}Bh$
$= \frac{1}{3}(12)(4) = 16$ cm^3

9. $B = \frac{1}{2}(b_1 + b_2)h$
$= \frac{1}{2}(3 + 5)4$
$= 16$ ft^2
$V = Bh$
$= 16(6) = 96$ ft^3

10. $B = 2(4) = 8$ in.^{2}
$P = 2(2) + 2(4)$
$= 4 + 8$
$= 12$ in.
$S = 2B + Ph$
$= 2(8) + 12(3)$
$= 16 + 36$
$= 52$ in.^{2}

11. $B = \frac{1}{2}bh = \frac{1}{2}(6)(2) = 6$ yd^2
$2^2 + 6^2 = c^2$
$4 + 36 = c^2$
$40 = c^2$
$\sqrt{40} = c$
$P = 2 + 6 + \sqrt{40}$
$= (8 + \sqrt{40})$ yd
$S = 2B + Ph$
$= 2(6) + (8 + \sqrt{40})4$
$= 12 + 32 + 4\sqrt{40}$
$= 44 + 4\sqrt{40}$
≈ 69.30 yd^2

12. Scale factor: $\frac{9}{6} = \frac{3}{2}$

13. $x =$ length of edge on base of Figure A in feet
$\frac{9}{6} = \frac{x}{4}$
$4 \cdot \frac{9}{6} = 4 \cdot \frac{x}{4}$
$6 = x$
$P = 6(6) = 36$ ft
$S = 2B + Ph$
$= 2(54\sqrt{3}) + 36(9)$
$= 108\sqrt{3} + 324$
≈ 511.06 ft^2

14. $V = Bh$
$= 54\sqrt{3}(9)$
$= 486\sqrt{3}$
≈ 841.78 ft^3

15. $S =$ surface area of Figure B in ft^2.

$$\left(\frac{2}{3}\right)^2 = \frac{S}{511.06}$$

$$\frac{4}{9} = \frac{S}{511.06}$$

$$511.06 \cdot \frac{4}{9} = S$$

$$227.14 \text{ ft}^2 \approx S$$

16. $V =$ volume of Figure B in ft^3.

$$\left(\frac{2}{3}\right)^2 = \frac{V}{841.78}$$

$$\frac{8}{27} = \frac{V}{841.78}$$

$$841.78 \cdot \frac{8}{27} = V$$

$$249.42 \text{ ft}^3 \approx V$$

17. $B = \pi r^2 = \pi(2)^2 = 4\pi \text{ ft}^2$

$C = 2\pi r = 2\pi(2) = 4\pi \text{ ft}$

$S = 2B + Ch$

$\quad = 2(4\pi) + 4\pi(0.25)$

$\quad = 8\pi + \pi$

$\quad = 9\pi$

$\quad \approx 28.27 \text{ ft}^2$

18. $V = Bh$

$\quad = 4\pi(8)$

$\quad = 32\pi$

$\quad \approx 100.53 \text{ ft}^3$

19. $B = \pi \left(\frac{d}{2}\right)^2 = \pi \left(\frac{8}{2}\right)^2 = 16\pi \text{ ft}^2$

$V = Bh$

$\quad = 16\pi(20)$

$\quad = 320\pi \approx 1005.31 \text{ ft}^3$

20. $V = \frac{4}{3}\pi \left(\frac{d}{2}\right)^3$

$\quad = \frac{4}{3}\pi \left(\frac{2160}{2}\right)^3$

$\quad = \frac{4}{3}\pi (1080)^3$

$\quad = 1{,}679{,}600{,}000\pi$

$\quad \approx 5{,}276{,}700{,}000 \text{ mi}^3$

Standardized Test Practice

1. A; $A = \pi r^2$

$\quad \approx (3.14)\left(\frac{2.5}{2}\right)^2$

$\quad \approx 4.9 \text{ m}^2$

2. C; $C = 2\pi r$

$\quad \approx 2(3.14)(2.5)$

$\quad \approx 15.7 \text{ m}$

3. B

4. A; $V = \frac{1}{3}Bh$

$\quad = \frac{1}{3}\pi \left(\frac{3}{2}\right)^2 (6)$

$\quad \approx 14.1 \text{ ft}^3$

5. C; $V = \frac{4}{3}\pi r^3$

$\quad = \frac{4}{3}\pi 5^3$

$\quad \approx 523.6 \text{ ft}^3$

6. B; $V_{\text{prism}} = lwh = 9.42(4)(16) = 602.88 \text{ cm}^3$

$V_{\text{cylinder}} = Bh = \pi \left(\frac{8}{2}\right)^2 (12) \approx 603.18 \text{ cm}^3$

$S_{\text{prism}} = 2B + Ph = 2(9.42)(4) + [2(9.42) + 2(4)](16)$

$\qquad\qquad = 75.2 + (26.84)(16) = 504.64 \text{ cm}^2$

$S_{\text{cylinder}} = 2B + Ch$

$\qquad\quad = 2(\pi)\left(\frac{8}{2}\right)^2 + \pi(8)(12) = 32\pi + 96\pi = 128\pi \approx 402.12 \text{ cm}^2$

7. B; $\dfrac{x}{7} = \dfrac{16}{10}$

$x = 11.2$ cm

8. B; Area$_{square} = 4^2 = 16$ m^2

Area$_{circle} = \pi r^2 = \pi(2^2) = 4\pi$ m^2

Area$_{region} = 16 - 4\pi \approx 3.4$ m^2

Cumulative **R E V I E W**

1. $\dfrac{8}{6} + \dfrac{1}{3} = \dfrac{8}{6} + \dfrac{1}{3} \cdot \dfrac{2}{2}$

$ = \dfrac{8}{6} + \dfrac{2}{6}$

$ = \dfrac{10}{6} = \dfrac{5}{3}$

2. $\dfrac{3}{4} \cdot \dfrac{8}{9} = \dfrac{\cancel{3} \cdot \cancel{4} \cdot 2}{\cancel{4} \cdot \cancel{3} \cdot 3}$

$ = \dfrac{2}{3}$

3. $\dfrac{7}{12} - \dfrac{5}{12} = \dfrac{2}{12}$

$ = \dfrac{1}{6}$

4. $\dfrac{12}{5} \div \dfrac{3}{5} = \dfrac{12}{5} \cdot \dfrac{5}{3}$

$ = \dfrac{4 \cdot \cancel{3} \cdot \cancel{5}}{\cancel{5} \cdot \cancel{3}}$

$ = 4$

5. $y + \dfrac{3}{4} = \dfrac{1}{2}$

$y + \dfrac{3}{4} - \dfrac{3}{4} = \dfrac{1}{2} - \dfrac{3}{4}$

$y = \dfrac{1}{2} \cdot \dfrac{2}{2} - \dfrac{3}{4}$

$y = \dfrac{2}{4} - \dfrac{3}{4}$

$y = -\dfrac{1}{4}$

6. $\dfrac{1}{3}m = \dfrac{1}{6}$

$3 \cdot \dfrac{1}{3}m = 3 \cdot \dfrac{1}{6}$

$m = \dfrac{3}{6}$

$m = \dfrac{1}{2}$

7. $\dfrac{4}{5} = 8a$

$\dfrac{4}{5} \div 8 = \dfrac{8a}{8}$

$\dfrac{4}{5} \cdot \dfrac{1}{8} = a$

$\dfrac{\cancel{4} \cdot 1}{5 \cdot \cancel{4} \cdot 2} = a$

$\dfrac{1}{10} = a$

8. $\dfrac{2}{7} = b - \dfrac{3}{2}$

$\dfrac{2}{7} + \dfrac{3}{2} = b - \dfrac{3}{2} + \dfrac{3}{2}$

$\dfrac{2}{7} \cdot \dfrac{2}{2} + \dfrac{3}{2} \cdot \dfrac{7}{7} = b$

$\dfrac{4}{14} + \dfrac{21}{14} = b$

$\dfrac{25}{14} = b$

9. $\dfrac{31}{40} \cdot \dfrac{26}{51} \approx 0.40$

10. $\dfrac{76}{55} + \dfrac{7}{35} \approx 1.58$

11. $\dfrac{93}{95} - \dfrac{54}{73} \approx 0.24$

12. $\dfrac{9}{92} \div \dfrac{26}{70} \approx 0.26$

13. $\dfrac{12}{36} = \dfrac{1}{3} = 0.\overline{3}$

$0.\overline{3} \cdot 100\% = 33.\overline{3}\%$

$ = 33\dfrac{1}{3}\%$

14. $\dfrac{8}{12} = \dfrac{\cancel{4} \cdot 2}{\cancel{4} \cdot 3}$

$ = \dfrac{2}{3} = 0.\overline{6}$

$0.\overline{6} \cdot 100\% = 66.\overline{6}\%$

$ = 66\dfrac{2}{3}\%$

15. $\dfrac{10}{25} = \dfrac{2 \cdot \cancel{5}}{5 \cdot \cancel{5}}$

$ = \dfrac{2}{5} = 0.4$

$0.4 \cdot 100\% = 40\%$

16. Secure: $55\% = \dfrac{55}{100} = \dfrac{\cancel{5} \cdot 11}{\cancel{5} \cdot 20} = \dfrac{11}{20}$

Somewhat secure: $28\% = \dfrac{28}{100} = \dfrac{\cancel{4} \cdot 7}{\cancel{4} \cdot 25} = \dfrac{7}{25}$

Not secure: $14\% = \dfrac{14}{100} = \dfrac{\cancel{2} \cdot 7}{\cancel{2} \cdot 50} = \dfrac{7}{50}$

Don't know: $3\% = \dfrac{3}{100}$

17. Secure: $\dfrac{11}{20}(500) = 275$

Somewhat secure: $\dfrac{7}{25} \cdot 500 = 140$

Not secure: $\dfrac{7}{50}(500) = 70$

Don't know: $\dfrac{3}{100}(500) = 15$

18. $\dfrac{100 \text{ mi}}{5 \text{ gal}} = 20$ mi/gal; rate

19. $\dfrac{18 \text{ people}}{24 \text{ people}} = \dfrac{18}{24} = \dfrac{\cancel{6} \cdot 3}{\cancel{6} \cdot 4} = \dfrac{3}{4}$; ratio

20. $\dfrac{99 \text{ chicks}}{100 \text{ chicks}} = \dfrac{99}{100}$; ratio

21.
$$\dfrac{3}{4} = \dfrac{x}{32}$$
$$32 \cdot \dfrac{3}{4} = 32 \cdot \dfrac{x}{32}$$
$$\dfrac{\cancel{4} \cdot 8 \cdot 3}{\cancel{4}} = x$$
$$24 = x$$

22.
$$\dfrac{18}{5} = \dfrac{3}{y}$$
$$\dfrac{5}{18} = \dfrac{y}{3}$$
$$3 \cdot \dfrac{5}{18} = 3 \cdot \dfrac{y}{3}$$
$$\dfrac{\cancel{3} \cdot 5}{\cancel{3} \cdot 6} = y$$
$$\dfrac{5}{6} = y$$

23.
$$\dfrac{z}{6} = \dfrac{5}{9}$$
$$6 \cdot \dfrac{z}{6} = 6 \cdot \dfrac{5}{9}$$
$$z = \dfrac{5 \cdot \cancel{3} \cdot 2}{\cancel{3} \cdot 3}$$
$$z = \dfrac{10}{3}$$

24.
$$\dfrac{24}{w} = \dfrac{3}{5}$$
$$\dfrac{w}{24} = \dfrac{5}{3}$$
$$24 \cdot \dfrac{w}{24} = 24 \cdot \dfrac{5}{3}$$
$$w = \dfrac{8 \cdot \cancel{3} \cdot 5}{\cancel{3}}$$
$$w = 40$$

25. $\dfrac{862 - 835}{835} = \dfrac{27}{835}$
$$\approx 0.0323$$
$$\approx 3.23\%$$

26. $\dfrac{862 - 14}{862} = \dfrac{848}{862}$
$$\approx 0.983$$
$$= 0.983 \cdot 100\%$$
$$= 98.3\%$$

27. $(6)3 = 18$

28. $\dfrac{6}{9} = \dfrac{2 \cdot \cancel{3}}{3 \cdot \cancel{3}} = \dfrac{2}{3}$

29. $x^2 = 121$
$$x = \sqrt{121}, -\sqrt{121}$$
$$x = 11, -11;$$
Rational

30. $84 = y^2$
$$y = \sqrt{84}, -\sqrt{84};$$
Irrational

31. $-8 = m^2 - 17$
$$9 = m^2$$
$$m = \sqrt{9}, -\sqrt{9}$$
$$m = 3, -3;$$
Rational

32. $h^2 + (18.6)^2 = 25^2$
$$h^2 + 345.96 = 625$$
$$h^2 = 279.04$$
$$h = \sqrt{279.04}$$
$$h \approx 16.7 \text{ in.}$$

33. $7^2 + 24^2 = c^2$
$$49 + 576 = c^2$$
$$625 = c^2$$
$$\sqrt{625} = c$$
$$25 = c$$

34. $5^2 + b^2 = 15^2$

$\quad 25 + b^2 = 225$

$\qquad b^2 = 200$

$\qquad b = \sqrt{200}$

$\qquad b \approx 14.14$

35. $a^2 + 13^2 = 15^2$

$\quad a^2 + 169 = 225$

$\qquad a^2 = 56$

$\qquad a = \sqrt{56}$

$\qquad a \approx 7.48$

36. $x + 14 \le 9$

$\qquad x \le -5$

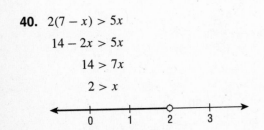

37.

$$\frac{2}{3} < -4y$$

$$\frac{2}{3} \div (-4) > \frac{-4y}{-4}$$

$$\frac{2}{3} \cdot \left(-\frac{1}{4}\right) > y$$

$$\frac{2(-1)}{3 \cdot 2 \cdot 2} > y$$

$$-\frac{1}{6} > y$$

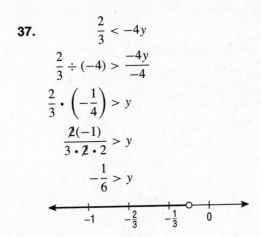

38. $-17 \le -12n + 19$

$\quad -36 \le -12n$

$\quad \dfrac{-36}{-12} \ge \dfrac{-12n}{-12}$

$\qquad 3 \ge n$

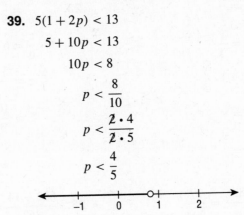

39. $5(1 + 2p) < 13$

$\quad 5 + 10p < 13$

$\qquad 10p < 8$

$\qquad p < \dfrac{8}{10}$

$\qquad p < \dfrac{2 \cdot 4}{2 \cdot 5}$

$\qquad p < \dfrac{4}{5}$

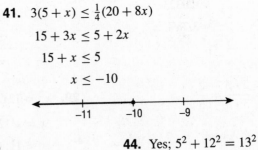

40. $2(7 - x) > 5x$

$\quad 14 - 2x > 5x$

$\qquad 14 > 7x$

$\qquad 2 > x$

41. $3(5 + x) \le \frac{1}{4}(20 + 8x)$

$\quad 15 + 3x \le 5 + 2x$

$\qquad 15 + x \le 5$

$\qquad x \le -10$

42. No; $5 + 9 \not> 14$

43. No; $2 + 4 \not> 6$

44. Yes; $5^2 + 12^2 = 13^2$

45. Any two of: $\overleftrightarrow{ED}, \overrightarrow{DH}, \overrightarrow{DM},$ $\overleftrightarrow{EM}, \overleftrightarrow{HM}$

46. Any five of: $\overline{CA}, \overline{CB}, \overline{CK},$ $\overline{CJ}, \overline{CE}, \overline{CF}$

47. $\overrightarrow{KG}$

48. Any two pairs of: $\angle ACB$ and $\angle KCE$, $\angle BCE$ and $\angle ACK$, $\angle DEC$ and $\angle FEH$, $\angle DEF$ and $\angle CEH$, $\angle LKC$ and $\angle JKH$, $\angle LKJ$ and $\angle CKH$, $\angle EHK$ and $\angle GHM$, $\angle EHG$ and $\angle KHM$

49. $\angle ACB$ and $\angle CED$, $\angle BCE$ and $\angle DEF$, $\angle ACK$ and $\angle CEH$, $\angle KCE$ and $\angle HEF$, $\angle LKC$ and $\angle KHE$, $\angle CKH$ and $\angle EHG$, $\angle LKJ$ and $\angle KHM$, $\angle JKH$ and $\angle MHG$

50. Any two pairs of: $\angle ACB$ and $\angle LKC$, $\angle ACK$ and $\angle LKJ$, $\angle BCE$ and $\angle CKH$, $\angle KCE$ and $\angle JKH$, $\angle CED$ and $\angle KHE$, $\angle CEH$ and $\angle KHM$, $\angle DEF$ and $\angle EHG$, $\angle HEF$ and $\angle MHG$

51. $\angle ACB$, $\angle CED$, $\angle FEH$, $\angle KCE$

52. Right

53. Obtuse

54. Acute

55. $x = 12$ cm; $y = 12$ cm

56. $x = 5$ m; $y = 5$ m

57. $x = 4$ in.; $y = 10$ in.

58. $10^2 = 8^2 + b^2$
$100 = 64 + b^2$
$36 = b^2$
$6 = b$
$P = 6 + 8 + 6 + 6 + 10$
$= 36$ units
$A = 8(6) + \frac{1}{2}(8)(6)$
$= 48 + 24$
$= 72$ units^2

59. $P = 8 + 4.5 + 4 + 4.5$
$= 21$ units
$2^2 + b^2 = (4.5)^2$
$4 + b^2 = 20.25$
$b^2 = 16.25$
$b = 4.03$
$A = \frac{1}{2}(8 + 4)(4.03)$
$= \frac{1}{2}(12)(4.03)$
≈ 24.18 units^2

60. $P = 17 + 16 + 17 + 16$
$= 66$ units
$A = 16(14)$
$= 224$ units^2

61. Yes

62. No. There is no relationship between BN and CM or between BB' and CC'.

63. Yes. In a reflection, the reflection line bisects each segment that joins an original point to its image.

64. Yes

65. No. D is farther from the center of rotation than F is; so $DD' > FF'$.

66. $A(2, 3) \rightarrow (2, 3 - 3) = (2, 0)$
$B(5, 3) \rightarrow (5, 3 - 3) = (5, 0)$
$C(4, 1) \rightarrow (4, 1 - 3) = (4, -2)$
$D(1, 1) \rightarrow (1, 1 - 3) = (1, -2)$

67. $A(2, 3) \rightarrow (2 + 2, 3) = (4, 3)$
$B(5, 3) \rightarrow (5 + 2, 3) = (7, 3)$
$C(4, 1) \rightarrow (4 + 2, 1) = (6, 1)$
$D(1, 1) \rightarrow (1 + 2, 1) = (3, 1)$

68. $A(2, 3) \rightarrow (2 + 1, 3 + 2) = (3, 5)$
$B(5, 3) \rightarrow (5 + 1, 3 + 2) = (6, 5)$
$C(4, 1) \rightarrow (4 + 1, 1 + 2) = (5, 3)$
$D(1, 1) \rightarrow (1 + 1, 1 + 2) = (2, 3)$

69. $\dfrac{24 \text{ in.}}{4 \text{ squares}} = 6$ in.

70. $\dfrac{36}{6} = 6$

71. Quilt: $P = 36(2) + 24(2)$ Piece: $P = 4(2) + 6(2)$
$= 120$ in. $= 20$ in.
$A = 36(24)$ $A = 4(6)$
$= 864$ in.^{2} $= 24$ in.^{2}

72. $\frac{120}{20} = 6$; this is the same as the scale factor.

73. $\frac{864}{24} = 36$; this is the same as the square of the scale factor.

74. $\frac{b}{60} = \tan 45°$

75. $\tan 45° = \dfrac{b}{60}$

$60 \tan 45° = 60 \cdot \dfrac{b}{60}$

$60 \text{ ft} = b$

76. $C = \pi d$ $A = \pi \left(\dfrac{d}{2}\right)^2$

$\quad = \pi(12)$

$\quad \approx 37.70 \text{ in.}$ $= \pi \left(\dfrac{12}{2}\right)^2$

$= 36\pi \approx 113.10 \text{ in.}^2$

77. $C = \pi d$ $A = \pi \left(\dfrac{d}{2}\right)^2$

$\quad = \pi(3.4)$

$\quad \approx 10.68 \text{ cm}$ $= \pi \left(\dfrac{3.4}{2}\right)^2$

$= 2.89\pi \approx 9.08 \text{ cm}^2$

78. $C = \pi d$ $A = \pi \left(\dfrac{d}{2}\right)^2$

$\quad = \pi(9.25)$

$\quad \approx 29.06 \text{ in.}$ $= \pi \left(\dfrac{9.25}{2}\right)^2$

$= 21.39\pi \approx 67.20 \text{ in.}^2$

79. $B = 13(5) = 65 \text{ in.}^2$

$P = 2(13) + 2(5) = 26 + 10 = 36 \text{ in.}$

$S = 2B + Ph$

$\quad = 2(65) + 36(6)$

$\quad = 130 + 216$

$\quad = 346 \text{ in.}^2$

$V = lwh = 13(5)(6) = 390 \text{ in.}^3$

80. $B = \pi r^2 = \pi(4.5)^2 = 20.25\pi$

$C = 2\pi r = 2\pi(4.5) = 9\pi$

$S = 2B + Ch$

$\quad = 2(20.25\pi) + 9\pi(4)$

$\quad = 40.5\pi + 36\pi$

$\quad = 76.5\pi$

$\quad \approx 240.33 \text{ cm}^2$

$V = Bh = 20.25\pi(4) = 81\pi \approx 254.47 \text{ cm}^3$

81. $a^2 + b^2 = c^2$

$3^2 + 4^2 = c^2$

$9 + 16 = c^2$

$25 = c^2$

$\sqrt{25} = c$

$5 = c$

$B = \frac{1}{2}bh = \frac{1}{2}(3)(4) = 6 \text{ in.}^2$

$P = 3 + 4 + 5 = 12 \text{ in.}$

$S = 2B + Ph$

$\quad = 2(6) + 12(3.5)$

$\quad = 12 + 42 = 54 \text{ in.}^2$

$V = Bh = 6(3.5) = 21 \text{ in.}^3$

82. $B = 6^2 = 36 \text{ ft}^2$

$V = \frac{1}{3}Bh = \frac{1}{3}(36)(4) = 48 \text{ ft}^3$

83. $V = \dfrac{4}{3}\pi r^3 = \dfrac{4}{3}\pi(9.5)^3$

$\quad = \dfrac{3429.5}{3}\pi \approx 3591.36 \text{ cm}^3$

84. $B = \pi r^2 = \pi(6)^2 = 36\pi \text{ in.}^2$

$V = \frac{1}{3}Bh = \frac{1}{3}(36\pi)(8) = 96\pi \approx 301.59 \text{ in.}^3$

Chapter 13
Exploring Linear Equations

ONGOING ASSESSMENT

1. $F = \frac{9}{5} \cdot C + 32$

    $F = \frac{9}{5} \cdot (-40) + 32$

    $F = -72 + 32$

    $F = -40$

    $-40°F$ and $-40°C$ are the same temperature.

EXERCISES

1. **a.** $(1, 2)$

    $2x + 3y = 7$

    $2(1) + 3(2) \overset{?}{=} 7$

    $2 + 6 \overset{?}{=} 7$

    $8 \neq 7$

    b. $(2, 1)$

    $2x + 3y = 7$

    $2(2) + 3(1) \overset{?}{=} 7$

    $4 + 3 \overset{?}{=} 7$

    $7 = 7$

    c. $(5, -1)$

    $2x + 3y = 7$

    $2(5) + 3(-1) \overset{?}{=} 7$

    $10 - 3 \overset{?}{=} 7$

    $7 = 7$

    d. $(4, -1)$

    $2x + 3y = 7$

    $2(4) + 3(-1) \overset{?}{=} 7$

    $8 - 3 \overset{?}{=} 7$

    $5 \neq 7$

    b. and **c.** are solutions of $2x + 3y = 7$.

2. **a.** No; r is raised to the second power.
    b. Yes; variables occur to the first power only.
    c. Yes; variables occur to the first power only.
    d. Yes; variables occur to the first power only.

3. $y = x + 5$

$x = -3;$ $y = -3 + 5 = 2 \Rightarrow (-3, 2)$
$x = -2;$ $y = -2 + 5 = 3 \Rightarrow (-2, 3)$
$x = -1;$ $y = -1 + 5 = 4 \Rightarrow (-1, 4)$
$x = 0;$ $y = 0 + 5 = 5 \Rightarrow (0, 5)$
$x = 1;$ $y = 1 + 5 = 6 \Rightarrow (1, 6)$
$x = 2;$ $y = 2 + 5 = 7 \Rightarrow (2, 7)$
$x = 3;$ $y = 3 + 5 = 8 \Rightarrow (3, 8)$

x	-3	-2	-1	0	1	2	3
y	2	3	4	5	6	7	8

4. $y = 3x - 3$

$x = -3;$ $y = 3(-3) - 3 = -12 \Rightarrow (-3, -12)$
$x = -2;$ $y = 3(-2) - 3 = -9 \Rightarrow (-2, -9)$
$x = -1;$ $y = 3(-1) - 3 = -6 \Rightarrow (-1, -6)$
$x = 0;$ $y = 3(0) - 3 = -3 \Rightarrow (0, -3)$
$x = 1;$ $y = 3(1) - 3 = 0 \Rightarrow (1, 0)$
$x = 2;$ $y = 3(2) - 3 = 3 \Rightarrow (2, 3)$
$x = 3;$ $y = 3(3) - 3 = 6 \Rightarrow (3, 6)$

x	-3	-2	-1	0	1	2	3
y	-12	-9	-6	-3	0	3	6

5. $y = 5x + 6$

$x = -3;$ $y = 5(-3) + 6 = -9 \Rightarrow (-3, -9)$
$x = -2;$ $y = 5(-2) + 6 = -4 \Rightarrow (-2, -4)$
$x = -1;$ $y = 5(-1) + 6 = 1 \Rightarrow (-1, 1)$
$x = 0;$ $y = 5(0) + 6 = 6 \Rightarrow (0, 6)$
$x = 1;$ $y = 5(1) + 6 = 11 \Rightarrow (1, 11)$
$x = 2;$ $y = 5(2) + 6 = 16 \Rightarrow (2, 16)$
$x = 3;$ $y = 5(3) + 6 = 21 \Rightarrow (3, 21)$

x	-3	-2	-1	0	1	2	3
y	-9	-4	1	6	11	16	21

6. $2x - y = 4$

$x = -3;$ $2(-3) - y = 4,$ $y = -10 \Rightarrow (-3, -10)$
$x = -2;$ $2(-2) - y = 4,$ $y = -8 \Rightarrow (-2, -8)$
$x = -1;$ $2(-1) - y = 4,$ $y = -6 \Rightarrow (-1, -6)$
$x = 0;$ $2(0) - y = 4,$ $y = -4 \Rightarrow (0, -4)$
$x = 1;$ $2(1) - y = 4,$ $y = -2 \Rightarrow (1, -2)$
$x = 2;$ $2(2) - y = 4,$ $y = 0 \Rightarrow (2, 0)$
$x = 3;$ $2(3) - y = 4,$ $y = 2 \Rightarrow (3, 2)$

x	-3	-2	-1	0	1	2	3
y	-10	-8	-6	-4	-2	0	2

7. $(0, -5)$

$$7x - y = 5$$
$$7(0) - (-5) \stackrel{?}{=} 5$$
$$0 + 5 \stackrel{?}{=} 5$$
$$5 = 5$$

Yes

8. $(2, 1)$

$$7x - y = 5$$
$$7(2) - 1 \stackrel{?}{=} 5$$
$$14 - 1 \stackrel{?}{=} 5$$
$$13 \neq 5$$

No

9. $(-1, 12)$

$$7x - y = 5$$
$$7(-1) - 12 \stackrel{?}{=} 5$$
$$7 - 12 \stackrel{?}{=} 5$$
$$19 \neq 5$$

No

10. $\left(\frac{1}{2}, -\frac{3}{2}\right)$

$$7x - y = 5$$
$$7\left(\frac{1}{2}\right) - \left(-\frac{3}{2}\right) \stackrel{?}{=} 5$$
$$\frac{7}{2} + \frac{3}{2} \stackrel{?}{=} 5$$
$$\frac{10}{2} \stackrel{?}{=} 5$$
$$5 = 5$$

Yes

11. $y = x - 8$

$x = -3;$ $y = -3 - 8,$ $y = -11 \Rightarrow (-3, -11)$
$x = -2;$ $y = -2 - 8,$ $y = -10 \Rightarrow (-2, -10)$
$x = -1;$ $y = -1 - 8,$ $y = -9 \Rightarrow (-1, -9)$
$x = 0;$ $y = 0 - 8,$ $y = -8 \Rightarrow (0, -8)$
$x = 1;$ $y = 1 - 8,$ $y = -7 \Rightarrow (1, -7)$
$x = 2;$ $y = 2 - 8,$ $y = -6 \Rightarrow (2, -6)$
$x = 3;$ $y = 3 - 8,$ $y = -5 \Rightarrow (3, -5)$

x	-3	-2	-1	0	1	2	3
y	-11	-10	-9	-8	-7	-6	-5

12. $y = 2x + 4$

$x = -3;$ $y = 2(-3) + 4,$ $y = -2 \Rightarrow (-3, -2)$
$x = -2;$ $y = 2(-2) + 4,$ $y = 0 \Rightarrow (-2, 0)$
$x = -1;$ $y = 2(-1) + 4,$ $y = 2 \Rightarrow (-1, 2)$
$x = 0;$ $y = 2(0) + 4,$ $y = 4 \Rightarrow (0, 4)$
$x = 1;$ $y = 2(1) + 4,$ $y = 6 \Rightarrow (1, 6)$
$x = 2;$ $y = 2(2) + 4,$ $y = 8 \Rightarrow (2, 8)$
$x = 3;$ $y = 2(3) + 4,$ $y = 10 \Rightarrow (3, 10)$

x	-3	-2	-1	0	1	2	3
y	-2	0	2	4	6	8	10

13. $4x + y = 20$

$x = -3;$ $4(-3) + y = 20,$ $y = 32 \Rightarrow (-3, 32)$
$x = -2;$ $4(-2) + y = 20,$ $y = 28 \Rightarrow (-2, 28)$
$x = -1;$ $4(-1) + y = 20,$ $y = 24 \Rightarrow (-1, 24)$
$x = 0;$ $4(0) + y = 20,$ $y = 20 \Rightarrow (0, 20)$
$x = 1;$ $4(1) + y = 20,$ $y = 16 \Rightarrow (1, 16)$
$x = 2;$ $4(2) + y = 20,$ $y = 12 \Rightarrow (2, 12)$
$x = 3;$ $4(3) + y = 20,$ $y = 8 \Rightarrow (3, 8)$

x	-3	-2	-1	0	1	2	3
y	32	28	24	20	16	12	8

14. $6x - y = 18$

$x = -3;$ $6(-3) - y = 18,$ $y = -36 \Rightarrow (-3, -36)$
$x = -2;$ $6(-2) - y = 18,$ $y = -30 \Rightarrow (-2, -30)$
$x = -1;$ $6(-1) - y = 18,$ $y = -24 \Rightarrow (-1, -24)$
$x = 0;$ $6(0) - y = 18,$ $y = -18 \Rightarrow (0, -18)$
$x = 1;$ $6(1) - y = 18,$ $y = -12 \Rightarrow (1, -12)$
$x = 2;$ $6(2) - y = 18,$ $y = -6 \Rightarrow (2, -6)$
$x = 3;$ $6(3) - y = 18,$ $y = 0 \Rightarrow (3, 0)$

x	-3	-2	-1	0	1	2	3
y	-36	-30	-24	-18	-12	-6	0

15. $x + y = 6$

$x = -3;$ $-3 + y = 6,$ $y = 9 \Rightarrow (-3, 9)$
$x = -2;$ $-2 + y = 6,$ $y = 8 \Rightarrow (-2, 8)$
$x = -1;$ $-1 + y = 6,$ $y = 7 \Rightarrow (-1, 7)$
$x = 0;$ $0 + y = 6,$ $y = 6 \Rightarrow (0, 6)$
$x = 1;$ $1 + y = 6,$ $y = 5 \Rightarrow (1, 5)$
$x = 2;$ $2 + y = 6,$ $y = 4 \Rightarrow (2, 4)$
$x = 3;$ $3 + y = 6,$ $y = 3 \Rightarrow (3, 3)$

x	-3	-2	-1	0	1	2	3
y	9	8	7	6	5	4	3

16. $x + 2y = 13$

$x = -3;$ $-3 + 2y = 13,$ $y = 8 \Rightarrow (-3, 8)$
$x = -2;$ $-2 + 2y = 13,$ $y = 7\frac{1}{2} \Rightarrow \left(-2, 7\frac{1}{2}\right)$
$x = -1;$ $-1 + 2y = 13,$ $y = 7 \Rightarrow (-1, 7)$
$x = 0;$ $0 + 2y = 13,$ $y = 6\frac{1}{2} \Rightarrow \left(0, 6\frac{1}{2}\right)$
$x = 1;$ $1 + 2y = 13,$ $y = 6 \Rightarrow (1, 6)$
$x = 2;$ $2 + 2y = 13,$ $y = 5\frac{1}{2} \Rightarrow \left(2, 5\frac{1}{2}\right)$
$x = 3;$ $3 + 2y = 13,$ $y = 5 \Rightarrow (3, 5)$

x	-3	-2	-1	0	1	2	3
y	8	$7\frac{1}{2}$	7	$6\frac{1}{2}$	6	$5\frac{1}{2}$	5

17. $6x + 2y = 24$

$x = -3;$ $6(-3) + 2y = 24,$ $y = 21 \Rightarrow (-3, 21)$
$x = -2;$ $6(-2) + 2y = 24,$ $y = 18 \Rightarrow (-2, 18)$
$x = -1;$ $6(-1) + 2y = 24,$ $y = 15 \Rightarrow (-1, 15)$
$x = 0;$ $6(0) + 2y = 24,$ $y = 12 \Rightarrow (0, 12)$
$x = 1;$ $6(1) + 2y = 24,$ $y = 9 \Rightarrow (1, 9)$
$x = 2;$ $6(2) + 2y = 24,$ $y = 6 \Rightarrow (2, 6)$
$x = 3;$ $6(3) + 2y = 24,$ $y = 3 \Rightarrow (3, 3)$

x	-3	-2	-1	0	1	2	3
y	21	18	15	12	9	6	3

18. $y = \frac{1}{3}x + 2$

$x = -3;$ $y = \frac{1}{3}(-3) + 2,$ $y = 1 \Rightarrow (-3, 1)$
$x = -2;$ $y = \frac{1}{3}(-2) + 2,$ $y = \frac{4}{3} \Rightarrow \left(-2, \frac{4}{3}\right)$
$x = -1;$ $y = \frac{1}{3}(-1) + 2,$ $y = \frac{5}{3} \Rightarrow \left(-1, \frac{5}{3}\right)$
$x = 0;$ $y = \frac{1}{3}(0) + 2,$ $y = 2 \Rightarrow (0, 2)$
$x = 1;$ $y = \frac{1}{3}(1) + 2,$ $y = \frac{7}{3} \Rightarrow \left(1, \frac{7}{3}\right)$
$x = 2;$ $y = \frac{1}{3}(2) + 2,$ $y = \frac{8}{3} \Rightarrow \left(2, \frac{8}{3}\right)$
$x = 3;$ $y = \frac{1}{3}(3) + 2,$ $y = 3 \Rightarrow (3, 3)$

x	-3	-2	-1	0	1	2	3
y	1	$\frac{4}{3}$	$\frac{5}{3}$	2	$\frac{7}{3}$	$\frac{8}{3}$	3

19.–20. $x =$ a number and $y =$ another number.

19. $6x - 4y = 12$

Sample answer:

$x = -1;$ $6(-1) - 4y = 12,$ $y = -\frac{9}{2} \Rightarrow \left(-1, -\frac{9}{2}\right)$
$x = 0;$ $6(0) - 4y = 12,$ $y = -3 \Rightarrow (0, -3)$
$x = 1;$ $6(1) - 4y = 12,$ $y = -\frac{3}{2} \Rightarrow \left(1, -\frac{3}{2}\right)$

20. $\frac{1}{2}x + 2y = 54$

Sample answer:

$x = 8;$ $\frac{1}{2}(8) + 2y = 54,$ $y = 25 \Rightarrow (8, 25)$
$x = 0;$ $\frac{1}{2}(0) + 2y = 54,$ $y = 27 \Rightarrow (0, 27)$
$x = -4;$ $\frac{1}{2}(-4) + 2y = 54,$ $y = 28 \Rightarrow (-4, 28)$

21. B; $x + y = 150°$

$x = 100°; \quad 100° + y = 150°, \quad y = 50° \quad \Rightarrow (100°, 50°)$
$x = 75°; \quad 75° + y = 150°, \quad y = 75° \quad \Rightarrow (75°, 75°)$
$x = 50°; \quad 50° + y = 150°, \quad y = 100° \Rightarrow (50°, 100°)$

22. D; $x + y = 210°$

$x = 200°; \quad 200° + y = 210°, \quad y = 10° \quad \Rightarrow (200°, 10°)$
$x = 105°; \quad 105° + y = 210°, \quad y = 105° \Rightarrow (105°, 105°)$
$x = 10°; \quad 10° + y = 210°, \quad y = 200° \Rightarrow (10°, 200°)$

23. C; $x + y = 180°$

$x = 100°; \quad 100° + y = 180°, \quad y = 80° \quad \Rightarrow (100°, 80°)$
$x = 90°; \quad 90° + y = 180°, \quad y = 90° \quad \Rightarrow (90°, 90°)$
$x = 80°; \quad 80° + y = 180°, \quad y = 100° \Rightarrow (80°, 100°)$

24. A; $x + y = 90°$

$x = 60°; \quad 60° + y = 90°, \quad y = 30° \Rightarrow (60°, 30°)$
$x = 45°; \quad 45° + y = 90°, \quad y = 45° \Rightarrow (45°, 45°)$
$x = 30°; \quad 30° + y = 90°, \quad y = 60° \Rightarrow (30°, 60°)$

25. $y = 2.54x$

$y = 2.54(12)$

$y = 30.48$ cm

26. $y = 2.54x$

$100 = 2.54x$

$\dfrac{100}{2.54} = x$

39.37 in. $\approx x$

27.

in.	1	5	10	15	20	25	30	35	40	45	50
cm	2.54	12.7	25.4	38.1	50.8	63.5	76.2	88.9	101.6	114.3	127

28. Infinite; there are an infinite number of possibilities for x, and each x has its own y.

29. $3x + 5y = 16 \qquad \dfrac{12x + 20y}{4} = \dfrac{64}{4}$

$\qquad\qquad\qquad\qquad 3x + 5y = 16$

Yes. When you divide both sides of the second equation by 4, you get the first equation.

30. $9x - 2y = 18 \qquad \dfrac{18x - 4y}{2} = \dfrac{30}{2}$

$\qquad\qquad\qquad\qquad 9x - 2y = 15$

No. When you divide both sides of the second equation by 2, you get $9x - 2y = 15$. Since the first equation is $9x - 2y = 18$, the expression $9x - 2y$ is equal to two different numbers.

31. $S = 0.76t + 2.6$

$\quad = 0.76(1) + 2.6$

$\quad = 0.76 + 2.6$

$\quad = 3.36$ million trucks

32. $S = 0.76t + 2.6$

$\quad = 0.76(4) + 2.6$

$\quad = 3.04 + 2.6$

$\quad = 5.64$ million trucks

33. B; $3(2) + 2(3) \overset{?}{=} 9$

$\qquad 6 + 6 \overset{?}{=} 9$

$\qquad 12 \neq 9$

34. C; $2x + 4y = 20$

$4y = 20 - 2x$

$0 = 20 - 2x - 4y$

35. $d = \frac{50}{60}t = \frac{5}{6}t$

t (min)	10	20	30	40	50
d (miles)	$8\frac{1}{3}$	$16\frac{2}{3}$	25	$33\frac{1}{3}$	$41\frac{2}{3}$

13.2 Exploring Graphs of Linear Equations

ONGOING ASSESSMENT

1. (5, 36)

2. *Sample answer:* Up until 1995, Club B has fewer members than Club A, but after 1995 Club B has more members.

EXERCISES

1. *Sample answer:* Begin by making a table of values: choose several values of x, substitute them into the original equation, and solve for y. Plot the solutions in a coordinate plane. Draw a line through the points.

2.

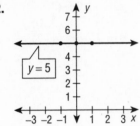

$y = 5$

$x = -1, \quad y = 5 \Rightarrow (-1, 5)$
$x = 0, \quad\ y = 5 \Rightarrow (0, 5)$
$x = 1, \quad\ y = 5 \Rightarrow (1, 5)$

3.

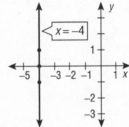

$x = -4$

$x = -4, \quad y = -1 \Rightarrow (-4, -1)$
$x = -4, \quad y = 0 \ \Rightarrow (-4, 0)$
$x = -4, \quad y = 1 \ \Rightarrow (-4, 1)$

4.

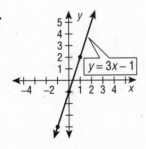

$y = 3x - 1$

$x = -1; \quad y = 3(-1) - 1, \quad y = -4 \Rightarrow (-1, -4)$
$x = 0; \quad\ \ y = 3(0) - 1, \quad\ \ y = -1 \Rightarrow (0, -1)$
$x = 1; \quad\ \ y = 3(1) - 1, \quad\ \ y = 2 \ \Rightarrow (1, 2)$

5.

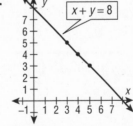

$x + y = 8$

$x = 3; \quad 3 + y = 8, \quad y = 5 \Rightarrow (3, 5)$
$x = 4; \quad 4 + y = 8, \quad y = 4 \Rightarrow (4, 4)$
$x = 5; \quad 5 + y = 8, \quad y = 3 \Rightarrow (5, 3)$

6. C **7.** A **8.** B **9.** C **10.** A **11.** B

12.

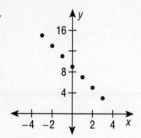

Yes; the relationship is linear.

13.

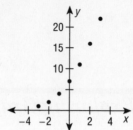

No; the relationship is not linear.

14.

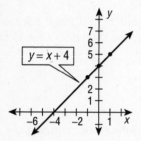

$y = x + 4$

$x = -1; \quad y = -1 + 4, \quad y = 3 \Rightarrow (-1, 3)$
$x = 0; \quad y = 0 + 4, \quad y = 4 \Rightarrow (0, 4)$
$x = 1; \quad y = 1 + 4, \quad y = 5 \Rightarrow (1, 5)$

15.

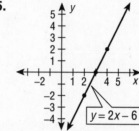

$y = 2x - 6$

$x = 2; \quad y = 2(2) - 6, \quad y = -2 \Rightarrow (2, -2)$
$x = 3; \quad y = 2(3) - 6, \quad y = 0 \Rightarrow (3, 0)$
$x = 4; \quad y = 2(4) - 6, \quad y = 2 \Rightarrow (4, 2)$

16.

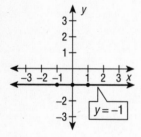

$y = -1$

$x = -1, \quad y = -1 \Rightarrow (-1, -1)$
$x = 0, \quad y = -1 \Rightarrow (0, -1)$
$x = 1, \quad y = -1 \Rightarrow (1, -1)$

17.

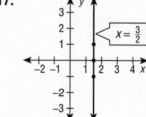

$x = \frac{3}{2}$

$x = \frac{3}{2}, \quad y = -1 \Rightarrow \left(\frac{3}{2}, -1\right)$
$x = \frac{3}{2}, \quad y = 0 \Rightarrow \left(\frac{3}{2}, 0\right)$
$x = \frac{3}{2}, \quad y = 1 \Rightarrow \left(\frac{3}{2}, 1\right)$

18.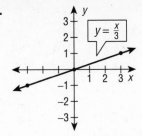

$y = \dfrac{x}{3}$

$x = -3; \quad y = \dfrac{-3}{3}, \quad y = -1 \Rightarrow (-3, -1)$

$x = 0; \quad y = \dfrac{0}{3}, \quad y = 0 \Rightarrow (0, 0)$

$x = 3; \quad y = \dfrac{3}{3}, \quad y = 1 \Rightarrow (3, 1)$

19.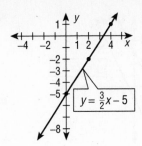

$y = \dfrac{3}{2}x - 5$

$x = 0; \quad y = \dfrac{3}{2}(0) - 5, \quad y = -5 \Rightarrow (0, -5)$

$x = 2; \quad y = \dfrac{3}{2}(2) - 5, \quad y = -2 \Rightarrow (2, -2)$

$x = 4; \quad y = \dfrac{3}{2}(4) - 5, \quad y = 1 \Rightarrow (4, 1)$

20.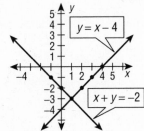

The point of intersection is $(1, -3)$.

$x + y = -2$

$x = -1; \quad -1 + y = -2, \quad y = -1 \Rightarrow (-1, -1)$
$x = 0; \quad 0 + y = -2, \quad y = -2 \Rightarrow (0, -2)$
$x = 1; \quad 1 + y = -2, \quad y = -3 \Rightarrow (1, -3)$

$y = x - 4$

$x = 4; \quad y = 4 - 4, \quad y = 0 \Rightarrow (4, 0)$
$x = 3; \quad y = 3 - 4, \quad y = -1 \Rightarrow (3, -1)$
$x = 2; \quad y = 2 - 4, \quad y = -2 \Rightarrow (2, -2)$

21.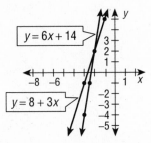

The point of intersection is $(-2, 2)$.

$y = 6x + 14$

$x = -3; \quad y = 6(-3) + 14, \quad y = -4 \Rightarrow (-3, -4)$
$x = -\dfrac{5}{2}; \quad y = 6\left(-\dfrac{5}{2}\right) + 14, \quad y = -1 \Rightarrow \left(-\dfrac{5}{2}, -1\right)$
$x = -2; \quad y = 6(-2) + 14, \quad y = 2 \Rightarrow (-2, 2)$

$y = 8 + 3x$

$x = -1; \quad y = 8 + 3(-1), \quad y = 5 \Rightarrow (-1, 5)$
$x = -2; \quad y = 8 + 3(-2), \quad y = 2 \Rightarrow (-2, 2)$
$x = -3; \quad y = 8 + 3(-3), \quad y = -1 \Rightarrow (-3, -1)$

22.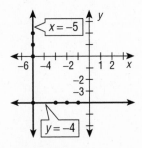

The point of intersection is $(-5, -4)$.

$x = -5$

$x = -5, \quad y = 0 \Rightarrow (-5, 0)$
$x = -5, \quad y = 1 \Rightarrow (-5, 1)$
$x = -5, \quad y = 2 \Rightarrow (-5, 2)$

$y = -4$

$x = -1, \quad y = -4 \Rightarrow (-1, -4)$
$x = -2, \quad y = -4 \Rightarrow (-2, -4)$
$x = -3, \quad y = -4 \Rightarrow (-3, -4)$

23. $x = 0$ is the y-axis and $y = 0$ is the x-axis.

24.

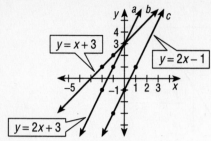

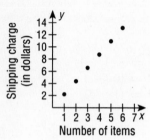

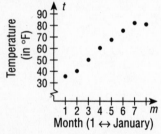

Lines a and c are parallel.

a. $y = 2x + 3$

$x = -2;$ $y = 2(-2) + 3,$ $y = -1 \Rightarrow (-2, -1)$
$x = -1;$ $y = 2(-1) + 3,$ $y = 1$ $\Rightarrow (-1, 1)$
$x = 0;$ $y = 2(0) + 3,$ $y = 3$ $\Rightarrow (0, 3)$

b. $y = x + 3$

$x = -2;$ $y = -2 + 3,$ $y = 1 \Rightarrow (-2, 1)$
$x = -1;$ $y = -1 + 3,$ $y = 2 \Rightarrow (-1, 2)$
$x = 0;$ $y = 0 + 3,$ $y = 3 \Rightarrow (0, 3)$

c. $y = 2x - 1$

$x = -1;$ $y = 2(-1) - 1,$ $y = -3 \Rightarrow (-1, -3)$
$x = 0;$ $y = 2(0) - 1,$ $y = -1 \Rightarrow (0, -1)$
$x = 1;$ $y = 2(1) - 1,$ $y = 1$ $\Rightarrow (1, 1)$

25.

For every increase of 1 by the number of items, there is a corresponding increase of $2.19 by the shipping charge.
Yes; the points lie on a line.

26.

m	1	2	3	4	5	6	7	8
t	35.9	40.9	50.3	60.4	68.4	76.7	82.0	81.1

Pattern: For an increase in m, there is an increase in t (with one exception).
No, the points do not all lie on the same line.

27. A

28. D; $y = cx + 1$

$5 = c(2) + 1$
$4 = 2c$
$2 = c$

29.

Number of rides, r	5	10	15	20	25	30	35
Cost with pass, $25.00	$25.00	$25.00	$25.00	$25.00	$25.00	$25.00	$25.00
Cost without pass, $1.25r$	$6.25	$12.50	$18.75	$25.00	$31.25	$37.50	$43.75

The monthly pass is a better buy for a person making more than 20 trips in a month.

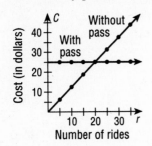

Spiral **R E V I E W**

1. $C = \pi d$
$\quad = \pi(7)$
$\quad \approx 22.0$ ft

$A = \pi \left(\dfrac{d}{2}\right)^2$
$\quad = \pi \left(\dfrac{7}{2}\right)^2$
$\quad = \pi(3.5)^2$
$\quad = 12.25\pi$
$\quad \approx 38.5$ ft^2

2. $C = \pi d$
$\quad = \pi(32)$
$\quad \approx 100.5$ in.

$A = \pi \left(\dfrac{d}{2}\right)^2$
$\quad = \pi \left(\dfrac{32}{2}\right)^2$
$\quad = \pi(16)^2$
$\quad = 256\pi$
$\quad \approx 804.2$ in.^{2}

3. $C = 2\pi r$
$\quad = 2\pi(8)$
$\quad = 16\pi$
$\quad \approx 50.3$ cm

$A = \pi r^2$
$\quad = \pi(8)^2$
$\quad = 64\pi$
$\quad \approx 201.1$ cm^2

4. $C = 2\pi r$ $A = \pi r^2$
$\quad = 2\pi(24)$ $= \pi(24)^2$
$\quad = 48\pi$ $= 576\pi$
$\quad \approx 150.8$ yd ≈ 1809.6 yd^2

5. $B = 3^2 = 9$ ft^2 $S = 2B + Ph$
$\quad P = 4(3) = 12$ ft $\quad = 2(9) + 12(3)$
$\qquad\qquad\qquad\qquad\quad = 18 + 36$
$\qquad\qquad\qquad\qquad\quad = 54$ ft^2

$\qquad\qquad\qquad\qquad V = lwh$
$\qquad\qquad\qquad\qquad\quad = 3(3)(3)$
$\qquad\qquad\qquad\qquad\quad = 27$ ft^3

6.

$15^2 + 20^2 = c^2$

$225 + 400 = c^2$

$625 = c^2$

$25 = c$

$B = \frac{1}{2}bh$

$= \frac{1}{2}(15)(20)$

$= 150 \text{ cm}^2$

$P = 15 + 20 + 25$

$= 60 \text{ cm}$

$S = 2B + Ph$

$= 2(150) + 60(40)$

$= 300 + 2400$

$= 2700 \text{ cm}^2$

$V = Bh$

$= 150 \cdot 40 = 6000 \text{ cm}^3$

7. $B = \pi r^2$

$= \pi(5)^2$

$= 25\pi \text{ in.}^2$

$C = 2\pi r$

$= 2\pi(5)$

$= 10\pi \text{ in.}$

$S = 2B + Ph$

$= 2(25\pi) + 10\pi(7)$

$= 50\pi + 70\pi$

$= 120\pi$

$\approx 376.99 \text{ in.}^2$

$V = Bh$

$= 25\pi(7)$

$= 175\pi$

$\approx 549.78 \text{ in.}^3$

8. $B = 16(10) = 160 \text{ in.}^2$

$P = 2(16) + 2(10) = 52 \text{ in.}$

$S = 2B + Ph$

$= 2(160) + 52(20)$

$= 320 + 1040$

$= 1360 \text{ in.}^2$

$V = lwh$

$= 16(10)(20)$

$= 3200 \text{ in.}^3$

9. $y = \frac{4}{5}x - 7$

$x = -3; \quad y = \frac{4}{5}(-3) - 7, \quad y = -\frac{12}{5} - \frac{35}{5} = -\frac{47}{5} \Rightarrow \left(-3, -9\frac{2}{5}\right)$

$x = -2; \quad y = \frac{4}{5}(-2) - 7, \quad y = -\frac{8}{5} - \frac{35}{5} = -\frac{43}{5} \Rightarrow \left(-2, -8\frac{3}{5}\right)$

$x = -1; \quad y = \frac{4}{5}(-1) - 7, \quad y = -\frac{4}{5} - \frac{35}{5} = -\frac{39}{5} \Rightarrow \left(-1, -7\frac{4}{5}\right)$

$x = 0; \quad y = \frac{4}{5}(0) - 7, \quad y = 0 - 7 = -7 \qquad \Rightarrow (0, -7)$

$x = 1; \quad y = \frac{4}{5}(1) - 7, \quad y = \frac{4}{5} - \frac{35}{5} = -\frac{31}{5} \Rightarrow \left(1, -6\frac{1}{5}\right)$

$x = 2; \quad y = \frac{4}{5}(2) - 7, \quad y = \frac{8}{5} - \frac{35}{5} = -\frac{27}{5} \Rightarrow \left(2, -5\frac{2}{5}\right)$

$x = 3; \quad y = \frac{4}{5}(3) - 7, \quad y = \frac{12}{5} - \frac{35}{5} = -\frac{23}{5} \Rightarrow \left(3, -4\frac{3}{5}\right)$

x	-3	-2	-1	0	1	2	3
y	$-9\frac{2}{5}$	$-8\frac{3}{5}$	$-7\frac{4}{5}$	-7	$-6\frac{1}{5}$	$-5\frac{2}{5}$	$-4\frac{3}{5}$

10. $-x - y = 12$

$x = -3; \quad -(-3) - y = 12, \quad y = -9 \Rightarrow (-3, -9)$

$x = -2; \quad -(-2) - y = 12, \quad y = -10 \Rightarrow (-2, -10)$

$x = -1; \quad -(-1) - y = 12, \quad y = -11 \Rightarrow (-1, -11)$

$x = 0; \quad -(0) - y = 12, \quad y = -12 \Rightarrow (0, -12)$

$x = 1; \quad -(1) - y = 12, \quad y = -13 \Rightarrow (1, -13)$

$x = 2; \quad -(2) - y = 12, \quad y = -14 \Rightarrow (2, -14)$

$x = 3; \quad -(3) - y = 12, \quad y = -15 \Rightarrow (3, -15)$

x	-3	-2	-1	0	1	2	3
y	-9	-10	-11	-12	-13	-14	-15

11. $6x - 8y = -4$

$x = -3; \quad 6(-3) - 8y = -4, \quad y = -\frac{7}{4} \Rightarrow \left(-3, -1\frac{3}{4}\right)$

$x = -2; \quad 6(-2) - 8y = -4, \quad y = -1 \Rightarrow (-2, -1)$

$x = -1; \quad 6(-1) - 8y = -4, \quad y = -\frac{1}{4} \Rightarrow \left(-1, -\frac{1}{4}\right)$

$x = 0; \quad 6(0) - 8y = -4, \quad y = \frac{1}{2} \Rightarrow \left(0, \frac{1}{2}\right)$

$x = 1; \quad 6(1) - 8y = -4, \quad y = \frac{5}{4} \Rightarrow \left(1, 1\frac{1}{4}\right)$

$x = 2; \quad 6(2) - 8y = -4, \quad y = 2 \Rightarrow (2, 2)$

$x = 3; \quad 6(3) - 8y = -4, \quad y = \frac{11}{4} \Rightarrow \left(3, 2\frac{3}{4}\right)$

x	-3	-2	-1	0	1	2	3
y	$-1\frac{3}{4}$	-1	$-\frac{1}{4}$	$\frac{1}{2}$	$1\frac{1}{4}$	2	$2\frac{3}{4}$

12. $\dfrac{x}{19} = \dfrac{100}{76} \cdot 19$

$x = 25$

Using a Graphing Calculator

1. $y = 2x - 3$

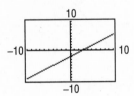

2. $y = 0.5x + 4$

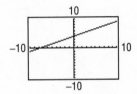

3. $y = -x + 5$

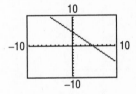

4. $y = 0.75x - 2$

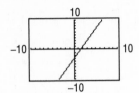

5. $y = 2x - 30$

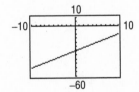

6. $y = -80x + 2000$

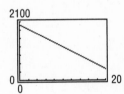

13.3 Exploring Intercepts of Graphs

ONGOING ASSESSMENT

1.

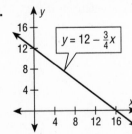

$y = 12 - \frac{3}{4}x$

$y + \frac{3}{4}x = 12$

$0 + \frac{3}{4}x = 12$

$x = 12 \cdot \frac{4}{3}$

$x = 16$

The x-intercept is 16. This means that it takes you 16 min to get home.

$y + \frac{3}{4}x = 12$

$y + \frac{3}{4}(0) = 12$

$y = 12$

The y-intercept is 12. This means that you start the trip 12 mi from home.

EXERCISES

1. *x*-intercept: 4
y-intercept: 2

2. *x*-intercept: 2
y-intercept: −1

3. *x*-intercept: −2
y-intercept: −2

4.

$y = 2x - 1$	*Rewrite original equation.*
$0 = 2x - 1$	*Substitute 0 for y.*
$1 = 2x$	*Add 1 to each side.*
$\frac{1}{2} = x$	*Divide each side by 2.*

5.

$5x + 3y = 9$	*Rewrite original equation.*
$5(0) + 3y = 9$	*Substitute 0 for x.*
$3y = 9$	*Simplify.*
$y = 3$	*Divide each side by 3.*

6. $x + y = 5$

x-intercept: $x + 0 = 5$
$x = 5$

y-intercept: $0 + y = 5$
$y = 5$

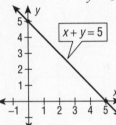

7. $x - y = 5$

x-intercept: $x - 0 = 5$
$x = 5$

y-intercept: $0 - y = 5$
$y = -5$

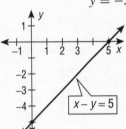

8. $y = \frac{5}{4}x + 3$

x-intercept:
$$0 = \frac{5}{4}x + 3$$
$$-3 = \frac{5}{4}x$$
$$\frac{4}{5} \cdot (-3) = \frac{4}{5} \cdot \frac{5}{4}x$$
$$-\frac{12}{5} = x$$

y-intercept: $y = \frac{5}{4}(0) + 3$
$y = 3$

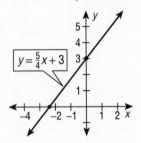

9. $-7x + 3y = -21$

x-intercept: $7x + 3(0) = -21$
$7x = -21$
$x = 3$

y-intercept: $7(0) + 3y = -21$
$3y = -21$
$y = -7$

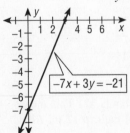

10. $y = 4x + 4$
$y = 4(0) + 4$
$y = 4$
The *y*-intercept is 4.
$y = 4x + 4$
$0 = 4x + 4$
$-4 = 4x$
$-1 = x$
The *x*-intercept is −1.

11. $y = -3x + 6$
$y = -3(0) + 6$
$y = 6$
The *y*-intercept is 6.
$y = -3x + 6$
$0 = -3x + 6$
$-6 = -3x$
$2 = x$
The *x*-intercept is 2.

12. $y = -\frac{2}{5}x - 2$

$y = -\frac{2}{5}(0) - 2$

$y = -2$

The y-intercept is -2.

$y = -\frac{2}{5}x - 2$

$0 = -\frac{2}{5}x - 2$

$2 = -\frac{2}{5}x$

$-5 = x$

The x-intercept is -5.

13. $y = \frac{5}{4}x - 5$

$y = \frac{5}{4}(0) - 5$

$y = -5$

The y-intercept is -5.

$y = \frac{5}{4}x - 5$

$0 = \frac{5}{4}x - 5$

$5 = \frac{5}{4}x$

$4 = x$

The x-intercept is 4.

14. $y = \frac{1}{2}x + 2$

y-intercept:

$y = \frac{1}{2}(0) + 2$

$y = 2$

Answer: A

15. $y = -\frac{1}{2}x - 2$

y-intercept: $y = -\frac{1}{2}(0) - 2$

$y = -2$

Answer: C

16. $3x + y = 6$

y-intercept: $3(0) + y = 6$

$y = 6$

Answer: B

17. $y = -3x + 6$

x-intercept: $0 = -3x + 6$

$6 = -3x$

$2 = x$

y-intercept: $y = -3(0) + 6$

$y = 6$

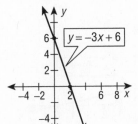

x	0	1	2	3	4
y	6	3	0	-3	-6

18. $y = 4x - 8$

x-intercept: $0 = 4x - 8$

$8 = 4x$

$2 = x$

y-intercept: $y = 4(0) - 8$

$y = -8$

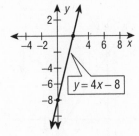

x	0	1	2	3	4
y	-8	-4	0	4	8

19. $x - y = 1$

x-intercept: $x - 0 = 1$

$x = 1$

y-intercept: $0 - y = 1$

$y = 1$

$y = -1$

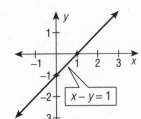

x	0	1	2	3	4
y	-1	0	1	2	3

20. $x + y = -3$

    x-intercept: $x + 0 = -3$

                    $x = -3$

    y-intercept: $0 + y = -3$

                    $y = -3$

$x + y = -3$

x	-3	-2	-1	0	1
y	0	-1	-2	-3	-4

21. $3x - 4y = 24$

    x-intercept: $3x - 4(0) = 24$

                     $3x = 24$

                     $x = 8$

    y-intercept: $3(0) - 4y = 24$

                     $4y = 24$

                     $y = -6$

$3x - 4y = 24$

x	8	4	0	-4	-8
y	0	-3	-6	-9	-12

22. $x + 5y = 5$

    x-intercept: $x + 5(0) = 5$

                     $x = 5$

    y-intercept: $0 + 5y = 5$

                     $5y = 5$

                     $y = 1$

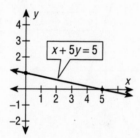

$x + 5y = 5$

x	-10	-5	0	5	10
y	3	2	1	0	-1

23. $y = -\frac{3}{2}x + 4$

    x-intercept:

              $0 = -\frac{3}{2}x + 4$

              $4 = -\frac{3}{2}x$

    $\left(-\frac{2}{3}\right) \cdot (-4) = \left(-\frac{2}{3}\right) \cdot \left(-\frac{3}{2}x\right)$

              $\frac{8}{3} = x$

    y-intercept: $y = -\frac{3}{2}(0) + 4$

                   $y = 4$

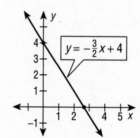

$y = -\frac{3}{2}x + 4$

x	-4	-2	0	2	4
y	10	7	4	1	-2

24. $y = \frac{4}{3}x + 6$

x-intercept: $\qquad 0 = \frac{4}{3}x + 6$

$$6 = \frac{4}{3}x$$

$$\frac{3}{4} \cdot (-6) = \frac{3}{4} \cdot \frac{4}{3}x$$

$$\frac{3 \cdot 2 \cdot 3}{2 \cdot 2} = x$$

$$\frac{9}{2} = x$$

y-intercept: $\quad y = \frac{4}{3}(0) + 6$

$$y = 6$$

x	-6	-3	0	3	6
y	-2	2	6	10	14

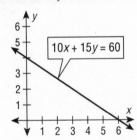

(graph labeled $y = \frac{4}{3}x + 6$)

25. $y = -3.64x + 2.18$

x-intercept: $\qquad 0 = -3.64x + 2.18$

$$2.18 = -3.64x$$

$$0.60 \approx x$$

y-intercept: $\quad y = -3.64(0) + 2.18$

$$y = 2.18$$

26. $y = 1.85x - 14.302$

x-intercept: $\qquad 0 = 1.85x - 14.302$

$$14.302 = 1.85x$$

$$7.73 \approx x$$

y-intercept: $\quad y = 1.85(0) - 14.302$

$$y \approx -14.30$$

27. $10x + 15y = 60$

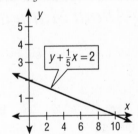

(graph labeled $10x + 15y = 60$)

x-intercept: $\quad 10x + 15(0) = 60$

$$10x = 60$$

$$x = 6$$

y-intercept: $\quad 10(0) + 15y = 60$

$$15y = 60$$

$$y = 4$$

The y-intercept means that you washed 4 sport utility vehicles, minivans, or trucks and *no* cars. The x-intercept means that you washed 6 cars and *no* sport utility vehicles, minivans, or trucks.

28. $y + \frac{1}{5}x = 2$

(graph labeled $y + \frac{1}{5}x = 2$)

x-intercept: $\quad 0 + \frac{1}{5}x = 2$

$$\frac{5}{1} \cdot \frac{1}{5}x = 2 \cdot \frac{5}{1}$$

$$x = 10$$

y-intercept: $\quad y + \frac{1}{5}(0) = 2$

$$y = 2$$

The y-intercept means that you start the trip 2 miles from school. The x-intercept means that it takes you 10 minutes to get to school.

29. *Sample answer:* The graph of an equation such as $x = 3$ (a vertical line), the graph of an equation such as $y = 3$ (a horizontal line), the graph of an equation such as $y = 2x$ (a line through the origin).

30. C; $y = 2x - 4$

$\qquad 0 = 2x - 4$

$\qquad 4 = 2x$

$\qquad 2 = x$

$(2, 0)$

31. A; $y = 3x - 6$

$\qquad y = 3(0) - 6$

$\qquad y = -6$

32. a. $4x + 6y = 400$

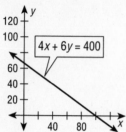

x-intercept: $4x + 6(0) = 400$

$\qquad\qquad\quad 4x = 400$

$\qquad\qquad\quad\ x = 100$

y-intercept: $4(0) + 6y = 400$

$\qquad\qquad\quad 6y = 400$

$\qquad\qquad\quad\ y = \frac{400}{6} = \frac{200}{3}$, or 66.67

b. Each solution represents the number of standing and seated passengers that the subway car can hold at a given time. The y-intercept means that there are about 66 seated passengers and no standing passengers. The x-intercept means that there are 100 standing passengers and no seated passengers.

c. Answers vary.

Communicating About Mathematics

1. For d number of days, the track brakes will be replaced B times.

2. $B = 40 \cdot \frac{4}{3}d = \frac{160}{3}d$

3. Each cable is replaced every $\frac{365}{3} \approx 121$ days. In 121 days, you will go through $\frac{121}{3} \approx 40$ brakes. Your cable car will go through about 40 track brakes before the cable is replaced again.

4.

The 2 represents the cost per ride.

5.

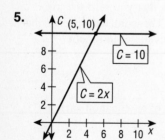

The point where $C = 10$ crosses $C = 2x$ is where the cost of the three-day pass is the same as the cost for 5 rides. A three-day pass is less expensive than paying per ride if you ride the cable car more than 5 times.

Lab 13.4

1.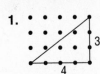

2. the line in part **b.**

3. a. $\frac{2}{3}$
   b. $\frac{4}{3}$
   Ex. 1: $\frac{3}{4}$
   The line in part **b** has the greatest slope.

4. *Sample answer:* The steepest line has the greatest slope.

5.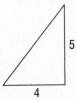

Slope $= \frac{5}{4}$

6.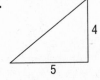

Slope $= \frac{4}{5}$

7.

Slope $= \frac{5}{3}$

8. The line in Exercise 7 is the steepest. The line in Exercise 6 is the least steep.

9. The line in Exercise 7 has the greatest slope. The line in Exercise 6 has the smallest slope. The steepest line has the greatest slope, and the least steep line has the smallest slope.

13.4 *Exploring Slope*

ONGOING ASSESSMENT

1. *Sample answer:*
$(-1, 0)$ and $(0, 3)$
$$m = \frac{y_2 - y_1}{x_2 - x_1}$$
$$= \frac{3 - 1}{0 - (-1)} = \frac{2}{1} = 2$$

2. *Sample answer:*
$(1, 5)$ and $(2, 7)$
$$m = \frac{y_2 - y_1}{x_2 - x_1}$$
$$= \frac{7 - 5}{2 - 1} = \frac{2}{1} = 2$$

3. Yes; because the points all lie on the same line, using any two points will produce the same slope.

EXERCISES

1.–3. $m = \dfrac{\text{Rise}}{\text{Run}}$

1. $m = \dfrac{4}{4} = 1$

2. $m = \dfrac{2}{3}$

3. $m = \dfrac{-2}{4} = -\dfrac{1}{2}$

4. $m = \dfrac{y_2 - y_1}{x_2 - x_1}$

$= \dfrac{2 - 3}{4 - (-1)}$

$= \dfrac{-1}{5}$

$= -\dfrac{1}{5}$

5.
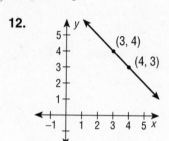

The line with a slope of 4 is steeper.

6. $m = 5$

7. $m = -6$

8.–10. $m = \dfrac{y_2 - y_1}{x_2 - x_1}$

8. $m = \dfrac{2 - 0}{2 - (-2)} = \dfrac{2}{4} = \dfrac{1}{2}$

9. $m = \dfrac{0 - 3}{2 - (-3)} = \dfrac{-3}{5} = -\dfrac{3}{5}$

10. $m = \dfrac{-2 - (-2)}{1 - (-3)} = \dfrac{0}{4} = 0$

11.
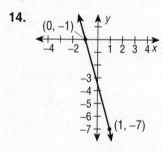

$m = \dfrac{5 - 5}{2 - 0} = \dfrac{0}{2} = 0$

12.

$m = \dfrac{3 - 4}{4 - 3} = \dfrac{-1}{1} = -1$

13.

$m = \dfrac{-2 - (-6)}{1 - (-1)} = \dfrac{4}{2} = 2$

14.

$m = \dfrac{-7 - (-1)}{1 - 0} = \dfrac{-6}{1} = -6$

15.–18. $m = \dfrac{y_2 - y_1}{x_2 - x_1}$

15. Slope of $\overleftrightarrow{AB} = \dfrac{-2 - 3}{1 - 3} = \dfrac{-5}{-2} = \dfrac{5}{2}$

Slope of $\overleftrightarrow{CD} = \dfrac{-1 - 4}{-3 - (-4)} = \dfrac{-5}{1} = -5$

No; the slopes are different.

16. Slope of $\overleftrightarrow{AB} = \dfrac{-2 - 1}{0 - 1} = \dfrac{-3}{-1} = 3$

Slope of $\overleftrightarrow{CD} = \dfrac{-2 - 1}{-3 - (-5)} = \dfrac{-3}{2} = -\dfrac{3}{2}$

No; the slopes are different.

17. Slope of $\overleftrightarrow{AB} = \dfrac{-2-3}{0-2} = \dfrac{-5}{-2} = \dfrac{5}{2}$

Slope of $\overleftrightarrow{CD} = \dfrac{8-3}{6-4} = \dfrac{5}{2}$

Yes; the slopes are the same.

18. Slope of $\overleftrightarrow{AB} = \dfrac{6-(-2)}{2-(-2)} = \dfrac{8}{4} = 2$

Slope of $\overleftrightarrow{CD} = \dfrac{4-(-4)}{-5-(-1)} = \dfrac{8}{-4} = -2$

No; the slopes are different.

19.–22. $m = \dfrac{\text{Rise}}{\text{Run}}$

19. $m = \dfrac{15}{70} = \dfrac{\cancel{5} \cdot 3}{\cancel{5} \cdot 14} = \dfrac{3}{14}$

20. $m = \dfrac{-2}{24} = -\dfrac{1}{12}$

21. $m = \dfrac{40}{180} = \dfrac{\cancel{20} \cdot 2}{\cancel{20} \cdot 9} = \dfrac{2}{9}$

22. $m = \dfrac{-25}{65} = \dfrac{-\cancel{5} \cdot 5}{\cancel{5} \cdot 13} = -\dfrac{5}{13}$

23. $a^2 + 8^2 = 10^2$

$a^2 + 64 = 100$

$a^2 = 36$

$a = 6$

$m = \dfrac{-6}{8}$

$= \dfrac{\cancel{2} \cdot (-3)}{\cancel{2} \cdot 4}$

$= -\dfrac{3}{4}$

24. $m = \dfrac{1}{1} = 1$

25. $8^2 + b^2 = 17^2$

$64 + b^2 = 289$

$b^2 = 225$

$b = 15$

$m = \dfrac{-8}{15}$

$= -\dfrac{8}{15}$

26.–28. $m = \dfrac{\text{Rise}}{\text{Run}}$

26. $m = \dfrac{7}{11}$

27. $m = \dfrac{8}{9}$

28. $m = \dfrac{24}{26} = \dfrac{12}{13}$

29. A; $\dfrac{4-0}{0-4} = \dfrac{4}{-4} = -1$

30. A; $\dfrac{-3-4}{2-(-3)} = -\dfrac{7}{5}$

31. a. Slope $= \dfrac{26}{50} = \dfrac{\cancel{2} \cdot 13}{\cancel{2} \cdot 25} = \dfrac{13}{25}$

b.

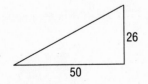

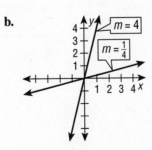

c. Answers vary.

d. Answers vary.

No; *sample answer:* you do not want an escalator with slope 4 because it would be too steep and you do not want an escalator with slope $\frac{1}{4}$ because it would not be steep enough.

1. $y = 4x + 12$

    x-intercept: $0 = 4x + 12$

                   $-12 = 4x$

                    $-3 = x$

    y-intercept: $y = 4(0) + 12$

                      $y = 12$

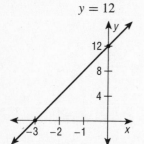

2. $y = -4x + 12$

    x-intercept: $0 = -4x + 2$

                   $-2 = -4x$

                    $\frac{1}{2} = x$

    y-intercept: $y = -4(0) + 2$

                      $y = 2$

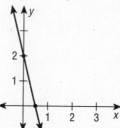

3. $3y = 12 + 3x$

    x-intercept: $3(0) = 12 + 3x$

                  $-12 = 3x$

                   $-4 = x$

    y-intercept: $3y = 12 + 3(0)$

                   $3y = 12$

                    $y = 4$

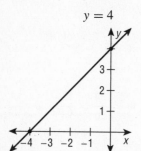

4. $2x + 3y = 6$

    x-intercept: $2x + 3(0) = 6$

                    $2x = 6$

                     $x = 3$

    y-intercept: $2(0) + 3y = 6$

                    $3y = 6$

                    $y = 2$

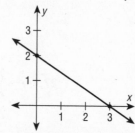

5. Rational; it is the quotient of two integers.

6. Irrational; $\sqrt{7} \approx 2.645751\ldots$; its decimal form neither repeats nor terminates.

7. Rational; the decimal terminates.

8. Rational; $\sqrt{\dfrac{64}{81}} = \dfrac{\sqrt{64}}{\sqrt{81}} = \dfrac{8}{9}$; it is the quotient of two integers.

9.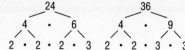

$24 = 2 \cdot 2 \cdot 2 \cdot 3 = 2^3 \cdot 3$

$36 = 2 \cdot 2 \cdot 3 \cdot 3 = 2^2 \cdot 3^2$

The LCM is $2^3 \cdot 3^2 = 72$.

10.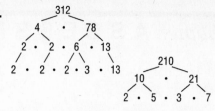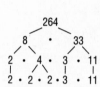

$312 = 2 \cdot 2 \cdot 2 \cdot 3 \cdot 13 = 2^3 \cdot 3 \cdot 13$

$210 = 2 \cdot 3 \cdot 5 \cdot 7$

The LCM is $2^3 \cdot 3 \cdot 5 \cdot 7 \cdot 13 = 10{,}920$.

11. $111 = 3 \cdot 37$

$55 = 5 \cdot 11$

The LCM is $3 \cdot 5 \cdot 11 \cdot 37 = 6105$.

12.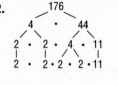

$176 = 2 \cdot 2 \cdot 2 \cdot \cdot 2 \cdot 11 = 2^4 \cdot 11$

$264 = 2 \cdot 2 \cdot 2 \cdot 3 \cdot 11 = 2^3 \cdot 3 \cdot 11$

The LCM is $2^4 \cdot 3 \cdot 11 = 528$.

13.

$\dfrac{a}{32} = \dfrac{18}{100}$

$\dfrac{a}{32} = 0.18$

$a = 32 \cdot 0.18$

$a = 5.76$

5.76 is 18% of 32.

14.

$\dfrac{15}{b} = \dfrac{45}{100}$

$\dfrac{b}{15} = \dfrac{100}{45}$

$b = 15 \cdot \dfrac{100}{45}$

$b = \dfrac{100}{3}$ or $33\dfrac{1}{3}$

15 is 45% of $33\frac{1}{3}$.

15.

$\dfrac{72}{36} = \dfrac{p}{100}$

$2 = \dfrac{p}{100}$

$100 \cdot 2 = p$

$200 = p$

72 is 200% of 36.

16.

$\dfrac{17}{40} = \dfrac{p}{100}$

$100 \cdot \dfrac{17}{40} = p$

$\dfrac{85}{2}$ or $42.5 = p$

17 is 42.5% of 40.

17. Yes; $12 + 24 = 36 > 30$,

$12 + 30 = 42 > 24$,

$24 + 30 = 54 > 12$

18. Yes; $21 + 26 = 47 > 46$,

$21 + 46 = 67 > 26$,

$26 + 46 = 72 > 21$

19. No; $13 + 14 = 27 \not> 29$

20. No; $18 + 18 = 36 \not> 38$

21. $\tan 57° = \dfrac{h}{50}$

$h = 50 \tan 57°$

≈ 77 yd

Mid-Chapter **ASSESSMENT**

1. $y = 28x$
$y = 28(2)$
$y = 56$ g

2. $y = 28x$
$700 = 28x$
25 oz $= x$

3. $y = 28x$
$y = 28(16)$
$y = 448$ g

Therefore, 1 lb = 448 g.
1 kg (1000 g) weighs more.

4. $(0, 7)$
$3x + 4y = 28$
$3(0) + 4(7) \overset{?}{=} 28$
$28 = 28$
Yes

5. $\left(9, -\frac{1}{4}\right)$
$3x + 4y = 28$
$3(9) + 4\left(-\frac{1}{4}\right) \overset{?}{=} 28$
$27 - 1 \overset{?}{=} 28$
$26 \neq 28$

No

6. $(8, 1)$
$3x + 4y = 28$
$3(8) + 4(1) \overset{?}{=} 28$
$24 + 4 \overset{?}{=} 28$
$28 = 28$

Yes

7.

x	1	6	11	16
y	8	6	4	2

$2x + 5y = 42$

$x = 1:\ 2(1) + 5y = 42$
$2 + 5y = 42$
$5y = 40$
$y = 8$

$x = 6:\ 2(6) + 5y = 42$
$12 + 5y = 42$
$5y = 30$
$y = 6$

$x = 11:\ 2(11) + 5y = 42$
$22 + 5y = 42$
$5y = 20$
$y = 4$

$x = 16:\ 2(16) + 5y = 42$
$32 + 5y = 42$
$5y = 10$
$y = 2$

8.

9. $8x + 2y = 32$

x-intercept: $8x + 2(0) = 32$
$8x = 32$
$x = 4$

y-intercept: $8(0) + 2y = 32$
$2y = 32$
$y = 16$

10. $4x + 5y = 20$

x-intercept: $4x + 5(0) = 20$
$4x = 20$
$x = 5$

y-intercept: $4(0) + 5y = 20$
$5y = 20$
$y = 4$

11. $12x + 8y = 24$

x-intercept: $12x + 8(0) = 24$
$12x = 24$
$x = 2$

y-intercept: $12(0) + 8y = 24$
$8y = 24$
$y = 3$

12.–15. $m = \dfrac{y_2 - y_1}{x_2 - x_1}$

12. $m = \dfrac{12 - 9}{4 - 2}$

$\qquad = \dfrac{3}{2}$

13. $m = \dfrac{6 - 2}{3 - 5}$

$\qquad = \dfrac{4}{-2} = -2$

14. $m = \dfrac{2 - (-5)}{-3 - 7}$

$\qquad = -\dfrac{7}{10}$

15. $m = \dfrac{10 - 7}{2 - 0}$

$\qquad = \dfrac{3}{2}$

16. Because they have the same slope, the lines in Exercises 12 and 15 are parallel.

17. B; $y = 3x - 3$

$\quad$ x-intercept:

$\quad$ $0 = 3x - 3$

$\quad$ $3 = 3x$

$\quad$ $1 = x$

$\quad$ y-intercept:

$\quad$ $y = 3(0) - 3$

$\quad$ $y = -3$

18. A; $3x + y = 3$

$\quad$ x-intercept:

$\quad$ $3x + 0 = 3$

$\quad$ $x = 1$

$\quad$ y-intercept:

$\quad$ $3(0) + y = 3$

$\quad$ $y = 3$

19. C; $y = -\frac{1}{3}x + 1$

$\quad$ x-intercept:

$\quad$ $0 = -\frac{1}{3}x + 1$

$\quad$ $\frac{3}{1} \cdot \frac{1}{3}x = 1 \cdot \frac{3}{1}$

$\quad$ $x = 3$

$\quad$ y-intercept:

$\quad$ $y = -\frac{1}{3}(0) + 1$

$\quad$ $y = 1$

Lab 13.5

Part A

1.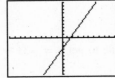

2. $(0, -3), (1.5, 0)$

3. $\dfrac{-3 - 0}{0 - 1.5} = \dfrac{-3}{-1.5} = 2$

4.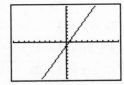

$(0, -1), (0.5, 0);\ \dfrac{-1 - 0}{0 - 0.5} = \dfrac{-1}{-0.5} = 2$

5.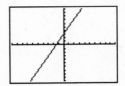

$(0, 3), (-1.5, 0);\ \dfrac{3 - 0}{0 - (-1.5)} = \dfrac{3}{1.5} = 2$

1.–5.

Equation	$y = 2x - 3$	$y = 2x - 1$	$y = 2x + 3$
Coordinates	$(0, -3), (1.5, 0)$	$(0, -1), (0.5, 0)$	$(0, 3), (-1.5, 0)$
Slope	2	2	2

6. The slopes are all 2. The slope of the line given by $y = mx + b$ is m.

7.–9.

Equation	$y = 2x + 3$	$y = -x + 3$	$y = \frac{1}{2}x + 3$
y-intercept	$(0, 3)$	$(0, 3)$	$(0, 3)$

9. The y-intercepts are all $(0, 3)$.

10. The y-intercept of the line given by $y = mx + b$ is b.

11. The slope of all of the graphs is -1.

12. The y-intercept of all of the graphs is -4.

13. The slope is -1 and the y-intercept is -4.

13.5 *The Slope-Intercept Form*

ONGOING ASSESSMENT

1. Move to the right 5 units and up 2 units; $(0 + 5, 3 + 2) = (5, 5)$

2. Move to the right 1 unit and up 3 units; $(0 + 1, 3 + 3) = (1, 6)$

3. Move to the right 3 units and down 2 units; $(0 + 3, 3 - 2) = (3, 1)$

4. Move to the right any number of units, but do not move up or down; $(0 + x, 3 - 0) = (x, 3)$

EXERCISES

1. *Sample answer:* It contains the slope, m, and the y-intercept, b.

2. Subtract $3x$ from each side to get $y = -3x + 5$.

3. The slope of the line is

$$m = \frac{\text{Rise}}{\text{Run}} = \frac{-3}{\frac{3}{2}}$$

$$= -3 \div \frac{3}{2} = -3 \cdot \frac{2}{3}$$

$$= -2.$$

The y-intercept is $b = 3$. The equation of the line is $y = mx + b = -2x + 3$. So, C is a correct choice and A, B, and D are not.

In E,

$$2x + y = 3$$
$$2x + y - 2x = 3 - 2x$$
$$y = 3 - 2x$$
$$= -2x + 3.$$

So, E is a correct choice.

In F,

$$2x - y = 3$$
$$2x - y - 2x = 3 - 2x$$
$$y = 3 - 2x$$
$$y = -3 + 2x$$
$$= 2x - 3.$$

So, F is not a correct choice.
Answer: C and E

4.–21. For $y = mx + b$, m is the slope and b is the y-intercept.

4. $y = -4x + 5$
Slope: -4
y-intercept: 5

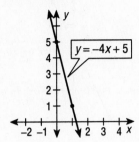

5. $y = \frac{1}{4}x - 1$
Slope: $\frac{1}{4}$
y-intercept: -1

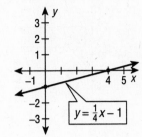

6. $3x + y = 2$
$\qquad y = 3x + 2$
Slope: 3
y-intercept: 2

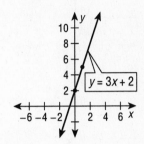

7. $2x + y = 8$
$\qquad y = -2x + 8$
Slope: -2
y-intercept: 8

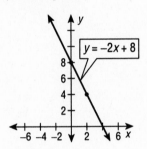

8. $y = x - 3$
Slope: 1
y-intercept: -3

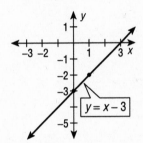

9. $y = -x + 3$
Slope: -1
y-intercept: 3

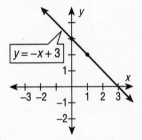

10. $y = -\frac{2}{3}x + 2$
Slope: $-\frac{2}{3}$
y-intercept: 2

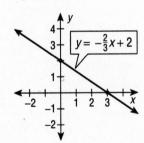

11. $y = 3x$
Slope: 3
y-intercept: 0

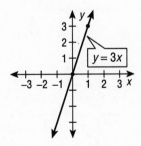

12. $y - 4x = 5$
$\qquad y = 4x + 5$
Slope: 4
y-intercept: 5

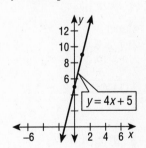

13. $\frac{5}{2}x + y = 0$

$\quad y = -\frac{5}{2}x$

Slope: $-\frac{5}{2}$

y-intercept: 0

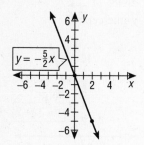

14. $2x + y = 1$

$\quad y = -2x + 1$

Slope: -2

y-intercept: 1

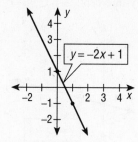

15. $-2x + y = 3$

$\quad y = 2x + 3$

Slope: 2

y-intercept: 3

16. $y = -2x + \frac{5}{2}$

Slope: -2

y-intercept: $\frac{5}{2} = 2\frac{1}{2}$

Answer: C

17. $y = 2x + \frac{5}{2}$

Slope: 2

y-intercept: $\frac{5}{2} = 2\frac{1}{2}$

Answer: A

18. $y = \frac{3}{4}x + 1$

Slope: $\frac{3}{4}$

y-intercept: 1

Answer: B

19. False;

$y - 2x = 5$

$\quad y = 2x + 5$

$m = 2$

$b = 5$

20. True;

$\frac{1}{4}x + y = 5$

$\quad y = -\frac{1}{4}x + 5$

$m = -\frac{1}{4}$

$b = 5$

21.

x	0	1	2	3	4
y	7	16.8	26.6	36.4	46.2

The speed increases 9.8 m/s every second.

22. Slope: 9.8

y-intercept: 7

The slope is the increase in speed per second; the y-intercept is the initial speed.

23.–25. For $y = mx + b$, the slope is m and the y-intercept is b.

23. Slope: $-\frac{2}{3}$

y-intercept: 1

$y = -\frac{2}{3}x + 1$

24. Slope: $-\frac{5}{2}$

y-intercept: 2

$y = -\frac{5}{2}x + 2$

25. Slope: $\frac{2}{5}$

y-intercept: -2

$y = \frac{2}{5}x - 2$

26. B; $y = -\frac{1}{2} + 3$

$4 \overset{?}{=} -\frac{1}{2}(-2) + 3$

$4 \overset{?}{=} 1 + 3$

$4 = 4$

$y = -\frac{1}{2} + 3$

$1 \overset{?}{=} -\frac{1}{2}(4) + 3$

$1 \overset{?}{=} -2 + 3$

$1 = 1$

27. D; $-2x + y = \frac{1}{2}$

$\quad y = 2x + \frac{1}{2}$

$m = 2$

28. a. $y = 2.5x + 1.25$

x	0	1	2	3	4	5	6
y	1.25	3.75	6.25	8.75	11.25	13.75	16.25

b.

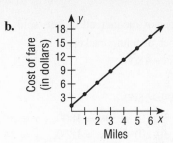

Sample answer: The slope, 2.50, represents the additional charge and the y-intercept, 1.25, represents the initial charge.

Lab 13.6

Part A

1. Answers vary.   **2.** Answers vary.   **3.** Answers vary.

Part B

4. Answers vary.

Part C

5. *Sample answer:* The points of each color are bunched together, separate from the other colors.

6. a. (Span, Height) and (Foot, Forearm)

   b. (Thumb, Wrist) and (Wrist, Neck)

7. Span = 5 feet   **8.** Foot = 10 inches   **9.** Thumb = $6 \div 2 = 3$ inches

13.6 *Problem Solving with Linear Equations*

ONGOING ASSESSMENT

1. $(150, 0)$

2. $(0, 300)$

3. If you sell only adult tickets, you need to sell 150 tickets. If you sell only child tickets, you need to sell 300 tickets.

EXERCISES

1. 1993

2. No; the line of best fit shows a 1996 population of 7.3 million not 7.4 million.

3. x = number of racquetball rackets sold

y = number of tennis rackets sold

$30x + 50y = 1800$

4. $30x + 50y = 1800$

$x = 10;$ $\quad 30(10) + 50y = 1800,$ $\quad y = 30 \Rightarrow (10, 30)$

$x = 20;$ $\quad 30(20) + 50y = 1800,$ $\quad y = 24 \Rightarrow (20, 24)$

$x = 30;$ $\quad 30(30) + 50y = 1800,$ $\quad y = 18 \Rightarrow (30, 18)$

$x = 40;$ $\quad 30(40) + 50y = 1800,$ $\quad y = 12 \Rightarrow (40, 12)$

x	10	20	30	40
y	30	24	18	12

5.

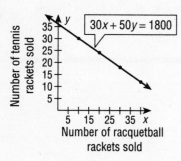

6. $30x + 50y = 1800$

x-intercept: $\quad 30x + 50(0) = 1800$

$$30x = 1800$$

$$x = 60$$

y-intercept: $\quad 30(0) + 50y = 1800$

$$50y = 1800$$

$$y = 36$$

If only one kind of racket is sold, selling 60 racquetball rackets or 36 tennis rackets is necessary to reach your goal.

7. a. About 33.5 cans

b. Answers vary.

8. a. $\boxed{\$1.50} \cdot \boxed{\begin{array}{c}\text{Number of}\\\text{carnations sold}\end{array}} + \boxed{\$3} \cdot \boxed{\begin{array}{c}\text{Number of}\\\text{roses sold}\end{array}} = \boxed{\$600}$

x = number of carnations sold

y = number of roses sold

$1.5x + 3y = 600$

b. $1.5x + 3y = 600$

$x = 100;$ $\quad 1.5(100) + 3y = 600,$ $\quad y = 150,$ $\quad \Rightarrow (100, 150)$

$x = 120;$ $\quad 1.5(120) + 3y = 600,$ $\quad y = 140,$ $\quad \Rightarrow (120, 140)$

$x = 140;$ $\quad 1.5(140) + 3y = 600,$ $\quad y = 130,$ $\quad \Rightarrow (140, 130)$

$x = 160;$ $\quad 1.5(160) + 3y = 600,$ $\quad y = 120,$ $\quad \Rightarrow (160, 120)$

x	100	120	140	160
y	150	140	130	120

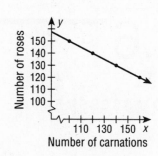

c. $1.5x + 3y = 600$

x-intercept: $\quad 1.5x + 3(0) = 600$ $\qquad$ y-intercept: $\quad 1.5(0) + 3y = 600$

$$1.5x = 600 \qquad\qquad\qquad 3y = 600$$

$$x = 400 \qquad\qquad\qquad\quad y = 200$$

If only one kind of flower is sold, selling 400 carnations or 200 roses is necessary to reach your goal.

9.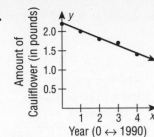

Year (0 ↔ 1990)

1996: 1.1 lb

10.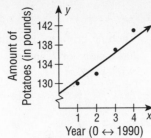

Year (0 ↔ 1990)

1996: 148 lb

11.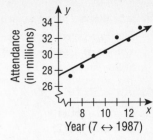

Year (7 ↔ 1987)

1995: About 35.2 million

12. B

13.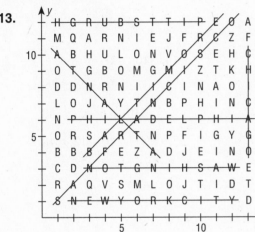

Atlanta: *y*-intercept: 11, $m = \dfrac{-6}{6} = -1$;

Baltimore: *y*-intercept: 1, $m = \dfrac{8}{8} = 1$;

Chicago: *y*-intercept: undefined, none;

Philadelphia: *y*-intercept: 6, $m = 0$;

Pittsburgh: *y*-intercept: 12, $m = 0$;

New York City: *y*-intercept: 1, $m = 0$;

San Francisco: *y*-intercept: 0, $m = \dfrac{11}{11} = 1$;

Washington, D.C.: *y*-intercept: 3, $m = 0$

13.7 *Graphs of Linear Inequalities*

ONGOING ASSESSMENT

1. Solutions of the inequality represent when the fund-raising dinner earned $1200 or more. Yes; a solution means that you met your goal.

EXERCISES

1. Yes

2. No

3. *Sample answer:*
(1, 1), (−2, 0), (0, 3)

4. $y > 2x - 4$
Slope: 2
y-intercept: −4

5.–8. A solid line consists of points that are on the graph, a dashed line consists of points that are not on the graph.

5. Solid

6. Dashed

7. Dashed

8. Solid

9. $y \le x + 3$

The line given by $y = x + 3$ has a slope of 1 and a y-intercept of 3.

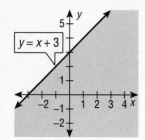

10. $y \ge \frac{1}{2}x - 1$

The line given by $y = \frac{1}{2}x - 1$ has a slope of $\frac{1}{2}$ and a y-intercept of -1.

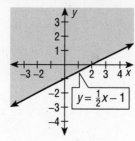

11. $x - y > 2$

$$y > -x + 2$$
$$y < x - 2$$

The line given by $y = x - 2$ has a slope of 1 and a y-intercept of -2.

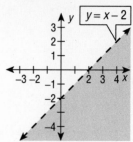

12. $x > -2$

The line given by $x = -2$ has no slope and no y-intercept; it is a vertical line.

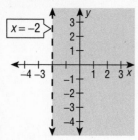

13. $(5, 5)$

$$4x + 6y \le 48$$
$$4(5) + 6(5) \overset{?}{\le} 48$$
$$20 + 30 \overset{?}{\le} 48$$
$$50 \not\le 48$$

No, $50 > 48$.

14. $(10, -2)$

$$4x + 6y \le 48$$
$$4(10) + 6(-2) \overset{?}{\le} 48$$
$$40 - 12 \overset{?}{\le} 48$$
$$28 \le 48$$

Yes

15. $(-2, 10)$

$$4x + 6y \le 48$$
$$4(-2) + 6(10) \overset{?}{\le} 48$$
$$8 + 60 \overset{?}{\le} 48$$
$$52 \not\le 48$$

No, $52 > 48$.

16. $(6, 4)$

$$4x + 6y \le 48$$
$$4(6) + 6(4) \overset{?}{\le} 48$$
$$24 + 24 \overset{?}{\le} 48$$
$$48 \le 48$$

Yes

17.–19. All the y-intercepts of Graphs A–C are 2.

17. B; the slope of Graph B is $\frac{1}{3}$, which is the slope given by $y = \frac{1}{3}x + 2$.

18. C; the slope of Graph C is -3, which is the slope given by $-3x - y = -2$.

19. A; the slope of Graph A is $-\frac{1}{2}$, which is the slope given by $x + 2y = 4$.

20. $y \le \frac{1}{4}x + 1$

The line given by $y = \frac{1}{4}x + 1$ has a slope of $\frac{1}{4}$ and a y-intercept of 1.

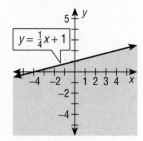

$(4, 0)$, $(4, 1)$, $(4, 2)$, $(0, -1)$

21. $y > -2x - 2$

The line given by $y = -2x - 2$ has a slope of -2 and a y-intercept of -2.

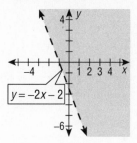

$(0, -1)$, $(0, 1)$, $(1, 1)$, $(1, 2)$

22. $x + y < 25$

$$y < -x + 25$$

The line given by $y = -x + 25$ has a slope of -1 and a y-intercept of 25.

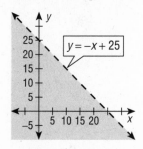

$(0, 24)$, $(1, 23)$, $(-1, 25)$, $(0, 0)$

23. $4x + 3y \ge 9$

$$3y \ge -4x + 9$$

$$y \ge -\frac{4}{3}x + 3$$

The line given by $y = -\frac{4}{3}x + 3$ has a slope of $-\frac{4}{3}$ and a y-intercept of 3.

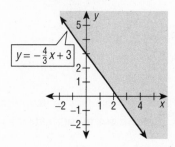

$(3, -1)$, $(3, 0)$, $(3, 1)$, $(0, 3)$

24. B

25. $2x + 5y < 30$

$$5y < -2x + 30$$

$$y < -\frac{2}{5}x + 6$$

The line given by $y = -\frac{2}{5}x + 6$ has a slope of $-\frac{2}{5}$ and a y-intercept of 6.
Sample answer: $(5, 3)$, $(-5, 6)$, $(0, 0)$, $(0, 5)$

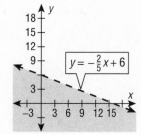

26. C; $x + y \le 26.2$.

The sum of the number of miles you walk and the number of miles you run could be equal to 26.2 if you finish the marathon, or could be less than 26.2 if you do not finish the marathon.

27. $x + y \leq 26.2$

$y \leq -x + 26.2$

The line given by $y = -x + 26.2$ has a slope of -1 and a y-intercept of 26.2.

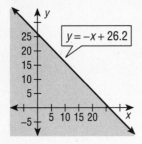

28. D

29. A. $x + y > 26.2 \Rightarrow$

You are sure you can finish the marathon and go farther.

B. $x + y \geq 26.2 \Rightarrow$

You are sure you can finish the marathon and perhaps go farther.

30. D

31. $h + 2.5 < 1.25h + 1.5$

$1 < 0.25h$

$4 < h$

The number of hours you can park so that Location A is less expensive than Location B;

Sample answer: It is cheaper to park farther away at Location A if you will be parking for more than 4 hours.

13.8 GEOMETRY CONNECTION: *The Distance and Midpoint Formulas*

ONGOING ASSESSMENT

1. $d = \sqrt{(x_2 - x_1)^2 + (y_2 - y_1)^2}$

$d = \sqrt{(57 - 20)^2 + (30 - 20)^2}$

$= \sqrt{37^2 + 10^2}$

$= \sqrt{1369 + 100}$

$= \sqrt{1469} \approx 38.33$ ft

$d = \sqrt{(94 - 57)^2 + (40 - 30)^2}$

$= \sqrt{37^2 + 10^2}$

$= \sqrt{1369 + 100}$

$= \sqrt{1469} \approx 38.33$ ft

The distances are the same.

2. *Sample answer:* yes; yes; a midpoint is halfway between the endpoints.

EXERCISES

1.
$$d = \sqrt{(x_2 - x_1)^2 + (y_2 - y_1)^2}$$
$$= \sqrt{(2 - 5)^2 + (0 - 4)^2}$$
$$= \sqrt{(-3)^2 + (-4)^2}$$
$$= \sqrt{9 + 16}$$
$$= \sqrt{25} = 5$$

$$\text{midpoint} = \left(\frac{x_1 + x_2}{2}, \frac{y_1 + y_2}{2}\right)$$
$$= \left(\frac{5 + 2}{2}, \frac{4 + 0}{2}\right)$$
$$= \left(\frac{7}{2}, 2\right)$$

2.
$$d = \sqrt{(x_2 - x_1)^2 + (y_2 - y_1)^2}$$
$$= \sqrt{(-1 - (-1))^2 + (-7 - (-3))^2}$$
$$= \sqrt{0^2 + (-4)^2}$$
$$= \sqrt{16} = 4$$

$$\text{midpoint} = \left(\frac{x_1 + x_2}{2}, \frac{y_1 + y_2}{2}\right)$$
$$= \left(\frac{-1 + (-1)}{2}, \frac{-3 + (-7)}{2}\right)$$
$$= (-1, -5)$$

3. $(x_1, y_1) = (2, 4), (x_2, y_2) = (-3, 3)$
$$d = \sqrt{(x_2 - x_1)^2 + (y_2 - y_1)^2}$$
$$= \sqrt{(-3 - 2)^2 + (3 - 4)^2}$$
$$= \sqrt{(-5)^2 + (-1)^2}$$
$$= \sqrt{25 + 1}$$
$$= \sqrt{26}$$
$$P = 2\left(\sqrt{26}\right) + 2\left(\sqrt{40}\right) \approx 22.85$$

$(x_1, y_1) = (-3, 3), (x_2, y_2) = (-1, -3)$
$$d = \sqrt{(-1 - (-3))^2 + (-3 - 3)^2}$$
$$= \sqrt{2^2 + (-6)^2}$$
$$= \sqrt{4 + 36}$$
$$= \sqrt{40}$$

4. $(x_1, y_1) = (2, 4), (x_2, y_2) = (-2, -2)$
$$\text{midpoint} = \left(\frac{x_1 + x_2}{2}, \frac{y_1 + y_2}{2}\right)$$
$$= \left(\frac{2 + (-2)}{2}, \frac{4 + (-2)}{2}\right)$$
$$= (0, 1)$$

$(x_1, y_1) = (-4, 3), (x_2, y_2) = (4, -1)$
$$\text{midpoint} = \left(\frac{-4 + 4}{2}, \frac{3 + (-1)}{2}\right)$$
$$= (0, 1)$$

5. Estimate: 8
$$d = \sqrt{(x_2 - x_1)^2 + (y_2 - y_1)^2}$$
$$= \sqrt{(-3 - 2)^2 + (-3 - 3)^2}$$
$$= \sqrt{(-5)^2 + (-6)^2}$$
$$= \sqrt{25 + 36}$$
$$= \sqrt{61} \approx 7.8$$

6. Estimate: 6
$$d = \sqrt{(x_2 - x_1)^2 + (y_2 - y_1)^2}$$
$$= \sqrt{(2 - (-3))^2 + (-3 - 1)^2}$$
$$= \sqrt{5^2 + (-4)^2}$$
$$= \sqrt{25 + 16}$$
$$= \sqrt{41} \approx 6.4$$

7. Estimate: 8

$$d = \sqrt{(x_2 - x_1)^2 + (y_2 - y_1)^2}$$
$$= \sqrt{(1 - 4)^2 + (-4 - 3)^2}$$
$$= \sqrt{(-3)^2 + (-7)^2}$$
$$= \sqrt{9 + 49}$$
$$= \sqrt{58} \approx 7.6$$

8. Estimate: $(-1, 0)$

$$\text{midpoint} = \left(\frac{x_1 + x_2}{2}, \frac{y_1 + y_2}{2} \right)$$
$$= \left(\frac{-4 + 2}{2}, \frac{2 + (-2)}{2} \right)$$
$$= \left(\frac{-2}{2}, \frac{0}{2} \right) = (-1, 0)$$

9. Estimate: $(-3, 0)$

$$\text{midpoint} = \left(\frac{x_1 + x_2}{2}, \frac{y_1 + y_2}{2} \right)$$
$$= \left(\frac{-2 + (-4)}{2}, \frac{3 + (-3)}{2} \right)$$
$$= \left(\frac{-6}{2}, \frac{0}{2} \right) = (-3, 0)$$

10. Estimate: $\left(\frac{5}{2}, 0 \right)$

$$\text{midpoint} = \left(\frac{x_1 + x_2}{2}, \frac{y_1 + y_2}{2} \right)$$
$$= \left(\frac{3 + 2}{2}, \frac{3 + (-3)}{2} \right)$$
$$= \left(\frac{5}{2}, 0 \right)$$

11. $\text{Center} = \left(\frac{x_1 + x_2}{2}, \frac{y_1 + y_2}{2} \right)$

$$= \left(\frac{1 + (-3)}{2}, \frac{3 + (-1)}{2} \right)$$
$$= \left(-\frac{2}{2}, \frac{2}{2} \right) = (-1, 1)$$
$$\text{diameter} = \sqrt{(x_2 - x_1)^2 + (y_2 - y_1)^2}$$
$$= \sqrt{(-3 - 1)^2 + (-1 - 3)^2}$$
$$= \sqrt{(-4)^2 + (-4)^2}$$
$$= \sqrt{16 + 16}$$
$$= \sqrt{32}$$
$$\approx 5.7 \text{ units}$$

12. $\text{Center} = \left(\frac{x_1 + x_2}{2}, \frac{y_1 + y_2}{2} \right)$

$$= \left(\frac{-1 + 3}{2}, \frac{-2 + 0}{2} \right)$$
$$= \left(\frac{2}{2}, \frac{-2}{2} \right) = (1, -1)$$
$$\text{diameter} = \sqrt{(x_2 - x_1)^2 + (y_2 - y_1)^2}$$
$$= \sqrt{(3 - (-1))^2 + (0 - (-2))^2}$$
$$= \sqrt{4^2 + 2^2}$$
$$= \sqrt{16 + 4}$$
$$= \sqrt{20}$$
$$\approx 4.5 \text{ units}$$

13. $\text{Center} = \left(\frac{x_1 + x_2}{2}, \frac{y_1 + y_2}{2} \right)$

$$= \left(\frac{-3 + 3}{2}, \frac{2 + 1}{2} \right)$$
$$= \left(0, \frac{3}{2} \right) = (0, 1.5)$$
$$\text{diameter} = \sqrt{(x_2 - x_1)^2 + (y_2 - y_1)^2}$$
$$= \sqrt{(3 - (-3))^2 + (1 - 2)^2}$$
$$= \sqrt{6^2 + (-1)^2}$$
$$= \sqrt{36 + 1}$$
$$= \sqrt{37}$$
$$\approx 6.1 \text{ units}$$

14. $(5, 6), (3, 1)$

15. $(0, -8)$, $(4, -2)$

16. Points: $A(10, 15)$, $B(80, 55)$

$$\text{midpoint} = \left(\frac{x_1 + x_2}{2}, \frac{y_1 + y_2}{2}\right)$$

$$= \left(\frac{10 + 80}{2}, \frac{15 + 55}{2}\right)$$

$$= \left(\frac{90}{2}, \frac{70}{2}\right) = (45, 35)$$

17. Points: $(38, 97)$, $(36, 87)$

$$\text{midpoint} = \left(\frac{x_1 + x_2}{2}, \frac{y_1 + y_2}{2}\right)$$

$$= \left(\frac{38 + 36}{2}, \frac{97 + 87}{2}\right)$$

$$= \left(\frac{74}{2}, \frac{184}{2}\right)$$

$$= (37, 92) \Rightarrow (37\text{N}, 92\text{W})$$

18. B; $(3, 2)$, and $(-4, -2)$

$$\text{midpoint} = \left(\frac{x_1 + x_2}{2}, \frac{y_1 + y_2}{2}\right)$$

$$= \left(\frac{3 + (-4)}{2}, \frac{2 + (-2)}{2}\right)$$

$$= \left(\frac{-1}{2}, \frac{0}{2}\right)$$

$$= \left(-\frac{1}{2}, 0\right)$$

19. C; $\text{distance} = \sqrt{(x_2 - x_1)^2 + (y_2 - y_1)^2}$

$$= \sqrt{(-4 - 3)^2 + (-2 - 2)^2}$$

$$= \sqrt{(-7)^2 + (-4)^2}$$

$$= \sqrt{49 + 16}$$

$$= \sqrt{65} \approx 8.06$$

20. Cable car turnaround: $(2, 6)$

Transamerica Pyramid: $(8, 1)$

$$\text{midpoint} = \left(\frac{x_1 + x_2}{2}, \frac{y_1 + y_2}{2}\right)$$

$$= \left(\frac{2 + 8}{2}, \frac{6 + 1}{2}\right)$$

$$= \left(\frac{10}{2}, \frac{7}{2}\right)$$

$$= (5, 3.5)$$

Washington Square is closest to the midpoint.

Chapter REVIEW

1. $y = -4x + 6$

x	-2	-1	0	1	2
y	14	10	6	2	-2

$x = -2$; $y = -4(-2) + 6 \Rightarrow y = 14$
$x = -1$; $y = -4(-1) + 6 \Rightarrow y = 10$
$x = 0$; $y = -4(0) + 6 \ \Rightarrow y = 6$
$x = 1$; $y = -4(1) + 6 \ \Rightarrow y = 2$
$x = 2$; $y = -4(2) + 6 \ \Rightarrow y = -2$

2. $6x + y = 16 \Rightarrow y = 16 - 6x$

x	-2	-1	0	1	2
y	28	22	16	10	4

$x = -2$; $y = 16 - 6(-2) \Rightarrow y = 28$
$x = -1$; $y = 16 - 6(-1) \Rightarrow y = 22$
$x = 0$; $y = 16 - 6(0) \ \Rightarrow y = 16$
$x = 1$; $y = 16 - 6(1) \ \Rightarrow y = 10$
$x = 2$; $y = 16 - 6(2) \ \Rightarrow y = 4$

3. $3x - y = 8 \Rightarrow y = 3x - 8$

x	−2	−1	0	1	2
y	−14	−11	−8	−5	−2

$x = -2; \quad y = 3(-2) - 8 \Rightarrow y = -14$
$x = -1; \quad y = 3(-1) - 8 \Rightarrow y = -11$
$x = 0; \quad y = 3(0) - 8 \Rightarrow y = -8$
$x = 1; \quad y = 3(1) - 8 \Rightarrow y = -5$
$x = 2; \quad y = 3(2) - 8 \Rightarrow y = -2$

4. $y = 5x - 7$

x	−2	−1	0	1	2
y	−17	−12	−7	−2	3

$x = -2; \quad y = 5(-2) - 7 \Rightarrow y = -17$
$x = -1; \quad y = 5(-1) - 7 \Rightarrow y = -12$
$x = 0; \quad y = 5(0) - 7 \Rightarrow y = -7$
$x = 1; \quad y = 5(1) - 7 \Rightarrow y = -2$
$x = 2; \quad y = 5(2) - 7 \Rightarrow y = 3$

5. $y = 2x + 10$

x	5	6	7	8	9	10
y	20	22	24	26	28	30

$x = 5; \quad y = 2(5) + 10 \Rightarrow y = \$20$
$x = 6; \quad y = 2(6) + 10 \Rightarrow y = \$22$
$x = 7; \quad y = 2(7) + 10 \Rightarrow y = \$24$
$x = 8; \quad y = 2(8) + 10 \Rightarrow y = \$26$
$x = 9; \quad y = 2(9) + 10 \Rightarrow y = \$28$
$x = 10; \quad y = 2(10) + 10 \Rightarrow y = \$30$

6. $y = 4x - 5$

x	−2	−1	0	1	2
y	−13	−9	−5	−1	3

$x = -2; \quad y = 4(-2) - 5 \Rightarrow y = -13$
$x = -1; \quad y = 4(-1) - 5 \Rightarrow y = -9$
$x = 0; \quad y = 4(0) - 5 \Rightarrow y = -5$
$x = 1; \quad y = 4(1) - 5 \Rightarrow y = -1$
$x = 2; \quad y = 4(2) - 5 \Rightarrow y = 3$

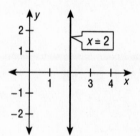

$y = 4x - 5$

7. $3x - y = 10 \Rightarrow y = -10 + 3x$

x	−2	−1	0	1	2
y	−16	−13	−10	−7	−4

$x = -2; \quad y = -10 + 3(-2) \Rightarrow y = -16$
$x = -1; \quad y = -10 + 3(-1) \Rightarrow y = -13$
$x = 0; \quad y = -10 + 3(0)5 \Rightarrow y = -10$
$x = 1; \quad y = -10 + 3(1)5 \Rightarrow y = -7$
$x = 2; \quad y = -10 + 3(2)5 \Rightarrow y = -4$

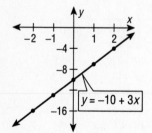

$y = -10 + 3x$

8. $x = 2$

For all values of y, x is 2.

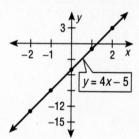

$x = 2$

9. $y = -3$

For all values of x, y is -3.

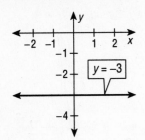

10. $3x + 4y = 24$

y-intercept:

$3(0) + 4y = 24$

$4y = 24$

$y = 6$

x-intercept:

$3x + 4(0) = 24$

$3x = 24$

$x = 8$

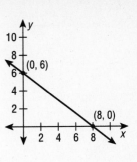

11. $5x - y = 10$

y-intercept:

$5(0) - y = 10$

$-y = 10$

$y = -10$

x-intercept:

$5x - 0 = 10$

$5x = 10$

$x = 2$

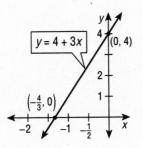

12. $y = -8x + 2$

y-intercept:

$y = -8(0) + 2$

$y = 2$

x-intercept:

$0 = -8x + 2$

$8x = 2$

$x = \frac{1}{4}$

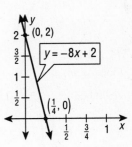

13. $y = 4 + 3x$

y-intercept:

$y = 4 + 3(0)$

$y = 4$

x-intercept:

$0 = 4 + 3x$

$-4 = 3x$

$-\frac{4}{3} = x$

14. $6x - 7 = -y$

$y = -6x + 7$

y-intercept:

$y = -6(0) + 7$

$y = 7$

x-intercept:

$0 = -6x + 7$

$6x = 7$

$x = \frac{7}{6}$

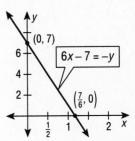

15. Slope $= \dfrac{y_2 - y_1}{x_2 - x_1}$

$= \dfrac{3 - 9}{6 - 4}$

$= \dfrac{-6}{2} = -3$

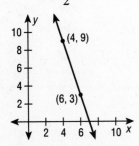

16. Slope $= \dfrac{y_2 - y_1}{x_2 - x_1}$

$= \dfrac{1 - 2}{8 - 1}$

$= -\dfrac{1}{7}$

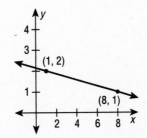

17. Slope $= \dfrac{y_2 - y_1}{x_2 - x_1}$

$= \dfrac{-2 - 5}{7 - 3}$

$= -\dfrac{7}{4}$

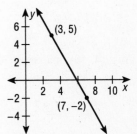

18. Slope $= \dfrac{y_2 - y_1}{x_2 - x_1}$

$= \dfrac{-2 - 6}{-1 - (-8)}$

$= -\dfrac{8}{7}$

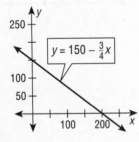

19. $y = -3x - 5$

Slope $= m = -3$

y-intercept $= b = -5$

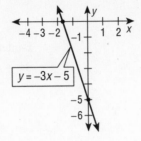

20. $y = 4 + 7x$

Slope $= m = 7$

y-intercept $= b = 4$

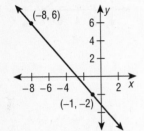

21. $9x + 3 = y$

Slope $= m = 9$

y-intercept $= b = 3$

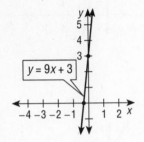

22. $4x + y = 3 \Rightarrow y = -4x + 3$

Slope $= m = -4$

y-intercept $= b = 3$

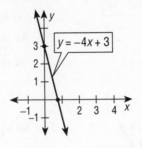

23. $3x + 4y = 600$

$4y = 600 - 3x$

$y = 150 - \dfrac{3}{4}x$

Subs, x	0	40	80	100	140	180	200
Pizzas, y	150	120	90	75	45	15	0

24. $y < 8x - 12$

$10 \overset{?}{<} 8(4) - 12$

$10 \overset{?}{<} 32 - 12$

$10 < 20$

Yes; $(4, 10)$ is a solution.

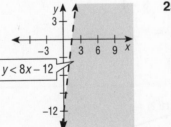

25. $2x - y \geq -16$

$-y \geq -16 - 2x$

$y \leq 16 + 2x$

Sample answer: $(0, 0)$, $(0, 4)$, $(4, 4)$, $(-6, -3)$

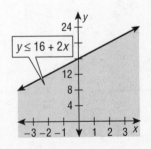

26. Points: $(5, 7)$, $(8, 12)$

$$d = \sqrt{(x_2 - x_1)^2 + (y_2 - y_1)^2}$$
$$= \sqrt{(8 - 5)^2 + (12 - 7)^2}$$
$$= \sqrt{3^2 + 5^2}$$
$$= \sqrt{9 + 25}$$
$$= \sqrt{34} \approx 5.83 \text{ units}$$

$$\text{midpoint} = \left(\frac{x_1 + x_2}{2}, \frac{y_1 + y_2}{2} \right)$$
$$= \left(\frac{5 + 8}{2}, \frac{7 + 12}{2} \right)$$
$$= \left(\frac{13}{2}, \frac{19}{2} \right)$$
$$= (6.5, 9.5)$$

27. Points: $(-2, 0)$, $(1, 9)$

$$d = \sqrt{(x_2 - x_1)^2 + (y_2 - y_1)^2}$$
$$= \sqrt{(1 - (-2))^2 + (9 - 0)^2}$$
$$= \sqrt{3^2 + 9^2}$$
$$= \sqrt{9 + 81}$$
$$= \sqrt{90} \approx 9.48 \text{ units}$$

$$\text{midpoint} = \left(\frac{x_1 + x_2}{2}, \frac{y_1 + y_2}{2} \right)$$
$$= \left(\frac{-2 + 1}{2}, \frac{0 + 9}{2} \right)$$
$$= \left(\frac{-1}{2}, \frac{9}{2} \right)$$
$$= (-0.5, 4.5)$$

28. Points: $(-3, 2)$, $(6, 4)$

$$d = \sqrt{(x_2 - x_1)^2 + (y_2 - y_1)^2}$$
$$= \sqrt{(6 - (-3))^2 + (4 - 2)^2}$$
$$= \sqrt{9^2 + 2^2}$$
$$= \sqrt{81 + 4}$$
$$= \sqrt{85} \approx 9.21 \text{ units}$$

$$\text{midpoint} = \left(\frac{x_1 + x_2}{2}, \frac{y_1 + y_2}{2} \right)$$
$$= \left(\frac{-3 + 6}{2}, \frac{2 + 4}{2} \right)$$
$$= \left(\frac{3}{2}, \frac{6}{2} \right)$$
$$= (1.5, 3)$$

29. Points: $(1, -7)$, $(-5, -6)$

$$d = \sqrt{(x_2 - x_1)^2 + (y_2 - y_1)^2}$$
$$= \sqrt{(-5 - 1)^2 + (-6 - (-7))^2}$$
$$= \sqrt{(-6)^2 + 1^2}$$
$$= \sqrt{36 + 1}$$
$$= \sqrt{37} \approx 6.08 \text{ units}$$

$$\text{midpoint} = \left(\frac{x_1 + x_2}{2}, \frac{y_1 + y_2}{2} \right)$$
$$= \left(\frac{1 + (-5)}{2}, \frac{-7 + (-6)}{2} \right)$$
$$= \left(\frac{-4}{2}, \frac{-13}{2} \right)$$
$$= (-2, -6.5)$$

Chapter ASSESSMENT

1. $2x + y = 6$

x	-3	-2	-1	0	1	2	3
y	12	10	8	6	4	2	0

$x = -3$ $2(-3) + y = 6$, $y = 12 \Rightarrow (-3, 12)$
$x = -2$ $2(-2) + y = 6$, $y = 10 \Rightarrow (-2, 10)$
$x = -1$ $2(-1) + y = 6$, $y = 8 \Rightarrow (-1, 8)$
$x = 0$ $2(0) + y = 6$, $y = 6 \Rightarrow (0, 6)$
$x = 1$ $2(1) + y = 6$, $y = 4 \Rightarrow (1, 4)$
$x = 2$ $2(2) + y = 6$, $y = 2 \Rightarrow (2, 2)$
$x = 3$ $2(3) + y = 6$, $y = 0 \Rightarrow (3, 0)$

2. x-intercept: 3
y-intercept: 6

3.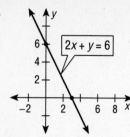

4. $(8, 3)$

$$x + 3y = 16$$
$$8 + 3(3) \stackrel{?}{=} 16$$
$$8 + 9 \stackrel{?}{=} 16$$
$$17 \neq 16$$

No

5. $(1, 5)$

$$x + 3y = 16$$
$$1 + 3(5) \stackrel{?}{=} 16$$
$$1 + 15 \stackrel{?}{=} 16$$
$$16 = 16$$

Yes

6. $(-2, 6)$

$$x + 3y = 16$$
$$-2 + 3(6) \stackrel{?}{=} 16$$
$$-2 + 18 \stackrel{?}{=} 16$$
$$16 = 16$$

Yes

7. $(5, 3)$

$$x + 3y = 16$$
$$5 + 3(3) \stackrel{?}{=} 16$$
$$5 + 9 \stackrel{?}{=} 16$$
$$14 \neq 16$$

No

8. $m = \dfrac{y_2 - y_1}{x_2 - x_1}$

$$= \dfrac{4 - 7}{2 - 3}$$
$$= \dfrac{-3}{-1}$$
$$= 3$$

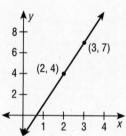

9. $m = \dfrac{y_2 - y_1}{x_2 - x_1}$

$$= \dfrac{-2 - 6}{3 - 4}$$
$$= \dfrac{-8}{-1}$$
$$= 8$$

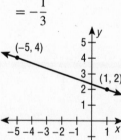

10. $m = \dfrac{y_2 - y_1}{x_2 - x_1}$

$$= \dfrac{4 - 2}{-5 - 1}$$
$$= \dfrac{2}{-6}$$
$$= -\dfrac{1}{3}$$

11. For $y = mx + b$, m is the slope and b is the y-intercept.

$$y = -2x + 4$$

Slope: -2

y-intercept: 4

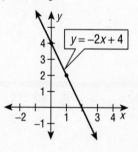

12.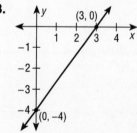

13.

14.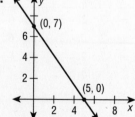

15. Slope: $= -\frac{3}{5}$
y-intercept: 3
$y = -\frac{3}{5}x + 3$

16. Slope: $\frac{2}{5}$
y-intercept: 2
$y = \frac{2}{5}x + 2$

17. Slope: $-\frac{4}{3}$
y-intercept: 4
$y = -\frac{4}{3}x + 4$

18. $y < 7x$
The line given by $y = 7x$ has a slope of 7 and a y-intercept of 0.

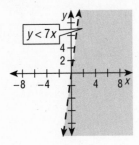

Answers vary.

19. $y \geq 2x + 2$
The line given by $y = 2x + 2$ has a slope of 2 and a y-intercept of 2.

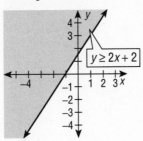

Answers vary.

20. $y > 5x - 7$

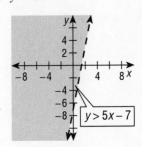

Answers vary.

21. Points: $(-3, -2), (5, 6)$

$d = \sqrt{(x_2 - x_1)^2 + (y_2 - y_1)^2}$

$= \sqrt{(5 - (-3))^2 + (6 - (-2))^2}$

$= \sqrt{8^2 + 8^2}$

$= \sqrt{64 + 64}$

$= \sqrt{128} \approx 11.31$ units

midpoint $= \left(\dfrac{x_1 + x_2}{2}, \dfrac{y_1 + y_2}{2} \right)$

$= \left(\dfrac{-3 + 5}{2}, \dfrac{-2 + 6}{2} \right)$

$= \left(\dfrac{2}{2}, \dfrac{4}{2} \right) = (1, 2)$

22. Points: $(1, 5), (8, 0)$

$d = \sqrt{(x_2 - x_1)^2 + (y_2 - y_1)^2}$

$= \sqrt{(8 - 1)^2 + (0 - 5)^2}$

$= \sqrt{7^2 + (-5)^2}$

$= \sqrt{49 + 25}$

$= \sqrt{74} \approx 8.6$ units

midpoint $= \left(\dfrac{x_1 + x_2}{2}, \dfrac{y_1 + y_2}{2} \right)$

$= \left(\dfrac{1 + 8}{2}, \dfrac{5 + 0}{2} \right)$

$= \left(\dfrac{9}{2}, \dfrac{5}{2} \right) = (4.5, 2.5)$

23. Points: $(4, -9), (-1, -7)$

$d = \sqrt{(x_2 - x_1)^2 + (y_2 - y_1)^2}$

$= \sqrt{(-1 - 4)^2 + (-7 - (-9))^2}$

$= \sqrt{(-5)^2 + 2^2}$

$= \sqrt{25 + 4}$

$= \sqrt{29} \approx 5.38$ units

midpoint $= \left(\dfrac{x_1 + x_2}{2}, \dfrac{y_1 + y_2}{2} \right)$

$= \left(\dfrac{4 + (-1)}{2}, \dfrac{-9 + (-7)}{2} \right)$

$= \left(\dfrac{3}{2}, \dfrac{-16}{2} \right) = (1.5, -8)$

24. C; $y = 4x$ when $y = 48$ and $x = 12$.   **25.** $y = 4(8) = 32$ mi/h

---

Standardized Test Practice

1. A; $A = 0.17(0) + 2.6 = 2.6$
(0, 2.6)

2. C

3. A;
  x-intercept:
$$0 = -\tfrac{1}{2}x + 3$$
$$\tfrac{1}{2}x = 3$$
$$x = 6$$
    (6, 0)

4. D; $\text{distance} = \sqrt{(x_2 - x_1)^2 + (y_2 - y_1)^2}$
$$= \sqrt{(3 - (-1))^2 + (-4 - 2)^2}$$
$$= \sqrt{4^2 + (-6)^2}$$
$$= \sqrt{16 + 36}$$
$$= \sqrt{52} \approx 7.21$$

5. B

6. A;
$$6x + 5y = 900$$
$$6(80) + 5y = 900$$
$$480 + 5y = 900$$
$$5y = 420$$
$$y = 84$$

7. D;
$$6x + 5y \geq 900$$
$$6(90) + 5(75) \geq 900$$
$$540 + 375 \geq 900$$
$$915 \geq 900$$

8. C; $\left(\dfrac{32.5 + 29.3}{2}, \dfrac{96.5 + 28.3}{2} \right) = (30.9, 62.4)$

Chapter 14
Exploring Data and Polynomials

| **14.1** | *Measures of Central Tendency* |

ONGOING ASSESSMENT

1. *Sample answer:* the median or mode, which are both $5.50 per hour. Thirteen of the 16 salaries are $5.50 per hour.

EXERCISES

1. a. median
   b. mode
   c. mean

3. Mean $= \dfrac{2 \cdot 3 + 4 \cdot 4 + 5 \cdot 5 + 4 \cdot 6 + 1 \cdot 7}{16}$

$= \dfrac{78}{16}$

$= 4\dfrac{7}{8}$

5. The mode is the number that occurs most often.
   Mode $= 5$

2. The numbers 3, 4, 5, 6, and 7 occur from 1 to 5 times each.

3, 3, 4, 4, 4, 4, 5, 5, 5, 5, 5, 6, 6, 6, 6, 7

4. The median is the average of the two middle numbers.
   Median $= \dfrac{5 + 5}{2} = 5$

6. Mean $= \dfrac{85 + 86 + 90 + 90 + 91 + 92}{6}$

$= \dfrac{534}{6}$

$= 89$

Median $= \dfrac{90 + 90}{2} = 90$

Mode $= 90$

7. Mean $= \dfrac{52.8 + 53.6 + 53.9 + 54 + 54.5 + 54.8 + 55.1}{7} = \dfrac{378.7}{7} = 54.1$

Median $= 54$ (the middle number)

Mode: Each number occurs once, so there is no mode.

8. Mean $= \dfrac{34 + 35 + 36 + 36 + 37 + 37 + 38 + 38 + 39 + 40}{10} = \dfrac{370}{10} = 37$

Median $= \dfrac{37 + 37}{2} = 37$

Mode: There is no mode because one number does not occur most often.

9. Mean $= \dfrac{55 + 56 + 57 + 58 + 59 + 60 + 60 + 60 + 62}{9} = \dfrac{527}{9} = 58\dfrac{5}{9}$

Median $= 59$ (the middle number)

Mode $= 60$

10. 20; 0, 0, 1, 2, 2, 2, 3, 3, 3, 3, 4, 4, 4, 4, 4, 4, 5, 5, 5, 6

11. Mean $= \dfrac{2 \cdot 0 + 1 \cdot 1 + 3 \cdot 2 + 4 \cdot 3 + 6 \cdot 4 + 3 \cdot 5 + 1 \cdot 6}{20} = \dfrac{64}{20} = 3.2$

Median $= \dfrac{3 + 4}{2} = \dfrac{7}{2} = 3.5$

Mode $= 4$

12. *Sample answer:* The numbers are responses to the question "How many hours do you usually watch TV on a Sunday?"

13.–15. Answers vary.

16. 5 three-year-old wolves

17. Mean $= \dfrac{12 \cdot 1 + 7 \cdot 2 + 5 \cdot 3 + 3 \cdot 4 + 3 \cdot 5 + 2 \cdot 6 + 1 \cdot 7}{33} = \dfrac{87}{33} = 2\dfrac{7}{11}$

Median $= 2$

Mode $= 1$

18. The mean or median, the mode is not good because it is the smallest number.

19. Mean $= \dfrac{7.1 + 6.9 + 6.7 + 6.5 + 6.3 + 6.9 + 6.8 + 6.5 + 6.3 + 6.1}{10}$

$= \dfrac{66.1}{10}$

$= 6.61$

Ordered data: 6.1, 6.3, 6.3, 6.5, 6.5, 6.7, 6.8, 6.9, 6.9, 7.1

Median $= \dfrac{6.5 + 6.7}{2} = \dfrac{13.2}{2} = 6.6$

Mode: None

20. The water tended to become more acidic. A chemical was added on the 5th or 6th day.

21.–22. *Sample answers:*

21. 13, 14, 15, 15, 16, 17

22. 8, 8, 8, 10, 10, 16

23. *Sample answer:* In 1996 in Seattle, Washington, half the houses cost as much as or more than $160,700 and half the houses cost as much or less than $160,700.

24. x = final test score

$$\frac{95 + 89 + 91 + 93 + x}{500} = \frac{93}{100}$$

$$\frac{x + 368}{500} = \frac{93}{100}$$

$$500 \cdot \frac{x + 368}{500} = 500 \cdot \frac{93}{100}$$

$$x + 368 = 465$$

$$x = 97$$

Final test score: 97

25. C; Ordered data: 10, 10, 11, 14, 16, 16, 16, 18, 19, 20

$$\text{Mean} = \frac{10 + 10 + 11 + 14 + 16 + 16 + 16 + 18 + 19 + 20}{10} = \frac{150}{10} = 15$$

$$\text{Median} = \frac{16 + 16}{2} = 16$$

$$\text{Mode} = 16$$

26. Answers vary.

14.2 *Stem-and-Leaf Plots*

ONGOING ASSESSMENT

1.

West		East
	6	4 8
0	5	0 3 5
7 7 6 3	4	0 5 8 9
9 5 4 4 2 2 2 1 1 0	3	1 1 5 7 9
9 7 4 0	2	1 6 7 9
8 3 2 2 1	1	1 4 5 5 6 6 9
7	0	

3 | 4 | 0 represents 43% and 40% rural population

2. The plot represents the opposite to that of Example 2: the eastern states tend to have more rural populations.

EXERCISES

1. 2, 2, 8, 10, 11, 15, 15, 16, 19, 20, 23, 25, 27, 31, 32, 34, 34, 36

2. Left side: 4.0, 4.2, 4.4, 5.2, 5.3, 5.7, 5.9, 6.0, 6.5, 6.5, 7.1, 7.3, 7.4, 7.8

Right side: 4.3, 5.2, 5.3, 5.5, 5.8, 5.9, 6.1, 6.4, 6.7, 7.0, 7.3, 7.4, 7.6

3.

6	5
5	0 2 4 5
4	1 3
3	0 2 2 3 4 8
2	1 4 8 9 9
1	0 7 8
0	1 2 2 5 6 8 8

6 | 5 represents 65

4. 20, 21, 21, 23, 35, 37, 39, 41, 48, 50, 52, 53, 64, 66, 66, 68

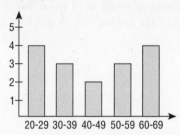

5. 84, 84, 85, 88, 90, 91, 101, 102, 107, 110, 113, 118, 118, 119, 124, 125, 126, 127

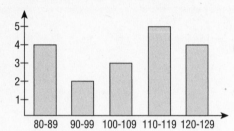

6. 13.5, 13.6, 14.3, 14.5, 14.9, 15.1, 15.9, 15.9, 16.1, 16.2, 16.3, 16.7, 17.2, 17.3, 17.4, 17.6, 17.8

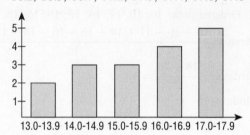

7.

10	0
9	0 2 3 5
8	0 1 3 4 5 5 9
7	1 7 8 9
6	6 7
5	2 9

5 | 2 represents 52

8.

(50-59 60-69 70-79 80-89 90-99 100-109)

9.

18	6
17	1 6
16	1 2 2 2 4 8
15	3 4 7
14	3 5 6 8
13	4 9

18 | 6 represents 186 mi/h

10.

1970		1995
	7	2
4 0	6	0 3 4 8 9
9 8 1	5	1 4 6 8
8 7 5 2 2	4	

8 | 5 | 4 represents 58 in 1970 and 54 in 1995

11. *Sample answer:* In 1970, the life expectancy was mostly in the 40s, where in 1995, it was mostly in the 50s and 60s.

12.

West		East
5 3 2 2	2	
1 1 1 1	2	1
0 0 0 0 0 0 0 0	2	
9 9 9 9 9 9 9	1	9 9 9 9 9 9 9 9 9
8 8	1	8 8 8 8 8 8 8 8
	1	7 7 7 7 7 7 7

1 | 2 | 1 represents 21% population west of the Mississippi and 21% population east of the Mississippi between 5 and 17 years old.

13. East: Mean = $\dfrac{7 \cdot 17 + 8 \cdot 18 + 9 \cdot 19 + 21}{25} = \dfrac{455}{25} = 18.2\%$

Median: 18%

Mode: 19%

West: Mean = $\dfrac{2 \cdot 18 + 7 \cdot 19 + 8 \cdot 20 + 4 \cdot 21 + 2 \cdot 22 + 23 + 25}{25} = \dfrac{505}{25} = 20.2\%$

Median: 20%

Mode: 20%

14. C; $\dfrac{0 + 5 + 10 + 10 + 15 + 15 + 20 + 25 + 25 + 35}{10} = \dfrac{160}{10} = 16$

15. Answers vary.

14.3 *Box-and-Whisker Plots*

ONGOING ASSESSMENT

1. 50%
2. 75%
3. 25%

EXERCISES

1. Smallest number: 6
Largest number: 56

2. 1st quartile: 21
2nd quartile: 34
3rd quartile: 44

3. 1st quartile: $\dfrac{8 + 10}{2} = 9$

2nd quartile: $\dfrac{17 + 21}{2} = 19$

3rd quartile: $\dfrac{29 + 31}{2} = 30$

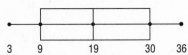

4. Ordered data: 6, 12, 15, 21, 25, 34, 39, 40, 46, 50, 52, 54, 56, 61, 66, 70

1st quartile: $\dfrac{21 + 25}{2} = 23$

2nd quartile: $\dfrac{40 + 46}{2} = 43$

3rd quartile: $\dfrac{54 + 56}{2} = 55$

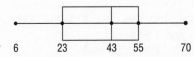

5. Smallest number: 14, Largest number: 96

6. 1st quartile: 40, 2nd quartile: 58, 3rd quartile: 77

7.–8. Because there are twenty numbers in the collection and all the numbers are different, ten numbers are less than 58 and ten numbers are greater than 58. Then five numbers are less than 40 and five numbers are greater than 77. Then ten numbers are between 40 and 77.

7. Since five numbers are less than 40, $\frac{5}{20}$ or 25% are less than 40.

8. Since ten numbers are between 40 and 77, $\frac{10}{20}$ or 50% are between 40 and 77.

9. Ordered data: 18, 24, 26, 29, 32, 36, 39, 40, 41, 41, 42, 44, 49, 50, 60, 62, 64, 67, 72, 82

1st quartile: $\dfrac{32 + 36}{2} = 34$

2nd quartile: $\dfrac{41 + 42}{2} = 41.5$

3rd quartile: $\dfrac{60 + 62}{2} = 61$

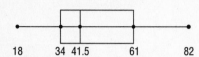

10. Ordered data: 3, 8, 10, 15, 18, 22, 29, 35, 50, 52, 60, 61, 62, 63, 65, 67, 72, 78, 80, 84

1st quartile: $\dfrac{18 + 22}{2} = 20$

2nd quartile: $\dfrac{52 + 60}{2} = 56$

3rd quartile: $\dfrac{65 + 67}{2} = 66$

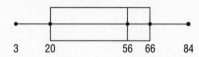

11. Ordered data: 1, 2, 5, 7, 10, 12, 14, 18, 19, 21, 24, 26, 30, 34, 37, 39

39 is the largest number, not 37. The 1st quartile is $\dfrac{7 + 10}{2}$ or 8.5, not 8. The 2nd quartile is $\dfrac{18 + 19}{2}$ or 18.5, not 18. The 2nd quartile should be located $\dfrac{18.5 - 8.5}{28 - 8.5}$ or $\dfrac{10}{19.5}$ of the way from 8.5 to 28, not where it is located now.

12. *Sample answer:* The median age is 31; 25% is under 14; 50% is under 31; 25% is over 51.

13. Mississippi's population is younger than Florida's and Rhode Island's, and is older than Alaska's and Utah's.

14. Ordered data: 1, 7, 13, 14, 14, 15, 16, 16, 20, 20, 20, 22, 25, 25, 28, 41, 55, 60

1st quartile: 14

2nd quartile: $\dfrac{20 + 20}{2} = 20$

3rd quartile: 25

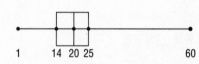

15. Receivers: 165, 180, 200, 225, 260, 280, 300, 325, 360, 380, 390, 400, 445, 460

1st quartile: 225

2nd quartile: $\dfrac{300 + 325}{2} = 312.5$

3rd quartile: 390

CD players: 140, 160, 170, 180, 195, 200, 230, 240, 245, 250, 255, 270, 280, 290

1st quartile: 180

2nd quartile: $\dfrac{230 + 240}{2} = 235$

3rd quartile: 255

Cassette decks: 150, 195, 200, 225, 230, 255, 260, 265, 280, 285, 290, 295

1st quartile: $\dfrac{200 + 225}{2} = 212.5$

2nd quartile: $\dfrac{255 + 260}{2} = 257.5$

3rd quartile: $\dfrac{280 + 285}{2} = 282.5$

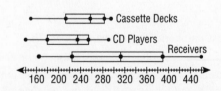

16. Receivers generally cost more than cassette decks, and cassette decks generaly cost more than CD players.

17. D; Most students who take algebra are about 15 years old.

18. C; The smallest and largest numbers are the most appropriate for a 100-point test.

19. B; Most 4th graders weigh about 65 pounds.

20. A; Scores of a baseball team are almost always less than 14.

21. C; Ordered data: 4, 8, 10, 14, 15, 16, 17, 19, 19, 19, 20, 21, 23, 24, 25, 27

3rd quartile: $\dfrac{21 + 23}{2} = 22$

22. B; Ordered data: 35, 39, 42, 43, 45, 46, 47, 48, 51, 51, 52, 55

1st quartile: $\dfrac{42 + 43}{2} = 42.5$

23. Answers vary.

Spiral **R E V I E W**

1. $(AB)^2 = 9^2 + 4^2$
$(AB)^2 = 81 + 16$
$(AB)^2 = 97$
$\quad AB = \sqrt{97} \approx 9.85$

2. Area $= \frac{1}{2}bh$
$\quad = \frac{1}{2}(9 \cdot 4)$
$\quad = \frac{1}{2}(36)$
$\quad = 18 \text{ units}^2$

3. $\sin A = \dfrac{4}{\sqrt{97}} \approx 0.406$

4. $\cos A = \dfrac{9}{\sqrt{97}} \approx 0.914$

5. $\tan A = \dfrac{4}{9} \approx 0.444$

6. $\sin B = \dfrac{9}{\sqrt{97}} \approx 0.914$

7. $\cos B = \dfrac{4}{\sqrt{97}} \approx 0.406$

8. $\tan B = \dfrac{9}{4} = 2.25$

9. Mean $= \dfrac{1.5 + 1.6 + 1.8 + 1.8 + 1.9 + 2.3 + 2.4 + 2.4 + 2.7 + 2.7 + 2.7 + 3.0 + 3.0 + 3.1}{14} = \dfrac{32.9}{14} = 2.35$

10. Median: $\dfrac{2.4 + 2.4}{2} = 2.4$

11. Mode: 2.7

12.
```
3 | 0 0 1
2 | 3 4 4 7 7 7
1 | 5 6 8 8 9
```
3 | 0 represents 3.0

13. $\dfrac{x}{13} = \dfrac{4}{12}$
$\dfrac{x}{13} = \dfrac{1}{3}$
$\quad x = \dfrac{13}{3}, \text{ or } 4\frac{1}{3}$

14. $\dfrac{b}{6} = \dfrac{6}{16}$
$\dfrac{b}{6} = \dfrac{3}{8}$
$\quad b = 6 \cdot \dfrac{3}{8}$
$\quad b = \dfrac{9}{4}$

15. $\dfrac{3}{2} = \dfrac{15}{r}$
$\dfrac{2}{3} = \dfrac{r}{15}$
$15 \cdot \dfrac{2}{3} = r$
$\quad 10 = r$

16. $\dfrac{4}{s} = \dfrac{21}{18}$
$\dfrac{s}{4} = \dfrac{18}{21}$
$\dfrac{s}{4} = \dfrac{6}{7}$
$\quad s = \dfrac{24}{7}, \text{ or } 3\frac{3}{7}$

17. $\sqrt{44.89} = 6.7 \text{ m}$
The garden is 6.7 m by 6.7 m.

Using a Calculator

1. Smallest number: 14
Largest number: 37
1st quartile: 19
2nd quartile: 27.5
3rd quartile: 34

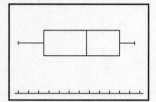

2. Smallest number: 52
Largest number: 82
1st quartile: 58
2nd quartile: 67
3rd quartile: 72

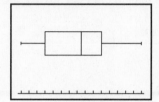

3. Smallest number: 21
Largest number: 56
1st quartile: 24
2nd quartile: 25.5
3rd quartile: 28

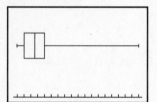

4. Smallest number: 34
Largest number: 52
1st quartile: 37
2nd quartile: 42.5
3rd quartile: 45

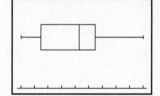

5.–7. *Sample answers:*

5. 1, 1, 1, 3, 13, 13, 13, 13, 13, 13, 13, 13, 17, 20, 20, 20

6. 2, 3, 4, 5, 6, 6, 7, 7, 9, 10, 11, 12, 14, 16, 18, 20

7. 1, 2, 3, 4, 5, 6, 7, 8, 9, 10, 11, 12, 13, 14, 15, 16

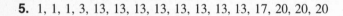

14.4 *Exploring Data and Matrices*

ONGOING ASSESSMENT

1. $\begin{bmatrix} 3+4 & -2+3 \\ 0+(-1) & 5+2 \end{bmatrix} = \begin{bmatrix} 7 & 1 \\ -1 & 7 \end{bmatrix}$

2. $\begin{bmatrix} -5-(-8) & 4-3 \\ 3-2 & 2-(-5) \end{bmatrix} = \begin{bmatrix} 3 & 1 \\ 1 & 7 \end{bmatrix}$

EXERCISES

1. 3 rows and 2 columns   **2.** −5   **3.** 3rd row and 1st column

4. $\begin{bmatrix} 0 = 0 & \frac{5}{4} = 1.25 & -1 \\ \frac{8}{5} = -1.6 & 2 & 3 \end{bmatrix}$

The matrices are equal because the corresponding entries are equal $\left(\frac{5}{4} = 1.25 \text{ and } -\frac{8}{5} = -1.6\right)$.

5. $\begin{bmatrix} 2 + (-4) & 3 + 1 & 0 + (-5) \\ -3 + (-6) & 0 + 7 & -1 + 2 \end{bmatrix} = \begin{bmatrix} -2 & 4 & -5 \\ -9 & 7 & 1 \end{bmatrix}$

6. $\begin{bmatrix} 2.1 - 1.8 & -1.5 - 4.8 \\ -3.5 - (-1.1) & 6.4 - (-0.8) \end{bmatrix} = \begin{bmatrix} 0.3 & -6.3 \\ -2.4 & 7.2 \end{bmatrix}$

7. $\begin{bmatrix} -2 + (-1) & 3 + 4 \\ 1 + (-6) & -5 + 0 \end{bmatrix} = \begin{bmatrix} -3 & 7 \\ -5 & -5 \end{bmatrix}$

$\begin{bmatrix} -2 - (-1) & 3 - 4 \\ 1 - (-6) & -5 - 0 \end{bmatrix} = \begin{bmatrix} -1 & -1 \\ 7 & -5 \end{bmatrix}$

8. $\begin{bmatrix} 5 + (-8) & 2 + 0 \\ -2 + (-9) & 7 + 3 \end{bmatrix} = \begin{bmatrix} -3 & 2 \\ -11 & 10 \end{bmatrix}$

$\begin{bmatrix} 5 - (-8) & 2 - 0 \\ -2 - (-9) & 7 - 3 \end{bmatrix} = \begin{bmatrix} 13 & 2 \\ 7 & 4 \end{bmatrix}$

9. $\begin{bmatrix} -4 + (-6) & -5 + 3 & 2 + 2 \\ 0 + 1 & -9 + (-1) & -3 + 4 \end{bmatrix} = \begin{bmatrix} -10 & -2 & 4 \\ 1 & -10 & 1 \end{bmatrix}$

$\begin{bmatrix} -4 - (-6) & -5 - 3 & 2 - 2 \\ 0 - 1 & -9 - (-1) & -3 - 4 \end{bmatrix} = \begin{bmatrix} 2 & -8 & 0 \\ -1 & -8 & -7 \end{bmatrix}$

10. $\begin{bmatrix} -4 + 4 & 4 + 7 \\ 5 + 2 & 3 + (-1) \\ -6 + (-3) & -2 + (-8) \end{bmatrix} = \begin{bmatrix} 0 & 11 \\ 7 & 2 \\ -9 & -10 \end{bmatrix}$

$\begin{bmatrix} -4 - 4 & 4 - 7 \\ 5 - 2 & 3 - (-1) \\ -6 - (-3) & -2 - (-8) \end{bmatrix} = \begin{bmatrix} -8 & -3 \\ 3 & 4 \\ -3 & 6 \end{bmatrix}$

11. $\begin{bmatrix} 3 + (-7) & 5 + 0 & -6 + 3 \\ -4 + (-1) & 0 + (-4) & -6 + 5 \\ 4 + 4 & 8 + (-2) & 1 + 9 \end{bmatrix} = \begin{bmatrix} -4 & 5 & -3 \\ -5 & -4 & -1 \\ 8 & 6 & 10 \end{bmatrix}$

$\begin{bmatrix} 3 - (-7) & 5 - 0 & -6 - 3 \\ -4 - (-1) & 0 - (-4) & -6 - 5 \\ 4 - 4 & 8 - (-2) & 1 - 9 \end{bmatrix} = \begin{bmatrix} 10 & 5 & -9 \\ -3 & 4 & -11 \\ 0 & 10 & -8 \end{bmatrix}$

12. $\begin{bmatrix} 4 + 12 & 2 + (-10) & 8 + (-6) \\ -2 + (-5) & 6 + 0 & -1 + 11 \\ 7 + (-1) & 9 + 2 & -1 + 3 \end{bmatrix} = \begin{bmatrix} 16 & -8 & 2 \\ -7 & 6 & 10 \\ 6 & 11 & 2 \end{bmatrix}$

$\begin{bmatrix} 4 - 12 & 2 - (-10) & 8 - (-6) \\ -2 - (-5) & 6 - 0 & -1 - 11 \\ 7 - (-1) & 9 - 2 & -1 - 3 \end{bmatrix} = \begin{bmatrix} -8 & 12 & 14 \\ 3 & 6 & -12 \\ 8 & 7 & -4 \end{bmatrix}$

13. $\begin{bmatrix} \frac{1}{3} + \frac{2}{3} & \frac{2}{3} + \frac{2}{3} & \frac{1}{3} + \frac{1}{3} \\ \frac{1}{4} + \frac{3}{4} & \frac{1}{4} + \frac{1}{4} & \frac{3}{4} + \frac{1}{2} \\ \frac{1}{5} + \frac{1}{5} & \frac{2}{5} + \frac{3}{5} & \frac{3}{5} + \frac{1}{5} \end{bmatrix} = \begin{bmatrix} 1 & \frac{4}{3} & \frac{2}{3} \\ 1 & \frac{1}{2} & \frac{5}{4} \\ \frac{2}{5} & 1 & \frac{4}{5} \end{bmatrix}$

$\begin{bmatrix} \frac{1}{3} - \frac{2}{3} & \frac{2}{3} - \frac{2}{3} & \frac{1}{3} - \frac{1}{3} \\ \frac{1}{4} - \frac{3}{4} & \frac{1}{4} - \frac{1}{4} & \frac{3}{4} - \frac{1}{2} \\ \frac{1}{5} - \frac{1}{5} & \frac{2}{5} - \frac{3}{5} & \frac{3}{5} - \frac{1}{5} \end{bmatrix} = \begin{bmatrix} -\frac{1}{3} & 0 & 0 \\ -\frac{1}{2} & 0 & \frac{1}{4} \\ 0 & -\frac{1}{5} & \frac{2}{5} \end{bmatrix}$

14.
$$\begin{bmatrix} 4.1+(-6.3) & 2.5+1.5 & -2.3+3.6 \\ 6.8+2.1 & 0.4+4.7 & -7.3+(-1.7) \\ -4.8+5.3 & 4.7+2.1 & -5.0+4.7 \end{bmatrix} = \begin{bmatrix} -2.2 & 4 & 1.3 \\ 8.9 & 5.1 & -9 \\ 0.5 & 6.8 & -0.3 \end{bmatrix}$$

$$\begin{bmatrix} 4.1-(-6.3) & 2.5-1.5 & -2.3-3.6 \\ 6.8-2.1 & 0.4-4.7 & -7.3-(-1.7) \\ -4.8-5.3 & 4.7-2.1 & -5.0-4.7 \end{bmatrix} = \begin{bmatrix} 10.4 & 1 & -5.9 \\ 4.7 & -4.3 & -5.6 \\ -10.1 & 2.6 & -9.7 \end{bmatrix}$$

15.

	Side 1	Side 2	Side 3
Triangle 1	5	7	10
Triangle 2	9	12	15
Triangle 3	0.9	4	4.1
Triangle 4	5	6	9.2

16.

Triangle 1:

$5^2 + 7^2 \overset{?}{=} 10^2$

$25 + 49 \overset{?}{=} 100$

$74 \neq 100$

Not right

Triangle 2:

$9^2 + 12^2 \overset{?}{=} 15^2$

$81 + 144 \overset{?}{=} 225$

$225 = 225$

Right

Triangle 3:

$0.9^2 + 4^2 \overset{?}{=} 4.1^2$

$0.81 + 16 \overset{?}{=} 16.81$

$16.81 = 16.81$

Right

Triangle 4:

$5^2 + 6^2 \overset{?}{=} 9.2^2$

$25 + 36 \overset{?}{=} 84.64$

$61 \neq 84.64$

Not right

17. Triangle 1: $5 + 7 + 10 = 22$

Triangle 2: $9 + 12 + 15 = 36$

Triangle 3: $0.9 + 4 + 4.1 = 9$

Triangle 4: $5 + 6 + 9.2 = 20.2$

18.

Income	Store 1	Store 2
May	32	35
June	35	33
July	30	41
August	37	36

Expenses	Store 1	Store 2
May	29	30
June	31	29
July	28	35
August	33	31

19. Pet Store 1: August

Pet Store 2: July

20. Income − Expenses = Profit

Profit	Store 1	Store 2
May	$32 − $29 = $3	$35 − $30 = $5
June	$35 − $31 = $4	$33 − $29 = $4
July	$30 − $28 = $2	$41 − $35 = $6
August	$37 − $33 = $4	$36 − $31 = $5

21. Store 1: $3 + 4 + 2 + 4 = 13$

Store 2: $5 + 4 + 6 + 5 = 20$

Store 2 had a greater profit.

22. $2a = -8 \qquad b = 3 \qquad c - 3 = 1 \qquad 2d = -5$

$\qquad a = -4 \qquad\qquad\qquad c = 4 \qquad d = -\frac{5}{2}$

23. $-4 = a + 2 \qquad 6 = 3b \qquad c - 1 = 7 \qquad -3d = 6c$

$-6 = a \qquad\quad 2 = b \qquad\quad c = 8 \qquad -3d = 6(8)$

$\qquad\qquad\qquad\qquad\qquad\qquad\qquad\qquad -3d = 48$

$\qquad\qquad\qquad\qquad\qquad\qquad\qquad\qquad d = -16$

24. B; $\begin{bmatrix} 3-2 & -2-4 \\ -1-(-1) & -6-5 \end{bmatrix} = \begin{bmatrix} 1 & -6 \\ 0 & -11 \end{bmatrix}$

25. Answers vary.

Communicating About Mathematics

1. $\dfrac{7680 + 14{,}048}{2} = \dfrac{21{,}728}{2} = 10{,}864$ feet

2. Mean $= (2 \cdot 30.6 + 32.3 + 32.7 + 2 \cdot 33.7 + 34.9 + 35.3 + 35.9 + 36.7 + 37.4 + 2 \cdot 37.8 +$
$38.8 + 39.5 + 2 \cdot 40.2 + 2 \cdot 40.4 + 40.6)/20$

$= \dfrac{729.5}{20} = 36.475$ h

Median $= \dfrac{36.7 + 37.4}{2} = 37.05$ h

Mode: none

The mean or median best represents the data.

3.

40	2 2 4 4 6
39	5
38	8
37	4 8 8
36	7
35	3 9
34	9
33	7 7
32	3 7
31	
30	6 6

40 | 2 represents 40.2 h. Pick numbers from 30 to 40 to lie on the stem because they represent the whole number portions of the decimals.

4. 1st quartile: 33.7

2nd quartile: $\dfrac{36.7 + 37.4}{2} = 37.05$

3rd quartile: $\dfrac{39.5 + 40.2}{2} = 39.85$

30.6   33.7   37.05   39.85 40.6

5.

$$\begin{array}{cc} 1996 & 1997 \\ \left[\begin{array}{cc} 30.7 & 30.6 \\ 30.9 & 30.6 \\ 31.7 & 32.3 \\ 31.9 & 32.7 \\ 32.6 & 33.7 \end{array}\right] \end{array}$$

Mid-Chapter ASSESSMENT

1. Mean $= \dfrac{80° + 81° + 82° + 83° + 85° + 87° + 87° + 89° + 89° + 87° + 84° + 81°}{12}$

$= \dfrac{1015°}{12}$

$= 84\dfrac{7}{12}°$

2. Ordered: 80°, 81°, 81°, 82°, 83°, 84°, 85°, 87°, 87°, 87°, 89°, 89°

Median $= \dfrac{84° + 85°}{2} = 84.5°$

3. Mode: 87°

4.

Jacksonville		Miami
	9	3
	8	
9 1	7	6 6
	6	2
7 6	5	6 7
	4	
9 7 6 3	3	
9 8 7 2	2	0 1 4 7 9
	1	8

1 | 7 | 6 represents 7.1 in. and 7.6 in.

5. Ordered data: 1.8, 2.0, 2.1, 2.4, 2.7, 2.9, 5.6, 5.7, 6.2, 7.6, 7.6, 9.3

Median: $\dfrac{2.9 + 5.6}{2} = 4.25$

6. Mean $= \dfrac{3.3 + 3.9 + 3.7 + 2.8 + 3.6 + 5.7 + 5.6 + 7.9 + 7.1 + 2.9 + 2.2 + 2.7}{12} \approx 4.28$ in.

7. 82°, 92°, 93°, 95°, 96°, 96°, 96°, 99°, 100°, 104°, 104°, 113°

8. 1st quartile: $\dfrac{93° + 95°}{2} = 94°$

9. 2nd quartile: 96°

10. 3rd quartile: $\dfrac{100° + 104°}{2} = 102°$

11.

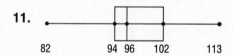

12. $\frac{9}{12} = 75\%$

13. 35

14. 64

15. 24

16. $\begin{bmatrix} 2+6 & 3+2 \\ 9+11 & 8+0 \end{bmatrix} = \begin{bmatrix} 8 & 5 \\ 20 & 8 \end{bmatrix}$

17. $\begin{bmatrix} 4-1 & 5-3 \\ 6-8 & 8-21 \end{bmatrix} = \begin{bmatrix} 3 & 2 \\ -2 & -13 \end{bmatrix}$

18. $\begin{bmatrix} 21-20 & 18-6 \\ 19-(-4) & 40-16 \end{bmatrix} = \begin{bmatrix} 1 & 12 \\ 23 & 24 \end{bmatrix}$

ONGOING ASSESSMENT

1.

Time	Substitution	Height
$t = 0$	$h = -16(0)^2 + 400 = 0 + 400$	400
$t = 1$	$h = -16(1)^2 + 400 = -16 + 400$	384
$t = 2$	$h = -16(2)^2 + 400 = -64 + 400$	336
$t = 3$	$h = -16(3)^2 + 400 = -144 + 400$	256
$t = 4$	$h = -16(4)^2 + 400 = -256 + 400$	144
$t = 5$	$h = -16(5)^2 + 400 = -400 + 400$	0

The ride would last approximately 5 seconds.

EXERCISES

1. Yes; each coefficient is a real number and each exponent is a whole number.

2. No; the negative exponent is not a whole number.

3. No; the negative exponent is not a whole number.

4. Yes; each coefficient is a real number and each exponent is a whole number.

5. No; the negative exponent is not a whole number.

6. Yes; each coefficient is a real number and each exponent is a whole number.

7. Yes; each coefficient is a real number and each exponent is a whole number.

8. Yes; each coefficient is a real number and each exponent is a whole number.

9. $4x - 2 + 3x^2 = 3x^2 + 4x - 2$
Terms: $3x^2, 4x, -2$

10. $10 - 5r^3 + 4r = -5r^3 + 4r + 10$
Terms: $-5r^3, 4r, 10$

11. $3p - 16p^2 - 12 + p^3 = p^3 - 16p^2 + 3p - 12$
Terms: $p^3, -16p^2, 3p, -12$

12. $t^2 + t - 5t + 2t^2 = t^2 + 2t^2 + t - 5t = 3t^2 - 4t$
Binomial

13. $12 - 6x^3 + 5x^3 - 7 = -6x^3 + 5x^3 + 12 - 7$
$$= -x^3 + 5$$
Binomial

14. $2n + 1 + 12n - 8 = 2n + 12n + 1 - 8$
$$= 14n - 7$$
Binomial

15. Yes; trinomial

16. Yes; binomial

17. Yes; monomial

18. No; because there is a fraction with a variable (x) in the denominator.

19. D **20.** C **21.** B **22.** A

23. $14m - 10m^2 + 5m^3 = 5m^3 - 10m^2 + 14m$

Terms: $5m^3, -10m^2, 14m$

24. $6x^3 - x - 2x^2 = 6x^3 - 2x^2 - x$

Terms: $6x^3, -2x^2, -x$

25. $5 - 11y - 8y^3 = -8y^3 - 11y + 5$

Terms: $-8y^3, -11y, 5$

26. $9z^2 - 7z + 3 - z^3 = -z^3 + 9z^2 - 7z + 3$

Terms: $-z^3, 9z^2, -7z, 3$

27. $2 - t^4 + t^2 + t = -t^4 + t^2 + t + 2$

Terms: $-t^4, t^2, t, 2$

28. $w + 4w^2 - 3 + 15w^3 = 15w^3 + 4w^2 + w - 3$

Terms: $15w^3, 4w^2, w, -3$

29. $y + 2y^2 - 3y = 2y^2 + y - 3y$

$\qquad = 2y^2 - 2y$

30. $x^3 - 3x + 5x - x^3 = x^3 - x^3 + 5x - 3x$

$\qquad\qquad = 0x^3 + 2x$

$\qquad\qquad = 2x$

31. $8 - 4x^2 + 10x^2 - 11 = 10x^2 - 4x^2 + 8 - 11$

$\qquad\qquad = 6x^2 - 3$

32. $x^2 + 7x + 10 + x^2 + 2x = x^2 + x^2 + 7x + 2x + 10$

$\qquad\qquad = 2x^2 + 9x + 10$

33. $2x^2 + 5x + 3 + 5x + 4 = 2x^2 + 5x + 5x + 3 + 4$

$\qquad\qquad = 2x^2 + 10x + 7$

34. $x^2 + 2x + 4 + 2x^2 + 4x + 6 = x^2 + 2x^2 + 2x + 4x + 4 + 6$

$\qquad\qquad = 3x^2 + 6x + 10$

35. $15 + 7s^3 - 21 - 3s^2 + s^3 = 7s^3 + s^3 - 3s^2 + 15 - 21$

$\qquad\qquad = 8s^3 - 3s^2 - 6$

36. $\frac{4}{3}m - 7 - \frac{2}{3}m + 8 = \frac{4}{3}m - \frac{2}{3}m + 8 - 7$

$\qquad\qquad = \frac{2}{3}m + 1$

37. $1.1r^2 - 2.9r + 1.8r^2 + 3.3r = 1.1r^2 + 1.8r^2 + 3.3r - 2.9r$

$\qquad\qquad = 2.9r^2 + 0.4r$

38. $-2(3p - 4p^3 + 6 - 9p) = -6p + 8p^3 - 12 + 18p$

$\qquad\qquad = 8p^3 + 18p - 6p - 12$

$\qquad\qquad = 8p^3 + 12p - 12$

39. Use $h = -16t^2 + 1053$.

$t = 0$
$h = -16(0)^2 + 1053$
$\quad = 1053$

$t = 1$
$h = -16(1)^2 + 1053$
$\quad = -16 + 1053$
$\quad = 1037$

$t = 2$
$h = -16(2)^2 + 1053$
$\quad = -64 + 1053$
$\quad = 989$

$t = 3$
$h = -16(3)^2 + 1053$
$\quad = -144 + 1053$
$\quad = 909$

$t = 4$
$h = 16(4)^2 + 1053$
$\quad = -256 + 1053$
$\quad = 797$

$t = 5$
$h = -16(5)^2 + 1053$
$\quad = -400 + 1053$
$\quad = 653$

$t = 6$
$h = -16(6)^2 + 1053$
$\quad = -576 + 1053$
$\quad = 477$

$t = 7$
$h = -16(7)^2 + 1053$
$\quad = -784 + 1053$
$\quad = 269$

$t = 8$
$h = -16(8)^2 + 1053$
$\quad = -1024 + 1053$
$\quad = 29$

$t = 9$
$h = -16(9)^2 + 1053$
$\quad = -1296 + 1053$
$\quad = -243$

(Since the height cannot be negative, the camera has already hit the water.)

t	0	1	2	3	4	5	6	7	8	9
h	1053	1037	989	909	797	653	477	269	29	−243

40. 797 ft

41.
$$h = -16t^2 + 1053$$
$$0 = -16t^2 + 1053$$
$$16t^2 = 1053$$
$$t^2 = 65.8125$$
$$t = \sqrt{65.8125} \approx 8.11 \text{ s}$$

42. B; $x^2 - 4x^3 + 5 - x + x^3 - 2x^2 = -4x^3 + x^3 + x^2 - 2x^2 - x + 5$
$$= -3x^3 - x^2 - x + 5$$

43. D; $4 + 5x^2 - 3x - 10x^3 = -10x^3 + 5x^2 - 3x + 4$

44. a. Answers vary.
b. Answers vary.

Lab 14.6

Part A

1. $2x^2 + 2x + 4$ **2.** $x^2 + 4x + 1$ **3.** $4x^2 + 2x + 7$ **4.** $3x^2 + 5x + 3$

5.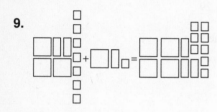

6.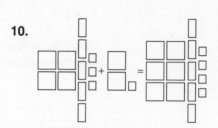

7.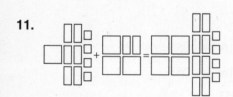

8.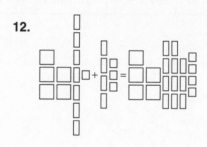

Part B

9.

(3x^2 + 2x + 7) + (x^2 + x + 1) = 4x^2 + 3x + 8

$$(3x^2 + 2x + 7) + (x^2 + x + 1) = 4x^2 + 3x + 8$$

10.

$$(4x^2 + 5x + 3) + (2x^2 + 1) = 6x^2 + 5x + 4$$

11.

$$(x^2 + 6x + 4) + (3x^2 + 2x) = 4x^2 + 8x + 4$$

12.

$$(5x^2 + 7x + 1) + (4x + 3) = 5x^2 + 11x + 4$$

13. $(3x^2 + x + 5) + (2x^2 + 3x + 2) = 5x^2 + 4x + 7$ **14.** $(x^2 + 3x + 10) + (3x^2 + 2x + 2) = 4x^2 + 5x + 12$

15. Add the coefficients of like terms.

14.6 *Adding and Subtracting Polynomials*

ONGOING ASSESSMENT

1. $(x^2 + 3x + 3) + (2x^2 - 2x + 4) = x^2 + 3x + 3 + 2x^2 - 2x + 4$

$$= 3x^2 + x + 7$$

2. $(3x^2 - x + 2) - (x^2 + 2x - 5) = 3x^2 - x + 2 - x^2 - 2x + 5$

$$= 2x^2 - 3x + 7$$

EXERCISES

1. $(3x^2 - 7x + 5) + (3x^2 - 10) = 3x^2 + 3x^2 - 7x + 5 - 10$

$$= 6x^2 - 7x - 5$$

2. $(n^2 + 8n - 7) - (-n^2 + 8n - 12) = n^2 - (-n^2) + 8n - 8n - 7 - (-12)$

$$= 2n^2 + 5$$

3.
$$2y^3 + \ y^2 - 4y + 3$$
$$\underline{+ \ \ \ y^3 - 5y^2 + 2y - 6}$$
$$3y^3 - 4y^2 - 2y - 3$$

4.
$$2y^3 + \ y^2 - 4y + 3$$
$$\underline{(y^3 - 5y^2 + 2y - 6)}$$
$$y^3 + 6y^2 - 6y + \ 9$$

5.
$$-4z^3 + z^2 \ \ \ \ \ \ + 7$$
$$\underline{+ \ \ \ 3z^3 \ \ \ \ \ \ - 6z - 5}$$
$$-z^3 + z^2 - 6z + 2$$

6.
$$4x^3 + 3x^2 + 4x + 3$$
$$\underline{(2x^3 + \ x^2 + 2x + 1)}$$
$$2x^3 + 2x^2 + 2x + \ 2$$

7. $(-x^2 + 9x - 5) + (6x^2 - 2x + 16) = -x^2 + 6x^2 + 9x - 2x - 5 + 16$

$$= 5x^2 + 7x + 11$$

8. $(-8a^3 + a^2 + 17) + (6a^2 - 3a + 9) = -8a^3 + a^2 + 6a^2 - 3a + 17 + 9$

$$= -8a^3 + 7a^2 - 3a + 26$$

9. $(-b^3 + 4b^2 - 1) - (7b^3 + 4b^2 + 3) = -b^3 - 7b^3 + 4b^2 - 4b^2 - 1 - 3$

$$= -8b^3 - 4$$

10. $(-5x^3 - 13x + 4) - (-3x^3 + x^2 + 10x - 9) = -5x^3 - (-3x^3) - x^2 - 13x - 10x + 4 - (-9)$

$$= -2x^3 - x^2 - 23x + 13$$

11.
$$x^3 + 4x^2 - 9x + 2$$
$$\underline{+ \ -2x^3 + 5x^2 + \ x - 6}$$
$$-x^3 + 9x^2 - 8x - 4$$

12.
$$2n^4 + 2n^3 - \ n^2 - 4n + 6$$
$$\underline{+ \ \ \ n^4 + 3n^3 - 3n^2 - 5n + 2}$$
$$3n^4 + 5n^3 - 4n^2 - 9n + 8$$

13.
$$3t^3 + 4t^2 + \ \ t - 5$$
$$\underline{(t^3 + 2t^2 - \ 9t + 1)}$$
$$2t^3 + 2t^2 + 10t - \ 6$$

14.
$$x^4 + 3x^3 + \ x^2 + 2x + 5$$
$$\underline{(x^4 + 2x^3 + 3x^2 + 4x - 4)}$$
$$x^3 - 2x^2 - 2x + \ 9$$

15. $(2x^2 + 9x - 4) + (-8x^2 + 3x + 6) + (x^2 - 5x - 7) = 2x^2 - 8x^2 + x^2 + 9x + 3x - 5x - 4 + 6 - 7$

$$= -5x^2 + 7x - 5$$

16. $(4x^2 + x - 17) - (x^2 - 15x + 7) - (-7x^2 + x + 6) = 4x^2 - x^2 - (-7x^2) + x - (-15x) - x - 17 - 7 - 6$

$$= 10x^2 + 15x - 30$$

17. Perimeter $= (4x + 1) + (x^2 + 3x - 4) + (2x^2 + x)$

$$= x^2 + 2x^2 + 4x + 3x + x + 1 - 4$$

$$= 3x^2 + 8x - 3$$

$x = 3$: $3(3)^2 + 8(3) - 3 = 27 + 24 - 3 = 48$

18. Perimeter $= (2x + 7) + (2x^2 - 4x + 5) + (x^2 + 5) + (3x^2 - 2x - 4)$

$$= 2x^2 + x^2 + 3x^2 + 2x - 4x - 2x + 7 + 5 + 5 - 4$$

$$= 6x^2 - 4x + 13$$

$x = 3$: $6(3)^2 - 4(3) + 13 = 54 - 12 + 13 = 55$

19. Area $= x(x + 9) - x(x - 2)$

$$= x^2 + 9x - x^2 + 2x$$

$$= 11x$$

$x = 5$: $11(5) = 55$

20. Area $= 15(2x - 5) - 9(x - 3)$

$$= 30x - 75 - 9x + 27$$

$$= 21x - 48$$

$x = 5$: $21(5) - 48 = 105 - 48$

$$= 57$$

21. Profit $= 12.50x - (2.50x + 500)$

$$= 12.50x - 2.50x - 500$$

$$= 10x - 500$$

22. $10x - 500 = 10(200) - 500$

$$= 2000 - 500$$

$$= 1500$$

23. $10x - 500 = 10(400) - 500 = 4000 - 500 = 3500$

No, you will make more than twice as much because $3500 > 2 \cdot 1500$.

24. D; $(2x^3 + 3x + 7) - (3x^3 - 2x^2 + 4x - 3) = 2x^3 + 3x + 7 - 3x^3 + 2x^2 - 4x + 3$

$$= -x^3 + 2x^2 - x + 10$$

25. a.

Miles, x	20	40	60	80
Mark Hartell: $18.1x$	362	724	1086	1448
Joel Zucker: $28.4x$	568	1136	1704	2272

b. $2272 - 1448 = 824$ min

c. $28.4x - 18.1x = 10.3x$; This represents the difference in the times it takes the two runners to run x miles.

14.7 GEOMETRY CONNECTION: Multiplying Polynomials

ONGOING ASSESSMENT

1. You are finding the area of the whole region (the rectangle).

$(x + 2x)(x + x + 2) = (3x)(2x + 2)$

$= 6x^2 + 6x$

2. $6x^2 + 6x = 8x^2$

$6x = 2x^2$

$6 = 2x$

$3 = x$

3. $6x^2 + 6x = 6(3)^2 + 6(3)$

$= 6(9) + 6(3)$

$= 54 + 18$

$= 72 \text{ units}^2$

EXERCISES

1. $4n(2n^2 - 3n + 5) = 4n(2n^2) - 4n(3n) + 4n(5)$

$= 8n^3 - 12n^2 + 20n$

2. $3y^2(y^2 + 2y - 5) = -3y^2(y^2) + (-3y^2)(2y) - (-3y^2)(5)$

$= -3y^4 - 6y^3 + 15y^2$

3. Rectangle: Area $= 4x(2x - 1)$

$= 2x(4x) - (4x)(1)$

$= 8x^2 - 4x$

Trapezoid: Use $A = \frac{1}{2}(b_1 + b_2)h$.

Area $= \frac{1}{2}[(x + 1) + (x + x + 1 + 2x)](4x)$

$= \frac{1}{2}(5x + 2)(4x)$

$= \frac{1}{2}(4x(5x) + 4x(2))$

$= \frac{1}{2}(20x^2 + 8x)$

$= 10x^2 + 4x$

Small triangle: Use $A = \frac{1}{2}bh$.

Area $= \frac{1}{2}(4x)(x)$

$= \frac{1}{2}(4x^2)$

$= 2x^2$

Large triangle: Use $A = \frac{1}{2}bh$.

Area $= \frac{1}{2}(4x)(2x)$

$= \frac{1}{2}(8x^2)$

$= 4x^2$

4. Area of entire region: $(8x^2 - 4x) + 2x^2 + (10x^2 + 4x) + 4x^2 = 24x^2$

5. Width $= 4x$

Length $= (2x - 1) + x + (x + 1) + 2x = 6x$

6. Area of entire region: $(4x)(6x) = 24x^2$

7. They are the same.

8. $2y(y^2 + 1) = 2y(y^2) + 2y(1)$

$= 2y^3 + 2y$

9. $4x(x^2 - 2x - 1) = 4x(x^2) - 4x(2x) - 4x(1)$
$$= 4x^3 - 8x^2 - 4x$$

10. $2(3x^2 + 6x - 8) = -2(3x^2) + (-2)(6x) - (-2)(8)$
$$= -6x^2 - 12x + 16$$

11. $8t^2(-6t - 5) = 8t^2(-6t) - 8t^2(5)$
$$= -48t^3 - 40t^2$$

12. $b^4(8b^2 + 10b - 1) = -b^4(8b^2) + (-b^4)10b - (-b^4)(1)$
$$= -8b^6 - 10b^5 + b^4$$

13. $2t(-4t^2 + 6t - 2) = 2t(-4t^2) + 2t(6t) - 2t(2)$
$$= -8t^3 + 12t^2 - 4t$$

14. $y(-7y^3 + 8y - 4) = y(-7y^3) + y(8y) - y(4)$
$$= -7y^4 + 8y^2 - 4y$$

15. $4z(2z^5 - z^3 + 10) = -4z(2z^5) - (-4z)(z^3) + (-4z)(10)$
$$= -8z^6 + 4z^4 - 40z$$

16. $n^3(-n^4 + n^3 - n^2 + n - 1) = n^3(-n^4) + n^3(n^3) - n^3(n^2) + n^3(n) - n^3(1)$
$$= -n^7 + n^6 - n^5 + n^4 - n^3$$

17. Triangle: Use $A = \frac{1}{2}bh$.
Area $= \frac{1}{2}(2x)(x) = x^2$

Trapezoid: Use $A = \frac{1}{2}[b_1 + b_2]h$.
Area $= \frac{1}{2}[(x - 2) + (2x - 2)]2x$
$$= \frac{1}{2}(3x - 4)2x$$
$$= (3x - 4)x$$
$$= 3x^2 - 4x$$

Rectangle: Use $A = lw$.
Area $= (2x)(x) = 2x^2$

Parallelogram: Use $A = bh$.
Area $= (x - 1)(2x) = 2x^2 - 2x$

18. Area of entire region: $x^2 + (2x^2 - 2x) + (3x^2 - 4x) + 2x^2 = 8x^2 - 6x$

19. Area of entire region: $(2x)[x + (x - 1) + (x - 2) + x] = (2x)(4x - 3) = 8x^2 - 6x$

20. The expressions are the same.

21. $n(n + 1) = n^2 + n$

22. $n^3(n - 2) = n^4 - 2n^3$

23. Area $= 2x(x) = 2x^2$

24. Area $= (3x + 1)(x) = 3x^2 + x$

25. Volume $= (3x + 1)(x)(2x)$
$$= (3x^2 + x)(2x)$$
$$= 6x^3 + 2x^2$$

26. Use $S = 2B + Ph$.
Surface area $= 2(3x + 1)(x) + [2(3x + 1 + x)]2x$
$$= 2(3x^2 + x) + (8x + 2)2x$$
$$= 6x^2 + 2x + 16x^2 + 4x$$
$$= 22x^2 + 6x$$

27. $22x^2 + 6x = 216$, so $11x^2 + 3x = 108$.
$x = 3$: $11(3)^2 + 3(3) \stackrel{?}{=} 108$
$$99 + 9 \stackrel{?}{=} 108$$
$$108 = 108$$
So $x = 3$.

Volume $= 6x^3 + 2x^2$
$$= 6(3)^3 + 2(3)^2$$
$$= 6(27) + 2(9)$$
$$= 162 + 18$$
$$= 180 \text{ units}^3$$

28. $3m(5m^3 + 7) = 3m(5m^3) + 3m(7)$
$$= 15m^4 + 21m$$

29. $4b(b^2 - 4) = 4b(b^2) - 4b(4)$
$$= 4b^3 - 16b$$

30. $7t^2(-t^3 + 3t^2 - 8t) = 7t^2(-t^3) + 7t^2(3t^2) - 7t^2(8t)$
$$= -7t^5 + 21t^4 - 56t^3$$

31. $3x^3(2x^2 - 5x + 9) = -3x^3(2x^2) - (-3x^3)(5x) + (-3x^3)(9)$
$$= -6x^5 + 15x^4 - 27x^3$$

32. C; $5z(6 - 2z^2) = 5z(6) - 5z(2z^2)$
$$= 30z - 10z^3$$

33. D; $-t(4t^2 - 2t - 1) = -t(4t^2) - (-t)(2t) - (-t)(1)$
$$= -4t^3 + 2t^2 + t$$

34. $4^0 = 1$

35. $2^{-1} = \dfrac{1}{2^1}$
$$= \dfrac{1}{2}$$

36. $3^3 \cdot 3^2 = 3^{3+2}$
$$= 3^5 = 243$$

37. $5^{-1} \cdot 5^4 = 5^{-1+4}$
$$= 5^3$$
$$= 125$$

38. $2(6 + x) = 2(6) + 2x$
$$= 12 + 2x$$

39. $3(t + 4) = -3t + (-3)(4)$
$$= -3t - 12$$

40. $5(2x + 3) = 5(2x) + 5(3)$
$$= 10x + 15$$

41. $4(3x - 5) = 4(3x) - 4(5)$
$$= 12x - 20$$

Spiral **R E V I E W**

1. $6^2 + 4^2 = c^2$ $9^2 + 6^2 = c^2$
$36 + 16 = c^2$ $81 + 36 = c^2$
$52 = c^2$ $117 = c^2$
$\sqrt{52} = c$ $\sqrt{117} = c$
$7.21 \approx c$ $10.82 \approx c$

2. $\dfrac{9}{6} = \dfrac{3}{2}$
$$= 1.5$$

3. Area of $\triangle ABC = \frac{1}{2}(6 \times 4)$
$$= \tfrac{1}{2}(24)$$
$$= 12 \text{ units}^2$$
Area of $\triangle DEF = \frac{1}{2}(9 \times 6)$
$$= \tfrac{1}{2}(54)$$
$$= 27 \text{ units}^2$$

Perimeter of $\triangle ABC = 6 + 4 + \sqrt{52}$
$$= 10 + \sqrt{52}$$
$$\approx 17.21$$
Perimeter of $\triangle DEF = 9 + 6 + \sqrt{117}$
$$= 15 + \sqrt{117}$$
$$\approx 25.82$$

4. $\dfrac{2}{3} + \dfrac{1}{6} = \dfrac{4}{6} + \dfrac{1}{6} = \dfrac{5}{6}$

5. $\dfrac{5}{8} - \dfrac{3}{4} = \dfrac{5}{8} - \dfrac{6}{8} = -\dfrac{1}{8}$

6. $\dfrac{12}{15} \times \dfrac{2}{5} = \dfrac{\cancel{3} \cdot 4 \cdot 2}{\cancel{3} \cdot 5 \cdot 5} = \dfrac{8}{25}$

7. $\dfrac{13}{21} \times \left(-\dfrac{4}{81}\right) = \dfrac{(-13)(-4)}{21 \cdot 81}$

$\qquad = \dfrac{52}{1701}$

8. $\dfrac{16}{21} \div \dfrac{4}{7} = \dfrac{16}{21} \times \dfrac{7}{4}$

$\qquad = \dfrac{\cancel{4} \cdot 4 \cdot \cancel{7}}{3 \cdot \cancel{7} \cdot \cancel{4}}$

$\qquad = \dfrac{4}{3}$

9. $\dfrac{6}{19} \div 2 = \dfrac{6}{19} \times \dfrac{1}{2}$

$\qquad = \dfrac{\cancel{2} \cdot 3 \cdot 1}{19 \cdot \cancel{2}}$

$\qquad = \dfrac{3}{19}$

10. $5y + 13 \geq 28$

$\qquad 5y \geq 15$

$\qquad\ \ y \geq 3$

11. $3 - 2r < 6$

$\qquad -2r < 3$

$\qquad\ \ r > -\dfrac{3}{2}$

12. $\qquad \dfrac{1}{2} < \dfrac{1}{4} - \dfrac{1}{3}s$

$\qquad \dfrac{1}{2} - \dfrac{1}{4} < -\dfrac{1}{3}s$

$\qquad\qquad \dfrac{1}{4} < -\dfrac{1}{3}s$

$\qquad -3 \cdot \dfrac{1}{4} > s$

$\qquad\qquad -\dfrac{3}{4} > s$

13. $4x + 3 \leq 2x$

$\qquad\ \ 3 \leq -2x$

$\qquad -\dfrac{3}{2} \geq x$

14. $(3x^2 + 2x + 1) + (x^2 + 2x + 3) = 3x^2 + x^2 + 2x + 2x + 1 + 3$

$\qquad\qquad\qquad\qquad\qquad\qquad = 4x^2 + 4x + 4$

15. $(6x^3 - x^2 + 2) + (3x^2 + 2) = 6x^3 - x^2 + 3x^2 + 2 + 2$

$\qquad\qquad\qquad\qquad\qquad = 6x^3 + 2x^2 + 4$

16. $V = Bh$

$\quad\ = (\pi r^2)h$

$\quad\ = (\pi \cdot 4.2^2)3.5$

$\quad\ \approx (55.4176)3.5$

$\quad\ \approx 193.9619 \text{ cm}^3$

Lab 14.8

1. $(x + 5)x = x^2 + 5x$ or
$x(x + 5) = x^2 + 5x$

2. $(x + 5)3 = 3x + 15$ or
$3(x + 5) = 3x + 15$

3. $(2x + 3)(x + 1) = 2x^2 + 5x + 3$

4. $(x + 5)(x + 1) = x^2 + 6x + 5$

5. $(3x + 2)(x + 2) = 3x^2 + 8x + 4$

6. $(2x + 4)(x + 2) = 2x^2 + 8x + 8$

7.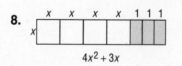
$6x^2 + 4x$

8.
$4x^2 + 3x$

9.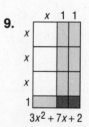
$3x^2 + 7x + 2$

10. 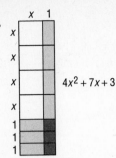 $4x^2 + 7x + 3$

11. $x^2 + 2x + 1$

12. 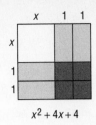 $x^2 + 4x + 4$

14.8 | *More About Multiplying Polynomials*

ONGOING ASSESSMENT

1. Horizontal: $(2x + 3)(x + 4) = (2x + 3)(x) + (2x + 3)(4)$

$= (2x)(x) + (3)(x) + (2x)(4) + (3)(4)$

$= 2x^2 + 3x + 8x + 12$

$= 2x^2 + 11x + 12$

Vertical:
$$
\begin{array}{r}
2x + 3 \\
x + 4 \\
\hline
8x + 12 \\
2x^2 + 3x \\
\hline
2x^2 + 11x + 12
\end{array}
$$

FOIL: $\overbrace{2x(x)}^{\text{First}} + \overbrace{2x(4)}^{\text{Outer}} + \overbrace{3(x)}^{\text{Inner}} + \overbrace{3(4)}^{\text{Last}} = 2x^2 + 8x + 3x + 12$

$= 2x^2 + 11x + 12$

2. Horizontal: $(3x + 5)(x + 2) = (3x + 5)(x) + (3x + 5)(2)$

$= (3x)(x) + (5)(x) + (3x)(2) + (5)(2)$

$= 3x^2 + 5x + 6x + 10$

$= 3x^2 + 11x + 10$

Vertical:
$$
\begin{array}{r}
3x + 5 \\
x + 2 \\
\hline
6x + 10 \\
3x^2 + 5x \\
\hline
3x^2 + 11x + 10
\end{array}
$$

FOIL: $\overbrace{3x(x)}^{\text{First}} + \overbrace{3x(2)}^{\text{Outer}} + \overbrace{5(x)}^{\text{Inner}} + \overbrace{5(2)}^{\text{Last}} = 3x^2 + 6x + 5x + 10$

$= 3x^2 + 11x + 10$

EXERCISES

1. $(x + 3)(3x + 2)$

$= (x + 3)(3x) + (x + 3)(2)$

$= (x)(3x) + (3)(3x) + (x)(2) + (3)(2)$

$= 3x^2 + 9x + 2x + 6$

$= 3x^2 + 11x + 6$

2. $(2x + 1)(4x + 5)$

$= (2x + 1)(4x) + (2x + 1)(5)$

$= (2x)(4x) + (1)(4x) + (2x)(5) + (1)(5)$

$= 8x^2 + 4x + 10x + 5$

$= 8x^2 + 14x + 5$

3. D; $(4x + 3)(3x + 2)$

$\quad = (4x + 3)(3x) + (4x + 3)(2)$

$\quad = (4x)(3x) + (3)(3x) + (4x)(2) + (3)(2)$

$\quad = 12x^2 + 9x + 8x + 6$

$\quad = 12x^2 + 17x + 6$

4. B; $(2x + 8)(6x + 2)$

$\quad = (2x + 8)(6x) + (2x + 8)(2)$

$\quad = (2x)(6x) + (8)(6x) + (2x)(2) + (8)(2)$

$\quad = 12x^2 + 48x + 4x + 16$

$\quad = 12x^2 + 52x + 16$

5. A; $(12x + 3)(x + 1)$

$\quad = (12x + 3)(x) + (12x + 3)(1)$

$\quad = (12x)(x) + (3)(x) + (12x)(1) + (3)(1)$

$\quad = 12x^2 + 3x + 12x + 3$

$\quad = 12x^2 + 15x + 3$

6. C; $(6x + 4)(2x + 4)$

$\quad = (6x + 4)(2x) + (6x + 4)(4)$

$\quad = (6x)(2x) + (4)(2x) + (6x)(4) + (4)(4)$

$\quad = 12x^2 + 8x + 24x + 16$

$\quad = 12x^2 + 32x + 16$

7. $(x + 6)(2x + 5)$

$\quad = (x + 6)2x + (x + 6)5$

$\quad = (x)(2x) + 6(2x) + (x)(5) + 6(5)$

$\quad = 2x^2 + 12x + 5x + 30$

$\quad = 2x^2 + 17x + 30$

8. $(3x + 4)(4x + 3)$

$\quad = (3x + 4)(4x) + (3x + 4)(3)$

$\quad = (3x)(4x) + 4(4x) + (3x)(3) + 4(3)$

$\quad = 12x^2 + 16x + 9x + 12$

$\quad = 12x^2 + 25x + 12$

9. $(x + 3)(8x + 12)$

$\quad = (x + 3)(8x) + (x + 3)(12)$

$\quad = (x)(8x) + (3)(8x) + (x)(12) + (3)(12)$

$\quad = 8x^2 + 24x + 12x + 36$

$\quad = 8x^2 + 36x + 36$

10. $(5x + 6)(x + 2)$

$\quad = (5x + 6)(x) + (5x + 6)(2)$

$\quad = (5x)(x) + (6)(x) + (5x)(2) + (6)(2)$

$\quad = 5x^2 + 6x + 10x + 12$

$\quad = 5x^2 + 16x + 12$

11. $(2x + 1)(9x + 7)$

$\quad = (2x + 1)(9x) + (2x + 1)(7)$

$\quad = (2x)(9x) + (1)(9x) + (2x)(7) + (1)(7)$

$\quad = 18x^2 + 9x + 14x + 7$

$\quad = 18x^2 + 23x + 7$

12. $(4x + 5)(5x + 4)$

$\quad = (4x + 5)(5x) + (4x + 5)(4)$

$\quad = (4x)(5x) + (5)(5x) + (4x)(4) + (5)(4)$

$\quad = 20x^2 + 25x + 16x + 20$

$\quad = 20x^2 + 41x + 20$

13. $(10x + 10)(2x + 2)$

$\quad = (10x + 10)(2x) + (10x + 10)(2)$

$\quad = (10x)(2x) + (10)(2x) + (10x)(2) + (10)(2)$

$\quad = 20x^2 + 20x + 20x + 20$

$\quad = 20x^2 + 40x + 20$

14. $(3x + 8)(3x + 2)$

$\quad = (3x + 8)(3x) + (3x + 8)(2)$

$\quad = (3x)(3x) + (8)(3x) + (3x)(2) + (8)(2)$

$\quad = 9x^2 + 24x + 6x + 16$

$\quad = 9x^2 + 30x + 16$

15. $(2x + 3)(4x + 1)$

$\quad = (2x + 3)(4x) + (2x + 3)(1)$

$\quad = (2x)(4x) + (3)(4x) + (2x)(1) + (3)(1)$

$\quad = 8x^2 + 12x + 2x + 3$

$\quad = 8x^2 + 14x + 3$

16. $(2x + 4)(7x + 9)$

$\quad = (2x + 4)(7x) + (2x + 4)(9)$

$\quad = (2x)(7x) + (4)(7x) + (2x)(9) + (4)(9)$

$\quad = 14x^2 + 28x + 18x + 36$

$\quad = 14x^2 + 46x + 36$

17. $(6x + 5)(3x + 5) = (6x + 5)(3x) + (6x + 5)(5)$

$\qquad\qquad\qquad = (6x)(3x) + (5)(3x) + (6x)(5) + (5)(5)$

$\qquad\qquad\qquad = 18x^2 + 15x + 30x + 25$

$\qquad\qquad\qquad = 18x^2 + 45x + 25$

18.
$$
\begin{array}{r}
3x + 2 \\
\underline{6x + 8} \\
24x + 16 \\
\underline{18x^2 + 12x} \\
18x^2 + 36x + 16
\end{array}
$$

19.
$$
\begin{array}{r}
9x + 6 \\
\underline{3x + 1} \\
9x + 6 \\
\underline{27x^2 + 18x} \\
27x^2 + 27x + 6
\end{array}
$$

20.
$$
\begin{array}{r}
x + 10 \\
\underline{4x + 15} \\
15x + 150 \\
\underline{4x^2 + 40x} \\
4x^2 + 55x + 150
\end{array}
$$

21.
$$
\begin{array}{r}
5x + 1 \\
\underline{x + 7} \\
35x + 7 \\
\underline{5x^2 + x} \\
5x^2 + 36x + 7
\end{array}
$$

22.
$$
\begin{array}{r}
6x + 1 \\
\underline{6x + 1} \\
6x + 1 \\
\underline{36x^2 + 6x} \\
36x^2 + 12x + 1
\end{array}
$$

23.
$$
\begin{array}{r}
3x + 10 \\
\underline{10x + 3} \\
9x + 30 \\
\underline{30x^2 + 100x} \\
30x^2 + 109x + 30
\end{array}
$$

24. $\text{Area} = (x + 12)(4x + 1)$

$\qquad\quad = (x + 12)(4x) + (x + 12)(1)$

$\qquad\quad = (x)(4x) + (12)(4x) + (x)(1) + (12)(1)$

$\qquad\quad = 4x^2 + 48x + x + 12$

$\qquad\quad = 4x^2 + 49x + 12$

When $x = 2$:

$4(2)^2 + 49(2) + 12 = 16 + 98 + 12$

$\qquad\qquad\qquad\quad = 126 \text{ units}^2$

25. Use $A = \frac{1}{2}bh$.

$\text{Area} = \frac{1}{2}(2x + 3)(5x + 14)$

$\qquad\quad = \frac{1}{2}[(2x + 3)(5x) + (2x + 3)(14)]$

$\qquad\quad = \frac{1}{2}[(2x)(5x) + (3)(5x) + (2x)(14) + (3)(14)]$

$\qquad\quad = \frac{1}{2}(10x^2 + 15x + 28x + 42)$

$\qquad\quad = \frac{1}{2}(10x^2 + 43x + 42)$

$\qquad\quad = 5x^2 + 21.5x + 21$

When $x = 2$:

$5(2)^2 + 21.5(2) + 21 = 20 + 43 + 21$

$\qquad\qquad\qquad\qquad = 84 \text{ units}^2$

26. Use $A = \frac{1}{2}(b_1 + b_2)h$.

$\text{Area} = \frac{1}{2}[(3x + 1) + (2x + 5)](x + 3)$

$\qquad\quad = \frac{1}{2}(5x + 6)(x + 3)$

$\qquad\quad = (5x + 6)(x) + (5x + 6)(3)$

$\qquad\quad = (5x)(x) + (6)(x) + (5x)(3) + (6)(3)$

$\qquad\quad = \frac{1}{2}[5x^2 + 6x + 15x + 18]$

$\qquad\quad = \dfrac{5x^2 + 21x + 18}{2}$

$\qquad\quad = 2.5x^2 + 10.5x + 9$

When $x = 2$: $2.5(2)^2 + 10.5(2) + 9 = 10 + 21 + 9$

$\qquad\qquad\qquad\qquad\qquad\qquad = 40 \text{ units}^2$

27. Width = $(4x + 2)$ feet
Height = $(7x + 4)$ feet
Mosaic area = 180 feet^2

$$(\text{Width})(\text{Height}) = \text{Area}$$
$$(4x + 2)(7x + 4) = 180$$
$$(4x + 2)(7x) + (4x + 2)(4) = 180$$
$$(4x)(7x) + (2)(7x) + (4x)(4) + (2)(4) = 180$$
$$28x^2 + 14x + 16x + 8 = 180$$
$$28x^2 + 30x + 8 = 180$$
$$28x^2 + 30x - 172 = 0$$
$$14x^2 + 15x - 86 = 0$$

$$x = 2: \quad 14(2)^2 + 15(2) - 86 \overset{?}{=} 0$$
$$56 + 30 - 86 \overset{?}{=} 0$$
$$0 = 0$$

Width = $(4x + 2)$
$$= 4(2) + 2$$
$$= 8 + 2$$
$$= 10 \text{ feet}$$

Height = $(7x + 4)$
$$= 7(2) + 4$$
$$= 14 + 4$$
$$= 18 \text{ feet}$$

28.

$$
\begin{array}{r}
x + 15 \\
2x + 1 \\
\hline
x + 15 \\
2x^2 + 30x \\
\hline
2x^2 + 31x + 15
\end{array}
\qquad
\begin{array}{r}
2x + 1 \\
x + 15 \\
\hline
30x + 15 \\
2x^2 + x \\
\hline
2x^2 + 31x + 15
\end{array}
$$

The products are equal. This illustrates the Commutative Property of Multiplication.

29. $2[(x + 3)(x + 5)] = 2(x^2 + 3x + 5x + 15)$
$$= 2(x^2 + 8x + 15)$$
$$= 2x^2 + 16x + 30$$
$$[2(x + 3)](x + 5) = (2x + 6)(x + 5)$$
$$= 2x^2 + 6x + 10x + 30$$
$$= 2x^2 + 16x + 30$$

The products are equal. This illustrates the Associative Property of Multiplication.

30. C

31. $(x + 1)(x + 1)$
$$= (x + 1)(x) + (x + 1)(1)$$
$$= (x)(x) + (1)(x) + (x)(1) + (1)(1)$$
$$= x^2 + x + x + 1$$
$$= x^2 + 2x + 1$$

32. $(x + 2)(x + 2) = (x + 2)(x) + (x + 2)(2)$
$$= (x)(x) + (2)(x) + (x)(2) + (2)(2)$$
$$= x^2 + 2x + 2x + 4$$
$$= x^2 + 4x + 4$$

33. $(x + 3)(x + 3) = (x + 3)(x) + (x + 3)(3)$
$$= (x)(x) + (3)(x) + (x)(3) + (3)(3)$$
$$= x^2 + 3x + 3x + 9$$
$$= x^2 + 6x + 9$$

34. $(x + 4)(x + 4) = (x + 4)(x) + (x + 4)(4)$
$$= (x)(x) + (4)(x) + (x)(4) + (4)(4)$$
$$= x^2 + 4x + 4x + 16$$
$$= x^2 + 8x + 16$$

35. $(x + 5)(x + 5) = (x + 5)(x) + (x + 5)(5)$
$$= (x)(x) + (5)(x) + (x)(5) + (5)(5)$$
$$= x^2 + 5x + 5x + 25$$
$$= x^2 + 10x + 25$$

36.
$$(x + 6)(x + 6) = (x + 6)(x) + (x + 6)(6)$$
$$= (x)(x) + (6)(x) + (x)(6) + (6)(6)$$
$$= x^2 + 6x + 6x + 36$$
$$= x^2 + 12x + 36$$

37.
$$(x + a)(x + a) = x^2 + 2ax + a^2$$
$$(x + 7)(x + 7) = x^2 + (2 \cdot 7)x + 7^2$$
$$= x^2 + 14x + 49$$

Chapter **R E V I E W**

1. Ordered data: 2, 3, 3, 4, 4, 4, 5, 5, 5, 5, 6, 6, 7, 8, 9

Mean: $\dfrac{2 + 3 + 3 + 4 + 4 + 4 + 5 + 5 + 5 + 5 + 6 + 6 + 7 + 8 + 9}{15} = \dfrac{76}{15} \approx 5.07$

Median: 5

Mode: 5

2. Ordered data: 20, 22, 23, 24, 24, 25, 26, 28, 29, 30

Mean: $\dfrac{20 + 22 + 23 + 24 + 24 + 25 + 26 + 28 + 29 + 30}{10} = \dfrac{251}{10} = 25.1$

Median: $\dfrac{24 + 25}{2} = 24.5$

Mode: 24

3. Ordered data: 40, 41, 41, 42, 44, 45, 46, 47, 48, 49

Mean: $\dfrac{40 + 41 + 41 + 42 + 44 + 45 + 46 + 47 + 48 + 49}{10} = \dfrac{443}{10} = 44.3$

Median: $\dfrac{44 + 45}{2} = 44.5$

Mode: 41

4. Ordered data: 71, 72, 72, 73, 75, 76, 77, 77, 78, 79

Mean: $\dfrac{71 + 72 + 72 + 73 + 75 + 76 + 77 + 77 + 78 + 79}{10} = \dfrac{750}{10} = 75$

Median: $\dfrac{75 + 76}{2} = 75.5$

Mode: none

5.

5	1 8
4	8
3	2 4
2	4 6 6
1	
0	5

0 | 5 represents 5

6.

18	2
17	
16	5 6
15	8
14	7
13	5
12	3

12 | 3 represents 123

7.

9	5 9
8	
7	1 2
6	1 7
5	
4	
3	1 3 5

3 | 1 represents 31

8.

9	4
8	
7	7
6	2 4
5	8
4	7
3	5 6
2	1 9

2 | 1 represents 21

9. Ordered data: 5, 8, 9, 12, 16, 18, 21, 22, 25, 27

1st quartile: 9

2nd quartile: $\dfrac{16 + 18}{2} = 17$

3rd quartile: 22

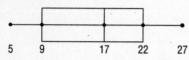

10. Ordered data: 0, 35, 47, 50, 67, 71, 82, 89, 95, 100

1st quartile: 47

2nd quartile: $\dfrac{67 + 71}{2} = 69$

3rd quartile: 89

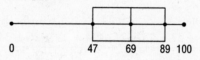

11. $\begin{bmatrix} 0+8 & -4+7 \\ 3+4 & 6+(-6) \end{bmatrix} = \begin{bmatrix} 8 & 3 \\ 7 & 0 \end{bmatrix}$

$\begin{bmatrix} 0-8 & -4-7 \\ 3-4 & 6-(-6) \end{bmatrix} = \begin{bmatrix} -8 & -11 \\ -1 & 12 \end{bmatrix}$

12. $\begin{bmatrix} 2+1 & -6+(-3) & 7+6 \\ 3+2 & 9+9 & -8+(-5) \end{bmatrix} = \begin{bmatrix} 3 & -9 & 13 \\ 5 & 18 & -13 \end{bmatrix}$

$\begin{bmatrix} 2-1 & -6-(-3) & 7-6 \\ 3-2 & 9-9 & -8-(-5) \end{bmatrix} = \begin{bmatrix} 1 & -3 & 1 \\ 1 & 0 & -3 \end{bmatrix}$

13. $10x - 7 + 3x + 7 = -10x + 3x - 7 + 7$

$\qquad\qquad\qquad\quad = -7x$

Monomial

14. $4t^2 - 6t + t^2 + 9t = 4t^2 + t^2 - 6t + 9t$

$\qquad\qquad\qquad\quad = 5t^2 + 3t$

Binomial

15. $3x^4 - 8x^3 + 2x^2 + 5x^3 = 3x^4 - 8x^3 + 5x^3 + 2x^2$

$\qquad\qquad\qquad\qquad\quad = 3x^4 - 3x^3 + 2x^2$

Trinomial

16. $3s^2 - 4s + 2s^2 + 2s - 9 = 3s^2 + 2s^2 - 4s + 2s - 9$

$\qquad\qquad\qquad\qquad\qquad = 5s^2 - 2s - 9$

Trinomial

17. $9 + 15r^3 - 7r^3 + 10 = 15r^3 - 7r^3 + 9 + 10$

$\qquad\qquad\qquad\qquad = 8r^3 + 19$

Binomial

18. $5m^2 + 4m^2 - 3m^2 = 6m^2$

Monomial

19. $(6x^2 - 3x - 7) + (x^2 - 9) = 6x^2 - 3x - 7 + x^2 - 9$

$\qquad\qquad\qquad\qquad\qquad = 7x^2 - 3x - 16$

20. $(2x^3 - 4x^2 + x - 1) - (-7x^2 - x) = 2x^3 - 4x^2 - (-7x^2) + x - (-x) - 1$

$\qquad\qquad\qquad\qquad\qquad\qquad\quad = 2x^3 + 3x^2 + 2x - 1$

21. $(4x^3 - 2x^2 - 5) - (-3x^3 + x^2 - 7) = 4x^3 + 3x^3 - 2x^2 - x^2 - 5 + 7$
$$= 7x^3 - 3x^2 + 2$$

22. $(5x^2 - 2x + 9) + (8x^2 - 3x - 2) = 5x^2 + 8x^2 - 2x - 3x + 9 - 2$
$$= 13x^2 - 5x + 7$$

23. $x(x^2 + x) = x(x^2) + x(x)$
$$= x^3 + x^2$$

24. $n^2(n^3 + 4) = n^2(n^3) + n^2(4)$
$$= n^5 + 4n^2$$

25. $x^2(3x + 7) = x^2(3x) + x^2(7)$
$$= 3x^3 + 7x^2$$

26. $t^3(5t^2 + 5t - 3) = t^3(5t^2) + t^3(5t) - t^3(3)$
$$= 5t^5 + 5t^4 - 3t^3$$

27. $(2z + 1)(6z + 5)$
$$= (2z + 1)(6z) + (2z + 1)(5)$$
$$= (2z)(6z) + (1)(6z) + (2z)(5) + (1)(5)$$
$$= 12z^2 + 6z + 10z + 5$$
$$= 12z^2 + 16z + 5$$

28. $(4x + 3)(4x + 3) = \overbrace{4x(4x)}^{\text{First}} + \overbrace{4x(3)}^{\text{Outer}} + \overbrace{3(4x)}^{\text{Inner}} + \overbrace{3(3)}^{\text{Last}}$
$$= 16x^2 + 12x + 12x + 9$$
$$= 16x^2 + 24x + 9$$

29. $(3p + 6)(p + 4) = 3p(p) + 3p(4) + 6(p) + 6(4)$
$$= 3p^2 + 12p + 6p + 24$$
$$= 3p^2 + 18p + 24$$

30. $(7x + 3)(x + 9) = 7x(x) + 7x(9) + 3(x) + 3(9)$
$$= 7x^2 + 63x + 3x + 27$$
$$= 7x^2 + 66x + 27$$

31. $(2s + 3)(8s + 7) = 2s(8s) + 2s(7) + 3(8s) + 3(7)$
$$= 16s^2 + 14s + 24s + 21$$
$$= 16s^2 + 38s + 21$$

32. $(x + 5)(3x + 9) = x(3x) + x(9) + 5(3x) + 5(9)$
$$= 3x^2 + 9x + 15x + 45$$
$$= 3x^2 + 24x + 45$$

Chapter ASSESSMENT

1.–3. Ordered data: 95.2, 162.7, 165.4, 173.6, 178.7, 181.5, 195.3, 196.3

1. 1st quartile: $\dfrac{162.7 + 165.4}{2} = 164.05$ million

2nd quartile: $\dfrac{173.6 + 178.7}{2} = 176.15$ million

3rd quartile: $\dfrac{181.5 + 195.3}{2} = 188.4$ million

2.

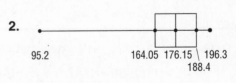

95.2   164.05   176.15   196.3
188.4

3. Mean: $\dfrac{77 + 79 + 84 + 93 + 93 + 96 + 99 + 99 + 99 + 102}{10} = \dfrac{921}{10} = 92.1$

Median: $\dfrac{93 + 96}{2} = 94.5$

Mode: 99

4. Ordered data: 22, 23, 32, 34, 34, 45, 65, 65, 67, 74, 98

Mean: $\dfrac{22 + 23 + 32 + 34 + 34 + 45 + 65 + 65 + 67 + 74 + 98}{11} = \dfrac{559}{11} \approx 50.82$

Median: 45

Mode: none

5.

9	8
8	
7	4
6	5 5 7
5	
4	5
3	2 4 4
2	2 3

9 | 8 represents 98

6. $\begin{bmatrix} 8+6 & 12+2 & 3+(-7) & (-5)+2 \\ 4+9 & 22+14 & 1+(-4) & 7+9 \end{bmatrix} = \begin{bmatrix} 14 & 14 & -4 & -3 \\ 13 & 36 & -3 & 16 \end{bmatrix}$

7. $\begin{bmatrix} 3-1 & 18-8 & 12-4 \\ 16-(-21) & 12-0 & 15-6 \end{bmatrix} = \begin{bmatrix} 2 & 10 & 8 \\ 37 & 12 & 9 \end{bmatrix}$

8. $2p^2 - p^3 + p + 2p^3 = 2p^3 - p^3 + 2p^2 + p$
$$= p^3 + 2p^2 + p$$
Trinomial

9. $3n^3 + 4 - n^2 - n^3 = 3n^3 - n^3 - n^2 + 4$
$$= 2n^3 - n^2 + 4$$
Trinomial

10. $m^2 + 8m^2 - 5m^2 - 7m^2 = -3m^2$
Monomial

11. $(3x^2 + 2x + 5) + (7x^2 - 4x + 2) = 3x^2 + 7x^2 + 2x - 4x + 5 + 2$
$$= 10x^2 - 2x + 7$$

12. $(4p^3 + 6p - 4) - (p^3 - p^2 + 6p - 5) = 4p^3 - p^3 - (-p^2) + 6p - 6p - 4 - (-5)$
$$= 3p^3 + p^2 + 1$$

13. $2y(3y^2 + 2y + 1) = 2y(3y^2) + 2y(2y) + 2y(1)$
$$= 6y^3 + 4y^2 + 2y$$

14. $(3p + 1)(2p + 3) = (3p + 1)(2p) + (3p + 1)(3)$
$$= (3p)(2p) + (1)(2p) + (3p)(3) + (1)(3)$$
$$= 6p^2 + 2p + 9p + 3$$
$$= 6p^2 + 11p + 3$$

15. $(4x + 5)(x + 7) = (4x + 5)(x) + (4x + 5)(7)$

$$= 4x(x) + 5(x) + 4x(7) + 5(7)$$
$$= 4x^2 + 5x + 28x + 35$$
$$= 4x^2 + 33x + 35$$

16. Small window: $(2x)(2x) = 4x^2$

Large window: $(2x)(2x + 1) = (2x)(2x) + (2x)(1) = 4x^2 + 2x$

17. $(8x)(2x + 3) - (4x^2 + 4x^2 + 2x) = 8x(2x) + 8x(3) - 4x^2 - 4x^2 - 2x$

$$= 16x^2 + 24x - 4x^2 - 4x^2 - 2x$$
$$= 8x^2 - 22x$$

18.

$$\begin{bmatrix} 108 - 100 & 164 - 150 \\ 480 - 450 & 325 - 300 \\ 648 - 600 & 1100 - 1000 \end{bmatrix} = \begin{matrix} \text{Interest} \\ \text{Bank 1} \ \text{Bank 2} \\ \begin{bmatrix} 8 & 14 \\ 30 & 25 \\ 48 & 100 \end{bmatrix} \end{matrix}$$

19.

$$\begin{bmatrix} \frac{8}{100} & \frac{14}{150} \\ \frac{30}{450} & \frac{25}{300} \\ \frac{48}{600} & \frac{100}{1000} \end{bmatrix} = \begin{bmatrix} 0.08 & \approx 0.093 \\ \approx 0.067 & \approx 0.083 \\ 0.08 & 0.1 \end{bmatrix} = \begin{matrix} \text{Percent of} \\ \text{Interest} \\ \text{Bank 1} \ \text{Bank 2} \\ \begin{bmatrix} 8 & \approx 9.3 \\ \approx 6.7 & \approx 8.3 \\ 8 & 10 \end{bmatrix} \end{matrix}$$

Standardized Test Practice

1. C; Ordered data: $1.00, $2.00, $3.75, $5.50, $5.50, $5.75, $5.75, $6.00, $6.00, $6.00, $6.25, $6.50

Mean: $\dfrac{1 + 2 + 3.75 + 5.5 + 5.5 + 5.75 + 5.75 + 6 + 6 + 6 + 6.25 + 6.5}{10} = \dfrac{50}{10} = \$5.00$

Median: $5.75

Mode: $6.00

2. D

3. A; $\begin{bmatrix} 1 - (-2) & -5 - 0 \\ -4 - (-1) & -3 - 6 \end{bmatrix} = \begin{bmatrix} 3 & -5 \\ -3 & -9 \end{bmatrix}$

4. C

5. B; $4n^2 - 3 + 4n + n^2 - 7n + 9 = 4n^2 + n^2 + 4n - 7n - 3 + 9$

$$= 5n^2 - 3n + 6$$

6. D; $x^2 - x + 5 + 3x - 4 + 2x^2 + 3x - 6 = 3x^2 + 5x - 5$

7. B; $x(x + 5) - x(x - 3) = (x^2 + 5x) - (x^2 - 3x)$

$$= x^2 + 5x - x^2 + 3x$$
$$= 8x$$

Standardized Test Practice Review

1. A; $3 \times 4 + 7 \times (9 - 2) = 3 \times 4 + 7 \times 7$
$$= 12 + 49$$
$$= 61$$

2. B; $4(x - 3) = 4(x) - 4(3) = 4x - 12$

3. A; $a^2 b = (-3)^2(-2) = 9(-2) = -18$

4. C; $4k - 12 = 2k + 12$
$$4k = 2k + 24$$
$$2k = 24$$
$$k = 12$$

5. B; $\dfrac{\text{Number of A's}}{\text{Number of letters}} = \dfrac{3}{10}$

6. C; 36: 1, 2, 3, 4, 6, 9, <u>12</u>, 18, 36
24: 1, 2, 3, 4, 6, 8, <u>12</u>, 24

7. C; $\frac{8}{12} \div \frac{4}{3} = \frac{8}{12} \cdot \frac{3}{4} = \frac{24}{48} = \frac{1}{2}$

8. A; $\dfrac{66 - 55}{55} = \dfrac{11}{55} = 0.20 = 20\%$ increase

9. D; $a^2 + b^2 = c^2$
$$6^2 + 9^2 = c^2$$
$$36 + 81 = c^2$$
$$117 = c^2$$
$$11 \approx c$$

10. B; $3 \times 5 = 15$ units

11. B; $3 + 4 + 5 = 12$ units

12. C; $C = 2\pi r$
$$\approx 2(3.14)(8)$$
$$\approx 50.24 \text{ units}$$

13. D; distance $= \sqrt{(x_2 - x_1)^2 + (y_2 - y_1)^2}$
$$= \sqrt{(-3 - 4)^2 + (2 - 6)^2}$$
$$= \sqrt{(-7)^2 + (-4)^2}$$
$$= \sqrt{49 + 16}$$
$$= \sqrt{65}$$
$$\approx 8.1$$

14. B; ordered data: 9, 14, 15, 15, 22, 26, 33, 38;
$$\dfrac{15 + 22}{2} = 18.5$$